World Swords
1400-1945
An Illustrated Price Guide for Collectors

Copyright © Studio Jupiter Military Publishing

FIRST EDITION 2006
SECOND EDITION 2013

ISBN-13: 978-0954591014

Design, Layout and Text by Harvey J. S. Withers

Published by
Studio Jupiter Military Publishing
128 Penns Lane
Sutton Coldfield
B72 1BP
West Midlands
United Kingdom

www.antiqueswordsonline.com

For
Debbie,
Imogen and Guy

With special thanks to the late Richard Holmes

Picture Acknowledgements:

Emmanuel College, Cambridge
Mike Robinson
Bob Erlandson
Mike Tremblay
Michael D. Long Ltd
Carl Koppeschaar
Garth Vincent
Rob Miller
Kroninklijke Bibliotheck - National Library of the Netherlands
James Bond
Rod Akeroyd
Richard Wheeler
Al Gregoritsch

HARVEY WITHERS

WORLD SWORDS
1400 - 1945
A PRICE GUIDE FOR COLLECTORS

Studio Jupiter Military Publishing
2013

Also by Harvey Withers

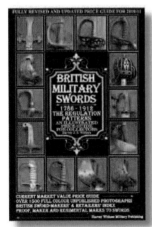

British Military Swords
1786-1912
The Regulation Patterns
An Illustrated Price Guide
for Collectors
ISBN: 978-0954591007

The Sword in Britain
An Illustrated History
Volume One
1600-1700
ISBN: 978-0-9545910-3-8

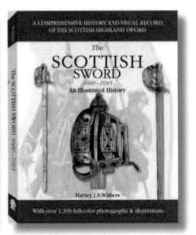

The Scottish Sword
1600-1945
An Illustrated History
ISBN: 978-1-58160-713-0

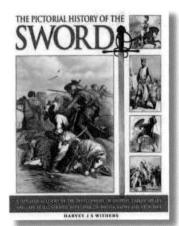

The Pictorial History of the
Sword
ISBN: 978-1-84476-839-4

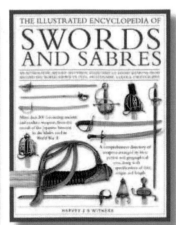

The Illustrated Encyclopedia of
Swords and Sabres
ISBN: 978-0-7548-1851-9

The Illustrated World
Encyclopedia of Knives,
Swords, Spears and Daggers
(with Dr Tobias Capwell)
ISBN: 978-0-7548-2331-5

For more information please go to:
www.antiqueswordsonline.com

CONTENTS

FOREWORD

I CAN WELL REMEMBER MY FIRST SWORD: an 1853 pattern trooper's sword to the 4th Light Dragoons, bought in a junk shop off London's Chinatown for the then princely sum of £5.00. It has long gone, traded up across the years as my interests changed and my wallet grew somewhat thicker, but how I wish I had kept it. It was that commodity I see too rarely these days, a 'sleeper', its blade thick with heavy grease and its scabbard and guard unpitted beneath thick black paint. Nobody had been near it with the dreaded buffing-wheel. Its label did not bear extensive research telling me that the 4th Light Dragoons had charged at Balaclava, and adjusting the price to match.

*O*ver the intervening half-century I have continued to collect swords, reining up when mortgages or prams placed a greater demand on my finances and spurring on when a new book or television series left me (all too briefly) feeling flush. I have tried to move on the more egregious rubbish and to retain some of the better pieces, and although the collection remains eclectic it focuses on French cavalry sabres, Georgian blue and gilt blades and 18th Century basket hilts. I still find the business of collecting pleasurable, and although I only ever bought things I liked, were I to fall under a bus tomorrow my family would, I think, find that my swords have appreciated rather better than stocks and shares.

I know Harvey Withers as a dealer – it was a really first-rate British gothic hilt with the rampant lion of the East India Company in its cartouche that first brought us together. I am delighted to write the foreword to this book because it gives what I would venture to call the average collector – somebody like me, who bounces around the subject as the years go by – a broad introduction to the types of swords that he might find on the market, and an indication of what he might expect to pay. This does not, of course, mean that I agree with every word in the pages that follow.

*B*ut this, of course, is part of the books' pleasure and interest. The more one knows about the subject, the easier it become to spot fakes (now depressingly frequent); to identify bargains (still not unknown, especially in country auctions); and to recognise that non-regulation military swords remain an area where a knowledgeable collector can still do well for himself. Talk to dealers (at least as anxious to sell as you are to buy, for this is a symbiotic relationship) and to other collectors. Recognise the prime importance of quality: there is a difference between getting a bargain and buying something that it was cheap when it emerged from the forge. Be sure how you feel about condition: I have bought swords that I could never really love because they were too far gone. Think hard before attempting restoration: it is always a wise precept never to do something to a sword that could not be undone. Knowledge lies at the heart of it all, and this book is invaluable for imparting that. I only wish that such an admirable general introduction had been available when I stepped into that shop, fiver clutched in vice-like grip, all those years ago.

Richard Holmes

INTRODUCTION

A BOOK THAT ENCOMPASSES ANTIQUE SWORDS from throughout the world and across so many centuries is obviously going to be an enterprise that has naturally enforced limits of scope and size. To include all swords from all nations during this timeframe is impossible. With this in mind, I have deliberately chosen to illustrate swords mainly from the continent of Europe and North America, although Japanese swords are featured, due to their obvious popularity within the collecting field.

*M*y primary task has been to feature a wide cross-section of the kind of antique military swords one might encounter on a regular basis at arms shows, auctions and online. I would like to think that this book will be used as both as an *entry level* work for the new collector, and also a good source of reference for those with more experience. I have included a brief description identifying each sword, combined with a market appraisal of its likely price for the collector. It is important to note that these prices are based on those found at antique arms shows in 2006, and is the *dealer's* selling price after they have added their profit margin. Prices paid at auction are likely to be lower as they are the natural hunting ground for the trade and from where most new items are brought into the market. Please remember that this is also a *"price guide"* and should be used accordingly i.e. as a *"rule of thumb"*. Condition and rarity are also critical factors and can dramatically increase or decrease the price of a sword. For the purposes of clarity and simplicity, I have chosen to include the approximate value of a sword in *good condition.* By this I mean that the sword has the following attributes:

- *a clean blade with only very minor pitting, stains or wear*
- *clear, crisp blade etching or engraving with little wear or rubbing*
- *grip covering (including twistwire) still present with only very minor losses to the fishskin, ivory or bone*
- *no damage or repairs to the hilt*
- *metal scabbard with only very light dents or dings*
- *light flaking or minor creases to leather scabbard and all stitching intact*
- *both blade and hilt solid, with no movement*
- *blade has not been taken out and re-seated*

*T*he vast majority of photographs in this book have never been published before and I hope that they will provide a new archive for the antique sword collector. I have also included many detailed close-up shots of both the sword hilt, blade and scabbard. This enables the collector to identify key features when considering the purchase of a sword. In my other role as a full time dealer in antique military swords, it might be useful to state that many of the swords featured in this book were actually bought and sold by the author in recent times. I believe that this immediacy gives the collector a realistic snapshot of what is available in the market today.

I have made every effort to correctly identify and value the swords featured in this book, but would like to take this opportunity to apologise for any unforeseen errors and omissions. The collecting of antique swords is nothing if not a steep learning curve, and I am always happy to receive correspondence that adds to my own knowledge base.

Harvey Withers
Sutton Coldfield
January 2006

COLLECTING SWORDS ~ the MARKET TODAY

THE PRESENT-DAY COLLECTOR OF ANTIQUE MILITARY SWORDS inhabits a commercial environment quite unlike that of past generations. The rapid global expansion of the internet has been the most important development within the antique collecting marketplace, creating a dynamic and ever-changing platform for the sourcing and selling of military antiques.

*D*edicated web sites have emerged to cater for the sword collector with both auctioneers and dealers quick to embrace the new technology. Customers now have the unique opportunity to both view and purchase antique swords directly from their own home computer. Internet auction sites such as e-Bay have also become an important hub for both the selling and buying of antique swords. Substantial numbers are traded every week and can be purchased with relative ease from almost anywhere in the world. The idea that a buyer would happily purchase any antique purely on the basis of a few photographs and a brief description would have seemed ludicrous only a few years ago, but this is exactly how antique swords are bring traded today. This form of business is ideal for those unable to attend regular auctions and antique arms shows, but it must be made clear that this form of trading is not painless and a number of important caveats must be remembered. One of the most crucial is to ask the seller a series of detailed questions. The answers given will prove useful if the sword arrives and it does not tally with the original auction description. In the case of E-Bay, always check the seller's feedback record as this illustrates the type of seller that you are dealing with and their previous history of transactions.

AUCTION HOUSES
*T*he main beneficiaries of this inflationary market are the auction houses who have realised that their business now has a global reach and can offer facilities for customers to view and bid for lots online. The time has long gone when only the bidder standing on the auction floor is guaranteed to take the lots home. Commission bids now frequently win the day. Many auction houses will also send prospective bidders digital pics of the lots via e-mail. Importantly, the emphasis is very much on the bidder to ask the appropriate questions concerning condition or provenance. Having said this, autioneers are still right in emphasising that nothing can replace actually seeing and handling a sword yourself.

E-COMMERCE
E-commerce can only expand further and looks set to be a major factor in the evolution of the market. This is not all benefit driven. It is an old adage in the antiques trade that demand invariably outstrips supply. This appears to be the current situation when trying to source good examples of antique military swords. Although it might seem that there is a reasonable quantity of swords available to buy via the internet and auctions, the actual *quality* of these pieces is sadly deteriorating. Examples in excellent condition are becoming extremely scarce. Added to this is the fact that prices are rising at an alarming rate.

INVESTMENT
*T*he investment value of antique swords is obvious, and with average yearly increases of around 15-20%, you will be hard pressed to find a better return in any financial market. To date, the market shows no sign of slowing down or reversing. Most collectors obviously do not wish to sell their coveted pieces, but it is reassuring to know that once bought, the value of a sword is likely to appreciate over time.

KNOWLEDGE
*T*he smart collector should constantly update their knowledge of the subject. The purchase of books and the building of a sound reference library is therefore essential. If possible, make a point of buying a relevant book whenever you attend an arms show. The ability to correctly identify and value a piece will always give you the upper hand, and might even allow you to occasionally purchase a bargain. Do not assume that the dealer on the other side of the table has more knowledge than you. They do sometimes let a special piece slip through because of their own ignorance!

ARMS SHOWS AND AUCTIONS

There is no substitute to visiting auctions, arms shows and museum collections. Go to as many as you can and follow some basic rules. When visiting an arms show, the most important rule is to *take your time* when inspecting a sword. Out of courtesy, always ask the dealer if you can inspect the sword. There is nothing more annoying to a dealer than to see their precious stock clumsily pawed by a novice collector. Always draw a sword out of a leather scabbard with the blade held vertically, point down, so as to avoid the danger of bending or breaking the leather at a weak point. If the sword comes with a scabbard, put both alongside and compare the blade length with the scabbard length. Sometimes there can be a great disparity in lengths. Scabbards are easily swapped around, although some would have been legitimately replaced during their service lives. Be wary of sword blades that do not fit snugly into the scabbard or are either loose or tight. Be also aware that with leather scabbards, a tight fit might actually be due to genuine leather shrinkage, so use sensible judgement. Look at the patination of both the hilt and metal scabbard. Matched patination is what you are looking for. A brightly cleaned metal scabbard and dark patinated hilt are obviously suspicious.

At many arms shows and auction houses the interior lighting can be quite poor. Large arenas are notorious venues where this disadvantage can hide damage, alteration and all manner of deceptions done to a sword. View the sword from as many angles as possible. Check that the blade has not been altered by looking at the tang button. It should not show any evidence of having been taken out and re-hammered back in. Unaltered tang buttons are invariably smooth and flush, with a dark age patination.

BUYING

When involved in the buying process, do not be afraid to haggle with the dealer but do not offer a silly price. This is both insulting and makes you look foolish. If you have any doubts about the authenticity of a piece, ask the dealer to confirm that it is genuine. Their response is normally enough to convince you either way. If the reply that you receive goes along the lines of; *"I have no idea what it is."*, be very cautious. For security of mind, ask for a written receipt or official invoice with the dealer's name, address and telephone number. The vast majority of dealers are honest and fair people so approach your purchases with a positive yet attentive mind. If attending an auction, always stick to your bid limit and don't get carried away. Remember also to factor in the buyer's commission when calculating your maximum bid.

FORGERIES

Spurious blade engraving or etching has become a recent and troubling phenomenon. In the case of British swords, I have seen an an ordinary mid-Victorian cavalry officer's sword transformed (by the addition of a notable and distinguished name or presentation inscription) to a potentially *"historic"* piece. Fortunately, the modern forger tends not to possess the skills of craftsmanship inherent in their forebears, and their attempts are usually quite crude when compared with the original blade decoration. Always compare the quality of the two. New collectors will always be caught out by these deceits, and it is only through constant viewing and handling of the genuine article, that you will be able to distinguish between the *right* and the *wrong* piece. Even seasoned collectors started out by buying *wrong* pieces. It is a tough process that all collectors have to go through. Experience is the only educator in this fascinating field of collecting.

PARTS OF A SWORD

1. POMMEL
2. BACKPIECE
3. GUARD / KNUCKLEBOW
4. GRIP
5. EAR
6. FERRULE
7. LANGET
8. DOUBLE LANGETS
9. QUILLON
10. ECUSSON
11. PAS-DE-ANE RING
12. TANG BUTTON
13. BOAT SHELL GUARD
14. SWORD KNOT SLIT / HOLE
15. CUP-HILT
16. SIDE RING

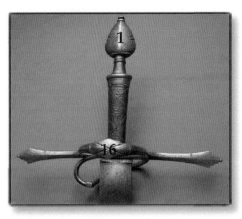

PARTS OF A SWORD

1. MOUTHPIECE
2. LOCKET
3. LOOSE RINGS
4. FROG BUTTON / LOOP
5. MIDDLE BAND
6. CHAPE
7. SHOE / DRAG

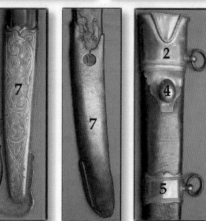

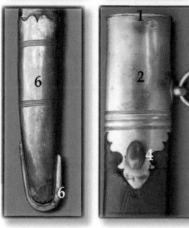

PARTS OF A SWORD

1. TANG
2. SHOULDER
3. FULLER
4. RICASSO
5. SPEAR POINT
6. QUILL-POINT
7. CLIPPED
8. HATCHET
9. PIPE BACK
10. SAWBACK
11. SINGLE-FULLERED
12. DOUBLE-FULLERED
13. UN-FULLERED
14. MULTI-FULLERED

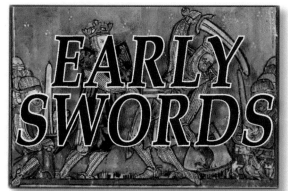

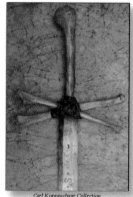

C.1650 GERMAN VEHMIC COURT SWORD

VALUE: $ 5250.00/£3285.00

German in origin, the blade is slightly ridged with both sides displaying hammered smith's marks, the upper third with the carved vehmic signs *"S+S+S+G"* (Strick und Stein), Rope and Stone, and *"Gras und Grein"* (Grass and Grief). The handle and guard is constructed from a human arm bone. In Volume VI of *"Justiz in alter Zeit"* (Justice in Old Times) by the Medieval Criminal Museum of Rothenburg ob der Tauber, it is written that:
"The sword...showed the power over life and death and was a symbol of the might of the tribunal. When saying an oath, the blade or the pommel was touched with the left hand, often with the tip pushed in the ground."

C.1485 ITALIAN KNIGHTLY SWORD

VALUE: $ 8000.00/£5000.00

Broad tapering blade with short double fullers. Both sides have stamped dot and sawtooth marks. Iron quillons are slightly bent toward the blade with chiselled groove decoration. Sharkskin grip covering with large, disk pommel and inset antique coin with the likeness of Julius Caesar on one side and a half round gem (serpentine) on the reverse.

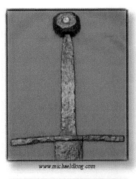

www.michaeldlong.com

www.michaeldlong.com

**C.1400 KNIGHTLY
SWORD**
VALUE: $ 4800.00/£ 3000.00

Carl Koppeschaar Collection

www.michaeldlong.com

Carl Koppeschaar Collection

**C.1680 GERMAN
EXECUTIONER'S
SWORD**
VALUE: $ 4800.00/£ 3000.00
With broad, flattened
double-edged blade rounded
at the tip and with half-length
fuller on each side. Blade is
decorated with a punishment
wheel and gibbet. The iron
hilt with much of the original
silvered finish and comprising
straight, swelling quillons of
octagonal section.

Carl Koppeschaar Collection

Carl Koppeschaar Collection

Carl Koppeschaar Collection

The battle between King Arthur and the Romans. By Permission: Kroninklijke Bibliotheck - National Library of the Netherlands.

THE MEDIEVAL SWORD IS INDICA-TIVE of a period in military history when the use of a sturdy and practical fighting weapon, was vital on the battlefield. Most examples are relatively plain in design and were produced with mortal combat, rather than public show in mind. Existing and genuine swords are now extremely scarce. Most are found in museums or established collections, but the collector can still occasionally purchase these swords from specialist auctions and private dealers. They do command very high prices, but the acquisition of one can be viewed as a unique window into a time when the carrying of such a highly prized and expensive blade conferred both status and power.

HISTORICAL BACKGROUND

The typical style of the *"Knightly Sword"* that has entered into our imagination was firmly established by the twelfth and thirteenth centuries. In general terms it comprised a long, broad-bladed sword with double fullers. A plain cross-bar hilt with wheel, brazil nut, ovoidal or mushroom-shaped pommel finished the profile. This sword design had remained virtually unchanged since the time of the Vikings, and over the next three centuries there was little change. Some blades are encountered with inlaid decoration, mostly in the form of large lettering or symbols, normally of a religious or mystical nature. Pommels of this period can also be found with inset heraldic devices, denoting particular royal or noble families. Rare specimens have pommels of agate, inlaid gold, or rock crystal.

Before the fourteenth century, soldiers worn a heavy chainmail vest and leather jerkin for protection. This allowed a relatively easy route of entry for a sword through the gaps provided between links. The emphasis was thus laid on the sword being a broad-bladed, slashing weapon. Lighter and shorter swords (falchions) could also do this work. When plate mail began to appear in the 1400's, the slashing swords of a previous generation could not penetrate between the closed metal. A new type of sword blade was needed. It had to be heavier and stronger (especially at the tip) to enable a powerful, downwards thrusting movement from the combatant. Blades therefore became longer and narrower. The grip was also extended to allow two-handed operation.

Attila being put to flight by Thorsimond, King of the Ostrogoths. By Permission: Kroninklijke Bibliotheck - National Library of the Netherlands.

COLLECTING MEDIEVAL SWORDS

Any serious collector of ancient and early swords will tell you that the scope for forgeries is great. For many years there has been a lively market both in their production and retailing. It is relatively easy to fake these swords as most genuine examples are in very poor condition, some just retaining the blade and lacking any hilt. It can be quite simple to age and corrode a new blade using specific chemicals. The result can be a sword that appears many centuries old. A recent phenomenon is the use of Victorian Sudanese *Kaskara* blades. They are very similar in profile to Viking and medieval blades. With carefully added ageing, they have been known to sell as original Viking or Medieval blades. A *"rule of thumb"* when buying medieval swords is that if it appears to be very cheap, it is more than likely to be a fake.

Roland kills the giant Farragut. By Permission: Kroninklijke Bibliotheck - National Library of the Netherlands.

Carl Koppeschaar Collection

Carl Koppeschaar Collection

Carl Koppeschaar Collection

Carl Koppeschaar Collection

C.1600 GERMAN "BASTARD" OR "HAND-AND-HALF" SWORD
VALUE: $8000.00/£5000.00

This is a truly superb example with a blackened hilt and broad, ribbon-like guards, consisting of straight, spatulate quillons supporting side-rings and arms. The centre of the side-ring is also linked to the end of the knuckle-guard by a loop-guard. With a large cone-shaped pommel of quadrilateral section. The large pommel would have acted as a perfect counterweight to the hilt and blade, producing a fine and effective balance to the sword. The blade is single-fullered, with a spear point and false edge. Grip is leather wrapped. Most swords of this great age are likely to have been re-gripped over their lifetime.

The battle between Alexander and King Porus.   By Permission: Kroninklijke Bibliotheck - National Library of the Netherlands.

Carl Koppeschaar Collection

Carl Koppeschaar Collection

Carl Koppeschaar Collection

Carl Koppeschaar Collection

C.1630 GERMAN "PAPPENHEIMER" RAPIER
VALUE: $8750.00/£5000.00

This is a sword of exceptionally high quality, with a double edged blade of hexagonal section and triple fullers. There is an illegible monogram to the blade and an orb stamped to both sides. Hilt is of heavy "Pappenheimer" type with surface decoration of fine filligree relief, inlaid with silver floral bands. Iron grip binding with braided ferrules.

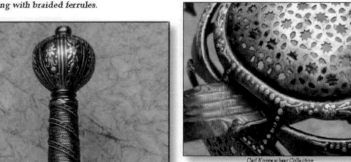

Carl Koppeschaar Collection

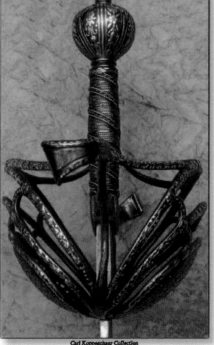

Carl Koppeschaar Collection

Carl Koppeschaar Collection

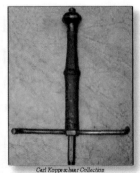

Carl Koppeschaar Collection

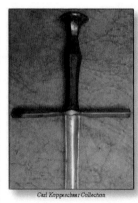

Carl Koppeschaar Collection

C.1500 GERMAN TWO-HANDED ESTOC
VALUE: $ 4000.00/£ 2500.00

Slender blade of stiff diamond section, struck with a mark on the ricasso, horizontally recurved quillons and a waisted, leather covered grip. The pommel is of polygonal form. The estoc (from the French for *thrust* or *point*) was a specialised weapon, developed as an antidote to the improved performance of armour. Cutting weapons had lost their effectiveness and this sword was designed as a crushing and thrusting tool. The strong blade point would be specifically targetted at rings of mail or crevices and joints in the armour. In a combat melee, this sword would probably have been far more use than the traditional double-edged broadsword.

Carl Koppeschaar Collection

C.1500 GERMAN ESTOC
VALUE: $ 4000.00/£ 2500.00

Heavy, strongly ridged triangular blade with a cross mark stamped on one side. Mushroom-shaped pommel.
Right:

C.1600 GERMAN TWO-HANDED SWORD
VALUE: $ 9600.00/£ 6000.00

Superb example with slightly ridged double-edged blade and massive iron hilt. The wide quillons and side rings have incised decoration, comprising spirals and lilies. With a large, conical pommel and leather on wood grip. The heavy pommel was designed to give the correct balance for what could be a unwieldy weapon. This impressive weapon was heavily copied by the Victorians.

Carl Koppeschaar Collection

Carl Koppeschaar Collection

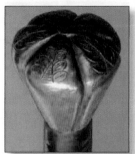

Carl Koppeschaar Collection

A Medieval Siege.

By Permission: *Kroninklijke Bibliotheek - National Library of the Netherlands.*

THE RAPIER IS ONE OF THE MOST elegant swords that a collector will encounter. Some pieces truly epitomise the supreme art and skills of the master sword makers of the sixteenth and seventeenth centuries. Prices for the best swords can be astronomical, but this is an area of collecting that can still turn up representative examples that do not break the bank balance. A new collector must be made immediately aware that there are many copies in the market, most notably those manufactured during the Victorian era, ostensibly to fill the great houses built throughout Britain during the Tudor and Medieval Revival period. These will be discussed later.

HISTORICAL BACKGROUND

*T*he rapier is first noted during the latter half of the fifteenth century, but only comes into major prominence during the early sixteenth century. It was primarily a sword designed to be worn by a gentleman and not particularly suitable for use during heavy combat on the battlefield. The traditional broadsword was still the preferred weapon of choice in this arena. During its height, rapiers were worn as the ultimate fashion accessory and signifier of rank. Great competition was placed at Court to be the nobleman with the most grandly ornate sword, and contemporary paintings vividly show the wide range of rapiers available to those willing to pay the vast sums needed to purchase such a *"trophy"* piece.

*T*he introduction of a more formalised system of fencing in Spain and Italy (and later, England), further enhanced the allure of the rapier and led to a gentleman's settling of accounts via the duel, a pastime frowned upon by the authorities, but one that continued well into the nineteenth century.

*S*pain is normally claimed as the first country to have introduced the rapier or *espada ropera* (dress sword), with Italy, Germany and England following soon afterwards.

*S*word blades were manufactured in Toledo and Valencia in Spain, Solingen and Passau, in Germany, and Milan and Brescia, in Italy. They would have been sent as un-hilted blades and hilted locally at their eventual destinations throughout Europe. Some blades are maker marked, although many are plain. Notable bladesmiths' names recurring on rapier blades include *PICCININO* (Italy), *CAINO* (Italy), *SACCHI* (Italy), *FERRARA* (Italy), *JOHANNES* (Germany), *WUNDES* (Germany), *TESCHE* (Germany), *SAHAGUN* (Spain), *RUIZ* (Spain), and *HERNANDEZ* (Spain). The names of respected bladesmiths were often forged by lesser rivals and it is sometimes rather difficult to know who actually made the blade.

TYPES OF RAPIER

*T*here are many differing styles of rapier, particularly with regard to the hilt. The evolution of hilt styles coincided with changes in the manner of combat and the lessening influence of plate armour. Previously, swords tended to be of simple, cross-hilted, cut and thrust form, with protection afforded by an armoured gauntlet. As full armour became less popular, the need to protect the hand became more important. This included the development of a thumb guard or ring to the hilt on early rapiers, leading to the adoption of side rings and later, the typical swept-hilt form most commonly attributed to the rapier. Early blades were of diamond section and extremely long. Some are known to have a blade length of over 40 inches.

General Ambrosio Spinola by Rubens (Brunswick Lundes Museum).

These early rapiers were designed to be used in conjunction with a left handed dagger in order to parry an opponent's blade. The rapier and dagger were normally crafted as a matching pair, although it is extremely rare to find any of these pairs still together. In style and proportions, the dagger was usually a smaller version of the rapier, with sweeping hilt quillons, large terminals, a plate guard and matched pommel. Spanish and Italian left-handed daggers tend to be more elaborate than English and German examples. Right-handed daggers with corresponding rapiers are known, but scarce.

As the sixteenth century progressed, blade lengths reduced making the rapier more manageable. Hilt design became ever more complex, with added emphasis laid on protecting the hand. In the 1620's, we see the addition of more side plates and shell guards. In Germany, the so-called *"Pappenheimer"* hilt, named after Gottfried Heinrich Graff Pappenheim, who carried this style of sword during the Thirty Years War (1618-1648), comprised a rapier hilt with large plates and recurved quillons. It was very popular in the Low Countries during this period. In time, the natural desire for more hand protection culminated with the design of the cup-hilt rapier. This featured a large bowl guard with pierced or scalloped shell decoration. It proved more popular in Spain and Italy, not being particularly favoured in England. Its very *"Spanish"* styling was probably regarded with great suspicion by this fiercely Protestant nation, although its use in the Low Countries was again frequent. Examples produced for the nobility are very fine, with exquisite chiselled hilt work in chased silver and gold. They very much represent the epitome of Renaissance craftsmanship.

COLLECTING RAPIERS

The demand for authentic rapiers has always been very high. Consequently, the market has had to contend with a large number of fakes or copies. As intimated earlier, many of these are not true fakes, in the sense that they were not *originally* produced to deceive, but in the hands of some unscrupulous or ignorant individuals, they are sold as the genuine article. Most are Victorian in date and manufactured to keep up with the demand for *"antique"* weaponry displayed in the new baronial or great houses. As many are well over a hundred years old, and probably uncleaned, they have now taken on the appearance of an antique sword, with appropriate wear, patination and pitting. Although the Victorian craftsman was noted for his metalworking skills, it is true to say that when compared with the original, there are a number of clear differences. At a basic level, the copies do not have the correct appearance of proportion. Hilt and blade lack the graceful lines of the period pieces, with the hilt bars tending to be over-sized and thick. Blades are also too heavy and completely un-balanced. Victorian examples were made in an age of machine tools, rather than the hand-wrought nature of the original. The Victorians also *"made up"* rapiers with parts (particularly blades) from genuine swords, combined with new hilts and pommels. This can make the task of identification even harder.

If you are buying a genuine rapier for the first time, it is very wise to ensure that you purchase from a source that can verify in writing and so guarantee, the authenticity of the piece. Reputable dealers and auction houses are therefore your recommended first port of call. Please note that if a rapier is described in an auction catalogue as *"in the style of"*, then it is definitely a copy.

"An Ambush" - *a Victorian interpretation.*

www.michaellong.com

C.1580 "HAND AND A HALF" SWORD
VALUE: $ 6400.00/£4000.00

This is of a type widely carried throughout most of Western Europe. The simple styling probably indicates a German (Saxon) origin. This example has a very elegant pear-shaped pommel with a flat, ribbon quillon, ending with a spear-shaped terminal. The blade is unusual in having engraved decoration. Most are completely plain.

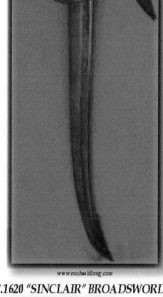

www.michaellong.com

C.1620 "SINCLAIR" BROADSWORD
VALUE: $ 4000.00/£2500.00

Probably of Southern German or Scandinavian origin, the name "Sinclair" is derived from the Scottish mercenary leader, Colonel George Sinclair, who led an ill-fated military expedition across Norway in 1612. Victorian collectors believed that he would have carried a similar sword, and that this style of hilt bore a resemblance to Scottish or Highland broadswords of the seventeenth century.

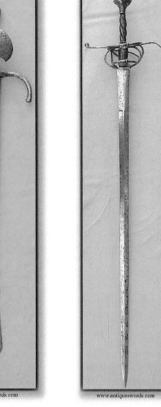

www.antiqueswords.com

www.antiqueswords.com

www.antiqueswords.com

www.antiqueswords.com

www.antiqueswords.com

www.antiqueswords.com

www.antiqueswords.com

www.antiqueswords.com

C.1500 ITALIAN CINQUEDEA
VALUE: $ 3300.00/£ 2000.00

Developed in northern Italy in the late 15th century, this short sword derives its name from the "five fingers" breadth of the blade. Original examples are extremely scarce. Be aware of the high quality fakes produced in Milan during the 1840's.

Right and right above:

C.1600'S ITALIAN FALCHION
VALUE: $ 5600.00/£ 3500.00

Based on an ancient classical blade design, the falchion was deemed obsolete by the end of 17th century.

C.1600-1630 ITALIAN BROADSWORD
VALUE: $5895.00/£3365.00

With typical "crab claw" quillons. Blade marked "Bartolomeus Scaachi".

Left and left above:

C.1600 SAXON LONGSWORD
VALUE: $6800.00/£3885.00

Rare example with large twisted pommel and recurved quillons.

22

C.1580 ITALIAN FALCHION SWORD
VALUE: $4000.00/ £2500.00

With distinctive and long, upward and downswept quillons. The wide, multi-fullered blade is deeply impressed with armourer's marks of stars and half circles. The large globular pommel is typical of the period.

Tower of London Collection, c.1910.

www.antiqueswords.com

C.1650 N. EUROPEAN HORSEMAN'S SWORD
VALUE: $1595.00/£995.00

Typical North European military sword with simple, two-bar hilt and large thumb ring. Blade is single-fullered and unmarked. There is an indistinct armourer's mark, heavily impressed to the inside of guard.

C.1690 ENGLISH RAPIER
VALUE: $1595.00/£995.00

Of transitional form with large, deeply ribbed pommel, well defined globular quillons and pas-de-ane ring.

C.1690 ENGLISH TRANSITIONAL RAPIER
VALUE: $1840.00/£1150.00

Fine chiselled steel hilt with pierced decoration to the shell guards.

www.antiqueswords.com

C.1690 FRENCH BROADSWORD
VALUE: $4500.00/£2825.00

Double-edged blade with two shallow fullers to blade, marked on both sides "Vaincre Oumourit". With curved quillons and small incised shell guard, egg-shaped pommel and baluster button.

C.1660 ENGLISH HOUNSLOW HANGER
VALUE: $2695.00/£1695.00

The Hounslow Works was established in 1629 by Benjamin Stone, at Hounslow Heath, near London. This particular style of sword was noted for its short, single-fullered blades. Imported German blades were ground and polished at his sword mill by skilled German immigrants from Solingen, who were paid on a piece-work basis.

C.1690 CONTINENTAL SWORD
VALUE: $1840.00/£1150.00

This Germanic hilt style was used extensively throughout Northern Europe during the 17th and 18th centuries. A distinctive characteristic of these swords are the double lobes to the knucklebow. Earlier examples have the knucklebow secured to the pommel by screws. With triple-fullered, broadsword blade.

C.1650 ENGLISH
"MORTUARY"
BROADSWORD
VALUE: $4150.00/£2595.00

C.1650 ENGLISH
"MORTUARY"
BROADSWORD
VALUE: $4150.00/£2595.00

C.1650 ENGLISH
"MORTUARY"
BROADSWORD
VALUE: $4195.00/£2595.00
Right:
C.1600 SPANISH RAPIER
VALUE: $1595.00/£995.00
Of very simple form.

C.1600 SHORT SWORD
VALUE: $2400.00/
£1500.00
The large shell guard is typical of swords from this period. This is an unusual sword, especially with regard to the pointed pommel. It also has unusually long, sweeping S-shaped quillons. It is more likely that this had both a hunting and military use. Blade is single-fullered with an impressed mark of an "L" to the blade forte. The significance of this is not known.

C.1680 GERMAN CUP-HILT RAPIER
VALUE: $3200.00/
£2000.00
With flattened sphere pommel and fluted ecusson. Ricasso stamped with maker's mark of crowned figure at prayer.

C.1635-1645 GERMAN
DISH-HILT ESTOC
VALUE: $5750.00/£3600.00
Elongated oviform pommel and button. Spirally fluted wire-bound grip, terminating in Turks' heads. Saucer-shaped guard is finely pierced and chiselled.

C.1650 CLAMSHELL HANGER
VALUE: $3035.00/£1895.00

A very good quality hanger with
incised decoration to the shell guard
and side bar. Finely turned horn grip.
Blade is maker marked on both sides.
Probably Italian or Swiss manufacture.
With leaping stag maker's mark on
each side of the forte.

A Sword Fight in Italy, c.1600. From an original print, 1794.

THE SCHIAVONA SWORD HAS A MOST DISTINCTIVE profile, exhibiting a cage-like basket hilt and unique *"cat's-head"* pommel. For the collector, there are many subtle varieties of hilt and pommel styles.

HISTORICAL BACKGROUND

The origin of the schiavona can be traced back to the swords carried by Slavonic mercenaries from Eastern Europe during the fifteenth and sixteenth centuries. These troops were mainly located in the Balkan or Dalmation region and vicariously employed by both Spain and the Republic of Venice during the sixteenth century. They gained an fearsome reputation for their rugged fighting spirit. The South German *bastard* sword is cited as the progenitor of the schiavona, although it is also thought that its distinctive hilt style lends itself to a possible Turkish origin. If we consider that the Dalmation mercenaries came from an area under sustained Ottoman rule, this possibility should not be ruled out.

The schiavona is probably more well known for its Venetian association. The Council of Ten or *Consiglio dei Dieci,* under which the Doge administered the Venetian State during the 1600's, hired many Dalamation mercenaries. A large store of schiavonas are still present in the Armoury of the Doge's Palace, in Venice. Most are stamped with the "CX" mark for the *Consiglio dei Dieci.*

There are different styles of schiavona hilt, but they all exhibit the common feature of having a leaf-shaped guard, and *"cat's head"* or *"katzenkopfknauf"* pommel in brass or iron. Early pieces are simpler in form with less complex baskets, whereas later schiavonas are usually of higher quality, with the hilt bars cast in one piece.

The sword proved very popular with European heavy cavalry during the seventeenth and eighteenth centuries. The long and wide blade proved very effective as a slashing weapon, allowing both cut and thrust. It was the standard cavalry sword for European horseman during this period, although the *"mortuary hilt"* was more popular in England, being the weapon of choice for most English cavalrymen during the English Civil War.

COLLECTING SCHIAVONAS

Many of the original schiavonas were manufactured in quantities for issue to cavalry troopers and some are of *"munition"* quality, although there are also superb examples in the market. Schiavonas have been known to be faked and special care must be taken.

A sword duel, c.1600.

www.guns.uk.com

C.1700'S VENETIAN SCHIAVONA BROADSWORD
VALUE: $4150.00/£2595.00

C.1700'S VENETIAN SCHIAVONA BROADSWORD
VALUE: $4150.00/£2395.00
A good example with broad blade and short central fuller stamped with a star. With a complex basket of 13 bars, inner guard and thumb ring. Grip is ribbed leather over wood.

C.1640 ENGLISH "MORTUARY" BROADSWORD
VALUE: $4150.00/£2595.00
In very good condition, with no apparent breaks to the hilt bars. Many swords of this type have damage to the hilt due to thinness of the hilt bars. Still retains the original screws attached to pommel bars. Underside of hilt with stylised, chiselled decoration. This example does not include the typical decoration of human faces often depicted on "mortuary" hilted swords.

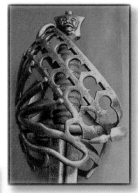

www.guns.uk.com

C.1700'S VENETIAN SCHIAVONA BROADSWORD
VALUE: $4150.00/£2595.00
With twin-faced brass pommel, fishskin grip and double-fullered blade. It is likely that the grip would have been bound in twistwire or banding.

www.guns.uk.com

www.antiqueswords.com

www.antiqueswords.com

C.1650 ENGLISH DISH-HILTED RAPIER
VALUE: $ 3200.00/£2000.00
Of a type carried during the English Civil War. With a slender, hollow ground single-edged blade. Hilt of classic English form with a chiselled dish guard, and secondary loop guard connected to the knucklebow by half S-bars.

www.antiqueswords.com

www.antiqueswords.com

C.1770 SPANISH "BILBO" BROADSWORD
VALUE: $1520.00/£2000.00

C.1650 ENGLISH RAPIER
VALUE: $ 3520.00/ £2200.00
Steel hilt with elaborate knucklebow and pierced hilt. Blade of diamond section and marked "SAHAGUM" to both sides.

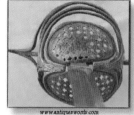

www.antiqueswords.com

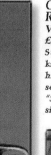

C.1620 - 1640 "PAPPENHEIMER" RAPIER
VALUE: $4800.00/£3000.00

www.michaellong.com

C.1700'S VENETIAN SCHIAVONA BROADSWORD
VALUE: $2400.00/£1500.00

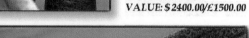

www.michaellong.com

www.michaeldlong.com

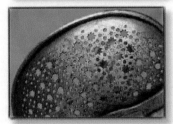

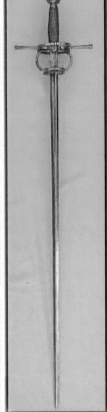

www.antiqueswords.com

www.antiqueswords.com

www.antiqueswords.com

C.1650 SPANISH RAPIER
VALUE: $4000.00/ £2500.00

Swept hilt rapier with large, globular pommel. Forte deeply stamped with armourer's mark.

C.1650 GERMAN CUP-HILT RAPIER
VALUE: $5600.00/ £3500.00

With large, fluted, egg-shaped pommel and pronounced tang button. The shallow cup-hilt exhibits well pierced raised decoration with scalloped edging. The form of the hilt is quite simple and functional, particularly the guard and pommel, and is a likely indicator of its Germanic origin. Italian and Spanish rapiers of this period tend to have more elaborate decoration to the hilt and pommel. The grip is bound with silver twistwire and Turk's head knots.

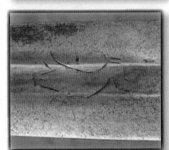

C.1660 N.EUROPEAN "WALLOON" SWORD
VALUE: $2560.00/£1600.00

This sword is commonly referred to as a "Walloon sword", in deference to its widespread use in the Low Countries. Examples differ with regard to the pierced shell guards. Some have just one guard, although most are double-guards. The sword featured has an armourer's mark to the quillon. It is reminiscent of marks attributed to Dutch armourers, particularly those working in Amsterdam.

www.antiqueswords.com

30

C.1680 N.EUROPEAN SWORD
VALUE: $1560.00/£975.00

C.1680 N.EUROPEAN SWORD
VALUE: $1560.00/£975.00

C.1640 N.EUROPEAN SWORD
VALUE: $1560.00/£975.00

www.firearmscollector.com

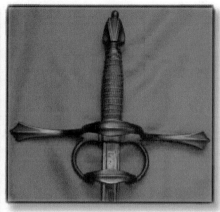

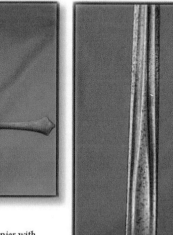

www.firearmscollector.com

C.1640 ENGLISH "MORTUARY" BACKSWORD
VALUE: $4150.00/£2595.00
Guard with typical hilt decoration of faces and swirling decoration.

C.1620 ITALIAN RAPIER
VALUE: $4800.00/£3000.00
High quality and elegant swept hilt rapier with double-loop ring-guards and exceptionally wide quillons. There is an excellent smooth and dark age patina to the hilt.

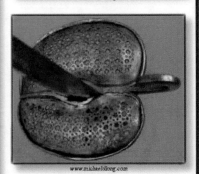

www.michaeldlong.com

www.antiqueswords.com

www.michaeldlong.com

C.1650 SPANISH CUP-HILT RAPIER
VALUE: $ 5600.00/£3500.00

Of typical form with a broad blade of flattened hexagonal section, tapering to a slender point, marked in the obverse fuller "P***R***O***M***P***R***O***M", and on the reverse, "M***O***R***P***M***P***O***R". The blade has a mark beneath the terminus of the short fuller, and is also struck with a maker's mark to the ricasso. The plain, spherical pommel with long baluster button, and wire wrapped grip with Turk's head knots.

www.antiqueswords.com

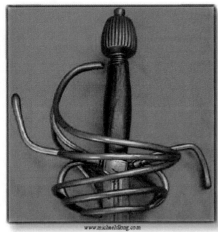

www.michaeldlong.com

www.michaeldlong.com

C.1650 GERMAN RAPIER
VALUE: $ 3200.00/£2000.00

This example exhibits a very complicated hilt configuration. With large, fluted pommel.

www.michaeldlong.com

C.1650 CONTINENTAL "WALLOON" SWORD
VALUE: $ 2700.00/£1695.00

Many of these so-called "Walloon" swords suffer from damaged guards, due to the fragility of the delicate piercing. This example is undamaged. Blade forte with deep maker's stamps. Probably of German origin.

www.michaeldlong.com

C.1620 GERMAN RAPIER
VALUE: $1400.00/ £800.00

Swept-hilt rapier with deeply incised blackened steel bars and fluted pommel. Although of near relic condition, the rapier is still of classic form, with sweeping guards and pierced dish. The double fullered blade is unmarked and Possibly a later replacement.

Carl Koppenschar Collection

www.michaeldlong.com

C.1600 ITALIAN CUP-HILT RAPIER
VALUE: $4000.00/£2500.00

Good example with pierced star decoration to the bowl. Deeply chiselled pommel and typically thin hilt guards.

www.antiqueswords.com

C.1650 CONTINENTAL "WALLOON" SWORD
VALUE: $ 3200.00/£2000.00

The sword is of typical form, with large, bulbous pommel, pierced shell guards and "bilobate" hilt. Grip is finely shaped and bound in brass twistwire. Blade is decorated and of crucifom shape.

www.antiqueswords.com

C.1680 "WALLOON" BROADSWORD
VALUE: $2880.00/£1800.00

C.1650 SHORT SWORD
VALUE: $ 3200.00/ £2000.00

Inlaid silver hilt, sometimes referred to as a "Pillow Sword".

C.1600 German Woodcut.

THE SCOTTISH BASKET HILT has become one of the most sought after swords for collectors. It is easy to understand why this is so. The shape and feel of an original Highland broadsword is like no other sword. Add to this the inevitable myth and romance associated with such swords, and you will find an area of collecting where competition to acquire good examples is very high indeed.

HISTORICAL BACKGROUND

*B*efore the introduction of the basket hilt, the Scottish Highlander already carried at least three distinct sword types. The first was the *claidheamh mor* (claymore), or classic *"big"* sword. This was used from the 1500's, and is of hand and a half length, with a long, broad blade. It has very recognisable quillons of diamond section, angled towards the blade. The terminus of the quillon is also decorated with brazed iron quatrefoils. In the late sixteenth and early seventeenth centuries, Highlanders also carried the *claidheamh da laimh* or two handed sword. It is similar to German or Swiss two - handed (*Zweihander*) swords carried by Landsknechte or mercenaries, and the few surviving examples have Scottish hilts with German blades. The hilt normally includes an oval shell guard and long, flattened, down-swept quillons. The third type of sword is referred to as the *"Lowland Sword"*. These have very long blades, with characteristic side rings to the hilt, globular pommels and quillons set at right angles to the blade, terminating in knobs.

*I*t must be remembered that it is a common mistake to refer to a Scottish basket hilt as a *"claymore"*. This is incorrect. They are two very different styles of sword. Having said this, Scottish commentators of the early 1600's referred to the basket hilt as a *"claymore"*, but it is still best to diffentiate.

*T*he geographical origin of this distinctly *"Scottish"* basket-hilted sword was not actually Scotland. Swords with basket hilts are likely to have originated in Germany, Scandinavia, and even England. Basket hilts of simple form were already known in England during the early 1500's. The development of an enclosed hilt was a natural consequence of the need for more protection to the hand

"Macduff" - from McIan's Highland Series.

at a time when the wearing of armour, and particularly the metal gauntlet, had become less common. Why the sword became associated with Highland use is not clear, although it is known that numbers of Scottish mercenaries fought for the English in Ireland during the sixteenth century, and it is probable that basket-hilted swords were brought back to Scotland and their design copied by local swordmakers. They were then known as *"Irish"* hilts.

*T*here are very few visual sources to enable us to determine exactly when the basket hilt began to be carried in the Highlands. The earliest known painting showing a Scottish clansman carrying this type of sword, is recorded as being c.1680. The painting is of a *"Highland Chieftain"* by Michael Wright and shows the subject carrying a broadsword with *"beaknose"* hilt. This comprised a series of welded ribbon-like strips of metal drawn together to form a beak at the front of the basket. The *"beaknose"* hilt was a specific Highland style and differed from English basket hilts in that the pommel was of *"coned form"* as opposed to the English *"apple"* shape. Pommel shape is an important indicator as to whether a basket hilt is either

Scottish or English. In these early basket hilts of the 1600's, there are some defining characteristics between the hilt styles of Scottish and English swords. The English hilt tended to have thinner, more spaced, bars, whereas Scottish hilts began to adopt wider, rectangular plates to either side of the hilt, coupled with decorative heart-shaped piercings.

*P*roblems of correct attribution do occur as we move into the eighteenth century and English sword makers began to imitate the Scottish style. These swords were sold to the British Army, and carried by both infantry soldiers and horsemen. Ironically, there are many so-called *"Scottish"* basket hilts described as such within the collecting market, that were actually produced in such *"Highland"* areas as London and Birmingham!

*W*here we do know of specific Highland makers, it is only because the maker has signed the hilt. These makers are normally categorised as falling into two schools of sword making; that of either the *Stirling* or *Glasgow* schools. They swords are universally acknowledged as being representative of the pinnacle of Scottish basket hilt sword making. The superb craftsmanship and detailing to the hilts marks them out as being of truly historic form. Father and son hilt-makers or *"Hammermen"*, John Allan Sr and Jnr (Stirling), and Walter Allan (Stirling), produced hilts of rare artistry, many with intricately inlaid brass

"MacBean" - from McIan's Highland Series.

circles, wavy lines and hatching. John Simpson of Glasgow was admitted as a Freeman of the Incorporation of Hammermen of Glasgow in 1711. His father was admitted in 1683 and became the King's Armourer in Scotland. This family produced some very fine basket hilts. The wide variety and breadth of quality that we see in Scottish basket hilts indicates the likelihood that many were produced as part of a *"cottage"* industry. Most blades were imported from the continent, principally Germany, with the hilts then manufactured in Scotland. Back-street workshops in Glasgow, Stirling, Edinburgh and other locations, produced the swords with a workforce comprising little more than one or two persons.

*A*fter the disaster of Culloden in 1746, the Scottish Highlander lost his right to bear arms, and the carrying of swords was outlawed. Most swords were not handed over to the English but hidden. The ban had a devastating effect on Scottish sword makers and the production of basket hilts went into decline. The subsequent raising of regiments for the British Army in Scotland initiated a requirement for basic military swords, but most of these were actually produced in England. They were still of basket hilt form. One of the most frequently encountered is the c.1750-1770 basket-hilted sword for privates in Highland regiments. It was of relatively poor manufacture, with a thin sheet metal guard and crude cut-outs in the junction plates. Grip was leather on wood. Blades were manufactured in London or Birmingham and are marked with a *"GR"*, crown, and maker's name to either *"Iefries"* (Jeffries, London) or *"Drury"* (Birmingham). Most Scottish-made basket-hilted swords after 1746 are likely to have been made for officers in the newly formed Highland regiments.

COLLECTING SCOTTISH BASKET HILTS

*I*t is not suprising that demand far outstrips supply when it comes to sourcing original Scottish basket-hilted swords. As mentioned, many *"Scottish"* basket hilts are actually English in origin, and it is worth taking time to study the literature on this subject in order that the new collector purchases the correct piece.

*P*rices are naturally very high for swords of the seventeenth and eighteenth centuries, and when a collection comes into the market via an auction house, estimates are frequently exceeded. Deep pockets are therefore a necessary evil.

*A*s with all early swords, care must be taken to avoid copies. They are limited in number but some are of high quality. If you are purchasing a basket hilt for the first time, it is probably wise to buy from either a reputable dealer or auction house.

C.1750 SCOTS/ENGLISH BASKET-HILTED BROADSWORD
VALUE: $ 1920.00/£ 1200.00
Simple basket-hilted sword, probably for use by a cavalry trooper.

C.1750 SCOTS/ENGLISH BASKET-HILTED BROADSWORD
VALUE: $ 1920.00/£ 1200.00

C.1650 SCOTTISH "RIBBON-HILT" BROADSWORD
VALUE: $ 6400.00/£ 4000.00
Also referred to as a "beak-nosed" sword. Its characteristics include broad, ribbon-like guards, affording excellent protection for the hand.

C.1720 SCOTTISH "STIRLING" BASKET-HILTED BROADSWORD
VALUE: $ 6100.00/£ 4000.00
Sometimes referred to as a "Stirling" or "Stuart" hilt, the use of the S-Bar is also a feature of many early 18th Century Scottish basket hilts. Blade is exceptionally wide with three central fullers.

C.1750 SCOTS/ENGLISH BROADSWORD
VALUE: $ 4000.00/£ 2500.00
A good quality example that is likely to have been issued to an English horseman. The single-fullered blade is of a type that was manufactured in England, most notably, Birmingham and London.

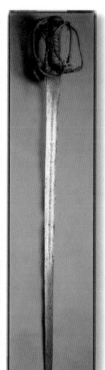

C.1600'S SCOTTISH HIGHLAND BROADSWORD
VALUE: $ 5600.00/£3500.00

Historically important and very early c.1600's Scottish basket-hilted broadsword. With a complex hilt design, retaining much original leather ragging to grip and traces to the hilt. The ragging would originally have covered all the hilt and was used to protect and preserve the iron hilt and grip. There are even small pieces of a tartan material still remaining to the hilt. Blade is extremely interesting and extensively marked. Deciphering has proved difficult as some letters are now worn away.
On one side the following letters are discernible:

.IVIICIFLORESO.ISLAL.WIEL.INDE.WERM.SO.

On the reverse side the following letters are discernible:

AV.IMVI.F.MI.SI.VS.CF.FSI.A.PONDE.IOVI.EST.BIENALE.MONDE.

The style of the wording appears to be French or Latin, and might indicate a connection with the active French and Scottish Jacobite alliance during this period.

"Highlander" - from McIan's Highland Series.

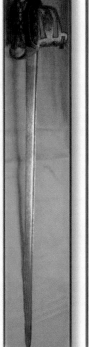

C.1750 ENGLISH HORSEMAN'S BASKET-HILTED BROADSWORD

VALUE: $ 3000.00 /£ 4800.00

John Harvey maker marked sword in a heavy iron scabbard. Rare to find an 18th Century broadsword with scabbard, albeit associated.

www.antiqueswords.com

C.1750 ENGLISH BASKET-HILTED BROADSWORD

VALUE: $ 3200.00/£ 2000.00

Of standard form but with a period or later replacement grip of iron studded bogwood.

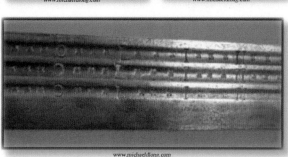

www.michaeldlong.com

C.1750 SCOTTISH BASKET-HILTED BROADSWORD

VALUE: $3995.00 /£2280.00

The stylised and imaginative decoration to the basket hilt is indicative of the *"Stirling"* school of swordsmiths or hammermen. The multi-fullered blade is impressed with a repeated Solingen maker's mark. The grip is bound with a later leather and brass twistwire covering. Rare examples are also found with the impressed initials of Walter Allen (c.1735-60), and his son, John Allan (J.A.S.), of Stirling.

C.1770 SCOTTISH BROADSWORD
VALUE: $ 3200.00/£2000.00
Basket-hilted backsword for use by Highland regiments during the 1770's, and also regular British Army troops serving in Scotland. Many of these swords were actually manufactured in either London or Birmingham. They are usually marked "G.R" and "IEFRIS", indicating the work of Nathaniel Jeffreys.

C.1770 SCOTTISH OFFICER'S BROADSWORD
VALUE: $8000.00/£5000.00
Very fine and complex hilt with detachable loops, and fishskin covered wire bound grip. Steel scabbard with two suspension loops and engraved with the maker's name - J. Read & Sons.

Above:
Blade is deeply marked with "running fox" stamp to Samuel Harvey. He is noted as working in Moor Street, Birmingham, around 1748. There were three generations of the Harvey family, and they are recorded as still producing swords c.1800.

C.1760 ENGLISH GRENADIER'S HANGER
VALUE: $ 2550.00/£1595.00
Maker marked to Samuel Harvey.

C.1740 ENGLISH CAVALRY OFFICER'S BROADSWORD
VALUE: $ 3200.00 /£2000.00
Of heavy hilt form with double-edged blade marked on one side with the running wolf mark of Passau and spurious "ANDREA", with the reverse marked "FERARA". The iron hilt exhibits very distinctive concentric circular bars. These swords were robust and functional, and copied Scottish basket hilt styles. They could not be compared with the quality of manufacture noted by some of the Scottish swordsmiths.

40

C.1720 SCOTTISH BASKET-HILTED BROADSWORD
VALUE: $4800.00/£3000.00

C.1720 SCOTTISH BASKET-HILTED BROADSWORD
VALUE: $4800.00/£3000.00
Of a type and style associated with the Glasgow *"school"*. This is highlighted by the wide and flat, chiselled bars. The Stirling *"school"* is known more for its rounded hilt bars.

C.1720 SCOTTISH BASKET-HILTED BROADSWORD
VALUE: $3200.00/£2000.00
Iron-hilted basket with distinctively crennelated side guards and side bars. With large, bun pommel and turned ivory grip. This could have been a period or possibly later replacement.

C.1740 SCOTTISH BASKET-HILTED BROADSWORD
VALUE: $4000.00/£2500.00

C.1740 ENGLISH HORSEMAN'S BROADSWORD
VALUE: $2700.00/£1695.00

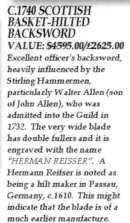

C.1740 SCOTTISH BASKET-HILTED BACKSWORD
VALUE: $4595.00/£2625.00
Excellent officer's backsword, heavily influenced by the Stirling Hammermen, particularly Walter Allen (son of John Allen), who was admitted into the Guild in 1732. The very wide blade has double fullers and it is engraved with the name *"HERMAN REISSER"*. A Hermann Reifser is noted as being a hilt maker in Passau, Germany, c.1610. This might indicate that the blade is of a much earlier manufacture.

C.1740 SCOTTISH BASKET-HILTED BROADSWORD
VALUE: $4000.00/£2500.00
With pronounced pommel cap.

C.1770 ENGLISH INFANTRY HIGHLAND BACKSWORD
VALUE: $3200.00/£2000.00

C.1770 ENGLISH INFANTRY HIGHLAND BACKSWORD
VALUE: $3200.00/£2000.00

www.michaeldlong.com

www.michaeldlong.com

C.1750 ENGLISH HORSEMAN'S BACKSWORD
VALUE: $3200.00/£2000.00

The decorative hilt lines and scalloped edges have been removed, and the pommel is smooth and plain. The blade is unusually decorated as most troopers' swords had plain blades.

C.1770 HIGHLAND INFANTRY SOLDIER'S BACKSWORD
VALUE: $2700.00/£1695.00

Rare example of an English infantry private's backsword. Of a type issued to soldiers in the 42nd regiment (Black Watch). Marked on the blade to Drury of London.

www.michaeldlong.com

www.michaeldlong.com

C.1650 SCOTTISH BROADSWORD
VALUE: $6400.00/£4000.00

Superb example of a typical "ribbon" hilted design with "beak" quillon.

C.1730 ENGLISH/ SCOTTISH HORSEMAN'S BACKSWORD
VALUE: $2595.00/£1480.00

An interesting example showing hilt design reminiscent of swords produced by John Allen of Stirling. It is possible that this is a Scottish hilt produced for English troopers.

C.1750 ENGLISH ROYAL HORSEGUARD'S BROADSWORD
VALUE: $3200.00/£2000.00

Extremely scarce trooper's sword of a type issued to the Regiment of Royal Horseguards. Back edge of the blade is struck with an "R".

C.1760 SCOTTISH/ ENGLISH BROADSWORD
VALUE: $3000.00/£1895.00

Steel basket pierced with hearts and dots. With bun-shaped pommel and horn grip, lacking original brass banding.

www.firearmscollector.com

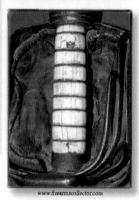

www.firearmscollector.com

www.guns.uk.com

C.1750 ENGLISH/ HORSEMAN'S BROADSWORD
VALUE: $ 2870.00/£ 1795.00
Distinctive and simple basket hilt of a grid pattern with welded bars. The very wide blade is likely to be much earlier and probably 17th Century.

C.1750 SCOTTISH BROADSWORD
VALUE: $ 3200.00/£ 2000.00
Three-fullered blade marked with crescent moons. Ivory grip with brass twistwire.

C.1790 SCOTTISH BROADSWORD
VALUE: $ 5600.00/£ 3500.00
Excellent double-edged blade, decorated with a stand of arms, and *"Vivat Rex Jacobus"* and *"Vivat Regum Carrissimus"*. Iron basket hilt with copper wire bound grip and brass pommel.

www.firearmscollector.com

C.1740 SCOTTISH BROADSWORD
VALUE: $ 4800.00/£ 3000.00
Good quality example with a finely formed basket hilt. Wire-bound fishskin grip and wide, three-fullered blade. The blade has a distinct armourer's mark struck in the centre of the blade just below the basket.

C.1720 SCOTTISH BROADSWORD
VALUE: $ 4000.00/£ 2500.00
Very wide and well tempered fighting blade marked to *"ANDRIA FERRARA"*. The pommel is of the typical bun type. Grip leather and brass twistwire has been added later.

www.michaeldlong.com

C.1660 ENGLISH HORSEMAN'S BROADSWORD
VALUE: $ 3200.00 /£2000.00

These early basket hilts were carried by both Scottish and English troops. The large bulbous iron pommel was used as a counter weight to allow a good balance to the sword whilst it was wielded in the field.

www.michaeldlong.com

www.guns.uk.com

www.guns.uk.com

Far left:
C.1745 SCOTTISH BASKETHILTED BROADSWORD
VALUE: $ 4000.00 /£2500.00

Marked "ANDREA FERRARA" to the blade. Of a type carried by the clans at Culloden.

Near left:
C.1750 ENGLISH HORSEMAN'S BROADSWORD
VALUE: $ 2550.00 /£1595.00

www.michaeldlong.com

C.1730 SCOTTISH BROADSWORD
VALUE: $ 4000.00/£2500.00

Highly unusual example with an openwork hilt and heart-shaped decoration to the bars, including a representation of a mythological(?) human head. The double-fullered blade is unmarked and plain. The use of a bun-shaped pommel is indicative of a basket hilt of the first quarter of the 1700's.

Scottish fighting sword types, 16th - 18th Century.

44

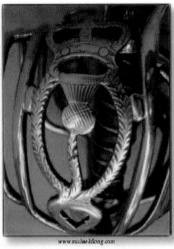
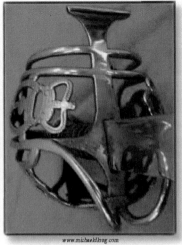

www.michaeldlong.com   *www.michaeldlong.com*   *www.michaeldlong.com*

C.1760 SCOTTISH BROADSWORD
VALUE: $4800.00/£3200.00

www.firearmscollector.com

C.1720 ENGLISH
BASKET-HILTED BROADSWORD
VALUE: $2070.00/£1295.00

This is a very simple design and typical of swords produced in both England and Germany for use by troops within the British Army. There is no pretense at style or decoration, and the hilt bars are somewhat crudely fashioned. Nevertheless, it would have afforded good protection for the hand. Unlike earlier basket hilts, the ovoid pommel has a pronounced capstan or tang button. Pre-1700 basket hilts tend to have a flattened or less pronounced pommel button. This example is without a grip but would probably have had a fishskin or leather covering, with brass twistwire or banding.

A Scottish Clan Chief c.1690 - a Victorian interpretation.

45

www.michaeldlong.com

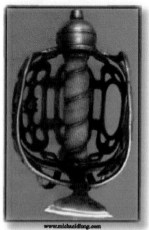

www.michaeldlong.com

C.1750 ENGLISH HORSEMAN'S BASKET-HILTED BROADSWORD
VALUE: $2070.00/£1295.00

www.michaeldlong.com

C.1750 SCOTTISH BASKET-HILTED BROADSWORD
VALUE: $4000.00/£2500.00
Excellent quality and intricately designed steel basket hilt. With large bun pommel.

"Mac Donald" - from McIan's Highland Series.

"Piper" - from McIan's Highland Series.

EUROPEAN HUNTING SWORDS

by
Mike Tremblay
(Michigan Antique Arms Collectors, Inc, 1987)

The *"Coup de Grace"*, or the action that gives a merciful death to a suffering animal (the *finishing stroke*), is a French term used throughout the nations of Europe, and was standard hunting terminology in the European courts.

The specialized European hunting sword came into being in conjunction with the development of the flintlock firearm during the mid-1600's. With the advent of these more sure-fire and accurate arms, and the changing style of the hunt, there was seldom a need for a sword to be used against an enraged boar or stag, but a hunting sword was needed for dispatching wounded or exhausted game brought to bay by the hounds.

This part of the hunt was referred as the *"L'Hallali"* and often hunters would creep up behind the game and cut the Achille's tendons, so the prey could not easily injure hounds or huntsmen.

Queen Elizabeth I at the hunt.

One of the many customs observed in the hunt was at the moment of dispatch. The hunter's companions would draw their swords at two finger's breadth from the scabbard, a symbolic action of ancient date, intended to increase vigilance if the wounded or exhausted quarry were insolent enough to resist the noble huntsman.

As the culminating feature of the stag hunt, Louis XIV of France introduced *"La Curee"*, or *the kill*. This was signalled by a tremendous triumphant fanfare on large circular horns. The hounds were then allowed at the same time to fight over the entrails. The tracker dog was encouraged to sink its teeth into the stag's skull. The trophies of the hunt were displayed for all to see.

From approximately 1650, the most common form of sword style was a short, fairly light weapon, probably derived from the small court sword. It had a shorter, broader blade, and was almost always single edged. The majority had straight blades, although a slightly curved blade was fairly common. A few also showed the clip-like edge at the point, but a short false edge towards the point was by far the most common.

These swords were sometimes fitted with shell-like guards, quillons, and knuckle guards, but they were never fitted with the pas d'ane, since this structure was only used in fencing. On very rare occasions such a sword might have been used to defend the wearer (very ineffectively) against a charging boar, bear or stag. They were more suited for dainty bleeding of game and never for the function of butchery.

The art of chopping up the animal (*"maitrice de veneur"*), of former times now belonged to the Court butcher and his attendants. These changes brought about the need for a handy and practical sword for mounted huntsmen who would sometimes ride through the forest at full gallop.

Although hunting swords were used throughout Western Europe, their most prolific usage occurred in the German speaking countries and France. These enthusiastic hunters held lavish hunts with rich costumes for the hunters, their horses, spectators, and even the hunt attendants. The new style hunting swords were sometimes referred to as hangers because they hung vertically from a sword belt or baldric (*"Couteau de Chase"*). They are also more commonly known as hirschfangers, which in German actually translates to *"deer catchers"*.

Hunting swords were prominently carried in the field and forest as part of the hunter's regular attire, and would probably be replaced by a court sword when the wearer left the hunting ground and changed into his court or town costume.

For around 150 years, specialized hunting swords, for the most part, were carried by the aristocracy and within the Royal Court. In keeping with their rich milieu, hunting swords, although fairly uniform in size, were individual in design and decoration, often splendidly decorated with no expense spared in their fabrication.

For centuries, cold steel enjoyed the reputation of being the chivalrous hunting weapon. The use of firearms for hunting was at first considered unsporting and many hunt masters forbade all but spear and sword for hunting game. Even the great hunter, Emperor Maximillian (1527–1576), had misgivings about firearms and predicted the extermination of all game unless the huntsmen continued to use the old practice of cold steel.

HILTS

Many different materials were at times incorporated into the construction of the hunting sword hilt, with a combination of two or three being quite common. Different metals were normally used in the manufacture of the hilt, either for the entire hilt or in conjunction with a grip of other composition. The basic materials used were silver, brass, bronze, steel, and later, German silver.

Silver was widely used in all European countries, but in England it was very common. Silver would be cast and sculptured with designs and motifs and, in most cases, hall-marked, enabling identification of the maker and place of manufacture. The brass and bronze hilt components were cast and chased sometimes in full relief (known as *"in the round"*). Some were left in their natural metal colour finish, but more often than not, a gold gilding was applied to their surfaces, which left them with a rich luxurious finish. Steel was also used extensively on hunting sword hilts, though some examples do exist that show fine engraving and chiselling, with a contrasting gold or blued foreground. German silver was a cheaper nineteenth century innovation used to replace more precious metals. One of the rarer metals used on a small number of sword hilts was *"shakudo"*, a copper and gold alloy. These were done in a Oriental style and were known as *"Peking Work"*. They were, in fact, of Japanese manufacture, made for export to the European market, and probably manufactured at the Dutch East India Company at Deshima, in Japan.

Some metal hilts had precious or semi-precious stones inset or were wrapped with silver or other wire. If the grips were not fabricated in metal as an intricate part, the most extensively used materials were stag horn (actually antler), ivory horn and wood. Ebony was also a popular choice for grips.

These materials could be left *"in-the-round"*, cut into flat panels or decorative strips. These would be left plain, carved around their exterior surfaces or have carving or engraving on part of their surfaces. Many times a central core was used, including wood, and then wrapped with ray or shark skin (shagreen), tortoise shell, wood veneer, velvet fabric, leather, mother-of-pearl etc. Silver or other wire was sometimes wrapped around the central core. A few of the rarer grips were made of enamelled painted porcelain, agate or jade.

BLADES

Although the hilts were furnished from many sources, the blade was normally obtained from Solingen, Germany, who seemed to have a virtual monopoly on hunting sword blades for almost three centuries. Some earlier blades had serrated back edges that on infrequent occasions, could be used for sawing through bone.

The Elizabethan Hunt.

The decoration of the earlier blades usually consisted of etched or engraved design, sometimes with a gold wash or gilt finish over the designs. Towards the middle of the eighteenth century, it became common practice to apply fire blueing to the blades. The etching or engravings might still be gold filled or have a gold wash around them with blueing covering the remainder of the blade, but only up to the extent of the designs where the blue would end with just a straight edge. By the end of the eighteenth

German hunters, c.1850.

century and into the nineteenth century, this blued area would be ended with scroll-like design rather than a straight edge. These decorated areas usually extended anywhere from one fourth to three fourths the length of the blade with the remaining portion being left in the bright.

SCABBARDS

The hunting sword scabbard was in itself a very skilled piece of work, with each one individually constructed and fitted in its own sword. The earlier scabbards were normally made of thin shaped pieces of wood, glued together to form a rigid base for an external covering of parchment, calfskin or morocco leather. From approximately the beginning of the 1800's, these scabbards would have been made of formed and hardened leather with no wood core.

Scabbard mounts normally consisted of the locket at the upper end and the chape at the tip. A stud was fixed to the locket that would catch in the eye of the frog attached to or formed as part of a waist or shoulder belt.

On some occasions a pair of clip-like projections were attached to the locket for a belt to be slipped through or a third mount was used somewhat below the locket with carrying rings on each for a two point suspension from the belt, with either chain or straps.

Scabbard mounts were made en-suite and often displayed very fine decoration. A pocket was sometimes constructed in the locket mount, which contained a small knife, a knife and fork, or a knife and fork with other utensils. The handles on these tools were designed to go with the rest of the outfit to form a matched set or trousse.

DECORATIVE THEMES

Naturally, on hunting sword hilts and blades, the hunting theme was most popular and comprised game animals, stag and boar, hunters on foot or mounted, stands of hunting implements, including spears, swords and horns. Diana (goddess of the hunt), or the miracle of St. Hubert (the patron saint of hunters) might also be worked into the decoration. Next to hunting themes, other motifs included mythical subjects, classical military scenes and numerous grotesque faces or masks. Stages of the moon, signs of the zodiac and astrological symbols with magical signs and numbers (added to bring luck to the hunter), are also common.

Although not a new innovation, a combination hunting sword with an in-built firearm gave the hunter a reserve shot in an emergency situation. Whatever advantage a combination weapon of this sort could offer was probably offset by its weight and clumsiness.

During the late nineteenth century, hunting swords became less functional and were carried mostly for fashion and ceremonial purposes. Purely show pieces were displayed at international exhibitions, with all manner of fantasy subjects worked into the hilt designs.

Hunting swords were still manufactured into the twentieth century and are even made today, although they have become more of a long knife with a quite standard shape, without knuckle guards and with fairly common etching styles to the blade. The Nazi regime in Germany brought about a resurgence to this style of sword with hunting associations and forestry services carrying hunting swords.

DATING

*T*he older hunting swords resemble more closely the short sword of the period, while the later hunting swords conform more to a knife-like style, with a very cruciform shape prominent after the beginning of the nineteenth century.

*T*hrough the seventeenth and the first part of the eighteenth centuries, a baroque style was used. Based on classical ideals it was ebullient in spirit and characterised by rich decorative effects and the use of prolific foliage, rounded contours and heavy symmetrical volutes.

*B*y the mid-eighteenth century, the rococo fashion was in vogue. An imaginative and vivacious style, it combined with fantasy and charm with motifs based on shell and rock forms, foliage, flowers, "C" scrolls and tortuous curves. In the beginning of the nineteenth century, neo-classicism was in favour, with more simple and restrained lines and curves with Greek or Roman decoration.

*A*ny person who decides to make hunting swords either most or part of their collection will find many varieties of these swords with almost each one a distinct example. Up until recently, hunting swords were priced very reasonably, but as with the militaria field in general, prices have risen quite steeply in recent times. They are an area of interest for a limited number of collectors, so good deals are still a possibility. Forgeries are not known as manufacture costs for these highly decorative pieces would be prohibitive. Collectors should look out for repairs, additions and marriage (where hilts and blades from different swords are assembled).

BOOK REFERENCES

The Hunting Book of Wolfgang Birkner - Translated by Atya and Ivo T. Havlu.

Der Hirshfanger - Gerhard Seifert.

A Handbook of Court and Hunting Swords 1660 – 1820 - P. Carrington-Pierce.

Hunting Weapons - Howard L. Blackmore.

Sport in Art from the Fifteenth to the Eighteenth Century - William A. Baillie-Grohman.

Hunting and Shooting from Earliest times to the Present Day - Michael Brander.

Hunting - Gunnar Busewitz.

The Metropolitan Museum of Art, Catalogue of European Court Swords and Hunting Swords, including the ELLIS, DE DINO RIGGS, and REUBELL collections - Bashford Dean.

Jagdwaffen und Jagderat des Historischen Museums zu Dresden Johannes Schobel/Aufnahmen Von Jurgen Karpinski - Deutsches Jagdmuseum Munchen - *Katalog 1977.*

Histoire des Armes de Chasse et de Leurs Empiois - P.L.Ducharte.

Baxter's Game Book - Ed. John Mowbrays.

Nove Secoli di Armi da Caccia - Lionello G. Boccia.

A Boar Hunt.

HUNTING SWORDS

www.michaellong.com

C.1700 SAWBACK HUNTING SWORD
VALUE: $ 1110.00/£ 695.00
Early example with sawback blade, horn grips and brass hilt mounts.

www.michaellong.com

C.1730 SAWBACK HUNTING SWORD
VALUE: $ 795.00/£ 495.00
C.1700's example with sawback blade, horn grips and highly decorative brass hilt mounts.

www.michaellong.com

C.1850 GERMAN HUNTING SWORD
VALUE: $ 1100.00/£ 695.00
Brass mounted hunting sword of typical form. Staghorn grip with applied brass acorn studs. The sword displays unusual stag head and hunting dog quillons. Blade with frost-etched hunting scenes.

www.michaellong.com

Hunting sword hilt, c.1800.

C.1750 ENGLISH HUNTING SWORD
VALUE: $ 695.00/ £1100.00

Hunting sword of simple form with staghorn handle and crudely cast brass shell guard and pommel mounts. Blade is impressed with the running fox mark of Samuel Harvey of Birmingham. The firm of Harvey was regarded with great renown in Birmingham, and witnessed four generations of swordmakers (Samuel, George, Joseph and William). Their years of business were c.1748-1897. The use of a running fox motif to the blade was deemed a gentle mockery of the contemporary use of the running wolf mark by German Solingen swordmakers.

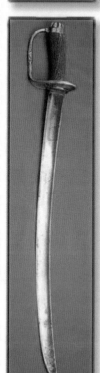

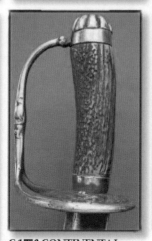

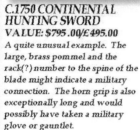

www.michaellong.com

C.1750 CONTINENTAL HUNTING SWORD
VALUE: $795.00/£495.00

A quite unusual example. The large, brass pommel and the rack(?) number to the spine of the blade might indicate a military connection. The horn grip is also exceptionally long and would possibly have taken a military glove or gauntlet.

C.1750 SPANISH HUNTING SWORD
VALUE: $ 630.00/£ 395.00

Of typical form with horn grip and silver twistwire. Brass hilt mounts. Blade is richly decorated and engraved "Toledo".

C.1750 GERMAN HUNTING SWORD
VALUE: $ 950.00/£595.00

Brass mounted hunting sword with decorative bone handle. Blade has engraved motifs including Turk's Head and mystical (caballistic) numbers (see above right).

www.antiqueswords.com

www.antiqueswords.com

www.antiqueswords.com

www.michaellong.com

www.michaellong.com

C.1900 GERMAN HUNTING SWORD
VALUE: $ 950.00/£595.00

With excellent frost etching to the blade.

C.1870 GERMAN HUNTING SWORD
VALUE: $ 630.00/£395.00

C.1800 FRENCH HUNTING SWORD
VALUE: $1215.00/£695.00

A fine example in excellent condition with much original fire-gilt remaining to the hilt and scabbard mounts. Hilt with horn grip and brass twist-wire. The blade is likely to have had extensive blue and gilt decoration. Scabbard mounts are also decorated with heavily chased and stylised floral motifs. It is rare to find such a complete piece.

French hunting scene, c.1650.

C.1750 FRENCH HUNTING SWORD
VALUE: $ 1270.00/£795.00
Good quality example with gilded blade.

*Blade detail to
hunting sword,
c.1750.*

*Blade detail to
hunting sword,
c.1850.*

Scottish hunters, c.1800.

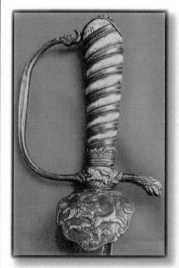

www.michaellong.com

www.michaellong.com

C.1750 HUNTING SWORD
VALUE: $ 950.00/£595.00

Good quality example with green stained horn grip and copper and silver wire banding. Solid brass shell guard with hunting scenes. Although the hunting sword was developed primarily as an edged weapon for hunters, it was also the weapon of choice for many military officers, both in the army and navy. The short blade length was especially suitable for use on board the deck of a ship, unlike a long-bladed sword that could easily be caught up in the numerous rigging and tackle on board ship. There are many contemporary portraits of British naval officers that clearly depict them as carrying a hunting sword. Likewise, army officers of this period also favoured a practical short sword, particularly during the Indian Wars of the 1750's, when many skirmishes took place within the restricted confines of the dense North American forests. The hunting sword was also carried during the American Revolutionary War.

www.michaellong.com

www.michaellong.com

C.1750 HUNTING SWORD
VALUE: $ 630.00/£ 395.00

Probably French or German with steel mounts to hilt and scabbard. Dog-head(?) quillons and tooled leather decoration to the scabbard. The grip is ebony with brass banding.

C.1750 HUNTING SWORD
VALUE: $ 630.00/£ 395.00

Silver-hilted with hallmarks to the crossguard. Grotesque lionshead pommel and stained ivory grip.

C.1770 HUNTING SWORD
VALUE: $ 250.00/ £400.00

Unusual hilt with folded brass pommel and curved horn(?) grips.

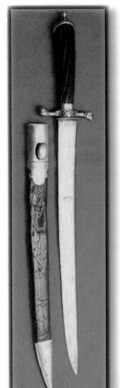

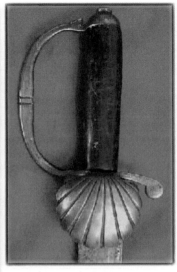

C.1750 HUNTING SWORD/ DIRK
VALUE: $630.00/£395.00

Of hunting sword form with a short blade and attractive spiral, ebony grip. Is unusual to find with original scabbard. The hilt quillons have stylised dog heads.

C.1750 HUNTING SWORD
VALUE: $950.00/£595.00

Of a type also carried by French infantry units. Simple in design and construction, with a smooth wood grip. It proved an inexpensive military hanger.

C.1770 HUNTING SWORD
VALUE: $4000.00/ £2500.00

Solid silver lionshead hilt with silver scabbard mounts. Grip comprises ivory and silver banding. The scabbard leather is likely to be a later replacement but retains the original mounts. Blade with faint decoration, including trophies of arms and foliage. Most of these lionshead hilts have a loose chain for the guard. It would have been attached to the mouth and extended down to the upturned quillon. There are no silver hallmarks visible.

Above:
C.1770 HUNTING SWORD
VALUE: $630.00/£395.00

Simple design with brass heart-shaped guard. Possibly American in origin and also associated with use as a naval cutlass.

Right:
C.1770 HUNTING SWORD
VALUE: $950.00/£595.00

With gilded ormulu decoration to the hilt.

www.michaeldlong.com

www.michaeldlong.com

www.michaeldlong.com

C.1780 HUNTING SWORD
VALUE: $ 1110.00/£ 695.00

With spiral carved horn grip and brass
crossguard cast with hunting dogs. Shell
guard comprising a winged angel motif.

**Sawback blade to
hunting sword. c.1700.**

Right and below:
C.1870 GERMAN
HUNTING SWORD
VALUE: $ 4000.00/£2500.00

Superb example of a
German presentation quality
late Victorian hunting sword.
Both hilt and scabbard mounts
are manufactured in cut steel
with recessed gilt highlighting.
Blade is plain with fishskin
covering to the scabbard. All
mounts are decorated with
classical motifs and stylised
hunting scenes.

C.1880 GERMAN
HUNTING SWORD
VALUE: $ 630.00/£ 395.00

Manufactured by J.A. Henckels
(see below).

www.antiqueswords.com

www.antiqueswords.com

**C.1700 GERMAN
HUNTING SWORD**
VALUE: $1430.00/£895.00
*Fine staghorn grip and blade
deeply stamped with a king's
head. It is possibly from the
workshop of Johannes Wundes
III (1660-1699).*

**1840 GERMAN
HUNTING TROUSSE**
VALUE: $950.00/£595.00
*With curved horn grips and
etched blade: "Fur Gott, Ehre,
Vaterland, Steyr, 1840".*

Above:
**Hilt detail to a c.1720 hunting
sword.**

**C.1880 GERMAN/
AUSTRIAN
HUNTING SWORD**
VALUE: $640.00/
£400.00
*Unmarked sawback
hunting sword with slab
horn grips. It was
probably carried by a
hunting aide. The large
and heavy sawback blade
is for chopping and
sawing through bone, and
would have been a very
effective hunting tool.*
Left:
**C.1880 POLISH
/RUSSIAN
HUNTING SWORD**
VALUE: $795.00/
£495.00
*Of possible Polish or
Russian origin. Hilt
comprises raised gold
collars and rings.*

**C.1700 HUNTING
SWORD**
VALUE: $1100.00/£695.00
*Unusual example with German
(Wundes) blade and brass and
staghorn grip with Scottish
thistle motif to quillon.*

www.antiqueswords.com

St. Hubert with stag.

By Permission: Kroninklijke Bibliotheek - National Library of the Netherlands.

Diana at the hunt.

By Permission: Kroninklijke Bibliotheek - National Library of the Netherlands.

Medieval hunter.

By Permission: Kroninklijke Bibliotheek - National Library of the Netherlands.

C.1750 HUNTING SWORD
VALUE: $ 950.00/£ 595.00

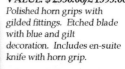

Above:
C.1780-1800 AUSTRIAN HUNTING SWORD
VALUE: $ 630.00/£ 395.00
With massive sabre-type blade and classical shellguard.

Below left:
C.1800 GERMAN HUNTING SWORD
VALUE: $ 2550.00/£ 1595.00
Polished horn grips with gilded fittings. Etched blade with blue and gilt decoration. Includes en-suite knife with horn grip.

www.guns.uk.com

C.1750 FRENCH HUNTING SWORD
VALUE: $ 630.00/£ 395.00
Delicately engraved blade and stained green ivory or bone grip.

C.1890-1900 FRENCH HUNTING SWORD
VALUE: $1100.00/£695.00
Ivory grip decorated with gold plated buttons. Acid etched blade of hunting scenes and marked "WK & C" to forte and "Stuttgart" to blade spine.

www.michaeldlong.com

C.1820-1860 FRENCH HUNTING SWORD
VALUE: $1595.00/£995.00
Carved horn grip with ornate brass fittings. Blade is marked "Coulaux de Klingenthal".

C.1890-1920 GERMAN HIRSHFANGER
VALUE: $1275.00/£795.00
Superior quality Senior Forester's hunting sword/ dagger with stag grip. Gold-plated fittings throughout hilt and scabbard. Blade engraved with hunting scenes and maker marked to Eichorn.

C.1800 FRENCH HUNTING SWORD
VALUE: $950.00/£595.00
Carved horn grip with silver gripwire. Blade is engraved with boars and stags in panels.

C.1770-1800 FRENCH HUNTING SWORD
VALUE: $2195.00/£1255.00
A very fine example in excellent condition. Ebony grip plates with silver buttons. All fittings are silver, including the hilt chain. Gilt-etched blade is highly decorated.
Left:
C.1760 FRENCH HUNTING SWORD
VALUE: $1040.00/£595.00
Large incised slab horn grip with steel hilt mounts and inner steel escutcheon engraved with a crown over "RP".

C.1870 GERMAN HUNTING SWORD
VALUE: $630.00/£395.00
With a heavy, single-edged blade and spear point. Grip is of staghorn with three plain studs of acorn design. The crossguard and shell guard is manufactured from thick gauge brass. The plain style of the sword indicates the simplication of design that was noted during the last years when hunting swords were in widespread use. They contrast sharply with the ornate examples noted in the late-eighteenth and early nineteenth centuries.

www.guns.uk.com

www.guns.uk.com

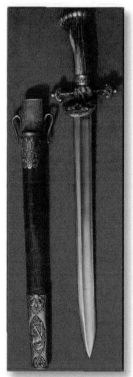

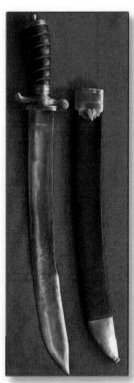

www.antiqueswords.com

www.michaellong.com

www.michaellong.com

www.michaellong.com

www.antiqueswords.com

C.1830-1860 GERMAN HIRSCHFANGER
VALUE: $1110.00/£695.00
Stag-horn grip surrounded by highly decorative brass fittings, including an ornate scabbard with lizard skin covering. Has an opening for an en-suite knife (missing). Blade marked with the Cross of Jerusalem. This identifies the sword as being manufactured by F.S. Jung of Solingen, Germany (1836-1862).

C.1820-1850 FRENCH HUNTING SWORD
VALUE: $1275.00/£795.00
Polished horn grip with braided wire wrap and brass fittings and leather on wood scabbard. Clean, unmarked blade.

C.1750-1790 GERMAN HUNTING SWORD
VALUE: $1100.00/ £695.00
Stag horn grip with brass plated pommel and scabbard mounts.

C.1800 GERMAN HUNTING SWORD AND .40 CAL. FLINTLOCK PISTOL COMBINATION
VALUE: $3200.00/£2000.00
Straight, single-edged sawtooth blade with double fullers. Typical horn handle with shallow flutes, steel knucklebow and pommel. Typical pierced shell guard.

C.1800 FRENCH HUNTING SWORD
VALUE: $1275.00/£795.00
Unusual piece with superbly carved part-lion, part-human ebony grip. Steel crossguard with hunting dog finials.

Right:
C.1760 FRENCH HUNTING SWORD
VALUE: $950.00/£595.00

www.guns.uk.com

Engraving of a hunt, c.1550 (probably Jost Amman).

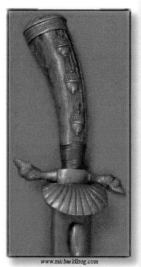

C.1870 GERMAN HUNTING SWORD
VALUE: $795.00/£495.00

C.1830 FRENCH HUNTING SWORD
VALUE: $2700.00/£1695.00

High quality hunting sword with cast gilt bronze hilt, elephant pommel and entwined animals to the grip. The damask blade features gilded panels, showing hunting scenes and trophies. The leather scabbard with embossed and gilded mounts. This is very much a dress sword and unlikely to have been used in the hunt.

C.1940 GERMAN HUNTING SWORD
VALUE: $1100.00/£695.00

With blackened steel finish and staghorn grip. Crossguard is engraved with a swastika motif. Blade is plain and the sword is complete with steel mounted leather scabbard and original black leather belt frog.

C.1935 GERMAN HUNTING SWORD
VALUE: $1275.00/£795.00

Nazi shooting association hunting sword.

1937 GERMAN HUNTING SWORD
VALUE: **$1595.00/£995.00**
Nazi commemorative hunting sword in honour of Hermann Goering. Signed to the blade and dated. Staghorn grip with brass mounts.

C.1850 GERMAN (BAVARIAN) HUNTING SWORD
VALUE: **$1595.00/£995.00**
Excellent quality example with plain blade and gilt brass decorative mounts to hilt and scabbard. Crowned "M" to scabbard chape is probably the royal cypher of Maximillian II of Bavaria (1848-1868).

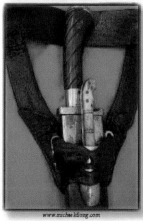

C.1820 HUNTING SWORD
VALUE: **$1100.00/£695.00**
Most hunting swords are not found with scabbard, let alone the original belt and sheath. Of simple form, the sword has a ribbed wood grip and brass mounts. The ivory hilted paring knife is probably associated.

C.1850 GERMAN HUNTING SWORD
VALUE: **$795.00/£495.00**

CAVALRY SWORDS

THE CAVALRY SWORD WAS THE PRINCIPAL and most effective weapon of the horseman. Unlike his infantry counterpart, who relied on pike, short hanger and later, musket and pistol, the cavalry soldier carried a firearm as his secondary line of defence. It was therefore crucial that he had a sword capable of having a devastating effect when used in combination with both the speed of the horse and the strength and skill of the rider. The sword needed to be heavy and robust, with a long cut and thrust blade, and large basket hilt affording adequate protection to the hand.

HISTORICAL BACKGROUND

*B*efore the Renaissance, horsemen tended to carry the same weapon as the foot soldier; that is a broad-bladed sword with a simple cross-hilt. This proved satisfactory as armour provided some protection against penetration by sword, arrow, axe or pike. The sword hand was covered with a gauntlet, so the shielding of the hand with a more protective hilt was not deemed as important. With the gradual withdrawl of armour over the next two centuries, swordmakers began to design specialised cavalry swords that protected the hand, but also allowed the horseman to despatch an enemy with a few timely and practised blade slashes and thrusts. The dichotomy between a long, straight, *"thrusting"* blade that was little more than a short spear, and a long, curved *"slashing"* blade, would tax the minds of both the military and swordmakers for the best part of four hundred years. The argument was only resolved at a much later time when the cavalry sword had become an obsolete and redundant weapon of the battlefield.

*T*he use of a straight-bladed, single-edged *"backsword"* for the cavalry had been well established by the 1600's. These swords were carried throughout Europe and became the mainstay for cavalry formations. It is only when we move into the eighteenth century that we see the growing influence of a more curved sabre. Its origins are thought to be Eurasian and Arabic. The Ottoman Turks had carried curved swords for many years. It is likely that the actual spread of the Ottoman Empire into Europe by the late 1600's, had a direct impact by enabling swordmakers to examine contemporary examples of this new form of sword and eventually interpreting them in more *"western"* sword styles.

*A*s European nations began to establish standing armies with separate infantry and cavalry regiments, so it was that within the cavalry regiments, the distinction between heavy and light cavalry was made. In general, the heavy cavalry carried a long, straight, thrusting blade and the light cavalry, a slightly shorter, slashing or slicing, curved blade.

*T*he straight, thusting blade was thought to be most effective during the initial charge and the sight of several hundred heavily armoured cuirassiers bearing down on an infantry square, was expected to cause a general panic and consequent fleeing of those soldiers on the ground. This was the case in some instances but a well trained and effective infantry square could withstand any onslaught. This was typified by the actions of the British Line Regiments at Waterloo.

Prussian cavalry, c.1760.

The curved sabre was carried by lighter cavalry troops, most notably the hussar or lancer regiments. The hussar soldier is thought to have originated in Eastern Europe, particuraly Hungary, Poland and the Balkan area. The Hungarian hussar of the 1700's used a large curved sabre, not so much in the *milieu* of the charge, but more specifically, when involved in a close-combat melee or in small skirmishes and chasing fleeing soldiers. This is where the curved sword was more practical as it could be wielded around the horse's head. A long, straight sword would not have had this manouverability.

The sheer variety and range of cavalry swords available to the collector is quite daunting, but it is clear that a number of core nations were instrumental in shaping the design and production of cavalry swords. Some are included here.

BRITAIN

Like most European nations of this period, English cavalry troops favoured a backsword during the 1600's. Common styles included an iron basket hilt with large apple-shaped pommel and a series of inter-twined bars. The design probably originated in Germany and went on to influence the Scottish hilt-makers. The so-called *"mortuary"* sword was another peculiarly English type carried at this time. It was described as such because of the application of decorative work to the hilt that featured a series of engraved human faces, supposedly those of Charles I, (executed in 1649). These swords were actually carried some time before this event, so the royal attribution is clearly unwarranted. Despite this inaccuracy, they are still regularly described as such.

The basket hilt continued to be the weapon of choice for the cavalryman well into the eighteenth century, although there was the parallel development of a more robust *"military"* version of the newly adopted smallsword. It had a bilobate counterguard and large ovoid pommel. By the mid-1700's we see a period when there were many differing styles of horseman's broadsword. This was partly due to the lack of any official regulations with regard to the appropriate sword that should be carried by the cavalry. Colonels of regiments were given the authority and funds to privately purchase swords for their soldiers. This led to some abuse, with poorly manufactured blades failing whilst in service. The centre of swordmaking at this time was Germany, where the blades were accepted to be of far better quality than the home-based English swordmakers. Measures had already been undertaken to bring over skilled German workers to establish rival firms, but it was only in the latter half of the eighteenth century, when any discernible competition from English firms started to affect imports. Even then, Germany had already effected a virtual stranglehold on the sword trade that was to last well into the nineteenth century.

This chaotic situation was addressed in 1788, when a universal sword for both the light and heavy cavalry was introduced. It took the form of a iron or steel basket hilt, with a long, straight, broad-fullered blade. The light cavalry version had a less enclosed basket, normally with three hilt bars. There was meant to be no differentiation in design for officers and men, although subtle differences in overall quality of finish can be discerned between the two. It was not a good design, with both versions badly balanced, cumbersome, and with over long blades. There was also no official system of proof at this time and blade quality was generally poor. It was back to the drawing board. In 1796, two completely new designs were issued to officers and men. Blades were now subject to official inspection and impressed stamps of a crown with inspector's number underneath, can be seen on troopers' blades from this period. The 1796 Pattern Heavy Cavalry Trooper's Sword has gained recent fame as the sword favoured by Captain Sharpe (of the Rifle Brigade), a colourful fictional character in the works of Bernard Cornwell. The practical necessity for such a large weapon by an infantry officer is a

French Cuirassiers, c.1870

little far fetched, but this does not get in the way of us enjoying his adventures! The sword is actually based on the Austrian Model 1769 Heavy Cavalry Trooper's Sword. The design of its light cavalry variant was heavily influenced by a young British cavalry officer by the name of John Gaspard Le Marchant. He had witnessed the equipment failings of the British cavalry during campaigns in the Low Countries during the 1780's, but with the fortunate patronage of King George III, was able to wield considerable influence within the military establishment, despite his junior officer status. His collaboration with the Birmingham swordmaker, Henry Osborn, produced the classic stirrup-hilted 1796 Pattern Light Cavalry Trooper's (and Officer's) Sword. Other 1796 patterns followed, including a boat shell-hilted dress sword and a series of half basket undress swords, both for the Heavy Cavalry.

The 1796 Pattern remained in use for many years and even after its obsolescence in 1821, it was still carried by militia units and native troops in India. The 1821 Pattern was a radical departure from previous designs. Again, both heavy and light cavalry versions were produced. The 1821 Pattern Light Cavalry Officer's Sword had a three-bar hilt with slightly curved pipe back, spear pointed blade. The blade was usually decorated. The light trooper's version was similar but with a plain blade and an *"ear"* to the grip backpiece. Heavy cavalry officers carried

Prussian Hussars, c.1813.

a sword with a steel bowl guard and *"honeysuckle"* piercings. Troopers carried a similar sword but with a plain bowl hilt.

The next major change occurred in 1853 when the differentiation between heavy and light cavalry troopers' swords was finally dropped in favour of a universal pattern. This was the 1853 Pattern Cavalry Trooper's Sword. It had the same guard and blade as the previous pattern but employed a new patent grip, designed by the swordmaker, Charles Reeves. It was quite revolutionary, as the full width of the tang was retained for the whole length of the grip, rather than the usual tapered form. It was then rivetted to leather grips. This new tang was stronger and more secure than earlier designs.

From the mid-nineteenth century, British cavalry swords went through a number of pattern changes. The historic argument of a thrusting versus a slashing sword continued, with many official committees sitting to ponder the question. The eventual result was an unsuitable compromise, with blades being neither fully straight or sufficiently curved. The patterns of 1864, 1882, 1885, 1890 and 1899, highlight the constant changes made to cavalry swords during this period.

The 1908 Pattern Cavalry Trooper's and the 1912 Cavalry Officer's Sword are probably the most radical of all known sword designs. They comprise a thin, rapier-like blade, enclosed bowl hilt and unique pistol grip. It was as far away from traditional sword design as could be possible, but finally resolved the argument of a thrusting versus slashing blade. This pattern was an unashamedly thrusting sword and designed for the cavalry charge. The grip of the trooper's version was manufactured in a new composite material, dermatine (the officer's sword retained a fishskin covering), and included a depression for the thumb, to enable the carrier to grip the sword in a fashion similar to the gripping of a lance. Despite the fact that King Edward VII described the new design as *"hideous"*, the 1908 Pattern went into production. The advent of the First War was thought to be the ideal testing ground for this pattern, but it actually sounded its deathknell. Confronted with the immoveable battlefield of the Western Front, the need for masses of cavalry on the move was now redundant. The last massed British cavalry charge was at the Battle of Mughar, near Jerusalem, on the 13th November 1917, where a combined force of the Buckinghamshire Hussars, supported by the Dorset and Berkshire Yeomanry Regiments, overran a significant Turkish position, capturing hundreds of prisoners.

FRANCE

As with most European countries in the seventeenth and early eighteenth centuries, the French cavalryman carried a sword similar to that of other nations. It would probably have been either brass or iron hilted with a long, straight blade. A sword based on the *"Walloon"* pattern (Model 1679) was carried by cavalry officers during the latter half of the seventeeth century. There followed a series of cavalry patterns based on this hilt form. In the mid-1700's, dragoons carried brass-hilted swords with single and S-Bar hilts. Unlike the English military, the French had already formalised a system of regulation sword models some years earlier, producing quite an extensive range of models for different branches of the cavalry.

In the 1770's, an attractive fan or shell-shaped hilt was adopted for both officers and troopers. Pommels were round or ovoid. Later examples during the Napoleonic period had a flat, cap pommel. Officers' blades were also blued.

Russian Lancer, c.1854.

The appearance of Napoleon Bonaparte coincided with a great revival of ancient classical designs, particularly in architecture. It was not lost on French swordmakers who turned out a series of superb, classically inspired cavalry swords. Napoleon shrewdly understood the importance of appearance amongst his army, and many new cavalry sword designs were introduced during this period. One of the most influential of designs was the Model ANIX Cuirassier Trooper's Sword. It was a heavy sword, with a four-bar cast brass hilt and long, two fullered and single-edged blade. It was a fearsome weapon and caused more fatal injuries to British troops than the hatchet-bladed swords of the British Heavy Cavalry regiments. The light cavalry soldier carried a elegant three-bar brass hilted sword with curved blade. An officer's version is also encountered. Hussar regiments favoured a stirrup-hilted light cavalry sword. Elite regiments such as the Imperial Guard Dragoons carried a sword with brass hilt, cap pommel and knucklebow, with two supplementary bars holding an oval, upon which was placed a silvered or brass flaming grenade badge. The *Mousquetaires de la Garde du Roi*, who acted as the royal bodyguard to Louis XVIII during the short period after Napoleon abdicated his throne, carried a very elegant sword, similar to the Imperial Guard Dragoons, but having a cross with fleur-de-lys and sun rays, within the hilt oval.

Swords issued to cavalry troopers were invariably marked on the spine of the blade with the year, month and place of manufacture. From the 1700's, the town of Klingenthal, in Alsace, became a centre of swordmaking for the French military. It was the official government manufactory, and produced an enormous quantity of military swords both before and after the French Revolution. Blades produced during the monarchy period are marked either with a Royal designation e.g. *"R^{le}"* or Imperial (Bonapartist) designation e.g. *"I$_{mp}{}^{le}$"*.

Dragoon, Imperial Russian Guard, c.1854.

including a version with hidden chape and another with multiple brass bandings. Other German states, including the Baden Dragoons and Saxon Cuirassiers, copied this form of broadsword and placed their own state arms within the hilt bars. Hussars carried a typical stirrup or three-bar hilted sword (Prussian Model 1791, Bavarian Model 1813, and Wurttemburg Model 1817).

Following the defeat of Napoleon in 1815, large numbers of French cuirassiers' swords were obtained by Prussia and used by Guard Cuirassier Regiments and the *Garde du Corps*, well into the nineteenth century. They are distinguished by Prussian regimental marks to the hilt and scabbard. In 1819, a new model of cuirassier's sword was introduced. It was heavily influenced by contemporary Russian patterns. A forward leaning or canted pommel is emblematic of this design.

German cavalry swords of the mid-nineteenth century were very similar to their French counterparts, with three or four-bar brass hilts, domed pommels and long, straight, single or double-fullered blades. Officers carried a gilt brass version. They were all sheathed in heavy steel scabbards. The light cavalry or *Uhlans*, carried a sword that was almost identical to the British 1796 Pattern Light Cavalry Trooper's Sword. This was the Model 1811 *"Blucher"* Cavalry Sabre. It comprised a steel stirrup hilt, single-fullered curved blade, and steel scabbard. This sword is common in the market and routinely confused with the British pattern. Factors that diffentiate the two include a much thicker knucklebow and different scabbard shoe to the Model 1811. They also tend to be regimentally stamped to the hilt and scabbard throat, sometimes with multiple crossings out, indicating long service lives in several regiments. The British 1796 Pattern Light Cavalry Sword is very rarely regimentally marked. The Model 1873 Pattern *Uhlan* Sword is a slightly less heavier version of the Model 1811. Apart from the elite cuirassiers who carried their own patterns, other German heavy cavalry regiments were issued with the Model 1852 Cavalry Sword, with steel, half basket hilt.

In 1889, a universal pattern of cavalry trooper's sword was developed for use by all cavalry regiments apart from the cuirassiers and Uhlans. It was also partly a response to the perceived need for a sword that reflected the newly unified nature of the German Empire. It comprised a blackened steel half basket hilt with a side guard upon which was inset the individual German state arms to which the

regiment belonged. When off duty, cavalry officers carried a gilt brass, stirrup-hilted dress sword with lionshead pommel. It was similar to infantry swords but featured a crossed sabres design in the hilt langet. If using a sword on active service, an ordinary cavalry officer carried a more ornate version of the 1889 Trooper's model, with either etched or blued decoration to the blade. Unlike most European swords of this period that had long dropped the use of gilding and blueing to blades, German swordmakers continued to decorate their blades in this manner right up until, and during the First World War.

Austria or the Austro-Hungarian Empire, had a range of differing cavalry swords that reflected the great ethnic and cultural diversity of its sphere of influence. They tend not to be as common as German swords, but are actually more interesting in their variety and breadth of design. Recent publications on this subject have revealed that the Austrian military needed little encouragment to design a new sword for every branch of both military and civilian service.

The Austrian cuirassier of the mid-1700's carried a heavy, hatchet-pointed, single-edged and disc-hilted broadsword (Model 1769) that became the future inspiration for the British 1796 Pattern Heavy Cavalry Trooper's Sword. The NCO's version had a lionshead pommel. Further modified versions are noted in 1775 and 1798. A Model 1768 Cavalry Sabre was

British Royal Horse Artillery, c.1864.

carried by hussars, and featured a stirrup hilt with wide, curving blade. The Model 1798 Cavary Sabre had a straight, single-edged blade with spear point and knuckleguard that widened into a pierced shell. Scabbards are likely to have been leather with iron mounts. Hussars continued to carry stirrup-hilted swords throughout the 1800's, following the design styles of other European armies. The Model 1837 Cavalry Sabre saw light cavalry officers carrying a very curved sword with an exaggerated stirrup hilt.

*A*ustria introduced a universal pattern of cavalry sword in 1845. It has a steel half bowl guard pierced with round holes. Some further changes were made in 1861 authorising its wear by both officers and men. Officers' versions are normally of higher quality with blade decoration. There was also a Model 1850 Cavalry Officer's and Trooper's Sword, followed by a Model 1858, Model 1861, Model 1869, Model 1875, and Model 1877. The collector can see from this that there is great scope for collecting Austrian cavalry swords! This list does not include the elite Guards' regiments, mounted infantry troops and regional forces.

*T*he Model 1904 Cavalry Trooper's Sword was the final pattern of cavalry sword issued to Austrian troops.

RUSSIA

*T*he Imperial Russian government had very tight control over sword manufacture until after the 1860's, when the market was opened to commercial sword-makers. They did this through a number of government administered sword factories. During the eighteenth century, the principal factories were located at Zlatoust and Tula. Skilled German swordmakers were also encouraged to work at Zlatoust, and their knowledge ensured that the swords produced would be of very high quality.

*T*he Russian Dragoon Trooper's Sword of the early 1700's was similar to German swords of the period, with a large protective brass shell guard upon which was engraved the monogram of Empress Elixaveta Petrovna (*"EPI"*). Dragoon swords of the mid-1700's also had a bird's head pommel. Cuirassiers carried a straight bladed sword with a wide, sweeping brass guard etched with the monogram of the reigning monarch. This was a feature on most Russian broadswords of the eighteenth century. Two patterns were issued in 1763; the Horse Guard's and Carabinier's Broadsword. The Horse Guard's sword had a three-bar hilt with the hilt branches placed horizontally on top of eachother. The Carabinier's sword included a large brass plate guard. The elite Chevalier Guards regiment carried an elaborate basket hilt with the

Bengal Lancers, c.1890.

Imperial Russian royal coat of arms placed within a hilt cartouche. Ordinary cavalry troopers carried a simplified version.

By the 1800's, the Russian military were being strongly influenced by French sword styles. A dragoon pattern was introduced in 1806 and a new sword for cuirassiers, in 1809. They copied the typical French design of a brass, three or four-bar-hilted sword. Many cuirassier swords issued to Russian forces post-1812, were actually captured French blades. The light cavalry also used captured French Model ANXI light cavalry swords and produced their own version which is almost identical (Model 1827).

As Russia grew both in prosperity and influence during the mid-1800's, it began to celebrate and promote its own cultural identity. This re-birth of nationalism was also felt in sword design and no more so than in cavalry swords. Recent experience of wars in the Caucausus, directly influenced a new style of *"Asiatic"* sword. It is known as the *"shashka"* and was first introduced in 1834. Its originated from Caucasian shashkas that had a plain grip, no knucklebow and a slightly curved, single-edged blade. It is strange that previously held beliefs in the concept of sword hand

protection were so easily abandoned. Subsequent models for both Cossack regiments and ordinary cavalry regiments were introduced in 1841 (with knucklebow), 1865 and 1868. A special commission was established in the late-nineteenth century to design a new universal type of cavalry sword. In 1881, it was formally adopted. It had a ribbed wooden grip, domed pommel and brass D-ring knucklebow. The blade was slightly curved. An interesting addition to this model was the attachment of special scabbard mounts to allow the carrying of a Model 1891 Moisin Nagant socket bayonet. This is not known on any other cavalry sword. The Model 1909 Cavalry Officer's sword had a ribbed composition grip with the Imperial Russian royal cypher (Nicholas II) on the pommel cap. The knucklebow, hilt bars and blade were also decorated.

Like their infantry and naval counterparts, presentation swords were a common feature within the cavalry regiments of the Imperial Russian Army. They are usually based on official sword patterns, but with profuse gilt (and sometimes solid gold) decoration to the hilt, blade and scabbard. Enamelled decorations or orders are also affixed to the hilt pommel and crossguard ecusson.

Charge of the Imperial Russian Chevalier Guards, Battle of Austerlitz, 1806.

UNITED STATES

The American War of Independence was a conflict in which the two opposing sides seemed quite mismatched in terms of edged weaponry. The colonists fighting against the English and her allies, would have carried very much the same swords as their enemies. Importantly, they are more likely to have used captured swords rather than domestically manufactured weapons. Blacksmiths did forge military blades but they were usually quite crude, although reasonably effective in the field. Plain hilts were also favoured, with the slotted type a popular choice. Blades tended to be flat and unfullered. In the absence of any official style of sword for the new "*Continental Army*", American swordmakers simply copied or interpreted patterns available at that time. The main priority was to produce swords quickly to fulfill a serious shortfall in serviceable weapons.

The American horseman's sword of the 1770's had a range of pommel shapes, including ball, urn, cap, ovoid, high domed and flat. Animal forms were also incorporated into the pommel and included horsehead, dog-head and lionshead. They were imitating English styles of the period but can be differentiated by their relative naivety. This is in itself a particular charm that makes these swords highly collectable. The stirrup-hilted, curved sabre and the basket hilt

Latvian cavalry troopers, c.1911.

were also favoured by cavalry troops, both officers and men. It was only after independence had been won that the new Administration could begin to consider introducing a distinctive "*American*" pattern of cavalry sword. The new American Congress did not want to rely on overseas countries for their swords and a domestic manufacturer was quickly sought. The Model 1798 Cavalry Trooper's Sword had a simple stirrup guard with a leather on wood covered grip and single-edged, curved blade. They were first supplied by Nathan Starr of Middleton, Connecticut, and afterwards, by the newly established Virginia Manufactory or State Armory. Updated versions of this sword were produced by Starr between 1814 and 1818.

By 1833, the N. P. Ames Sword Company of Springfield, Massachusetts, began manufacturing a standard steel, three-bar- hilted cavalry sword with slightly curved blade. It was a short-lived pattern and in 1840, a cavalry trooper's sword of French style, was introduced. It had a typical heavy cast brass, three -bar hilt, and slightly curved blade with steel scabbard, grudgingly known by its users as the "*wristbreaker*". It was replaced in 1860 by a lighter version, and updated in 1872 and 1906. Officers carried a more elaborate version of these patterns with etched blades and embossed hilts. The Model 1913 "*Patton*" hilt cavalry trooper's sword is based on a design by Lieutenant George S. Patton, later to become the famous US General. It owes more than a passing nod to the British 1908 Pattern Cavalry Trooper's Sword and differed only in having a bird's head pommel and slightly lower basket guard. The straight blade is again a little wider than the British version and also double-fullered. Scabbards are either wood with canvas or nickel-plated steel.

COLLECTING CAVALRY SWORDS

The cavalry sword, particularly the trooper's, endured a very hard service life. Collectors should therefore be tolerant and not expect pristine examples of these swords. Scabbards are also the natural loser when it comes to service wear. Many are found dented near the end where the scabbard bounced against other equipment during the gallop.

There are copies of various patterns of cavalry swords, most notably the US Model 1860 Cavalry Trooper's Sword, Model 1913 Cavalry Trooper's Sword, Russian Model 1881 Cossack shasquas and British 1912 Pattern Cavalry Officer's Sword. The French Model XI Heavy Cavalry Cuirassier's Sword is also heavily copied.

C.1780 CAVALRY OFFICER'S SWORD
VALUE: $1910.00/£1195.00
Fine example with delicate S-Bar cut steel hilt. Blade is also quite narrow. Although possibly used in the field, this might have also been a dress piece.

C.1780 HEAVY CAVALRY OFFICER'S SWORD
VALUE: $2700.00/£1695.00
A much heavier and more robust example than that shown opposite. This is the pre-cursor to the 1788 Pattern Heavy Cavalry Officer's Sword. Has a heavy and wide, single-fullered blade with open basket hilt, white sharkskin grip and brass twistwire. The pommel is of a large bun type, later replaced by the more typical ovoid, plain or fluted pommel.

1788 PATTERN HEAVY CAVALRY TROOPER'S SWORD
VALUE: $1910.00/£1195.00
This sword was the first officially regulated cavalry pattern in the British Army. It is found in both trooper and officer's versions. The trooper's sword has a typically plain blade with either a leather or fishskin grip. Hilt is of half basket form.

www.michaelclong.com

www.michaelclong.com

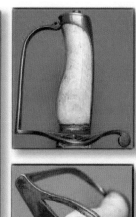

www.michaelclong.com

C.1790 HEAVY CAVALRY OFFICER'S SWORD
VALUE: $2550.00/£1595.00
An interesting example of a non-regulation officer's sword. It is possible that this was carried by an officer in the Horse Guards.

www.michaelclong.com

C.1760 HORSEMAN'S SWORD
VALUE: $2075.00/£1295.00
This sword would have been carried by a dragoon. It was a new departure from previous Scottish inspired basket hilts.

C.1800 CAVALRY OFFICER'S SWORD
VALUE: $1595.00/£995.00

Battle of Waterloo, 1815.

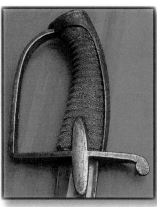

1788 PATTERN LIGHT CAVALRY OFFICER'S SWORD
VALUE: $2550.00/£1595.00
The light cavalry versions feature a stirrup hilt and broad, slightly curved blade. Both officers' and troopers' swords are very similar and it is sometimes difficult to distinguish between the two, although officer's swords tend to have decorated blades and a better standard of finish. The scabbard mounts are iron, with a leather (sometimes, fishskin) insert.

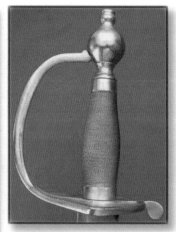

C.1780 CAVALRY OFFICER'S SWORD
VALUE: $1275.00/£795.00

C.1800 CAVALRY OFFICER'S SWORD
VALUE: $1520.00/£950.00

1796 PATTERN LIGHT CAVALRY OFFICER'S SWORD
VALUE: $1110.00/£695.00

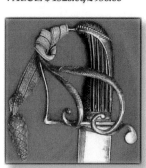

Left:
C.1800 CAVALRY OFFICER'S SWORD
VALUE: $1910.00/£1195.00
Fine example with chased gilt-brass multiple S-Bar hilt, ribbed and chequered ebony grip, and later (Victorian) sword knot. This style of sword does not conform to any authorised pattern and it is possible that it was carried by a Yeomary Officer. They tended to carry more unorthodox and unofficial swords.

Officer, 23rd Light Dragoons, 1812.

77

www.michaelllong.com

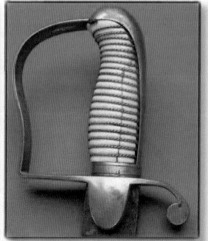

www.michaelllong.com

www.michaelllong.com

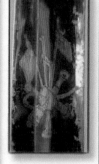

www.michaelllong.com

1796 PATTERN HEAVY CAVALRY OFFICER'S UNDRESS SWORD
VALUE: $ 4480.00/£2000.00

This is a very scarce sword. It was manufactured by Woolley & Co. of Birmingham (1785-1825). It has a steel half basket guard with triangular piercings. Handle is of ribbed leather on a wood core, with an eared steel back-strap. The hatchet blade is straight and single-edged.

Officer, Scots Greys(?), c.1820.

1796 PATTERN LIGHT CAVALRY OFFICER'S SWORD
VALUE: $ 3200.00/ £2000.00

Probably for use by a Yeomanry Officer.

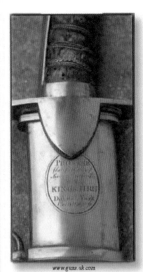

www.guns.uk.com

www.guns.uk.com

Detail of scabbard throats from 1796 Pattern Infantry Officers' swords. Makers are John Prosser (London) and Henry Osborn (Birmingham).

1796 PATTERN HEAVY CAVALRY TROOPER'S SWORD
VALUE: $2875.00/ £1795.00

This sword still retains its original hilt langets. Many examples had these removed, including the inner edge of the disc-guard that tended to fray the uniform. In the 1840's, the Royal Navy used a large number of old 1796 Heavy Cavalry troopers' blades for seamans' cutlasses.

www.guns.uk.com

www.michaeldlong.com

1788 PATTERN LIGHT CAVALRY OFFICER'S SWORD
VALUE: $1275.00/£795.00

www.michaeldlong.com

C.1780 CAVALRY OFFICER'S SWORD
VALUE: $2875.00/£1795.00

Blade detail from 1803 Pattern Infantry Officer's Sword.

Capture of the French Eagle by Sergeant Ewart of the Scots Greys, Waterloo, 1815.

1788 PATTERN LIGHT CAVALRY OFFICER'S SWORD
VALUE: $1275.00/£795.00

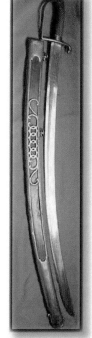

C.1800 VOLUNTEER LIGHT CAVALRY OFFICER'S SWORD
VALUE: $1275.00/£795.00

1796 PATTERN LIGHT CAVALRY TROOPER'S SWORD
VALUE: $720.00/£450.00

Maker's name to blade forte.

1788 PATTERN LIGHT CAVALRY OFFICER'S SWORD
VALUE: $1695.00/£970.00
Unusual variant with ribbed walnut(?) grip. Most British examples of this pattern have either fishskin or leather wrap to the grips. This sword might have been produced for an officer of a volunteer cavalry regiment as they were required to purchase their own swords, uniform and equipment. This sometimes led to more ornate and unusual embellishment that would not have been seen (or probably tolerated) in regular army units.

C.1800 VOLUNTEER LIGHT CAVALRY OFFICER'S SWORD
VALUE: $1910.00/£1195.00
Many volunteer or yeomanry cavalry regiments adopted this style of sword. They are normally identified by the use of a gilt-brass hilt and ivory grip.

80

Above and above right:
1796 PATTERN LIGHT CAVALRY OFFICER'S SWORD
VALUE: $1275.00/£795.00

Of unusual form, with a curved backstrap and pommel. Blade is engraved to both sides with the following:

> NO ME SAQUES
> SIN RASON
> NO ME ENBAINES
> SIN HONOR

This translates as:

> DO NOT USE ME
> WITHOUT REASON
> DO NOT DRAW ME
> WITHOUT HONOUR

This motto was popular during the eighteenth century.

1796 PATTERN LIGHT CAVALRY TROOPER'S SWORD
VALUE: $795.00/£495.00

1796 PATTERN LIGHT CAVALRY OFFICER'S SWORD
VALUE: $1095.00/£625.00

The langets have been removed from this hilt, probably to ease removal of the sword from the scabbard. It also retains the original steel and leather mounted scabbard.

1796 PATTERN LIGHT CAVALRY TROOPER'S SWORD
VALUE: $795.00/£495.00

1796 PATTERN LIGHT CAVALRY OFFICER'S SWORD
VALUE: $1110.00/£695.00

Interesting example with a pronounced "beak" pommel and plain, pipe back blade. Hilts of this style have sometimes been associated with Scottish regiments, although very few have relevant engraving or markings to hilt or blade to enable positive identification.

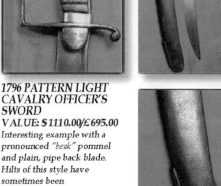

Death of Sir Edward Pakenham, New Orleans, 1815.

C.1800 YEOMANRY CAVALRY OFFICER'S SWORD

VALUE: $1520.00/£950.00

A high quality example, and very much typical of the non-regulation style of sword carried by yeomanry officers. With decorative gilt brass and leather scabbard.

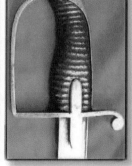

1788 PATTERN CAVALRY TROOPER'S SWORD

VALUE: $950.00/£595.00

1796 PATTERN CAVALRY OFFICER'S SWORD

VALUE: $950.00/£595.00

Blade is plain and with a hatchet point. Standard steel stirrup hilt. With leather binding and silver twistwire to the grip.

1796 PATTERN CAVALRY TROOPER'S SWORD

VALUE: $950.00/£595.00

Note the "ear" to backstrap.

1796 PATTERN HEAVY CAVALRY OFFICER'S DRESS SWORD

VALUE: $1110.00/£695.00

Plain blade is marked "Runkel" within the central fuller. Grip is minus the usual silver twistwire. Typical boat shell hilt and ovoid pommel.

Above and below left:

C.1820 CAVALRY OFFICER'S SWORD

VALUE: $1750.00/£1095.00

Late Georgian example of a stirrup-hilted officer's sword. With typical swirling floral decoration. Blade features the royal cypher of King George IV (1820-1830).

C.1800 YEOMANRY CAVALRY OFFICER'S SWORD

VALUE: $950.00/£595.00

With finely chequered ivory grip and brass stirrup hilt with lionshead pommel. Blade is wide, single-fullered and slightly curved.

www.michaeldlong.com

1796 PATTERN HEAVY CAVALRY TROOPER'S SWORD
VALUE: $2875.00/£1795.00

This particular example is marked on the hilt to the 2nd Dragoon Guards (Scots Greys). This regiment was immortalised in Lady Butler's painting, *"Scotland Forever"*, which depicts their famous charge at Waterloo. Many examples of this sword are encountered with the narrow langets removed. This was normally done whilst in service and served little purpose. Another modification is the cutting away of the sharp inner edge of the disc guard as it tended to fray the wearer's jacket. Originally, the blade had a hatchet point, but many examples were altered to a spear point for functionality.

1788 PATTERN LIGHT CAVALRY OFFICER'S SWORD
VALUE: $2700.00/£1695.00

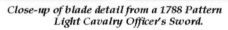

Close-up of blade detail from a 1788 Pattern Light Cavalry Officer's Sword.

Quartermaster J. Kirk, Leicestershire Yeomanry, 1841.

1796 PATTERN LIGHT CAVALRY OFFICER'S SWORD
VALUE: $4800.00/£3000.00

*Superb example of a volunteer cavalry officer's sword with very fine blue and gilt blade.
Manufactured by Henry Osborn of Birmingham (1785-1849). During the late-eighteenth and early
nineteenth century, Birmingham became the centre for swordmaking, particularly for Officers
swords. Within a relatively short period of time they were being compared favourably with the
quality of workmanship displayed by the former London swordsmiths. Birmingham had the
capacity to produce all parts for the swords, from the blade and hilt, to the scabbard. This was done
through a local network of craftsmen and women. Blade engravers and gilders, scabbard makers,
grip binders and leather workers were all called into the production of an elegant officer's sword.
Many worked from home on a piece-work basis. Women and children were especially skilful at this
detailed work. The use of mercury in the application of blue and gilt decoration to the blade caused
the early and untimely death of many workers, but wages were relatively high and great risks were
accepted and taken.*

1796 PATTERN LIGHT CAVALRY OFFICER'S SWORD
VALUE: $ 3200.00/£2000.00

This is one of the most popular British Army pattern swords for the collector, but it is rare to find an example in such good condition, and particularly one that retains most of its original blue and gilt decoration to the blade. The hilt is steel with leather and silver twistwire to the grip. Some grips are also bound in fishskin. The blade decoration is usually predictable, with motifs such as the "GR" royal cypher of King George III, royal coat of arms (both pre-1801 and post-1801), royal crown, Britannia, stands of arms and trophies. The blade is not maker marked.

The Union Brigade at Waterloo.

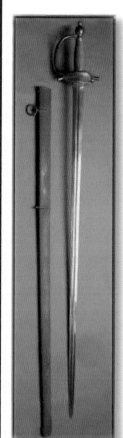

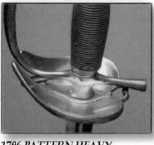

1796 PATTERN HEAVY CAVALRY OFFICER'S SWORD
VALUE: $ 1595.00/£ 995.00
With typical boat shell hilt.

A contemporary watercolour commemorating the 1804 Birmingham Sword Trials, an event arranged to highlight the superior quality of British blades over their German rivals.

1796 PATTERN LIGHT CAVALRY OFFICER'S SWORD
VALUE: $ 1795.00/ £ 2875.00
Blade spine marked to the German born blade importer, J.J. Runkel, who eventually became a naturalised Briton. The gilded coat of arms shown is the pre-1801 version.

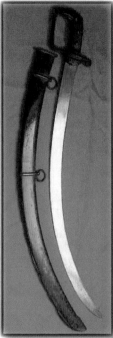

1796 PATTERN HEAVY CAVALRY OFFICER'S SWORD
VALUE: $4000.00/£2500.00

This is a very attractive sword and features the first use of what has subsequently been termed as a *"ladder"* or *"honeysuckle"* design to the hilt. It became the standard for British heavy cavalry officers' swords throughout the Victorian period. Extremely rare examples feature a blue and gilt decorated blade, but most are plain with a hatchet point. Blades are almost identical to the 1796 Pattern Heavy Cavalry Trooper's Sword and invariably maker marked to John Prosser of London (1797-1860).

Left, above and below:
C.1800 CAVALRY OFFICER'S SWORD
VALUE: $1750.00/£1095.00

Elegant example of a non-regulation officer's sword with a typical neo-classical hilt. Both hilt and scabbard still retain the original black paint finish. Blade has finely engraved decoration.

1796 PATTERN CAVALRY OFFICER'S SWORD
VALUE: $2550.00/£1595.00

A silver mounted officer's sword of 1796 Pattern Cavalry Officer's type. Blade is single-fullered and plain. It also appears never to have been engraved. The langets are engraved *"Eundring onv"* and *"CLS"*. Identification has so far proved impossible. The grip is ribbed ivory. It is likely that it was carried by a Yeomanry Officer. They had quite a leeway when it came to choice of sword, and officers with wealth lost no opportunity to purchase a sword befitting their social status.

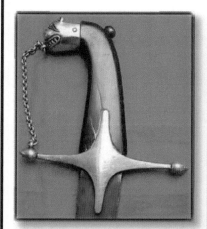

1796 PATTERN CAVALRY OFFICER'S SWORD
VALUE: $995.00/£570.00

A very clean officer's sword with pronounced pommel of *"beak-head"* form. Plain steel, clip-point blade. With its original steel scabbard. Fishskin and silver twistwire to the grip.

C.1800 INDIAN OFFICER'S SWORD
VALUE: $1275.00/£795.00

An unusual tiger's-head hilt, probably of Indian native manufacture. The blade is imported and marked with the name of swordmaker, Thomas Gill of Birmingham.

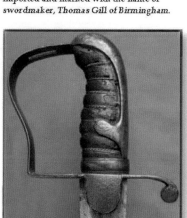

1796 PATTERN CAVALRY OFFICER'S SWORD
VALUE: $950.00/£595.00

Of typical form, with a steel, stirrup hilt and leather and silver twistwire grip.

C.1800 YEOMANRY OFFICER'S SWORD
VALUE: $1110.00/£695.00

A large sword that is likely to been carried by an officer in a mounted Yeomanry regiment.

C.1800 CAVALRY OFFICER'S SWORD
VALUE: $950.00/£595.00

Of non-regulation form, with a very detailed lionshead pommel and backstrap.

C.1800 CAVALRY OFFICER'S SWORD
VALUE: $ 1910.00/£ 1195.00

Fine all steel cavalry officer's sword with spadroon hilt and large, chequered ebony grip. It would originally have had an impressive blue and gilt blade. Some traces still remain within the etching. Manufactured in Birmingham and named on the scabbard throat to Woolley and Co.

C.1800 CAVALRY OFFICER'S SWORD
VALUE: $ 8000.00/£ 5000.00

Superb solid silver Georgian presentation quality sabre to a senior British cavalry officer. Napoleonic horse-head swords are extremely rare. This example does not bear any silver hallmarks, although similar styled swords have been noted with Irish hallmarks. The blade is marked to the famous military sword importer, J.J. Runkel. John Justus Runkel was a German immigrant who beame a British subject in 1796. He became a major importer of German manufactured blades, and in the early years of the nineteenth century, was said to be handling hundreds of blades every month. This goes some way to explain why there are so many British Napoleonic blades still available to the collector with his name prominently engraved to the blade.

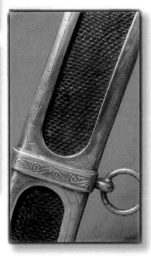

1788 PATTERN LIGHT CAVALRY TROOPER'S SWORD
VALUE: $ 1435.00/£ 895.00

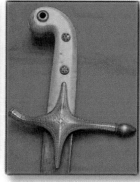

C.1800 CAVALRY OFFICER'S SWORD
VALUE: $ 795.00/£495.00
With typical period S-Bar curved hilt bars.

C.1800 INDIAN CAVALRY TROOPER'S SWORD
VALUE: $ 795.00/£495.00
Scarce example of a native made trooper's sword with Indian manufactured blade and hilt. Possibly issued to mounted native troops of the British East India Company. Blade is of rather crude manufacture.

C.1800 CAVALRY OFFICER'S MAMELUKE SWORD
VALUE: $ 1110.00/£695.00
Unusual example with distinctive crossguard and quillons.

1788 PATTERN HEAVY CAVALRY TROOPER'S SWORD
VALUE: $1740.00/£995.00
The first officially regulated pattern of heavy cavalry sword for troopers. Blades are typically plain with grip coverings of leather or fishskin Gill or Runkel are common maker's names found on the blade forte.

C.1800 CAVALRY OFFICER'S SWORD
VALUE: $ 795.00/£495.00

Royal Horse Artillery, 1815.

Battle of Waterloo, 1815.

www.guns.uk.com

C.1800 CAVALRY OFFICER'S SWORD
VALUE: $1995.00 /£1295.00

A high quality example of a cavalry officer's sword. With acanthus-leaved decoration to the stirrup hilt and a faceted backstrap. Ribbed ivory and brass twistwire to the grip. Complete with original gilt brass mounted leather scabbard. The hilt quillons are of a typically neo-classical style. Probably Yeomanry.

www.firearmscollector.com

www.antiqueswords.com

C.1800 CAVALRY OFFICER'S/ TROOPER'S SWORD
VALUE: $1435.00/£895.00

Hilt is of early spadroon type, soon to be replaced by the more common stirrup design. Blade is double-fullered and plain. Grip is of ribbed ebony.

www.guns.uk.com

www.michaeldlong.com

C.1800'S CAVALRY OFFICER'S MAMELUKE SWORD
VALUE: $1910.00/£1195.00

www.firearmscollector.com

1796 PATTERN HEAVY CAVALRY OFFICER'S PRESENTATION (UNDRESS) SWORD
VALUE: $4595.00/£2625.00

Very fine presentation example with excellent detail to the ivory and brass grip. The blue and gilt decoration extends to the length of blade. With typical boat shell hilt. Scabbard with leather and brass mounts.

C.1830 CAVALRY OFFICER'S MAMELUKE SWORD
VALUE: $950.00/£565.00

C.1800'S CAVALRY OFFICER'S MAMELUKE SWORD
VALUE: $1100.00/£695.00

With green horn slab grips and simple cut steel mounts.

www.guns.uk.com

C.1830 CAVALRY OFFICER'S MAMELUKE SWORD
VALUE: $ 4150.00/£ 2595.00

A high quality example. Blade forte is etched with maker's name, Widdowson & Veale, 73 Strand, London (1835-1909). The vogue for mameluke swords was initiated by both French and British cavalry officers during the Napoleonic campaigns in Egypt and the Near East. They really came into vogue after 1815 and were primarily adopted by lancer regiments. The use of velvet covered scabbards is quite typical for these swords.

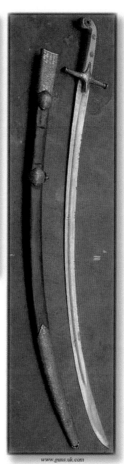

www.guns.uk.com

www.guns.uk.com

www.michaeldlong.com

C.1800 CAVALRY OFFICER'S MAMELUKE SWORD
VALUE: $ 3195.00/£ 1995.00

Unusual Georgian officer's mameluke sword, with *"Prepare the Way For My Soul"* etched for three quarters on both sides of the pipeback blade. Complete with decorated gilt brass scabbard. Well executed tooled decoration to the ivory grip.

www.guns.uk.com

C.1830 CAVALRY OFFICER'S MAMELUKE SWORD
VALUE: $ 4150.00/£ 2595.00

High quality piece marked to the *"Kings Hussars"* on blade.

Royal Artillery, 1815.

www.antiqueswords.com

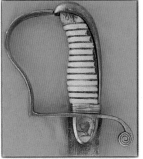

www.antiqueswords.com

www.firearmscollector.com

www.antiqueswords.com

www.firearmscollector.com

C.1800 YEOMANRY CAVALRY OFFICER'S PRESENTATION SWORD
VALUE: $ 3520.00/£ 2200.00
With gilt brass stirrup hilt of 1796 Pattern type, the scabbard is also engraved with a presentation inscription:

"KING AND COUNTRY
PRESENTED TO
ALBERT G. FLEETWOOD
BY THE MEN OF THE
BIRMINGHAM
LIGHT HORSE
MARCH 1806 A.D."

The blade bears the crowned "GR" cypher and is marked *"WARRANTED"*. Langet is engraved with a lion holding a crescent moon with inscription:

"PATIENTIA ET SPE"
(BY PATIENCE AND HOPE)

1796 PATTERN LIGHT CAVALRY OFFICER'S SWORD
VALUE: $ 3195.00/ £ 1995.00
Blade retains most of the original blue and gilt decoration.

www.antiqueswords.com

The Battle of Vimiera, 1808.

C.1850 CAVALRY OFFICER'S MAMELUKE SWORD
VALUE: $ 1100.00/£ 695.00
Early Victorian piece with excellent blade, retaining all original polish.

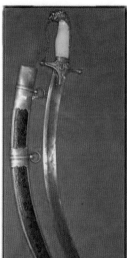

www.firearmxcollector.com

C.1800 CAVALRY OFFICER'S SWORD
VALUE: $ 4795.00/£ 2995.00
Rare example in exceptional condition with solid silver lionshead pommel, curved blade and silver and leather mounted scabbard. Grip is comprised of finely chequered ivory. With personal dedication engraved to the scabbard throat.

www.firearmxcollector.com

C.1850 CAVALRY OFFICER'S MAMELUKE SWORD
VALUE: $ 1100.00/£ 695.00

C.1850 CAVALRY OFFICER'S MAMELUKE SWORD
VALUE: $ 1100.00/£ 695.00

The British Army, c.1820.

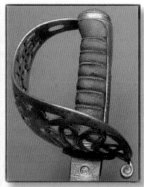

Blade spine is stamped with the Wilkinson Sword serial number 24957. This indicates that the sword was sold in 1882 to an officer named Yardley. The facility to check the Wilkinson archives is still available.

1820 PATTERN (LIFE GUARDS) CAVALRY TROOPER'S SWORD
VALUE: $1910.00/£1195.00
A scarce sword. Bowl guard is incised with 1st Life Guard's regimental device.

1848 PATTERN (ROYAL HORSE GUARDS) CAVALRY TROOPER'S SWORD
VALUE: $1910.00/£1195.00
With *"honeysuckle"* hilt.

1821 PATTERN HEAVY CAVALRY OFFICER'S SWORD
VALUE: $1100.00/£695.00
A clean, late - Victorian example.

C.1850 WARWICKSHIRE RIFLE VOLUNTEER OFFICER'S SWORD
VALUE: $1100.00/£695.00
A non-regulation sword, specially commisioned for the Warwickshire Rifle Volunteers. Officers of this regiment were required to purchase their own swords and this gave rise to a great variety of styles.

C.1830 LIFE GUARDS OFFICER'S DRESS SWORD
VALUE: $1100.00/£795.00
This type of sword was carried by both the Life Guards regiments (1st and 2nd) and used for evening or formal occasions.

Storming of Delhi, 1857.

www.michaeldlong.com

1834/1874 PATTERN (LIFE GUARDS) OFFICER'S STATE SWORD

VALUE: $ 2700.00/£ 1695.00

This is one of the most attractive British Army pattern swords, and is still carried by officers of the regiment. It was meant for both dress and undress. First adopted by the 1st Life Guards in 1834, all regiments of the Household Cavalry Division adopted this pattern in 1874. The brass hilt cyphers are marked with "1LG" (1st Life Guards), "2LG" (2nd Life Guards), and "RHG" (Royal Horse Guards). Many examples have the owner's monogram and regimental battle honours etched to the blade. Wilkinson made a substantial number of these swords and some can still be traced via the blade's serial number and the company's sales records. In recent years, a number of copies of these swords have been produced in India and Pakistan. They feature a very poor acid etched blade with "VR" royal cypher. The grip is covered in pigskin and brass twistwire, unlike the correct fishskin covering of the originals.

www.guns.uk.com

www.guns.uk.com

www.michaeldlong.com

www.michaeldlong.com

www.guns.uk.com

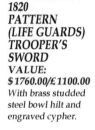

www.guns.uk.com

1820 PATTERN (LIFE GUARDS) TROOPER'S SWORD

VALUE: $ 1760.00/£ 1100.00

With brass studded steel bowl hilt and engraved cypher.

www.guns.uk.com

1853 PATTERN CAVALRY TROOPER'S SWORD
VALUE: $ 950.00/£ 595.00

This pattern was a unique attempt to marry the characteristics of both a heavy and light cavalry trooper's sword. It first saw service during the Crimean War.

Hilt markings to the 2nd Dragoons (Scots Greys).

1821 PATTERN HEAVY CAVALRY TROOPER'S SWORD
VALUE: $ 895.00/ £ 1435.00

The introduction of this pattern of sword heralded the arrival of a true cut and thrust weapon for the British Army. It featured a curved, spear-pointed single fullered blade, double-edged towards the end. The wide bowl guard was not particularly favoured by troops as, although it afforded good protection for the hand, it was seen to be too thin and weak when used in actual combat.

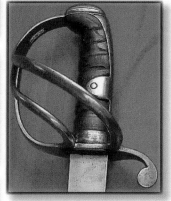

1821 PATTERN LIGHT CAVALRY TROOPER'S SWORD
VALUE: $ 795.00/£ 495.00

The 1821 patterns are relatively difficult to find, particularly the heavy version. This may be due to their inherent fragility (the hilt bars of the light version were prone to break) and its subsequent discarding during a long service life. The scabbard was also deemed too weak and liable to breakage and repair.

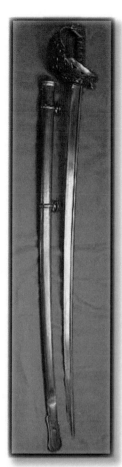

1821 PATTERN HEAVY CAVALRY OFFICER'S SWORD
VALUE: $1100.00/£695.00
This sword is defined by its very distinctive *"honeysuckle"* pattern pierced hilt. The pipe back blade was also a new development and was believed to add extra strength.

1821 PATTERN HEAVY CAVALRY OFFICER'S SWORD
VALUE: $1100.00/£695.00
This is a later Victorian (c.1890) piece with some modifications, including a single-fullered blade, smaller gaps between hilt piercings, a thicker gauge of metal and a longer, wider grip. The pommel is also less pronounced than earlier versions.

Battle of Maharajpore, 1843.

11th Hussars, c.1854.

Royal Horse Artillery, c.1828.

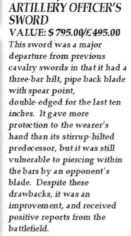

1821 PATTERN LIGHT CAVALRY/ROYAL ARTILLERY OFFICER'S SWORD

VALUE: $795.00/£495.00

This sword was a major departure from previous cavalry swords in that it had a three-bar hilt, pipe back blade with spear point, double-edged for the last ten inches. It gave more protection to the wearer's hand than its stirrup-hilted predecessor, but it was still vulnerable to piercing within the bars by an opponent's blade. Despite these drawbacks, it was an improvement, and received positive reports from the battlefield.

Early examples have quite a pronounced and stepped pommel. They tend to be from the reigns of King George IV and William IV (1820's-1830's). Later Victorian swords have a far less exaggerated pommel.

99

1892 PATTERN HOUSEHOLD CAVALRY TROOPER'S SWORD
VALUE: $1435.00/£895.00

The elaborately pierced hilt includes the intertwined letters "HC" (Household Cavalry). The initial 1882 Pattern featured both a long and short-bladed version. The long sword was intended for ordinary troopers whilst the shorter blade was to be carried by bandsmen and trumpeters. The difference in length between the two was around four inches. The supposed need for two differing lengths was abandoned in 1892 when a universal pattern was introduced.

1864 PATTERN CAVALRY TROOPER'S SWORD
VALUE: $1595.00/ £995.00

This pattern is extremely rare. It is known that in 1878, 12,000 were in stock and ready to be used for the Second Afghan War. The use of a bowl guard, rather than the more traditional three-bar hilt, was seen as proof that a more protective hilt was required. Despite this perceived improvement, many regiments actually discarded the 1864 Pattern in favour of the former 1853 Pattern, due to its awkward handling and the tendency for the edge of the bowl guard to fray the uniform. The placing of two sword knot slits at the back of the hilt is not seen on any other British military regulation sword.

Above:
Scabbard throat marked to the 1st Life Guards. Enfield manufactured and dated to 1900.

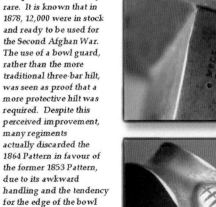

1899 PATTERN CAVALRY TROOPER'S SWORD
VALUE: $ 950.00/£595.00

Royal Horse Artillery, c.1897.

1882/1885/1890 PATTERN CAVALRY TROOPER'S SWORD
VALUE: $895.00/£510.00

Many of these swords were manufactured in German by Weyersberg and Kirschbaum (see hilt forte pictured below), due to the inability of British swordmakers to fulfill government orders. They feature the company's knight's head stamp to the blade forte. The Maltese Cross motif cut into the hilt is also a distinctive feature of this pattern. It was purely decorative and served no practical purpose. The fact that we encounter three differing patterns of this sword only highlights the crisis experienced within the British Army to find a sword both durable and effective. The 1882 pattern is, found in both *"long"* and *"short"* patterns.

"The Charge", c.1915.

1912 PATTERN CAVALRY OFFICER'S SWORD
VALUE: $1110.00/£695.00

This is the Officer's version of the earlier 1908 Cavalry Trooper's Sword and incorporated superb decorative styling to the bowl guard. The new hilt design was noticeably different, with a flowing style, heavily influenced by the contemporary Art Nouveau movement. The rapier-type blade is almost identical to the trooper's version, except for the etched decoration. Some of these swords were made with plain blades, particularly during WW1, due to economy measures. Some examples have the hilt completely covered in leather. This acted as a protector for the hilt and also removed the possibility of giving away an officer's position because of glare from the sun.

www.michaeldlong.com

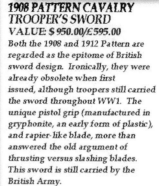

1908 PATTERN CAVALRY TROOPER'S SWORD
VALUE: $ 950.00/£595.00

Both the 1908 and 1912 Pattern are regarded as the epitome of British sword design. Ironically, they were already obsolete when first issued, although troopers still carried the sword throughout WW1. The unique pistol grip (manufactured in gryphonite, an early form of plastic), and rapier-like blade, more than answered the old argument of thrusting versus slashing blades. This sword is still carried by the British Army.

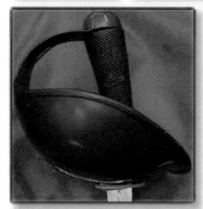

1908 PATTERN INDIAN CAVALRY TROOPER'S SWORD
VALUE: $ 595.00/£395.00

Rare Indian trooper's sword issue to native forces, with a smaller grip and chequered walnut grip. It is likely that this example has been re-painted during its lifetime as it shows little wear. Economy models produced during WW1 feature a dermatine grip.

British Cavalryman, c.1914.

FRENCH CAVALRY SWORDS

Right:

C.1805-1810 OFFICER OF HORSE TROOP'S SWORD

VALUE: $ 4150.00/£2595.00

This sabre was inspired by the classic pattern of 1784, and would have been carried by a cuirassier, dragoon or mounted artillery officer.

Mike Robinson Collection

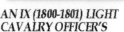

Mike Robinson Collection

AN IX (1800-1801) LIGHT CAVALRY OFFICER'S SWORD

VALUE: $ 4000.00/£2500.00

Adopted for use by Officers of Hussars, Light Artillery, Chasseurs a Cheval, and Lancers. The scabbard is silver plated, indicating a high status owner. Grip is made of black, chequered ebony with blue and gold wash to blade. The guard is of stirrup type with two faceted side branches and large oval langets engraved along edge. Much of the original blue and gilt is still present and the engravings are quite clear. The brass pommel is made up of a very typical, albeit modified, Phrygian helmet. This motif was used extensively on French military swords of this period. This model of sabre was carried by French cavalry officers from 1801 through to 1815, and into the Restoration.

Mike Robinson Collection

C.1800 LIGHT CAVALRY OFFICER'S SWORD

VALUE: $ 4150.00/£2595.00

This was made during the Consulate Period (1799-1804) but could very well have been carried until 1815. It is of high quality manufacture and suprisingly light for its size. Unusually, just about all of the blueing still remains to the blade that features a distinctive clipped point.

C.1770 CAVALRY OFFICER'S SWORD

VALUE: $1910.00/£1195.00

With turned and fluted decoration to the pommel, reminiscent of smallswords of this period. Blade is engraved to both sides *"Vive Le Roi"*.

C.1790 CAVALRY TROOPER'S SWORD

VALUE: $1100.00/£ 695.00

Brass, three-bar hilt of simple form with twisted copper wire to grip. Blade is curved and plain.

C.1790 HUSSAR OFFICER'S SWORD
VALUE: $795.00/£495.00

Mike Robinson Collection

C.1792-1798 HUSSAR SOUS OFFICER'S SWORD
VALUE: $2075.00/£1295.00
Of a type used by Hussars until superceded by the Model XI. Brass pommel of bird's head form with the hilt marked *"Dumont"* on the knucklebow.

Right and right above:
C.1792-1798 HUSSAR SOUS OFFICER'S SWORD
VALUE: $3200.00/£2000.00
Excellent example of a First Empire sword inspired by the vogue for classical styling. Grip is manufactured of ebony, with finely chequered, geometric designs.

Mike Robinson Collection

C.1804-1815 LIGHT CAVALRY OFFICER'S SWORD
VALUE: $3510.00/£2195.00

Mike Robinson Collection

www.antiqueswords.com

Left:
C.1805-1815 LIGHT CAVALRY OFFICER'S SWORD
VALUE: $3200.00/£2000.00

Mike Robinson Collection

SUPERIOR OFFICER DE CHASSEUR'S SILVER-HILTED SWORD
VALUE: $3510.00/£2195.00
Chasseurs were originally formed from guides of both infantry and cavalry units. Due to its short length, this could also be a *"walking out"* sword.

French Lancer, c.1812.

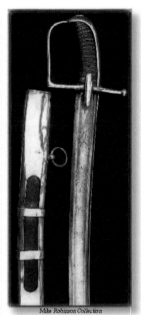

Mike Robinson Collection

C.1798 HUSSAR OFFICER'S SWORD

VALUE: $2700.00/£1695.00

Similar to swords carried by Napoleon's Consular Guard, who later became the Imperial Guard.

C.1800'S CAVALRY OFFICER'S SWORD

VALUE: $4000.00/£2500.00

Officer's version of the cuirassier trooper's sword with plain, damascus blade and superb brass mounted scabbard.

Right:

C.1815 OFFICER'S AND TROOPER'S SWORD OF THE GARDE-DU-ROI

VALUE: $2625.00/£1500.00

Hilt with royal coat of arms of Louis XVIII, and carried by an officer of his personal guard, when he returned after the first abdication of Napoleon in 1814. Blade is marked with a panoply of arms and *"Garde Du Corps Du Roi"*. Spine of blade is also marked *"Manufacture Royale De Klingenthal Janvier 1815"*.

Mike Robinson Collection

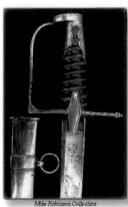

Mike Robinson Collection

C.1801-1815 HUSSAR'S SWORD A L'ALLEMANDE

VALUE: $4150.00/£2595.00

These swords were originally carried by officers of German Hussar regiments during the reign of Louis XIV. It was widely used during the Napoleonic Wars. The style of pommel is attributed to General Officers.

Mike Robinson Collection

1790 PATTERN CHASSEUR À CHEVAL TROOPER'S SWORD

VALUE: $2395.00/£1495.00

At the start of the French Revolution, the Dragoons and Chasseurs a Cheval were both equipped with the 1784 Pattern Sword. However, the Chasseurs wanted to distinguish themselves from other regiments and adopted this sword soon afterwards. Because of heavy usage during the Revolution and Napoleonic Wars, original examples still surviving are very rare.

Mike Robinson Collection

C.1801-1815 HUSSAR OFFICER'S SWORD

VALUE: $1910.00/£1195.00

Carried by all branches of Napoleon's light cavalry, including hussars.

Mike Robinson Collection

C.1810 HUSSAR OFFICER'S SWORD

VALUE: $1595.00/£995.00

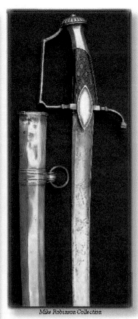

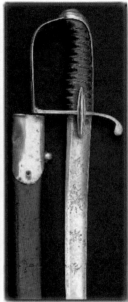

Mike Robinson Collection

Mike Robinson Collection

Mike Robinson Collection

Mike Robinson Collection

C.1795-1798 CARABINIERS TROOPER'S SWORD
VALUE: $4310.00/£2695.00

A rare piece. This pattern of sword was used by the Carabiniers from 1795 until 1809 when it was replaced by a subsequent pattern. The Carabiniers were considered the elite of the French heavy cavalry. There were only two regiments of Carabiniers. Blade is engraved on both sides with "CARABINIERS DE LA REPUBLIQUE FRANCOISE". Brass half basket hilt with large embossed flaming bomb.

C.1805-1812 CUIRASSIER OFFICER'S SWORD - "DE BATAILLE"
VALUE: $4150.00/£2595.00

The French cuirassier formed the heavy cavalry of Napoleon's army. This officer's sword is patterned from the dragoon officer sword of 1783. It was adopted for use by cuirassier officers around 1805. In 1812, a new pattern was adopted for use by all mounted cavalry officers. Blade retains much original blue and gilt finish. This pattern is currently being copied. Some of these can easily fool the novice.

C.1784-1804 DRAGOON OFFICER'S SWORD - "DE BATAILLE" MODEL 1784
VALUE: $2700.00/£1695.00

The blade is blued and gilded, and likely to have been carried by a cuirassier or dragoon officer during the Revolutionary, Consulate and the First Empire periods.

C.1783-1815 LIGHT CAVALRY OFFICER'S SWORD
VALUE: $1910.00/£1195.00

This sword would have been carried by either a mounted or light cavalry officer. Hilt is of pronounced stirrup-type, with long double langets and raised centres. Blade with traces of original engraving.

Battle of Toulouse, 1814.

Marechal de France, c.1812.

AN XIII CUIRASSIER'S
BROADSWORD
VALUE: $1910.00/£1195.00

AN XIII CUIRASSIER'S
BROADSWORD
VALUE: $1910.00/£1195.00

AN XIII CUIRASSIER'S
BROADSWORD
VALUE: $1910.00/£1195.00
This sword was manufactured in July 1810, in Klingenthal. The French army tended not to mark their swords with exact regimental designations, although some are found with such markings. It is thought that large quantities were captured by the Prussians when they invaded France in 1814 and used by their own cavalry regiments. This particular example is marked "3.K.191". indicating use by the 3rd East Prussian Kuirassiers.

C.1800 HUSSAR OFFICER'S MAMELUKE SWORD
VALUE: $1595.00/£995.00

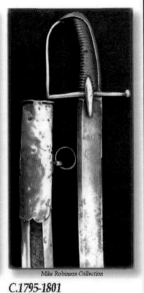

CUIRASSIER TROOPER'S BROADSWORD
VALUE: $1595.00/£910.00
Early, unmarked example with pronounced curved grip.

C.1800 LIGHT CAVALRY OFFICER'S SWORD
VALUE: $1435.00/£895.00
Unmarked, single-fullered blade. The quillon is stamped with the number "3".

C.1800 HUSSAR OFFICER'S SWORD
VALUE: $1435.00/£895.00
Of lightweight construction and used by both hussars and mounted infantry. Blade is German and marked to blade spine: *"Schaberg fils de Francoise Frabriquant a Solingen"*.

C.1795-1801 HUSSAR OFFICER'S SWORD
VALUE: $3035.00/£1895.00
Wide, single-fullered, curved blade. Ribbed leather grip and typical brass D-shaped guard. With pronounced and long lozenge langet. Scabbard is brass with a leather insert.

C.1801-1815 HUSSAR TROOPER'S SWORD
VALUE: $1435.00/£895.00
Brass, three-bar hilt with central tang rivet to grip.

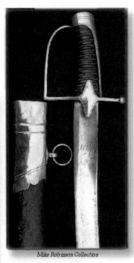

C.1800 HUSSAR/ CHASSEURS À CHEVAL SOUS OFFICER'S SWORD
VALUE: $3035.00/£1895.00
The lozenge shaped langet is typical of Chasseurs à Cheval swords.

Napoleon's entry into Moscow, 1812.

Mike Robinson Collection

C.1798-1803 KINGDOM OF SARDINIA HEAVY CAVALRY TROOPER'S SWORD

VALUE: $ 3035.00/£1895.00

This sword was used by the French Army during campaigns from 1798-1803. These included important battles such as Marengo (1800). They were originally intended to arm the Italian cavalry of the Kingdom of Sardinia and stored at Turin Armoury. Between 1798-1803, the French confiscated these sabres and issued them to cuirassiers.

Mike Robinson Collection

Left:
1792 PATTERN CHASSEUR À CHEVAL OFFICER'S SWORD
VALUE: $2595.00/£1480.00

Mike Robinson Collection

1792 PATTERN CHASSEUR À CHEVAL OFFICER'S SWORD
VALUE: $ 3035.00/£1895.00

www.guns.uk.com

C.1800 CAVALRY OFFICER'S SWORD
VALUE: $ 3035.00/£1895.00

Highly unusual example with crouching lion pommel, walrus ivory grip and copper wire binding. Blade retaining traces of blue and gilt decoration.

French Lancers at Quatre Bras, Waterloo, 1815.

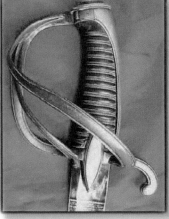

C.1830 LIGHT CAVALRY OFFICER'S SWORD
VALUE: $1195.00/£680.00

This sword is of a type carried by both French and continental cavalry officers. The blade was manufactured in Solingen, Germany. It is virtually impossible with these swords to directly attribute them to any particular country. The German sword trade was a great exporter of swords to both European countries and the growing United States. Commercial pattern books were made available to customers, both private and governmental. German swordmakers were adept at copying contemporary military designs and selling them at competitive prices. This made them quite unpopular to indigenous makers.

C.1880 HEAVY CAVALRY OFFICER'S SWORD
VALUE: $1110.00/£695.00

With straight, double-fullered blade and steel scabbard. Horn grip.

www.michaelllong.com

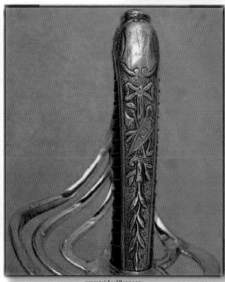
www.michaelllong.com

www.michaelllong.com

C.1870 CAVALRY OFFICER'S SWORD
VALUE: $ 950.00/ £595.00

Excellent officer's sword with deep decorative chiselling to the four-bar hilt. Horn grip with brass twistwire. Blade is nickel-plated and plain. Hilt backstrap with engraved personal monogram.

MODEL 1854 CUIRASSIER TROOPER'S SWORD
VALUE: $1040.00/£595.00

French Cavalry Troopers, c.1890.

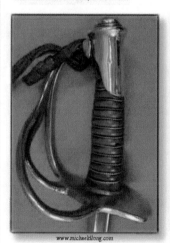

www.michaeldlong.com

C.1870 CAVALRY OFFICER'S SWORD
VALUE: $795.00/£495.00
With plain blade and green horn grip and brass twistwire. Probably a private purchase.

www.michaeldlong.com

C.1890 CAVALRY OFFICER'S SWORD
VALUE: $635.00/£395.00
Engraved to *"Klingenthal"* on spine of blade and complete with nickel-plated scabbard.

www.michaeldlong.com

MODEL 1882 DRAGOON TROOPER'S SWORD
VALUE: $950.00/£595.00
A good example of a late-Victorian French cavalry trooper's sword. Manufactured at Chattelerault. Engraved to the blade spine with *"1883 Dragon Mdl 1882"*. Three-bar cast brass hilt.

www.michaeldlong.com

www.michaeldlong.com

www.michaeldlong.com

MODEL 1816 CUIRASSIER TROOPER'S SWORD
VALUE: $1435.00/£895.00

This sword is an amalgam of a dated 1813 cuirassier blade, combined with a Model 1816 hilt. It has changed from earlier Imperial French examples in that the hilt branches are now fully incorporated into the guard. This set the trend for both light and heavy cavalry swords throughout Europe and North America.

www.michaeldlong.com

DATED 1831 CUIRASSIER TROOPER'S SWORD
VALUE: $1895.00/£1195.00

Here we see the utilization of an earlier First Empire hilt with a later (1831) broadsword blade. Both hilt and scabbard have matching numbers.

French Cuirassier Troopers in training, c.1910.

GERMAN CAVALRY SWORDS

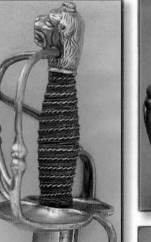

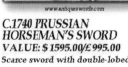

www.antiqueswords.com

www.antiqueswords.com

C.1740 PRUSSIAN HORSEMAN'S SWORD
VALUE: $ 1595.00/£ 995.00

Scarce sword with double-lobed, bilobate guard and thumb-ring. Lionshead pommel and wooden grip wrapped with copper and brass wire, terminating in a Turks's head. Single-fullered, slightly curved blade with flat spine, etched with a hand holding a sabre extending from a cloud, sunburst, crescent moon and stars.

The blade has been shortened by approximately ten inches during its working life. This is very much a transitional sword, exhibiting earlier "Walloon" patterns e.g. double-lobed, bilobate counterguard, but losing the guard's complex, pierced holes.

C.1740'S HORSEMAN'S SWORD
VALUE: $ 1595.00/£ 995.00

C.1720'S CAVALRY OFFICER'S SWORD
VALUE: $2695.00/£1695.00
Rare and early officer's lionshead four-bar brass hilt. Engraved, single-fullered blade. Possibly from the German state of Hesse.

Prussian Hussar Officer, c.1812.

Hanover Officer, 1866.

Hanover Officer, 1866.

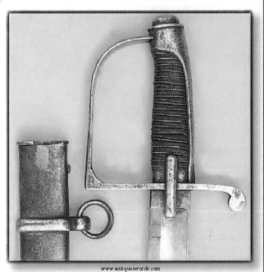

www.antiqueswords.com

C.1830 SAXON/ITALIAN TROOPER'S SWORD
VALUE: $950.00/£595.00
This sword has also been described as an Italian Mounted Artillery Trooper's Sword. It is possible that German makers exported this sword to other countries, including Italy.

www.michaelong.com

www.michaelong.com

Left:
PRUSSIAN MODEL 1889 CAVALRY TROOPER'S SWORD
VALUE: $795.00/ £495.00
Nickel-plated hilt with folding guard and composite grip.

Right:
PRUSSIAN MODEL 1882 CUIRASSIER TROOPER'S SWORD
VALUE: $1110.00/ £695..00
This sword is very similar in design to contemporary French Heavy Cuirassier swords. Regimentally marked to blade forte.

C.1830 PRUSSIAN MOUNTED ARTILLERY TROOPER'S SWORD
VALUE: $1275.00/£795.00
With iron hilt and scabbard mounts, clip-point blade and pronounced long langets. Pre-1830 German cavalry troopers' swords are scarce (especially in good condition) as most enlisted men and NCO's received government issued swords and they were constantly re-issued.

www.michaelong.com

www.guns.uk.com

www.guns.uk.com

1806 PATTERN BAVARIAN TROOPER'S SWORD
VALUE: $1435.00/£895.00
Rare example with a heavy, broad-fullered, slightly curved blade. Steel, three-bar hilt. Contained in its steel scabbard with original leather carrying straps and belt. Unlike British and French cavalry swords of the Napoleonic period, German swords are quite scarce. One of the reasons for this could be the relatively large number of individual nation states within Germany during the 1800's, and before re-unification in 1871. Numbers of swords issued would consequently have been much smaller, with few surviving.

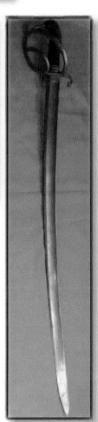

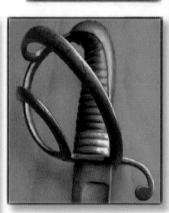

MODEL 1826 BAVARIAN CHEVAULEGER TROOPER'S SWORD
VALUE: $950.00/£595.00
Regimentally marked to the 3rd Regiment on the underside of the hilt.

117

PRUSSIAN MODEL 1811 "BLUCHER" TROOPER'S SWORD
VALUE: $1100.00/£695.00

The sword is very similar to the British 1796 Pattern Light Cavalry Trooper's Sword, and was heavily influenced by this earlier sword. It is also often mistakenly identified as such. It was promoted by General Blucher of the Prussian Army and had a very long service life. They are invariably regimentally marked and show evidence of having passed through many regiments, due to the multiple crossing through of regimental designations to the hilt and scabbard throat.

www.michaeldlong.com

www.michaeldlong.com

PRUSSIAN MODEL 1811 "BLUCHER" TROOPER'S SWORD
VALUE: $1100.00/£695.00

German Cavalry, c.1910.

Adjutant, 5th Garde Regiment, c.1910.

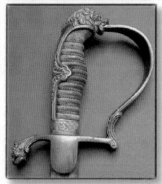

German Cavalryman, c.1910.

C.1900 PRUSSIAN CAVALRY OFFICER'S SWORD
VALUE: $ 950.00/ £595.00

Good quality pre-WW1 cavalry officer's sword with *"jewelled"* eyes to the lionshead pommel. Typical, lightly etched blade with stands of trophies and scrolling foliage. Fishskin and silver wire grip. Hilt cartouche displays crossed sabres. The lionshead quillon is very finely detailed.

Prussian Hussar Trooper, c.1870.

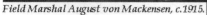

Field Marshal August von Mackensen, c.1915.

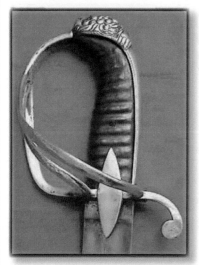

C.1840'S CAVALRY OFFICER'S SWORD

VALUE: $795.00/ £495.00

With a double-fullered and very curved, plain blade. Pommel is of simple lionshead form. Leather wrap to the grip. It is unlikely to have had any twistwire. Interestingly, the hilt design echoes the Napoleonic period rather than the mid-nineteenth century.

www.antiqueswords.com

PRUSSIAN MODEL 1889 TROOPER'S SWORD

VALUE: $ 950.00/£595.00

Left:
PRUSSIAN MODEL 1889 OFFICER'S SWORD

VALUE: $1100.00/£695.00

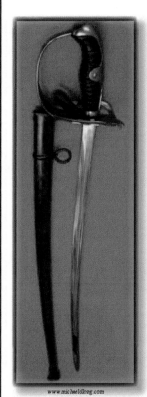

www.michaeldlong.com

www.michaeldlong.com

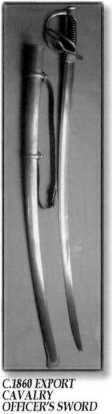

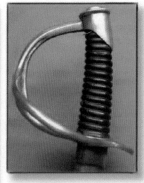

www.michaeldlong.com

MODEL 1867/1881 CAVALRY OFFICER'S SWORD
VALUE: $ 635.00/£ 395.00
With steel hilt, folding guard and nickel-plated blade.

C.1860 EXPORT CAVALRY OFFICER'S SWORD
VALUE: $ 635.00/ £ 395.00

This sword is an example of a type of sword produced in large quantities by German swordmakers for export to both European and American markets during the mid-nineteenth century. One of the biggest markets was the United States, or more particularly, both the Union and Confederate States during the Civil War. These swords tend to be unmarked, perhaps signifying the reluctance of German swordmakers to identify or allign themselves with any particular combatant. It also allowed them to sell to both warring governments.

German Lancers, c.1915.

UNITED STATES' CAVALRY SWORDS

General Jacob Brown.

General David Humphreys.

Al Gregoritsch Collection

C.1775 HORSEMAN'S SWORD
VALUE: $ 2395.00/£ 1495.00

Of very basic form and comprising a thin, stirrup guard and slotted counterguard. Wooden grip would originally have had either copper or wire banding. The blade is flat, slightly curved, and unfullered.

C.1780'S HORSEMAN'S SWORD
VALUE: $ 2875.00/£ 1795.00

This sword is sometimes known as an *"American Light Horse Sabre"*, due to many examples bearing this designation to the blade or hilt. These swords were actually manufactured in Germany and exported to the United States during the post-Revolutionary period. This example has an unmarked blade, save for an armourer's mark of three stars to each side of the blade. Variations include an iron mounted version with leather or fishskin grips.

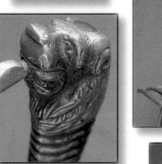

Battle of Bull Run, 1861.

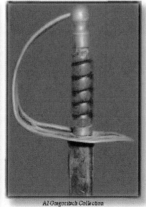

Al Gregoritsch Collection

C.1775 HORSEMAN'S SWORD
VALUE: $2075.00/£1275.00
With D-Guard and brass, slotted hilt.

Al Gregoritsch Collection

C.1785-1800 HORSEMAN'S SWORD
VALUE: $2395.00/£1495.00
A typically crude sword of American manufacture. With wide, three-fullered blade and solid brass, eaglehead hilt. Hilt is of brass. Blade is unfullered and unmarked. The eagle was not fully adopted as a national symbol until 1782, but the use of animal motifs (including lions and dogs) on sword pommels, was already in widespread use by the 1770's.

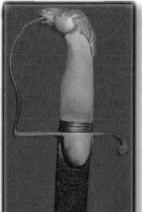

Al Gregoritsch Collection

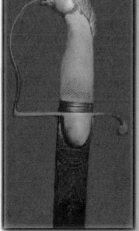

Al Gregoritsch Collection

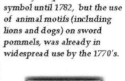

Al Gregoritsch Collection

Al Gregoritsch Collection

Above:
C.1780 HORSEMAN'S SWORD
VALUE: $1595.00/£995.00
Of typical crude manufacture (probably local blacksmith), with single-fullered blade and hatchet point. This style of sword was produced in many local communities in response to the need during the Revolutionary War for hastily produced edged weapons. Foreign imports were difficult to source due to the British blockade of ports, and these basic swords were both serviceable and expendable.

Above and right:
C.1805 CAVALRY OFFICER'S SWORD
VALUE: $1910.00/£1195.00
This sword is essentially an identical example of a type carried by British cavalry officers during this period, particularly Yeomanry officers. It would have been manufactured in Birmingham, England, and then exported to the United States. The blade is decorated with blue and gilt military motifs, including stands of arms, and an American eagle.

Left and below:
C.1840 NON-REGULATION CAVALRY OFFICER'S SWORD
VALUE: $1595.00/£995.00

A scarce piece with blade decoration of stands of arms and floral designs. Ricasso stamped with "J.B.S." and "B". Three-bar solid brass hilt and leather grip. Of a type carried during the Mexican and Civil War.

Right:
C.1820 MOUNTED ARTILLERY OFFICER'S SWORD
VALUE: $795.00/£495.00

Double-fullered, curved blade, with etched decoration. Original leather wrap to grip. Iron stirrup guard with slot for sword knot.

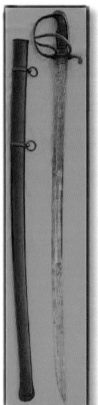

www.antiqueswords.com

www.antiqueswords.com

www.antiqueswords.com

C.1820-1840 MOUNTED ARTILLERY OFFICER'S SWORD
VALUE: $950.00/£595.00

Typical gilt brass stirrup hilt with carved bone grips. Blade still retains around 50% of the blue and gilt decoration, including stands of arms and a shield with stars. The grip has a length-wise age crack. This is very common with ivory grips due to natural age shrinkage and poor storage. During the early 1800's the supply of ivory became restricted and bone was subsequently used as a replacement.

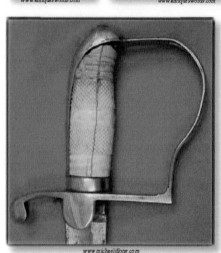

www.michaeldlong.com

C.1810 CAVALRY OFFICER'S SWORD
VALUE: $1595.00/£995.00

Chequered and ribbed ivory grip with gilt brass stirrup hilt. The blade retains much of the original blue and gilt decoration.

www.michaeldlong.com

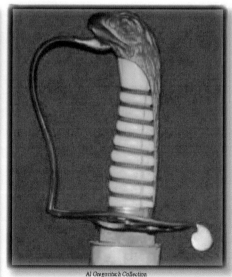

Al Gregoritsch Collection

C.1810 MOUNTED ARTILLERY OFFICER'S SWORD
VALUE: $1435.00/£895.00

MODEL 1840 CAVALRY TROOPER'S SWORD
VALUE: $ 795.00/£495.00
Manufactured in Germany by Friedrich Potter of Solingen. Small numbers are known to have been exported to the United States during the early part of the Civil War. They have a distinctive rabbit's head motif to the ricasso and were sold to Union forces.

MODEL 1860 CAVALRY TROOPER'S SWORD
VALUE: $ 950.00/£595.00
A relatively scarce sword by Mansfield and Lamb, Forestdale, Rhode Island.

MODEL 1840 CAVALRY TROOPER'S SWORD
VALUE: $ 950.00/£595.00
Manufactured by sword importer, C.R. Kirschbaum and Co., Solingen, Germany.

MODEL 1860 CAVALRY TROOPER'S SWORD
VALUE: $ 950.00/£595.00
This is part of a special contract, manufactured by Emerson and Silver, for the State of New Jersey, and then sold on to the U.S. Government.

MODEL 1840 CAVALRY TROOPER'S SWORD
VALUE: $ 950.00/£595.00
Manufactured by W. H. Horstmann and Sons, Philadelphia, Pennsylvania.

Battle of Gettysburg, 1863.

MODEL 1853 CAVALRY TROOPER'S SWORD (IMPORT)
VALUE: $2075.00/£1295.00

Scarce and unusual Model 1853 Cavalry Trooper's Sword. Completely unmarked and possibly issued to Confederate troops during the American Civil War. It was manufactured in Britain or Germany and imported to the US. With a plain blade and hatchet point. Home-made(?) iron and brass mounted leather scabbard. Most of these swords were purchased by agents from both Union and Confederate governments. They travelled throughout Europe sourcing swords.

Robert E. Lee and Stonewall Jackson.

Patriotic Postcard, c.1910.

www.michaeldlong.com

www.michaeldlong.com

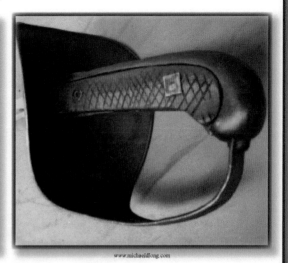

www.michaeldlong.com

MODEL 1913 CAVALRY TROOPER'S SWORD
VALUE: $ 1100.00/£ 695.00

This sword was based on a design by the future General George S. Patton, and submitted whilst he was an army lieutenant. Strongly influenced by the British 1908 Pattern Cavalry Trooper's Sword, it is very similar to its successful British counterpart, serving primarily as an effective thrusting weapon. Grips were manufactured in bakelite or thermo-plastic. It is found with either a wood and canvas scabbard covering, or nickel-plated steel. The quality of manufacture was very high. This sword is currently being copied.

www.michaeldlong.com

www.michaeldlong.com

www.michaeldlong.com

www.michaeldlong.com

Captain of Cavalry, c.1900.

OTHER NATIONS' CAVALRY SWORDS

ITALY

www.antiquezwords.com

ITALIAN MODEL 1871/ 1909 TROOPER'S SWORD
VALUE: $ 475.00/£295.00
Of simple manufacture, with a thin, steel basket hilt and smooth wood grip. Blade is of single-fullered, pipe back form. Scabbard is also of thin metal and is likely to have proved rather unserviceable.

www.antiquezwords.com

C.WW2 ITALIAN OFFICER'S SWORD
VALUE: $ 950.00/£595.00
With nickel-plated finish to the hilt, blade and scabbard. Grip is of composite material. This example is in virtually untouched condition, and also retains the original leather sword knot and hanger. One of the most innovative aspects of these swords is the placing of a thumb-hole underneath the hilt quillon. This allowed the thumb's full extension and consequently, a more solid grip when the closed hand is around the grip. It is interesting to note that the general quality of these Victorian and twentieth century swords is not very high, with thin sheet metal used for the hilt and scabbard.

www.michaelllong.com

www.michaelllong.com

www.michaelllong.com

C.WW2 ITALIAN OFFICER'S SWORD
VALUE: $ 475.00/ £295.00
Steel hilt with composite grip. Blade is etched with the royal coat of arms of the House of Savoy and is without any facist designations.

IMPERIAL RUSSIA

The Storming of Kars, 1877.

MODEL 1826 CUIRASSIER TROOPER'S SWORD
VALUE: $2395.00/£1495.00

The blade edge is dated 1831 and arsenal marked to the forte and hilt bars. Many French manufactured Napoleonic cuirassier and light cavalry swords were captured and re-used by Russian forces, particularly after the campaigns in Russia post-1812.

MODEL 1827 LIGHT CAVALRY TROOPER'S SWORD
VALUE: $1595.00/£995.00

Imperial Russian Cavalry Trooper, c.1900.

1881 PATTERN DRAGOON TROOPER'S SWORD
VALUE: $1435.00/£895.00

Dated to 1914, and used extensively during the First World War, these swords were produced in large quantities for the Imperial Russian Army. Other versions feature a provision for the attachment of a Moisin-Nagant socket bayonet to the scabbard throat. Many are regimentally marked and it is common to see examples defaced. This was initiated by post-revolutionary Bolsheviks who routinely erased any traces of the Imperial dynasty.

www.michaeldlong.com

www.michaeldlong.com

1881 PATTERN COSSACK TROOPER'S SHASQUA
VALUE: $1435.00/£895.00

With typical Cossack style solid brass bird's head hilt and pommel. Blade is dated on the forte to 1918, and it is likely that it would have been carried by both White Russian and Bolshevik forces during the Russian Civil War (1918-1922). Despite its association with the former Imperial Monarchy, this distinctive sabre remained a design constant for Russian and subsequently, Soviet cavalry, from the Revolution onwards.

SOVIET UNION

Bolshevik commander, Russian Civil War, c.1921.

C.WWII SOVIET 1881 PATTERN COSSACK TROOPER'S SHASQUA
VALUE: $1100.00/£695.00
This sword is identical to those carried by troopers during the Imperial era, except for the addition of a soviet star to the hilt pommel. The scabbard has been adapted to carry the Moisin Nagant Model 1891 Socket Bayonet.

Soviet officers , c.1925.

Soviet propaganda , c.1945.

Soviet propaganda , c.1940.

POLAND

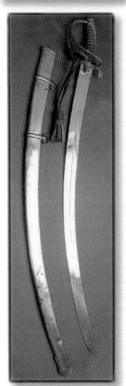

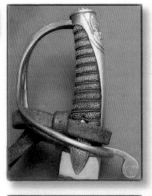

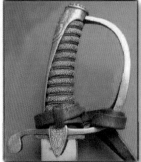

US WW1 recruiting poster for soldiers of Polish origin.

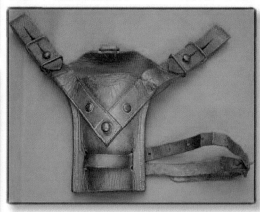

Sword frog for Model 1921 Cavalry Officer's sword.

MODEL 1917 CAVALRY OFFICER'S SWORD

VALUE: $ 3195.00/ £1995.00

This is an extremely scarce sword and very few examples have survived the brief interwar period when Poland was a self governing republic. This sword has an unmarked, nickel-plated blade. Some can be found with patriotic etchings and mottos. All Polish military swords of this period are rare.

Polish Cavalry, c.1920.

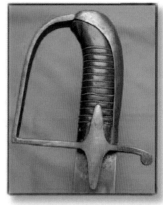

1921 PATTERN CAVALRY OFFICER'S SWORD
VALUE: $ 3195.00/ £1995.00

Examples of pre-communist Polish swords are extremely rare, and especially those issued between the years 1918-1930. Few appear on the market.

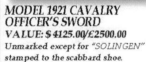

MODEL 1921 CAVALRY OFFICER'S SWORD
VALUE: $ 4125.00/£2500.00

Unmarked except for "SOLINGEN" stamped to the scabbard shoe.

Polish Officers, c.1925.

1921 PATTERN
CAVALRY OFFICER'S
SWORD
VALUE: $ 3500.00/£2195.00

1934 PATTERN
CAVALRY TROOPER'S
SWORD
VALUE: $ 2700.00/£1695.00

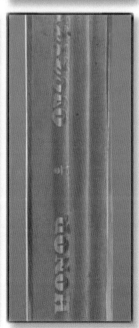

Detail from a patriotic postcard, c.1918.

TURKEY

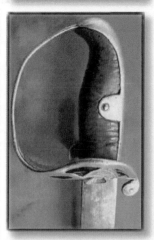

C.1890 CAVALRY TROOPER'S SWORD
VALUE: $1100.00 /£695.00
With solid brass hilt and crescent moon inset to the hilt cartouche.

CHILE

www.michaelilong.com

C.1900 CAVALRY OFFICER'S SWORD
VALUE: $950.00/£595.00
Of German manufacture and no doubt produced specially for the South American market. German arms manufacturers built up a large arms trade with countries such as Chile, Argentina and Brazil. The grip is reminiscent of the German Model 1889 Cavalry Trooper's Sword. Hilt, blade and scabbard are heavily plated, indicating probable parade use.

www.michaelilong.com

www.michaelilong.com

Above:
Knight's Head maker's mark of Weyersberg, Kirschbaum.

Battle of Plevna, 1877.

SWEDEN

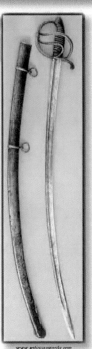

www.antiqueswords.com

www.antiqueswords.com

1867 PATTERN CAVALRY TROOPER'S SWORD
VALUE: $695.00/£400.00

This sword was heavily influenced by contemporary sword designs, particularly the Austrian Model 1850 Cavalry Trooper's Sword. Quality of manufacture is very high (as is shown with most Swedish edged weapons). Solid brass pierced hilt with both holes and slots. It is also regimentally marked to the hilt crossguard and the scabbard. Blade is single-fullered and straight.

1815 PATTERN CAVALRY TROOPER'S SWORD
VALUE: $795.00/£455.00

Clip-point, single-fullered curved blade and iron, three-bar hilt. Blade is plain and unmarked. Scabbard is manufactured in iron.

www.michaeldlong.com

www.michaeldlong.com

www.michaeldlong.com

www.michaeldlong.com

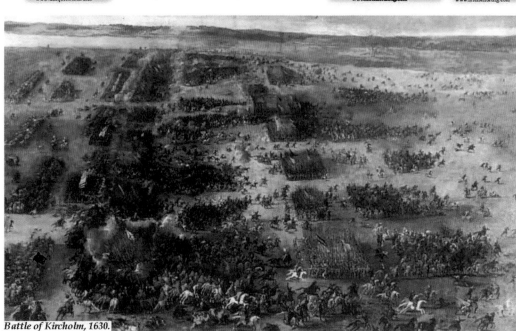

Battle of Kircholm, 1630.

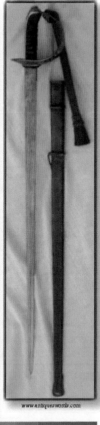

www.antiqueswords.com

1893 PATTERN CAVALRY TROOPER'S SWORD
VALUE: $ 950.00/£595.00

Many examples are found with regimental marks to the hilt and scabbard (see below). The use of punched holes to the brass bowl guard became popular during the mid-1800's and can be seen on many Austro-Hungarian sabres of this period. Grip is bound with leather and is without twistwire. Scabbard is of blued steel. The overall quality of the manufacture is very high. This sword is quite common in the collecting market.

Swedish Army, c.1920.

SPAIN

SPANISH C.1840'S CAVALRY TROOPER'S SWORD
VALUE: $1045.00/ £600.00

This is a very heavy-bladed weapon, with a thick unfullered blade. Many of the swords manufactured in Toledo for the Spanish military during the nineteenth century have this type of flat blade. They have great weight and would have inflicted serious wounds if wielded correctly, but their combat flexibility must be doubted. They are invariably dated to the blade.

SPANISH C.1800 CAVALRY OFFICER'S SWORD
VALUE: $785.00/ £450.00

Scarce Spanish Napoleonic Cavalry Officer's Sword with large gilt brass boat shell hilt and faceted ovoid pommel. The unfullered blade is engraved with patriotic inscriptions. Original copper twistwire to the grip.

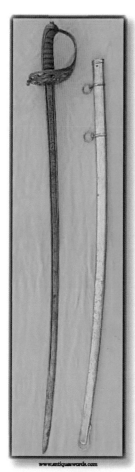

www.antiqueswords.com

www.antiqueswords.com

C.1860'S CAVALRY OFFICER'S SWORD
VALUE: $ 1100.00/£ 695.00

The quality of the workmanship to the hilt and blade is very high, with deep etching to the length of its double-fullered blade. The hilt still retains a light wash of fire-gilt. Hilt design and particularly the swirling acanthus-leafed decoration to the hilt, is also reminiscent of British cavalry officers' swords of this period. Sword design was very much influenced by other European countries. Most Spanish military swords of this period were manufactured in Toledo, and blades are invariably marked *"Toledo"*, combined with the date.

www.michaeldlong.com

1870 CAVALRY OFFICER'S SWORD
VALUE: $ 950.00/ £595.00

www.michaeldlong.com

www.gunsuk.com

www.gunsuk.com

www.michaeldlong.com

www.michaeldlong.com

www.michaeldlong.com

C.1890 CAVALRY TROOPER'S SWORD
VALUE: $ 475.00/£ 295.00

140

PORTUGAL

SERBIA (YUGOSLAVIA)

Detail from c.1900's Serbian cavalry officer's sword. With finely etched blade. Nickel-plated lionshead pommel and composite grip.

C.1790 HEAVY CAVALRY OFFICER'S SWORD
VALUE: $ 2550.00/£1595.00

Of very simple and relatively crude manufacture. Blade is single-fullered and normally found with the engraved coat of arms of the Portugese Royal Family. A scarce sword.

C.1920'S CAVALRY TROOPER'S SWORD
VALUE: $ 950.00/£595.00

The sword hilt is very reminiscent of contemporary German cavalry designs, and it is likely that this was manufactured in Germany and exported.

Battle of Solferino, 1859.

Champigny, 1870.

BRAZIL

ETHIOPIA

**C.1900'S CAVALRY
TROOPER'S SWORD**
VALUE: $ 630.00/£ 395.00

The Spanish-American War, 1898.

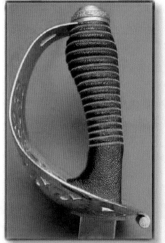

**ETHIOPIAN CAVALRY
OFFICER'S SWORD**
VALUE: $ 950.00/£ 595.00
Thought to be for a cavalry
officer in the Ethiopian Army.
Purchased from the London Military
outfitter, Hawkes and Co., and
probably part of a special order.
Sword is a hybrid of the British
1821/1912 Cavalry Officer's Sword.
Mid-twentieth century(?).

SWITZERLAND

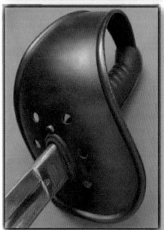

MODEL 1867
CAVALRY
TROOPER'S SWORD
VALUE: $ 950.00/
£595.00

Swiss Cavalry Trooper, 1890.

C.1920'S CAVALRY TROOPER'S
SWORD
VALUE: $ 475.00/£295.00
Based on contemporary Russian cavalry
shasquas, these swords were probably imported
from either Russia, Turkey or Germany.

PERSIA (IRAN)

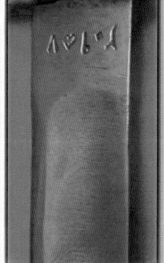

MEXICO

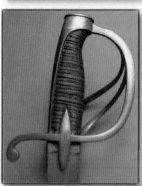

Battle of Buena Vista, 1846.

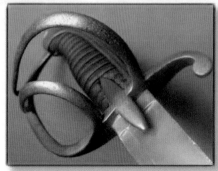

C.1840'S CAVALRY OFFICER'S SWORD
VALUE: $ 1275.00/£795.00

This is very typical of swords carried throughout Europe during this period. It is likely to have been manufactured in Germany and imported into Mexico. Trade links between Germany and the Mexican State were quite strong during this period and it is probable that agents for the sword companies were present in the country. Leather and copper twistwire to the grip. Steel, three-bar hilt and scabbard. Blade features stylised decoration, including floral motifs, crossed cannons and the Mexican national coat of arms of an eagle clutching serpent in mouth. The crossed cannons might also indicate a mounted artillery function.

UNIDENTIFIED

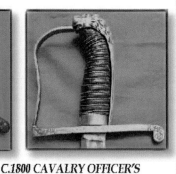

C.1800 CAVALRY OFFICER'S SWORD
VALUE: $2700.00/£1695.00

An attractive design with brass hilt and slab horn grip. Blade is single-fullered and plain, with no markings present. The rather flamboyant boat shell guard is reminiscent of Spanish rapiers of the period, and it could be reasonably attributed to this country. Scabbard is leather and brass mounted.

French Mounted Artillery, c.1840.

C.1800 CAVALRY OFFICER'S SWORD
VALUE: $1100.00/£695.00

Likely to be North European, possibly German.

Left and above left:
C.1800 CAVALRY OFFICER'S SWORD
VALUE: $1435.00/£895.00

This sword could be either North European or possibly German. They tend not to be marked and blades are heavy and single-fullered.

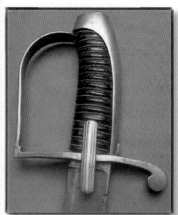

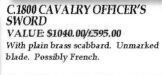

C.1800 CAVALRY OFFICER'S SWORD
VALUE: $1040.00/£595.00

With plain brass scabbard. Unmarked blade. Possibly French.

THE INFANTRY SWORD WAS one of the standard edged weapons issued to those fighting on foot. The range of swords available to the collector is truly immense and one could probably spend a lifetime accumulating infantry swords from just one specific period and nation.

HISTORICAL BACKGROUND

The origins of the *"infantry"* sword can be traced back to the ancient world, when nation states first developed the knowledge needed to produce strong blades of bronze and later, iron. The ordinary foot soldier of these times tended to use the sword as a secondary weapon, with the spear or long pike, the first line of attack. The sword was normally a short and wide-bladed thrusting sword, characterised by the Roman *Gladius*. The earlier Greeks favoured a falchion type sword with a single-edged blade. These short swords were also ideal for close combat situations where masses of troops were pressed together and a long-bladed weapon would have been quite impractical.

During the Middle Ages, the sword for those who fought on foot was similar to that carried by the horseman; that is a long, wide-bladed and double-edged broadsword. It must be remembered that most ordinary soldiers did not actually carry swords. They were an expensive item to produce and more basic percussive weapons such as the axe, polearm, club and flail, were more commonly carried onto the field of battle.

The true *"infantry"* sword (in collector's terms) fits more comfortably into a period during the last three hundred years when massed infantry formations were regulated into more formal and national structures of regiments.

BRITAIN

The English infantryman of the 1700's carried a brass-hilted hanger or short sword. It was of simple form with a three-bar hilt, globular pommel and ribbed cast brass grip. The blade was usually flat, single-fullered and sheathed in a black leather and brass mounted scabbard. A number of these hangers were re-issued to county militia regiments when no longer needed by the regular army. They are marked accordingly to the underside of the guard. Many are marked to *Huntingdon(shire)*.

Officers did not carry a regulation infantry sword until 1786. Before this, a spontoon or short staff weapon, was carried into battle. Its fighting capabilities must surely have been in doubt, and it appears to have served more as a symbol of rank and signpost to gain attention when rallying the troops. In 1786, a specific pattern of sword for infantry officers was introduced. The Order issued by George III stipulated that this new pattern must be a *"...strong cut and thrust weapon with blade 32in long and 1in wide at the shoulder, the hilt to be steel, gilt or silver according to the buttons of the uniform"*. The breadth of interpretation allowed within this Order seems quite wide, but it is generally agreed that the sword referred to is of *"spadroon"* type with a five-ball or beaded guard. Plain guards are also found. This style of sword is frequently encountered by the collector and the relatively large number of examples extant must indicate some kind of uniformity within the Army. Grips were either ivory, ebony or dark horn. A metal *"cigar band"* was placed around the centre of the grip. This normally bore an engraved royal crown,

French Imperial Guard, c.1810.

146

"GR", or even a regimental badge. Some are also left blank. Blades from this early pattern tend not to be decorated although some are known. The 1786 Pattern actually refers more to the type of blade required (i.e. straight and *"cut and thrust"*), rather than the hilt. Thus we see a later version with fixed shell guard and Adam-style urn pommel. Both pommel and quillon are decorated with acanthus leaves. This variation was standardised in the 1796 Pattern Infantry Officer's Sword, a weapon regarded by many collectors as epitomising the English Napoleonic infantry officer. The original inspiration for the design came from Prussian military smallswords of the 1750's. It is abundantly clear that this rather flimsy-bladed sword would not have stood up to a charging horseman's broadsword, but these were times when elegant appearance took precedence over awkward practicality. Protection for the hand was minimal with just a single knucklebow. There hilt included a double shell guard with one folding guard (to prevent chafing of the uniform) and the grip was bound in either silver wire or applied sheet silver. Blades were lavishly decorated with blue and gilt highlighted engraving, featuring the royal coat of arms, "GR" cypher, stands of trophies and scrolling foliage. There is another version with completely plain hilt and blade. It is thought that this was possibly carried by NCO's. Very few examples remain that still display their original blue and gilt decoration as the blue and gilt was easily rubbed away. Because of the fragility of the leather and gilt brass mounted scabbard, most swords are long separated from their sheath and have suffered consequent wear and tear.

The image of the dashing light cavalryman or hussar had engendered a strong feeling within the British Army of the 1800's for swords that reflected this gallant *"espirit de corps"*. Not to be outdone, the Army introduced a new pattern of infantry sword based on a light cavalry model. The 1803 Pattern Infantry Officer's Sword had a curved, single-edged blade with lionshead pommel and gilt brass knucklebow. Above the knucklebow a "GR" royal cypher and crown. Placed above that was either a strung bugle, denoting use by a rifle company officer, or a flaming grenade, for a grenadier company officer. The blade was normally decorated in blue and gilt, although the author has seen many plain bladed examples of this pattern. It must be remembered that not all officers had the financial means to purchase the best swords available. Where they did, the surviving examples are superb. Infantry or flank officers' swords with stirrup hilts are also quite common. The curved blades of these swords would seem to indicate a cavalry function but

Prussian Pioneer Troops, c.1830.

actual measurement of the blade lengths shows that it would not have been long enough for a mounted cavalryman.

The 1796 and 1803 Pattern Infantry Officer's Sword had a long service life, and it was not until 1822 when a new pattern replaced them. It was very different in design and featured a pipe back blade with a *"Gothic"* gilt brass half basket hilt. The *"Gothic"* refers to the similarity of the hilt design to Gothic windows, a reference to the contemporary vogue for all things medieval. Within the hilt was placed a cartouche with the reigning monarch's royal cypher. The original pipe back blade was replaced in the 1840's by the single-fullered *"Wilkinson"* blade. Blue and gilt blade decoration became unpopular, and blades were etched rather than engraved. The scabbard was either leather and gilt brass mounted, brass or plain steel. They also found in steel. The 1845 Pattern followed with the removal of the folding guard and a new blade. In 1892, the blade changed to a purely thrusting type, combined with a completely new hilt design. This comprised a solid sheet steel, half basket guard impressed with the royal crown and cypher. In 1895 and 1897, there were minor modifications to the hilt, including the addition of a turned down inner edge to the guard to avoid fraying of the officer's uniform. The Rifle Regiment and Foot Guards' Regiments carried a steel half basket-hilted sword (1827 Pattern and 1854 Pattern, respectively). In 1857, the Royal Engineers were designated an attractive gilt brass half basket-hilted sword which they carried until 1892.

FRANCE

The French military had a far greater variety of infantry swords than most of their European neighbours. The idea of rank was very important and there were many different designs of sword carried, from the infantry private, sergeant, captain and through to General Officer. The early years after the Revolution created a series of very distinctive infantry swords, including those carried by the *Garde National* and *Garde Nationale Chasseur*. They featured pommels with helmets of neo-classical form and half basket brass guards that carried emblems placed in cartouche.

A common type of sword carried by most French infantry soldiers during the Napoleonic Wars (alongside the musket and socket bayonet) was the *"sabre*

briquet", a brass-hilted short hanger. It had a curved single-edged blade with brass and leather mounted scabbard. This sword was widely copied throughout Europe and adopted by many countries during the early to mid-1800's. It was noticeably rejected by Britain for a time, although a *Gladius* sword was introduced very briefly for the Land Transport Corps during the 1850's.

Napoleon Bonaparte was always keen to reward his best regiments with either honours or special uniform and equipment privileges. An example of this was the weapon carried by the *Sappers of the Old Guard*. They were given a special uniform of bearskin, felling axe, apron, and more importantly, a large brass, cockerel-hilted sword. They were also allowed to grow a beard! This sword is currently being copied and examples are of reasonably high quality and can easily fool the beginner.

In the early 1800's, a very distinctive and clasically inspired infantry sidearm was introduced. It had a wide, leaf-shaped blade combined with a scaled brass grip. This Model 1816 and the later Model 1833 Foot Artillery Sidearm, was based on the Ancient Roman *Gladius* Sword. It is best known to collectors as the *"cabbage chopper"*. Vast quantities were produced. It seems ubiquitous at arms shows and auctions. The standard of manufacture of these swords was very high, but its military effectiveness must be questioned. The carrying of a sword for the ordinary ranks in the French Army declined during the latter part of the nineteenth century, as the reliance on the musket, rifle and bayonet became dominant. This was not so for officers.

British Infantry Officer, c.1790.

Infantry officers had always carried a straight-bladed sword throughout the eighteenth century. It usually took the form of a smallsword with stylised pommel and stirrup guard. These pommel styles ranged from plain ovoid to classical helmet and lionshead. The shellguard was also classically inspired, with embossed decoration of victory wreaths, stands of trophies, and figures in classical poses. This style continued throughout the Napoleonic Wars. Blades were also frequently finished in blue and gilt. The vogue for the classical continued in the design of other infantry swords, including a wide range of curved sabres of light cavalry form. There was no great official desire to regulate these swords and officers were allowed a great deal of freedom to choose whatever style of sword they wished to carry.

This laxity was to change with the introduction of the

Model 1821 and 1845 Infantry Officer's Sword. It was a radical departure from previous designs and proved to be the inspiration for many other countries. It comprised a decorated brass hilt with single knucklebow guard and a slightly curved, single-edged blade. Grips are of ribbed horn. The Model 1845 continued into a knucklebow into a pierced shell guard with floral decoration. The blade is a little straighter and found in both pipe back and quill-pointed form. Scabbards were leather with gilt brass mounts. The standard of manufacture is normally very high and they tend to be maker marked to the blade forte. Another change in 1855 led to a more plainer, single-fullered blade. This sword was carried until 1882, when a steel or nickel-plated steel, four-bar-hilted sword was introduced. It had a much narrower blade and came with a steel scabbard. It was carried until 1923, when a universal pattern of sword for all officers of the French Army was issued. This is an attractive sword with a gilt brass, shallow bowl hilt, and single knucklebow. The sides of the bowl guard are pierced and decorated with leaf patterns.

Officer, Kings Own Scottish Borderers, c.1910.

GERMANY AND AUSTRIA

The German states of the eighteenth and nineteeth centuries generally followed patterns and styles prevalent throughout Europe at that time. In keeping with the French and English infantry private of the mid-1700's, a short, brass-hilted infantry hanger was carried, particularly by Prussia. It is virtually indistinguishable from the English version, although you tend to find that the Prussian examples are regimentally marked.

By 1818, a pattern of hanger, identical to the French *"sabre briquet"*, was being produced in large numbers by German swordmakers. The German states favoured the short sword for infantry soldiers and there are quite a variety of models to be sourced, particulary pioneer swords. The heyday of these swords appears to be the mid-late nineteenth century. They also served a function as a dress sidearm, particularly the Model 1860/71 Infantry Sidearm, where a range of sword knots denoted particular rank.

By 1800, officers were already wearing a sword similar in design to the British 1796 Pattern Infantry Officer's Sword. The British had actually copied the pattern from a Prussian design of the 1750's. Hilt design was also influenced by French infantry swords of the period. Sword blades commonly have engraved decoration, including state coat of arms and royal cyphers. Blue and gilt was also used extensively. There was no real attempt at uniformity of pattern and different states adopted their own styles of infantry sword. The Saxon Model 1867 Infantry Officer's Sword had a gilt brass hilt very similar to both French and Russian infantry swords of the period. It was not until 1889, when a standardised pattern of infantry sword was introduced. This sword had a straight, single-edged blade with a gilt brass hilt that incorporated the badge of each German state. The grip was fishskin and brass or silver twistwire. The cap pommel was quite slanted and there are examples where the owner's intitials have been engraved at the top. The scabbard was either steel or black painted steel.

Infantryman, British Army c.1880.

Towards the end of the nineteenth century, infantry and artillery officers began to carry a stirrup-hilted sword with lionshead pommel, quillon and lions-mane backstrap. The langets included a motif to represent the particular branch of service e.g. crossed cannons for the artillery. The lionshead pommel had *"jewelled"* eyes. The variety of blades is enormous, ranging from typically plain to profusely etched, blued and damascus finishes. It was worn primarily as a dress sword. This type of sword took over from the 1889 Pattern after the defeat of the German

Empire in the First War, and was carried up until the end of the Second World War. All symbols of the Imperial Monarchy were erased from the swords.

The stirrup-hilted sword is also found with a plain, "*dovehead*" pommel, including examples worn by infantry or artillery NCO's. In the case of the Nazis, the crossguard on the lionshead and eagle-head stirrup-hilted sword was altered to allow the placing of an eagle and swastika motif.

The Austrian infantry officer of the 1800's followed the same path as his English and German counterparts in favouring a smallsword. It had a gilt brass hilt, with double boat shell guard and rounded pommel. The blade was straight and double-edged. Blades were normally engraved wth the royal cypher and double-headed eagle of the Habsburg monarchy. It must be remembered that Austrian infantry officers of the Napoleonic period also carried a wide range of unofficial swords, including wide-bladed and curved

General, US Army, c.1910.

"*hussar*" type sabres that were extremely popular throughout Europe during this time.

The Model 1837 Infantry Officer's Sword introduced a more regulation sword for infantry officers, although it was still of smallsword form and not adopted by all officers. It was quite plain, with a brass, double shell hilt and ovoid pommel. The sword was quite inadequate as both a fighting weapon and one that afforded protection to the wearer's hand. An unofficial version was soon adopted by officers that was very different to the original model. It had a steel stirrup hilt and wide shell guard. The military authorities seemed to tolerate this adaptation of an official pattern.

The Model 1850 and subsequently, the Model 1861 Infantry Officer's sword was the first fully standardised weapon for the infantry. Again, it was of simple design, with sheet steel curved knuckleguard, terminating with two slots for a sword knot and a downturned scroll quillon. There are also versions of this sword for ordinary troops and NCO's, with shorter and wider blades. The Model 1861 Infantry Officer's Sword was carried for many years and saw service until the end of the First World War.

From the mid-1700's, ordinary soldiers had carried a range of hangers, mainly of brass, stirrup-hilted form. Blades were short, curved and flat backed. They were carried in leather scabbards with concealed throat and chape mounts. Saw-backed pioneer swords were also favoured. The Model 1853/89 (sometimes referred to as the Model 1862) Pioneer Falchion is a distinctive and common weapon amongst collectors. It has a massive hatchet blade, steel crospiece and horn grip (later, wooden). Scabbard is wood covered with blackened horse leather.

RUSSIA

From the mid-1700's, Russia embarked on a sustained period of contact and rapprochement with the West. This involved a wide range of activities from changes in administration to architecture, dress, and importantly, military organisation. The Czars had looked with envy at the disciplined troops of Frederick the Great of Prussia, and wanted the same attitude to be instilled within their own ranks. To do this, they needed to change the whole *look* of the Army which, in turn, would hopefully change the military approach of both the officers and rank and file. One of the methods of doing this was by adopting Western military dress and weapons.

By 1800, the Russian infantry officer was carrying a military smallsword of European type. The Model 1786 Infantry Officer's Sword had a slightly curved, double-edged blade with brass, heart-shaped guard and ovoid pommel. It was contained within a leather and brass mounted scabbard. Subsequent patterns (Model 1796 and Model 1798) had straight, single-edged blades with typical period double shell guards and pronounced, upward quillons. The acanthus-leaved decoration to the hilt was also similar to British infantry officers' swords of that time. In 1826, the overt influence of French sword design brought about the Model 1826 Infantry Officer's Sword. It is based on the French Model 1821 Infantry Officer's Sword, with slightly curved, single-edged blade, gilt brass hilt, domed pommel, single knucklebow and narrow shell guard. The model was also updated in 1855.

In 1913, the infantry officer changed to a sword of Model 1909 shasqua or cavalry type.

Lower ranks in the infantry carried a range of hangers based on European designs of the period. Simple brass-hilted short swords with shell guards would have been carried during the mid-1700's. As the century progressed, the Russian infantry carried the same style of brass hilted hanger as that carried by Prussian and English troops. In 1817, a brass-hilted "sabre briquet" hanger was issued. It is virtually identical to the original French version. A large pioneer hanger was issued in 1827, with a massive sawback blade and heavy cast brass hilt. It must have been a cumbersome burden for any soldier to carry. A Gladius short sword (for the artillery) of French design was also introduced in 1834 and 1848.

UNITED STATES

The ordinary foot soldier and officer of the campaigning American forces during the War of Independence, would have carried a wide variety of weapons, with many captured and some home produced. It was very much what could be had by either fair means or foul. The short hanger or hunting sword was typically favoured by the infantry, especially when fighting in the dense forests of North America. Smallswords were also carried by American officers but it is unlikely that they would have been the first weapon of choice for combat.

The eagle-head sword was very popular with American infantry officers just after the War. Many of these swords were actually supplied by British swordmakers, most notably William Ketland and Henry Osborn of Birmingham. Frederick W. Widmann, a German born swordmaker, made distinctive and high quality eagle-head swords in Philadelphia during the 1830's and 1840's. Indian-head and helmet pommel swords were also very popular during this period.

Regulation infantry swords began to appear in the 1830's. A smallsword of English style with gilt brass boat shell hilt, ovoid pommel and straight blade, was introduced in 1832 for officers of the Infantry, Artillery and Ordnance. There then followed a number of regulation swords including the Model 1840 Militia Staff Officer's Sword, with its distinctive outstretched eagle crossguard, and eagle pommel. The blade was straight, double-edged, with short central fuller. Decoration included drums, cannons, floral sprays, "US", eagles and crossed pikes.

Militia officers carried a wide variety of swords. Differences of design usually centre around the pommel type and blade decoration. Some have a helmet pommel in the style of French infantry swords, and other examples feature an eagle. The grip was either bone or ivory, with fluted or hatched patterns. Scabbards are found in iron, leather and plain gilt brass, usually with elaborately engraved decoration.

Russian troops storm the fortress of Kars, 1877.

Militia swords of presentation grade would have had grips of inlaid or engraved brass, silver or gold, with corresponding decoration to the hilt and scabbard mounts.

The Army also carried patterns specific to their departments. These include the Model 1834 Revenue Cutter Service Sword, Model 1840 Engineer's Sword, Model 1840 Commissary Officer's Sword, Model 1832 and Model 1840 Medical Staff Officer's Sword.

In the mid-nineteenth century and in keeping with the contemporary vogue for all things French, the US military adopted a completely new sword for infantry officers. The Model 1850 Foot Officer's Sword is an almost exact copy of the French Model 1845 Infantry Officer's Sword. The blade is slightly curved and single-edged, with double fullers. A large number of these swords were imported from Europe and can be found with maker marks of well known German sword-makers such as Clauberg, Schnitzler and Kirschbaum and Weyersberg. American makers such as Ames and Horstmann (Philadelphia) also produced some very fine examples with etched blades. Scabbards are usually leather and brass mounted. The Model 1850 Staff and Field Officer's Sword is of the same pattern as the Model 1850 Foot Officer except that it has as an additional branch to the hilt, with a *"US"* set between the hilt bars. Some imported swords do not have the *"US"* within the guard. These models were carried extensively throughout the American Civil War by the Union side. Confederate infantry swords imitated the Union models and many were imported from Europe. There was a sword manufacturing base in the South, but quality of finish was generally poor and few examples still survive. This has made them extremely scarce and prone to the faker's art.

A universal pattern of sword for all branches of the army was introduced in 1902. It is still carried today. In comparison with its elegant predecessors, it is quite a disappointment, with a nickel-plated three-bar *"bird-head"* hilt and horn (later bakelite or thermoplastic) grip with finger grooves. Blade is single-edged and slightly curved. Most are etched with military motifs and sometimes the owner's name. Scabbard is nickel-plated steel. They are plentiful within the collecting market, although presentation models with more elaborate blades and scabbards, do command premium prices.

Within the lower ranks of the infantry, musicians and NCO's carried a pattern of 1840, with brass D-guard hilt, straight blade and ovoid pommel. The NCO's sword had a small shell guard and was longer than the musician's sword. The Model 1832 Foot Artillery Sword is a copy of the French *Gladius* sword with the exception that an eagle has been engraved into the pommel.

COLLECTING INFANTRY SWORDS

The same rules apply to collecting infantry swords as they do to any other branch of service, although it must be noted that there do appear to be far more copies of infantry swords circulating in the market. American swords of the Civil War period are extensively copied and fake British pattern swords have recently been seen in the market.

Battle of Lexington, 1775.

BRITISH INFANTRY SWORDS

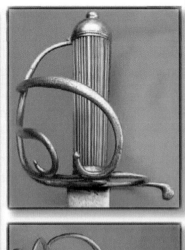

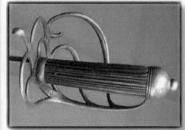

C.1750 INFANTRY OFFICER'S HANGER
VALUE: $895.00/£510.00
Finely made example with ribbed green horn grip and steel mounts.

C.1780 INFANTRY OFFICER'S SPADROON
VALUE: $1275.00/£795.00
With cut steel hilt mounts and ivory and copper banded grip.

C.1750 INFANTRYMAN'S HANGER
VALUE: $1275.00/£795.00
Marked to Samuel Harvey of Birmingham (1748-1800).

C.1770 INFANTRY OFFICER'S SPADROON
VALUE: $950.00/£595.00
The steel crossguard has a typical heart motif to the side guard. This design was very popular during the late-eighteenth century.

www.michaeldlong.com

www.michaeldlong.com

C.1750 INFANTRYMAN'S HANGER
VALUE: $1295.00/£795.00

This hanger was probably first issued to regular army units, then taken out of service and used by local militia units; in this case, Huntingdon (Cambridgeshire). It is of a type carried during the American Revolutionary War. The running wolf mark (copied from the German Passau swordmakers) is deeply impressed on the blade, with a "SH", indicating manufacture by Samuel Harvey of Birmingham.

www.gunsuk.com

www.michaeldlong.com

www.michaeldlong.com

C.1770 INFANTRYMAN'S HANGER
VALUE: $1595.00/£995.00

Rare infantryman's hanger with original leather and brass mounted scabbard. Most examples are without scabbard. Note the elongated belt hook to the scabbard throat.

Private, Royal Scots Fusiliers, 1742.

C.1790 INFANTRY OFFICER'S SWORD
VALUE: $2550.00/£1595.00

Rare example to the 42nd Royal Highlanders (Black Watch).

C.1800 GRENADIER OFFICER'S SWORD
VALUE: $1435.00/£895.00

Spadroon sword to an officer in a Grenadier regiment, indicated by the flaming grenade motif to side bar. These swords are quite scarce.

Private, Cameronians, 1815.

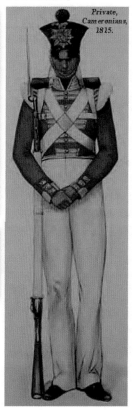

154

Left and below left:

C.1770 INFANTRY OFFICER'S HANGER
VALUE: $ 1910.00/£1195.00
Fine quality example with silver hilt mounts. Grip is turned ebony with copper banding and silver twistwire. Slightly curving, single - fullered plain blade. Hilt of slotted form. This style of sword was also popular with naval officers.

Right:

C.1780 INFANTRY OFFICER'S SWORD
VALUE: $ 1275.00/£795.00
Spadroon hilt with cut steel mounts and ribbed ivory grip. *"Cigar band"* to hilt grip.

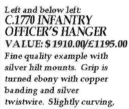

1786/1796 PATTERN INFANTRY NCO'S SWORD
VALUE: $ 950.00/£595.00
The plain hilt mounts and blade indicate that this would have been issued to NCO's. The officer's version is more elaborate with a decorated hilt and blade.

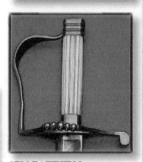

1786 PATTERN INFANTRY OFFICER'S SWORD (SPADROON HILT)
VALUE: $ 1040.00/£650.00
With diamond insert to hilt guard.

1786 PATTERN INFANTRY OFFICER'S SWORD (SPADROON HILT)
VALUE: $1100.00/£695.00

1786 PATTERN INFANTRY OFFICER'S SWORD (SPADROON HILT)
VALUE: $895.00/£510.00

1786 PATTERN INFANTRY OFFICER'S SWORD (SPADROON TYPE)
VALUE: $ 1275.00/£795.00
This is the first official British regulation infantry officer's sword. With gilt brass hilt mounts and distinctive five-ball or *"beaded"* side guard. Ribbed ivory grip and cushion pommel.

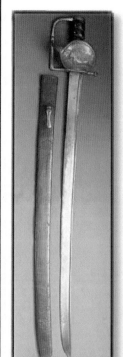

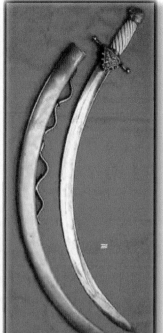

**C.1750-1800
YEOMAN
WARDER'S SWORD**
VALUE: $1910.00/
£1195.00
Carried by Yeoman
Warders from the Tower of
London. Shell guard with
royal House of Hanover
horse. Later examples
have a crowned pommel.

**C.1810 INFANTRY OFFICER'S
SWORD**
VALUE: $1050.00/£600.00
Unusual and extravagant example
with lionshead pommel, turned ivory
grip and very curved blade. Brass
scabbard with applied snake design to
the edge. This could be a private
purchase for a militia officer. The
blade is etched with the maker's name
of Richard Kennedy of Birmingham
and London. They are noted as being
in business from 1810-1899.

**C.1780 INFANTRY
OFFICER'S SWORD**
VALUE: $1100.00/£695.00

C.1770 INFANTRY MILITIA SWORD
VALUE: $1110.00/£695.00

It is likely that this sword was originally issued to the Regular Army and then re-issued to the Hereford Militia regiment after its serviceable life was deemed to be over. The blade is stamped with a running fox (rather than the running wolf mark of Solingen, Germany). It is stamped with the initials "JD", indicating probable manufacture by James Drury of London. The blade forte has a government inspector's mark.

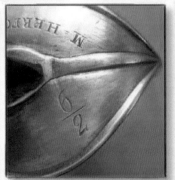

C.1800 INFANTRY OFFICER'S SWORD
VALUE: $1910.00/£1195.00

Rare and fine example of a senior infantry officer's sword. With typical Georgian styling, including urn pommel and chased decoration to the delicate shell guards. It is based on the 1796 Pattern Infantry Officer's Sword, but is far more elegant in proportions. Complete with a rarely seen original bullion sword knot.

C.1800 HONOURABLE ARTILLERY COMPANY OFFICER'S SWORD
VALUE: $ 950.00/ £595.00

Of distinctive design. With folding dishguard, large engraved cruciform quillons and knucklebow branching off. The grip would have probably been covered in silver or brass twistwire. The blade is plain and single-fullered. It is very similar to the 1796 Pattern Infantry Officer's Sword. The Honourable Artillery Company is still an essential and effective part of the British Army.

C.1800 GENERAL OFFICER'S SWORD
VALUE: $ 1910.00/£1195.00

This sword bears some resemblance to the British 1796 Pattern Heavy Cavalry Officer's Dress Sword. The hilt proportions are smaller, especially the narrow, rapier-type blade. The blade was probably too thin to be very effective as a cavalry weapon. Previous authors have attributed this sword to General Officers as similar examples are noted in contemporary paintings.

C.1800 INFANTRY PRIVATE'S SWORD
VALUE: $ 1595.00/£995.00

An excellent example and especially so because it comes with its original scabbard. The blade maker is Thomas Craven of Birmingham. The broad arrow and "BO" stamp to the forte are the official designation of the Board of Ordnance, the government regulated body given the task of approving and inspecting weapons for the British Army.

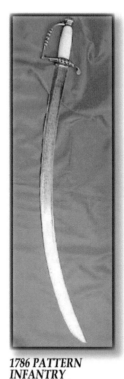

1786 PATTERN INFANTRY OFFICER'S SWORD (SPADROON TYPE)
VALUE: $ 2350.00/£ 1595.00

This pattern of sword was adopted soon after the official abolition of the officer's spontoon, or half pike. This had become little more than a symbol of authority in the field of battle rather than an effective combat weapon. King George III approved the introduction of a straight-bladed, single-fullered sword. To find an early regulation sword with original scabbard is rare.

1786 PATTERN INFANTRY OFFICER'S SWORD
VALUE: $ 2235.00/£ 1395.00

This pattern replaced the earlier 1786 Pattern spadroon version. It is the more commonly encountered sword, with a gilt brass double shell-guard and urn-shaped pommel, normally with acanthus-leaved decoration. The blue and gilt blade is etched with royal cypher, royal coat of arms and stands of trophies. The guard is rigid. It would later be changed to a folding guard in subsequent versions.

1786 PATTERN INFANTRY OFFICER'S SWORD
VALUE: $ 1275.00/£ 795.00

Five-ball or *"beaded"* gilt brass hilt.

1786 PATTERN INFANTRY OFFICER'S SWORD
VALUE: $ 950.00/£ 595.00

Battle of Vitoria, 1813.

1796 PATTERN INFANTRY OFFICER'S SWORD

VALUE: $ 3035.00/£ 1895.00

This is a pattern of infantry sword commonly encountered by collectors. The 1796 Pattern was the mainstay of the British Infantry Officer for over twenty five years and quantities produced were very large. The design influenced many other countries, including the United States of America, where the Model 1840 Non-Commissioned Officer's Sword bears a striking resemblance. It had obvious fighting defects, including lack of protection to the hand and a rather weak blade. It is not a scarce sword for the collector but most eamples are in poor condition with worn blades, lacking scabbards and quillons. The example shown has a very fine blue and gilt blade and original scabbard. It is rare to find one in such condition.

1st Guards, 1808.

Above:
C.1790 SCOTTISH FENCIBLE'S BROADSWORD
VALUE: $ 3200.00/£2000.00
This style of sword is normally attributed to Scottish volunteer battalions raised during the Napoleonic Wars. It is also sometimes referred to as a "Bredalbane Fencibles" sword. This is because they are invariably engraved to the regiment on the basket hilt. Blade is double-fullered and probably of much earlier form. It was not unusual for owners of Scottish broadswords to keep an older blade and replace with later hilts.

Above right:
C.1790 SCOTTISH INFANTRY/FENCIBLE BROADSWORD
VALUE: $ 3200.00/£2000.00
Many of the blades for these functional swords were manufactured in Birmingham by such makers as Harvey and Thomas Gill.

Sergeant William Duff,
42nd Highlanders,
Black Watch, c.1816.

SCOTTISH 1798 PATTERN HIGHLAND OFFICER'S BROADSWORD
VALUE: $2700.00/£1695.00
Good example with typical single-fullered, plain blade. Many examples are found with the blade marked *"Runkel"*, the well known Napoleonic German blade importer, based in London.

C.1780 HIGHLAND OFFICER'S SWORD
VALUE: $2075.00/£1295.00
Scottish Infantry Officer's half basket hilt. Blade is marked with a *"G"* to the forte, indicating possible manufacture by Thomas Gill of Birmingham. The letter *"G"* is seen on many swords of the period.

SCOTTISH 1798 PATTERN HIGHLAND OFFICER'S BROADSWORD
VALUE: $2700.00/£1695.00
This is the first regulation Scottish Highland Officer's broadsword. There are few contemporary details indicating the exact form this sword was supposed to take. According to *"The View of the Standing Regulations for the Colours, Clothing etc., of the Infantry"* (1802), it was to be *"according to a particular pattern at the Comptroller's Office"*. Hilt and scabbard mounts were of gilded copper or brass.

C.1815 SCOTTISH LIGHT COMPANY OFFICER'S SWORD
VALUE: $1910.00/£1195.00
Sword of the 21st Regiment of Foot (Royal North British Fusiliers). The regiment is more commonly known by their later designation, The Royal Scots Fusiliers.

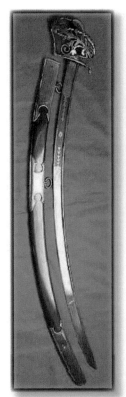

C.1800 SCOTTISH SENIOR OFFICER'S LIGHT INFANTRY SWORD
VALUE: $8000.00/£5000.00

Superb example of a senior Scottish Light Infantry or Flank Officer's Sword. Is probably a unique piece, with gilt brass half basket hilt, elegantly overlaid with thistles and foliage. The blue and gilt decoration to the blade is also highly unusual. It is most likely that this was a captured senior French officer's blade mounted on an English hilt. The scabbard has gilt metal mounts with blued metal body, rather than the usual leather. There are no apparent maker's marks to blade or hilt. This is not unusual, even with such a high quality piece.

British Army, c.1815.

C.1800'S SCOTTISH BANDSMAN'S(?) MAMELUKE SWORD
VALUE: $ 1595.00/£ 995.00

This is a very unusual example, faintly marked "75" to the hilt ecusson. This designation is likely to indicate use by the 75th (Highland) Regiment of Foot, later to become the Gordon Highlanders. Of very basic and crude manufacture with a wide, single-fullered and curved blade.

C.1850 SCOTTISH BANDSMAN'S SWORD
VALUE: $ 1435.00/£ 895.00

The Indian Mutiny, Lucknow, 1857.

C.1780 SCOTTISH INFANTRY OFFICER'S SWORD
VALUE: $ 3035.00/£ 1895.00

Non-regulation example with steel three-bar hilt and Scottish thistle and royal crown in cartouche. Blade is of typical smallsword type with deeply incised etching, highlighted with gilding. Decoration is very typical of the styling found on period hunting swords and civilian smallswords. Blade might be a replacement.

Officer,
Argyll and
Sutherland
Highlanders,
1851.

SCOTTISH 1828/1831 PATTERN HIGHLAND INFANTRY OFFICER'S BROADSWORD
VALUE: $1435.00/£895.00

Above and right:
SCOTTISH 1828/1831 PATTERN HIGHLAND INFANTRY OFFICER'S BROADSWORD (LEVEE)
VALUE: $1435.00/£895.00

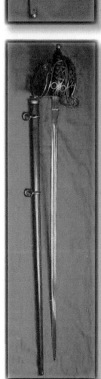

SCOTTISH 1828/1831 PATTERN HIGHLAND INFANTRY OFFICER'S (GORDON HIGHLANDERS) BROADSWORD
VALUE: $2595.00/£1480.00

The dates of 1828 and 1831 are frequently used to describe the year of introduction for this broadsword. This is somewhat confusing for the collector, but is basically describing the same pattern of sword i.e. the 1828 Pattern, but with minor on-going changes, mainly of a scabbard or regimental nature. The year 1828 actually refers to a circular sent to highland regiments announcing the new pattern of sword which, the 1831 Dress Regulations, confirmed in more formal terms. There is a later Victorian field service version of the scabbard with brown leather and nickel plated throat and ball chape. Scabbards were previously manufactured in black leather with steel mounts. Most examples date from the late Victorian era and feature a steel or nickel plated steel scabbard with ball chape. Later basket hilts enabled the owner to unscrew the bun pommel and replace the basket with a dress cross-hilt.

Officer,
Cameron
Highlanders,
1854.

165

Seaforth Highlanders

Highland Light Infantry

C.1880 SCOTTISH HIGHLAND INFANTRY OFFICER'S CROSS-HILTED BROADSWORD (ROYAL SCOTS FUSILIERS)
VALUE: $ 1435.00/£895.00

The Scottish officer's cross-hilted broadsword made its debut during the mid-nineteenth century. It had already been accepted that the standard basket hilt was not a comfortable sword to carry, both in combat and undress situations. The cross-hilt remedied this problem. Each regiment tended to adopt their own hilt design and these can be identified by observing the pommel, hilt quillons and langets. Examples include the Seaforth and Argyll and Sutherland Highlanders, who carried a hilt with bun pommel and ball quillons. Like the regulation basket hilt, the cross-hilt could be disassembled, with the pommel, grip and cross-bar interchangeable with the basket hilt. The cross-hilt had a relatively short life and most examples are late-Victorian and early Edwardian in date. The Black Watch never chose to carry a cross-hilt.

London Scottish

Left:
C.WW1 LONDON SCOTTISH OFFICER'S CROSS-HILTED BROADSWORD
VALUE: $ 1275.00/£795.00

**C.1850 ROYAL SCOTS
NCO'S SWORD**
VALUE: $1435.00/£895.00

**SCOTTISH 1857
PATTERN FIELD
OFFICER'S SWORD**
VALUE: $1435.00/£895.00

**C.1850 ROYAL SCOTS
FUSILIERS OFFICER'S
SWORD**
VALUE: $2075.00/£1295.00
Rare officer's sword to the Royal
Scots Fusiliers. It is very difficult to
date precisely as the title "Royal Scots
Fusiliers" was not officially
adopted until 1887, but the pipe
back blade and 1822 Pattern hilt,
would suggest a much earlier origin.
Blade shows faint traces of
decoration. To find one with
original scabbard is very unusual.

Drum Major, c.1890.

**C.WWI LONDON SCOTTISH
OFFICER'S BASKET - HILTED
SWORD**
VALUE: $1910.00/£1195.00

167

1803 PATTERN INFANTRY/FLANK OFFICER'S SWORD
VALUE: $ 3200.00/£2000.00

By 1800, this type of curved sabre had already been adopted, (albeit unofficially), by many light infantry officers. It is one of the most attractive of British pattern swords. Subtle variations are noted to the knucklebow and lionshead pommel. The knucklebow can also feature either a strung bugle or flaming grenade above the royal cypher, denoting use by both grenadiers and rifle companies. Blades were normally found with lavish blue and gilt decoration. Examples with ivory grips are likely to have been carried by more senior officers.

1803 PATTERN INFANTRY/FLANK OFFICER'S SWORD
VALUE: $ 1910.00/£1195.00

Death of Colonel Donellan, Battle of Talavera, 1809.

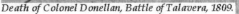

C.1830 PIONEER'S SAWBACK SWORD
VALUE: $1110.0/£695.00

This is a sword that appears not to have had any known official designation or acknowledgement. It is the forerunner of the 1856 Pattern Pioneer's Sword. The lionshead pommel is very much indicative of Georgian military styling, as is the pronounced stirrup hilt. Condition is crucial. Not many of these swords are found with their original scabbards and, consequently, examples tend to have very worn blades. Regimental markings are also normally absent.

1856 PATTERN PIONEER'S SAWBACK SWORD
VALUE: $795.00/£495.00

This sword was based on the British Army's perceived need for an effective battlefield tool. Pioneers were a crucial part of any British infantry regiment. Their role included the preparation of defensive works and constructing military accommodation. The sawback blade was also used to cut down trees and clear a pathway for troops. This type of blade had already seen service in many other armies, including Russia, Austria and Prussia.

The Indian Mutiny, 1857.

Ensign Pennycuik defending his father's body at the Battle of Chillianwalla, 1849.

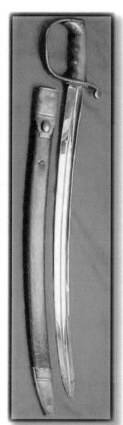

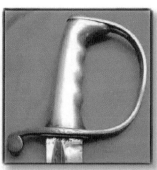

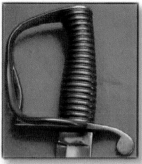

C.1850 "DUNDAS" ROYAL ARTILLERY SWORD
VALUE: $1275.00/£795.00

Developed by Colonel W.B. Dundas, who originally served as a lieutenant with the Royal Artillery during the Napoleonic Wars. It was designed to be carried by soldiers manning field guns. It is a heavy sword, with solid brass hilt and thick blade. Its service life was relatively short, probably from around 1845 to 1860, and numbers produced were small. This sword, although associated with the Royal Artillery, is also likely to have been issued as an all-purpose hanger for different service branches, including Customs, Police and Prison Officers. Many are unmarked or stamped with a *"BO"* - Board of Ordnance.

C.1860 ARMY HOSPITAL CORPS PRIVATE'S SWORD
VALUE: $950.00/£595.00

Curiously, all ranks within the military medical establishment carried some form of edged weapon, and this included privates or medical orderlies. There is no official recognition of this sword. Hilt and grip are manufactured in cast iron, thus making the sword quite heavy and unwieldy.

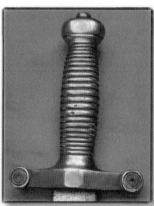

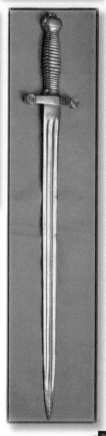

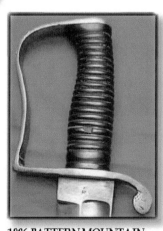

1896 PATTERN MOUNTAIN ARTILLERY SWORD
VALUE: $1110.00/£695.00

This sword was carried by troops of mountain artillery batteries, particularly in northern Indian and Afghanistan. It is often confused with the British 1796 Pattern Light Cavalry Trooper's Sword.

C.1855 LAND TRANSPORT CORPS DRIVER'S SWORD
VALUE: $395.00/£225.00

Formed towards the end of the Crimean War, the Land Transport Corps was an attempt to provide a more organised system of transport for the British Army. This sword is intriguing because there appears to be little evidence that it was actually carried by soldiers of the L.T.C, although this is how it is described in most publications. No examples that the author has seen bear this designation. The design was based on contemporary gladius-style short swords carried throughout Europe (particularly France).

C.1820 BANDSWORD
VALUE: $ 630.00/£ 395.00

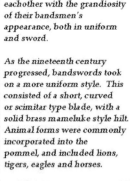

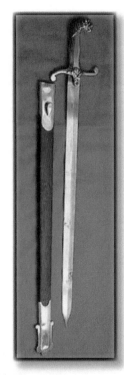

UP UNTIL THE 1820'S, the position of the bandsman in the British Army was quite unique. Bands were comprised of civilians and were not normally required to join their regiments on overseas or active service. During the late - eighteenth and early nineteenth century, the responsibility for the upkeep of the musician was entirely that of the regiment. Consequently, a wide variety of sword designs were produced with some regiments trying to outdo eachother with the grandiosity of their bandsmen's appearance, both in uniform and sword.

As the nineteenth century progressed, bandswords took on a more uniform style. This consisted of a short, curved or scimitar type blade, with a solid brass mameluke style hilt. Animal forms were commonly incorporated into the pommel, and included lions, tigers, eagles and horses.

C.1850 BUGLER'S PRESENTATION SWORD
VALUE: $ 1110.00/ £ 695.00
Silver plated example with presentation inscription to grip. Most of these swords were produced in brass and presentation swords are very scarce. It was presented to a bugler in a volunteer company.

C.1820 BANDSWORD
VALUE: $ 1110.00/£ 695.00

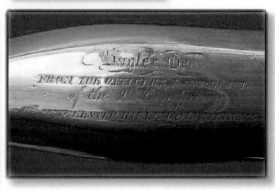

1856 PATTERN DRUMMER'S/BUGLER'S SWORD (FOR RIFLE REGIMENTS)
VALUE: $635.00/£395.00

1856 PATTERN DRUMMER'S/BUGLER'S SWORD (FOR INFANTRY REGIMENTS)
VALUE: $635.00/£395.00

1895 PATTERN DRUMMER'S/BUGLER'S SWORD (FOR INFANTRY REGIMENTS)
VALUE: $635.00/£395.00

Unlike bandsmen, drummers and buglers were enlisted soldiers and could be ordered to fight alongside their fellow soldiers. Swords tend to be regimentally marked to both hilt and scabbard.

Bugler, Sherwood Foresters, c.1890.

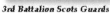

3rd Battalion Scots Guards

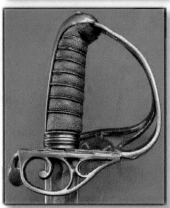

George IV

William IV

Victoria

General Officer

1822 PATTERN INFANTRY OFFICER'S SWORD
VALUE: $1100.00/ £695.00

The 1822 Pattern Infantry Officer's Sword was a radical departure from previous designs. The half basket hilt was soon to become the standard form for British infantry swords until the end of the nineteenth century. Distinctive features of the sword include the *"Gothic"* style pierced hilt, so-called after its resemblance to the shapes of windows in Gothic architecture. Extremely elegant in design, the slender pipe-backed blade was sheathed in a black leather scabbard with decorated gilt brass mounts. It is also found with brass and steel scabbards. The royal cypher was placed within an oval hilt cartouche. During its lifetime, the cyphers of three monarchs (George IV, William IV, and Victoria) are noted for this pattern.

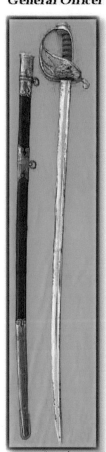

www.antiqueswords.com

1827 PATTERN RIFLE OFFICER'S SWORD

VALUE: $795.00/£495.00

Originally raised as the King's Royal Rifle Corps in 1755, the Rifle Brigade was officially formed in 1800. Initially, officers carried a lighter version of the 1796 Pattern Light Cavalry Sword, later adopting the 1803 Pattern Infantry Officer's Sword, with strung bugle motif placed within the knucklebow. The regiment was always noted for its individuality, both in uniform and tactics, and it is no wonder that they eventually gained their own distinctive pattern of sword. The 1827 Pattern is defined by an all-steel hilt coupled with the replacement of the usual royal cypher with a strung bugle in the hilt cartouche. Post-Victorian examples tend to feature a nickel-plated hilt and scabbard. Most swords are from volunteer/militia units (marked accordingly on the blade) raised during the Victorian era.

1827 PATTERN NCO'S SWORD

VALUE: $795.00/ £495.00

Meeting of British Rifle Volunteers, c.1850's.

C.1870 HONOURABLE ARTILLERY COMPANY OFFICER'S SWORD
VALUE: $ 950.00/£595.00

Established in 1537, the Honourable Artillery Company is the oldest regiment in the British Army. It was primarily a citizen militia, and raised in times of national emergency, including the Armada, English Civil War and Napoleonic Wars. Up until the Victorian era, officers would have followed regular infantry sword patterns. As this was a volunteer army, they would have had to pay for all service equipment, including their own swords. This sword highlights the strong influence of French sword design at this time, particularly with regard to the knucklebow and angled or canted pommel.

1845/1854 PATTERN INFANTRY OFFICER'S SWORD
VALUE: $ 795.00/£495.00

This is the successor to the 1822 Pattern Infantry Officer's Sword. There are two main changes. The blade was of the *"Wilkinson"*, single-fullered type, and the fold down guard has been removed.

Sword sharpening, c.1900.

General and Staff Officer's Sword with crossed batons to the ecusson.

1831 PATTERN GENERAL/STAFF OFFICER'S MAMELUKE SWORD

VALUE: $1435.00/ £895.00

The introduction of the 1831 Pattern followed a vogue for mameluke style swords during the 1800's. It is still worn by British General Officers and Lord Lieutenants. There is also a version formerly carried by the British Indian Political Service. It features a royal coat of arms in the crossguard ecusson.

General Tyndall, c.1870.

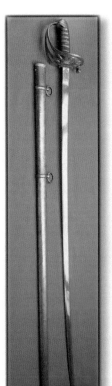

1854 PATTERN FOOT GUARD'S OFFICER'S (SCOTS GUARDS) SWORD
VALUE: $1100.00/ £695.00

This sword is specific to the regiments of Foot Guards. The hilt cartouche features the badges of the Grenadier Guards, Coldstream Guards, Irish, Scots and Welsh Guards. It is virtually identical in design to the 1827 Pattern Rifle Officer's Sword. It has a steel (later nickel-plated) hilt. Many are found in the light or picquet weight version and exhibit very slender blades. What makes these swords particularly attractive is that most blades are fully etched for most of their length with the particular regiment's numerous battle honours. Some examples also include the owner's initials or family crest which can possibly aid identification. Examples by Henry Wilkinson are especially sought after and can be more easily traced.

Welsh Guards

Coldstream Guards

Irish Guards

Grenadier Guards

Officer, Grenadier Guards, c.1900.

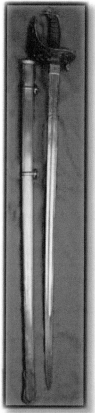

1857 PATTERN ROYAL ENGINEERS' OFFICER'S SWORD
VALUE: $ 1100.00/£ 695.00

Royal Engineers' officers carried standard infantry pattern swords from 1786. In the Victorian era, the Royal Engineers established a specific and unique role for themselves and underlined their independence with a new design of sword. It is one of the most attractive of British Victorian sword designs and features a pierced gilt brass bowl hilt, with deep scrolled acanthus-leafed decoration. This pattern of sword was carried until the late-nineteenth century when it was replaced by the 1892/1895, and finally, the 1897 Pattern Infantry Officer's Sword.

1889 PATTERN STAFF SERGEANT'S INFANTRY SWORD
VALUE: $ 950.00/£ 595.00

This sword was specifically designed for staff sergeants and features a heavy, flat-backed blade. A straight steel scabbard with fixed rings was unique to this pattern.

British Army Officer, c.1860.

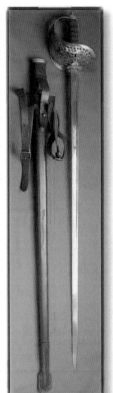

1895/1897 PATTERN INFANTRY OFFICER'S SWORD
VALUE: $ 795.00/£495.00

This sword was a great improvement on previous patterns, with better protection to the wearer's hand through its new three-quarter basket hilt. This pattern lacked a fold-down inner guard to prevent fraying of the uniform. It was added in the 1897 Pattern (see below left).

Battle of Laings Nek, South Africa, 1881.

www.antiquesswords.com

www.antiquesswords.com

1905 PATTERN SERGEANT'S (NCO'S) SWORD
VALUE: $ 1275.00/£ 795.00

In 1905, the British military authorities deemed it necessary to produce another staff sergeant's sword. This was very much an ad-hoc design and may have been a short-term response to swords lost during the recent Boer War. It was quite an hybrid, with the cut-down blade of a 1899 Pattern Cavalry Trooper's Sword, and a 1897 Pattern Staff Sergeant's hilt. Grip with fishskin and steel rivets. The sword is rarely seen and numbers produced were relatively small.

1889 PATTERN SERGEANT'S (NCO'S) SWORD
VALUE: $ 950.00/£ 595.00

Sword is marked to the Welch Fusiliers.

MODEL 1870 LEADCUTTER SWORD
VALUE: $ 1275.00/£ 795.00

These swords were never meant for combat but designed solely for the purpose of improving the swordsman's cutting technique and strength. Lead bars with varying degrees of thickness were either suspended or placed upright on a stool, and cuts made in a chopping motion. When the swordsman had become proficient in cutting the lead bars, he could then move on to a sheep's carcass or legs of lamb. The Model 1870 is the only known official pattern. In practical terms, just one size and blade weight was not sufficient to accurately test swordsmen with differing arm strengths. This was resolved with the use of varied blade weights, numbered from 1 to 4. The *"Number 4"* blade weighs in at well over four pounds. These swords are often mistaken for naval cutlasses.

1899 PATTERN GYMNASIUM SWORD
VALUE: $475.00/£295.00

The ability to wield a sword effectively was always a vital factor in the basic training of a military swordsman. Up until the Crimean War, training included a series of pre-ordained parries and thrusts laid down in military manuals, most notably, Le Marchant's, *"Sword Exercise of the Cavalry"* (1796). The appropriate regulation sword would be used and much thrusting and slashing inflicted on straw-filled dummies. As the nineteenth century progressed and the British Army became more standardised and scientific in its approach to warfare, one of the natural consequences was a belief that swordmanship could be improved by leaning towards the athletic and methodical approach found within the art of fencing. In parallel with the regulation swords used for practice, a new series of patterns based on fencing sabres were also introduced. These included the 1864 Pattern, 1895 Pattern, 1899 Pattern, 1904 Pattern, 1907 Pattern and the 1911 Pattern. Pre-1899 examples are extremely scarce.

1907 PATTERN GYMNASIUM SWORD
VALUE: $475.00/£295.00

1911 PATTERN GYMNASIUM SWORD
VALUE: $295.00/£170.00

C.1900 ARMY GYMNASIUM SWORD
VALUE: $315.00/£195.00

SCOTS GREYS

ROYAL HORSE GUARDS

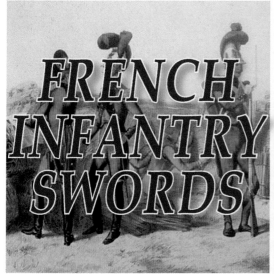

FRENCH INFANTRY SWORDS

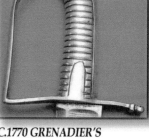

C.1770 GRENADIER'S HANGER
VALUE: $1275.00/£795.00

This style of hanger followed an official pattern of 1767 that required the introduction of a *"grenadier sabre"*. Swords of this style were already in circulation but this sword standardised the pattern. The ribbed grip to the brass hilt and reversed langet is typical of French swords during this period. Collectors often believe that the langet has been cut flush with the hilt guard but this is not the case. This example is in excellent condition with a single-edged and slightly curved blade. They are rarely found with the original scabbard.

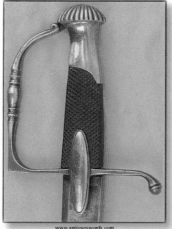

www.antiqueswords.com

C.1800 FLANK OFFICER'S SWORD
VALUE: $1275.00/ £795.00

Typical French infantry officer's sword with classical styling, including a slightly canted domed and fluted pommel with double langets. Grip is of chequered ebony. It is likely that the scabbard would have been composed of leather with plain brass mounts.

C.1800 FLANK OFFICER'S SWORD
VALUE: $1110.00/ £695.00

This sword shows an exaggerated neo-classical hilt style and is quite unusual in having a cut steel hilt. Many French infantry swords of this period are manufactured in brass. Blade is straight, unmarked and plain.

C.1800 GRENADIER'S HANGER
VALUE: $950.00/£595.00

REGIMENTAL EAGLE

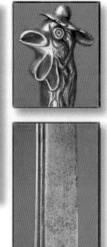

FRENCH C.1800 SAPPER'S SWORD
VALUE: $1910.00/£1195.00
With typical cockerel-headed pommel. Crossed sappers' axes within the hilt cartouche. Wide, double-fullered blade.

FRENCH C.1770 GRENADIER'S SWORD
VALUE: $950.00/£595.00

C.1780'S NATIONAL VOLUNTEER OFFICER'S SWORD (FOLDING GUARD)
VALUE: $2235.00/£1395.00
Of a type noted in French swords of the Revolutionary and Napoleonic period. The "single" guard is folded out into three bars during combat. Because of the relative shortness of the blade, hilts of this type are also seen in French naval swords of the period.

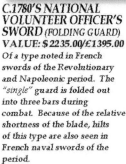

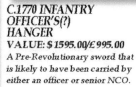

C.1780 INFANTRY HANGER
VALUE: $950.00/£595.00
With an unmarked blade. The half langet and simple quillon style are similar to French infantry and artillery hangers of the Pre-Revolutionary period.

C.1770 INFANTRY OFFICER'S(?) HANGER
VALUE: $1595.00/£995.00
A Pre-Revolutionary sword that is likely to have been carried by either an officer or senior NCO.

C.1805 SAPEUR'S ("PIONEERS OF THE OLD GUARD") SWORD
VALUE: $2235.00/ £1395.00

One of the most distinctive of French infantry swords. It was only issued to pioneers and featured a cockerel's-head pommel and ram's-head quillons. Very few are seen with the original scabbard. Many examples have a saw-tooth blade. Copies are known.

Imperial Guard, c.1805.

Battle of Baylen, 1808.

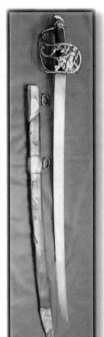

C.1790 VOLUNTEER GUARD OFFICER'S SWORD
VALUE: $3200.00/£2000.00

C.1815 SUPERIOR INFANTRY OFFICER'S SWORD
VALUE: $1435.00/£895.00
Decorative and stylish sword with gilt brass hilt mounts and mother-of-pearl banded grip. An inlaid panel to the grip depicts a winged Victory holding a laurel wreath above her head. The Victory motif is repeated to the shell guard.

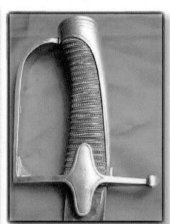

C.1810 INFANTRY OFFICER'S SWORD
VALUE: $1595.00/£995.00

Battle of Austerlitz, 1805.

C.1820 GENERAL OFFICER'S SWORD
VALUE: $ 1595.00/£ 995.00

From the Restoration Period, and of very high quality. This would have been carried by a very senior officer. The blue and gilt decoration to the blade is still extremely bright. The mother-of-pearl grips are also intact and without damage.

C.1850-1871 GENDARMERIE WARRANT OFFICER'S SWORD
VALUE: $ 635.00/£ 375.00

With plain, double-fullered blade. Cast brass shell guard with French Eagle and banners.

Below left and right:

C.1800 INFANTRY OFFICER'S SWORD
VALUE: $ 1595.00/ £ 995.00

From the Consulate Period. With very fine pattern-welded damask blade. Blade would originally have been blued for half its length.

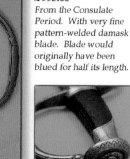

C.1825 INFANTRY OFFICER'S SWORD
VALUE: $ 950.00/£ 595.00

With unusual dogs-head pommel and sweeping, classically styled shellguard. This style of sword emerged during the Restoration period, particularly during the reigns of Charles X (1824-1830) and Louis Phillipe (1830-1848). Grip is of finely chequered ebony.

C.1800 INFANTRY GUARD OFFICER'S SWORD
VALUE: $1100.00/£ 695.00

Typical plumed helmet pommel and boat shell hilt.

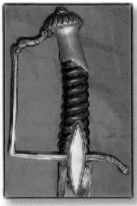

**C.1800 INFANTRY
OFFICER'S SWORD**
VALUE: $2075.00/£1295.00
The pronounced double langet,
geometric styling to the
stirrup hilt and the canted,
fluted, domed pommel, are all
indicative of the great influence
of neo-classical French design at
the height of the First Empire.
The slightly curved blade still
retains some original blue and
gilt decoration. The horn grip
is deeply ribbed. Scabbard with
leather and brass mounts.

**C.1820 INFANTRY
OFFICER'S SWORD**
VALUE: $1100.00/£695.00
Solid brass hilt with distinctive
tortoiseshell slab grips.

**MODEL 1816 MUSICIAN'S
SWORD**
VALUE: $560.00/£350.00

French Army outside Moscow, 1812.

www.michaeldlong.com

C.1800 INFANTRY OFFICER'S SWORD (WITH FOLDING HILT)
VALUE: $1595.00/ £995.00

With scalloped folding hilt bar that could be retracted when not in combat use. These folding or "attack" hilts were quite common in the French Army (and Navy) during the Napoleonic Wars. It proved less popular with British and allied armies. They are found with both lionshead and plain pommels (see above left).

www.michaeldlong.com

C.1800 SENIOR INFANTRY OFFICER'S SWORD
VALUE: $3200.00/£2000.00

Superb quality example with finely chequered ivory grip and gilt brass mounts. Decoration is of high classical form.

www.michaeldlong.com

C.1790 INFANTRY/ MILITIA OFFICER'S SWORD
VALUE: $1435.00/ £895.00

Revolutionary period infantry officer's sword. Probably for a militia officer and engraved with military symbols and the Phrygian Cap of the French Revolution.

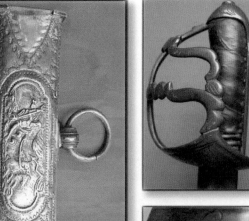

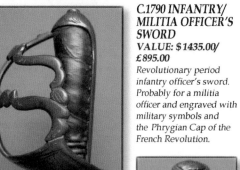

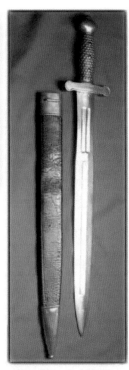

MODEL 1831 INFANTRY SWORD
VALUE: $525.00/£300.00
Heavily influenced by the classical styling of the period and based on an ancient Roman Gladius. Sword. These swords were made in very large quantities. Condition is a prime factor and many are without scabbards. Blades can therefore suffer much corrosion. Most examples are dated and maker marked (see below).

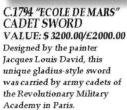

C.1794 "ECOLE DE MARS" CADET SWORD
VALUE: $ 3200.00/£2000.00
Designed by the painter Jacques Louis David, this unique gladius-style sword was carried by army cadets of the Revolutionary Military Academy in Paris.

Sortie from Paris, 1871.

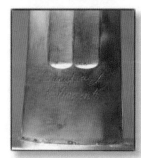

MODEL 1816 ARTILLERY SWORD
VALUE: $ 1435.00/£895.00

Capture of Son-Tai, 1883.

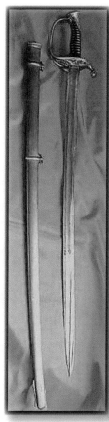

MODEL 1845/1855 INFANTRY OFFICER'S SWORD
VALUE: $595.00/£340.00

The standard infantry officer's sword from the 1840's through to the 1900's. The quality of French-made examples of this sword are normally very high, particularly the quill-point blade. It had a great influence on the design of other nations' infantry swords, most notably the United States, where the US Model 1850 Staff and Field Officer's Sword and Model 1852 Naval Officer's Sword, are almost identical copies. Blades are usually maker marked with the French arsenal at Chatelleraut.

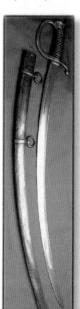

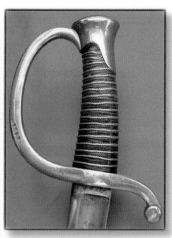

MODEL 1829 MOUNTED ARTILLERYMAN'S SWORD
VALUE: $ 950.00/£ 595.00

This sword design was heavily copied by other nations, including the United States, in the form of the Model 1840 Light Artillery Sword.

www.michaeldlong.com

HILT DETAIL TO MODEL 1845 INFANTRY OFFICER'S SWORD

MODEL 1882 INFANTRY OFFICER'S SWORD
VALUE: $495.00/£280.00
The sword of General Georges Comte de Villebois-Marevil, commander of a European unit in the Boer Army during the Anglo-Boer War (1899-1902). Killed in action.

Zouave Captain, c.1855.

Zouave Captain, c.1870.

Zouave Captain, c.1910.

MODEL 1845/1855 INFANTRY OFFICER'S SWORD
VALUE: $795.00/£495.00

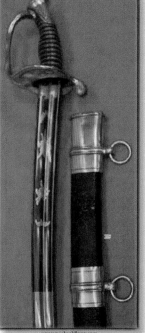

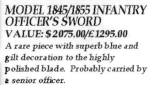

www.michaelllong.com

MODEL 1845/1855 INFANTRY OFFICER'S SWORD
VALUE: $2075.00/£1295.00
A rare piece with superb blue and gilt decoration to the highly polished blade. Probably carried by a senior officer.

Below; left and right:
C.1850 INFANTRY OFFICER'S SWORD
VALUE: $1395.00/£800.00
Likely to be a special order piece as the hilt style and scabbard mounts are not traditional. The two stars on underside of the guard indicate the rank of Brigadier General.

www.michaelllong.com

MODEL 1882 INFANTRY OFFICER'S SWORD
VALUE: $475.00/£295.00

www.michaelllong.com

www.michaelllong.com

www.michaelllong.com

www.michaelllong.com

www.michaelllong.com

GERMAN INFANTRY SWORDS

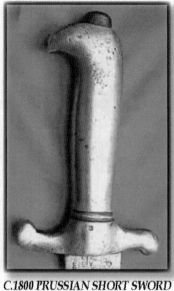

C.1800 PRUSSIAN SHORT SWORD
VALUE: $475.00/£295.00
Solid brass bird's-head pommel. With most German military swords, hilt crossguards and scabbard throats tend to be regimentally marked.

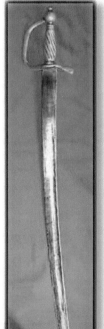

MODEL 1816 INFANTRY HANGER
VALUE: $1100.00/£695.00
This sword design had a very long service life and was also carried by a number of other European countries, including Britain, Denmark and Sweden. Its style is very much that of the mid-eighteenth century. Blades are sometimes found with the engraved royal cypher of the reigning German state monarch.

MODEL 1817/1869 INFANTRY HANGER
VALUE: $560.00/£350.00
This hanger was based on the common French Napoleonic "sabre-briquet". Large numbers were captured by German forces during the Napoleonic Wars and subsequently used by their troops. It was also extensively copied and manufactured by German swordmakers and carried throughout the nineteenth century by many other European nations. Condition is usually a factor with this type of sword and many are in a poor state and without scabbard.

German Army, c.1866.

C.1800 BAVARIAN INFANTRY OFFICER'S SWORD
VALUE: $2695.00/ £1695.00

Superb example of a Bavarian Napoleonic infantry officer's sword. With cut steel hilt and five ball or beaded knucklebow. Fluted and domed pommel. Cigar-band to the chequered ebony grip, incorporating a royal cypher. Blade with cypher of King Maximillian I.

www.michaeldlong.com

www.michaeldlong.com

C.WW1 TRAIN BATTALION OFFICER'S SWORD
VALUE: $350.00/£200.00

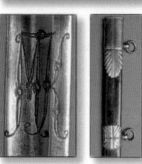

MODEL 1852 INFANTRY HANGER
VALUE: $635.00/£395.00

This infantry hanger is found in a number of variations, including sawback and shortened cadet forms. Most will have a regimental designation stamped to both the hilt crossguard and the scabbard top mount. Inspectors' marks are also present on the sword mounts. This sword was based on the Model 1849 Artillery Sword with a smooth grip, rather than the later spiral grooved examples. Although not uncommon, it is seldom seen with the original scabbard. Like most short infantry hangers of this period, it was probably of little practical use.

MODEL 1855 PRUSSIAN INFANTRY PIONEER'S SHORT SWORD
VALUE: $560.00/£350.00

C.1860 PRUSSIAN INFANTRY SIDEARM
VALUE: $495.00/£280.00
Hilt and scabbard throat is regimentally marked.

C.1850 INFANTRY SHORT SWORD
VALUE: $395.00/£225.00
The exact German state designation of this piece is unknown but it is noted as having a very distinctive *"beak"* pommel. The blade is marked as being of German manufacture. The solid brass ribbed grip is reminiscent of the type found on French and German *"sabre briquet"* sidearms, but lacks the typical stirrup hilt.

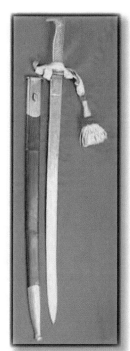

www.antiqueswords.com

www.antiqueswords.com

MODEL 1871 PRUSSIAN INFANTRY SIDEARM
VALUE: $ 635.00/£ 395.00

C.1900'S BAVARIAN BORDER GUARD'S SHORT SWORD
VALUE: $ 1275.00/£ 795.00
This is a rare sword. The blade is etched with the Bavarian state motto, "In Treue Fest" (In True Faith).

www.michaeldlong.com

www.michaeldlong.com

Prussian Army, c.1871.

www.michaeldlong.com

C.1900 SAXON INFANTRY OFFICER'S SWORD
VALUE: $ 720.00/£ 450.00

MODEL 1889 PRUSSIAN INFANTRY OFFICER'S SWORD
VALUE: $ 635.00/£ 395.00
With hilt cartouche of Emperor Wilhelm II.

www.antiqueswords.com

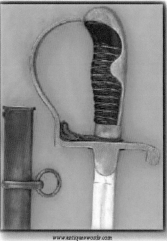

www.antiqueswords.com

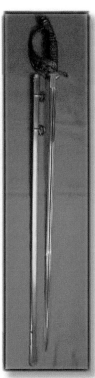

MODEL 1889 WURTTEMBURG INFANTRY OFFICER'S SWORD
VALUE: $ 795.00/£495.00

With the state of Wurttemburg coat of arms to the hilt cartouche. Because of the differing number of German states that carried this model of sword, there are also varying degrees of rarity to examples. Prussian examples are far more common.

www.antiqueswords.com

C.1920 WEIMAR PRUSSIAN INFANTRY NCO'S SWORD
VALUE: $ 720.00/£450.00

The solid brass hilt is of typical *"dovehead"* form. The grip is manufactured from a composite or plastic and wrapped in brass twistwire. The underside of the crossguard is stamped with an official acceptance mark and serial number. Blade is nickel-plated and plain.

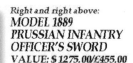

C.1890 INFANTRY SHORT SWORD
VALUE: $ 635.00/£395.00

Although not unit marked, this is likely to be of German or Dutch origin. The blade forte is stamped with the company initials and King's Head motif for Weyersberg, Schnitzler and Kirschbaum, Solingen, Germany. They produced a large number of swords for export throughout Europe during the nineteenth century.

Right and right above:
MODEL 1889 PRUSSIAN INFANTRY OFFICER'S SWORD
VALUE: $ 1275.00/£455.00

A luxury version of the standard model with heavy floral embellishments to the gilt hilt. Blade is plain and retains a mirror polish. Grip with standard fishskin and brass twistwire. Many German officers chose to have their personal initials (monogram) or family coat of arms engraved at the top of the hilt backstrap / pommel (particularly with regard to this model).

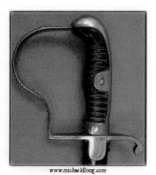

www.michaelclong.com

C. WWI ARTILLERY OFFICER'S SWORD
VALUE: $475.00/£295.00

www.michaelclong.com

C. WWI SAXON ARTILLERY NCO'S SWORD
VALUE: $475.00/£295.00

www.antiqueswords.com

SAXON MODEL 1874 ARTILLERYMAN'S SWORD
VALUE: $525.00/£300.00
Manufactured by "WK & C" (Weyersberg, Kirschbaum and Company), indicating post-1883 manufacture.

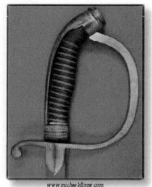

www.michaelclong.com

C. WWI BAVARIAN(?) ARTILLERY SWORD
VALUE: $475.00/£295.00

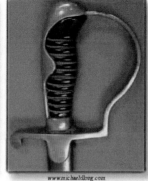

www.michaelclong.com

C.1920 PRUSSIAN ARTILLERY SWORD
VALUE: $495.00/£295.00

German Coastal Infantry, c.1910.

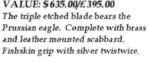

www.antiqueswords.com

C.1890 PRUSSIAN DOVE-HEAD OFFICER'S SWORD
VALUE: $635.00/£395.00
The triple etched blade bears the Prussian eagle. Complete with brass and leather mounted scabbard. Fishskin grip with silver twistwire.

www.antiqueswords.com

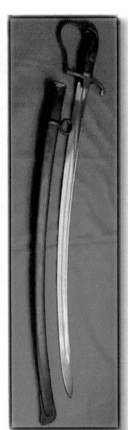

PRUSSIAN 1918 ARTILLERYMAN'S SWORD
VALUE: $ 795.00/£ 495.00

Dated to the spine and with regimental designation to hilt crossguard and scabbard. The stamps to the spine include the crowned *"W"* for Wilhelm II, date mark for 1918, maker's mark of *"RC"* (unknown) and official inspector's mark.

www.antiqueswords.com

C.WWI PRUSSIAN ARTILLERY OFFICER'S SWORD
VALUE: $ 635.00/£ 395.00

www.antiqueswords.com

Hanover Army, 1866.

Hanover Army, 1866.

Cavalry Trooper, c.1914.

www.michaeldlong.com

**MODEL 1889
WURTTEMBURG
INFANTRY OFFICER'S
SWORD**
VALUE: $ 795.00/£ 495.00

www.michaeldlong.com

www.michaeldlong.com

German Balloon Unit, c.1910.

**PRUSSIAN MODEL 1889
INFANTRY OFFICER'S
SWORD**
VALUE: $ 1275.00/£ 795.00
Scarce example with Garde
Regiment badge and royal
cypher of Emperor Wilhelm
II applied to the fishskin and
brass twistwire grip.

GERMAN 1888 ARTILLERY OFFICER'S PRESENTATION GRADE SWORD
VALUE: $2075.00/£1295.00

Very high quality presentation grade officer's sword. Deeply etched blade inset with blue and gilt panels. Crossguard is engraved with the owner's initials and his monogram to the langet. The company of Ewald Cleff was based in Solingen and had a long business history, producing both swords and bayonets from 1867-1966. During WW2, it combined manufacture with Hugo Koeller. Their main products were bayonets and daggers.

www.michaeldlong.com

www.michaeldlong.com

C.WWI SAXON ARTILLERY TRAIN BATTALION OFFICER'S SWORD
VALUE: $ 795.00/£ 495.00

www.michaeldlong.com

www.michaeldlong.com

www.michaeldlong.com

C.1890 BAVARIAN(?) ARTILLERYMAN'S SWORD
VALUE: $ 560.00/£ 350.00

www.antiqueswords.com

www.michaeldlong.com

Above:
Detail of langet from late-war example. Owner's monogram to the reverse langet. Note the relative crudity of the engraving.
Left:
C.WWII INFANTRY OFFICER'S SWORD
VALUE: $ 795.00/£ 495.00

www.michaeldlong.com

C.WWI SAXON MINING OFFICIAL'S SWORD
VALUE: $ 1100.00/£ 695.00

www.michaeldlong.com

PRUSSIAN 1920 ARTILLERY OFFICER'S SWORD
VALUE: $ 635.00/£ 395.00

www.michaelilong.com

**C.WWII INFANTRY
OFFICER'S SWORD
VALUE: $795.00/£495.00**
With maker's mark to blade
forte, indicating the Puma
factory at Solingen.

www.michaelilong.com

www.michaelilong.com

**C.WWII
INFANTRY
OFFICER'S
SWORD
VALUE:
$950.00/£595.00**
Excellent example
with lionshead
pommel and gilt
hilt mounts. Most
infantry officer's
swords of this
period feature
simulated
"jewelled" eyes.
Blades are mostly
nickel-plated and
plain. The grip is
made of celluloid
with silver
twistwire.
Scabbards are
black, painted
steel.

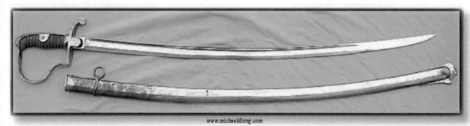

www.michaelilong.com

**C.WWI
PRUSSIAN
ARTILLERY
OFFICER'S
SWORD
VALUE:
$795.00/£495.00**
Plated blade and
scabbard.

German Infantry NCO's, c.1939.

German Infantry Officer, c.1940.

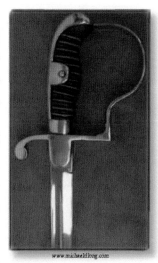

**C.WWI INFANTRY NCO'S
OFFICER'S SWORD**
VALUE: $400.00/£250.00

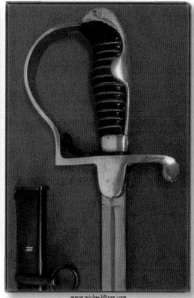

www.michaelilong.com

German infantry take the oath of allegiance, c.1940.

www.michaelilong.com

www.michaelilong.com

www.michaelilong.com

www.michaelilong.com

www.michaelilong.com

**C.WWII INFANTRY OFFICER'S
SWORD (NCO)**
VALUE: $560.00/£350.00
With brass stirrup hilt and crossguard. Black
composition grip and brass twistwire. The
underside of the guard is stamped with Waffen-
amt marks. These are repeated on the scabbard
throat. With black painted steel scabbard.

UNITED STATES' INFANTRY SWORDS

www.antiqueswords.com

C.1820-1840 INFANTRY OFFICER'S SWORD
VALUE: $1435.00/£895.00
Typical eagle-head pommel with floral cast crossbar and eagle langets.

www.antiqueswords.com

www.antiqueswords.com

C.1770 INFANTRY OFFICER'S SWORD
VALUE: $2075.00/ £1295.00
A very early example of the style of sword carried by American infantry officers during the Revolutionary War. The brass hilt has a lionshead pommel and typical slotted guard. The blade is of rather crude manufacture and single-fullered.

www.antiqueswords.com

C.1840-1850 INFANTRY (MILITIA) OFFICER'S SWORD
VALUE: $1435.00/£895.00
Good quality example with fluted bone grip and brass hilt mounts and chain. Scabbard is silvered brass.

Al Gregoritsch Collection

Al Gregoritsch Collection

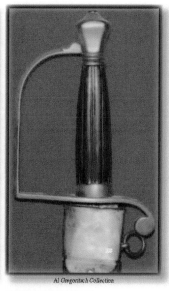

Al Gregoritsch Collection

Al Gregoritsch Collection

C.1770 INFANTRY OFFICER'S SWORD
VALUE: $2395.00/£1495.00

Unmarked silver hilt with ivory or bone grip and silver banding. Oval pommel with typical gadrooned styling. Blade is plain, slightly curved and three-fullered. The guard is quite thin and does not exhibit the overall quality found in most English and French infantry officers' short sabres of the period.

C.1790 INFANTRY OFFICER'S SWORD
VALUE: $2235.00/£1395.00

Although this sword was produced only a few years after the Revolutionary War, it exhibits more definitive and independent characteristics of a sword manufactured and aimed primarily for the home market. The blade is decorated with an American eagle, stands of trophies and is maker(?) marked on the blade to "Wells, NY".

Battle of Bunker Hill, 1775.

Al Gregoritsch Collection

Left:
C.1770 INFANTRY OFFICER'S SWORD
VALUE: $1435.00/£895.00
Typically plain officer's fighting sword with a finely ribbed ivory grip. Hilt mounts are of iron. Blade is single-fullered.

Al Gregoritsch Collection

C.1785-1800 INFANTRY OFFICER'S SWORD
VALUE: $1200.00/£750.00
Swords of this style were produced both in the USA and England during this period.

Al Gregoritsch Collection

C.1820-1840 INFANTRY OFFICER'S SWORD
VALUE: $1660.00/£950.00
The adoption of a uniquely decorated shell guard for these swords coincided with the growing awareness of a specific identity for the new United States. With this awareness came a series of motifs and national symbols, including the reclining American Indian shown in this example. The grips are mother-of-pearl. The sword also retains its very scarce original knot. The engraved blade has traces of blue and gilt decoration.

Al Gregoritsch Collection

George Washington - from a patriotic postcard, c.1900's.

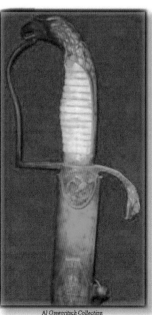

Al Gregoritsch Collection

Left and right above:
C.1810-1820 ARTILLERY OFFICER'S SWORD
VALUE: $2075.00/ £1295.00
The style of this eagle-head sword is distinctively French and it is likely that the sword was actually an import from the Paris swordmaker, Le Page. Henri Perin Le Page was an assistant to the famous Nicholas Boutet, of the Imperial Manufactory at Versailles. The Le Page family had been arms makers and dealers since 1665. They built up an enviable reputation for superb quality, particularly with regard to pistols.

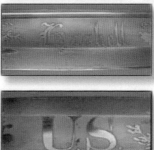

Union Soldiers - detail from a lithograph, c.1900's.

MODEL 1850 STAFF AND FIELD OFFICER'S SWORD
VALUE: $ 3195.00/£1995.00

This model of sword was directly influenced by contemporary French infantry officers' swords. Many of these swords were actually produced in Europe and imported into the USA, some in parts (to be assembled and finished by American firms), and others complete but with the addition of a US sword retailer's name to the blade forte. This example was wholly manufactured in the USA by the Ames Sword Company and is in exceptional condition. It is also named to the blade.

**MODEL 1840
MUSICIAN'S SWORD**
VALUE: $ 635.00/£ 395.00

**MODEL 1840 MOUNTED
ARTILLERY TROOPER'S
SWORD**
VALUE: $ 1100.00/£ 695.00
Of American manufacture and
marked on the blade forte, "AMES
MFG. Co. CHICOPEE, MASS".
and "CONN. 1862". This type
of sword was a virtual copy of
the French Model 1829 Artillery
Trooper's Sword.

**MODEL 1840 NCO'S
SWORD**
VALUE: $ 635.00/£ 395.00

MODEL 1860 (STAFF & FIELD)
OFFICER'S SWORD
VALUE: $ 795.00/£ 495.00

**MODEL 1840 NCO'S
SWORD**
VALUE: $ 635.00/£ 395.00
A very crisp sword complete
with original scabbard. It has
a longer scabbard than the
musician's version, and a
kidney-shaped counter-guard.
Left:
**MODEL 1850 FOOT
OFFICER'S SWORD**
VALUE: $ 795.00/£ 495.00

www.antiquerswords.com

US CIVIL WAR OFFICER'S PRESENTATION SWORD
VALUE: $ 4000.00/£2500.00

Presentation grade officer's sword with solid silver grip and fire gilt knucklebow and guard. Blade is maker marked to *"Clauberg, Solingen"*. Spine is also marked *"Iron Proof"*. There are remnants of an inscription to the blade, now illegible. Silver hilt mounts with heavy patination. Scabbard is bronze with solid silver mounts.

www.antiquerswords.com

MODEL 1860 STAFF AND FIELD OFFICER'S SWORD
VALUE: $ 635.00/£ 395.00

An unpopular sword when first introduced due to its thin and flimsy blade, it is another American sword heavily influenced by contemporary French designs. Civil war pieces can normally be determined by the higher quality of the blade etching and overall craftsmanship and detail of the piece.

C.1890 OFFICER'S SWORD
VALUE: $ 795.00/£495.00

Non-regulation officer's sword. The exact branch of service for which this sword would have been carried is unknown, although it might possibly be artillery. The solid brass stirrup hilt is unlike most contemporary swords carried by the US military. The blade forte is marked *"Ridabock & Co, New York"*.

www.michaeldlong.com

www.michaeldlong.com

www.michaeldlong.com

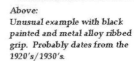

www.michaeldlong.com

www.michaeldlong.com

MODEL 1902 INFANTRY OFFICER'S SWORD
VALUE: $475.00/£295.00

This was a completely new design for all infantry officers. Early examples have a ribbed horn grip, with bakelite or thermoplastic, for the later models. This sword is still carried by US Army Officers and is a very common sword for collectors, due to its relative affordability in the market. Blades are usually etched with military motifs, eagle ,"US", and floral patterns. Many swords are also etched with the owner's name and date.

www.michaeldlong.com

Above:
Unusual example with black painted and metal alloy ribbed grip. Probably dates from the 1920's/1930's.

Brigadier General, c.1905.

Major General, c.1905.

www.michaeldlong.com

**MODEL 1902 INFANTRY
OFFICER'S SWORD
VALUE: $475.00/£295.00**

Army Patriotic Postcard, c.1910.

www.michaeldlong.com

www.michaeldlong.com

www.michaeldlong.com

American Infantry Officers, c.1918.

www.michaeldlong.com

OTHER NATIONS' SWORDS

ITALY

C.1850 INFANTRY OFFICER'S SWORD
VALUE: $795.00/£455.00

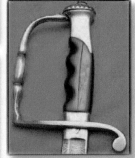

C.1850 INFANTRY OFFICER'S SWORD
VALUE: $ 635.00/£395.00
Of a style influenced by contemporary French sword designs. This sword has been attributed to an Italian origin, due to the rather simple hilt style. The same attribution has been made to the sword below.

C.1820 INFANTRY OFFICER'S SWORD
VALUE: $475.00/£295.00

C.1850 INFANTRY OFFICER'S SWORD
VALUE: $ 950.00/£595.00
This sword is interesting as the hilt style is more reminiscent of Napoleonic swords but is actually considerably later. The presence of a large thumb-ring is also quite unusual.

TURKEY

C.1900 ARTILLERY OFFICER'S SWORD
VALUE: $ 950.00/£595.00

With the opening up and consequent modernisation of the nation towards the West during the nineteenth century, the Ottoman Empire adopted many European influences both in military dress and equipment. This was especially so with regard to swords. Many swords were manufactured in Germany and based on official German patterns of the period.

C.1880 INFANTRY OFFICER'S SWORD
VALUE: $ 635.00/£395.00
Hilt design of typical French style.

Senior Turkish Army Officers, 1895.

C.1900 SENIOR OFFICER'S MAMELUKE SWORD
VALUE: $1195.00/£680.00

An example of a specially commisioned mameluke sword for a senior Turkish officer. Stylistically, it is very similar to mamelukes produced for British Army Officers and Royal Equerries. Although not maker marked, it is highly likely that the sword was manufactured by a British swordmaker.

C.1915 NCO'S SHORT SWORD
VALUE: $795.00/ £495.00

With brass and steel scabbard.

INFANTRY OFFICER'S SWORD
VALUE: $475.00/£295.00

Likely to be of twentieth century manufacture.

IMPERIAL RUSSIA

MODEL 1855 INFANTRY OFFICER'S SWORD
VALUE: $1275.00/£795.00
The hilt shows the typical canted pommel that is a distinctive feature of Imperial Russian swords. Blade is plain and slightly curved.

MODEL 1909 INFANTRY OFFICER'S SWORD
VALUE: $2075.00/£1295.00
With ribbed plastic composite grip. The royal cypher of Nicholas II on the pommel has been deliberately ground away. This universal pattern of sword was carried by both infantry and cavalry officers. The scabbard is of cavalry type, indicating that this sword could also have been used by a cavalry officer.

Battle of Plevna, 1877.

Battle of Inkerman, 1854.

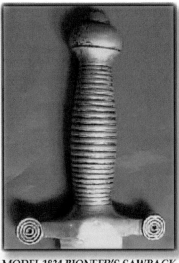

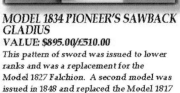

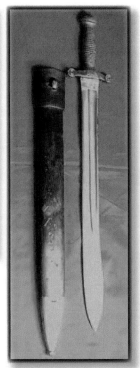

MODEL 1834 PIONEER'S SAWBACK GLADIUS
VALUE: $895.00/£510.00

This pattern of sword was issued to lower ranks and was a replacement for the Model 1827 Falchion. A second model was issued in 1848 and replaced the Model 1817 Hanger. The sawback blade was removed in this version.

Left and above left:
MODEL 1817 INFANTRYMAN'S HANGER
VALUE: $1100.00/£695.00

This design imitated the numerous contemporary variations of infantry hangers available throughout Europe in the 1800's. Most were inspired by patterns carried by the French Army during the Napoleonic Wars. The Russian military was always swift to copy and use, captured French swords. This example indicates Russian manufacture.

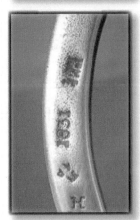

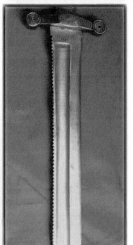

Above and above right:
MODEL 1827 PIONEER SAWBACK FALCHION
VALUE: $1435.00/£895.00

Of massive proportions, it seems unlikely that this sword was of great practical use. Its heavy weight and unwieldy nature would certainly have made it unpopular with the average soldier. Copies are currently being manufactured.

SWEDEN

C.1820 INFANTRY OFFICER'S SWORD
VALUE: $ 1275.00/£795.00
Swedish infantry officers, like many of their contemporary European counterparts, adopted a smallsword as their principal weapon. Most blades are engraved with the royal coat of arms. The example below shows the royal cypher of Oscar I (1799-1859).

www.michaeldlong.com

MODEL 1856 HANGER
VALUE: $ 635.00/£ 395.00

ARGENTINA

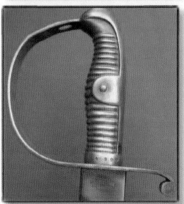

C.1820 INFANTRY OFFICER'S SWORD
VALUE: $ 1275.00/£795.00

C.1900 INFANTRY SIDEARM
VALUE: $ 475.00/ £295.00
Manufactured in Germany for export.

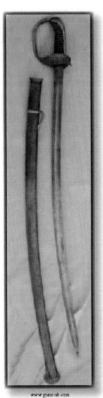

www.guns.uk.com

C.1880 SHARPSHOOTER'S SWORD
VALUE: $ 950.00/£595.00

A scarce example. The gilt brass guard is decorated with panoplies of arms, victory wreath, and the royal arms of Sweden (three crowns). Blade is slightly curved and plain. The scabbard includes an unusual brass, single hook or ring attachment for the sword belt. Similar attachments have also been noted on Dutch Infantry swords.

Swedish troops, c.1850.

MODEL 1848 INFANTRY FACINE SHORT SWORD
VALUE: $ 635.00/£395.00

Of unusual design, with a machete-type blade. Hilt is of stained wood with brass rivets and pommel hole for sword knot.

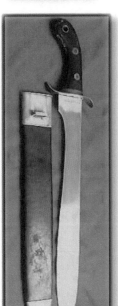

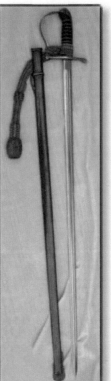

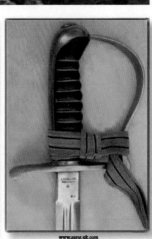

www.guns.uk.com

MODEL 1899 INFANTRY OFFICER'S SWORD
VALUE: $795.00/£455.00

HOLLAND

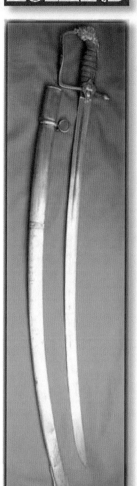

MODEL 1852 FUSILIER OFFICER'S SWORD
VALUE: $1435.00/£895.00

With the royal cypher of King Wilhelm III (1817-1890) to the knucklebow. No maker's mark is visible. The slightly curved and single-fullered blade is plain. Note the unusual scabbard ring.

Below left and right:
C.1900 INFANTRY OFFICER'S SWORD
VALUE: $635.00/£395.00

Celluloid and brass twistwire to the grip.

www.antiqueswords.com

C.WWII DUTCH FASCIST OFFICER'S SWORD
VALUE: $2075.00/£1295.00

A rare sword carried by Dutch SS Volunteers.

C.1880 MUSICIAN'S(?)/ ARMY CADET'S SWORD
VALUE: $475.00/£295.00

The sword has been described both as a sword for army musicians and also army cadets. Grip is of ribbed horn. Hilt of solid brass with lionshead pommel. The blade is finely etched with scrolling foliage and maker(?) marked to "Y.P. Mol Breda". It is of short sword length and probably worn more as a decorative sidearm. Scabbard of black leather with plain brass mounts.

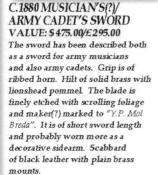

Dutch Infantry, c.1900.

REPUBLIC OF IRELAND

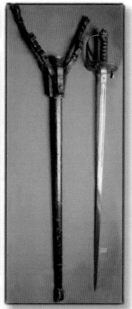

PERSIA (IRAN)

C.1930'S INFANTRY OFFICER'S SWORD
VALUE: $ 1910.00/£1195.00

An extremely rare sword that is seldom seen in the market. The Army of the Irish Republic was quite small, especially the officer corps, and swords were produced in very limited quantities. It is based on a British military sword design and features the *Fianna Fail* badge to the hilt cartouche. The blade is decorated with Celtic motifs.

C.1900'S PERSIAN INFANTRY OFFICER'S SWORD
VALUE: $ 475.00/£295.00

Most examples date from the post-Victorian era and are of German manufacture.

SPAIN

www.michaeldlong.com

MODEL 1800 INFANTRY OFFICER'S SWORD
VALUE: $ 1435..00/£895.00

C.1750 COLONIAL SHORT SWORD
VALUE: $ 1100.00/£695.00

These crudely manufactured swords were produced in Spanish colonies and used throughout South and North America, the Phillipines and Cuba. They tended to be produced in very small quantities by rural/local blacksmiths. The hand forged blades are normally unmarked. This example has an iron hilt, with incised decoration to the hilt bars and quillons. Blade is triple-fullered. Grip of ribbed and stained hardwood.

MODEL 1843 ARTILLERY/ ENGINEER'S SHORT SWORD
VALUE: $1040.00/£650.00

Weighing in at over three pounds with its sheath, this short sword was manufactured by the *Fabrica de Nacional de Toledo*. The handle is a solid brass casting with flaming grenade motif to the hilt pommel. Most examples are without scabbard and in poor condition. An officer's version is also known. It is identical except that the standard pommel is replaced with a lionshead.

These swords are sometimes found with sawback blades, indicating a Pioneer function.

MODEL 1867 INFANTRY OFFICER'S SWORD
VALUE: $ 560.00/£ 350.00
The style of this sword has been heavily influenced by contemporary French swords.

MODEL 1843(?) PIONEER OFFICER/NCO'S SWORD
VALUE: $ 880.00/£ 550.00

C.1860'S ARTILLERY OFFICER'S SWORD
VALUE: $ 950.00/£ 595.00
Dated to 1861 and manufactured in Toledo.

www.michaellong.com

www.michaellong.com

C.1860 INFANTRY OFFICER'S SWORD
VALUE: $ 795.00/£ 495.00

CHINA

C.1900 CHINESE INFANTRY OFFICER'S SWORD
VALUE: $1435.00/£895.00

There has been a lot of debate regarding this sword and it is frequently mis-identified as for use by German infantry officers during the Boxer Rebellion of 1900. There is no direct evidence for this viewpoint, and it is not known as an official regulation pattern within the German Army. It is now thought that this sword was actually manufactured in Germany for Chinese officers. It is based on the Model 1889 German Infantry Officer's Sword.

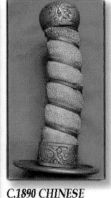

C.1890 CHINESE SHORT SWORD
VALUE: $950.00/£595.00

Of relatively simple manufacture, with plain, unfullered blade. The grip is of fishskin with copper banding. Scabbard is brass mounted, white fishskin.

Chinese Army, c.1900.

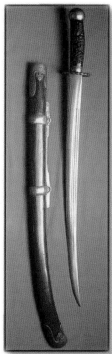

C.1890 CHINESE BROADSWORD
VALUE: $1435.00/ £895.00

Very high quality example of a late-Victorian broadsword. Deeply carved wood grip with decorative brass scabbard fittings. Hardwood scabbard with good age toning.

C.1890 CHINESE SHORT SWORD
VALUE: $635.00/£395.00

This is typical of many 19th Century examples. With ribbed hardwood grip, yellow lacquered scabbard and decorated brass mounts. The blade is unfullered.

SERBIA
(YUGOSLAVIA)

DENMARK

C.1900 SERBIAN OFFICER'S SWORD
VALUE: $1100.00/£695.00
Etched with Belgrade maker's name.

C.1820 INFANTRY HANGER
VALUE: $795.00/£455.00
This short hanger was very common during the 1800's and carried by a number of European countries. Many are stamped with regimental designations to the guard or scabbard throat.

MEXICO

CZECHOSLOVAKIA

C.1840 MEXICAN INFANTRY OFFICER'S SWORD
VALUE: $ 1275.00/£795.00
European styled stirrup hilt with pipe back blade engraved with Mexican national motif of eagle and snake. Sword was probably manufactured in Europe, possibly Germany.

www.michaeldlong.com

www.michaeldlong.com

C.1920 CZECH NCO'S SWORD
VALUE: $ 795.00/£495.00

FINLAND

MODEL 1921 FINNISH INFANTRY OFFICER'S SWORD
VALUE: $1275.00/£795.00

Czech patriotic postcard, 1920.

AUSTRIA

MODEL 1889(?) STATE OFFICIAL'S SWORD

VALUE: $1275.00/£795.00

An attractive and sought after sword with richly decorated and elaborate gilt brass hilt and scabbard. The hilt features the double-headed eagle of the Austro-Hungarian royal family. The embossed royal cypher of Emperor Franz Josef I is on the scabbard locket. Most blades are found with Vienna maker marks. Grip is fishskin and brass twistwire.

Austrian Army, c.1860.

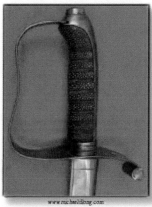

www.michaeldlong.com

MODEL 1853/1889 INFANTRY PIONEER'S SWORD
VALUE: $ 795.00/£495.00

Issued to technical troops and designed for clearing of woodland and creating fascines. The lack of a serrated cutting edge means that it was unlikely to have been of much practical use, although quite intimidating.

www.michaeldlong.com

MODEL 1861 INFANTRY OFFICER'S SWORD
VALUE: $560.00/£350.00

Considering this sword was used during the mid-nineteenth century, it lacks virtually any decoration or styling. There is a shorter version for NCO's. Blades also tend to be plain.

SWITZERLAND

Austrian Army Pioneer, c.1900.

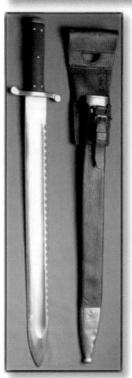

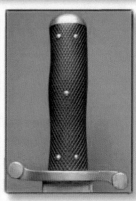

MODEL 1875 PIONEER'S SWORD
VALUE: $695.00/£395.00

A rare sword, seldom found in the market. Scabbard is leather and brass mounted. Grip is composed of chequered leather.

COLLECTORS OF NAVAL SWORDS

are at a slight disadvantage in that the choice of swords in the market is more limited. Navies were always smaller than the army and consequently, fewer swords were manufactured. The acquistion of a fine example is therefore all the more fulfilling.

HISTORICAL BACKGROUND

The history of naval swords and more precisely, the tracing of distinct patterns and types carried whilst on board a ship, is likely to have its origins in the sixteenth and seventeenth century. Up until then, officers and sailors generally carried the same swords as those wielded on land. Over time, navies became more organised, especially by centralised governments, and their roles changed from legalised privateers to official enforcers of a state's military and commercial interests. This led to formal changes in the administration, equipping and appearance of both the ship and also its crew. Whereas before, ships functioned more as embarkers and disembarkers of troops, the appearance of proper *"fighting ships"* in the seventeenth and eighteenth centuries, meant that close, hand to hand engagements became more commonplace. A sword was therefore needed that would be both practical and effective during these onboard naval melees.

GREAT BRITAIN

From the late 1500's, a style of weapon known as a *"curtleax"*, or *"coute-lace"*, was carried on board British ships, although this is thought to have been more of an axe than a sword. Despite this, the name was established and as we move into the eighteenth century, ships' captains began to refer to a *"cutt lashe"*. This was probably just an anglicisation of the earlier descriptions. Cutlasses were provided for the seaman by the Board of Ordnance. Quantities were small in relation to the numbers of seaman on board a ship and not every seaman was issued with a cutlass. Standards of manufacture were also pretty poor. Most cutlasses were manufactured from one piece of sheet steel, opened out into two discs for hand protection. Blades were either straight or slightly curved. Cutlass manufacture was undertaken by a number of English swordmakers and quality varied greatly.

In 1804, an official pattern of cutlass was ordered. This was the *"figure of eight"* or double disc-hilted cutlass. It is probably this cutlass that is most commonly associated with British seaman during the Napoelonic Wars. It also featured a cast iron, ribbed grip and straight blade. Subsequent patterns followed until 1900. In 1936, the cutlass was withdrawn from naval use, except for ceremonial purposes.

Man-o-War, c.1800.

Before the standardisation of officers' naval swords after 1805, the British Royal Navy officer had great leeway as to what edged weapon he carried whilst on board ship. During the latter part of the seventeenth century, the rapier was abandoned by naval officers in favour of short, hunting type hangers. These short swords were far more practical whilst fighting amongst the rigging and confined space of a ship's deck. Many contemporary paintings show British naval officers carrying these swords. In keeping with fashions of the day, a naval officer might also carry a smallsword. They were identical to those carried by civilians or army officers, although some rare examples carry nautical motifs to the hilt. By the late-eighteenth century, the hunting hanger was dropped in favour of an infantry sword with slotted guard. Many of these exhibit an anchor inset into the guard or engraved to the pommel.

In 1786, the British Army formally adopted a pattern sword for infantry officers. Naval officers soon copied this style. The cut and thrust blade was straight

with either a *"beaded"* or *"five-ball"* hilt and cushion pommel. A gilt brass *"cigar band"* with etched anchor was placed in the centre of the ivory or ebony grip. Some examples also have a cut-out anchor placed in the centre of the side-ring. Other sword types include those with S-Bar hilt (with anchor in cartouche), and stirrup hilt. These swords copied contemporary army and cavalry swords.

The 1805 Pattern brought in a more recognisable *naval* style of sword. It featured a gilt brass lionshead pommel and engraved fouled anchor to the langets. Blades were straight and single-fullered. In keeping with their army counterparts, many blades would have displayed blue and gilt blade decoration, including flags, trophies, anchors, and buoys. Few have survived intact with this decoration.

In 1827, the naval sword changed completely and officers adopted a solid, gilt brass half basket hilt. Again, the Royal Navy was influenced by the Army, and the design closely follows the 1822 Pattern Infantry Officer's Sword. The grip was of white fishskin (black for warrant officers). Blades were initially of pipe back and spear point form, later changing to the single fullered *"Wilkinson"* type. It is this later type that is more commonly encountered. Other naval sword designs include a mameluke hilt for Flag Officers, an open basket hilt, plain *"dove-head"* pommels for warrant officers, and the Scottish, multi-fullered or *"Claymore"* blade, especially popular in the late nineteenth century. The 1827 Pattern is still carried by British Royal Navy Officers.

FRANCE

The standardisation of cutlasses came a little earlier for the French Navy, with the introduction of a Model 1771 Cutlass (modified in 1782/83). The hilt was brass with a ribbed grip and prominent pommel cap. It was similar to contemporary grenadier hilts, but differed slightly in having a three-bar hilt. The year XI (1802-1803) witnessed a new model that has become very familiar to collectors (although not as common as its British counterpart). The large, half basket guard was of blackened iron with an octagonal grip and a slightly curved and a wide-fullered blade. A later model (1833) saw the addition of an engraved anchor to the blade. The last pattern of French cutlass was the Model 1872. It comprised a hilt of steel plate, shaped grip and a perforated guard.

French officers of the eighteenth century followed the British practice of carrying swords similar to those in the army. Around 1800, a more uniform sword was

British Naval Captain, c.1850.

hilt bars. A number of grades or orders were presented, An enammelled cross of either the Order of St. George or St. Anne (before 1869), was attached to the hilt pommel. Specific bullion sword knots were also worn and graded according to the level of Order attained. This style of naval sword remained unchanged until the Revolution of 1917. Thereafter, all Imperial designations were removed and the sword became more plain in design, although some officers were known to place a hammer and sickle or red star device to the hilt pommel.

A specific pattern of naval cutlass for seaman was not issued until 1810. Before then, naval ratings carried a short hanger of *"briquet"* form. It was normally worn from a shoulder belt. The 1810 Pattern was ostensibly carried by bombadiers and gunners. The blade is of yataghan style with brass hilt crossguard, wooden grip and swollen pommel. It is more of a hanger than a cutlass and does not have the bowl guard or disc hilt more commonly associated with naval cutlasses of this period. The 1856 Pattern Boarding Cutlass is traditional in style and imitates British cutlasses of the period. It has a blackened iron hilt, iron ribbed grip and blackened steel scabbard mounts. Cutlass design remained unchanged until 1940, when a new pattern

German U-Boat, c.1915.

was introduced for naval students. It had a double-edged, slightly curved blade, steel hilt with pronounced guard and a ribbed wooden grip. The actual need for this cutlass seems rather tenuous, although the military still insisted on it being carried when outside the naval school. After 1958, it was only worn on ceremonial occasions.

UNITED STATES

American naval officers, both during and after the American Revolutionary War, carried swords of English and French style. Most were actually exported from these countries to the United States. In 1841, a specific *"eagle-head"* naval officer's sword was introduced. This followed sword styles prevalent in the army. The Model 1852 Naval Officer's sword copied European solid half-basket-hilted naval swords and is still carried today. Cutlasses of English style were issued in 1797 and 1808. The Model 1841 and Model 1860 *"Ames"* cutlasses were quite distinct styles, the former derived from the French Artillery gladius short sword, and the latter, an interpretation of the French Model 1801 Cutlass, albeit with brass furniture, rather than blackened sheet iron. This cutlass had a long service life and was only replaced in 1917, by a rather ugly cutlass based on the Dutch army *"klewang"* cutlass. There are two versions. The early model has a solid iron bowl guard. The 1941 variation has a guard with separate hilt branches.

COLLECTING NAVAL SWORDS

One of the major factors in collecting naval swords especially early examples, is overall condition. The effect of saltwater on exposed steel blades can be very deleterious, and many swords are found in a poor state. Hilts survive better because they tended to be made of brass. Some Napoleonic naval blades were richly decorated with blue and gilt, but it is rare to come across a naval sword of this period that still retains this decoration. Early cutlasses are normally found with severely corroded blades and hilts. This indicates that they were probably used, rather than left in storage. A bit of wear or *"history"* to a sword should never be frowned upon.

British infantry swords of 1786 (Spadroon) Pattern have been altered into more valuable naval officers' swords, by the inclusion of a spurious anchor within the side-ring and crosspiece. Anchors can also be easily engraved onto plain brass, stirrup hilted cavalry officers' swords. The American Model 1852 Naval Officer's Sword is rare and has been extensively faked. The quality of reproduction, especially blade etching, is usually poor.

BRITISH NAVAL SWORDS

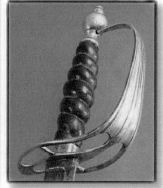

C.1770 NAVAL OFFICER'S SWORD
VALUE: $1910.00/£1195.00
Of typical form for the period, with slotted hilt and ovoid pommel engraved with a fouled anchor. Most blades are short and curved, without decoration and typically single-fullered. Grip is manufactured from hardwood or ebony.

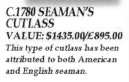

C.1780 SEAMAN'S CUTLASS
VALUE: $1435.00/£895.00
This type of cutlass has been attributed to both American and English seaman.

Right:
C.1780-1800 SEAMAN'S CUTLASS
VALUE: $1100.00/£695.00

Right:
C.1780 SILVER-HILTED NAVAL OFFICER'S SWORD
VALUE: $3200.00/ £2000.00
With a typical late-eighteenth century lionshead pommel and fouled anchor inset within a slotted hilt. Smooth part-ribbed ivory grip. Blade is of short hanger form, slightly curved and plain. No silver hallmarks present.

C.1800 NAVAL OFFICER'S SWORD
VALUE: $2075.00/£1295.00

C.1800 NAVAL OFFICER'S SWORD
VALUE: $2700.00/£1695.00

C.1800 NAVAL OFFICER'S SWORD
VALUE: $3035.00/£1895.00

The introduction of a spadroon-hilted officer's sword within British Army regiments, was quickly copied by the Royal Navy. These swords are exceptionally rare and few survive. They are typically found with a gilt brass, five-ball hilt. Like their army counterparts, the ribbed ivory grip has an engraved *"cigar band"* to the centre. It normally features a fouled anchor.

Battle of Trafalgar, 1805.

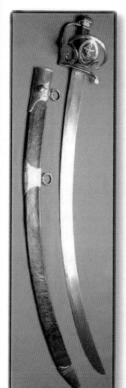

C.1800 S-BAR HILTED NAVAL OFFICER'S SWORD
VALUE: $8000.00/£5000.00

Superb example of a c.1800's S-Bar-hilted officer's sword. Silver plated hilt and scabbard mounts. Maker marked on scabbard throat to Tatham of London (1800-1860). The S-Bar is a rare naval variant with a side bar that emerges from the knucklebow and joins the side-ring with the curl of a s-shape. Features include an anchor in cartouche and lionshead or cushion pommel. The fighting blade is plain and wide. Grip is of ribbed ebony. Although this is not a solid silver-hilted sword, they are known with English hallmarks. Very few decent examples of British Napoleonic naval officers' swords enter the market, and those that do command very high prices, especially if they have retained their original blue and gilt blade. The smaller size of the Royal Navy in comparison with the Army limits the numbers available.

British ships at anchor, c.1800.

1805 PATTERN NAVAL OFFICER'S SWORD
VALUE: $ 4000.00/£2500.00

With ribbed ivory grip and gilt-brass lionshead pommel. The blade appears to be from an earlier broadsword, possibly Scottish. Many officers used old family blades and had them re-hilted to their current service hilt.

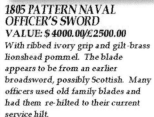

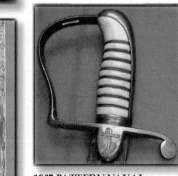

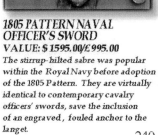

1805 PATTERN NAVAL OFFICER'S SWORD
VALUE: $ 1595.00/£ 995.00

The stirrup-hilted sabre was popular within the Royal Navy before adoption of the 1805 Pattern. They are virtually identical to contemporary cavalry officers' swords, save the inclusion of an engraved, fouled anchor to the langet.

Seaman, c.1830.

Midshipman, c.1830.

Petty Officer, c.1855.

Mate, c.1833.

Flag Officer, c.1833.

Officer, Naval Brigade, 1854.

240

C.1830 NAVAL SEAMAN'S CUTLASS
VALUE: $ 795.00/£495.00
A non-regulation example, possibly for merchantmen.

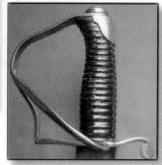

1804 PATTERN NAVAL SEAMAN'S CUTLASS
VALUE: $ 1275.00/£795.00
This was the first regulation naval cutlass issued to British seaman. Many examples are impressed with a royal cypher ("GR") to the blade.

C.1800'S NAVAL SEAMAN'S CUTLASS
VALUE: $ 1100.00/ £695.00
A hybrid of the 1804 Pattern hilt.

C.1830 COASTGUARD(?) CUTLASS
VALUE: $ 635.00/£395.00

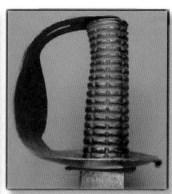

1804 PATTERN NAVAL SEAMAN'S CUTLASS
VALUE: $ 2550.00/£1595.00
Complete with original scabbard.

Left:

C.1800 SEAMAN'S CUTLASS
VALUE: $895.00/ £795.00

These cutlasses are also thought to have been used by British Coastguard units during the first half of the nineteenth century. It is unusual to find one with its original leather and brass mounted scabbard.

C.1820 WARRANT OFFICER'S SWORD
VALUE: $1435.00/ £895.00

Gilt brass stirrup hilt with engraved fouled anchor to the langets. The use of of a black fishskin grip was normally designated for Warrant Officers. It is also seen on swords carried by merchant marine officers.

C.1820 CUSTOMS OFFICER'S SWORD
VALUE: $1910.00/ £1195.00

A rare example with ribbed ivory grip, sword knot and Custom's badge to hilt langet, repeated on the blade. Blade is of pipe back form and slightly curved. Scabbard is leather and gilt-brass mounts. Customs' officers' swords are rarely encountered.

Action between the "Chesapeake" and "Shannon", 1813.

LLOYDS PATRIOTIC FUND PRESENTATION SWORD (FIFTY POUNDS)
VALUE: $ 128000.00/ £80000.00

Probably the most sought after of all British naval swords, the Lloyds Presentation swords are known for the superb quality of their workmanship. Swords are typically decorated in blue and gilt for the entire length of the blade, and both hilt and scabbard are elaborately worked with fire-gilt finish throughout. In this example, all surfaces are decorated, with a large blued panel detailing the recipient's act of heroism. Grip is of both chequered and ribbed ivory, and the scabbard has leather inserts. These swords would have been produced with a felt lined display case. In many cases these have become separated from the sword. The maker is noted as Richard Teed of the Strand, London, in business from 1797-1821.

FROM THE PATRIOTIC FUND AT LLOYDS TO LIEUT. THO. ROBT PYE OF THE
MARINES OF H.M.S. BOADECEA SEVERELY WOUNDED IN A GALLANT ATTACK ON THE
ENEMY AT ST.PAULS IN THE ISLE OF BOURBON ON THE 21ST OF SEPTR 1809.

Embarkation at Balaklava, 1854.

Grand Naval Review, Spithead, 1856.

C.1800 NAVAL WARRANT OFFICER'S DRESS SWORD
VALUE: $ 1435.00/£895.00
This sword exhibits the typical design features of a Georgian sword, including a neo-classical knucklebow.

C.1820 WARRANT OFFICER'S DRESS SWORD
VALUE: $ 1435.00/£895.00

1805 PATTERN NAVAL OFFICER'S SWORD
VALUE: $ 2550.00/£1595.00

British Sailors, c.1800.

1805 PATTERN NAVAL OFFICER'S SWORD
VALUE: $ 1535.00/£995.00
Of typical form, with ivory grip and brass twistwire. Hilt would originally have had a gilt brass finish, now worn away. A finely detailed anchor is engraved to the langet.

Above and right:
C.1820 WARRANT OFFICER'S DRESS SWORD
VALUE: $ 1435.00/£895.00

1827 PATTERN NAVAL OFFICER'S SWORD
VALUE: $1910.00/£1195.00

The year 1827 brought about a radical change in the design of British naval officers' swords. The Napoleonic stirrup hilt was replaced with a solid gilt-brass, half-basket hilt. It was based on the 1822 Pattern Infantry Officer's Sword. Early examples have a wide, pipe back, quill-pointed blade. In 1846, Henry Wilkinson manufactured a single-fullered blade and this is how most swords are found.

The death of Lord Nelson, Trafalgar, 1805.

1845/1858 PATTERN NAVAL CUTLASS
VALUE: $ 950.00/ £595.00

The 1845 Pattern was chosen following the appraisal of four cutlasses presented to the Board of Admiralty in 1842. Based on the 1821 Pattern Heavy Cavalry Trooper's Sword, it took another three years before sufficient quantities were manufactured. This was due to the scarcity of domestic sword cutlers, many of whom had been driven out of business following the Napoleonic Wars. Suppliers were eventually found, including makers such as Reeves, Heighington, and the government manufactory at Enfield. They are normally maker marked to the blade edge.

C.1830 WARRANT OFFICER'S SWORD
VALUE: $ 1595.00/£995.00

This open half-basket sword is a scarce piece. It very much resembles contemporary 1845/1854 Pattern infantry swords. The "Gothic" hilt is also identical to the army version. It is probable that the maker simply replaced the usual royal crown and "VR" cartouche, with a crown and anchor. The hilt might have come from existing manufacturer's stocks of army pattern hilts. This design of sword was only manufactured for a couple of years.

1889 PATTERN NAVAL CUTLASS
VALUE: $ 795.00/£495.00

Following repeated complaints within the service about the inadequacy of naval cutlasses, coupled with a series of very negative press stories regarding the unnecessary deaths of British sailors in combat due to the bending and breaking of blades, a new design of cutlass was ordered. The cutlass had a straight blade and the bowl hilt was manufactured in bright steel, in contrast to the usual black painted cast iron. This pattern is probably the most common British naval cutlass in the collecting market.

Cutlass Drill, c.1910.

1900 PATTERN NAVAL CUTLASS
VALUE: $795.00/£495.00

This is the final official cutlass pattern for the Royal Navy. It is basically the 1889 Pattern, but with the grip changed from ribbed steel to one in which two strips of leather are riveted against the tang. By the time it was introduced, the need for a cutlass had all but disappeared and most are found in very good condition and complete with scabbard. It is likely that many were actually unissued. In 1936, the wearing of cutlasses was formally abolished in the Royal Navy.

British Naval Officer, c.1870.

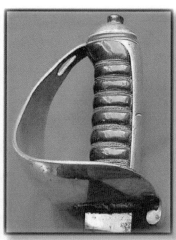

C.1890 NAVAL CUTLASS
VALUE: $1100.00/£695.00

This example is unmarked but swords of this type have been associated with naval use, particularly coastguard duties. Some are maker marked to Wilkinson Sword. It might even have a merchant marine origin as there were many different cutlass designs produced by commercial swordmakers during the Victorian period, both in Germany and England.

Lieutenant William Blewett Fawckner, R.N., 1879.

C.1910 WARRANT OFFICER'S SWORD
VALUE: $ 595.00/
£950.00
Warrant Officers carried a specific pattern with a black, fishskin grip and plain pommel, lacking the typical lionshead.

C.1900 WARRANT OFFICER'S SWORD
VALUE: $ 950.00/
£595.00

H.M.S. Majestic, 1895.

H.M.S. Diadem, 1896.

H.M.S. Commonwealth, 1903.

FRENCH NAVAL SWORDS

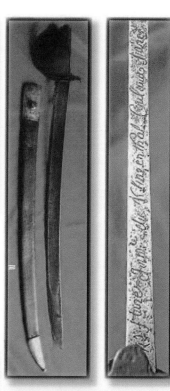

C.1780 NAVAL OFFICER'S CUTLASS
VALUE: $2075.00/£1295.00

A rare sword that is likely to have originally been carried by a naval officer of the pre-Revolutionary period. The blade has had some engraving removed. It is presumed that the engraving contained references to the recently deposed royal family.

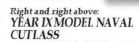

Right and right above:
YEAR IX MODEL NAVAL CUTLASS
VALUE: $2075.00/£1295.00

It is rare to find decent examples of this cutlass, and especially so with original scabbard. The spine of the blade is marked to the Klingenthal sword factory in Alsace, and indicates manufacture c.1806, during the reign of Emperor Napoleon I. Smooth, tubular grip with large bowl guard. Blade is engraved along the fuller with an anchor. There is a later example from the 1830's that saw the removal of the more elaborate turned over quillon. Scabbards would have been leather with brass mounts. The short and wide blade was very effective during close combat on board ship.

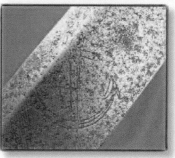

251

C.1800 NAVAL(?) OFFICER'S CUTLASS
VALUE: $2550.00/£1595.00

This is quite a speculative piece. Opinion is divided as to whether this is an actual naval or army sword. The short blade seems to indicate naval use, as does the typically wide, cutlass-type blade.

Battle of Walcheren, 1809.

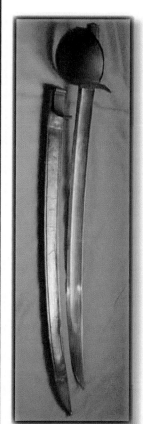

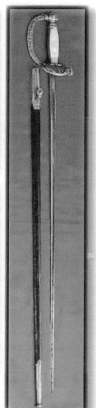

MODEL 1833 NAVAL CUTLASS
VALUE: $1100.00/£695.00

Battle of Trafalgar, 1805.

C.1820 NAVAL OFFICER'S SWORD
VALUE: $1435.00/£895.00
Likely to be from the Restoration Period.

FRENCH MODEL 1837 OFFICER'S SWORD
VALUE: $1435.00/£895.00

One of the most attractive of French naval swords from the nineteenth century, the hilt features a ribbed horn grip and heavily decorated guard with dolphin-head quillon. Blades tend to be plain and highly polished. Copies are known to have been produced in India and Pakistan. On first inspection they appear quite plausible, but they tend not to have the crisp hilt definition of the original and scabbards are poorly made. Blade markings to the blade spine are also crude and probably applied with an electric engraving tool.

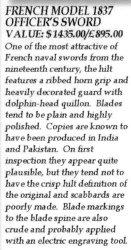

FRENCH MODEL 1837 OFFICER'S SWORD
VALUE: $1435.00/£895.00

Detail from a French warship, c.1905.

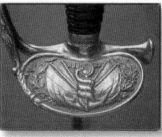

MODEL 1889 NAVAL OFFICER'S SWORD
VALUE: $ 950.00/£595.00

Rare French Surgeon Officer's Dress Sword. Is unusual in having a browned metal and brass mounted scabbard. Most are found with leather and brass mounts.

"La Gloire", c.1900.

Right:
C.1830 NAVAL OFFICER'S SWORD
VALUE: $ 950.00/ £595.00

Rare and very clean example, likely to be from the reign of Louis Phillipe (1830-1848). Brass hilt with anchor and laurels to the shell guard. Ball pommel has an engraved fleur-de-lys. Ribbed, slab grips are mother of pearl. Blade is plain and of trefoil form. Scabbard would have been leather and brass mounted. Because of the fragility of these very thin scabbards, most have not survived. The grips can also suffer consequent age damage, including splitting and loss.

www.michaeldlong.com

www.michaeldlong.com

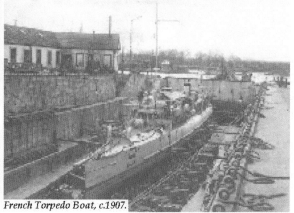

French Torpedo Boat, c.1907.

255

OTHER NATIONS' NAVAL SWORDS

UNITED STATES

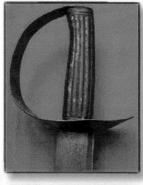

C.1770 "AMERICAN" NAVAL CUTLASS
VALUE: $ 1275.00/£795.00

The following cutlasses are of a type usually attributed to domestic American manufacture during the Revolutionary War period. The crude hilt and unfullered, handforged blades, were hastily produced in local blacksmith's forges and then issued to seaman of the fledgling American Navy. They are invariably unmarked and exact identification is always difficult.

C.1770 "AMERICAN" NAVAL CUTLASS
VALUE: $995.00/£570.00

C.1770 "AMERICAN" NAVAL CUTLASS
VALUE: $1095.00/£625.00

An unusual design with elaborate curled quillons. The blade could be from an earlier sword.

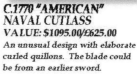

www.michaeldlong.com

www.michaeldlong.com

www.michaeldlong.com

C.WW2 NAVAL OFFICER'S SWORD
VALUE: $ 560.00/£ 350.00

www.michaeldlong.com   www.michaeldlong.com

US Navy Parade, c.1917.

Admiral, US Navy, c.1905.

Rear Admiral, US Navy, c.1905.

Commander, US Navy, c.1905.

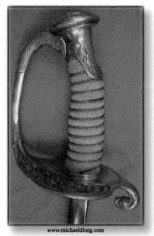

www.michaeldlong.com

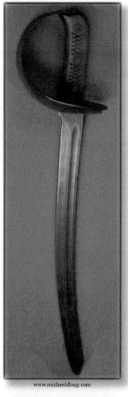

www.michaeldlong.com

www.michaeldlong.com

C.WW2 NAVAL OFFICER'S SWORD
VALUE: $ 560.00/£ 350.00
Many of these wartime swords are marked on the blade to the original owner. Post-war swords tend to deteriorate with regard to overall quality of manufacture.

US sailors, c.1917.

USS Texas, c.1910.

MODEL 1917 NAVAL CUTLASS
VALUE: $ 400.00/£ 250.00
This cutlass was issued to ordinary seaman and carried on US warships until declared obsolete in 1949. The hilt and clipped-point blade was blued. Chequered wood grip, secured with copper rivets. The short, curved blade was designed for cut and thrust action. The design of this cutlass is very similar to the contemporary Dutch cutlass or "Klewang".

GERMANY

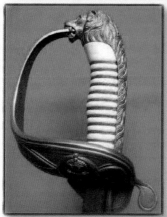

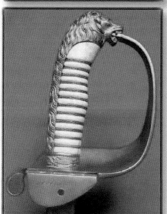

C. WWI GERMAN NAVAL OFFICER'S SWORD
VALUE: $ 1435.00/£895.00

The sword bears a great resemblance to contemporary British naval officers' swords of the period. It differs in having a bone, ivory or celluloid (with later pieces) grip, as opposed to the choice of white fishskin for their British counterpart. The blade is of pipe back form. The fold-down guard of this sword is engraved with the owner's name.

German Marine, c.1914.

S.M.S. Magdeburg, c.1912.

259

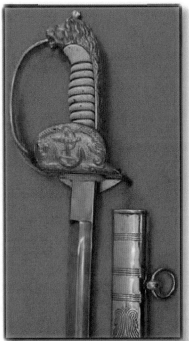

www.michaeldlong.com

C.1920'S NAVAL OFFICER'S SWORD
VALUE: $1100.00/£695.00
Good example of an inter-war sword. They tend to be clearly marked with an official government acceptance stamp to the fold-down guard. Official marks are also noted on the scabbard throat and shoe (chape).

Right:
C.1925 NAVAL OFFICER'S SWORD
VALUE: $1100.00/£695.00
From the Weimar period. Grip is manufactured in either bone or ivory.

www.michaeldlong.com

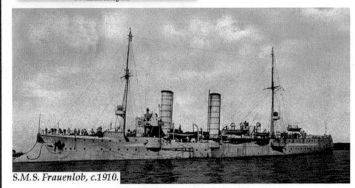

S.M.S. Frauenlob, c.1910.

S.M.S. Von der Tann, c.1914.

German Sailor, c.1914.

AUSTRIA (HUNGARY)

MODEL 1850/1871 NAVAL OFFICER'S SWORD
VALUE: $ 1435.00/£ 895.00

An attractive model with elaborate gilt brass hilt comprising the Austro-Hungarian double-headed eagle, mermaids and a fouled anchor. The hilt backstrap features a stylised Neptune. This example is rare as it retains the original sword knot.

The Battle of Lissa, 1866.

MODEL 1891 NAVAL CADET'S SWORD
VALUE: $ 1275.00/£ 795.00

Designed as a purely decorative item, this short sword is quite a scarce piece. It features a simple crosspiece with dolphin quillon and raised anchor motif to the backpiece. The grip is fishskin and brass twistwire.

The "Kaiser" ramming the "Re di Portogallo", 1866.

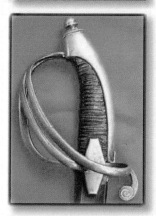

IMPERIAL RUSSIA

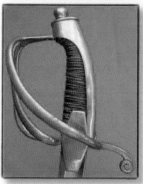

Vice Admiral Nikolay Skridlov, 1904.

MODEL 1855 NAVAL OFFICER'S SWORD

VALUE: $1095.00/£625.00

This pattern replaced the 1811 sabre. Early examples feature a pipe back blade. Post-1914 swords are also embossed to the backstrap with a floral pattern and the cypher of Emperor Nicholas II. Many of these cyphers were disfigured after the 1917 Revolution.

www.michaeldlong.com

www.michaeldlong.com

Vice Admiral Stepan Osipovitz Makarov, 1904.

www.michaellong.com

www.michaellong.com

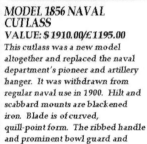

www.michaellong.com

MODEL 1856 NAVAL CUTLASS
VALUE: $1910.00/£1195.00

This cutlass was a new model altogether and replaced the naval department's pioneer and artillery hanger. It was withdrawn from regular naval use in 1900. Hilt and scabbard mounts are blackened iron. Blade is of curved, quill-point form. The ribbed handle and prominent bowl guard and pommel are similar to British naval cutlasses of this period.

A naval engagement, Russo-Japanese War, 1904.

Kronstadt naval base, c.1855.

A naval engagement, Russo-Japanese War, 1904.

A naval engagement, Russo-Japanese War, 1904.

SPAIN

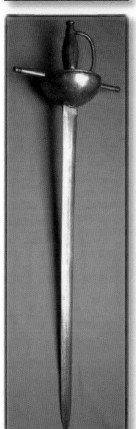

SPANISH C.1750 PRIVATEER'S CUTLASS
VALUE: $1910.00/£1195.00

This style of sword was favoured by Spanish privateers and comprised a cut-down cup-hilt rapier of Bilbo form. It is of very sturdy manufacture with a small walnut grip and incised chequering.

DENMARK

www.michaeldlong.com

www.michaelddlong.com

www.michaeldlong.com

C.1945 NAVAL OFFICER'S SWORD
VALUE: $1100.00/£695.00

SIAM (THAILAND)

C.1900 SIAMESE NAVAL OFFICER'S SWORD
VALUE: $1040.00/ £650.00

Although there are no obvious naval motifs evident on this sword, the use of white fishskin to the grip and a navy blue and silver bullion sword knot, could be indicative of a naval origin. The choice of an elephant's head pommel is probably unique in world naval swords.

TURKEY

C.1870 NAVAL OFFICER'S SWORD
VALUE: $1435.00/ £895.00

The hilt is very reminiscent of European swords of the period and highlights western influences within the Ottoman Empire. It is also likely that the sword was manufactured in Europe, possibly Germany.

Turkish Naval Mutiny, 1909.

UNIDENTIFIED

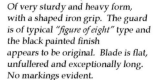

Naval Signals

C.1830 NAVAL CUTLASS
VALUE: $635.00/£395.00

Of very sturdy and heavy form, with a shaped iron grip. The guard is of typical *"figure of eight"* type and the black painted finish appears to be original. Blade is flat, unfullered and exceptionally long. No markings evident.

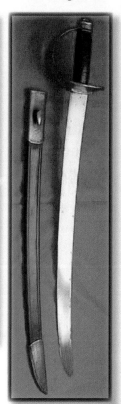

C.1850 NAVAL CUTLASS
VALUE: $475.00/£295.00

Possibly a composite. Blade with German maker's mark.

SWEDEN

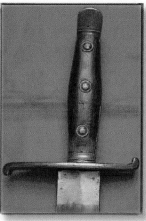

C.1800'S NAVAL CUTLASS
VALUE: $1435.00/£895.00

An unusual design offering minimal protection to the hand, this cutlass features a very wide, single-fullered blade. The long grip is manufactured from a light wood, probably birch, and has age darkened over the years. The grip is secured with steel studs. Flanged brass pommel. The blade is unmarked but there is an impressed letter to the grip. It is likely that the sword would have been issued with a scabbard.

MODEL 1685 INFANTRYMAN'S SWORD (CUTLASS CONVERSION)
VALUE: $2075.00/£1295.00

A very early example of a regulation infantry sword, converted later for naval use. Blade length has been reduced and the knucklebow removed. Hilt is iron, with brass twistwire to the grip. Each side of the blade is deeply struck with three armourer's marks.

Swedish naval battery, c.1905.

HOLLAND

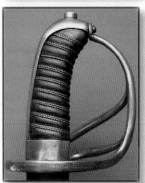

1759 DUTCH EAST INDIA COMPANY HANGER
VALUE: $1910.00/£1195.00
Unusual piece that has probably lost its original knucklebow. Dated blade and DEIC symbol.

DUTCH C.1780'S NAVAL CUTLASS
VALUE: $1435.00/£895.00
The blade is dated to 1786 on one side with crossed anchors to the obverse. With brass three-bar hilt. Leather and brass twistwire to the grip. It is unusual to find a naval cutlass of this early period complete with its original scabbard.

MODEL 1837 NAVAL OFFICER'S SWORD
VALUE: $1435.00/£895.00

www.michaeldlong.com

www.michaeldlong.com

Of a style reminiscent of contemporary European naval officer's swords, particularly French examples. This sword has a ribbed ivory grip. Blade is of pipe back form. Brass guard is richly decorated with an extravagant design, including clamshell quillons. Anchor and royal crown inset into hilt cartouche.

THE SMALLSWORD OFFERS THE COLLECTOR an infinite variety of styles and decoration. Materials used in the construction of smallswords included iron, steel, brass, silver and gold. The craftsmen who produced smallswords (primarily for the civilian market), were only limited by the client's financial means. Thus we see a terrific range of quality and ornamentation.

HISTORICAL BACKGROUND

The smallsword was a natural development of the earlier rapier sword, and its evolution was of a gradual and transitional nature. During the mid-seventeenth century, the need to carry a large, long-bladed weapon diminished, and gentlemen began to adopt a form of sword referred to as a *"Town"* or *"Walking"* sword. In England, this change was due partly to a period of relative social stability after the English Civil War, and the belief that you did not need to go abroad as fully armed as in previous years. The dagger that normally accompanied the rapier was also dropped and a lighter, more flexible sword introduced. This was believed to be more practical when involved in any form of combat, particularly the duel, and was also considered more comfortable to wear alongside civilian dress. It must be remembered that a sword served not only a weapon of defence. It was also very much an ornament of fashion, and prey to transient vogues. What was worn at Court was soon copied. During the late seventeenth century, the dominant influence was French design. It became a powerful stimulus in smallsword design.

The flat, rapier blade of the 1600's was superceded by an important technological breakthrough in the early 1700's, when a group of German swordmakers developed the *clochimarde* blade. It was of trefoil or three-sided form and hollow ground. It had a very distinctive shape, being wide at the blade forte (up to eight inches), and then dramatically narrower for the remainder of the blade. This new hilt style included a shell guard, quillons, knucklebow, pommel and grip. The addition of *pas d'ane* rings formed downward quillons that reached the base of the shell guard. Blades of the early 1700's are thus easily dateable and identifiable by these attributes of design. The actual popularity of *clochimarde* blades was quite short and by the mid-1700's, blades were already changing. The technical knowledge needed to produce these hollow ground blades was jealously guarded by the German swordmakers, despite successful attempts by the English Government to bring over German workers who established a manufactory at Shotley Bridge in County Durham during the 1600's. This project eventually failed, although one of the unforeseen by-products was the retention in England of one of its German workers, a certain Herman Mohll. His family were later to become a major force in British swordmaking and are best known amongst collectors by their anglicised name; Mole.

As the eighteenth century progressed, the smallsword soon became the weapon of choice for military officers. Officers tended to purchase more than one sword, and the "military" smallsword was likely to have been carried on more formal or *"walking out"* occasions, with a more robust fighting sword carried into battle. With the onset of the Napoleonic Wars, the use of the smallsword by the military began to decline and its everyday use was relegated to diplomats and those attending Court. Presentation smallswords were also popular during the 1800's, and there are some very fine examples awarded to British naval officers.

COLLECTING SMALLSWORDS

The collecting of smallswords has no major pitfalls excepting the usual warnings associated with any antique sword purchase. Having said this, one of the most basic areas to be be wary about when looking at a smallsword concerns the blade length. Smallswords have very thin, tapering blades, liable to breakage, particularly near the point. One should always check to see if there has been any loss to the blade length. The elegant proportions of a smallsword can be ruined by the loss of a few inches to the blade length. The average length of a smallsword blade should be around thirty two inches.

Sword-play during the eighteenth century.

C.1700 ENGLISH SMALLSWORD
VALUE: $ 1910.00/ £1195.00

Of early form. With the transitional elements of earlier sword styles, including a long, rapier-type blade. The deeply chiselled guard is more styled in the seventeeth century, but the plain round pommel and pas-de-ane, show the growing emergence of the true smallsword. Grip of brass and silver twistwire.

www.michaelllong.com

www.michaelllong.com

www.michaelllong.com

C.1770 SILVER-HILTED SMALLSWORD
VALUE: $ 1910.00/£1195.00

C.1770 SILVER-HILTED SMALLSWORD
VALUE: $ 2075.00/£1295.00

www.michaelllong.com

www.michaelllong.com

A Duel, c.1730.

C.1730 INLAID SILVER SMALLSWORD
VALUE: $1910.00/£1195.00
Inlaid with silver to the hilt, guard and pommel. The blade is plain and of cruciform shape.

C.1700 DUTCH SMALLSWORD
VALUE: $1910.00/£1195.00
This example highlights the distinctive influence of the Roccoco during this period. This is seen in the heavily decorated neo-classical shellguard, featuring mythical figures, theatrical masks and the head of a fantastic grotesque to the quillon. The large bulbous pommel mimics earlier rapiers, and shows the transitional nature of the smallsword during this period. The blade is of trefoil form and plain. Grip is bound with silver twistwire. Overall quality of the hilt detail is exceptionally fine.

C.1780 SMALLSWORD
VALUE: $1435.00/£895.00
With a very fine fire gilt and iron hilt. Complete with its original white leather scabbard. The grip appears to be bone and is likely to be a later(?) replacement.

C.1780 MOURNING SMALLSWORD
VALUE: $695.00/£400.00
These swords were manufactured specifically for wear during funerals. This sword is quite plain with a smooth iron hilt. The hilt has also been given a japanned black finish.

C.1720 SMALLSWORD
VALUE: $1100.00/£695.00
Featuring chinese motifs to the hilt.
With early *"clochimarde"* blade.

C.1760 SMALLSWORD
VALUE: $635.00/£395.00

C.1760 SMALLSWORD
VALUE: $1295.00/£795.00
An unusual smallsword with rarely seen and excellent cross-ribboned decoration to the hilt. The intertwined engraving to the blade forte is a feature of mid-late eighteenth century smallswords. It is also noted on hunting hangers of the period.

C.1750 SMALLSWORD
VALUE: $1100.00/£695.00

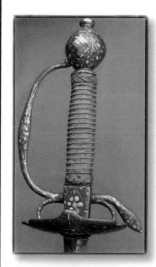

C.1680 RAPIER/SMALLSWORD
VALUE: $2235.00/£1395.00

A very fine piece with inlaid silver decoration to an iron hilt. This sword is of transitional form, indicated by the large, bulbous pommel (seen on earlier rapiers) and the smallsword dish hilt guard and pas-de-ane.

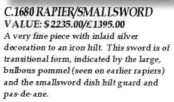

C.1680 RAPIER/SMALLSWORD
VALUE: $2075.00/£1295.00

The fencing master, Domenico Angelo, c.1760.

C.1750 SMALLSWORD
VALUE: $ 3035.00/£1895.00
A very fine quality iron hilt with deeply inlaid gilt decoration, including extravagantly scrolled foliage. The grip is bound with silver twistwire and banding. Original scabbards are virtually unknown.

C.1770 SMALLSWORD
VALUE: $ 795.00/£495.00
Brass hilt with copper banding and twistwire. The original knucklebow is missing.

Right and below right:
C.1780 ENGLISH SILVER-HILTED SMALLSWORD
VALUE: $ 1435.00/£895.00
A very delicate and elegant example of a gentleman's sword. With a solid silver open work hilt. Blade is plain and of trefoil form.

www.michaeldlong.com

www.michaeldlong.com

www.michaeldlong.com

The Boar Thrust, c.1750.

www.michaeldlong.com www.michaeldlong.com

275

C.1750 BRASS-HILTED SMALLSWORD
VALUE: $ 635.00/£ 395.00

C.1760 ENGLISH SMALLSWORD
VALUE: $ 1100.00/£ 695.00
A good example of an English brass-hilted smallsword with distinctive gadrooning decoration to the hilt.

Below:
C.1760 CONTINENTAL SMALLSWORD
VALUE: $ 2075.00/£ 1295.00
An important example with very high quality and complex cut steel and gold decoration to hilt.

www.antiqueswords.com

C.1750 CUT STEEL SMALLSWORD
VALUE: $ 950.00/£ 595.00

www.michaeklilong.com

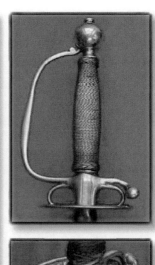

C.1770 ENGLISH SILVER HILTED SMALLSWORD
VALUE: $ 1595.00/£ 995.00

www.gams.uk.com

C.1760 ENGLISH SILVER-HILTED SMALLSWORD
VALUE: $1395.00/£800.00
Exceptional quality with finely chiselled pommel and knucklebow.

www.michaeklilong.com

www.michaeklilong.com

C.1800 ENGLISH CUT STEEL SMALLSWORD
VALUE: $1595.00/£995.00

Probably for use at Court, the sword includes a cut steel sectioned hilt and polished steel studs. The blade has fine blue and gilt decoration with standing arms and foliage. The use of such martial motifs might point towards this sword being carried by a military officer, although this is not totally clear. These cut steel smallswords were particularly in vogue during the early 1800's.

C.1780 ENGLISH SILVER-HILTED SMALLSWORD
VALUE: $2075.00/£1295.00

An interesting piece that displays a wealth of details to the hilt guard. The presence of an anchor might indicate its adoption by a naval officer. Until the introduction of a universal pattern of British naval officer's sword in 1805, officers tended to choose their own style of sword. Smallswords were a popular choice. There do not appear to be any silver hallmarks. Smallsword hallmarks are normally found on the knucklebow, underside of the dishguard or branches of the pas-de-ane.

www.michaeldlong.com

Above and below:
C.1750 SMALLSWORDS
VALUE: $1100.00/£695.00

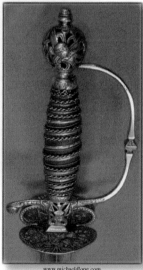

www.michaeldlong.com

Above:
English smallsword silver scabbard lockets, c.1770.

www.guns.uk.com

www.michaeldlong.com

www.michaeldlong.com

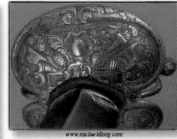

C.1800 ENGLISH SILVER-HILTED SMALLSWORD
VALUE: $2075.00/£1295.00

With excellent blue and gilt blade. Leather and silver scabbard.

C.1750 ENGLISH SILVER-HILTED SMALLSWORD
VALUE: $1910.00/£1195.00

Hallmarked for London (1750).

C.1800 ENGLISH SILVER-HILTED SMALLSWORD
VALUE: $1910.00/£1195.00

With typical delicately pierced decoration to the shell guard. Both pommel and guard have urn motifs.

C.1780 FRENCH(?) SILVER-HILTED SMALLSWORD
VALUE: $2075.00/£1295.00

With deeply impressed hallmarks.

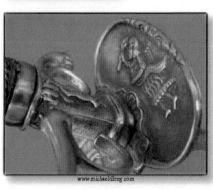

Left:
C.1780 CONTINENTAL SILVER-HILTED SMALLSWORD
VALUE: $1000.00/£1600.00

With elaborately curved boat shell hilt and deeply cut fanned decoration.
Right:
Hilt detail to a c.1760 smallsword.

www.antiqueswords.com

www.antiqueswords.com

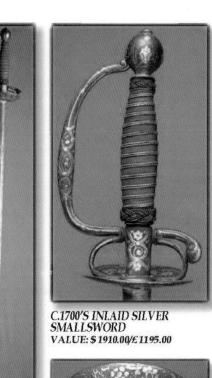

C.1850 BAVARIAN MILITARY COURTSWORD
VALUE: $ 635.00/£ 395.00
With mother-of-pearl slab grips and gilt brass hilt mounts. The shell guard features the Bavarian lion amidst martial trophies.

C.1830 FRENCH MILITARY SMALLSWORD
VALUE: $ 635.00/£ 395.00
From the period of Napoleon II (Restoration) and carried by a senior NCO.

C.1700'S INLAID SILVER SMALLSWORD
VALUE: $ 1910.00/£ 1195.00

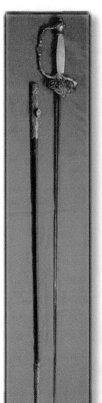

C.1850 CONTINENTAL SMALLSWORD
VALUE: $895.00/ £510.00
French in style and likely to have been worn at Court, possibly by a diplomat.

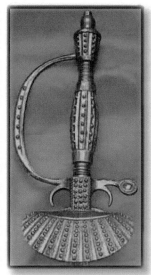
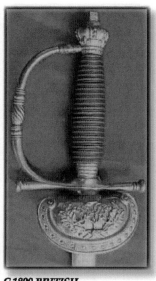
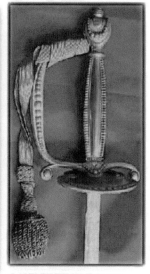

C.1800 BRITISH CUT STEEL MOURNING/ COURTSWORD
VALUE: $475.00/£295.00

C.1890 BRITISH DIPLOMATIC CORPS COURTSWORD
VALUE: $475.00/£295.00

C.1870 BRITISH ROYAL HOUSEHOLD COURTSWORD
VALUE: $475.00/£295.00

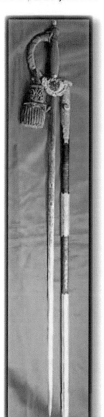

SCOTTISH COMPANY OF ARCHERS (ROYAL BODYGUARD OF SCOTLAND) COURTSWORD
VALUE: $1275.00/£795.00

A fine quality example with frost etched blade and heavy bullion sword knot. Founded in 1676 as a private archery club, the Company first acted as a royal bodyguard when George IV first visited Scotland in 1822. This tradition has continued to this day and most members are drawn from ex-military, political and noble families.

MODEL 1855 IMPERIAL RUSSIAN CIVIL SERVANT'S COURTSWORD
VALUE: $ 2710.00/£1695.00
Later examples feature an imperial crown to the pommel.

"The Salute". A duellist before the combat.

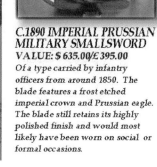

C.1890 IMPERIAL PRUSSIAN MILITARY SMALLSWORD
VALUE: $ 635.00/£ 395.00
Of a type carried by infantry officers from around 1850. The blade features a frost etched imperial crown and Prussian eagle. The blade still retains its highly polished finish and would most likely have been worn on social or formal occasions.

C.1890 SIAMESE OFFICER'S COURTSWORD
VALUE: $ 635.00/£ 395.00

C.1860 GERMAN STATES MILITARY COURTSWORD
VALUE: $ 795.00/£ 495.00

C.1800 SMALLSWORD
VALUE: $ 635.00/£ 395.00

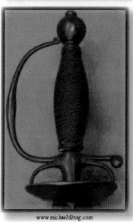

C.1800'S FRENCH MILITARY SMALLSWORD
VALUE: $ 950.00/£ 595.00
For an officer of senior status.

C.1750 ENGLISH MOURNING SMALLSWORD
VALUE: $ 635.00/£ 395.00

C.1900 GERMAN MILITARY COURTSWORD
VALUE: $ 795.00/£ 495.00

C.1690 AUSTRIAN(?) SMALLSWORD
VALUE: $ 795.00/£ 495.00
With carved ivory grip.

AIR FORCE SWORDS

THE COLLECTOR OF AIR FORCE SWORDS has a somewhat limited field of choice. Most original examples tend to date from the 1920's, and corresponded with the early growth of national airforces, particularly within Europe and North America. These pre-WW2 airforce swords are extremely scarce and tend to command high prices.

One of the most common airforce swords to appear in the market is the British 1920 Pattern Royal Air Force Officer's Sword. This was the last official regulation pattern sword of the British Army. Designed by Wilkinson Sword, the pattern was based on the 1897 Pattern Infantry Officer's sword (worn by Royal Engineer Officers). This was an acknowledgment of the Royal Engineers' Balloonist Unit (raised in 1878), and the precursor to the future Royal Flying Corps and Royal Air Force. British airmen during WW1 would originally have been posted from army or naval units. They would have therefore carried a dress sword appropriate to their relevant branch of service prior to joining the Royal Flying Corps.

The 1920 Pattern is most elegant in design, with an eagle-head pommel and crowned winged albatross to the hilt cartouche. Grip was white sharkskin.

The Italian and German airforces produced swords of unique design, with both nations drawing heavily on the art deco influences prevalent during the 1920's and 1930's. The Italian Air Force officer's sword has an impressive sweeping eagle-head hilt, and the German Model 1934 Air Force Officer's Sword, displays a very modernistic hilt design.

COLLECTING AIR FORCE SWORDS

The British 1920 Pattern Air Force Officer's sword has been the subject of attention by the forgers, and copies are currently being produced in India and Pakistan. As with most modern copies from this part of the world, they do not match in any shape or form the quality of the original. Whereas the original period swords have genuine white sharkskin grips, these fakes have a simulated sharkskin grip made of plastic resin. The blade etching is also crude and fuzzy. It is probably best to look out for examples maker marked and numbered to Wilkinson Sword as they were the principal manufacturers of this pattern. The serial number on the blade edge is also traceable via the company records. Copies tend to be unmarked, although I have noticed a recent trend of faking the Wilkinson Star of David company logo to the blade forte, both on these airforce swords and other British regulation pattern swords.

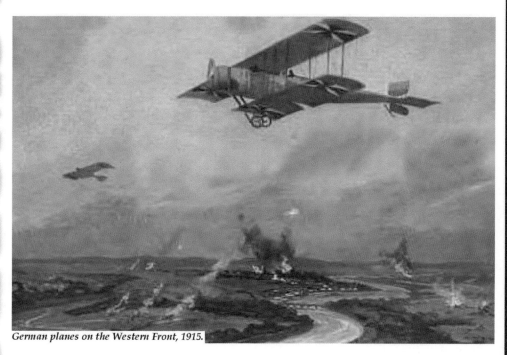

German planes on the Western Front, 1915.

1921 PATTERN BRITISH ROYAL AIR FORCE OFFICER'S SWORD
VALUE: $1435.00/£895.00

www.antiqueswordz.com

www.antiqueswordz.com

C.1930'S SPANISH AIR FORCE OFFICER'S SWORD
VALUE: $2550.00/£1595.00
Extremely rare sword that is likely to have been carried by an officer on the Nationalist side. It is doubtful that this was an official model.

French monoplane, c.1916.

German monoplanes. A fanciful interpretation, c.1914.

C.1930'S ITALIAN AIR FORCE OFFICER'S SWORD
VALUE: $ 795.00/ £ 1275.00
This sword was carried by a pilot officer below the rank of Colonel. The grips are usually manufactured in either painted wood or ebony.

C.1930'S ITALIAN AIR FORCE OFFICER'S SWORD
VALUE: $ 1435.00/£ 895.00
Rare sword with blue and gilt decoration to the blade. Manufactured by Eichorn, Germany.

285

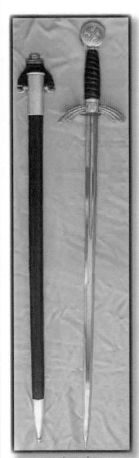

www.antiqueswords.com

www.antiqueswords.com

www.antiqueswords.com

www.antiqueswords.com

GERMAN MODEL 1934 LUFTWAFFE OFFICER'S SWORD
VALUE: $1100.00/£695.00

A uniquely designed sword with very strong contemporary art deco influences. Hilt and scabbard mounts are manufactured in aluminium. Blade forte is engraved with the knight's head maker mark for W.K.C. (Weyersberg, Kirschbaum and Company).

www.antiqueswords.com

Senior Luftwaffe officers.

Early Soviet airman.

French airmen, c.WW1.

THE JAPANESE SWORD IS BOTH A FUNCTIONAL weapon of armed combat and also an object of great aesthetic beauty. It displays qualities of artistry and craftsmanship that can be understood and appreciated by those who would normally declare no actual interest in swords. This is what makes it unique in many respects when compared with swords produced purely as tools of war.

HISTORICAL BACKGROUND

The origin of the Japanese sword can be traced back to nearly two millenia. Very early swords (c.300AD) have been found in Japanese burial mounds. They show signs of being heavily influenced by Japan's near neighbours, Korea and China. Blades were long and single-edged, with simple *tsuba* mounts. Warriors at this time were predominantly horsemen and needed a long-bladed sword that could be used effectively at the gallop. Many of the swords carried by these Japanese clansmen were imported and not manufactured in Japan. The development of home-based swordmaking came later.

As we move into the early Middle Ages, the classical *samurai* sword style became more recognisable. This was augmented by the gradual change of the blade from straight to slightly curved. During the Heian Period (795-1185), Japanese swordsmiths began to mark their own work on the blade tang, so enabling the collector to identify date of manufacture, and also name and province of the maker. The appearance of a more varied *hamon* or pattern to the blade is also seen during this period. Heian blades are regarded as some of the most perfect ever produced. Consequently, they have acquired an almost mythical status, with most surviving examples far beyond the reach of most collectors. Other important periods of sword manufacture include the *Kamakura Period* (1185-1392), *Yoshino or Namboku Cho Period* (1333-1393), *Muromachi Period* (1392-1477), *Edo Period* (1603-1867) and *Showa Period* (1926-1989). The carrying of samurai swords in public was outlawed in 1867, resulting in a rapid decline in the number of working swordsmiths. With the revival of Japanese nationalism during the *Showa Period*, a parallel revival in swordmaking was witnessed. This came to an abupt end with the defeat of Japan in 1945, but Japanese swordmaking has revived again in recent years with a great demand for particular swordsmiths.

After the demise of the samurai class in the late- nineteenth century, Japan entered into an unprecedented period of contact with the West. This was reflected in dramatic changes in sword design for regular army forces. Although the traditional *samurai* sword was still being made during this period (albeit in small numbers), military swords from the 1870's -1900's were heavily influenced by European designs, most notably those carried by the French military. Some officers' swords were virtual copies of French swords. This is evident when viewing hilt styles.

One of the most common Japanese sword styles is the *kyu-gunto* pattern. It retains the long grip associated with the *samurai* sword, but has a knucklebow and pommel of European design. There are many variations of this pattern, with a version for both officers and ncos. From the 1920's, many officers reverted back to the classic *samurai* sword form or new *shin-gunto* pattern. Most examples in the market date from this period. Blades were either machine-made, hand-forged or earlier family or ancestral blades attached to new hilts. They were carried by all branches of the Imperial Army. Large numbers were destroyed at the end of WW2, but significant quantities were also brought home as souvenirs and are common at arms shows.

Woodblock by Tsukioka Yoshitoshi (1839-1892).

287

COLLECTING JAPANESE SWORDS

*I*t is often remarked that a new collector must try to read as much as possible about their chosen subject *before* making any kind of major purchase. This fact is absolutely essential when considering the purchase of a Japanese *samurai* sword. This is a specialised field of collecting and can be quite complicated, with many levels of price, quality, age and category. It is advisable to study the subject in reasonable depth in order that you have a basic idea of what you want. The internet has spawned many collectors' clubs and forums. These can be invaluable when asking important questions and can also save you making some basic errors. It is also vital that you know how to handle and care for a *samurai* sword. If a blade is not treated with care, it can seriously deteriorate, as can any inherent value. This is the same for delicate hilt and scabbard fittings. Do not attempt any kind of restoration if you do not have the necessary skills. Polishing a samurai sword is best left to the professionals. It takes years of training and special skills to do this job.

*I*f you are making a first purchase, it might be best to acquire your sword from a reputable dealer or auction house. You might possibly have to pay a little bit more but you can at least be comforted in the knowledge that you will be buying from a source that has a reputation in the market to protect. You will also receive an official invoice that provides a safeguard if you have any problems in the future. Try to avoid buying online, unless you value the seller's reputation. Japanese blades are difficult to photograph and you might find that problems only become apparent when the sword has already been purchased.

*M*any first-time sword collectors with surplus funds tend to go on an initial spending spree. There is no denying that this can be great fun and you might also believe that you have got some great bargains. In reality, this *"blunderbus"* approach can leave you stock rich but quality poor. In the case of Japanese swords, one needs to be collect with great care and discernment. It is far better to have a small collection of fine pieces than a ragbag of average swords.

FORGERIES

*J*apanese swords have always been a target of the faker and this trend has grown considerably in recent years. Most of the fakes are now being produced in China and sold via internet auction sites. The quantities are huge and the market has been saturated. To the experienced collector they are laughably poor, but to the first-timer they are tempting because of their very low price. This fact should always raise alarm bells. The quality of these swords is very bad, with crude attempts to age and distress the sword. The sight of red rust normally indicates that a sword has been left out in the rain for a few weeks to enhance the ageing process. Sellers of these swords will always declare that they are genuine, have been in China for many years and were formerly carried by Japanese forces in WW2. Their auctions are nearly always private (another warning bell), so prospective buyers cannot access the no doubt poor feedback lodged by previously disgruntled purchasers. Profit is gained by charging extortionate amounts for shipping. The sword itself probably costs only a few pounds to manufacture. The best *"rule of thumb"* is to never buy a sword that is being sold out of China and especially so if it is a private auction. It will *definitely* be a fake.

Samurai battle - nineteenth century woodblock.

Below:
C.1941 GENDAI KATANA
VALUE: $4050.00/£2315.00

An important gendai work signed Okishiba Yoshisada tsukuru kore. It is dated on the reverse of the tang - Showa 19th year, 6th month, lucky day, March, 1941. Blade retains just about all the original polish and displays exceptionally fine hamon.

www.antiqueswords.com

Right:
KATANA - EARLY SHINTO
VALUE: $4160.00/ £2600.00

Early Shinto, probably Owari-Seki, or possibly Echizen. Old iron fuchi/ kashira and iron menuki in swallow motif. Tsuba cut out in the form of sea birds and waves. Unsigned. Slightly shortened from the tang. Beautiful blade with combination of suguha and choji; lots of activity.

www.antiqueswords.com

Below left:
C.1800 JAPANESE WAKAZASHI
VALUE: $7000.00/ £4380.00

Good, early blade with strong hamon grain pattern hada. Scabbard is black leather on wood with overlaid malachite.

www.antiqueswords.com   www.antiqueswords.com   www.antiqueswords.com   www.antiqueswords.com

C.1550-1650 KATANA
VALUE: $2235.00/£1395.00

Late Koto or early Shinto, 1550-1650. Single-hole nakago, partially punched and drilled, indicating early technique. Ubu tang, without signature. Old rust deterioration to base of nakago, with nice brownish-black patina. Copper habaki, of good quality, and may have been originally covered with gold or silver foil. Well-forged plain iron tsuba, possibly cleaned at some point. Shakudo fuchi with fine diamond pattern surface, and horn kashira. Black battle-wrap with dark snake or lizard skin. Exposed menuki are a combination of leaves, berries and stems (probably early nineteenth century). Saya with three copper fittings are also likely to be nineteenth century.

www.michaeldlong.com

~ Japanese Swords ~

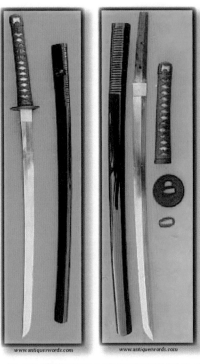

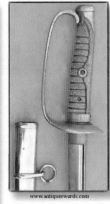

WAKAZASHI - LATE KOTO OR EARLY SHINTO
VALUE: $4575.00/£2615.00

The blade is noteworthy as having a Notare Ba (crashing wave) hamon with Tobiyaki (floating jewels) and drifting sand formation in the temper line. It has a very good, healthy blade with beautiful temper and no flaws. Suriage (sword with shortened tang) blade. The two-hole nakago and partial signature reads *"hitachi no kami fujiwara"*. The blade is probably by Munishige from Settsu Province, who was most active in 1686. He was also noted for making very sharp blades, and worked in Edo (Tokyo). The scabbard appears to be original, but has probably been relacquered during its lifetime. Tsuka has old iron fuchi kashira. Wrap with military gunto menuki. The hand forged Tsuba is of old iron, c.1750. It is also engraved with a wood pattern design. Habaki is silver-plated.

www.antiqueswords.com

C.1870'S ARMY OFFICER'S SHIN GUNTO
VALUE: $ 5275.00/ £ 3295.00

Excellent white same grip with original wire. Nickel mounts and chromed scabbard. Koto period blade nagasa. Blade is grooved to both sides.

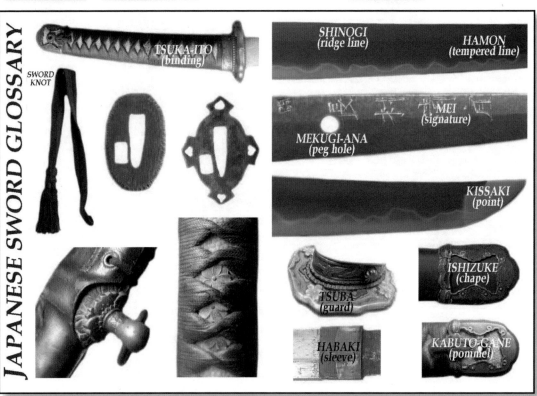

JAPANESE SWORD GLOSSARY

- **TSUKA-ITO** (binding)
- **SWORD KNOT**
- **SHINOGI** (ridge line)
- **HAMON** (tempered line)
- **MEI** (signature)
- **MEKUGI-ANA** (peg hole)
- **KISSAKI** (point)
- **TSUBA** (guard)
- **ISHIZUKE** (chape)
- **HABAKI** (sleeve)
- **KABUTO-GANE** (pommel)

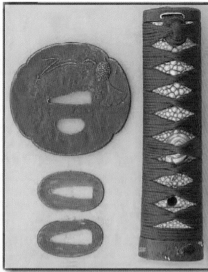

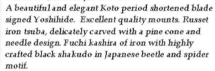

www.antiqueswords.com

www.antiqueswords.com

www.antiqueswords.com

www.antiqueswords.com

C.1500 WAKAZASHI
VALUE: $ 6395.00/£ 3995.00

A beautiful and elegant Koto period shortened blade signed Yoshihide. Excellent quality mounts. Russet iron tsuba, delicately carved with a pine cone and needle design. Fuchi kashira of iron with highly crafted black shakudo in Japanese beetle and spider motif.

www.antiqueswords.com

www.antiqueswords.com

Left:
C.1600-1650 WAKAZASHI
VALUE: $4595.00/ £2625.00

Probably from Chikuzen province. With its original samurai mounts and very good early polish. In near mint condition. Sugaha temper running the full length of the blade through to the tip. No flaws of any kind. Double fullers to both sides of blade through nakago on both sides. Nakago signed Nobukuni and inlaid with gold. Seppa of gold foil over copper; menuki appear to be of solid gold in the form of tigers. Gold foil habaki and solid shakudo tsuba with gold foil edge. Matching fuchikashira of shakudo with gold floral motif.

Far left:
C.1600-1650 WAKAZASHI
VALUE: $2595.00/ £1480.00

Japanese Woodblock, c.1880.

291

SHIN-SHINTO PERIOD KATANA
VALUE: $7360.00/ £4600.00

A very fine example exhibiting a temper gunome suguha with nie and nioi, and a combination of mokume and itame hada. No visible flaws are present on the blade. White wrap with matching same. Matching iron fuchi kashira with berry and leaf motif. There is also a foxy-red copper lobster menuki. The tachi-style iron tsuba is designed with cut-out boars-eyes matching the scabbard toe. The Saya is covered in brown textured lacquer.

Right:
C.1600'S KO-KATANA
VALUE: $1865.00/ £1165.00

www.antiqueswords.com

www.antiqueswords.com

www.michaeldlong.com

www.michaeldlong.com

www.antiqueswords.com

www.michaeldlong.com

www.michaeldlong.com

C.1930 KYU-GUNTO ARMY SWORD
VALUE: $570.00/£325.00

Detail from a Samurai battle scene, c.1880.

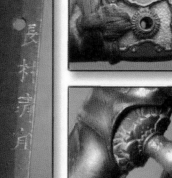

SHOWA PERIOD (C.WWII) ARMY OFFICER'S KATANA
VALUE: $1800.00/ £1125.00

High quality example with an exceptional hand forged blade, retaining all original polish. Scabbard is leather covered for field service use.

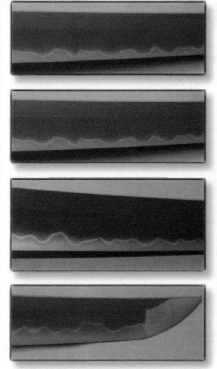

Detail from Samurai woodblock, c.1880.

THE CORRECT CARE AND PRESERVATION of an antique sword is not an easy task. Many a fine sword has been ruined by overzealous cleaning, and poor attempts at amateur *"restoration"*. If you are new to this field of collecting, the basic rule is:

IF YOU ARE NOT SURE ABOUT HOW TO PRESERVE YOUR SWORD, OR FEEL THAT YOU DO NOT HAVE THE NECESSARY SKILLS TO COMPLETE THE PROCESS, ASK SOMEONE WHO DOES

This *"someone"* might be a fellow collector with experience of restoration, or a dealer who might be able to advise you. As time goes by, you will meet people who can offer sound advice. They will be speaking from years of experience, including mistakes that they themselves made at the start!

If the restoration job is quite complex, it is always better to hand over your sword to an expert restorer and let them do the tricky work. Expert restorers can be found through word of mouth via dealers and collectors, and some advertise through related militaria journals and magazines. There is also a lively circle of dealers and collectors who speak to eachother through internet web sites devoted to collecting edged weapons (www.swordforum.com is a particularly useful resource), and they are always more than happy to exchange tips and contacts.

You might think that after paying a considerable sum for your sword, the very last thing that you may wish to do is spend even more cash. This attitude is wrong. If you intend to keep and preserve a fine collection of antique military swords, a little extra spent on preservation will be a sound investment for the future.

Saying this, I do not mean to frighten away the collector by saying that they cannot or should not do any kind of preservation work. Far from it. An expert should normally be called in when there are complex or detailed areas of preservation or restoration work to be addressed, particularly when this might require the sword to be taken apart or broken parts to be repaired. I have visited too many auction rooms and fairs to see the results of amateur botched repairs to hilts, blades and scabbards. Here are some basic emergency procedures that are relatively simple to undertake and ensure that the sword does not deteriorate any further.

BLADES & METAL SCABBARDS/FITTINGS

One of the first problems that you might encounter concerns the accumulation of corrosion e.g. rust. The use of a *"Break Free"* oil which dislodges the rust is recommended, but not on blades with blue and gilt finish, as it has been known to loosen the gilding. Alcohol or kerosene is also light enough to clean these delicate blades. When completely wiped clean of these substances, a covering of fine carabellum wax should be applied. This provides a protective seal which keeps out moisture. There are a number of specialist waxes on the market. I recommend *Museum*

Wax or *Renaissance Wax*. All these products are available from specialist hardware or gun supply shops, and a quick trawl through the internet will also locate a number of merchants who can probably supply mail order.

Vaseline petroleum jelly or pure mineral oil/gel will also protect the blade from future moisture, but it is important to stress that you will need to inspect the sword on a regular basis to see if any rust or corrosion has returned. Some swords can have very heavy areas of rust where the use of *"Break Free"* oil might not be very effective and other options need to be considered. In these cases, a very fine abrasive might be used, but you must decide whether the blade etching or hilt/scabbard plating might be damaged or worn by this method. It all comes down to how you want the sword to look. There are some collectors who cannot resist removing the age or patina of a sword because they believe that a highly polished sword is more attractive. Thankfully, these individuals are not great in number. The collector will continue to see swords that have been polished to a gleaming state and there is little you can do to return it to an original age patina. Do not let this be a reason not to buy a particular sword. I would rather acquire a highly polished but rare piece, than none at all!

Another important point to remember is that constant handling of the sword will endanger its condition, especially when moisture from your hands comes into contact with the blade. Any collector of Japanese swords will testify to the permanent damage that can result from fingermarks that have not been immediately removed from a blade. The wearing of lint free cotton gloves might sound a bit drastic but it ensures that the sword is kept dry. Purchase two pairs so that there is a spare pair on hand when that inquisitive friend pays a visit.

HILTS, SCABBARDS AND LEATHER/FISHSKIN GRIPS

A toothbrush and some ammonia detergent or soapy water is pretty effective in rooting out dirt and grime from recesses in hilts and scabbard mounts. The main priority is to preserve the original gilding (if present), so do not use any abrasives in this area. Use a good leather care product on grips and scabbards to avoid drying out. It should also have a high wax content as it will act as a long term anti-drying sealant. For fishskin grips, I recommend a little baby oil or olive oil to allow the material to breathe again. Do not rub too hard on grips as they can be very flaky and pieces can easily come away. Regular inspection of leather fittings should be done in conjunction with the inspection of the metal parts. Try not to display swords with leather scabbards or fragile grips too near areas of heat and direct sunlight.

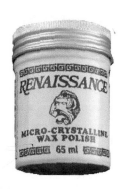

SELECT BIBLIOGRAPHY

Here is a selected list of books that will prove useful for the collector of antique swords. Unfortunately, many are now out of print but they are well worth hunting for. If you have access to the internet, the use of an online out of print book finding service might possibly turn up these publications. Where possible, I have included the ISBN.

P.G.W. Annis - Naval Swords. British and American Naval Edged Weapons 1660-1815, Arms and Armour Press, 1970.

J.D. Aylward - The Smallsword in England, Hutchinson, 1960.

H.T. Bosanquet -The Naval Officer's Sword, H.M.S.O., 1955.

Richard F. Burton - The Book of the Sword, Dover Publications Inc., New York, 1987.
ISBN 0-486-25434-8

Anthony D. Darling - Weapons of the Highland Regiments, Museum Restoration Service, 1998.
ISBN 0-919316-33-6

Vladimir Dolinek and Jan Durdik - The Encyclopedia of European Historical Weapons, Hamlyn, 1993.
ISBN 0-600-57538-1

Nick Evangelista - The Encyclopedia of the Sword, Greenwood Press, 1995.
ISBN 0-313-27896-2

Charles ffoulkes and E. C. Hopkinson - Sword, Lance and Bayonet, Arms and Armour Press, 1967.

James D. Forman - The Scottish Dirk, Museum Restoration Service, 1993.

William Gilkerson - Boarders Away. With Steel - Edged Weapons and Polearms 1626-1826, Andrew Mowbray Publishers, 1991.
ISBN 0-917218-50-7

J. F. Hayward - Swords and Daggers, H.M.S.O., 1964.

W.E. May and A.N. Kennard - Naval Swords and Firearms (British), H.M.S.O., 1962.

A.N. Kulinsky - European Edged Weapons, Atlant, St. Petersburg, 2003.
ISBN 5-901555-13-9

National Trust for Scotland - Culloden. The Swords and the Sorrows, NTS Trading Company, 1996.
ISBN 0-901625-58-2

W.E. May and P.G. Annis - Swords for Sea Service, H.M.S.O., 1970.

George C. Neumann - Swords and Blades of the American Revolution, Rebel Publishing Co., Inc., 1991.
ISBN 0-9605666-9-4

A.V.B. Norman - The Rapier and Smallsword, 1460-1820, Arms and Armour Press, 1980.
ISBN 0-405-13089-9

Ewart Oakshott - Records of the Medieval Sword, The Boydell Press, 1991.
ISBN 0-85115-566-9

Ewart Oakshott - European Weapons and Armour, The Boydell Press, 1980.
ISBN 0-85115-789-0

Harold Peterson - The American Sword 1775-1945, Riling Arms Books, 1996.
ISBN 0-9603094-1-1

Brian Robson - Swords of the British Army - The Regulation Patterns, 1788 to 1914, National Army Museum, 1996.
ISBN 0-901721-33-6

Ian D. Skennerton - British Service Sword and Lance Patterns, Ian Skennerton, 1994.
ISBN 0-646190-36-9

Ian D. Skennerton and Robert Richardson - British and Commonwealth Bayonets, Ian Skennerton, 1984.
ISBN 0-949749-04-4

Ian D. Skennerton - The Broad Arrow. British and Empire Factory Production, Proof, Inspection, Armourers, Unit and Issue Markings, Ian Skennerton, 2001.
ISBN 0-949749-43-5

Leslie Southwick - London Silver-Hilted Swords. Their makers, suppliers and allied traders, with directory, Royal Armouries, 2001.
ISBN 0-948092-47-5

George Cameron Stone - A Glossary of the Construction, Decoration and Use of Arms and Armor in all Countries and in all Times, Jack Brussel, 1961.

Eduard Wagner - Cut and Thrust Weapons, Spring Books, London, 1967.

John Wallace - Scottish Swords and Dirks. An Illustrated Reference Guide to Scottish Edged Weapons, Arms and Armour Press, 1970.

Gerald Weland - A Collectors Guide to Swords, Daggers and Cutlasses, Chartwell Books Inc., 1998.
ISBN 1-55521-726-5

Frederick Wilkinson - Swords and Daggers. An Illustrated Reference Guide for Collectors, Arms and Armour Press, 1985.
ISBN 0-85368-673-4

Frederick Wilkinson - Swords and Daggers, Ward Lock and Co., Ltd, 1967.

John Wilkinson-Latham - British Military Swords from 1800 to the present day, Crown Publishers, Inc, 1967.

John Wilkinson-Latham - British Cut and Thrust Weapons, David and Charles Publishers, 1971.

R.J. Wilkinson-Latham - Pictorial History of Swords and Bayonets, Ian Allan, 1973.

Terence Wise - European Edged Weapons, Almark Publishing, 1974.

Harvey J. S. Withers - British Military Swords 1786-1912. The Regulation Patterns. An Illustrated Price Guide for Collectors, Studio Jupiter Military Publishing, 2003.
ISBN 0-9545910-0-3

SELECT BIBLIOGRAPHY

earth and rule from the throne of David in Jerusalem for 1000 years. After that time God will allow Satan to be released to test mankind one final time. God will then defeat Satan forever by casting him into the lake of fire, and Christ will establish his eternal kingdom on the new earth.

The Importance of the Millennial Kingdom

From the moment God made his first covenant with Abraham, God committed himself to establish a theocratic kingdom in which humanity would ultimately enjoy the restoration of the peace and righteousness Adam and Eve lost in the garden. The church has often lost sight of God's commitment to establish such a kingdom and has often set out to change and rule the world on its own. Yet the Bible clearly promises that God's kingdom will come on earth and will be ruled by the Messiah.

Scripture describes in detail the Gentile empires that will rule the world prior to the Messiah's return (see Da 7—8). Though there would be many nations who would challenge one another for supremacy, only four Gentile empires would successfully govern the world during the centuries of human history. The fourth empire, Rome, would be revived as a ten-nation confederacy under the control of the antichrist. This evil world empire will gain its power and supremacy from Satan. Only Jesus Christ, as the conquering Messiah returning from heaven with his mighty army, will destroy this enemy of God. Christ will then establish his millennial kingdom of righteousness and peace and rule from the throne of David in Jerusalem (see Isa 9:7). (For further information, see the article on "The Four World Empires on p. 954 and the article on "The Battle of Armageddon" on p. 1468.)

When Christ comes to establish his kingdom, he will descend to earth on the Mt. of Olives (see Zec 14:4), opposite the temple mount. A great earthquake will split the earth from the Mediterranean through the Mt. of Olives to the Dead Sea. Ezekiel adds that the Messiah will enter the temple through the eastern gate (see Eze 43:2, 4–5). This gate would be sealed to preserve it for the coming Messiah, the Prince (see 44:2–3).

True to Ezekiel's prophecy, this eastern gate to the temple has been shut now for many centuries, sealed by the Muslims when they rebuilt the walls of Jerusalem four hundred years ago. Accumulated rubble and a Muslim graveyard now occupy the area that used to be the eastern gate to the temple. The Muslims believe that walking through a graveyard would defile a priest or holy man, and therefore the placement of a cemetery in such a strategic place would prevent the Messiah fulfilling Ezekiel's prophecy. What the Muslims failed to recognize by their attempt to prevent the Messiah's entry into the temple is that God's plans are beyond understanding and his power beyond human control. Scripture records that the Messiah will enter the temple via the eastern gate, and this prophecy will be fulfilled.

The Character of the Millennial Kingdom

Some people have supposed that the end of the Millennium would also signal the end of the kingdom of Christ. Yet the Bible teaches that Christ's kingdom is an eternal kingdom that will be established "with judgment and with justice from henceforth even for ever" (Isa 9:7). The

Millennium is simply the beginning of the eternal kingdom of Christ. John referred to this first period of Christ's thousand-year rule six times in Revelation 20. Both the OT and NT prophesy that the eternal kingdom begins with the return of the Messiah in glory.

The spiritual character of the millennial kingdom will reflect the nature of Christ. Following the rebellion of Adam and Eve, Satan was given power to rule over this world. He became "the god of this world" (2Co 4:4), and a curse was placed on its inhabitants and on the ground. However, in the millennial kingdom of Christ, the righteousness and justice of God will finally be restored. Any sin will be dealt with judicially by Christ as he rules with "a rod of iron" (Rev 12:5). Yet even in this ideal condition, the Bible indicates that humanity will rebel.

When God releases Satan from his thousand-year imprisonment, Satan will roam freely again on the earth for "a little season" (20:3). He will gather the rebels of all nations for a last great battle against God and the beloved city of Jerusalem. Yet Satan will be defeated and condemned forever to the "lake of fire and brimstone" (20:10). At that time God will renew the earth and the heavens with fire in the same way that he cleansed the world from the effects of sin with the flood in Noah's day. (For further information, see the article on "A New Heaven and a New Earth" on p. 1488.) Then Israel and the surviving Gentile nations will enjoy the blessings of God throughout eternity under the righteous rule of Christ.

The Blessings of the Millennial Kingdom

The covenant God made with Abraham, the kingdom promises he spoke to David and his descendants, the justice his prophets yearned for—all these will be finally realized in the millennial kingdom of Christ. The promises made to Israel of peace, justice, prosperity and eternal blessings will become a reality. In addition, the Lord will fulfill his promise of a new covenant with Israel in which he will give them a new heart, a willingness to obey, forgiveness of sin, the presence of his Spirit, and a peaceful existence in their land (see Eze 36:26–28).

One of the greatest blessings that will flow from the millennial kingdom of God will be the introduction of a true and lasting world peace. For the first time in human history, soldiers will put down their weapons. Armies will be unnecessary. Under the direction of Jesus Christ, the resurrected believers of the church will provide the leadership necessary to create a just society for all people. Governmental corruption will disappear. Mercy, justice, integrity, peace and righteousness will be the hallmarks of this kingdom.

The earth will also reap the benefits of Christ's righteous rule. The curse that was placed upon the earth following the sin of Adam and Eve will be lifted when the kingdom is established. The desert "shall rejoice, and blossom as the rose" (Isa 35:1), and the earth will produce abundantly. According to Isa 33:24, all sickness will be eliminated. The deaf and the blind will be cured (see Isa 29:18). Even the devastated land of "Lebanon shall be turned into a fruitful field" (Isa 29:17) as the Messiah renews the land from the curse of sin.

Though we do not know when Christ will establish this kingdom, the Bible promises that this kingdom will one day be a reality. May we always be looking for that reality every time we pray "Thy kingdom come. Thy will be done in earth, as it is in heaven" (Mt 6:10).

unto them: and *I saw* ᶜthe souls of them that were beheaded for the witness of Jesus, and for the word of God, and ᵈwhich had not worshipped the beast, ᵉneither his image, neither had received *his* mark upon their foreheads, or in their hands; and they lived and ᶠreigned with Christ a thousand years.

F
W 5 But the rest of the dead lived not again until the thousand years were finished. This *is* the first resurrection.

6 Blessed and holy *is* he that hath part in the first resurrection: on such ᵃthe second death hath no power, but they shall be ᵇpriests of God and of Christ, ᶜand shall reign with him a thousand years.

The loosing of Satan

V 7 And when the thousand years are expired, ᵃSatan shall be loosed out of his prison,

8 And shall go out ᵃto deceive the nations which are in the four quarters of the earth, ᵇGog and Magog, ᶜto gather them

together to battle: the number of whom *is* as the sand of the sea.

9 ᵃAnd they went up on the breadth of the earth, and compassed the camp of the saints about, and the beloved city: and fire came down from God out of heaven, and devoured them.

10 ᵃAnd the devil that deceived them was cast into the lake of fire and brimstone, ᵇwhere the beast and the false prophet *are*, and ᶜshall be tormented day and night for ever and ever.

The great white throne judgment

11 And I saw a great white throne, and him that sat on it, from whose face ᵃthe earth and the heaven fled away; ᵇand there was found no place for them.

12 And I saw the dead, ᵃsmall and great, stand before God; ᵇand the books were opened: and another ᶜbook was opened, which is *the book* of life: and the dead were judged out of those things

H
J
S

Center column references:
4 ᶜch. 6:9 ᵈch. 13:12 ᵉch. 13:15 ᶠRom. 8:17; 2 Tim. 2:12; ch. 5:10
6 ᵃch. 2:11 ᵇIs. 61:6; 1 Pet. 2:9; ch. 1:6 ᶜver. 4
7 ᵃver. 2
8 ᵃver. 3,10 ᵇEzek. 38:2 & 39:1 ᶜch. 16:14
9 ᵃIs. 8:8; Ezek. 38:9
10 ᵃver. 8 ᵇch. 19:20 ᶜch. 14:10
11 ᵃ2 Pet. 3:7; ch. 21:1 ᵇDan. 2:35
12 ᵃch. 19:5 ᵇDan. 7:10 ᶜPs. 69:28; Dan. 12:1; Phil. 4:3; ch. 3:5

F *Heb 11:35* ◄   **W** *1Co 15:21–26* ◄
V *Rev 19:15–16* ◄

H *Rev 19:20* ◄► *Rev 21:8*   **J** *Jude 6* ◄
S *Rev 3:14–16* ◄► *Rev 21:7–8*

---

on earth (see 5:10). Those who died unrepentant for their sins will be resurrected to stand before the great white throne at the end of the Millennium. This resurrection of the wicked dead will be the second resurrection and will result in the punishment of the wicked in hell after their judgment before Christ (see 20:13–14).

John states that the first resurrection is resurrection unto eternal life in heaven. Those who are "blessed and holy" (20:6) will participate in this resurrection and will have no fear of hell because their sins are forgiven. All those who participate in this first resurrection will also "reign with him a thousand years" (20:6). This includes the OT saints, those who were raised when Christ rose (see Mt 27:52–53), the raptured church, the 144,000 Jewish witnesses and the "great multitude" (7:9,14) of believers who come out of the tribulation. For further information, see the article on "The Resurrection of the Body" on p. 1206.

20:7–10 John continues with his description of Satan's release after the thousand years. The armies of the nations of the world, made up of those who are born during the Millennium and who never accept the Messiah as their Lord, join with Satan in one final attempt to overthrow God.

Note that Gog and Magog are different peoples from those who take part in the battle described in Eze 38—39. Ezekiel described a battle that takes place prior to the Battle of Armageddon. The weapons, allies, motive, participants and the method of destruction used by God differ between these two battles that take place over a thousand years apart. God will destroy Satan's armies in this battle with fire from heaven (20:9) and will cast Satan into the lake of fire to be tormented forever (20:10).

20:11–15 John describes the final judgment that will occur after the completion of the Millennium. All of the wicked dead, from Cain to the last rebel killed at the end of the Millennium, will be resurrected to stand before God's great white throne to receive judgment for their sins. All those who refused Christ's mercy will face his holy and severe judgment. They will be condemned to hell for eternity and suffer eternal separation from God.

Since all of these people are destined for an eternity in hell, some say the purpose of God's record book (20:12) may be to show that this punishment is deserved. Others contend that Scripture teaches a principle of judgment on the basis of works and that this book of deeds will determine each individual sinner's punishment in hell (see Ps 62:12; Jer 17:10; Lk 12:47–48; 20:47; Ro 2:6; 1Pe 1:17). Note that "the book of life" (20:12) was also opened to prove to the wicked dead that though some of them claimed to be Christians, their claim was counterfeit, and their name was not recorded in God's book of life. Anyone not named in "the book of life" (20:12) will be cast into hell. For further information, see the article "The Great White Throne Judgment" on p. 1484.

The Great White Throne Judgment

J OHN RECEIVED A clear vision of the final judgment before God's great white throne. This judgment will occur after the Millennium. Satan will be loosed from his imprisonment and lead the rebels of the earth in one final rebellion against God. Following this rebellion all of the earth's unrepentant sinners who have ever lived will be judged by God and sentenced to hell (see Rev 20:11–15).

The Time of the Judgment
John prophesied that this judgment would occur in heaven at the end of the millennial reign of the Messiah. God will test the men and women born in the Millennium by unleashing Satan for a short time to prove that, apart from Christ's redemption, people will still choose to rebel rather than serve God. After the defeat of Satan's final rebellion at the end of the Millennium, the Lord will resurrect the bodies and souls of all wicked men and women. They will stand in judgment with the sinful angels who participated in Satan's rebellion against God. This great tribunal will seal the final judgment of all the wicked dead who have died from the beginning of the world until the end of Satan's final rebellion. While the Scriptures do not reveal the length of time the trial will take, the length of the sentence for each defendant will be eternity without end. The devil will be cast into the lake of fire forever, demonstrating the ultimate victory of Christ over sin and evil.

Who Will Be Judged?
Many writers have suggested that all people, both believers and nonbelievers, would appear at this final judgment before the throne of God to determine their destination of hell or heaven. They suggest that this judgment will occur simultaneously because Daniel prophesied that "many of them that sleep in the dust of the earth shall awake, some to everlasting life, and some to shame and everlasting contempt" (Da 12:2). Yet John's vision indicates that only "death and hell delivered up the dead which were in them" (Rev 20:13) and that only unrepentant sinners who reject God's salvation will appear before this great white throne. Though this is an apparent contradiction, a careful reading of the passage in Daniel reveals that Daniel is not declaring that the two resurrections will take place simultaneously. Rather, Daniel simply records the fact that two different groups will be resurrected and judged.

The apostle Paul confirms a separate appearance for those who accept Jesus Christ as their Savior "before the judgment seat of Christ" (2Co 5:10). This judgment of believers occurs at the rapture 1000 years before the great white throne judgment and will determine the believers' rewards for faithful service to God. There is no punishment for believers at this judgment seat because our sins are dealt with forever at the cross.

John's words describe a resurrecting of the wicked from the sea, death and *hades*. The "sea" and "death" refers to the fact that the bodies of those unrepentant sinners who died in the seas as well as those who were buried on land in the grave will all be resurrected by God to stand in judgment. Note also the reference to a resurrection from *hades*. Those souls of the OT who had rejected God's truth and died were confined to the part of *hades* known as a "place of torment" (Lk 16:28). The statement that *hades* will give up its wicked dead confirms that the souls of sinners will be delivered from *hades* to God's final judgment. No sinner will be left out. The wicked dead will stand before God to hear their sentence, and they will be delivered to hell in their resurrected bodies that cannot be destroyed or die.

The only wicked people who will not be judged at the great white throne judgment are those who have already been judged by God at an earlier point in time. These individuals include the antichrist, the false prophet and those evil people who survive the Battle of Armageddon (see Rev 19:20). These evil ones will be judged at the judgment of the Gentile nations described in Mt 25. Christ referred to these evil people as the "goats" (Mt 25:33), the wicked Gentiles who will enthusiastically join in the persecution of the tribulation believers. Christ promised that these "goats" would be cursed and sent "into everlasting fire, prepared for the devil and his angels" (25:41). Since these wicked individuals have already been judged by Christ and sentenced to hell following the Battle of Armageddon, they will not appear to be judged a second time a thousand years later at the great white throne judgment in heaven. (For further information, see the article on "The Battle of Armageddon" on p. 1468 and the article on "The Judgments of God" on p. 1222.)

A Just Punishment

All those who appear at the great white throne judgment are already destined to an eternity in hell because they have not "believed in the name of the only begotten Son of God" (Jn 3:18). Since they are summoned to stand before the Judge they will therefore receive individual sentences. Scripture clearly states that each person is responsible for his or her own actions and that God deals individually with sinners (see Ps 28:4; 62:12; Pr 24:12, 29; Ecc 12:14; Jer 17:10; 32:19; Mt 16:27; Ro 2:6). Though their fate is already sealed by their sin and rejection of Christ, God's holiness and justice will provide all with their own appointed judgment. The wicked will receive punishment according to their sinful works as every single deed, thought and act is reviewed at God's throne when the books that record the deeds of humanity are opened. Even careless words will bring added judgment, for "every idle word that men shall speak, they shall give account thereof in the day of judgment" (Mt 12:36).

Note that John mentions that two books will be opened at this tribunal. One book is the record book of sinful humanity's deeds. The other book is "the book of life" (Rev 20:12). The wicked will be judged from this book too. Why? The book of life contains only the names of those who have accepted the salvation of Christ. There may be some at the great white throne judgment who will protest to the Judge that they are Christians. They will claim that some great mistake has been made or that they were members of the church for years or that they have done great things for God during their life on earth. Yet Christ warned that "not every one that saith unto me, Lord, Lord, shall enter into the kingdom of heaven" (Mt 7:21).

Only God knows the true heart of any person. Unless we truly repent, turn from our sinful rebellion and accept Christ as our Lord and Savior, we shall never experience the salvation of Christ and have our names recorded in the book of life. No amount of good works or theological knowledge will qualify us to enter heaven's gates. The only acceptable price for salvation and pardon from hell is the blood of Christ shed on the cross for each one of us.

which were written in the books, ᵈaccording to their works.

13 And the sea gave up the dead which were in it; ᵃand death and ᶠhell delivered up the dead which were in them: ᵇand they were judged every man according to their works.

14 And ᵃdeath and hell were cast into the lake of fire. ᵇThis is the second death.

15 And whosoever was not found written in the book of life ᵃwas cast into the lake of fire.

The new Jerusalem

N **21** AND ᵃI saw a new heaven and a new earth: ᵇfor the first heaven and the first earth were passed away; and there was no more sea.

2 And I John saw ᵃthe holy city, new Jerusalem, coming down from God out of heaven, prepared ᵇas a bride adorned for her husband.

3 And I heard a great voice out of heaven saying, Behold, ᵃthe tabernacle of God *is* with men, and he will dwell with them, and they shall be his people, and God himself shall be with them, *and be* their God.

S 4 ᵃAnd God shall wipe away all tears from their eyes; and ᵇthere shall be no more death, ᶜneither sorrow, nor crying, neither shall there be any more pain: for the former things are passed away.

5 And ᵃhe that sat upon the throne said, ᵇBehold, I make all things new. And he said unto me, Write: for ᶜthese words are true and faithful.

L 6 And he said unto me, ᵃIt is done. ᵇI W am Alpha and Omega, the beginning and the end. ᶜI will give unto him that is

athirst of the fountain of the water of life freely.

7 He that overcometh shall inherit ᶠall S things; and ᵃI will be his God, and he shall be my son.

8 ᵃBut the fearful, and unbelieving, H and the abominable, and murderers, and whoremongers, and sorcerers, and idolaters, and all liars, shall have their part in ᵇthe lake which burneth with fire and brimstone: which is the second death.

9 And there came unto me one of ᵃthe P seven angels which had the seven vials full of the seven last plagues, and talked with me, saying, Come hither, I will show thee ᵇthe bride, the Lamb's wife.

10 And he carried me away ᵉin the E spirit to a great and high mountain, and showed me ᵇthat great city, the holy Jerusalem, descending out of heaven from God,

11 ᵃHaving the glory of God: and her light *was* like unto a stone most precious, even like a jasper stone, clear as crystal;

12 And had a wall great and high, *and* had ᵃtwelve gates, and at the gates twelve angels, and names written thereon, which are *the names* of the twelve tribes of the children of Israel:

13 ᵃOn the east three gates; on the north three gates; on the south three gates; and on the west three gates.

14 And the wall of the city had twelve foundations, and ᵃin them the names of the twelve apostles of the Lamb.

15 And he that talked with me ᵃhad a golden reed to measure the city, and the gates thereof, and the wall thereof.

16 And the city lieth foursquare, and

Center cross-reference column:

12 ᵈJer. 17:10 & 32:19; Mat. 16:27; Rom. 2:6; ch. 2:23

13 ᵃch. 6:8 ᵇver. 12 ᶠOr, *the grave*

14 ᵃ1 Cor. 15:26 ᵇch. 21:8

15 ᵃch. 19:20

21:1 ᵃIs. 65:17; 2 Pet. 3:13 ᵇch. 20:11

2 ᵃIs. 52:1; Gal. 4:26; Heb. 11:10 & 12:22; ch. 3:12 ᵇIs. 54:5; 2 Cor. 11:2

3 ᵃLev. 26:11; Ezek. 43:7; 2 Cor. 6:16

4 ᵃIs. 25:8 ᵇ1 Cor. 15:26; ch. 20:14 ᶜIs. 35:10 & 61:3 & 65:19

5 ᵃch. 4:2,9 & 20:11 ᵇIs. 43:19; 2 Cor. 5:17 ᶜch. 19:9

6 ᵃch. 16:17 ᵇch. 1:8 ᶜIs. 12:3; John 4:10 & 7:37

7 ᵃZech. 8:8; Heb. 8:10 ᶠOr, *these things*

8 ᵃ1 Cor. 6:9; Gal. 5:19; Eph. 5:5; 1 Tim. 1:9; Heb. 12:14 ᵇch. 20:14

9 ᵃch. 15:1 ᵇch. 19:7

10 ᵃch. 1:10 ᵇEzek. 48

11 ᵃch. 22:5

12 ᵃEzek. 48:31-34

13 ᵃEzek. 48:31-34

14 ᵃMat. 16:18; Gal. 2:9; Eph. 2:20

15 ᵃEzek. 40:3; Zech. 2:1

Letter cross-references:

N *1Jn 2:17* ◄ ► *Rev 22:3–5*
S *Rev 7:17* ◄   L *Rev 3:20* ◄ ► *Rev 22:17*
W *Rev 3:20* ◄ ► *Rev 22:17*

S *Rev 20:12–13* ◄ ► *Rev 21:27*
H *Rev 20:9–15* ◄ ► *Rev 21:27*
P *Rev 19:11* ◄
E *Rev 17:3* ◄ ► *Rev 22:17*

21:1 John's vision of the "new heaven and a new earth" (21:1) reveals the fulfillment of Peter's prophecy that the first heaven and the first earth will be burned with fire and cleansed from the effects of sin (see 2Pe 3:7, 10, 12, 13). Note the absence of the oceans on the new earth. This may indicate climactic changes to the new earth as well as changes to its surface.

Though the earth will be burned with fire, Scripture seems to indicate that it will not be totally annihilated. The Bible indicates that the earth was created to last forever (see Ps 78:69; 104:5; Ecc 1:4).

For further information, see the article "A New Heaven and a New Earth" on p. 1488.

21:2–27 The new Jerusalem is the capital city of heaven, and the description of this glorious city reveals the wonders that await those who love Jesus Christ. After sin is eliminated from the universe following the judgments after the Millennium, this new Jerusalem will descend to the cleansed earth. God will dwell with his people in holiness on this renewed earth. For more information, see the article on "The New Jerusalem" on p. 1492.

A New Heaven and a New Earth

BOTH ISAIAH AND John were given visions of the transformation of the heavens and the earth that will occur at the end of the Millennium (see Isa 65:17; Rev 21:1). The effects of humanity's sins have polluted the earth and the heavens since the days of Adam and Eve. God cleansed the earth with a worldwide flood during the time of Noah, but that cleansing was only a temporary one. God promised that he will purify the earth and the heavens again at the end of the Millennium, removing every vestige of sin and its effects and ushering in a time of purity in God's eternal kingdom (see 2Pe 3:10–13).

A Renovation by Fire

Though Isaiah and John glimpsed the new heavens and the new earth, the apostle Peter described a fiery destruction as the means for their renovation. This refining will be God's last judgment on earth at the end of the Millennium after God defeats Satan's final rebellion. Some suggest that this refining will involve a total annihilation of the earth (see Mk 13:31). Others contend that the earth will continue forever (see Ps 72:5; 78:69; Ecc 1:4). These scholars believe that God will merely destroy the surface of the earth with fire in much the same way that he destroyed the earth's surface with the flood in Noah's day. Whatever way God chooses to cleanse the earth, Peter encouraged believers to anticipate the new heavens and new earth, for in them "dwelleth righteousness" (2Pe 3:13).

In past generations some people scoffed at Peter's words that "the elements shall melt with fervent heat" (2Pe 3:10). Scientists believed that the elements were impervious to destruction. Yet the discovery of thermonuclear reactions changed those beliefs. These nuclear chain reactions convert elements into energy, producing power and heat. In fact, a continuous series of nuclear chain reactions produces the ball of fire—our sun—that gives us daylight. Peter's words may well have foreshadowed a worldwide nuclear holocaust as a means of God's cleansing for the earth.

The Redemption of Creation

In a sense, the creation of the new heavens and new earth will be a return to the conditions found in the Garden of Eden. In that glorious time of innocence, Adam and Eve had lived in perfect, peaceful harmony with God and his creation. Yet from the moment of Adam and Eve's rebellion against God, all of creation has lived under the curse of sin. Adam's descendants were deprived of immortality and intimate communion with God. The earth itself was cursed because of Adam's sin and forced to travail under the dominion of the wicked serpent, Satan. Peaceful coexistence was shattered; all who chose violence and murder were cursed. Even the eternal, perfect universe felt the shock of sin's calamity. Designed by God to renew itself, the universe was flawed by sin and began to decay, run down and degenerate to a more and more disorganized state.

The apostle Paul prophesied the redemption of all creation when Christ creates the new heavens and the new earth (see Ro 8:21). When Christ removes the curse of sin, decay will be replaced by sustainable growth; disease and death will be replaced with eternal health and immortality. Peaceful coexistence will be restored so that "the wolf also shall dwell with the lamb, and the leopard shall lie down with the kid; and the calf and the young lion and the fatling together; and a little child shall lead them" (Isa 11:6; see 11:7; 65:25). When the Messiah reigns, the redeemed of the Lord will live once more in perfect harmony in a peaceful world under the rule of a loving God.

The People of the New Earth

The new earth will be inhabited. Some have thought that the nations will not exist in the future, but the Scriptures teach that the Gentile nations and Israel will exist forever under the rule of the Messiah (see Rev 21:24). God's kingdom on the new earth will be populated with the descendants of those who survived the great tribulation and the Battle of Armageddon. The resurrected saints of the church will reign over the nations under the rule of the Messiah forever. God's new heavens and new earth will be far greater than we can imagine (see 1Co 2:9–10) and filled with righteousness and justice forever.

the length is as large as the breadth: and he measured the city with the reed, twelve thousand furlongs. The length and the breadth and the height of it are equal.

17 And he measured the wall thereof, an hundred *and* forty *and* four cubits, *according to* the measure of a man, that is, of the angel.

18 And the building of the wall of it was *of* jasper: and the city *was* pure gold, like unto clear glass.

19 ªAnd the foundations of the wall of the city *were* garnished with all manner of precious stones. The first foundation *was* jasper; the second, sapphire; the third, a chalcedony; the fourth, an emerald;

20 The fifth, sardonyx; the sixth, sardius; the seventh, chrysolite; the eighth, beryl; the ninth, a topaz; the tenth, a chrysoprasus; the eleventh, a jacinth; the twelfth, an amethyst.

21 And the twelve gates *were* twelve pearls; every several gate was of one pearl: ªand the street of the city *was* pure gold, as it were transparent glass.

22 ªAnd I saw no temple therein: for the Lord God Almighty and the Lamb are the temple of it.

23 ªAnd the city had no need of the sun, neither of the moon, to shine in it: for the glory of God did lighten it, and the Lamb *is* the light thereof.

24 ªAnd the nations of them which are saved shall walk in the light of it: and the

kings of the earth do bring their glory and honour into it.

25 ªAnd the gates of it shall not be shut at all by day: for ᵇthere shall be no night there.

26 ªAnd they shall bring the glory and honour of the nations into it.

27 And ªthere shall in no wise enter **H** into it any thing that defileth, neither **S** *whatsoever* worketh abomination, or *maketh* a lie: but they which are written in the Lamb's ᵇbook of life.

The water and tree of life

22 AND HE showed me ªa pure river of water of life, clear as crystal, proceeding out of the throne of God and of the Lamb.

2 ªIn the midst of the street of it, and **H** on either side of the river, *was there* ᵇthe tree of life, which bare twelve *manner of* fruits, *and* yielded her fruit every month: and the leaves of the tree *were* ᶜfor the healing of the nations.

3 And ªthere shall be no more curse: **N** ᵇbut the throne of God and of the Lamb shall be in it; and his servants shall serve him:

4 And ªthey shall see his face; and ᵇhis name *shall be* in their foreheads.

5 ªAnd there shall be no night there;

Margin references:
19 ª Is. 54:11
21 ª ch. 22:2
22 ª John 4:23
23 ª Is. 24:23 & 60:19,20
24 ª Is. 60:3 & 66:12
25 ª Is. 60:11 ᵇ Is. 60:20; Zech. 14:7; ch. 22:5
26 ª ver. 24
27 ª Is. 35:8 & 52:1 & 60:21; Joel 3:17; ch. 22:14 ᵇ Phil. 4:3
22:1 ª Ezek. 47:1; Zech. 14:8
2 ª Ezek. 47:12; ch. 21:21 ᵇ Gen. 2:9; ch. 2:7 ᶜ ch. 21:24
3 ª Zech. 14:11 ᵇ Ezek. 48:35
4 ª Mat. 5:8; 1 Cor. 13:12; 1 John 3:2 ᵇ ch. 14:1
5 ª ch. 21:23

H *Rev 21:8* ◄ ► *Rev 22:15*
S *Rev 21:7–8* ◄ ► *Rev 22:12*　　 H *3Jn 2* ◄
N *Rev 21:1–5* ◄

22:1–7 The angel showed John "a pure river of water of life" (22:1) that flowed from God's throne in the new Jerusalem. Note that 22:2 indicates that the "tree of life" bears fruit every month, suggesting that a way to mark time will exist in eternity. This passage also indicates that there will be food in heaven. Scripture records that believers will participate in a literal marriage supper of the Lamb (see 19:9; Isa 25:6; Lk 22:18) and even the angels in heaven partake of manna (see Ps 78:22–25).

Access to the tree of life was restricted when Adam and Eve sinned in the garden (see Ge 3:22). In the new Jerusalem the curse of sin has been removed and access to this tree is restored. Some believe that the leaves of the tree of life will be used to grant immortality to those who have been born during the Millennium. These adherents suggest that while resurrected believers receive an incorruptible body (1Co 15:51–55), those born during the Millennium will need to partake of the leaves of the tree to heal their bodies so that they may live eternally.

Other scholars believe that the absence of hunger, thirst, sickness and sorrow (7:9–17; 21:4) indicates that the need for healing is removed in the new Jerusalem. These scholars contend that this reference to the tree and its leaves is merely symbolic of continuous blessing and the restoration to fullness of life for eternity.

The angel also showed John that the curse of sin would be removed forever, allowing the holy throne of God to reside in the new Jerusalem. God's people will live and reign forever in the presence of God.

Note, too, that the Lord promises a blessing to anyone who "keepeth the sayings of the prophecy of this book" (22:7). Several such blessings are granted throughout the book of Revelation (see 1:3; 14:13; 16:15; 19:9; 20:6; 22:7, 14). When John fell at the angel's feet to worship him because of this marvelous message (22:8), the angel constrained him, telling John that he was only a servant of God and reminding John that only God should be worshiped (22:9).

and they need no candle, neither light of the sun; for [b]the Lord God giveth them light: [c]and they shall reign for ever and ever.

Epilogue

E   6 And he said unto me, [a]These sayings *are* faithful and true: and the Lord God of the holy prophets [b]sent his angel to show unto his servants the things which must shortly be done.

C   7 [a]Behold, I come quickly: [b]blessed *is* he that keepeth the sayings of the prophecy of this book.

  8 And I John saw these things, and heard *them*. And when I had heard and seen, [a]I fell down to worship before the feet of the angel which showed me these things.

  9 Then saith he unto me, [a]See *thou do it* not: for I am thy fellowservant, and of thy brethren the prophets, and of them which keep the sayings of this book: worship God.

E   10 [a]And he saith unto me, Seal not the sayings of the prophecy of this book: [b]for the time is at hand.

N   11 [a]He that is unjust, let him be unjust still: and he which is filthy, let him be

filthy still: and he that is righteous, let him be righteous still: and he that is holy, let him be holy still.

  12 [a]And, behold, I come quickly; and [b]my reward *is* with me, [c]to give every man according as his work shall be.

  13 [a]I am Alpha and Omega, the beginning and the end, the first and the last.

  14 [a]Blessed *are* they that do his commandments, that they may have right [b]to the tree of life, [c]and may enter in through the gates into the city.

  15 For [a]without *are* [b]dogs, and sorcerers, and whoremongers, and murderers, and idolaters, and whosoever loveth and maketh a lie.

  16 [a]I Jesus have sent mine angel to testify unto you these things in the churches. [b]I am the root and the offspring of David, *and* [c]the bright and morning star.

  17 And the Spirit and [a]the bride say, Come. And let him that heareth say, Come. [b]And let him that is athirst come. And whosoever will, let him take the water of life freely.

  18 For I testify unto every man that

C
S

S

H

C
E
L
W

Center column references

5 [b]Ps. 36:9 [c]Dan. 7:27; Rom. 5:17; 2 Tim. 2:12

6 [a]ch. 19:9 [b]ch. 1:1

7 [a]ch. 3:11 [b]ch. 1:3

8 [a]ch. 19:10

9 [a]ch. 19:10

10 [a]Dan. 8:26 [b]ch. 1:3

11 [a]Ezek. 3:27; Dan. 12:10; 2 Tim. 3:13

12 [a]ver. 7 [b]Is. 40:10 [c]ch. 20:12

13 [a]Is. 41:4

14 [a]Dan. 12:12; 1 John 3:24 [b]ch. 2:7 [c]ch. 21:27

15 [a]1 Cor. 6:9; Gal. 5:19; Col. 3:6 [b]Phil. 3:2

16 [a]ch. 1:1 [b]ch. 5:5 [c]Num. 24:17; Zech. 6:12; 2 Pet. 1:19

17 [a]ch. 21:2,9 [b]Is. 55:1; John 7:37

E *Rev 5:1* ◄ ► *Rev 22:10*
C *Rev 3:11* ◄ ► *Rev 22:12*
E *Rev 22:6–7* ◄   N *Rev 13:9* ◄

C *Rev 22:7* ◄ ► *Rev 22:20*
S *Rev 21:27* ◄ ► *Rev 22:14–15*
S *Rev 22:12* ◄   H *Rev 21:27* ◄
C *Eph 6:17* ◄   E *Rev 21:10* ◄
L *Rev 21:6* ◄   W *Rev 21:6* ◄

22:12–13 Christ's promise to all believers is that he will return soon. Since centuries have passed since John penned this book, God apparently views time differently than we do (see 2Pe 3:8). Yet God keeps his promises (see 1Ki 8:56), and Christ will return. When he comes, he will reward those who have been faithful witnesses for him (see 1Co 3:8, 14;

2Ti 4:8; Heb 6:10; Jas 1:12). Note that in this passage Christ reaffirms his supremacy as the God of the universe (22:13; see 1:8).

22:18–19 Revelation ends with a prophetic warning for all who would dare alter God's words in this book. God also warned about adding or subtracting from the OT (see Dt 4:2; 12:32; Pr 30:6).

Possible Sequence of Future Events

				The Tribulation Period		The Millennium		Eternity
Rebirth of Israel	Israel Captured Temple Mount		Rapture		Christ's Victory at Battle of Armageddon	Satan Bound in Bottomless Pit		Great White Throne	A New Heaven & A New Earth
1948	**1967**							
		Nations Surround Israel	Invasion of Israel	Antichrist Signs 7 Year Treaty with Israel	Antichrist Defiles Temple			Final War of Gog & Magog

The New Jerusalem

THE LAST PORTION of the book of Revelation deals with a new heaven, a new earth and a new Jerusalem. Scholars differ on the exact interpretation to give to John's vision of this major city. Some scholars view this vision of the new Jerusalem as a fuller picture of Jerusalem during the Millennium. Others view this city as a symbol of eternity encompassing all of the aspects of eternal life. Still other scholars who interpret Biblical prophecy literally contend that the new Jerusalem is a literal city, the eternal home of the resurrected saints of God. It is this latter interpretation to which we will turn our focus.

The City of God

At the end of the Millennium, after sin has been eliminated from the universe and Satan has been banished forever to the lake of fire, God will cleanse the earth with fire. As a holy God, the Lord could never establish his eternal throne on earth until sin and evil and its effects were eradicated. After this cleansing of the earth, the new Jerusalem will descend from heaven (see Rev 3:12).

The Bible describes the new Jerusalem in very real, physical terms and sometimes calls it by other names. The author of Hebrews calls it "mount Sion," "the city of the living God," and "the heavenly Jerusalem" in order to distinguish it from the earthly Jerusalem that will continue to exist forever (see Heb 12:22). The apostle Paul uses a similar phrase, "Jerusalem which is above" (Gal 4:26), to make the same distinction for his readers.

The exact location of this marvelous city is unclear. It may exist as a real entity in another dimension, or possibly, somewhere out in distant space. The Bible does not give us enough information to locate it, though it consistently refers to heaven and the heavenly city as existing in an upward direction, north from the earth. John notes that when the city is revealed, it comes "down out of heaven from my God" (Rev 3:12). During this present age the new Jerusalem is still in the heavens. It will descend to its eternal location only after the earth is cleansed.

Some suggest that the new Jerusalem's eternal position will be over the earth so that the light of the city, which is the light of God's presence, will shine on the earth beneath. This shining from above onto the earth beneath will enable "the nations of them which are saved [to] walk in the light of it: and the kings of the earth do bring their glory and honour into it" (21:24).

A Description of the New Jerusalem

The apostle John describes the dimensions of the new Jerusalem. The distance along each side is 1,500 miles. Some writers suggest that this holy city must be either a pyramid or cube in shape, rising in tiers as a huge mountain 1,500 miles up into the sky. Its walls are 216 feet tall (see 21:17), and there are 12 gates in this wall that are used for entering and leaving the city. (A pyramidal city could logically rest on a base 216 feet high with 12 gates.) Even John had to go to the top of a high mountain in order to see all of the "great city, the holy Jerusalem, descending out of heaven from God" (21:10).

The materials described in the new Jerusalem are precious stones and metals. The walls will be laid in twelve foundation layers of jasper crystal. Each layer will be 18 feet high and embellished with every manner of precious stone. Each of the twelve foundation layers will bear the name of one of the twelve apostles in honor of their faithfulness (see 21:14). These layers are decorated with jasper, sapphire, chalcedony, emerald, sardonyx, sardius, chrysolyte, beryl, topaz, chrysoprasus, jacinth and amethyst (see 21:19–20). The twelve gates will be named in honor of the twelve tribes of Israel, indicating God's unbreakable covenant with his chosen people. These twelve gates will be "twelve pearls; every several gate was of one pearl: and the street of the city was pure gold, as it were transparent glass" (21:21). For further information on the composition and character of the heavenly Jerusalem, see the article on "Heaven" on p. 1226.

The Inhabitants of the New Jerusalem

John declared that in addition to his vision he heard a "great voice out of heaven saying, Behold, the tabernacle of God is with men, and he will dwell with them, and they shall be his people, and God himself shall be with them, and be their God" (21:3). God the Father, Son and Holy Spirit will eternally make the new Jerusalem his home. He will dwell in it with his heavenly hosts and surround himself with his beloved.

New Jerusalem is also the home of the resurrected church and of the departed saints of the OT. All Christians who died will be present in this heavenly city in the glorious, eternal, resurrection bodies they received at the rapture of the church. After the judgment seat of Christ and the marriage supper of the Lamb, Christ's bride will settle into her permanent home in the new Jerusalem. Jesus promised he would prepare the new Jerusalem as a home for his church (see Jn 14:2). He has kept his promise and prepared the new Jerusalem, adorned with jewels, for the church in the same careful, expectant manner that a bride prepares for her prospective husband.

When Jesus defeated Satan at the cross he also freed the souls of the OT saints that rested in Abraham's bosom (see Lk 16:22). Unfallen angels, the tribulation saints and "the spirits of just men made perfect" (Heb 12:23) will be citizens of the heavenly new Jerusalem too.

The inhabitants of the new Jerusalem will retain their individual and national characteristics. Nations will continue to exist as political entities and will continue to have rulers who will administer their political affairs. These nations will "even go up from year to year to worship the King, the LORD of hosts, and to keep the feast of tabernacles" (Zec 14:16).

Life in the New Jerusalem

The new Jerusalem will have "no need of the sun, neither of the moon, to shine in it: for the glory of God did lighten it, and the Lamb is the light thereof" (Rev 21:23). In this bright and glowing city, life will be joyful and free of pain or tears (see 21:4). The martyrs for the faith will be "before the throne of God, and serve him day and night in his temple: and he that sitteth on the throne shall dwell among them" (7:15).

The river of life will flow through the new Jerusalem, and the tree of life will grow along its banks (see 22:1–2). Time will continue to be marked in eternity because the tree of life will bear "her fruit every month" (22:2). John also indicates that we will enjoy food in this heavenly city (see 22:2).

What a joy this city will be for the saints of God. John's vision regarding the heavenly city, the new Jerusalem, was a confirmation of all of the promises made to believers for the last six thousand years. The OT saints kept their eyes focused on "a city which hath foundations, whose builder and maker is God" (Heb 11:10) and earned Christ's commendation for their faithfulness. When the resurrected and redeemed of the Lord possess this city as their eternal inheritance in an everlasting relationship with God who is living among them, they will have attained heaven at last.

heareth the words of the prophecy of this book, [a]If any man shall add unto these things, God shall add unto him the plagues that are written in this book:

19 And if any man shall take away from the words of the book of this prophecy, [a]God shall take away his part [1]out of the book of life, and out of [b]the holy city,

and *from* the things which are written in this book.

20 He which testifieth these things [c] saith, [a]Surely I come quickly. [b]Amen. [c]Even so, come, Lord Jesus.

21 [a]The grace of our Lord Jesus Christ *be* with you all. Amen.

18 [a]Deut. 4:2; Prov. 30:6

19 [a]Ex. 32:33; Ps. 69:28 [b]ch. 21:2
[1]Or, *from the tree of life*

20 [a]ver. 12 [b]John 21:25 [c]2 Tim. 4:8

21 [a]Rom. 16:20

C *Rev 22:12* ◄

22:20–21   John ends this marvelous prophecy with Christ's awesome promise to return quickly. As prophecies are fulfilled in our generation, we need to stay alert (see Mk 13:33) and awaken each day with the realization that "now is our salvation nearer than when we believed" (Ro 13:11). With John we can prayerfully say, "Even so, come, Lord Jesus" (22:20).

STUDY HELPS

Index to Subjects

Index to Articles

Concordance

Index to Color Maps

Index to Subjects

The index to subjects will help you find information on a variety of subjects covered in the notes of the *Prophecy Study Bible*. References to articles are indicated by **A**. References to book introductions are indicated by **I**.

Q-R

Index to Articles

Introduction
to the KJV Concordance

For each verse quoted in this concordance, an italicized single letter is used to designate the word entry. The texts chosen for each word are in Bible book order under the entry. Occasionally the verses under a word entry contain different forms of that entry (for example, under the word ABASE, entries may contain "abased" or "abasing"). Those alternate forms of the word have been placed in parentheses after the key word. The context of each verse will help the reader understand which form of the word fits the italicized letter.

Concordance Abbreviations for the Books of the Bible

Genesis . . . . .Gen.	Isaiah . . . . .Is.	Romans . . . . .Rom.
Exodus . . . . Ex.	Jeremiah .Jer.	1 Corinthians . . . . .1 Cor.
Leviticus . . . . Lev.	Lamentations . . . . .Lam.	2 Corinthians . . . . .2 Cor.
Numbers . . . . .Num.	Ezekiel .Ezek.	Galatians . . . . .Gal.
Deuteronomy . . . . .Deut.	Daniel . . . . .Dan.	Ephesians . . . . .Eph.
Joshua . . . . .Josh.	Hosea . . . . .Hos.	Philippians . . . . .Phil.
Judges . . . . .Judg.	Joel . . . . .Joel	Colossians . . . . .Col.
Ruth .Ruth	Amos . . . . .Amos	1 Thessalonians . . . . .1 Thes.
1 Samuel . . . . .1 Sam.	Obadiah . . . . .Obad.	2 Thessalonians . . . . .2 Thes.
2 Samuel . . . . .2 Sam.	Jonah . . . . .Jonah	1 Timothy . . . . .1 Tim.
1 Kings . . . . .1 Ki.	Micah . . . . .Mic.	2 Timothy . . . . .2 Tim.
2 Kings . . . . .2 Ki.	Nahum .Nah.	Titus . . . . .Tit.
1 Chronicles . . . . .1 Chr.	Habbakuk . . . . .Hab.	Philemon . . . . .Philem.
2 Chronicles . . . . .2 Chr.	Zephaniah . . . . .Zeph.	Hebrews . . . . .Heb.
Ezra . . . . .Ezra	Haggai .Hag.	James . . . . .Jas.
Nehemiah . . . . .Neh.	Zechariah . . . . .Zech.	1 Peter . . . . .1 Pet.
Esther . . . . .Esth.	Malachi . . . . .Mal.	2 Peter . . . . .2 Pet.
Job . . . . .Job	Matthew . . . . .Mat.	1 John . . . . .1 John
Psalm . . . . .Ps.	Mark . . . . .Mark	2 John . . . . .2 John
Proverbs . . . . .Prov.	Luke . . . . .Luke	3 John . . . . .3 John
Ecclesiastes . . . . .Eccl.	John . . . . .John	Jude . . . . .Jude
Song of Solomon . . . . .Sol.	Acts . . . . .Acts	Revelation . . . . .Rev.

KJV Concordance

ABASE (ABASED, ABASING)
Job   40: 11 every one that is proud, and *a*
Dan.   4: 37 walk in pride he is able to *a*
Mat.   23: 12 exalt himself shall be *a*

ABHOR (ABHORRED, ABHORREST, ABHORRETH, ABHORRING)
Lev.   26: 11 my soul shall not *a* you
Deut.   23: 7 shalt not *a* an Edomite
        32: 19 when the Lord saw it he *a* them
1 Sam.   2: 17 for men *a* the offering
Job   19: 19 my inward friends *a* me
        30: 10 they *a* me, they flee
Ps.   5: 6 Lord will *a* the bloody
        10: 3 covetous, whom the Lord *a*
        22: 24 nor *a* the affliction of the afflicted
        89: 38 cast off and *a* . . . thine anointed
        106: 40 he *a* his own inheritance
        119: 163 I hate and *a* lying
Prov.   22: 14 *a* of the Lord shall fall
Is.   49: 7 him whom the nation *a*
        66: 24 be an *a* unto all flesh
Lam.   2: 7 Lord hath *a* his sanctuary
Amos   5: 10 they *a* him that speaketh
Mic.   3: 9 house of Israel that *a* judgment
Zech.   11: 8 their soul also *a* me
Rom.   2: 22 thou that *a* idols

ABIDE
Num.   35: 25 *a* in it unto the death of the high
Ps.   15: 1 who shall *a* in thy tabernacle
        61: 4 I will *a* in thy tabernacle
Mal.   3: 2 who may *a* the day of his
Luke   19: 5 I must *a* at thy house
John   14: 16 Comforter, that he may *a* with you
        15: 4 *a* in me and I in you
        15: 10 ye shall *a* in my love, *a* in his
1 Cor.   3: 14 if any man's work *a*
Phil.   1: 24 to *a* in the flesh is needful

ABIDETH (ABIDING)
Ps.   55: 19 even he that *a* of old
Eccl.   1: 4 the earth *a* for ever
John   3: 36 wrath of God *a* on him
        8: 35 the Son *a* for ever
        12: 34 Christ *a* for ever
        15: 5 he that *a* in me bringeth forth
1 Pet.   1: 23 word of God *a* for
1 John   3: 24 hereby we know he *a*

ABLE
Ex.   18: 21 *a* men, such as fear God,
Deut.   16: 17 every man give as he is *a*
Dan.   3: 17 God is *a* to deliver
Mat.   3: 9 God is *a* of these stones to raise
        9: 28 believe ye I am *a* to do this?
John   10: 29 no man is *a* to pluck them
Rom.   14: 4 God is *a* to make him stand
1 Cor. 10: 13 tempted above that ye are *a*
2 Cor.   9: 8 *a* to make all grace abound
2 Tim.   1: 12 *a* to keep that which
        3: 15 are *a* to make thee wise
Heb.   5: 7 *a* to save him from death
        7: 25 *a* to save to the uttermost
Jas.   1: 21 *a* to save your souls
Jude   1: 24 *a* to keep you from falling

ABOLISH (ABOLISHED)
Is.   51: 6 righteousness shall not be *a*
Ezek.   6: 6 your works may be *a*
Eph.   2: 15 having *a* in his flesh
2 Tim.   1: 10 Jesus Christ hath *a* death

ABOMINABLE
Lev.   7: 21 or any *a* unclean thing
Is.   14: 19 thy grave like an *a* branch
Jer.   44: 4 do not this *a* thing that I hate
Nah.   3: 6 I will cast *a* filth on
Rev.   21: 8 unbelieving and *a* shall

ABOMINATION (ABOMINATIONS)
2 Ki.   21: 2 the *a* of the heathen

Ezra   9: 14 join people of these *a*
Prov.   6: 16 seven things are an *a* to Lord
        11: 1 a false balance is *a* to the Lord
        12: 22 lying lips are *a* to the Lord
        15: 8 sacrifice of wicked is an *a*
        16: 5 proud in heart is an *a* to Lord
        20: 23 divers weights are an *a* to the Lord
Is.   1: 13 incense is an *a* unto me
Jer.   7: 10 delivered to do all these *a*
Ezek.   16: 2 cause Jerusalem to know her *a*
Mat.   24: 15 see the *a* of desolation
Luke   16: 15 is *a* in the sight of

ABOUND (ABOUNDED, ABOUNDING)
Prov.   28: 20 faithful shall *a* with blessings
Mat.   24: 12 because iniquity shall *a*
Rom.   3: 7 truth of God hath more *a*
        6: 1 in sin that grace may *a*
1 Cor. 15: 58 always *a* in the work
Eph.   1: 8 he hath *a* toward us
Phil.   1: 9 that your love may *a*
        4: 12 both to *a* and to suffer
Col.   2: 7 *a* therein with thanksgiving
1 Thes.   3: 12 the Lord make you *a* in love
2 Pet.   1: 8 things be in you and *a*

ABOVE
Ex.   20: 4 that is in the heaven *a*
John   3: 31 cometh from *a* is *a* all
        8: 23 I am from *a*; ye are of this world
        19: 11 power given thee from *a*
Eph.   4: 6 one God who is *a* all
Col.   3: 1 seek those things which are *a*
Jas.   1: 17 every perfect gift is from *a*
        3: 15 wisdom from *a* is pure

ABSENT
2 Cor.   5: 6 in body we are *a* from the Lord
Col.   2: 5 though I be *a* in the flesh

ABSTAIN
Acts   15: 20 that they *a* from pollutions of idols
1 Thes.   5: 22 *a* from all appearance of evil
1 Pet.   2: 11 *a* from fleshly lusts

ABUNDANCE
Deut.   28: 47 for the *a* of all things
Eccl.   5: 10 he that loveth *a* with increase
Mat.   12: 34 out of the *a* of the heart the mouth
        13: 12 and he shall have more *a*
Luke   12: 15 life consisteth not in *a* of

ABUNDANT (ABUNDANTLY)
Ex.   34: 6 *a* in goodness and truth
Job   12: 6 whose hand God bringeth *a*
Is.   55: 7 he will *a* pardon
John   10: 10 might have life more *a*
2 Cor.   9: 12 is *a* also by many thanksgivings
1 Tim.   1: 14 grace of our Lord exceeding *a*
Tit.   3: 6 shed on us *a* through Jesus
1 Pet.   1: 3 his *a* mercy hath begotten
2 Pet.   1: 11 shall be ministered unto you *a*

ACCEPT (ACCEPTED, ACCEPTEST, ACCEPTETH, ACCEPTING)
Gen.   4: 7 shalt thou not be *a*
Deut.   33: 11 *a* the work of his hands
2 Sam. 24: 23 Lord thy God *a* thee
Job   42: 8 servant Job, him will I *a*
Eccl.   9: 7 God now *a* thy works
Ezek.   43: 27 I will *a* you, saith the Lord
Hos.   8: 13 but the Lord *a* them not
Luke   4: 24 no prophet is *a* in his own
Acts   10: 35 worketh righteousness is *a*
2 Cor.   5: 9 we may be *a* of him
        6: 2 behold, now is the *a* time
Eph.   1: 6 made us *a* in the beloved

ACCEPTABLE (ACCEPTABLY)
Ps.   19: 14 meditation of my heart, be *a*
Is.   49: 8 in an *a* time I heard thee
        61: 2 proclaim the *a* year of the Lord
Dan.   4: 27 let my counsel be *a*

Rom.   12: 1 sacrifice holy *a* to God
Eph.   5: 10 proving what is *a* to God
1 Pet.   2: 5 *a* to God by Jesus Christ

ACCESS
Rom.   5: 2 we have *a* by faith
Eph.   2: 18 we both have *a* by one Spirit

ACCOMPLISH (ACCOMPLISHED, ACCOMPLISHING)
Is.   40: 2 her warfare is *a* that her
John   19: 28 all things were now *a*
Heb.   9: 6 *a* the service of God

ACCORD
Acts   1: 14 continued with one *a* in prayer
        2: 1 with one *a* in one place

ACCOUNT (ACCOUNTED)
Ps.   22: 30 it shall be *a* to the Lord
        144: 3 that thou makest *a* of him
Mat.   12: 36 give *a* thereof in the day of judgment
Luke   16: 2 give an *a* of thy stewardship
        20: 35 they which shall be *a* worthy to obtain
                that world
Rom.   14: 12 give *a* of himself to God
Gal.   3: 6 *a* to him for righteousness
Heb.   13: 17 as they that must give *a*

ACCURSED
Deut.   21: 23 hanged is *a* of God.
Is.   65: 20 one hundred years old shall be *a*
Rom.   9: 3 wish myself *a* from Christ
1 Cor. 12: 3 the Spirit of God calleth Jesus *a*

ACCUSATION
Mat.   27: 37 over his head his *a*
Luke   6: 7 might find an *a* against him

ACCUSE (ACCUSETH, ACCUSING)
Prov.   30: 10 *a* not a servant unto his master
Luke   3: 14 neither *a* any falsely
John   5: 45 that I will *a* you to the Father
Rev.   12: 10 which *a* them before our God

ACCUSERS
2 Tim.   3: 3 trucebreakers, false *a*

ACKNOWLEDGE (ACKNOWLEDGING)
Ps.   32: 5 I *a* my sin unto thee, and mine
        51: 3 For I *a* my transgression
Prov.   3: 6 in all thy ways *a* him
Jer.   3: 13 only *a* thine iniquity
        14: 20 we *a* our wickedness
2 Tim.   2: 25 to the *a* of the truth

ACKNOWLEDGMENT
Col.   2: 2 to the *a* of the mystery of God

ACQUAINT (ACQUAINTED)
Is.   53: 3 man of sorrows, and *a* with grief

ACQUIT
Job   10: 14 wilt not *a* me from mine iniquity
Nah.   1: 3 will not at all *a* the wicked

ACT (ACTS)
Deut.   11: 3 his miracles, and his *a*
        11: 7 great *a* of the Lord
Judg.   5: 11 rehearse the righteous *a*
Ps.   106: 2 who can utter the mighty *a*
        145: 4 declare thy mighty *a*

ADD (ADDED, ADDETH)
Lev.   5: 16 shall *a* the fifth part thereto
Deut.   4: 2 shall not *a* unto the word
        29: 19 *a* drunkenness to thirst
Ps.   69: 27 *a* iniquity to their iniquity
Is.   30: 1 that they may *a* sin to sin
Jer.   45: 3 Lord *a* grief to my sorrow
Mat.   6: 27 can *a* one cubit unto his stature
Acts   2: 41 there were *a* unto them about
2 Pet.   1: 5 *a* to your faith virtue
Rev.   22: 18 if any man *a* unto these things

ADDER
Gen.   49: 17 an *a* in the path
Ps.   91: 13 tread upon the lion and *a*

ADMONISH (ADMONISHED, ADMONISHING)
Eccl.　12:12　by these, my son be *a*
Col.　　3:16　*a* one another in psalms
1 Thes.　5:12　over you and *a* you
2 Thes.　3:15　*a* him as a brother
Heb.　　8:　5　as Moses was *a* of God

ADMONITION
1 Cor.　10:11　they were written for our *a*
Eph.　　6:　4　up in the nurture and *a* of the Lord
Tit.　　3:10　after first and second *a* reject

ADOPTION
Rom.　　8:15　ye have received the Spirit of *a*
Gal.　　4:　5　we might receive the *a* of sons
Eph.　　1:　5　us unto the *a* of children

ADORN (ADORNED, ADORNETH)
Is.　　61:10　as a bride *a* herself
1 Tim.　2:　9　women *a* themselves in modest
1 Pet.　3:　5　holy women *a* themselves
Rev.　　21:　2　as a bride *a* for her husband

ADULTERER (ADULTERERS)
Lev.　20:10　the *a* and adulteress shall surely
Job　24:15　eye also of the *a* waits for twilight
Is.　57:　3　seed of the *a* and the whore
Jas.　　4:　4　ye *a* and adulteresses know

ADULTERY (ADULTERIES)
Prov.　6:32　committeth *a* with a woman lacks
Mat.　　5:28　committed *a* in his heart
　　　15:19　out of the heart proceed *a*
2 Pet.　2:14　having eyes full of *a*

ADULTEROUS
Prov.　30:20　such is the way of an *a* woman
Mat.　12:39　*a* generation seeketh after a sign
Mark　8:38　this *a* and sinful generation

ADVERSARY (ADVERSARIES)
Ex.　23:22　I will be an *a* to thy *a*
1 Ki.　　5:　4　is neither *a* nor evil
Mat.　　5:25　agree with thine *a*
1 Tim.　5:14　give no occasion to *a*
Heb.　10:27　shall devour the *a*
1 Pet.　5:　8　your *a* the devil as a

ADVERSITY
2 Sam.　4:　9　redeemed my soul from all *a*
2 Chr.　15:　6　God did vex with all *a*
Ps.　　10:　6　I shall never be in *a*
　　　31:　7　thou hast known my soul in *a*
Prov.　17:17　brother is born for *a*
Eccl.　7:14　in the day of *a* consider
Is.　　30:20　give you the bread of *a*

ADVOCATE
1 John　2:　1　we have an *a* with the Father

AFAR
Ps.　139:　2　understandest thoughts *a* off
Jer.　23:23　Lord, and not a God *a* off
Eph.　　2:17　preached peace to you *a*
Heb.　11:13　having seen promises *a*

AFFECTIONS (AFFECTIONED)
Rom.　12:10　be kindly *a* one to another
Gal.　　5:24　have crucified flesh with the *a*

AFFLICT (AFFLICTED)
Gen.　15:13　they shall *a* them four hundred years
Ex.　22:22　shall not *a* any widow
Num.　30:13　every binding oath to *a* the soul
2 Sam.22:28　*a* people thou wilt save
Job　　6:14　to him that is *a* pity should be showed
Ps.　　22:24　nor abhorred the affliction of the *a*
　　　119:67　before I was *a* I went astray
　　　140:12　wilt maintain the cause of the *a*
Prov.　15:15　all days of the *a* are evil
Is.　　49:13　and will have mercy upon his *a*
　　　53:　4　smitten of God and *a*
　　　53:　7　he was oppressed and he was *a*
Lam.　3:33　doth not *a* willingly

AFFLICTION (AFFLICTIONS)
Ex.　　3:　7　seen the *a* of my people
2 Ki.　14:26　For the Lord saw the *a* of Israel
Job　　5:　6　*a* cometh not forth of dust
　　　36:　8　and be holden in cords of *a*
Ps.　25:18　look upon my *a* and pain
　　　34:19　many are the *a* of the righteous
　　107:10　being bound in *a* and iron
Is.　48:10　chosen thee in the furnace of *a*
　　　63:　9　in all their *a* he was afflicted

Hos.　　5:15　in their *a* they will seek
Amos　6:　6　not grieved for the *a* of Joseph
Obad.　1:13　not have looked on their *a*
Nah.　　1:　9　*a* shall not rise up the second time
Zech.　1:15　and they helped forward the *a*
Acts　　7:10　delivered him out of all his *a*
　　　20:23　bonds and *a* abide me
Phil.　　4:14　communicate with my *a*
2 Tim.　1:　8　partaker of the *a* of the gospel
Heb.　10:32　endured a great fight of *a*
　　　11:25　choosing rather to suffer *a*
Jas.　　1:27　to visit the fatherless and widows in *a*

AFRAID
Lev.　26:　6　and none shall make you *a*
Ps.　56:11　Not be *a* what man can do
Is.　12:　2　I will trust, and not be *a*
Mark　5:36　Be not *a*, only believe
Luke　12:　4　Be not *a* of them that kill
1 Pet.　3:　6　ye do well, and are not *a*

AGE
Ps.　39:　5　mine *a* is as nothing before thee
Heb.　5:14　meat to those of full *a*

AGED
Tit.　　2:　2　that the *a* men be sober, grave

AGES
Eph.　　2:　7　that in the *a* to come he might
　　　3:21　Christ Jesus throughout all *a*
Col.　　1:26　mystery which hath been hid from *a*

AGREE (AGREED)
Amos　3:　3　walk together, except they be *a*?
Mat.　　5:25　*a* with thine adversary quickly
　　　18:19　if two shall *a* on earth
1 John　5:　8　these three *a* in one

ALIEN (ALIENS)
Ex.　18:　3　been an *a* in a strange land
Ps.　69:　8　an *a* unto my mother's children
Eph.　　2:12　being *a* from the commonwealth

ALIENATED
Eph.　　4:18　being *a* from the life of God

ALIVE
1 Sam.　2:　6　The Lord killeth and maketh *a*
Luke　15:24　my son was dead and is *a*
Rom.　6:11　*a* unto God through Jesus
　　　7:　9　I was *a* without the law once
1 Cor.　15:22　in Christ shall all be made *a*
Rev.　　2:　8　which was dead and is *a*

ALMIGHTY
Gen.　17:　1　I am the *A* God; walk
　　　35:11　I am God *A*: be fruitful and
Ex.　　6:　3　by the name of God *A*
Num.　24:　4　saw the vision of the *A*
Ruth　1:20　the *A* hath dealt very bitterly
Job　21:15　what is the *A*, that we should
　　　27:10　delight himself in the *A*
Ps.　91:　1　under the shadow of the *A*
Rev.　　1:　8　and which is to come, the *A*
　　　4:　8　holy, holy, Lord God *A*

ALMS
Mat.　　6:　1　not your *a* before men
Luke　12:33　sell that ye have, give *a*
Acts　　3:　2　to ask *a* of them that entered
　　　24:17　I came to bring *a* to my nation

ALONE
Gen.　　2:18　not good for man to be *a*
Num.　23:　9　lo, the people shall dwell *a*
Ps.　136:　4　to him *a* who doeth great wonders
Gal.　　6:　4　rejoicing in himself *a*

ALTAR (ALTARS)
Gen.　　8:20　builded an *a* unto the Lord
　　　12:　7　there builded he an *a*
　　　35:　1　make there an *a* unto God
Ex.　17:15　Moses built an *a*
Deut.　12:　3　ye shall overthrow their *a*
Josh.　22:10　built there an *a* by Jordan
Judg.　6:25　throw down the *a* of Baal
1 Ki.　13:　2　cried against the *a* in the word
Ps.　26:　6　so will I compass thine *a*
　　　43:　4　then will I go to the *a* of God
Mat.　　5:23　if thou bring thy gift to the *a*
1 Cor.　9:13　they that wait at the *a* are partakers
Heb.　13:10　we have an *a* whereof
Rev.　　9:13　the golden *a* which is before God

ALWAYS
Gen.　　6:　3　my spirit shall not *a* strive
1 Chr.　16:15　mindful *a* of the covenant
Job　27:10　will he *a* call on God
Ps.　　9:18　needy shall not *a* be forgotten
　　　16:　8　I set the Lord *a* before me
Prov.　28:14　happy is man that feareth *a*
Is.　57:16　neither will I be *a* wroth
Mat.　26:11　have the poor *a* with you
　　　28:20　I am with you *a*, to the end
Luke　18:　1　men ought *a* to pray
John　8:29　I do *a* things that please
2 Cor.　6:10　yet *a* rejoicing; as poor, yet
Phil.　　4:　4　rejoice in the Lord *a*
Col.　　4:　6　your speech be *a* with grace

AMBASSADOR (AMBASSADORS)
Prov.　13:17　a faithful *a* is health
2 Cor.　5:20　we are *a* for Christ
Eph.　　6:20　I am an *a* in bonds

AMEN
2 Cor.　1:20　promises of God in him *a*
Rev.　22:20　*A* Even so, come, Lord Jesus

ANCHOR
Heb.　　6:19　as an *a* of the soul

ANCIENT (ANCIENTS)
Job　12:12　with the *a* is wisdom
Dan.　　7:　9　the *a* of days did sit

ANGEL
Gen.　24:　7　send his *a* before thee
　　　48:16　the *a* which redeemed me
Ps.　34:　7　*a* of the Lord encampeth round
Is.　63:　9　*a* of his presence saved
Dan.　　6:22　sent his *a* and shut the lions' mouths
Acts　　5:19　*a* of the Lord by night opened
　　　12:　7　*a* of the Lord came upon him
　　　23:　8　Sadducees say that there is no . . . *a*

ANGELS (ANGELS')
Gen.　28:12　*a* of God ascending and
Ps.　　8:　5　a little lower than the *a*
　　　78:25　man did eat *a* food
Mat.　　4:11　*a* came and ministered
　　　18:10　their *a* do always behold the face of
　　　24:31　send his *a* with a great sound
Mark　12:25　are as the *a* in heaven
Luke　15:10　joy in the presence of the *a*
　　　20:36　equal unto the *a*
John　1:51　the *a* of God ascending and
Col.　　2:18　beguile worshipping of *a*
1 Tim.　3:16　seen of *a*, preached
Heb.　　2:16　took not the nature of *a*
　　　13:　2　entertained *a* unawares
2 Pet.　2:11　*a* which are greater in power
Rev.　　1:20　*a* of the seven churches

ANGER
Ex.　32:22　let not the *a* of my lord wax
Deut.　29:24　meaneth the heat of this great *a*
Josh.　7:26　from fierceness of his *a*
Neh.　　9:17　slow to *a*, and of great kindness
Ps.　27:　9　put not thy servant away in *a*
　　　30:　5　his *a* endureth but a moment
　　　85:　4　cause *a* towards us to cease
　　　90:　7　we are consumed by thine *a*
　　103:　8　slow to *a*, and plenteous in mercy
Prov.　15:　1　grievous words stir up *a*
Eccl.　7:　9　*a* resteth in the bosom of fools
Joel　2:13　slow to *a*, and of great kindness
Mic.　7:18　retaineth not his *a* for
Eph.　　4:31　let all *a* be put away
Col.　　3:　8　put off all these; *a*, wrath
Jas.　　1:19　slow to *a*, slow to wrath

ANGRY
Deut.　1:37　Also the Lord was *a* with me
Ps.　　2:12　kiss the Son lest he be *a*
　　　7:11　God is *a* with the wicked every day
Prov.　14:17　He that is soon *a* dealeth foolishly
　　　22:24　no friendship with an *a* man
　　　29:22　an *a* man stirreth up strife
Eccl.　7:　9　be not hasty to be *a*
Mat.　　5:22　whosoever is *a* with his brother
Eph.　　4:26　be ye *a* and sin not

ANGUISH
Jer.　　6:24　*a* hath taken hold of us
John　16:21　remembereth no more the *a*, for joy

ANOINT
Ex. 28:41 shalt *a* them and consecrate them
Ps. 23: 5 thou *a* my head with oil
Mat. 6:17 when thou fastest, *a* thy head
Jas. 5:14 *a* him with oil

ANOINTED
1 Sam. 2:10 exalt the horn of his *a*
     24: 6 seeing he is the *a* of the Lord
1 Chr. 16:22 touch not my *a*
2 Chr. 6:42 turn not away the face of thine *a*
Ps. 28: 8 Lord is the saving strength of his *a*
     45: 7 *a* thee with the oil of gladness
     89:38 hast been wroth with thine *a*
    132: 17 ordained a lamp for mine *a*
Acts 4:27 Jesus, whom thou hast *a*
     10:38 how God *a* Jesus of Nazareth
2 Cor. 1:21 who hath *a* us is God

ANSWER
Deut. 20:11 if it make thee *a* of peace
Job 9: 3 he cannot *a* him one of a thousand
     14:15 thou shalt call and I will *a*
Ps. 91:15 call upon me and I will *a* him
    143: 1 in thy faithfulness *a* me
Prov. 15: 1 soft *a* turneth away wrath
     26: 4 *a* a fool according to his folly
Is. 58: 9 call, and the Lord shall *a*
Jer. 33: 3 Call unto me, and I will *a* thee
Ezek. 14: 7 I the Lord will *a* him by myself
Luke 21:14 meditate not what to *a*
Rom. 11: 4 what saith the *a* of God
Col. 4: 6 know how to *a* every man
1 Pet. 3:15 ready to give an *a* to
     3:21 the *a* of a good conscience

ANSWERED (ANSWERETH)
Ps. 18:41 to the Lord, but he *a* not
     81: 7 I *a* thee in the secret place
Prov. 18:13 he that *a* a matter before he
Eccl. 10:19 money *a* all things

ANT (ANTS)
Prov. 6: 6 Go to the *a*, thou sluggard

ANTICHRIST (ANTICHRISTS)
1 John 2:22 he is *a*, that denieth the Father
2 John 1: 7 this is a deceiver and an *a*

APOSTLE (APOSTLES)
Mat. 10: 2 names of the twelve *a*
Luke 11:49 I will send prophets and *a*
Rom. 11:13 I am an *a* of Gentiles
1 Cor. 9: 1 am I not an *a*? Am I not free
     15: 9 I am the least of the *a*
2 Cor. 11:13 such are false *a*; deceitful workers
Eph. 2:20 built upon the foundation of the *a*
     4:11 gave some *a*, some prophets
Heb. 3: 1 consider the *a* and high priest
Rev. 18:20 and ye holy *a* and prophets
     21:14 names of the twelve *a* of the Lamb

APOSTLESHIP
Rom. 1: 5 we have received grace and *a*
Gal. 2: 8 to the *a* of the circumcision

APPAREL
Is. 63: 1 that is glorious in his *a*
Zeph. 1: 8 such as are clothed with strange *a*
1 Tim. 2: 9 adorn themselves in modest *a*

ADORNING
1 Pet. 3: 3 let it not be that outward *a*

APPEAR (APPEARED)
Ex. 23:15 none shall *a* before me empty
Deut. 16:16 all thy males *a* before the Lord
1 Sam. 2:27 plainly *a* unto the house of thy father
Ps. 42: 2 when shall I *a* before God
Mat. 6:16 may *a* to men to fast
     23:27 which indeed *a* beautiful outward
2 Cor. 5:10 we must all *a* before the judgment
Tit. 2:11 bringeth salvation hath *a* to all men
Heb. 9:24 to *a* in the presence of God
1 Pet. 5: 4 when the chief shepherd shall *a*
1 John 3: 2 not yet *a* what we shall be

APPEARANCE
1 Sam.16: 7 man looketh on the outward *a* but the
              Lord
John 7:24 judge not according to *a*
1 Thes. 5:22 abstain from all *a* of evil

APPEARING
2 Tim. 1:10 manifest by the *a* of Jesus
     4: 1 judge the quick and the dead at his *a*
1 Pet. 1: 7 unto praise at the *a* of Jesus

APPLE
Deut. 32:10 kept him as the *a* of his eye
Prov. 7: 2 my law as the *a* of thine eye

APPOINT (APPOINTED)
Gen. 30:28 *a* me thy wages, and I will give
Job 7: 1 an *a* time to man upon earth
Is. 61: 3 *a* to them that mourn in Zion
1 Thes. 5: 9 God hath not *a* us to wrath
Heb. 9:27 *a* unto men once to die

APPROACH (APPROACHING)
Lev. 18: 6 none of you shall *a* to any
Ps. 65: 4 the man whom thou . . . causest to *a*
Heb. 10:25 as ye see the day *a*

APPROVE (APPROVED, APPROVEST, APPROVETH, APPROVING)
Lam. 3:36 man in his cause, the Lord *a* not
Acts 2:22 a man *a* of God among you
Rom. 2:18 *a* the things that are more excellent
     14:18 acceptable to God, and *a* of men
2 Cor. 6: 4 in all things *a* ourselves
Phil. 1:10 may *a* things that are excellent

ARISE (ARISETH)
Ps. 44:26 *A* for our help, and redeem
     68: 1 let God *a*, let his enemies be
    112: 4 Unto the upright there *a* light
Amos 7: 2 by whom shall Jacob *a*
Mal. 4: 2 shall the Sun of righteousness *a*

ARM (ARMS)
Ex. 15:16 by the greatness of thine *a*
Deut. 33:27 underneath are the everlasting *a*
Job 40: 9 hast thou an *a* like God
Ps. 44: 3 never did their own *a* save them
     89:13 Thou hast a mighty *a*: strong
     98: 1 his holy *a*, hath gotten him victory
Is. 40:10 his *a* shall rule for him
     40:11 gather the lambs with his *a*
     51: 5 on my *a* shall they trust
     51: 9 put on strength, O *a* of the Lord
     53: 1 is the *a* of the Lord revealed
     63:12 led them by his glorious *a*
Luke 1:51 he hath shown strength with his *a*
1 Pet. 4: 1 *a* yourselves likewise with the same

ARMIES
1 Sam.17:26 defy the *a* of the living God
Rev. 19:14 *a* which were in heaven followed

ARMOUR
Rom. 13:12 put on the *a* of light
Eph. 6:11 put on the whole of God

ARROGANCY
1 Sam. 2: 3 let not *a* come out of your mouth
Prov. 8:13 pride and *a*, and the evil way

ARROW (ARROWS)
2 Ki. 13:17 the *a* of Lord's deliverance
Ps. 45: 5 thine *a* are sharp in the heart
     91: 5 nor for the *a* that flieth by day
Lam. 3:12 set me as a mark for the *a*

ASCEND (ASCENDED, ASCENDING)
Gen. 28:12 angels *a* and descending
Ps. 24: 3 shall *a* into the hill of the Lord
    139: 8 if I *a* up into heaven
John 1:51 *a* and descending upon the Son of man
Eph. 4: 8 when he *a* up on high
Rev. 11:12 *a* up to heaven in a cloud

ASCRIBE
Deut. 32: 3 *a* ye greatness unto our God
Job 36: 3 *a* righteousness to my Maker

ASHAMED
Gen. 2:25 man and his wife, and were not *a*
Ps. 25: 2 let me not be *a*
Ezek. 16:61 shalt remember thy ways and be *a*
Mark 8:38 be *a* of me and my word
Rom. 1:16 I am not *a* of the gospel
     9:33 believeth on him shall not be *a*
2 Tim. 2:15 workman that needeth not to be *a*

ASHES
Gen. 18:27 which am but dust and *a*
Job 42: 6 repent in dust and *a*
Ps. 102: 9 I have eaten *a* like bread

ASK (ASKETH)
Jer. 50: 5 They shall *a* the way to Zion
Mat. 7: 7 *a* and it shall be given
     7:11 good things to them that *a* him
     20:22 ye know not what ye *a*
Luke 12:48 of him they will *a* more
John 14:14 whatsoever ye *a* in my name
     16:24 *a* and ye shall receive
Eph. 3:20 above all that we *a* or think
Jas. 1: 5 wisdom let him *a* of God
     4: 2 ye have not, because ye *a* not
1 John 5:14 *a* anything according to his will

ASLEEP
1 Cor. 15: 6 but some are fallen *a*
1 Thes. 4:13 concerning them which are *a*

ASP (ASPS)
Job 20:14 it is the gall of *a* within him
Is. 11: 8 play on the hole of the *a*
Rom. 3:13 poison of *a* is under their lips

ASS
Zech. 9: 9 lowly, and riding upon an *a*
Mat. 21: 5 meek, and sitting upon an *a*

ASSEMBLY (ASSEMBLIES)
Ps. 22:16 the *a* of the wicked have inclosed me
     89: 7 to be feared in the *a* of the saints

ASSEMBLING
Heb. 10:25 forsake not the *a* of ourselves

ASSURANCE
Is. 32:17 effect of righteousness quietness and *a*
Col. 2: 2 riches of the full *a* of understanding
Heb. 6:11 the full *a* of hope unto the end

ASTRAY
Ps. 119:176 gone *a* like a lost sheep
Is. 53: 6 all we like sheep have gone *a*
Mat. 18:12 one of them be gone *a*
1 Pet. 2:25 ye were as sheep going *a*

ATTAIN (ATTAINED)
Ps. 139: 6 high, I cannot *a* unto it
Prov. 1: 5 man of understanding shall *a*
Phil. 3:12 as though I had already *a*

ATTEND (ATTENDED)
Ps. 55: 2 *a* unto me, and hear me
     86: 6 *a* to the voice of my supplication
Prov. 4:20 my son, *a* to my words

AUTHOR
1 Cor. 14:33 God is not the *a* of confusion
Heb. 12: 2 Jesus the *a* and finisher of our faith

AUTHORITY (AUTHORITIES)
Mat. 7:29 taught as one having *a*
John 5:27 *a* to execute judgment
Tit. 2:15 exhort, and rebuke with all *a*

AVAILETH
Gal. 5: 6 neither circumcision *a* any thing
Jas. 5:16 prayer of a righteous man *a* much

AVENGE (AVENGED, AVENGETH, AVENGING)
Lev. 19:18 thou shalt not *a*, nor bear
Judg. 5: 2 praise the Lord for the *a* of Israel
Is. 1:24 I will *a* me of my enemies
Luke 18: 7 shall not God *a* his elect
Rom. 12:19 *a* not yourselves, but rather
Rev. 6:10 dost thou not *a* our blood
     18:20 God hath *a* you on her

AVENGER
Ps. 8: 2 still the enemy and the *a*
     44:16 by reason of the enemy and *a*
1 Thes. 4: 6 the Lord is the *a* of all

AWAKE (AWAKED, AWAKEST)
Ps. 73:20 when thou *a* thou shalt despise
     78:65 Lord *a* as one out of sleep
    139: 18 when I *a* I am still with
1 Cor. 15:34 *a* to righteousness; and sin not
Eph. 5:14 *a* thou that sleepest; and arise

AWE
Ps. 4: 4 stand in *a*, and sin not
     33: 8 of the world stand in *a* of him

AXE (AXES)
Deut. 19: 5 a stroke with the *a* to cut down
1 Ki. 6: 7 neither hammer nor *a* nor any tool
2 Ki. 6: 5 the *a* head fell into the water

Jer. 46:22 come against her with *a*
Mat. 3:10 *a* laid to root of trees

BABE (BABES)
Ps. 8: 2 out of the mouth of *b*
Is. 3: 4 princes and *b* shall rule over them
Luke 1:41 the *b* leaped in her womb
1 Cor. 3: 1 as unto *b* in Christ
1 Pet. 2: 2 as newborn *b*, desire the sincere

BACKBITERS (BACKBITETH, BACKBITINGS)
Ps. 15: 3 He that *b* not with his tongue
Rom. 1:30 *b*, haters of God, despiteful
2 Cor. 12:20 strifes, *b*, whisperings, swellings

BACKSLIDER
Prov. 14:14 *b* in heart shall be filled

BACKSLIDING (BACKSLIDINGS)
Jer. 2:19 thy *b* shall reprove thee
5: 6 and their *b* are increased
Hos. 11: 7 my people are bent to *b*
14: 4 I will heal their *b*

BAG
Deut. 25:13 have in thy *b* divers measures
Hag. 1: 6 earneth wages to put it into a *b*

BALANCE
Job 31: 6 be weighed in an even *b*
Ps. 62: 9 to be laid in the *b*
Prov. 11: 1 false *b* is abomination to
Is. 40:12 and the hills in a *b*
Hos. 12: 7 *b* of deceit are in hand
Mic. 6:11 count pure with wicked *b*

BALDNESS
Lev. 21: 5 not make *b* upon their head
Deut. 14: 1 nor make any *b* between your eyes
Ezek. 7:18 *b* upon all their heads

BALM
Jer. 8:22 is there no *b* in Gilead

BANNER (BANNERS)
Ps. 20: 5 we will set up our *b*
Sol. 2: 4 his *b* over me was love
Is. 13: 2 Lift ye up a *b* upon the high

BAPTISM (BAPTISMS)
Mat. 20:22 be baptized with the *b* that I am
21:25 the *b* of John, whence was it
Mark 1: 4 preach the *b* of repentance
11:30 the *b* of John, was it from heaven
Luke 7:29 being baptized with the *b* of John
Acts 10:37 after the *b* which John preached
13:24 before his coming the *b* of repentance
18:25 knowing only the *b* of John
19: 4 verily baptized with the *b* of repentance
Rom. 6: 4 buried with him by *b*
Eph. 4: 5 One Lord, one faith, one *b*
1 Pet. 3:21 even *b* doth also now save us by

BAPTIZE
Mat. 3:11 I indeed *b* you with water
Mark 3:16 he shall *b* you with the Holy Ghost
Luke 3:16 he shall *b* you with the Holy Ghost
John 1:26 I *b* with water: but there

BAPTIZED (BAPTIZING)
Mat. 28:19 all nations *b* them in the name
Mark 1: 8 I indeed have *b* you with water
16:16 he that believeth and is *b*
Luke 3: 7 came forth to be *b* of him
John 4: 1 Jesus *b* more disciples
Acts 1: 5 ye shall be *b* with the Holy Ghost
2:38 repent and be *b* every one
8:13 Simon believed and was *b*
8:48 Peter commanded them to be *b*
16:15 she was *b* and her household
16:33 was *b* he and all his straight way
22:16 arise and be *b* wash away
Rom. 6: 3 Jesus Christ were *b* into his death
1 Cor. 1:13 were ye *b* in the name of Paul
10: 2 were all *b* unto Moses in the cloud
12:13 are all *b* into one body
15:29 do which are *b* for the dead
Gal. 3:27 as have been *b* into Christ

BARE
Ex. 19: 4 how I *b* you on eagles' wings
Is. 53:12 he *b* the sin of many
1 Pet. 2:24 *b* our sins in his own body

BARN (BARNS)
Prov. 3:10 shall thy *b* be filled with plenty

Mat. 6:26 neither do they reap, nor gather into *b*
13:30 gather the wheat into my *b*

BARREN
Gen. 11:30 But Sarai was *b*; she had no child
29:31 opened her womb; but Rachel was *b*
Ex. 23:26 cast their young nor be *b*
1 Sam. 2: 5 so that the *b* hath borne seven
Ps. 113: 9 maketh the *b* woman to keep house
Luke 1: 7 because that Elisabeth was *b*

BASTARD (BASTARDS)
Deut. 23: 2 A *b* shall not enter into the congregation
Heb. 12: 8 are ye *b* and not sons

BATTLE
Gen. 14: 8 *b* of four kings against
2 Chr. 25: 8 be strong for the *b*: God shall
Ps. 140: 7 covered my head in the day of *b*
Eccl. 9:11 not the *b* to the strong
Rev. 16:14 *b* of the great day of God

BEAM (BEAMS)
Mat. 7: 3 the *b* that is in thine own eye

BEAR
Gen. 4:13 punishment greater than I can *b*
Ps. 75: 3 I *b* up the pillars of it
91:12 *b* thee up in their hands
Prov. 18:14 wounded spirit who can *b*
Lam. 3:27 he *b* the yoke in his youth
Mic. 7: 9 I will *b* the indignation of Lord
Luke 13: 9 and if it *b* fruit, well
14:27 whosoever doth not *b* his cross
John 15: 8 that ye *b* much fruit
Rom. 15: 1 strong *b* the infirmities of the weak
1 Cor. 3: 2 hitherto ye were not able to *b*
Gal. 6: 2 *b* ye one another's burdens
6:17 I *b* in my body the marks
Heb. 9:28 offered to *b* the sins of many

BEAREST (BEARETH, BEARING)
Ps. 126: 6 *b* precious seed, shall doubtless
Mat. 13:23 which also *b* fruit, and bringeth
John 15: 2 every branch that *b* fruit
Rom. 2:15 conscience also *b* witness
13: 4 *b* the not sword in vain
1 Cor. 13: 7 *b* all things, believeth all things
Heb. 13:13 without the camp, *b* his reproach

BEARD (BEARDS)
2 Sam. 19:24 nor trimmed his *b*, nor washed

BEAR (BEARS)
2 Ki. 2:24 there came forth two she *b*
Prov. 17:12 Let a *b* be robbed of her whelps
Amos 5:19 from a lion and a *b* met him

BEAST (BEASTS)
Gen. 1:24 and *b* of the earth after his kind
Ps. 49:12 like the *b* that perish
73:22 I was as a *b* before thee
Dan. 7: 3 four great *b* came up from the sea
1 Cor. 15:32 I fought with the *b* at Ephesus
Rev. 4: 6 were four *b* full of eyes before and
13: 1 saw a *b* rise up out of the sea
14: 3 and before the four *b*
19: 4 four *b* fell down and worshipped God

BEAT (BEATEN, BEATETH)
Prov. 23:14 Thou shalt *b* him with the rod
Luke 12:47 shall be *b* with many stripes

BEAUTY
Ex. 28: 2 thy brother for glory and for *b*
2 Chr. 20:21 praise the *b* of holiness
Ps. 29: 2 the Lord in the *b* of holiness
27: 4 to behold the *b* of the Lord
39:11 makest his *b* to consume
96: 9 the Lord in the *b* of holiness
Prov. 20:29 *b* of old men is the gray head
31:30 favour is deceitful and *b* is vain
Is. 61: 3 give unto them *b* for ashes

BEAUTIFY
Ps. 149: 4 he will *b* the meek with salvation

BEAUTIFUL
Eccl. 3:11 every thing *b* in his time
Sol. 6: 4 Thou art *b*, O my love
Is. 64:11 Our holy and our *b* house
Ezek. 16:13 thou was exceeding *b*
Mat. 23:27 which indeed appear *b* outside
Acts 3: 2 temple which is called *b*

Rom. 10:15 How *b* are the feet of them

BED (BEDS)
Ps. 41: 3 make his *b* in sickness
Sol. 1: 1 on my *b* I sought him
Amos 6: 4 lie on *b* of ivory
Heb. 13: 4 and the *b* undefiled but whoremongers

BEG (BEGGED, BEGGING)
Ps. 37:25 forsaken, nor his seed *b* bread
109: 10 children be continually vagabonds and *b*
Prov. 20: 4 therefore shall he *b* in harvest

BEGINNING
Ps. 111:10 fear of the Lord is the *b* of wisdom
Col. 1:18 who is the *b*, the firstborn
2 Pet. 2:20 end is worse than the *b*

BEGOTTEN
Ps. 2: 7 this day have I *b* thee
John 1:14 as of the only *b* of the Father
3:16 that he gave his only *b* Son
1 Pet. 1: 3 *b* us again unto a lively hope
1 John 4: 9 sent his only *b* Son into the world
5: 1 loveth him that is *b* of him
Rev. 1: 5 Christ the first *b* of the dead

BEGUILE (BEGUILED)
Gen. 3:13 The serpent *b* me, and I did eat
Col. 2: 4 lest any man should *b* you

BEHELD
Luke 10:18 I *b* Satan as lightning fall
John 1:14 we *b* his glory, the glory as of
Rev. 11:12 in a cloud and their enemies *b* them

BEHIND
Neh. 9:26 cast thy law *b* their backs
Ps. 139: 5 thou hast beset me *b* and before
Phil. 3:13 forgetting those things which are *b*

BEHOLD
Job 19:27 mine eyes shall *b* and not another
Ps. 17:15 I will *b* thy face in righteousness
27: 4 desired to *b* the beauty of Lord
Is. 32: 1 *b* a king shall reign in righteousness
40:10 *b* the Lord will come with strong hand
42: 1 my servant, whom I uphold; mine
48:10 *b* I have refined thee but not with
49: 1 *b* Lord's hand is not shortened
Mat. 18:10 their angels do always *b* the face of
John 17:24 they may *b* my glory
19: 5 Pilate saith unto them, *b* the man
19:26 unto his mother, Woman *b* thy son
1 Pet. 3: 2 while they *b* your chaste conversation
Rev. 1: 7 *b* he cometh with clouds
1:18 *b* I am alive for evermore
3:20 *b* I stand at the door, and knock
4: 2 a *b* a throne was set in heaven
21: 5 *b* I make all things new

BEHOLDETH (BEHOLDING)
Ps. 33:13 from heaven; he *b* all the sons of men
119: 37 turn away mine eyes from *b* vanity
Prov. 15: 3 *b* the evil and the good
Jas. 1:23 like unto a man *b* his natural face
1:24 he *b* himself and goeth his way

BEING
Ps. 104:33 to my God while I have my *b*
Acts 17:28 and move, and have our *b*

BELIAL
1 Sam. 2:12 sons of Eli were sons of *B*
2 Cor. 6:15 what concord hath Christ with *B*

BELIEVE
Ex. 4: 1 behold, they will not *b* me
Deut. 1:32 ye did not *b* the Lord
2 Chr. 20:20 *b* in the Lord your God
Mat. 9:28 *b* ye that I am able to do this
Mark 1:15 repent and *b* the gospel
9:24 Lord, I *b* help thou mine unbelief
Luke 8:13 which for a while *b* and in time
24:25 slow of heart to *b* all
John 4:48 signs and wonders, ye will not *b*
6:69 we *b* and are sure thou art that Christ
7:39 that *b* on him should receive
8:24 if ye *b* not I am he, ye die
10:26 ye *b* not, because ye are not
11:27 I *b* that thou art the Christ
12:36 *b* in the light while ye have
14: 1 ye *b* in God, *b* also in me

17:20 pray for them who shall *b*
20:25 hand into his side, I will not *b*
20:31 written that ye might *b*
Acts 8:37 I *b* Jesus Christ is the Son
 16:31 *b* on the Lord Jesus Christ
Rom. 3: 3 for what if some did not *b*
 Jesus Christ unto all them that *b*
2 Cor. 4: 4 blinded the mind of them that *b* not
Phil. 1:29 not only to *b* but suffer
2 Thes. 2:13 worketh also in you that *b*
1 Tim. 4:10 especially those that *b*
2 Tim. 2:13 we *b* not, yet he abideth faithful
Heb. 10: 9 *b* to the saving of the soul
 11: 6 cometh to God must *b* that he is
Jas. 2:19 devils also *b* and tremble
1 John 3: 8 on the name of his Son Jesus Christ
 4: 1 beloved, *b* not every spirit

BELIEVED
Gen. 15: 6 *b* in Lord, and he counted
Ps. 78:32 and *b* not for his wondrous works
Jonah 3: 5 people of Nineveh *b* God
Mat. 21:32 publicans and harlots *b* him
John 4:53 himself *b* and his house
 17: 8 have *b* that thou didst send me
Acts 4:32 that *b* were of one heart
Rom. 4:18 against hope *b* in hope
 10:14 in whom they have not *b*
 13:11 salvation nearer than when we *b*
Eph. 1:13 after that ye *b* ye were sealed
2 Thes. 2:12 who *b* not the truth
2 Tim. 1:12 for I know whom I have *b*

BELIEVERS
Acts 5:14 and *b* were the more

BELIEVEST (BELIEVING)
Luke 1:20 because thou *b* not my words
John 1:50 I saw thee under the fig tree, *b* thou
 14:10 *b* thou not that I am in the Father
 20:31 *b* ye might have life
Acts 8:37 if thou *b* with all thine heart
 16:34 *b* in God with all his house
Rom. 15:13 all joy and peace in *b*
1 Pet. 1: 8 yet *b* ye rejoice with joy

BELIEVETH
Prov. 14:15 the simple *b* every word
Mark 9:23 things possible to him that *b*
 16:16 he that *b* shall be saved
Luke 24:41 while they yet *b* not for joy
John 3:15 *b* in him shall not perish
 3:36 *b* on the Son hath everlasting life
 5:24 *b* on him that sent me
 6:35 *b* on me shall never thirst
 6:40 and *b* on him, may have everlasting life
 7:38 that *b* on me out of his belly shall flow
 11:26 he that *b* in me shall never die
 12:46 *b* on me should not abide in darkness
 14:12 *b* on me the works that I do
Rom. 1:16 unto salvation to every one that *b*
 3:26 justifier of him that *b* in Jesus
 9:33 *b* on him shall not be ashamed
 10: 4 for righteousness to every one that *b*
1 Cor. 7:12 brother hath a wife that *b* not
 13: 7 *b* all things, hopeth all things
1 Pet. 2: 6 *b* on him shall not be confounded
1 John 5: 1 whosoever *b* that Jesus is the Christ

BELLY
Gen. 3:14 upon thy *b* shalt thou go
Job 15: 2 fill his *b* with the east wind
 20:15 God cast them out of his *b*
Ps. 17:14 whose *b* thou fillest
 22:10 art my God from my mother's *b*
 44:25 our *b* cleaveth to the earth
Jonah 1:17 was in the *b* of fish
 2: 1 prayed to God out of the fish's *b*
John 7:38 out of his *b* shall flow
1 Cor. 6:13 meats for the *b* and the *b* for
Phil. 3:19 whose god is their *b*, and whose glory
Rev. 10: 9 it shall make thy *b* bitter

BELONG (BELONGETH)
Gen. 40: 8 interpretations *b* to God
Deut. 29:29 secret things *b* to the Lord
Ps. 3: 8 salvation *b* to the Lord
 47: 9 shields of the earth *b* to God
 62:11 heard this; that power *b* unto God

68:20 to God *b* the issues from death
Dan. 9: 9 to the Lord *b* mercies and forgivenesses
Mark 9:41 because ye *b* to Christ
1 Cor. 7:32 for the things that *b* to the Lord

BELOVED
Deut. 21:15 two wives, one *b* and another hated
Ps. 127: 2 Lord giveth his *b* sleep
Sol. 4:16 let my *b* come into his garden
Dan. 10:11 O Daniel, a man, greatly *b*
Mat. 3:17 this is my *b* Son, in whom
 17: 5 this is my *b* Son, in whom
Rom. 11:28 they are *b* for the fathers' sake
Eph. 1: 6 made us accepted in the *b*
Col. 3:12 as the elect of God holy and *b*
 4:14 Luke the *b* physician

BEND (BENDETH, BENDING, BENT)
Ps. 11: 2 the wicked *b* their bow
 37:14 and have *b* their bow, to cast
 58: 7 when he *b* his bow to shoot
Jer. 9: 3 *b* their tongues like a bow
Zech. 9:13 I have *b* Judah for me

BENEFACTORS
Luke 22:25 authority upon them are called *b*

BENEFITS
Ps. 68:19 who daily loadeth us with *b*
 103: 2 forget not all his *b*
 116:12 render to Lord for all his *b*

BEREAVED
Gen. 43:14 If I be *b* of my children
Jer. 18:21 let their wives be *b* of their children
Hos. 13: 8 a bear that is *b* of her whelps

BESEECH (BESOUGHT)
2 Sam.12:16 David therefore *b* God for the child
Mal. 1: 9 *b* God that he will be gracious
2 Cor. 5:20 as though God did *b* you by us

BESET
Ps. 139: 5 Thou hast *b* me behind and before
Heb. 12: 1 sin which doth so easily *b* us

BESTOW (BESTOWED)
John 4:38 whereon ye *b* no labour
1 Cor. 12:23 *b* more abundant honour
 13: 3 *b* all my goods to feed the poor
 15:10 his grace which was *b* on me
2 Cor. 8: 1 grace of God *b* on the churches
Gal. 4:11 have *b* upon you labour in vain
1 John 3: 1 love the Father hath *b* on us

BETRAY (BETRAYETH)
Mat. 24:10 be offended, and shall *b* one another
 26:21 one of you shall *b* me
Mark 13:12 brother shall *b* the brother to death
 14:18 which eateth with me shall *b* me
Luke 22:21 the hand of him that *b* me is with me
John 13:21 one of you shall *b* me

BETROTH
Hos. 2:19 I will *b* thee unto me for ever

BETTER
1 Sam. 1: 8 am I not *b* to thee than ten sons
Prov. 15:16 *b* is little with fear of the Lord
 15:17 *b* is a dinner of herbs where love
 16: 8 *b* is a little with righteousness
 17: 1 *b* is a dry morsel, and quietness
 27:10 *b* is a neighbour near than
Eccl. 4:13 *b* is a poor and wise child than
 7: 1 *b* is a good name than precious
 7: 2 *b* to go to the house of mourning
 7: 3 *b* is sorrow than laughter
 7: 8 the patient in spirit is *b* than
 9:16 wisdom is *b* than strength
Sol. 1: 2 for thy love is *b* than wine
1 Cor. 9:15 it were *b* for me to die
Phil. 1:23 with Christ; which is far *b*
 2: 3 esteem others *b* than themselves
Heb. 1: 4 made so much *b* than the angels
 7:22 Jesus made a surety of a *b* testament
 8: 6 mediator of a *b* covenant
 11:16 now they desire a *b* country
 11:35 might obtain a *b* resurrection
 12:24 blood speaketh *b* than Abel

BEWARE
Mat. 7:15 *b* of false prophets,
 16: 6 *b* of the leaven of Pharisees
Luke 12:15 *b* of covetousness: for a man's life

Phil. 3: 2 *b* of dogs, *b* of evil
Col. 2: 8 *b* lest any man spoil
2 Pet. 3:17 *b* lest ye also being led away

BILL
Deut. 24: 1 let him write her a *b* of divorcement
Luke 16: 6 take thy *b*, and sit down

BIND
Job 31:36 I would *b* it as a crown
Ps. 105:22 *b* his princes at pleasure
Prov. 3: 3 *b* them about thy neck
Is. 8:16 *b* up the testimony,
Mat. 12:29 first *b* the strong man
 16:19 thou shalt *b* on earth

BIRD (BIRDS)
Gen. 15:10 but the *b* divided he not
Ps. 104:17 *b* make their nests
 124: 7 soul is escaped as a *b*
Eccl. 10:20 *b* of the air shall carry the voice
Is. 46:11 ravenous *b* from the
Jer. 5:27 as a cage is full of *b*
Mat. 8:20 the *b* of the air have nests

BIRTH
Eccl. 7: 1 of death than the day of one's *b*
Is. 66: 9 shall I bring to the *b*,
Gal. 4:19 whom I travail in *b* again

BIRTHRIGHT
Gen. 25:31 sell me this day thy *b*
 27:36 he took away my *b*;
 43:33 the firstborn according to his *b*
Heb. 12:16 for one morsel of meat sold his *b*

BISHOP (BISHOPS)
Phil. 1: 1 at Philippi, with *b* and deacons
1 Tim. 3: 1 desire the office of *b*
Tit. 1: 7 for a *b* must be blameless
1 Pet. 2:25 shepherd and *b* of souls

BITE (BITETH)
Prov. 23:32 at last it *b* like a serpent
Amos 9: 3 command the serpent, and he shall *b* thee
Mic. 3: 5 prophets *b* with their teeth
Gal. 5:15 if ye *b* and devour one another

BITTER
Ex. 1:14 made their lives *b* with hard bondage
 12: 8 with *b* herbs they shall eat it
Deut. 32:32 grapes of gall, their clusters are *b*
Job 3:20 life given to the *b* in soul
Ps. 64: 3 to shoot their arrows even *b* words
Prov. 27: 7 every *b* thing is sweet
Is. 5:20 woe to them that put *b* for sweet
Col. 3:19 wives and be not *b* against them
Jas. 3:14 if ye have *b* envying and strife
Rev. 10: 9 and it shall make thy belly *b*

BITTERNESS
1 Sam. 1:10 she was in *b* of soul, and prayed
2 Sam. 2:26 it will be *b* in the end
Prov. 14:10 heart knows its own *b*
Rom. 3:14 whose mouth full of cursing and *b*
Eph. 4:31 let all *b* . . . be put away from you
Heb. 12:15 root of *b* springing up trouble you

BLACK
Sol. 1: 5 look not upon me because I am *b*
Mat. 5:36 canst not make one hair white or *b*

BLAME (BLAMED)
2 Cor. 6: 3 that the ministry be not *b*
Eph. 1: 4 we should be holy and without *b*

BLAMELESS
Gen. 44:10 and ye shall be found *b*
Mat. 12: 5 profane the sabbath, and are *b*
Luke 1: 6 in ordinances of the Lord *b*
1 Cor. 1: 8 *b* in the day of our Lord
Phil. 3: 6 righteous which is in the law *b*
1 Thes. 5:23 soul and body be preserved *b* unto the
1 Tim. 3: 2 bishop then must be *b*, the husband
 3:10 office of a deacon being found *b*
2 Pet. 3:14 of him in peace, without spot and *b*

BLASPHEME (BLASPHEMED, BLASPHEMETH)
Lev. 24:16 *b* the name of the Lord
Ps. 74:10 shall the enemy *b* thy name forever
Is. 52: 5 my name continually every day is *b*
Mark 3:29 *b* against Holy Ghost hath never
Luke 12:10 unto him that *b* against the Holy
Rom. 2:24 is *b* among the Gentiles through you

1 Tim.   1:20 that they may learn not to *b*
Rev.   16:11 and *b* the God of heaven

BLASPHEMER (BLASPHEMERS)
1 Tim.   1:13 who was before a *b*, and a persecutor
2 Tim.   3: 2 covetous, boasters, proud, *b*

BLASPHEMY
2 Ki.   19: 3 day of trouble, and of rebuke, and *b*
Mat.   12:31 and *b* shall be forgiven unto men
Mark   7:22 an evil eye, *b*, pride, foolishness
Col.   3: 8 off all these; anger, wrath, malice, *b*
Rev.   2: 9 I know the *b* of them which say

BLEMISH
Ex.   12: 5 Your lamb shall be without *b*
Lev.   1: 3 let him offer a male without *b*
Dan.   1: 4 children in whom was no *b*
Eph.   5:27 that it should be holy and without *b*
1 Pet.   1:19 as of a lamb without *b* and without

BLESS
Gen.   12: 3 I will *b* them that *b* thee
Ex.   24: 1 pleased the Lord to *b* Israel
Num.   6:24 Lord *b* thee and keep thee
Deut.   8:10 thou shalt *b* the Lord thy God
Ps.   5:12 Thou, Lord wilt *b* the righteous
  16: 7 I will *b* the Lord
  29:11 will *b* his people with peace
  63: 4 Thus will I *b* thee while I live
  67: 1 be merciful to us and *b* us
  104: 35 *b* the Lord, O my soul
  132: 15 I will abundantly *b* her
  134: 3 the Lord *b* thee out of Zion
  145: 2 Every day will I *b* thee
Rom.   12:14 *b* them that persecute
1 Cor.   4:12 being reviled we *b*

BLESSED
Gen.   1:22 God *b* them, saying,
  2: 3 God *b* the seventh day
Ex.   20:11 the Lord *b* the sabbath day
Ps.   1: 1 *b* is the man that walketh not in the
  32: 1 is he whose transgression is
  33:12 *b* is the nation whose God is
  34: 8 *b* is the man that trusteth in him
  41: 1 *b* is he that considereth the poor
  65: 4 *b* is the man whom thou choosest
  84: 5 *b* is the man whose strength is in thee
  112: 1 *b* is the man *that* feareth the Lord
Prov.   8:32 *b* are they that keep my ways
  10: 7 memory of the just is *b*
Is.   30:18 *b* are all they that wait
Jer.   17: 7 *b* is the man that trusteth in the Lord
Mat.   5: 3 *b* are the poor in spirit
  5: 4 *b* are they that mourn
  5: 5 *b* are the meek
  5: 6 *b* are they which do hunger and thirst
  5: 7 *b* are the merciful
  5: 8 *b* are the pure in heart
  5: 9 *b* are the peacemakers
  5:10 *b* are they which are persecuted
  11: 6 *b* is he whosoever not offended in me
  13:16 *b* are your eyes for they see
  21: 9 *b* is he that cometh in the name of the
      Lord
Mark   10:16 his arms and *b* them
Luke   1:28 *b* art thou among women
  1:48 all generations shall call me *b*
  11:28 *b* are they that hear the word
John   20:29 *b* are they that have not seen, and
Acts   20:35 it is more *b* to give
Rom.   4: 7 *b* are they whose iniquities are . . .
1 Tim.   6:15 *b* and only Potentate
Jas.   1:12 *b* is the man that endureth temptation
Rev.   14:13 *b* are the dead which die in the Lord
  19: 9 *b* are they which are called unto the
      marriage supper
  22: 7 *b* is he that keepeth the sayings
  22:14 *b* are they that do his commandments

BLESSEDNESS
Gal.   4:15 where is then the *b* ye spake of

BLESSING (BLESSINGS)
Gen.   12: 2 name great; and thou shalt be a *b*
  27:36 now he hath taken away my *b*
  49:25 bless thee with *b* of heaven above
Deut.   11:26 set before you a *b* and a curse
  23: 5 turned curse into a *b*

Neh.   9: 5 name, which is exalted above all *b*
Ps.   3: 8 thy *b* is upon thy people
  129: 8 the *b* of the Lord be upon you
Prov.   28:20 faithful man shall abound with *b*
Is.   65: 8 destroy it not, for a *b* is in it
1 Cor.   10:16 cup of *b* which we bless
Eph.   1: 3 hath blessed us with all spiritual *b*
Jas.   3:10 same mouth proceedeth *b* and cursing

BLIND
Job   29:15 I was eyes to the *b*,
Ps.   146: 8 openeth the eyes of the *b*
Is.   42: 7 to open the *b* eyes, to bring out
Mat.   11: 5 the *b* receive their sight
  23:16 woe unto you ye *b* guides
Luke   4:18 recovery of sight to the *b*
Rev.   3:17 not that thou art . . .is

BLINDED
John   12:40 he hath *b* their eyes and hardened
2 Cor.   4: 4 god of this world *b* the minds
1 John   2:11 that darkness hath *b* his eyes

BLOOD
Gen.   4:11 receive thy brother's *b* from thy hand
Job   16:18 cover thou not my *b*,
Ps.   72:14 precious is their *b* in his sight
Ezek.   3:18 his *b* will I require at thine hand
Mic.   3:10 they build up Zion with *b*
Mat.   26:28 This is my *b* of the new testament
  27: 8 that field was called the field of *b*
  27:25 his *b* be on us and on our children
John   1:13 born not of *b* nor of flesh
  6:54 drinketh my *b* hath eternal life
Acts   17:26 made of one *b* all nations
Rom.   3:25 through faith in his *b*
1 Cor.   11:27 guilty of the body and *b* of the Lord
Eph.   1: 7 redemption through his *b* even
      forgiveness
Col.   1:20 peace through the *b* of the cross
Heb.   9:20 This is the *b* of the testament
  10:19 into the holiest by the *b* of Jesus
  12: 4 ye have not yet resisted unto *b*
1 Pet.   1: 2 sprinkling of the *b* of Jesus
  1:19 with the precious *b* of Christ
1 John   1: 7 *b* of Jesus Christ cleanseth us
Rev.   1: 5 washed us in his own *b*
  6:10 dost thou not avenge our *b*
  16: 6 thou hast given them *b* to drink
  17: 6 drunken with the *b* of saints

BLOODGUILTINESS
Ps.   51:14 deliver me from *b*, O God

BLOSSOM (BLOSSOMED)
Is.   5:24 their *b* shall go up as dust
  27: 6 Israel shall *b* and bud
  35: 1 the desert shall *b* as the rose
Ezek.   7:10 rod hath *b*, pride hath
Hab.   3:17 the fig tree shall not *b*

BLOT (BLOTTED, BLOTTETH)
Ex.   32:32 *b* me out of thy book
2 Ki.   14:27 he would *b* out the name of Israel
Neh.   4: 5 let not their sin be *b* out
Job   31: 7 if any *b* hath cleaved to mine hands
Ps.   51: 1 *b* out my transgressions
  109: 13 let their name be *b* out
Is.   43:25 I am he that *b* out thy transgressions
Jer.   18:23 neither *b* out their sin from thy sight
Acts   3:19 that your sins may be *b* out

BOAST (BOASTETH)
Ps.   34: 2 my soul shall make her *b* in the Lord
Prov.   27: 1 *b* not thyself of tomorrow
Eph.   2: 9 not of works lest any man should *b*
Jas.   3: 5 *b* as he that putteth it off

BODY
Deut.   28:11 in the fruit of thy *b*, and in
Mat.   6:22 light of the *b* is the eye
  10:28 fear not them which kill the *b*
  26:26 take, eat: this is my *b*
John   2:21 spake of the temple of his *b*
Rom.   6: 6 *b* of sin might be destroyed
  7: 4 dead to the law by the *b* of Christ
  7:24 me from the *b* of this death
  8:23 the redemption of our *b*
1 Cor.   5: 3 absent in *b*, but present in spirit
  6:19 *b* is the temple of Holy Ghost
  7: 4 wife hath not power of her own *b*

  11:29 not discerning the Lord's *b*
  12:14 the *b* is not one member, but many
  12:27 ye are the *b* of Christ
  15:44 it is raised a spiritual *b*
2 Cor.   5: 6 home in *b* absent from the Lord
  12: 2 whether in *b* or out I cannot
Eph.   4:12 for edifying the *b* of Christ
  5:23 he is the saviour of the *b*
Phil.   1:20 Christ magnified in my *b*
  3:21 shall change our vile *b*
Col.   1:18 head of the *b* the church
  2:23 humility, and neglecting of the *b*
Heb.   10: 5 but a *b* hast thou prepared
  13: 3 yourselves also in the *b*
Jas.   3: 6 tongue defileth the whole *b*
1 Pet.   2:24 bare our sins in his own *b*

BODIES
Rom.   8:11 quicken your mortal *b* by your spirit
  12: 1 present your *b* a living sacrifice
1 Cor.   6:15 your *b* are the members of Christ
Eph.   5:28 love wives as their own *b*

BODILY
1 Tim.   4: 8 *b* exercise profiteth little

BOLD (BOLDLY)
Prov.   28: 1 righteous are *b* as a lion
2 Cor.   10: 1 being absent am *b* toward you
  11:21 if any is *b* I am *b* also
Heb.   4:16 come *b* to throne of grace

BOLDNESS
Eph.   3:12 in whom we have *b* and
Heb.   10:19 *b* to enter into the holiest

BOND (BONDS)
Ezek.   20:37 bring you into the *b* of the covenant
1 Cor.   12:13 whether we be *b* or free
Gal.   3:28 there is neither *b* nor free
Eph.   4: 3 unity of Spirit in the *b* of peace
  6:20 I am an ambassador in *b*
Phil.   1:16 to add affliction to my *b*
Col.   3:11 *b* nor free but Christ is all

BONDAGE
Rom.   8:15 spirit of *b* again to fear
1 Cor.   7:15 brother or a sister is not under *b*

BONE (BONES)
Gen.   2:23 this is now *b* of my bones
Ex.   12:46 neither shall ye break a *b* thereof
Ps.   6: 2 heal me, my *b* are vexed
  22:14 all my *b* are out of joint
  32: 3 my *b* waxed old
  34:20 he keepeth all his *b*: not one of
  51: 8 *b* which thou hast broken may
Eccl.   11: 5 how the *b* do grow in the womb
Ezek.   37: 1 valley which was full of dry *b*
Mat.   23:27 are within full of dead men's *b*
John   19:36 *b* of him shall not be broken

BOOK (BOOKS)
Ex.   32:32 blot me out of thy *b*
Job   19:23 O that they were printed in a *b*
Ps.   139:16 in thy *b* all my members were written
Eccl.   12:12 of making many *b* there is no end
John   21:25 could not contain the *b* that should be
Phil.   4: 3 whose names are in the *b* of life
Heb.   10: 7 the volume of the *b* it is written
Rev.   3: 5 name out of the *b* of life
  20:15 not found written in the *b* of life
  22:19 words of the *b* of this prophecy

BORN
Job   5: 7 Yet man is *b* unto trouble
Prov.   17:17 brother is *b* for adversity
Eccl.   3: 2 a time to be *b* and a time to die
Is.   9: 6 unto us a child is *b* unto us
Mat.   26:24 better if he had not been *b*
Luke   7:28 among those that are *b* of women
John   3: 3 except a man be *b* again
  3: 5 *b* of water and of the Spirit
  3: 7 said unto thee ye must be *b* again
1 Cor.   15: 8 as of one *b* out of due time
Gal.   4:23 bond woman was *b* after the flesh
1 John   3: 9 is *b* of God doth not commit
  4: 7 everyone that loveth if *b* of God

BORROWER
Prov.   22: 7 the *b* is servant to the lender
Is.   24: 2 as with the lender so with the *b*

BOSOM

Deut.	13:	6 wife of thy *b*; or thy friend
Ps.	35:13	my prayer returned into my own *b*
	74:11	pluck thy hand out of thy *b*
	89:50	how I do bear in my *b*
Prov.	5:20	and embrace the *b* of a stranger
	19:24	hideth his hands in his *b*
Eccl.	7: 9	anger resteth in the *b* of fools
Is.	40:11	his arm, and carry them in his *b*
Jer.	32:18	fathers into the *b* of their children
Luke	16:22	carried by the angels into Abraham's *b*

BOTTLE (BOTTLES)

Ps.	56: 8	put thou my tears into thy *b*
Jer.	13:12	every *b* filled with wine
Mat.	9:17	do men put new wine into new *b*
Mark	2:22	no man putteth new wine into new *b*

BOUGHT

Deut.	32: 6	is not he thy father that hath *b* thee?
1 Cor.	6:20	For ye are *b* with a price
	7:23	Ye are *b* with a price

BOUND

Gen.	22: 9	b Isaac his son,
Prov.	22:15	foolishness is *b* in the heart
Is.	61: 1	prison to them that are *b*
Mat.	16:19	bind on earth shall be *b* in heaven
Acts	20:22	I go *b* in the spirit
	21:13	ready not to be *b* only,
Rom.	7: 2	wife is *b* to her husband
1 Cor.	7:39	the wife is *b* by law
2 Tim.	2: 9	word of God is not *b*

BOW (BOWS)

Gen.	9:13	I do set my *b* in the clouds
Josh.	24:12	not with thy sword nor with thy *b*
1 Sam.	2: 4	the *b* of the mighty men are broken
Ps.	11: 2	lo, the wicked bend their *b*
	37:15	their *b* shall be broken
	44: 6	I will not trust in my *b*
Jer.	9: 3	bend their tongue like their *b* for lies
Lam.	2: 4	bent his *b* like an enemy
Hos.	1: 5	break the *b* of Israel
	7:16	turned like a deceitful *b*

BOW (BOWED, BOWETH)

Judg.	7: 5	every one that *b* down upon his knees
2 Ki.	19:16	Lord, *b* down thine ear
Ps.	31: 2	b down thine ear to me
	38: 6	I am *b* down greatly; I go mourning
	95: 6	let us worship and *b* down
	145:14	raiseth up all that be *b* down
Is.	2:11	haughtiness of men shall be *b* down

BOWELS

Gen.	43:30	his *b* did yearn upon his brother
2 Chr.	21:18	the Lord smote him in his *b*
Ps.	71: 6	took me out of my mother's *b*
Jer.	31:20	my *b* are troubled for him
Acts	1:18	in the midst and, all his *b* gushed out
Col.	3:12	put on the *b* of mercies
Philem.	1: 7	b of the saints are refreshed
1 John	3:17	shutteth up his *b* of compassion

BRAKE

Job	29:17	b the jaws of the wicked
Ps.	105:16	b the whole staff of bread
	107:14	b their bands in sunder
Jer.	31:32	my covenant they *b* although I was
Ezek.	17:16	and whose covenant he *b*, even with him
Dan.	6:24	b all their bones to pieces
Mat.	14:19	he blessed and *b*, and gave the loaves
	15:36	and gave thanks, and *b* them
	26:26	blessed it, and *b* it and gave it
Mark	6:41	and blessed, and *b* the loaves
	14:22	took bread, and blessed and *b* it
Luke	22:19	took bread, and gave thanks, and *b* it
	24:30	took bread, and blessed it, and *b*
1 Cor.	11:24	he *b* it and said, Take,

BRANCH

Job	14: 7	the tender *b* thereof will not cease
Prov.	11:28	righteous shall flourish as a *b*
Is.	4: 2	shall the *b* of the Lord be beautiful
	11: 1	a *b* shall grow out of
Jer.	23: 5	I will raise unto David a righteous *B*
Zech.	3: 8	bring forth my servant the *B*
	6:12	behold the man whose name is the *B*
Mal.	4: 1	leave neither root nor *b*
Mat.	24:32	fig tree; when his *b* is yet tender

BRANCHES

John	15: 4	As the *b* cannot bear fruit of itself
	15: 6	cast forth as a *b* and is withered

BRANCHES

Job	15:30	flame shall dry up his *b*
Ps.	80:11	sent her *b* unto the river
Is.	17: 6	four or five in the outmost fruitful *b*
Jer.	11:16	the *b* of it are broken
Dan.	4:14	hew down the tree, and cut off his *b*
Hos.	14: 6	his *b* shall spread and his beauty
Zech.	4:12	what be these two olive *b*
John	15: 5	I am the vine, ye are the *b*
Rom.	11:16	root be holy, so are the *b*

BRASS

Num.	21: 9	And Moses made a serpent of *b*
Deut.	28:23	that is over thy head shall be *b*
Job	41:27	he esteemeth *b* as rotten wood
Is.	48: 4	thy neck iron, and thy brow *b*
Dan.	2:32	his belly and his thighs of *b*
1 Cor.	13: 1	I am become as sounding *b* and
Rev.	1:15	his feet like unto fine *b*

BREACH (BREACHES)

Gen.	38:29	this *b* be upon thee: therefore his
Ps.	60: 2	heal the *b* thereof; for it shaketh
	106: 23	his chosen stood before him in the *b*
Is.	30:13	this iniquity shall be to you as *b*
	58:12	shalt be called the repairer of the *b*

BREAD

Gen.	3:19	sweat of thy face shalt thou eat *b*
	28:20	will give me *b* to eat
Ex.	12:15	shall ye eat unleavened *b*
	16: 4	I will rain *b* from heaven
Lev.	21: 6	b of their God they do offer
Num.	21: 5	soul loatheth this light *b*
Deut.	8: 3	man doth not live by *b*
	16: 3	b therewith even the *b* of affliction
1 Sam.	2: 5	hired themselves for *b*
Neh.	9:15	gavest them *b* from heaven
Ps.	37:25	nor his seed begging *b*
	80: 5	feedest them with *b* of tears
	102: 9	I have eaten ashes like *b*
	105:16	he brake the whole staff of *b*
	127: 2	to eat the *b* of sorrows
	132: 15	satisfy her poor with *b*
Prov.	9:17	b eaten in secret is pleasant
	20:17	b of deceit is sweet to a man
	25:21	be hungry, give him *b* to eat
	31:27	she eateth not *b* of idleness
Eccl.	9:11	neither yet *b* to the wise
	11: 1	cast thy *b* upon the waters
Is.	30:20	Lord give you *b* of adversity
	55: 2	money for that which is not *b*
	58: 7	deal thy *b* to the hungry
Ezek.	18: 7	hath given his *b* to the hungry
Amos	4: 6	want of *b* in all your places
Mat.	4: 4	not live by *b* alone
	6:11	Give us this day our daily *b*
	7: 9	son ask *b* will he give a stone
	15:26	meet to take the children's *b*
	26:26	took *b* and blessed it
Mark	7: 5	but eat *b* with unwashen hands
Luke	7:33	neither eating *b* nor drinking wine
	15:17	servants of my father's have *b* enough
John	6:32	Moses gave you not that *b*
	6:35	I am the *b* of life
	6:50	this is the *b* that cometh down
	13:18	he that eateth *b* with me
Acts	2:42	breaking of *b* and in prayer
	20: 7	came together to break *b*
	27:35	he took *b* and gave thanks
1 Cor.	10:16	b we break is it not the communion
	5: 8	with the unleavened *b* of sincerity and truth
	10:17	we many are one *b* and one body
	11:26	for as often as ye eat this *b*
2 Thes.	3:12	they work, and eat their own *b*

BREAK

Ezra	9:14	should we again *b* thy commandments
Job	19: 2	and *b* me in pieces with words
Ps.	2: 3	let us *b* their bands asunder
	2: 9	shalt *b* them with a rod of iron
	10:15	b thou the arm of the wicked
	58: 6	b their teeth in their mouth
Eccl.	3: 3	a time to *b* down,

BREAK

Is.	14: 7	they *b* forth into singing
	42: 3	bruised reed shall be not *b*
	45: 2	I will break in pieces the gates
	55:12	the hills shall *b* forth
Jer.	14:21	b not thy covenant with us
	33:20	if ye can *b* my covenant of the day
Ezek.	17:15	b the covenant and be delivered
Dan.	7:23	tread it down, and *b* it into pieces
Hos.	1: 5	that I will *b* the bow of Israel
Zech.	11:10	that I might *b* my covenant which I
Mat.	5:19	b one of these least commandments
	6:19	thieves *b* through and steal
1 Cor.	10:16	bread which we *b*, is

BREAKETH (BREAKING)

Job	9:17	he *b* me with a tempest
Ps.	29: 5	voice of the Lord *b* the cedars
	46: 9	b the bow and cutteth the spear
	119: 20	my soul *b* for the longing
Prov.	25:15	a soft tongue that *b* the bone
Jer.	23:29	like a hammer that *b* rocks
Luke	24:35	known of them in *b* of bread
Acts	2:42	and in *b* of bread, and in prayer

BREAST (BREASTS)

Gen.	49:25	blessings of the *b*, and of the womb
Ps.	22: 9	I was upon my mother's *b*
Prov.	5:19	let her *b* satisfy thee
Sol.	1:13	all night between my *b*
	4: 5	thy *b* are like two roes
	7: 7	thy *b* to clusters of grapes
	8: 8	a little sister, and she hath no *b*
Is.	28: 9	from the milk and drawn from the *b*
	66:11	satisfied with the *b* of her consolation
Ezek.	16: 7	thy *b* are fashioned, and thine hair
Hos.	2: 2	adulteries from between her *b*
Joel	2:16	the children, and those that suck *b*
Rev.	15: 6	their *b* girded with golden girdles

BREASTPLATE (BREASTPLATE)

Ex.	28: 4	garments which they shall make; a *b*
Eph.	6:14	having on the *b* of righteousness
1 Thes.	5: 8	putting on the *b* of faith and love
Rev.	9:17	having *b* of fire and of jacinth

BREATH

Gen.	2: 7	into his nostrils the *b* of life
Job	15:30	by the *b* of his mouth
	17: 1	my *b* is corrupt, my days are extinct
	33: 4	b of the Almighty hath given me life
	37:10	by the *b* of God frost is given
	41:21	his *b* kindleth coals
Ps.	104:29	thou takest away their *b*
	146: 4	b goeth forth, he returneth
Is.	11: 4	b of his lips shall he slay
	30:28	his *b*, as an overflowing stream
	30:33	the *b* of the Lord doth kindle it
	33:11	your *b* as fire shall devour you
Dan.	5:23	in whose hand thy *b* is
Acts	17:25	giveth to all life and *b*

BREATHE (BREATHED, BREATHING)

Ps.	27:12	such as *b* out cruelty
Ezek.	37: 9	come *b* upon these slain
John	20:22	he *b* on them, and saith unto
Acts	9: 1	b out threatenings and slaughter

BRETHREN

Gen.	45:16	Joseph's *b* are come: and it pleased
	50:15	Joseph's *b* saw their father was dead
Deut.	17:20	be not lifted up above his *b*
	25: 5	if *b* dwell together, and one of them die
1 Chr.	4: 9	more honourable than his *b*
Job	6:15	my *b* dealt deceitfully
	19:13	put my *b* far from me
Ps.	22:22	declare thy name unto my *b*
	69: 8	become a stranger to my *b*
	133: 1	for *b* to dwell in unity
Prov.	6:19	soweth discord among *b*
Hos.	13:15	though he be fruitful among his *b*
Mat.	12:48	my mother, who are my *b*
	19:29	forsaken houses, or *b* or sisters
	23: 8	even Christ and all ye are *b*
	25:40	the least of these my *b*
	28:10	go tell my *b* that they
Mark	10:29	man that hath left house or *b*
Luke	14:26	hate not . . . *b*, sisters,
	21:16	betrayed by both by parents and *b*
John	7: 5	neither did his *b* believe

| | 20:17 | go to my *b* and say, I ascend |

Acts 10:23 certain *b* from Joppa accompanied
15: 3 caused great joy to all the *b*
15:40 by the *b* unto the grace of God
18:27 *b* wrote exhorting the disciples
Rom. 8:29 the firstborn among many *b*
9: 3 accursed from Christ for my *b*
1 Cor. 6: 5 to judge between his *b*
8:12 when ye sin so against the *b*
15: 6 seen of above five hundred *b* at once
Gal. 2: 4 false *b* unawares brought in
1 Tim. 4: 6 If thou put the *b* in remembrance
5: 1 a father and the younger men as *b*
Heb. 2:11 is not ashamed to call them *b*
1 Pet. 1:22 Spirit unto unfeigned love of the *b*
3: 8 love as *b* be pitiful,

BRIBE (BRIBES)
1 Sam. 8: 3 turned aside after lucre, and took *b*
Ps. 26:10 right hand is full of *b*

BRIDE
Is. 61:10 as a *b* adorneth herself
Jer. 2:32 can a *b* forget her attire
John 3:29 hath *b* is the bridegroom
Rev. 21: 2 as a *b* adorned for her husband
21: 9 show thee the *b* the Lamb's wife

BRIDEGROOM
Ps. 19: 5 as *b* coming out of the chamber
Is. 62: 5 as a *b* rejoiceth over the bride
Joel 2:16 let the *b* go forth of his chamber
Mat. 9:15 as long as the *b* is with them
25: 1 went forth to meet the *b*
John 2: 9 the governor of the feast called the *b*
Rev. 18:23 voice of the *b* and of the

BRIDLE (BRIDLETH)
Job 30:11 loose the *b* before me
Ps. 32: 9 must be held in with bit and *b*
39: 1 I will keep my mouth as with a *b*
Is. 37:29 put my *b* in thy lips
Jas. 1:26 *b* not his tongue, but deceiveth
3: 2 able to *b* the whole body

BRIER (BRIERS)
Judg. 8:16 and thorns of the wilderness and *b*
Is. 55:13 instead of *b* shall come up myrtle
Ezek. 2: 6 though *b* and thorns be with thee
Heb. 6: 8 that which beareth thorns and *b* is rejected

BRIGHT
Job 37:11 he scattereth his *b* cloud
Ezek. 1:13 the fire was *b* and out of
Nah. 3: 3 up both the *b* sword and the glittering
Rev. 22:16 of David, and the *b* and morning star

BRIGHTNESS
Is. 59: 9 for *b* but we walk in darkness
Ezek. 10: 4 full of the *b* of the Lord's glory
28: 7 they shall defile thy *b*
Dan. 12: 3 shine as the *b* of the firmament
Hab. 3: 4 and his *b* was as the light
Acts 26:13 a light above the *b* of the sun
2 Thes. 2: 8 Lord with the *b* of his coming
Heb. 1: 3 being the *b* of his glory

BRIMSTONE
Gen. 19:24 rained upon Sodom and upon Gomorrah *b*
Is. 34: 9 dust thereof into *b*, land burning
Luke 17:29 it rained fire and *b* from heaven
Rev. 19:20 cast into a lake of fire and *b*

BRING
Gen. 1:24 the earth *b* forth the living creature
Job 33:30 to *b* back his soul from the pit
Ps. 92:14 they shall still bring forth fruit in old age
Eccl. 11: 9 God will *b* thee into judgment
Is. 43: 5 I will *b* thy seed from the east
46:13 I *b* near my righteousness
Hos. 2:14 *b* her into wilderness and speak
Zeph. 3: 5 every morning doth he *b* his judgment
Mat. 1:21 she shall *b* forth a son
Luke 2:10 I *b* you good tidings of great joy
3: 8 *b* forth fruits worthy of repentance
8:14 this life, and *b* no fruit to perfection
John 12:24 if it die it *b* much fruit
15: 2 that it may *b* forth more fruit
1 Cor. 1:28 *b* to nought things that are
4: 5 *b* to light the hidden things

1 Pet. 3:18 that he might *b* us to God

BRINGETH
Ps. 1: 3 *b* forth fruit in his season
Mat. 3:10 every tree which *b* not forth good fruit
7:19 every tree that *b* not forth good fruit
Luke 6:43 a good tree *b* not forth corrupt fruit
Jas. 1:15 when lust hath conceived, it *b* forth sin

BROAD
Mat. 7:13 *b* is the way that leadeth to destruction

BROKEN
Gen. 17:14 he hath *b* my covenant
Ps. 34:18 nigh unto them that are of a *b* heart
51: 8 bones which thou hast *b* rejoice
51:17 a *b* spirit, a *b* and a contrite heart
147: 3 He healeth the *b* in heart, and bindeth
Prov. 17:22 but a *b* spirit drieth the bones
Eccl. 4:12 a threefold cord is not quickly *b*
Is. 61: 1 sent me to bind up the *b* hearted
Jer. 2:13 hewed them out cisterns, *b* cisterns
Hos. 5:11 Ephraim is oppressed and *b* in judgment
Mat. 21:44 fall on this stone shall be *b*

BROOK
Is. 19: 6 the *b* of defence shall be emptied

BROTHER
Prov. 17:17 a *b* is born for adversity
18:19 a *b* offended is harder to be won
18:24 a friend that sticketh closer than a *b*
27:10 neighbour that is near, than a *b* far off
Mat. 10:21 *b* shall deliver up *b* to death
Mark 13:12 *b* shall betray the *b* to death
1 Cor. 7:15 A *b* or sister is not under bondage
8:11 knowledge shall the weak *b* perish
1 Thes. 4: 6 no man go beyond and defraud his *b*
2 Thes. 3:15 admonish him as a *b*
Jas. 1: 9 let the *b* of low degree rejoice

BROTHERLY
Rom. 12:10 affectioned one to another with *b* love
Heb. 13: 1 let *b* love continue
2 Pet. 1: 7 to godliness *b* kindness; and to *b*

BROUGHT
Ps. 79: 8 mercies prevent us: we are *b* low
90: 2 before the mountains were *b* forth
106: 43 *b* low for their iniquities
Is. 1: 2 nourished and *b* up children
66: 7 before she travailed, she *b* forth
Gal. 2: 4 because of false brethren unawares *b*
1 Tim. 6: 7 we *b* nothing into this world, and it
Jas. 1:18 earth *b* forth her fruit

BRUISE (BRUISED)
Gen. 3:15 it shall *b* thy head, and thou shalt
Is. 42: 3 a *b* reed shall he not break
53: 5 He was *b* for our iniquities
Ezek. 23: 3 there they *b* the teats of their virginity
Luke 4:18 to set at liberty them that are *b*
Rom. 16:20 God of peace shall *b* Satan

BRUTISH
Ps. 92: 6 a *b* man knoweth not; neither doth a
Prov. 12: 1 but he that hateth reproof is *b*
Jer. 10:14 every man is *b* in his knowledge

BUILD (BUILDETH)
Josh. 6:26 cursed be the man that . . . *b* this city
Ps. 102:16 when the Lord shall *b* up Zion, he shall
127: 1 except the Lord *b* the house they labour
Prov. 14: 1 Every wise woman *b* her house: but
Eccl. 3: 3 a time to *b* up
Mic. 3:10 they *b* up Zion with blood
Acts 20:32 his grace, which is able to *b* you up
1 Cor. 3:10 foundations and another *b* thereon

BUILDER
Ps. 118:22 stone which the *b* refused is become head
Mat. 21:42 stone which the *b* rejected
Mark 12:10 stone which the *b* rejected
Heb. 11:10 foundations whose *b* and maker is God

BUILDING
1 Cor. 3: 9 God's husbandry, ye are God's *b*
Eph. 2:21 all the *b* fitly framed together

BUILT
Mat. 7:24 wise man which *b* his house upon a rock
Eph. 2:20 ye are *b* on the foundation of
Heb. 3: 4 he that *b* all things is God
1 Pet. 2: 5 *b* up a spiritual house, an holy

BULLS
Ps. 22:12 many *b* have compassed me
68:30 rebuke the multitude of *b*
Heb. 9:13 if the blood of *b* and goats

BULLOCK (BULLOCKS)
Ps. 51:19 they offer *b* on thine altar
Is. 1:11 delight not in the blood of *b*
Jer. 31:18 as a *b* unaccustomed to the yoke: turn

BULRUSH (BULRUSHES)
Ex. 2: 3 took for him an ark of *b*
Is. 58: 5 Is it to bow down his head as a *b*

BULWARKS
Ps. 48:13 mark ye well her *b*
Is. 26: 1 will God appoint for walls and *b*

BURDEN
Ex. 18:22 shall bear the *b* with thee
Deut. 1:12 how can I bear your *b*
2 Sam. 15:33 thou shalt be a *b* unto
2 Ki. 5:17 two mules' *b* of earth
Neh. 13:19 no *b* brought in on the sabbath day
Ps. 38: 4 a *b* too heavy for me
55:22 cast thy *b* upon the Lord
Is. 9: 4 thou hast broken the yoke of his *b*
13: 1 the *b* of Babylon, which Isaiah
Ezek. 12:10 this *b* concerneth the prince in Jerusalem
Nah. 1: 1 the *b* of Nineveh.
Hab. 1: 1 the *b* which Habakkuk the prophet
Zech. 9: 1 the *b* of the word of the Lord
Mat. 11:30 my yoke is easy, my *b* is light
Gal. 6: 5 every man bear his own *b*

BURDENED
2 Cor. 5: 4 in this tabernacle do groan being *b*
8:13 not that other men be eased and ye *b*

BURDENS
Ex. 1:11 taskmasters to afflict them with their *b*
Mat. 23: 4 bind heavy *b* and grievous to be born
Gal. 6: 2 bear one another's *b* and fulfil

BURN (BURNED, BURNETH)
Gen. 44:18 let not thine anger *b*
Ex. 3: 2 the bush *b* with fire
Lev. 1: 9 the priest shall *b* all on the altar
Deut. 32:22 shall *b* unto the lowest hell
Ps. 46: 9 he *b* the chariot in the fire
Is. 9:18 wickedness *b* as the fire
Mal. 4: 1 day cometh shall *b* as an oven
Luke 3:17 chaff he will *b* with fire
24:32 did not our heart *b* within us?
1 Cor. 3:15 if man's work shall be *b*, he shall
7: 9 it is better to marry than to *b*
13: 3 I give my body to be *b*
Heb. 6: 8 whose end is to be *b*
Rev. 21: 8 lake which *b* with fire

BURNING (BURNINGS)
Ex. 21:25 *b* for *b*, wound for wound
Is. 3:24 of sackcloth and *b* instead of beauty
33:14 shall dwell with everlasting *b*
Jer. 20: 9 word was in mine heart as a *b* fire
Ezek. 1:13 their appearance was like *b* coals of fire
Luke 12:35 loins be girded about, and your lights *b*
John 5:35 He was a *b* and a shining light
Rev. 4: 5 there were seven lamps of fire *b*

BURNT
Gen. 8:20 and offered *b* offerings on the altar
1 Sam 15:22 great delight in *b* offerings and sacrifices
Ps. 51:16 thou delightest not in *b* offering
Jer. 7:21 put your *b* offerings unto your sacrifices
Mat. 22: 7 and *b* up their city
Heb. 10: 6 In *b* offerings and sacrifices
2 Pet. 3:10 works that are therein shall be *b*

BURST
Jer. 2:20 broken thy yoke, and *b* thy bands
Mark 2:22 new wine doth *b* the bottles
Acts 1:18 he *b* asunder in the midst

BURY (BURIED, BURYING)
Gen. 23: 4 *b* my dead out of my sight
Mat. 8:21 first to go and *b* my father
1 Cor. 15: 4 he was *b* and rose again
Col. 2:12 *b* with him in baptism,

BUSHEL
Mat. 5:15 and put it under a *b*;

Luke   11:33 neither under a *b*, but on a
BUSINESS
Ps.   107:23 in ships, that do *b* in great waters
Luke   2:49 must be about my Father's *b*
Rom.   12: 11 not slothful in *b*
BUTTER
Ps.   55: 21 words were smoother than *b*
Is.   7:15 *b* and honey shall he eat
BUY (BUYETH)
Prov.   23:23 *b* the truth, and sell it not
Is.   55: 1 *b* and eat, yea, *b* wine
Mat.   13:44 selleth all and *b* that field
Jas.   4:13 *b* and sell, and get gain
Rev.   3:18 I counsel thee to *b* gold
        13:17 no man might *b* or sell
BYWORD
Deut.   28:37 and a *b* among all nations
1 Ki.   9: 7 Israel shall be a . . . *b* among
Job   17: 6 he hath made me also a *b* of the prophet
Ps.   44:14 makest us a *b* among the heathen
CALAMITY (CALAMITIES)
Deut.   32:35 the day of their *c* is at hand
Job   6: 2 my *c* laid in the balances
Ps.   18:18 prevented me in the day of my *c*
       141:   5 my prayer shall be in their *c*
Prov.   1:26 I will laugh at your *c*
        17: 5 glad at *c* shall not be unpunished
        19:13 a foolish son is the *c* of his
Jer.   18:17 not the face in the day of their *c*
Ezek.   35: 5 the sword in the day of their *c*
Obad.   1:13 my people in the day of their *c*
CALF (CALVES)
Ex.   32: 4 made a molten *c*
Neh.   9:18 they had made them a molten *c*
Ps.   29: 6 them also to skip like a *c*
Is.   11: 6 *c* and the young lion
Hos.   8: 5 thy *c*, O Samaria, hath cast thee
Luke   15:23 bring hither the fatted *c*
Rev.   4: 7 the second beast like a *c*
CALL
Gen.   2:19 to see what he would *c* them
        30:13 daughters will *c* me blessed
Deut.   4: 7 God is in all things that we *c* upon
         4:26 I heaven and earth to witness
1 Sam.   3: 6 for thou didst *c* me
        18:24 and I will *c* on the name of the Lord
2 Ki.   5: 11 and *c* on the name of the Lord
Job   5: 1 *c* now if there be any to answer
Ps.   50:15 And *c* upon me in the day of trouble
        77: 6 I *c* to remembrance my song
        80:18 quicken us and we will *c* on thy name
       116:   4 then I *c* upon the name of the Lord
       145: 18 nigh to all that *c* upon him
Is.   5:20 woe unto them that *c* evil good
        22:12 Lord God of hosts *c* to weeping
        58: 9 *c* and Lord will answer
Jer.   25:29 I will *c* for a sword upon all
Jonah   1: 6 arise, *c* upon thy God
Zech.   13: 9 shall *c* upon thy name
Mal.   3: 12 all nations shall *c* you blessed
Mat.   9:13 I am not come to *c* the righteous
        23: 9 *c* no man your father
Luke   1:48 all generations will *c* me blessed
         6:46 why *c* ye me Lord, Lord and
John   4:16 *c* thy husband and come hither
        13:13 ye *c* me Master and Lord
        15:15 I *c* you not servants, but friends
Acts   2: 21 shall *c* on the name of the Lord
         2:39 as many as the Lord shall *c*
Rom.   9:25 I will *c* them my people
        10:12 rich in mercy to all that *c* on him
1 Cor.   1: 2 *c* upon the name of Jesus Christ
2 Cor.   1:23 I *c* God for a record upon my soul
Jas.   5:14 *c* for the elders of the
1 Pet.   1:17 if ye *c* on the Father
CALLED
Gen.   21:17 angel of God *c* to Hagar
        22: 11 angel of Lord *c* to Abraham
Ex.   3: 4 God *c* him out of the bush
Judg.   15:18 sore athirst and *c* on the Lord
2 Ki.   8: 1 Lord hath *c* for a famine
        21:26 David *c* upon the Lord and he
2 Chr.   6:33 have built is *c* by my name

          7:14 which are *c* by my name
Ps.   17: 6 I have *c* upon thee
        18: 6 in my distress I *c* upon the Lord
        88: 9 I have *c* daily upon thee
Prov.   1:24 I have *c* and ye refused
Is.   41: 2 who *c* him to his foot
        42: 6 I the Lord *c* thee in righteousness
        49: 1 the Lord *c* me from the womb
        51: 2 I *c* him alone, and blessed him
        61: 3 might be *c* trees of righteousness
        65:12 when I *c* ye did not answer
Jer.   15:16 I am *c* by thy name
        34:15 House which is *c* by my name
Lam.   3:55 I *c* upon thy name, O Lord
Dan.   9:19 people are *c* by thy name
Hos.   11: 1 I *c* my son out of Egypt
Mark   14:72 Peter *c* to mind the word
Luke   15:19 not worthy to be *c* thy son
John   10:35 if he *c* them gods to whom
        15:15 but I have *c* you friends
Acts   9: 21 destroy them which *c* on this name
        11:26 disciples were *c* Christians first
        13: 2 for the work whereto I *c* them
        15:17 Gentiles upon whom my name is *c*
        24: 21 of the dead I am *c* in question
Rom.   1: 1 *c* to be an apostle
         1: 6 ye also the *c* of Jesus Christ
         8:28 the *c* according to his purpose
         9:24 whom he *c*, not of Jews only
1 Cor.   1: 9 ye were *c* unto the fellowship
         1:26 not many wise, not many noble are *c*
         5: 11 if any man that is *c* a brother
        15: 9 not meet to be *c* an apostle
Gal.   1: 6 *c* you into the grace of Christ
         1:15 God who *c* me by his grace
         5:13 ye have been *c* to liberty
Eph.   2: 11 who are *c* uncircumcision
         4: 4 are *c* in one hope of your calling
Col.   3:15 peace of God to which ye are *c*
1 Thes. 2:12 who hath *c* you unto his Kingdom
         4: 7 God hath not *c* us to uncleanness
1 Tim.   6:12 life, whereunto thou art *c*
2 Tim.   1: 9 *c* us with holy calling
Heb.   3:13 while it is *c* today
        11:16 not ashamed to be *c* their God
Jas.   2: 7 name by the which ye are *c*
1 Pet.   1:15 as he that *c* you is holy
         2: 9 *c* you out of darkness
         5: 10 God *c* us to his eternal glory
1 John   3: 1 we should be *c* sons of God
Rev.   17:14 that are with him are *c* and chosen
        19: 9 are *c* unto the marriage supper
CALLETH
Ps.   42: 7 deep *c* unto deep at
       147:   4 stars, he *c* them by all
Is.   59: 4 none *c* for justice nor
Amos   5: 8 that *c* for waters of the sea
John   10: 3 he *c* his own sheep by name
Gal.   5: 8 cometh not of him that *c* you
1 Thes. 5:24 faithful is he that *c* you
CALLING
Is.   41: 4 *c* the generations from
Acts   22:16 *c* on the name of the Lord
Rom.   11:29 the gifts and *c* of God
1 Cor.   7:20 let every man abide in the same *c*
Eph.   1:18 know what is the hope of his *c*
         4: 4 called in one hope of your *c*
Phil.   3:14 prize of the high *c* of God
2 Thes. 1: 11 count worthy of this *c*
2 Tim.   1: 9 called us with a holy *c*
Heb.   3: 1 partakers of the heavenly *c*
2 Pet.   1: 10 make your *c* and election sure
CAMEL
Mat.   3: 4 John had his raiment of *c*'s hair
        19:24 it is easier for a *c* to go through
        23:24 strain at a gnat, and swallow a *c*
CAMP
Ex.   14:19 angel of God which went before the *c*
Num.   11: 31 let the quails fall by the *c*
Deut.   23:14 therefore shall thy *c* be holy
Judg.   13:25 began to move him at times in the *c*
Heb.   13:13 go unto him without the *c*
Rev.   20: 9 compassed the *c* of the saints

CANDLE (CANDLES, CANDLESTICK, CANDLESTICKS)
Ex.   25: 31 shalt make a *c* of pure gold
Job   18: 6 his *c* shall be put with him
Ps.   18:28 Lord will light my *c*
Prov.   20:27 spirit of man is the *c* of the Lord
        24:20 *c* of the wicked shall be put out
        31:18 her *c* goeth not out by night
Dan.   5: 5 wrote over against the *c* upon the
                 plaster
Zeph.   1:12 I will search Jerusalem with *c*
Zech.   4: 2 behold a *c*, all of gold
Mat.   5:15 do men light a *c* and put it
Luke   15: 8 light a *c* and sweep the house
Rev.   1:20 seven *c* are the seven churches
        18:23 light of the *c* shine no more
        22: 5 they need no *c*, neither light
CAPTAIN
Josh.   5:14 as *c* of the Lord's host
2 Chr. 13:12 God himself is our *c*
Heb.   2: 10 make the *c* of their salvation perfect
CAPTIVE
Gen.   14:14 his brother was taken *c*
Judg.   5:12 arise, Barak, lead thy captivity *c*
Is.   51:14 The *c* exile hasteneth that he may
Jer.   22:12 whither they have led him *c*
Amos   7: 11 Israel shall surely be led away *c*
2 Tim.   2:26 are taken *c* by him at his will
         3: 6 lead *c* silly women
CAPTIVITY
Deut.   30: 3 Lord thy God will turn thy *c*
Job   42: 10 the Lord turned the *c* of Job
Ps.   14: 7 Lord bringeth back the *c*
        68:18 thou hast led *c* captive
       126:   1 I turned again the *c* of Zion
Jer.   15: 2 such as are for *c*, to the
Zeph.   2: 7 shall visit them and turn away their *c*
Rom.   7:23 bringing me into *c* to the law of sin
2 Cor. 10: 5 bringing into *c* every thought
Eph.   4: 8 he led *c* captive and gave gifts
Rev.   13: 10 he that leadeth into *c* shall go
CARE (CARED, CARETH)
Ps.   142: 4 no man *c* for my soul
Mat.   13:22 and the *c* of this world and the
John   10:13 hireling *c* not for the sheep
        12: 6 not that he *c* for the poor
1 Cor.   7:32 is unmarried *c* for things of the Lord
         9: 9 God take *c* for oxen
2 Cor. 11:28 daily, the *c* of all the churches
1 Tim.   3: 5 how shall he take *c* of the church
1 Pet.   5: 7 *c* upon him for he *c* for you
CAREFUL
Luke   10:41 Martha, thou art *c* and troubled
Phil.   4: 6 be *c* for nothing; but in every thing
Tit.   3: 8 might be *c* to maintain good works
CARNAL
Rom.   7:14 law is spiritual, but I am *c*
         8: 7 the *c* mind is enmity against God
        15:27 minister to them in *c* things
1 Cor.   3: 1 as unto spiritual, but as unto *c*
2 Cor. 10: 4 weapons of our warfare are not *c*
Heb.   7:16 not after the law of a *c* commandment
         9: 10 *c* ordinances imposed on them until
CARNALLY
Rom.   8: 6 to be *c* minded is death
CARPENTER'S
Mat.   13:55 Is not this the *c* son?
Mark   6: 3 Is not this the *c*, the son of Mary
CARRY (CARRIED)
Num.   11:12 say unto me *c* them in thy bosom
Eccl.   10:20 bird of the air shall *c* the voice
Is.   40: 11 *c* them in his bosom and shall gently
Luke   10: 4 *c* neither purse nor scrip, nor shoes
        16:22 *c* by the angels into Abraham's bosom
John   21:18 *c* thee whither thou wouldest not
Eph.   4:14 *c* about with every wind
Heb.   13: 9 *c* about with divers doctrines
Rev.   17: 3 *c* me away in the spirit
CAST
Gen.   21: 10 *c* out this bondwoman
Ex.   34:24 I will *c* out the nations before thee
2 Sam.   1: 21 shield is vilely *c* away
Neh.   9:26 *c* thy law behind their backs

Job   8: 20 God will not *c* away perfect man
    22: 29 when men are *c* down
Ps.   2: 3 let us *c* away their cords from us
    22: 10 *c* upon thee from the womb
    42: 5 why art thou *c* down
    55: 22 *c* thy burden on the Lord
    71: 9 *c* me not off in the time of old age
    94: 14 the Lord will not *c* his people
Prov.   1: 14 *c* in thy lot among us
    16: 33 the lot is *c* into the lap
Eccl.   11: 1 *c* thy bread upon the waters
Is.   14: 19 thou art *c* out of thy grave
    26: 19 the earth shall *c* out the dead
    38: 17 hast *c* all my sins behind thy back
    41: 9 I will not *c* thee away
    66: 5 *c* you out for my name's sake
Jer.   7: 15 I will *c* you out of my sight
    31: 37 I will *c* off all the seed of Israel
Ezek.   18: 31 *c* away all your transgressions
Jonah   2: 4 I am *c* out of thy sight
Mic.   7: 19 *c* their sins into the sea
Mal.   3: 11 vine shall not *c* her fruit
Mat.   3: 10 hewn down and *c* into the fire
    7: 5 *c* the beam out of thine own eye
    7: 6 neither *c* pearls before swine
    12: 24 *c* out devils but by Beelzebub
    13: 42 *c* them into a furnace
    21: 12 *c* out them that sold and bought
    22: 13 *c* him into outer darkness
    25: 30 *c* the unprofitable servant into
Mark   9: 28 why could not we *c* him out?
    11: 23 be thou *c* into the sea
    12: 8 *c* him out of the vineyard
    16: 17 in my name shall they *c* out devils
Luke   6: 22 *c* out your name as evil
John   6: 37 I will in no wise *c* out
    8: 7 let him first *c* a stone
    12: 31 prince of this world be *c* out
Rom.   11: 1 hath God *c* away his people
    13: 12 let us *c* off the works of darkness
2 Cor.   4: 9 *c* down but not destroyed
    7: 6 comforteth those that are *c* down
Heb.   10: 35 *c* not away your confidence
1 Tim.   5: 12 they *c* off their first faith
Rev.   12: 9 and the great dragon was *c* out
    20: 3 *c* him into the bottomless pit

CASTETH
Mat.   9: 34 he *c* out devils through Beelzebub
1 John   4: 18 perfect love *c* out fear

CASTING
2 Cor.   10: 5 *c* down imaginations and every high
1 Pet.   5: 7 *c* all your care upon him

CATTLE
Ps.   50: 10 the *c* upon a thousand hills
    104: 14 grass to grow for the *c*

CATCH (CAUGHT)
Ps.   10: 9 he lieth in wait to *c* the poor
    35: 8 his net that he hid *c* himself
Luke   5: 10 henceforth thou shalt *c* men
Acts   8: 39 Spirit of the Lord *c* away Philip
2 Cor.   12: 4 he was *c* up into paradise
1 Thes.   4: 17 remain shall be *c* up together with

CAUSE
Ex.   9: 16 for this *c* have I raised thee up
    22: 9 of both parties shall come before
Deut.   1: 17 the *c* that is too hard for you
Job   5: 8 to God would I commit my *c*
Ps.   9: 4 maintained my right and my *c*
    10: 17 wilt *c* thine ear to hear
    35: 23 judgment even unto my *c*, my God
    85: 4 *c* thine anger towards us to cease
Prov.   3: 30 with a man without *c*
    18: 17 that is first in his own *c*
    25: 9 debate thy *c* with thy neighbour
Is.   3: 12 which lead thee, *c* thee to err
    51: 22 pleadeth the *c* of his people
Jer.   3: 12 not *c* my anger to fall
    5: 28 the *c* of the fatherless
Lam.   3: 36 to subvert a man in his *c*
    37: 5 *c* breath to enter into you
Dan.   9: 17 *c* thy face to shine upon thy
Mat.   5: 22 without *c* shall be in danger
    19: 3 put away his wife for every *c*

John   15: 25 hated me without *c*
1 Cor.   11: 30 this *c* many are weak and sickly
2 Cor.   4: 16 for which *c* we faint not
Eph.   5: 31 For this *c* shall a man
1 Tim.   9: 1 for this I obtained mercy

CAUSED (CAUSETH)
Prov.   18: 18 the lot *c* contentions to cease
Mat.   5: 32 *c* her to commit adultery

CAVE (CAVES)
Gen.   19: 30 he dwelt in a *c*, he and his
Josh.   10: 16 hid themselves in a *c*
John   11: 38 grave. It was a *c*
Heb.   11: 38 wandered in the *c* of the earth

CEASE (CEASETH)
Gen.   8: 22 day and night shall not *c*
Ps.   37: 8 *c* from anger and wrath
    46: 9 he maketh wars to *c*
Prov.   19: 27 *c* to hear instruction
    23: 4 *c* from thine own wisdom
    26: 20 where there is no talebearer, the strife *c*
1 Cor.   13: 8 tongues, they shall *c*
Eph.   1: 16 *c* not to give thanks for

CEASING
Rom.   1: 9 without *c* I make mention
1 Thes.   5: 17 pray without *c*
2 Tim.   1: 3 without *c* I have remembrance

CEDAR (CEDARS)
Ps.   29: 5 voice of the Lord breaketh *c*
    92: 12 grow like a *c* in Lebanon
Sol.   5: 15 countenance excellent as *c*
Is.   9: 10 we will change them into *c*
Ezek.   17: 3 took the highest branch of the *c*
    31: 3 the Assyrian was a *c* in Lebanon

CHAFF
Ps.   1: 4 the *c* which the wind driveth away
    35: 5 be as *c* before the wind
Is.   5: 24 the flame consumeth the *c*
    17: 13 chased as the *c* of mountains
    41: 15 make the hills as *c*
Jer.   23: 28 what is the *c* to the wheat
Dan.   2: 35 became like *c* of the summer
Hos.   13: 3 as the *c* that is driven
Zeph.   2: 2 before the day pass as the *c*
Mat.   3: 12 burn up the *c* in unquenchable
Luke   3: 17 the *c* he will burn with fire

CHAIN (CHAINS)
Ps.   73: 6 compasseth them as a *c*
    149: 8 to bind their kings with *c*
Prov.   1: 9 thy head and *c* about thy neck
Is.   3: 19 Lord will take away thy *c*
    16: 11 I put a *c* on thy neck
Acts   12: 7 Peter's *c* fell from his
    28: 20 I am bound with this *c*
2 Tim.   1: 16 was not ashamed of my *c*
2 Pet.   2: 4 delivered into the *c* of darkness
Rev.   20: 1 a great *c* in his hand

CHAMBER (CHAMBERS)
Job   9: 9 Pleiades, and the *c* of the south
Ps.   19: 5 bridegroom coming out of his *c*
    104: 3 beams of his *c* in the waters
Prov.   7: 27 going down to the *c* of death
Is.   26: 20 enter thou into thy *c* and shut
Joel   2: 16 bridegroom go forth of his *c*
Mat.   24: 26 he is in the secret *c*

CHANCE
2 Sam.   1: 6 I happened by *c* upon Mount Gilboa
Eccl.   9: 11 time and *c* happeneth to them all

CHANGE (CHANGED, CHANGETH)
Job   17: 12 the night into day
Jer.   13: 23 can the Ethiopian *c* his skin
Dan.   2: 21 he *c* times and seasons
Mal.   3: 6 I am the Lord, I *c* not
Rom.   1: 23 *c* the glory of the uncorruptible God
    1: 25 *c* the truth of God into a lie
Phil.   3: 21 Christ shall *c* our vile bodies
Heb.   1: 12 they shall be *c*: but thou art

CHARGE (CHARGED)
Gen.   26: 5 obeyed my voice and kept my *c*
    28: 6 as he blessed him he gave him a *c*
Ex.   6: 13 gave them a *c* unto the children
Job   1: 22 nor *c* God foolishly
    4: 18 *c* his angels with folly

Ps.   35: 11 to my *c* things that I knew not
    91: 11 give his angels *c* over thee
Sol.   2: 7 I you, O daughters of Jerusalem
Mat.   4: 6 He shall give his angels *c*
Luke   4: 10 He shall give his angels *c*
Acts   7: 60 lay not to their *c*
    16: 24 such a *c* thrust into the inner prison
    23: 29 nothing laid to his *c* worthy of
Rom.   8: 33 lay to the *c* of God's elect
1 Cor.   9: 18 make the gospel without *c*
1 Thes.   2: 11 *c* every one as a father
1 Tim.   1: 18 this *c* I commit to thee
    6: 13 I give thee *c* in the sight of God
    6: 17 *c* them that are rich
2 Tim.   4: 16 be laid to their *c*

CHARIOT (CHARIOTS)
Gen.   41: 43 the second *c* which he
    14: 25 took off their *c* wheels
Josh.   17: 16 of the valley have *c* of iron
1 Ki.   10: 26 Solomon gathered together *c* and
2 Ki.   14: 2 *c* of fire
Ps.   20: 7 some trust in *c*,
    68: 17 the *c* of God are twenty thousand
    104: 3 who maketh the clouds his *c*
Is.   31: 1 stay on horses and trust in *c*
Hab.   3: 8 and thy *c* of salvation
Rev.   9: 9 sound of wings as of *c*

CHARITY
1 Cor.   8: 1 knowledge puffeth up but *c* edifieth
    13: 2 have not *c* I am nothing
    13: 13 faith, hope, *c* . . . but the greatest is *c*
Col.   3: 14 above all these things put on *c*
1 Thes.   3: 6 tidings of your faith and *c*
2 Thes.   1: 3 *c* of every one aboundeth
1 Tim.   1: 5 end of commandment is *c*
    4: 12 be thou an example in *c*
2 Tim.   2: 22 follow righteousness, faith, *c*
    3: 10 known my doctrine, faith, *c*
Tit.   2: 2 aged men be sound in *c*
1 Pet.   4: 8 fervent *c* among yourselves for *c*
    5: 14 greet one another with a kiss of *c*
2 Pet.   1: 7 to brotherly kindness, *c*
3 John   1: 6 borne witness of thy *c*
Jude   1: 12 spots in your feasts of *c*
Rev.   2: 19 I know thy works and *c*

CHASTE
2 Cor.   11: 2 as a *c* virgin to Christ
Tit.   2: 5 young women discreet, *c*
1 Pet.   3: 2 they behold your *c* conversation

CHASTEN (CHASTENED, CHASTENEST)
Deut.   8: 5 as man *c* his son so the Lord
2 Sam.   7: 14 I will *c* him with the rod
Ps.   69: 10 *c* my soul with fasting
    94: 12 blessed is the man whom thou *c*
    118: 18 the Lord hath *c* me sore
Prov.   13: 24 loveth him *c* him betimes
    19: 18 *c* thy son while there is hope
1 Cor.   11: 32 we are *c* of the Lord
2 Cor.   6: 9 as *c* and not killed
Heb.   12: 6 whom the Lord loveth he *c*
    12: 10 fathers for few days *c*
Rev.   3: 19 as many as I love, I *c*

CHASTENING
Job   5: 17 despise not thou *c* of the Lord
Is.   26: 16 when thy *c* was upon
Heb.   12: 11 no *c* for present seemeth joyous

CHASTISE
Lev.   26: 28 will *c* you seven times
Hos.   7: 12 I will *c* as their congregation
    10: 10 my desire that I should *c* them

CHASTISEMENT
Is.   53: 5 *c* of our peace was upon him
Jer.   30: 14 with the *c* of a cruel
Heb.   12: 8 without *c* then are ye bastards

CHEEK
Mic.   5: 1 judge of Israel, with a rod upon the *c*
Mat.   5: 39 smite thee on the right *c*, turn
Luke   6: 29 smiteth thee on the one *c* offer

CHEER (CHEERETH)
Deut.   24: 5 and shall *c* up his wife
Judg.   9: 13 leave my wine, which *c* God and man
Eccl.   11: 9 let thy heart *c* thee
Mat.   9: 2 Son, be of good *c*, thy sins be

John　16:33 be of good c, I have overcome

CHERISHETH
Eph.　5:29 own flesh but nourisheth and c it
1 Thes. 2: 7 as a nurse c her children

CHICKENS
Mat.　23:37 gathereth her c under her wings

CHIEF
Job　40:19 he is the c of the ways of God
Ps.　78:51 the c of their strength
Mat.　20:27 whoso will be c among you
Luke　22:26 is c, as he that serveth
Eph.　2:20 himself being the c corner stone
1 Tim.　1:15 sinners, of whom I am c
1 Pet.　2: 6 in Sion a c corner stone

CHILD
2 Sam.12:16 David besought God for a c
1 Ki.　3: 7 I am not but a little c
　　　3:25 divide the living c in two
Ps.　131: 2 quieted as a c that is weaned
Prov.　20:11 even a c is known by his doings
　　　22: 6 train up a c in the way he
　　　22:15 bound in the heart of the c
Eccl.　4:13 better is as poor and wise c
Is.　9: 6 for unto us a c is born
　　　11: 6 and a little c shall lead them
　　　11: 8 and the sucking c shall play
　　　65:20 for the c shall die an hundred
Hos.　11: 1 when Israel was a c I loved
Mat.　18: 5 receive one such little c in my name
Luke　9:48 shall receive this c in
　　　18:17 as a little c shall in no wise
Rev.　12: 5 a man c who was to rule

CHILDBEARING
1 Tim.　2:15 she shall be saved in c

CHILDISH
1 Cor.　13:11 a man, I put away c things

CHILDREN
Gen.　3:16 thou shalt bring forth c
Ex.　1: 7 c of Israel were fruitful
　　　13:15 firstborn of my c I redeem
　　　20: 5 iniquity of the fathers upon the c
Num.　14:33 your c shall wander forty years
Deut.　6: 7 teach them diligently unto thy c
1 Ki.　2: 4 thy c take heed to their way
2 Ki.　17:31 Sepharvites burnt their c
Ps.　17:14 they are full of c and leave
　　　82: 6 all of you are c of the Most High
　　　89:30 his c forsake my law
　　127: 4 mighty men so are c of the youth
　　128: 3 thy c like olive plants
Prov.　17: 6 glory of c are their fathers
　　　31:28 her c rise and call her blessed
Is.　54:13 thy c shall be taught of the Lord
Jer.　31:15 Rahel weeping for her c
Lam.　4: 4 the young c ask for bread
Nah.　3:10 her young c also were dashed in pieces
Mal.　4: 6 turn the hearts of fathers to the c
Mat.　2:18 Rachel weeping for her c,
　　　3: 9 raise up the c unto Abraham
　　　5: 9 be called the c of God
　　　8:12 but the c of the kingdom
　　　11:19 wisdom is justified of her c
Luke　6:32 c sitting in the marketplace
　　　6:35 ye shall be c of the Highest
　　　16: 8 for the c of this world are in
　　　20:34 the c of this world marry
　　　20:36 c of God being the c of the resurrection
John　12:36 ye may be the c of light
Acts　2:39 promise unto you and to your c
　　　3:25 ye are the c of the prophets
Rom.　8:17 if c then heirs; heirs of God
　　　9: 7 seed of Abraham, are they all c
1 Cor.　14:20 in malice be ye c in understanding
2 Cor.　12:14 c ought not to lay up
Gal.　4: 3 we, when we were c, were in bondage
　　　4:28 are the c of the promise
Eph.　2: 3 by nature the c of wrath
　　　4:14 no more c tossed to and fro
　　　5: 8 walk as c of light
　　　6: 1 c, obey your parents
　　　6: 4 fathers provoke not your c
Col.　3:20 c, obey your parents
　　　3:21 provoke not your c to anger

1 Thes.　5: 5 ye are all c of light
Heb.　2:14 as the c are partakers of flesh
　　　12: 5 speaketh unto you as unto c
1 John　5: 2 that we love the c of God

CHOKE (CHOKED)
Mat.　13: 7 thorns sprung up and c them
Mark　4:19 things entering in c the word
Luke　8:14 and are c with cares and riches

CHOOSE (CHOOSEST, CHOOSING, CHOSE)
Num.　17: 5 the man's rod whom I shall c
Deut.　17:15 whom the Lord thy God shall c
　　　30:19 therefore c life, that both thou
Josh.　24:15 c you this day whom ye will serve
Neh.　9: 7 Lord God didst c Abraham
Ps.　65: 4 blessed is the man whom thou c
Prov.　1:29 did not c the fear of the Lord
Is.　7:15 refuse evil and c good
　　　56: 4 c the things that please me
Phil.　1:22 what I shall c I wot not
Heb.　11:25 c rather to suffer affliction

CHOSEN
1 Ki.　8:48 city which thou hast c
Job　36:21 iniquity c rather than affliction
Ps.　105:43 with joy and his c with gladness
　　119: 30 I have c the way of truth
　　119: 73 I have c his precepts
Prov.　16:16 rather to be c than silver
Is.　41: 8 Jacob, whom I have c, the seed
　　　44: 1 Israel, whom I have c
　　　48:10 I have c thee in the furnace of
　　　58: 5 is it such a fast that I have c
Mat.　20:16 many be called, but few c
Luke　10:42 Mary hath c that good part
　　　23:35 Christ the c of God
John　13:18 I know whom I have c
　　　15:16 Ye have not c me
Acts　9:15 for he is a c vessel unto me
1 Cor.　1:27 God hath c the foolish
Eph.　1: 4 c us in him before the foundation
1 Pet.　2: 4 c of God, and precious
Rev.　17:14 called, and c and faithful

CHRIST
Mat.　16:16 thou art the C the Son
　　　23: 8 one is your master, even C.,
Mark　9:41 because ye belong to C
Luke　2:26 not die before seeing C
　　　4:41 the devils knew he was C
　　　24:26 ought not C to have suffered
　　　24:46 it behooved C to suffer and rise
John　4:25 Messias cometh which is called C
　　　7:41 shall C come out of Galilee?
　　　11:27 I believe that thou art the C
Acts　8: 5 Samaria, and preached C unto them
Rom.　5: 6 C died for the ungodly
　　　6: 8 if we be dead with C
　　　8: 1 them which are in C Jesus
　　　8: 9 have not the Spirit of C, he is none of
　　　8:17 heirs of God and joint heirs with C
　　　12: 5 many, one body in C
　　　15: 3 for C pleased not himself; but
1 Cor.　1:24 C the power of God and
　　　2: 2 save Jesus C, and him crucified
　　　3:23 ye are C's, and C is God's
　　　5: 7 C our passover is sacrificed
　　　15:14 if C be not risen, then is
　　　15:19 if in this life only we have hope in C
2 Cor.　5:17 if any man be in C
　　　12: 2 I knew a man in C above fourteen years
Gal.　1:22 churches which were in C
　　　2:20 I am crucified with C
　　　3:13 C hath redeemed us from the curse
　　　3:28 ye are all one in C Jesus
　　　4:19 travail till C be formed in you
　　　5: 6 in C Jesus neither circumcision nor
Eph.　1: 1 faithful in C Jesus
　　　2: 5 quickened us together with C
　　　2:10 created in C Jesus unto good works
　　　3:17 that C dwell in your hearts
　　　4:20 ye have not so learned C, if so
　　　5:14 dead, and C shall give thee light
　　　5:23 wife, as C is head of the church
Phil.　1:13 so that my bonds in C are manifest in all
　　　1:21 to live is C and to die

　　　2: 1 if there be any consolation in C
　　　2: 11 confess that C Jesus is Lord
　　　3: 8 that I may win C
　　　4:13 I can do all things through C
Col.　1:27 C in you hope of glory
　　　2:20 if ye be dead with C
　　　3: 3 and your life is hid with C in God
1 Thes.　4:16 the dead in C shall rise first
1 Tim.　1:15 C Jesus came into world to save
2 Tim.　2: 3 as a good soldier of C Jesus
　　　3:12 will live godly in C Jesus shall suffer
Heb.　13: 8 C Jesus the same yesterday
Rev.　20: 4 reigned with C a thousand years

CHRISTIAN (CHRISTIANS)
Acts　11:26 were called C first at Antioch
　　　26:28 persuadest me to be a C

CHURCH
Mat.　16:18 this rock I will build my c
Acts　2:47 the Lord added to the c daily
1 Cor.　4:17 teach every where in the c
　　　14: 4 he that prophesieth edifieth the c
Eph.　1:22 head over all things to the c
　　　3:10 heavenly places known by the c
　　　5:25 as Christ loved the c and gave
　　　5:27 present to himself a glorious c
Phil.　3: 6 Concerning zeal, persecuting the c
Col.　1:18 he is head of the body, the c
　　　1:24 for his body's sake, which is the c
1 Tim.　3: 5 take care of the c of God
3 John　1: 6 witness of thy charity before the c

CHURCHES
1 Cor.　14:34 women keep silence in the c
1 Thes.　2:14 became followers of the c of God
2 Thes.　1: 4 glory in you in the c of God
Rev.　1: 4 seven c which are in Asia
　　　2: 7 hear what the Spirit saith unto the c
　　　22:16 testify these things in the c

CIRCUMCISE (CIRCUMCISED)
Gen.　17:10 every male shall be c
　　　21: 4 Abraham c his son Isaac, being eight
Deut.　30: 6 the Lord will c thy heart
Josh.　5: 2 c again the children of Israel
Jer.　4: 4 c yourselves to the Lord
Acts　15: 1 the c cannot be saved
　　　15:24 ye must be c and keep
　　　16: 3 c him because of the Jews
Col.　2:11 in whom also ye are c

CIRCUMCISION
John　7:22 Moses therefore gave unto you c
Acts　7: 8 God gave the covenant of c
Rom.　2:25 c verily profiteth if thou keep the
　　　2:29 c is that of the heart, in the spirit
　　　3: 1 what profit is there of c?
　　　3:30 which shall justify the c by faith
　　　4: 9 cometh this blessedness on the c only?
　　　15: 8 Christ was minister of the c
1 Cor.　7:19 c is nothing, but the keeping
Gal.　2: 7 as the gospel of c was unto Peter
　　　5: 6 neither c availeth nor uncircumcision
Phil.　3: 3 we are the c which worship
Col.　2:11 the c made without hands

CISTERN (CISTERNS)
Prov.　5:15 waters out of thine own c
Jer.　2:13 hewed them out c, broken c

CITY
Josh.　21:13 to be a c of refuge
Neh.　1: 1 to dwell in Jerusalem the holy c
Ps.　48: 2 the c of the great King
　　127: 1 except the Lord keep the c
Prov.　16:32 than he that taketh a c
Is.　1:21 is the faithful c become a harlot
　　　22: 2 a tumultuous c a joyous c
　　　26: 1 We have a strong c, salvation
　　　33:20 Zion, c of our solemnities
Jer.　29: 7 seek the peace of the c
Lam.　1: 1 How doth the c sit solitary
Dan.　9:24 upon thy holy c to finish
Amos　4: 7 to rain on one c not on
Zeph.　2:15 this is the rejoicing c
Zech.　8: 3 shall be called the c of truth
Mat.　4: 5 devil taketh him into the holy c
　　　5:14 c on a hill cannot be hid
　　　5:35 the c of the great king

27:53 resurrections and went into the holy *c*
Luke 10: 8 whatsoever *c* ye enter
10:12 tolerable for Sodom than for that *c*
19:41 he beheld the *c* and wept over it
Heb. 11:10 he looked for a *c* which
12:22 to the *c* of the living God
Rev. 3:12 name of the *c* of my God
11: 2 holy *c* shall they tread
21: 2 John saw the holy *c*
21:23 *c* had no need of the sun
22:19 and out of the holy *c*

CITIZENS
Eph. 2:19 fellow *c* with the saints

CLAY
Job 10: 9 that thou hast made me as *c*
38:14 it is turned as *c* to the seal
Is. 45: 9 shall the *c* say to him
64: 8 we are the *c*, thou our potter
Jer. 18: 6 the *c* is in the potter's hands
Dan. 2:33 feet part of iron, part of *c*
John 9: 6 made *c* of spittle and anointed
Rom. 9:21 power over the *c*

CLEAN
Gen. 7: 2 of every *c* beast thou shalt
Lev. 10:10 unholy and between unclean and *c*
Job 14: 4 bring a *c* thing out of unclean
17: 9 he that hath *c* hands shall be
Ps. 19: 9 the fear of the Lord is *c*
24: 4 that hath *c* hands and
51:10 in me a *c* heart, O God
73: 1 such as are of a *c* heart
Prov. 16: 2 ways of man are *c* in his own
Jer. 13:27 wilt thou not be made *c*
Ezek. 36:25 *c* water upon you, and ye shall be *c*
Mat. 8: 3 I will, be thou *c*
23:25 make *c* the outside of the cup
Luke 11:41 all things are *c* to you
John 13:11 said he, Ye are not all *c*
Rev. 19: 8 fine linen, *c* and white

CLEANNESS
Ps. 18:24 according to the *c* of my hands

CLEANSE (CLEANSED, CLEANSETH)
Ps. 19:12 *c* me from secret faults
51: 2 *c* me from my sin
73:13 I have *c* my heart in vain
119: 9 young man *c* his way
Jer. 33: 8 I will *c* them from all
Ezek. 36:33 *c* you from all iniquities
Mat. 10: 8 heal the sick, *c* the lepers
11: 5 lame walk, the lepers are *c*
Acts 10:15 what God hath *c*, that call not
2 Cor. 7: 1 let us cleanse ourselves from
Eph. 5:26 *c* with washing of water
Jas. 4: 8 *c* your hands, ye sinners
1 John 1: 7 blood of Jesus Christ *c* us

CLEAVE (CLEAVETH)
Gen. 2:24 and shall *c* unto his wife
Deut. 4: 4 ye that did *c* to the Lord
Josh. 23: 8 but *c* unto the Lord your God
Ps. 22:15 my tongue *c* to my jaws
44:25 our belly *c* unto the earth
137: 6 tongue *c* to the roof of my mouth
Mat. 19: 5 and shall *c* to his wife
Mark 10: 7 mother and *c* to his
Rom. 12: 9 *c* to that which is good

CLOAK
Is. 59:17 clad with zeal as a *c*
Mat. 5:40 let him have thy *c* also
1 Pet. 2:16 liberty for a *c* of maliciousness

CLOSET
Mat. 6: 6 when thou prayest, enter thy *c*

CLOTHE (CLOTHED)
Gen. 3:21 God make coats of skins and *c* them
Ps. 35:26 let them be *c* with shame
109: 18 he *c* himself with cursing
132: 9 priests be *c* with righteousness
Is. 61:10 *c* with garments of salvation
Zech. 3: 3 Joshua was *c* with filthy garments
Mat. 6:30 God so *c* the grass of
11: 8 a man *c* in soft raiment
25:36 naked, and ye *c* me: I
2 Cor. 5: 4 not unclothed, but *c*
1 Pet. 5: 5 be *c* with humility: for

Rev. 3: 5 be *c* with white raiment
12: 1 a woman *c* with the sun
19:14 *c* in fine linen, clean and white

CLOTHING
Ps. 45:13 her *c* is of wrought gold
Prov. 31:25 strength and honour are her *c*
Is. 59:17 garment of vengeance for *c*
Mat. 7:15 which come to you in sheep's *c*
Acts 10:30 stood before me in bright *c*

CLOUD (CLOUDS)
Gen. 9:13 set my bow in the *c*
Ex. 14:20 it was a *c* and darkness to them
19: 9 I come unto thee in a thick *c*
Ps. 36: 5 faithfulness reacheth to the *c*
57:10 and thy truth unto the *c*
104: 3 who maketh *c* his chariot
Is. 44:22 blotted out as a thick *c*
Mat. 24:30 coming in the *c* of heaven
1 Cor. 10: 1 our fathers were under the *c*
1 Thes. 4:17 with them in the *c*, to meet
Heb. 12: 1 so great a *c* of witnesses
Rev. 11:12 ascended up to heaven in a *c*

COAL (COALS)
Job 41:21 his breath kindleth *c*
Ps. 18: 8 *c* were kindled by it
140: 10 let burning *c* fall upon them
Prov. 6:28 can one go upon hot *c*
25:22 heap *c* of fire upon his head
Sol. 8: 6 thereof are *c* of fire
Is. 6: 6 a live *c* in his hands
47:14 shall not be a *c* to warm
Lam. 4: 8 visage is blacker than *c*
John 18:18 who had made a fire of *c*
Rom. 12:20 heap *c* of fire on his head

COAT (COATS)
Gen. 3:21 God make *c* of skin
37: 3 made him a *c* of many colors
Mat. 10:10 neither two *c*, neither shoes
Luke 3:11 he that hath two *c* let him
John 19:23 the *c* was without seam

COLD
Gen. 8:22 and *c* and heat, and summer and
Mat. 24:12 the love of many shall wax *c*
Rev. 3:15 thou art neither *c* nor hot

COME
Ex. 20:24 where I record my name, I will *c*
Job 22:21 good shall *c* unto thee
Ps. 40: 7 lo I *c*: in the volume of
65: 2 to thee shall all flesh *c*
Eccl. 9: 2 all things *c* alike to all
Is. 1:18 *c* let us reason together
35: 4 God will *c* and save you
55: 1 that thirsteth *c* ye to the waters
Jer. 3:22 we *c* to thee for thou art Lord
Hos. 6: 1 *c* let us return unto the Lord
Hab. 2: 3 it will surely *c* it will not tarry
Mal. 3: 1 Lord shall suddenly *c* to his temple
Mat. 8:11 many shall *c* from east and west
11:28 *c* unto me all ye that labour and
16:24 if any man will *c* after me
22: 4 all things ready, *c* to marriage
Luke 14:20 married a wife, I cannot *c*
John 1:39 saith unto them *c* and see
6:44 no man can *c* to me, except
7:37 if any man thirst, let him *c*
14:18 comfortless, I will *c* to
Acts 1:11 this Jesus shall so *c* as
1 Cor. 11:26 Lord's death till he *c*
Heb. 4:16 *c* boldly unto the throne of
Rev. 6: 1 four beasts, saying *c* and see
18: 4 *c* out of her, my people
22:17 the Spirit and the bride say, *c*

COMETH
Ps. 118:26 *c* in the name of the Lord
Mat. 3:11 he that *c* after me is
Luke 6:47 whoso *c*, heareth, doeth, is
John 3:31 he that *c* from above
6:35 *c* to me shall never hunger
Jas. 1:17 gift *c* down from the Father

COMING
Ps. 19: 5 as a bridegroom *c* out of his
121: 8 the Lord shall preserve thy *c* in
Mal. 3: 2 who may abide the day of his *c*

John 1:27 *c* after me is preferred before
1 Cor. 1: 7 waiting for the *c* of our
15:23 that are Christ's at his *c*
1 Thes. 3:13 at the *c* of our Lord
2 Thes. 2: 1 by the *c* of our Lord
Jas. 5: 8 for the *c* of the Lord
2 Pet. 3:12 hasting unto the *c* of the day

COMELY
Job 41:12 his power, nor his *c* proportion
Ps. 33: 1 praise is *c* for the upright
Sol. 1: 5 I am black but *c*
1 Cor. 12:24 *c* parts have no need

COMELINESS
Is. 53: 2 he hath no form nor *c*

COMFORT (COMFORTED)
Gen. 5:29 this same shall *c* us concerning
Job 7:13 my bed shall *c* me
Ps. 23: 4 thy rod and thy staff they *c* me
119: 50 is my *c* in my affliction
Is. 40: 1 *c* ye *c* ye my people
49:13 Lord hath *c* his people
51: 3 for the Lord shall *c* Zion
61: 2 to *c* all that mourn
Jer. 31:13 I will *c* and make them rejoice
31:15 Rahel weeping . . . refused to be *c*
Mat. 9:22 be of good *c*, thy faith hath
Acts 9:31 walking in the *c* of the Holy Ghost
Rom. 1:12 I may be *c* together with you
1 Cor. 14:31 all prophesy one by one all be *c*
2 Cor. 1: 4 we may be able to *c*
Phil. 2: 1 if any *c* of love, if any
Col. 4:11 have been a *c* unto me
1 Thes. 3: 7 *c* over you by your faith
4:18 *c* one another with
5:14 *c* the feeble minded, support the weak
2 Thes. 2:17 Lord Jesus *c* your hearts and

COMFORTERS
Job 16: 2 miserable *c* are ye all
Ps. 69:20 for, but I found none

COMFORTLESS
John 14:18 I will not leave you *c*

COMMAND (COMMANDETH, COMMANDING)
Deut. 28: 8 Lord shall *c* thy blessing upon thee
Ps. 42: 8 Lord will *c* his lovingkindness
Mat. 4: 3 these stones be made bread
John 15:14 if ye do whatsoever I *c*
Acts 17:30 now *c* all men to repent
1 Cor. 7:10 unto the married I *c*
1 Tim. 4: 3 *c* to abstain from meats, which God

COMMANDED
Ps. 111: 9 he hath *c* his covenant for ever
133: 3 Lord *c* the blessing, even life
Mat. 28:20 whatsoever I have *c* you
2 Cor. 4: 6 God who *c* the light to

COMMANDMENT
Ps. 119:96 thy *c* is exceeding broad
Prov. 6:23 the *c* is a lamp; and law is light
Hos. 5:11 willingly walked after the *c*
Mat. 22:38 is the first and great *c*
John 10:18 this *c* I received of my Father
12:50 his *c* is life everlasting
13:34 a new *c* give I unto
15:12 this is my *c* that ye love one
Rom. 7: 8 sin taking occasion by the *c*
1 Tim. 1: 5 end of the *c* is charity
2 Pet. 2:21 turn from the holy *c*
1 John 3:23 this is his *c* that we believe

COMMANDMENTS
Ex. 34:28 words of the covenant the ten *c*
Ps. 111: 7 all his *c* are sure
119: 6 I have respect unto all thy *c*
119: 35 make me to go in the path of thy *c*
119: 66 have believed thy *c*
119:127 I love thy *c* above gold
119:131 I longed for thy *c*
Mat. 22:40 two *c* hang all the law
Luke 1: 6 walking in all the *c*
Col. 2:22 after the *c* and doctrines of men
1 John 3:24 he that keepeth his *c* dwelleth
2 John 1: 6 that we walk after his *c*

COMMEND (COMMENDED, COMMENDETH)
Luke 23:46 to thy hands I *c* my spirit

Rom. 3: 5 our unrighteousness *c* the righteousness
5: 8 God *c* his love toward us
2 Cor. 10:18 not he that *c* self is approved

COMMIT (COMMITTED, COMMITTETH)
Ex. 20:14 thou shalt not *c* adultery
Job 5: 8 to God would I *c* my cause
Ps. 10:14 the poor *c* himself unto thee
31: 5 to thy hand I *c* my spirit
37: 5 *c* thy way unto the Lord
Prov. 16: 3 *c* thy works unto the Lord
Mat. 5:27 thou shalt not *c* adultery
Luke 12:48 to whom men have *c* much
John 5:22 *c* all judgment to the Son
8:34 who *c* sin is servant of
Rom. 1:32 *c* such things are worthy of death
1 Cor. 9:17 dispensation of the gospel is *c*
Gal. 2: 7 uncircumcision was *c* unto me
1 Tim. 1:11 God's which was *c* to my trust
2 Tim. 1:12 which I have *c* unto him against
1 Pet. 4:19 *c* the keeping of their souls
1 John 3: 8 who *c* sin is of the devil
3: 9 born of God doth not *c* sin

COMMON
Jer. 31: 5 and shall eat them as *c* things
Mark 12:37 the *c* people heard him gladly
Acts 2:44 together and had all things *c*
10:15 God hath cleansed, that call not *c*
1 Cor. 10:13 such as is *c* to man

COMMUNE (COMMUNED)
Ex. 25:22 I will *c* with thee from above
Ps. 4: 4 *c* with your own heart
Luke 6:11 they *c* one with another

COMMUNICATE (COMMUNICATED)
Phil. 4:14 ye did *c* with my affliction
1 Tim. 6:18 ready to distribute, willing to *c*
Heb. 13:16 do good and to *c* forget not

COMMUNICATION (COMMUNICATIONS)
1 Cor. 15:33 evil *c* corrupt good manners
Eph. 4:29 let no corrupt *c* proceed
Col. 3: 8 filthy *c* out of your mouth

COMMUNION
1 Cor. 10:16 is it not the *c* of the blood of
2 Cor. 6:14 what *c* hath light with darkness?

COMPANY
Prov. 29: 3 keepeth *c* with harlots
Sol. 6:13 as it were the *c* of two armies
Acts 6: 7 a great *c* of the priests
Rom. 15:24 first filled with your *c*
Heb. 12:22 an innumerable *c* of angels

COMPANION (COMPANIONS)
Ps. 45:14 the virgins, her *c* that follow
122: 8 for my brethren and *c* sakes
Prov. 13:20 *c* of fools shall be destroyed
Is. 1:23 are rebellious and *c* of thieves
Mal. 2:14 thy *c* and thy wife of the covenant
Rev. 1: 9 your brother and *c* in tribulation

COMPARE (COMPARED, COMPARING)
Ps. 89: 6 who in heaven can be *c*
Prov. 3:15 desire are not to be *c* unto her
Sol. 1: 9 *c* thee, O my love to a company
Is. 40:18 what likeness will ye *c* unto him
Rom. 8:18 not worthy to be *c* with the glory
2 Cor. 10:12 *c* ourselves with some that commend

COMPASS (COMPASSED, COMPASSEST, COMPASSETH)
Ps. 5:12 with favour *c* him as
18: 4 sorrows of death *c* me
26: 6 innocency: so will I *c* thy altar
32:10 mercy shall *c* him about
73: 6 pride *c* them about as a chain
116: 3 sorrows of death *c* me
118: 10 all nations *c* me about
139: 3 thou *c* my path and my lying
Jer. 31:22 woman shall *c* a man
Jonah 2: 3 and the floods *c* me about
Hab. 1: 4 wicked doth *c* the righteous

COMPASSION (COMPASSIONS)
Ex. 2: 6 babe wept. And she had *c*
Deut. 30: 3 Lord turn captivity and have *c*
Ps. 78:38 being full of *c* forgave
111: 4 Lord is gracious and full of *c*
Jer. 12:15 return and have *c* on

Lam. 3:22 consumed because his *c* fail not
Mic. 7:19 he will have *c* on us
Zech. 7: 9 and show mercy and *c* every man
Mat. 9:36 he was moved with *c*
15:32 I have *c* on the multitude
20:34 Jesus had *c* on them
Mark 1:41 Jesus, moved with *c* put forth
5:19 friends, tell how the Lord had *c* on
9:22 canst do any thing have *c* on us
Luke 7:13 Lord had *c* and said, Weep not
15:20 off, his father saw him, and had *c*
Rom. 9:15 on whom I will have *c*
1 Pet. 3: 8 having *c* one of another

COMPEL (COMPELLED, COMPELLEST)
Luke 14:23 and *c* them to come in
Acts 26:11 I *c* them to blaspheme
2 Cor. 12:11 I am a fool ye *c* me
Gal. 2:14 *c* Gentiles to live as Jews

COMPREHEND (COMPREHENDED)
John 1: 5 the darkness *c* it not
Eph. 3:18 be able to *c* with all saints

CONCEAL (CONCEALETH, CONCEALED)
Gen. 37:26 slay our brother and *c* his blood
Ps. 40:10 not *c* thy lovingkindness and thy
Prov. 12:23 a prudent man *c* knowledge

CONCEIT (CONCEITS)
Prov. 18:11 and as an high wall in his own *c*
26: 5 lest he be wise in his own *c*
28:11 rich man is wise in his own *c*
Rom. 11:25 should be wise in your own *c*

CONCEIVE (CONCEIVED)
Gen. 30:38 should *c* when they came to drink
Num. 11:12 have I *c* all this people?
Job 15:35 they *c* mischief, and bring forth
Ps. 7:14 hath *c* mischief, and brought forth
51: 5 in sin did my mother *c* me
Is. 59: 4 they *c* mischief, and bring forth
7:14 a virgin shall *c* and bear a son
Mat. 1:20 *c* in her is of the Holy Ghost
Luke 1:31 thou shalt *c* in thy womb
2:21 so named before he was *c*
Acts 5: 4 why hast thou *c* in thy heart
Jas. 1:15 when lust hath *c* it bringeth

CONCORD
2 Cor. 6:15 what *c* hath Christ with Belial

CONCUBINE (CONCUBINES)
2 Sam.16:21 go in unto thy father's *c*

CONCUPISCENCE
Col. 3: 5 affection, evil *c*, and covetousness
1 Thes. 4: 5 not in the lust of *c*, even

CONDEMN (CONDEMNED, CONDEMNETH)
2 Chr. 36: 3 *c* the land in a hundred talents
Job 9:20 own mouth shall *c* me
Ps. 37:33 nor *c* him when judged
94:21 righteous and *c* the innocent blood
Is. 50: 9 Lord will help me, who shall *c*?
Prov. 17:15 he that *c* the just, even
Mat. 12:37 by thy words thou shalt be *c*
Luke 6:37 *c* not and ye shall not be condemned
John 3:17 into the world to *c* the world
8:11 neither do I *c* thee, go and sin
Rom. 8: 3 for sin, *c* sin in the flesh
8:34 who is he that *c*? It is Christ
14:22 Happy is he that *c* not himself
1 Cor. 11:32 we should not be *c* with the world
Tit. 2: 8 sound speech cannot be *c*

CONDEMNATION
Luke 23:40 seeing thou art in the same *c*
John 3:19 this is the *c*, that light is
Rom. 5:16 judgment by one to *c*, but free
8: 1 no *c* to them which are in
1 Tim. 3: 6 fall into *c* of the devil
Jas. 1: 1 we shall receive the greater *c*
5:12 swear not, lest ye fall into *c*

CONFESS (CONFESSED, CONFESSETH, CONFESSING)
Lev. 5: 5 he shall *c* that he hath
26:40 if they *c* their iniquity
1 Ki. 8:35 *c* thy name, and turn
Neh. 1: 6 *c* the sins of the children
Ps. 32: 5 I will *c* my transgressions unto
Prov. 28:13 whoso *c* and forsaketh them shall
Dan. 9:20 *c* my sin and the sin of my

Mat. 3: 6 baptized in the Jordan *c* their sins
10:32 shall *c* me before men
Luke 12: 8 him will the Son of Man also *c*
Rom. 10: 9 *c* with thy mouth the Lord Jesus;
Jas. 5:16 *c* your faults one to another
1 John 1: 9 if we *c* our sins, he is faithful
4:15 *c* Jesus is the Son of God

CONFESSION
2 Chr. 30:22 making *c* to the Lord God
Rom. 10:10 mouth *c* is made unto salvation
1 Tim. 6:13 Pontius Pilate witnessed a good *c*

CONFIDENCE (CONFIDENCES)
Ps. 118: 8 than to put *c* in man
Prov. 3:26 the Lord shall be thy *c*
Jer. 2:37 the Lord hath rejected thy *c*
Ezek. 29:16 no more the *c* of Israel
Mic. 7: 5 put ye not *c* in a guide,
Eph. 3:12 in whom we have access with *c*
Phil. 3: 3 we have no *c* in the flesh
Heb. 3: 6 if we hold fast the *c*
1 John 3:21 then have we *c* toward God

CONFIRM (CONFIRMED)
Is. 35: 3 and *c* the feeble knees
44:26 that *c* the word of his servant
Rom. 15: 8 to *c* the promises made unto
1 Cor. 1: 8 shall also *c* you unto the end
2 Cor. 2: 8 *c* your love toward
Heb. 6:17 of his counsel *c* it by an oath

CONFORMED
Rom. 8:29 predestined to be *c* to the image
12: 2 be not *c* to this world

CONFOUND (CONFOUNDED)
Gen. 11: 7 and there *c* their language
Mic. 3: 7 and the diviners *c*: yea, they
7:16 nations shall see and be *c*
Acts 2: 6 multitude came together and were *c*
1 Cor. 1:27 foolish things of the world to *c*
1 Pet. 2: 6 believeth shall not be *c*

CONFUSION
Ps. 71: 1 let me never be put to *c*
Is. 24:10 the city of *c* is broken
1 Cor. 14:33 God is not the author of *c*

CONGREGATION
Ex. 16: 2 the whole *c* of the children
27:21 tabernacle of the *c*
Lev. 14:27 I bear with this evil *c*
Josh. 9:15 princes of the *c* sware
Ps. 22:25 be of thee in the great *c*
Is. 14:13 the mount of the *c* in the sides
Lam. 1:10 heathen not enter the *c*,

CONQUER (CONQUERING)
Rev. 6: 2 he went forth *c*

CONQUERORS
Rom. 8:37 we are more than *c* through him

CONSCIENCE
John 8: 9 convicted by their own *c*
Acts 23: 1 in all good *c* before God
24:16 a *c* void of offence
Rom. 2:15 their *c* also bearing witness
9: 1 my *c* also bearing me witness
1 Tim. 3: 9 of faith in a pure *c*
4: 2 having their *c* seared with hot
2 Tim. 1: 3 my forefathers with pure *c*
Tit. 1:15 their mind and *c* is defiled
Heb. 9:14 purge *c* from dead works
1 Pet. 3:21 answer of a good *c* toward God

CONSENT (CONSENTING)
Acts 8: 1 was *c* unto his death
Rom. 7:16 I *c* unto the law

CONSIDER (CONSIDERED, CONSIDEREST)
1 Sam.12:24 *c* how great things he
Job 1: 8 hast thou *c* my servant Job
Ps. 8: 3 when I *c* thy heavens
31: 7 thou hast *c* my trouble
41: 1 blessed is he that *c* the poor
77: 5 have *c* days of old, the years
Eccl. 7:13 *c* the work of God
Is. 1: 3 my people doth not *c*
Hag. 1: 5 saith the Lord, *c* your ways
Mat. 6:28 *c* the lilies of the field
7: 3 *c* not the beam
Rom. 4:19 *c* not his own body dead

CONSOLATION (CONSOLATIONS)
Job 15: 11 are the c of God small
Is. 66: 11 with the breasts of her c
Luke 2: 25 waiting for the c of Israel
6: 24 are rich, have received your c
Acts 4: 36 being interpreted the son of c
Rom. 15: 5 God of c grant you to
2 Cor. 1: 5 our c aboundeth by Christ
Phil. 2: 1 if therefore any c in Christ

CONSTRAIN (CONSTRAINED)
2 Cor. 5: 14 for the love of Christ c
Gal. 6: 12 they c you to be circumcised

CONSUME (CONSUMED)
Ex. 3: 2 bush was not c
33: 3 lest I c thee in the way
Deut. 5: 25 this great fire will c us
Ps. 78: 33 their days did he c in vanity
90: 7 we are c by thine anger
119: 139 my zeal hath c me, because
Prov. 5: 11 thy flesh and body are c
Lam. 3: 22 of the Lord's mercies not c
Gal. 5: 15 not c one of another
2 Thes. 2: 8 Lord shall c with the spirit of
Jas. 4: 3 c it upon your lusts

CONSUMING
Deut. 4: 24 thy God is a c fire
Heb. 12: 29 our God is a c fire

CONTAIN
John 21: 25 itself could not c the books
1 Cor. 7: 9 if they cannot c, let them marry

CONTEND (CONTENDETH)
Deut. 2: 9 neither c with them in battle
Job 40: 2 he that c with the Almighty
Is. 49: 25 I will c with them that c
57: 16 I will not c for ever
Jude 1: 3 earnestly c for the faith

CONTENTION (CONTENTIONS)
Prov. 13: 10 only by pride cometh before c
18: 6 A fool's lips enter into c and
Jer. 15: 10 borne me a man of c
Phil. 1: 16 preach Christ of c
1 Thes. 2: 2 gospel of God with much c

CONTENTIOUS
Prov. 18: 18 lot causeth c to cease
19: 13 and the c of a wife are a
21: 19 than with a c and an angry woman
27: 15 rainy day and a c woman are alike
Rom. 2: 8 are c, and do not obey
1 Cor. 11: 16 but if any man seem to be c

CONTENT
Josh. 7: 7 would to God we had been c
Prov. 6: 35 neither will he rest c
Luke 3: 14 be c with your wages
Phil. 4: 11 therewith to be c
1 Tim. 6: 8 food and raiment let us be c
Heb. 13: 5 be c with such things

CONTENTMENT
1 Tim. 6: 6 but godliness with c is great gain

CONTINUAL (CONTINUALLY)
Ps. 34: 1 his praise c in my mouth
52: 1 goodness of God endureth c
73: 23 I am c with thee
Prov. 6: 21 bind c upon thine heart
Is. 58: 11 the Lord shall guide thee c
Hos. 12: 6 wait on thy God c
Acts 6: 4 give ourselves c to prayer
Heb. 13: 15 sacrifice of praise to God c

CONTINUANCE
Ps. 139: 16 which in c were fashioned
Rom. 2: 7 to them who by patient c in well doing

CONTINUE
1 Sam.12: 14 c following the Lord your God
Ps. 36: 10 O c thy lovingkindness unto
John 8: 31 c in my word, then are ye my disciples
15: 9 c ye in my love
Acts 13: 43 to c in the grace of God
Rom. 6: 1 shall we c in sin that grace
Col. 1: 23 if ye c in faith grounded
4: 2 c in prayer, and watch
1 Tim. 2: 15 if they c in faith and charity
Heb. 13: 1 let brotherly love c

CONTINUED (CONTINUETH, CONTINUING)
Luke 6: 12 c all night in prayer
22: 28 c with me in my temptations
Acts 2: 42 c stedfastly in the apostles' doctrine
1 Tim. 5: 5 c in supplication and prayer
Heb. 8: 9 because they c not in my covenant

CONTRARY
Lev. 26: 21 if ye walk c unto me
Acts 18: 13 to worship God c to the law
Rom. 11: 24 grafted c to nature
1 Tim. 1: 10 other thing that is c to sound doctrine

CONVERSATION
Ps. 37: 14 such as be of upright c
50: 23 ordereth his c aright
2 Cor. 1: 12 we have had our c in the world
Eph. 4: 22 the former c the old man
Phil. 1: 27 c be as becometh the gospel
3: 20 our c is in heaven
Heb. 13: 5 let your c be without covetousness
Jas. 3: 13 show out of good c his works
1 Pet. 1: 15 holy in all manner of c
2: 12 c honest among the Gentiles
3: 1 won by c of the wives
2 Pet. 2: 7 with the filthy c of the wicked
3: 11 in all holy c and godliness

CONVERT (CONVERTED)
Ps. 51: 13 sinners be c to thee
Is. 6: 10 c and be healed
Mat. 13: 15 be c and I should heal them
18: 3 except ye be c and become as
Luke 22: 32 when thou art c strengthen
Acts 3: 19 be c and your sins blotted out

CONVERTS
Is. 1: 27 her c with rightousness

CORD (CORDS)
Job 30: 11 he hath loosed my c,
36: 8 be holden in c of affliction
Ps. 129: 4 asunder of c of the wicked
Prov. 5: 22 holden with the c of his sins
Is. 54: 2 spare not, lengthen thy c, and strengthen
Hos. 11: 4 c of a man, bands of love

CORN
Gen. 41: 49 gathered c as the sand of the sea
Josh. 5: 11 eat of the old c of the land
Neh. 13: 5 the tithes of the c, the new wine
Ps. 72: 16 handful of c in the earth
78: 24 given them c of heaven to eat
Is. 62: 8 no more than give c to enemies
Mat. 12: 1 began to pluck the ears of c
John 12: 24 except a c of wheat fall
1 Cor. 9: 9 ox that treadeth out the c

CORNER (CORNERS)
Lev. 19: 9 shalt not reap the c of thy field
Job 38: 6 who laid the c stone
Ps. 118: 22 is become the head of the c
144: 12 daughters may be as c stones
Prov. 21: 9 it is better to dwell in a c
Is. 28: 16 a precious c stone
Mat. 21: 42 same has become the head of the c
Acts 4: 11 has become the head of the c
Eph. 2: 20 himself being the chief c stone
1 Pet. 2: 6 in Sion a chief c stone

CORRECT (CORRECTED, CORRECTETH)
Job 5: 17 happy is the man whom God c
Ps. 39: 11 with rebukes dost c man
Prov. 3: 12 whom the Lord loveth he c
29: 17 c thy son, and he shall give
Jer. 10: 24 c me, but with judgment
Heb. 12: 9 our flesh which c us

CORRECTION
Prov. 3: 11 but be not weary of his c
22: 15 rod of c shall drive foolishness
23: 13 withhold not c from the child
Hab. 1: 12 established them for c
2 Tim. 3: 16 Scripture profitable for c

CORRUPT
Ps. 38: 5 wounds stink and are c
Mat. 6: 19 moth and rust doth c
7: 17 but a c tree bringeth forth
1 Cor. 15: 33 evil communications c good manners
Eph. 4: 22 the old man which is c

1 Tim. 6: 5 men of c minds and destitute

CORRUPTIBLE
1 Cor. 9: 25 do it to obtain a c crown
15: 53 For this c must put in
1 Pet. 1: 18 redeemed with c things

CORRUPTION
Ps. 16: 10 Holy one to see c
Jonah 2: 6 brought up my life from c
Acts 2: 31 his flesh did see c
13: 34 now no more to return to c
1 Cor. 15: 42 It is sown in c, it is raised
Gal. 6: 8 shall of the flesh reap c
2 Pet. 1: 4 having escaped through c

COST
1 Chr. 21: 24 offer burnt offering without c
Luke 14: 28 and counteth the c, whether we

COUNCIL
Mat. 5: 22 shall be in danger of the c
10: 17 they will deliver you up to the c
Acts 4: 15 them to go aside out of the c

COUNSEL
Num. 31: 16 through the c of Balaam
Job 12: 13 he hath c and understanding
21: 16 c of the wicked far from me
38: 2 who is this that darkeneth c
Ps. 1: 1 walketh not in the c of the ungodly
33: 10 c of the Lord stands for ever
55: 14 we took sweet c together
Prov. 1: 25 set at nought all my c
8: 14 c is mine and sound wisdom
11: 14 where no c is the people fall
20: 18 purpose established by c
24: 6 by wise c make war, in multitude
27: 9 a man's friend by hearty c
Is. 11: 2 the spirit of c and might
Jer. 32: 19 great in thy c and mighty in thy work
Zech. 6: 13 c of peace between them
Acts 2: 23 delivered by the determinate c
5: 38 if this c be of men it

COUNSELLOR (COUNSELLORS)
2 Sam.15: 12 Ahithophel the Gilonite, David's c
1 Chr. 26: 14 Zechariah his son, a wise c
Ps. 119: 24 thy testimonies are my c
Prov. 11: 14 in a multitude of the c safety
Is. 1: 26 restore the c as at the beginning
9: 6 called Wonderful, C, the mighty God
Dan. 3: 24 spake and said unto his c
Mark 15: 43 Joseph of Arimathaea, an honourable c

COUNT (COUNTED)
Gen. 15: 6 c to him for righteousness
Ex. 12: 4 shall make your c for the lamb
Ps. 106: 31 and that was c unto him for
Is. 40: 17 c to him less than nothing
Hos. 8: 12 law c as a strange thing
10: 29 c the blood of the covenant unholy
Acts 20: 24 neither c I my life dear
Rom. 4: 3 it was c unto him for righteousness
Phil. 3: 7 those I c loss for Christ
Jas. 1: 2 c it all joy when ye fall

COUNTENANCE
Num. 6: 26 Lord lift up his c upon thee
1 Sam.16: 7 look not on his c or height
Job 29: 24 the light of my c they cast not
Ps. 4: 6 the light of thy c upon
90: 8 secret sins in the light of thy c

COUNTRY
Prov. 25: 25 good news from a far c
Heb. 11: 16 they desire a better c

COURAGE
Num. 13: 20 and be ye of good c
Josh. 1: 6 be strong and of good c
Ps. 27: 14 Wait on the Lord: be of good c
Is. 41: 6 Be of good c

COURAGEOUS
Josh. 23: 6 be ye therefore very c
2 Sam.13: 28 be c and be valiant

COURSE (COURSES)
1 Chr. 23: 6 divided them into c among the sons
Ps. 82: 5 foundations of the earth are out of c
Acts 20: 24 finish my c with joy
2 Thes. 3: 1 word may have free c and
2 Tim. 4: 7 I have finished my c

Jas.   3: 6 setteth on fire the c of nature
COURT (COURTS)
Ex.   27: 9 make the c of tabernacle
Ps.   65: 4 that he may dwell in thy c
       84: 10 for a day in thy c is better
      100:      enter his c with praise
Is.   62: 9 drink it in the c of my holiness
COVENANT
Gen.   9: 9 I establish my c with you
       15: 18 Lord made a c with Abraham
       17: 7 will establish my c between me and thee
Ex.   2: 24 God remembered his c with Abraham
        6: 4 have established my c with them
       19: 5 obey my voice indeed, and keep my c
       34: 27 I have made a c with thee
Num. 10: 33 the ark of the c of the Lord
       25: 13 c of an everlasting priesthood
Deut.   5: 2 made a c with us in Horeb
        7: 9 which keepeth c and mercy
Josh.   7: 11 also transgressed my c
Judg.   2: 1 never brake the c with you
        2: 20 people hath transgressed my c
2 Sam. 23: 5 made with me an everlasting c
1 Ki.   8: 23 who keepest c and mercy
       11: 11 thou hast kept my c and statues
2 Ki. 18: 12 but transgressed his c, and all
1 Chr. 16: 15 be ye mindful always of his c
2 Chr. 6: 14 the earth; which keepest my c
Neh.   1: 5 that keepeth c and mercy for them
        9: 32 who keepest c and mercy
Job   31: 1 I made a c with mine eyes
Ps.   25: 10 keep his c and testimonies
       50: 5 made a c with me by sacrifice
       89: 3 I have made a c with my chosen
      103: 18 to such as keep his c
      105: 10 to Israel for an everlasting c
      106: 45 he remembered for them his c
      132: 12 if thy children keep my c
Prov.   2: 17 forgetteth the c of her God
Is.   28: 15 we have made a c with death
       42: 6 give thee for a c of the people
       54: 10 nor the c of my peace be removed
       55: 3 I will make an everlasting c with
Jer.   14: 21 break not the c with us
       31: 31 will make a new c with the house
       50: 5 to the Lord in a perpetual c
Ezek. 16: 60 I will remember my c
Dan.   9: 4 keeping the c and mercy to them
Hos.   8: 1 they have transgressed my c
       10: 4 swearing falsely in making a c
Amos   1: 9 remembered not thy brotherly c
Mal.   2: 14 thy companion, the wife of the c
Luke   1: 72 to remember his holy c
Rom.   9: 4 adoption, and glory and c
Eph.   2: 12 strangers from the c of promise
Heb.   8: 6 the mediator of a better c
       13: 20 through the blood of an everlasting c
COVER (COVERED, COVEREST, COVERETH)
Ex.   33: 22 I will c thee with my hand
Deut. 33: 12 Lord shall c him all day
Job   31: 33 if I c my transgressions
Ps.   32: 1 is forgiven whose sin is c
       73: 6 violence c them as a garment
       91: 4 c thee with his feathers
      104: 2 c thyself with light as with
Prov. 10: 12 but love c all sins
Is.   11: 9 as the waters c the sea
Lam.   3: 44 c thyself with a cloud
Hos.   10: 8 say to the mountains, c us
Rom.   4: 7 and whose sins are c
1 Cor. 11: 7 man ought not to c his head
1 Pet. 4: 8 charity shall c a multitude of
COVET (COVETED)
Ex.   20: 17 thou shalt not c thy neighbor's house
1 Cor. 12: 31 c earnestly the best gifts
       14: 39 c to prophesy and forbid not
COVETOUS
Ps.   10: 3 blesseth the c, whom the Lord
1 Cor. 6: 10 nor the c inherit the kingdom of God
1 Tim. 3: 3 but patient, not a brawler, not c
2 Pet. 2: 14 heart they have exercised with c
COVETOUSNESS
Ex.   18: 21 fear God, men of truth, hating c

Ps.   119: 36 thy testimonies and not to c
Luke   12: 15 and beware of c: for man's life
Col.   3: 5 and c which is idolatry
Heb.   13: 5 let your conversation be without c
CREATE (CREATED)
Gen.   1: 1 God c the heavens and the earth
Ps.   51: 10 c in me a clean heart
      104: 30 forth thy spirit, they are c
Is.   4: 5 will c upon every dwelling place
       43: 7 I have c him for my glory
       57: 19 I c the fruit of the lips, peace
Jer.   31: 22 c a new thing in the earth
Eph.   2: 10 c in Christ Jesus to good works
Col.   3: 10 after the image of him that c him
1 Tim. 4: 3 which God c to be received
Rev.   4: 11 thou hast c all things
CREATION
Rom.   1: 20 of him from the c of the world
        8: 22 the whole c groaneth
CREATOR
Eccl. 12: 1 remember now thy C in the days
1 Pet. 4: 19 in well doing as unto a faithful C
CREATURE
Gen.   1: 20 moving c that hath life
Rom.   8: 20 c was made subject to vanity
2 Cor. 5: 17 man in Christ is a new c
Gal.   6: 15 availeth anything but a new c
Col.   1: 15 the firstborn of every c
1 Tim. 4: 4 every c of God is good
CROOKED
Deut. 32: 5 are a perverse and c generation
Eccl.   1: 15 c cannot be made straight
Is.   40: 4 the c shall be made straight
Luke   3: 5 the c shall be made straight
Phil.   2: 15 a c and perverse generation
CROSS
Mat.   10: 38 taketh not up his c and followeth
Luke   14: 27 whosoever doth not bear his c
John   19: 17 bearing his c went forth
1 Cor. 1: 17 lest the c of Christ be of none
Gal.   5: 11 is the offence of the c ceased
        6: 14 glory save in the c of our Lord Jesus
Phil.   2: 8 even death on the c
        3: 18 enemies of the c of
Col.   1: 20 peace through the blood of his c
Heb.   12: 2 before him endured the c
CROWN (CROWNS)
Lev.   8: 9 the golden plate, the holy c
Esth.   1: 11 the king with the c royal
Ps.   89: 39 thou hast profaned his c
Prov. 12: 4 virtuous woman is a c
       14: 24 c of the wise is their riches: but
       14: 17 children's children are the c of
Is.   28: 5 Lord of hosts for the c of glory
1 Cor. 9: 25 to obtain a corruptible c
Phil.   4: 1 joy and c, so stand fast
2 Tim. 4: 8 laid up for me a c of righteousness
Jas.   1: 12 receive the c of life which Lord
Rev.   2: 10 I will give thee a c of life
        3: 11 that no man take thy c
        4: 4 on their heads c of gold
       12: 3 seven c upon his heads
       13: 1 upon his horns ten c
       19: 12 on his head were many c
CROWNED (CROWNETH)
Ps.   8: 5 and hast c him with glory
      103: 4 c thee with lovingkindness
Prov. 14: 18 prudent are c with knowledge
Heb.   2: 9 c with glory and honor
CRUCIFY (CRUCIFIED)
Mat.   20: 19 to scourge and to c him
       28: 5 ye seek Jesus, which was c
Rom.   6: 6 the old man is c with him
1 Cor. 1: 23 but we preach Christ c
2 Cor. 13: 4 though he was c through weakness
Gal.   2: 20 I am c with Christ, I live
        5: 24 that are Christ's have c the flesh
        6: 14 world is c to me, I to world
Heb.   6: 6 they c the Son of God afresh
CRUEL
Prov. 11: 17 he that is c troubleth
Sol.   8: 6 jealousy is c as the grave

Is.   13: 9 c both with wrath and fierce anger
Jer.   6: 23 they are c and have no mercy
Heb.   11: 36 had a trial of c mockings
CRUMBS
Mat.   15: 27 dogs eat the c which fall
Luke   16: 21 with the c which fell
CRY (CRIED, CRIEST, CRIETH)
Gen.   4: 10 brother's blood c unto me
       18: 20 Because the c of Sodom and Gomorrah
Ex.   22: 23 I will surely hear their c
Ps.   9: 12 forgetteth not the c of the humble
       22: 5 c to thee and were delivered
      138: 3 I c thou answeredst me
Prov.   1: 20 wisdom c without; she uttereth
        2: 3 if thou c after knowledge
Jer.   7: 16 neither lift up c nor prayer
Lam.   2: 18 their heart c unto the Lord
Mic.   6: 9 Lord's voice c to the city
Luke   18: 7 c day and night to him
       19: 40 peace, the stones would c out
Rom.   8: 15 where by we c, Abba Father
CRYING
Prov. 19: 18 thy soul spare for his c
Mat.   3: 3 voice of one c in the wilderness
Rev.   21: 4 neither sorrow nor c, neither
CUP
Gen.   40: 11 Pharaoh's c was in my hand
Ps.   16: 5 mine inheritance and of my c
       23: 5 with oil; my c runneth over
      116: 13 take the c of salvation
Prov. 23: 31 when it giveth colour in the c
Is.   51: 17 the dregs of the c of trembling
Jer.   16: 7 give them the c of salvation
       25: 15 the wine c of this fury
Ezek. 23: 31 give her c into her hand
Hab.   2: 16 c of the Lord's right hand
Mat.   10: 42 a c of cold water only
       20: 22 able to drink of the c that I
       23: 25 make clean outside of the c and
       26: 39 let this c pass from me
John   18: 11 c which the Father hath given
1 Cor. 10: 16 c of blessing which
       11: 25 this c is the new testament
Rev.   16: 19 unto her the c of the wine
CURSE
Gen.   8: 21 not again c the ground
       27: 13 Upon me be thy c, my son
Lev.   19: 14 thou shalt not c the deaf
Deut. 11: 26 before you a blessing and a c
       23: 5 turned the c into a blessing
Job   1: 11 he will c thee to thy face
        2: 9 retain integrity? c God and die
Ps.   109: 28 let them not c but bless
Prov. 11: 26 the people shall c him
       26: 2 so the c causeless shall not come
Eccl. 10: 20 c not the king in his chamber
Is.   65: 15 for a c unto my chosen
Jer.   15: 10 every one of them doth c me
       26: 6 city a c to all the nations
Mal.   2: 2 I will c your blessings
        3: 9 ye are cursed with a c
Mat.   5: 44 bless them that c you,
Rom.   12: 14 bless, and do not c
CURSED (CURSING)
Deut. 30: 19 life and death, blessing and c
Job   3: 1 I opened Job his mouth and c his day
Jer.   48: 10 c be he that doeth the work of the
CURTAIN
2 Sam. 7: 2 God dwelleth within the c
Ps.   104: 2 stretchest out the heavens like a c
CUSTOM (CUSTOMS)
Rom.   13: 7 c to whom c; fear to
CUT
Lev.   22: 24 or crushed, or broken, or c
Ps.   37: 28 the wicked shall be c off
       76: 12 He shall c off the spirit
      129: 4 he hath c asunder the cords
Prov.   2: 22 but the wicked shall be c off
Zech. 11: 10 c it asunder that I might break
Mat.   5: 30 hand offend thee, c it
       18: 8 thy foot offend thee, c it off
Rom.   11: 22 thou also shalt be c off

CYMBAL (CYMBALS)
2 Sam. 6: 5 and on cornets and on c
Ps. 150: 5 Praise him upon the loud c
1 Cor. 13: 1 as sounding brass, or a tinkling c

DAMNED
Mark 16:16 believeth not shall be d
Rom. 14:23 doubteth, is d if he eat

DAMNATION
Mat. 23:14 ye shall receive the greater d
23:33 can ye escape the d of hell
Mark 3:29 is in danger of eternal d
John 5:29 forth to resurrection of d
1 Cor. 11:29 eateth and drinketh d

DANCE (DANCED, DANCES)
Ex. 15:20 with timbrels and with d
2 Sam. 6:14 And David d before the Lord
Ps. 149: 3 let them praise his name in the d
Mat. 14: 6 the daughter of Herodias d

DARE
Rom. 5: 7 some would even d to die

DARK
Num. 12: 8 and not in d speeches
Job 24:16 in the d dig through houses
Ps. 18:11 d waters and thick clouds of the
74:20 for the d places of the earth
78: 2 I will utter d sayings
88:12 thy wonders known in the d?
Prov. 1: 6 of the wise and their d sayings
Is. 45:19 in a d place of the earth
Lam. 3: 6 set me in the d places

DARKENED
Ex. 10:15 so that the land was d
Ps. 69:23 let eyes be d that they see not
Mat. 24:29 shall the sun be d
Rom. 1:21 their foolish heart was d
11:10 Let their eyes be d that they may
Eph. 4:18 having the understanding d

DARKLY
1 Cor. 13:12 now we see through a glass d

DARKNESS
Gen. 1: 2 d was upon the face of the deep
1 Sam. 2: 9 wicked shall be silent in d
2 Sam.22:29 Lord will lighten my d
Ps. 104:20 makest d., and it is night
107: 10 such as sit in d and in
Is. 5:20 d for light, and light for d
9: 2 walked in d have seen
Mat. 4:16 sat in d saw a great light
6:23 whole body full of d
8:12 cast out into outer d
John 1: 5 light shineth in the d
3:19 men loved d rather than light
12:35 light lest d come upon
Acts 26:18 turn them from d to light
Rom. 13:12 cast off the works of d
2 Cor. 4: 6 light to shine out of d
Eph. 5:11 the unfruitful works of d
6:12 the rulers of the d of this world
1 Thes. 5: 4 but ye brethren are not in d
1 Pet. 2: 9 called you of d
2 Pet. 2: 4 delivered into chains of d
1 John 1: 5 in him is no d at all
2: 8 d is past, and the true light shineth

DASH (DASHED)
2 Ki. 8:12 wilt d their children, and rip up
Ps. 2: 9 d in pieces like a potter's vessel
91:12 lest thou d thy foot against a stone
137: 9 d thy little ones against the stones
Is. 13:18 bows shall d the young men

DAY
Gen. 1: 5 and God called the light d
Ps. 19: 2 d unto d uttereth speech
84:10 a d in thy courts is better than
118: 24 this is the d which the Lord
Is. 13: 9 the d of the Lord cometh
34: 8 the d of the Lord's vengeance
Jer. 46:10 the d of the Lord of Hosts
Joel 1:15 the d of the Lord is at hand
Amos 5:18 that desire the d of the Lord
6: 3 put far away the evil d
Nah. 1: 7 a strong hold in the d of trouble
Hab. 3:16 I might rest in the d of trouble

Zeph. 2: 3 be hid in the d of the Lord's anger
Zech. 4:10 despised the d of small things
Mal. 4: 5 the great and dreadful d
Mat. 6:34 sufficient to the d is the evil
Mark 6:11 in the d of judgment than for
John 8:56 Abraham rejoiced to see my d
1 Cor. 1: 8 blameless in the d of our Lord
1 Thes. 5: 5 children of the d
2 Pet. 1:19 d star arise in your hearts
Rev. 1:10 the Spirit on the Lord's d

DAYS
Gen. 49: 1 which shall befall you in the last d
Job 7: 6 my d are swifter than a
7:16 let me alone, my d are vanity
8: 9 d on earth as a shadow
Ps. 39: 4 to know the end, and measure of my d
90:12 teach us to number our d
102: 3 my d are consumed like smoke
102: 23 in the way; he shortened my d
Eccl. 12: 1 while the evil d come not
Is. 2: 2 it shall come to pass in the last d
Jer. 30:24 in the latter d ye shall consider
Dan. 10:14 befall thy people in the latter d
Hos. 5: 3 his goodness in the latter d
Eph. 5:16 time because the d are evil
2 Tim. 3: 1 that in the last d perilous
Jas. 5: 3 treasure together in the last d
1 Pet. 3:10 love life and see good d
2 Pet. 3: 3 come in the last d scoffers

DEACONS
1 Tim. 3: 8 likewise must the d be grave

DEAD
Gen. 20: 3 behold thou art but a d man
Num. 16:48 stood between d and living
Ps. 88:10 shall the d arise and praise
115: 17 the d praise not the Lord
Mat. 8:22 let the d bury their own d
22:32 not the God of the d but of the
Luke 8:52 she is not d but sleepeth
John 5:25 d hear the voice of the Son of God
11:25 though d yet shall he live
Rom. 6: 8 now if we be d with Christ
6:11 d indeed unto sin, but alive
Gal. 2:19 I through the law am d to the law
Eph. 2: 1 who were d in trespasses and sins
Col. 2:13 being d in your sins and the
1 Thes. 4:16 d in Christ rise first
2 Tim. 2:11 d with him, we shall live
Heb. 11: 4 by it he being d yet speaketh
Rev. 14:13 blessed are the d which die

DEAF
Lev. 19:14 thou shalt not curse the d
Is. 35: 5 ears of the d shall be unstopped
42:18 hear, ye d and look, ye blind
Mat. 11: 5 the d hear, the dead are raised up

DEATH
Gen. 21:16 not see the d of the child
Num. 23:10 let me die the d of the righteous
Ps. 6: 5 in d no remembrance of thee
89:48 liveth and shall not see d
116: 15 Lord is the d of his saints
118: 18 he hath not given me over unto d
Prov. 2:18 her house inclineth to d
8:36 all they that hate me love d
18: 21 d and life in the power of the tongue
Is. 25: 8 he will swallow up d in victory
28:15 we have made a covenant with d
Jer. 8: 3 chosen rather than life
21: 8 you a way of life, a way of d
Mat. 16:28 which shall not taste of d
26:38 exceeding sorrowful even unto d
John 5:24 is passed from d unto life
8:51 he shall never see d.,
12:33 what d he should die
Acts 2:24 having loosed the pains of d
Rom. 5:12 sin entered, and d by sin
6: 9 d hath no more dominion over
6:21 for the end of those things is d
7: 5 to bring forth fruit unto d
8: 2 free from the law of sin and d
8:38 nor life shall separate us from
1 Cor. 3:22 or life, or d or things
11:26 ye show the Lord's d till he come

15: 21 by man came d by man also
15:54 d is swallowed up in victory
2 Cor. 1: 9 sentence of d in ourselves
2:16 we are the savour of d unto d
4:11 delivered to d for Jesus' sake
Phil. 2: 8 d even the d of the cross
Heb. 2: 9 should taste d for every man
2:15 through fear of d are subject to
11: 5 should not see d.,
Jas. 1:15 sin finished bringeth d
1 Pet. 3:18 put to d in the flesh
1 John 3:14 but is passed from d unto life
5:16 there is a sin unto d: I do not
Rev. 1:18 I have the keys of hell and d
2:10 be faithful unto d and I will
20: 6 on such second d hath no power
21: 4 there shall be no more d nor

DEBATE
Prov. 25: 9 d thy cause with thy neighbour
Rom. 1:29 full of envy, murder, d
2 Cor. 12:20 lest there be d envyings

DEBT (DEBTS)
Mat. 6:12 forgive us our d
Rom. 4: 4 reckoned of grace, but of d

DEBTOR (DEBTORS)
Ezek. 18: 7 restored the d his pledge
Luke 7:41 creditor which had two d
Rom. 1:14 I am d both to the Greeks
8:12 brethren, we are d; not to the
Gal. 5: 3 he is a d to do the whole law

DECEIT
Ps. 72:14 redeem thy soul from d
101: 7 worketh d shall not dwell
Prov. 20:17 bread of d is sweet to man
Is. 53: 9 neither was any d in his mouth
Col. 2: 8 spoil through philosophy and vain d

DECEITFUL (DECEITFULLY)
Ps. 35:20 they devise d matters against
55:23 d men shall not live half their days
Prov. 11:18 wicked worketh a d work
14:25 but a d witness speaketh lies
27: 6 kisses of an enemy are d
Jer. 17: 9 heart d above all things
2 Cor. 4: 2 handling the word of God d
Eph. 4:22 corrupt according to the d lusts

DECEITFULNESS
Mat. 13:22 d of riches, choke the word

DECEIVE (DECEIVED, DECEIVING, DECEIVETH)
Deut. 11:16 that your heart be not d
Prov. 26:19 the man that d his neighbor
Is. 44:20 a d heart hath turned
Jer. 20: 7 O Lord, thou hast d me
Mat. 24: 4 take heed no man d you
Rom. 7: 11 sin d me, and by it slew me
1 Cor. 3:18 let no man d himself
Gal. 6: 3 when he is nothing, he d himself
1 Tim. 2:14 and Adam was not d but the woman
1 John 1: 8 no sin, we d ourselves
Rev. 12: 9 d the whole world

DECEIVER (DECEIVERS)
Gen. 27:12 shall seem to him as a d
2 John 1: 7. many d are entered into the world

DECLARE (DECLARED, DECLARETH)
Ps. 22:22 I will d thy name unto brethren
38:18 I will d mine iniquity and
78: 6 may d them to their children
145: 4 shall d thy mighty acts
Is. 53: 8 who shall d his generation
Amos 4:13 d to man his thought
Acts 20:27 not shunned to d all counsel
Rom. 1: 4 d to be the Son of God
Heb. 11:14 say such things d plainly
1 John 1: 3 seen and heard d we unto you

DECREE (DECREED)
Luke 2: 1 went out a d from Caesar
1 Cor. 7:37 and hath d in his heart

DEDICATE (DEDICATED)
2 Sam. 8:11 King David did d unto the Lord
Ezek. 44:29 and every d thing in Israel

DEDICATION
Num. 7:84 this was the d of the altar
Neh. 12:27 the d of the wall of Jerusalem

John　10:22 the feast of the *d*, and it was
DEED (DEEDS)
Judg. 19:30 no such *d* done nor seen
Neh. 13:14 wipe not out my good *d*
Ps. 28: 4 give them according to their *d*
John 3:19 because their *d* were evil
Rom. 2: 6 every man according to his *d*
8:13 do mortify the *d* of the body
15:18 obedient by word and *d*
Col. 3:17 whatsoever ye do in word or *d*
1 John 3:18 in tongue but in *d* and in truth
DEEP
Gen. 1: 2 was upon the face of the *d*
7:11 fountains of the great *d*
Job 42: 7 *d* calleth unto *d* at the noise
1 Cor. 2:10 yea, the *d* things of God
DEFENCE
Job 22:25 the Almighty shall be thy *d*
Ps. 59: 9 upon thee; for God is my *d*
89:18 for the Lord is our *d*
Eccl. 7:12 for wisdom is a *d*, and money
Is. 4: 5 on all the glory shall be the *d*
19: 6 brooks of *d* shall be emptied
33:16 place of *d* shall be the munitions
DEFER (DEFERRED, DEFERRETH)
Prov. 13:12 hope *d* maketh the heart sick
19:11 discretion of a man *d* his anger
DEFILE (DEFILED, DEFILETH)
Lev. 18:25 and the land is *d*, therefore
Dan. 1: 8 he would not *d* himself
Mark 7: 2 his disciples eat bread with *d*
1 Cor. 3:17 if any *d* the temple of God
Rev. 3: 4 have not *d* their garments
21:27 not enter any thing that *d*
DEFRAUD (DEFRAUDED)
Lev. 19:13 thou shalt not *d* thy neighbor
DELICATE (DELICATES)
Deut. 28:56 tender and *d* woman among you
Is. 47: 1 no more be called tender and *d*
Jer. 6: 2 a comely and *d* woman
DELICATELY
Prov. 29:21 he that *d* bringeth up his servant
Luke 7:25 gorgeously apparelled, and live *d*
DELIGHT (DELIGHTED, DELIGHTETH)
Gen. 34:19 he had *d* in Jacob's daughter
Num. 14: 8 If the Lord *d* in us
Deut. 10:15 Lord had a *d* in thy fathers
1 Sam.15:22 as great *d* in burnt offerings
Esth. 6: 6 whom the king *d* to honour
Job 22:26 thy *d* in the Almighty
Ps. 1: 2 his *d* is in the law
16: 3 saints in whom is all my *d*
40: 8 I *d* to do thy will, O my God
94:19 thy comforts *d* my soul
147: 10 he *d* not in the strength of the horse
Prov. 3:12 the son in whom he *d*
11: 1 just weight is his *d*
11:20 in their way is his *d*
15: 8 prayer of the upright is his *d*
Sol. 2: 3 under his shadow with *d*
Is. 1:11 I *d* not in the blood of bullocks
42: 1 elect in whom my soul *d*
58: 2 take *d* in approaching to God
Mic. 7:18 for ever, because he *d* in mercy
Rom. 7:22 I *d* in the law of God
DELIGHTS
Ps. 119:92 thy law had been my *d*
Sol. 7: 6 how pleasant, O love, for *d*
DELIGHTSOME
Mal. 3:12 ye shall be a *d* land
DELIVER
Ex. 3: 8 come down to *d* them
Job 5:19 *d* thee in six troubles
Ps. 33:19 to *d* their soul from death
50:15 I will *d*, and thou
74:19 *d* not the soul of thy turtledove
Ezek. 34:10 I will *d* my flock from their mouth
Dan. 3:17 our God is able to *d* us
Hos. 11: 8 how shall I *d* thee, Israel
Rom. 7:24 shall *d* me from the body
1 Cor. 5: 5 to *d* such a one to Satan
2 Tim. 4:18 Lord shall *d* me from every evil

2 Pet. 2: 9 Lord knoweth how to *d* the godly
DELIVERED
Prov. 28:26 walketh wisely shall, he shall be *d*
Is. 38:17 *d* it from the pit of corruption
Ezek. 3:19 but thou hast *d* thy soul
Dan. 12: 1 thy people shall be *d*
Joel 2:32 name of the Lord shall be *d*
Mat. 11:27 all *d* to me of my Father
Rom. 4:25 who was *d* for our offences
8:32 *d* him up for us all
2 Cor. 1:10 who *d* us from so great a death
4:11 *d* to death for Jesus' sake
1 Thes. 1:10 *d* us from the wrath to come
Jude 1: 3 faith once *d* to the saints
DELIVERANCE
Gen. 45: 7 save your lives by a great *d*
2 Ki. 13:17 the arrow of the Lord's *d*
Esth. 4:14 *d* arise to the Jews from another
Ps. 32: 7 about with songs of *d*
Luke 4:18 to preach *d* to the captives
DEN (DENS)
Ps. 10: 9 as a lion in his *d*
104: 22 lay them down in their *d*
Jer. 7:11 become a *d* of robbers in your eyes
10:22 desolate and a *d* of dragons
Dan. 6:24 cast them into the *d* of lions
Mat. 21:13 have made it a *d* of thieves
DENY (DENIED, DENYING)
Prov. 30: 9 lest I be full, and *d* thee
Mat. 10:33 shall *d* me before men
16:24 let him *d* himself and take up
26:34 cock crow thou shalt *d* me
Mark 14:30 thou shalt *d* me thrice
1 Tim. 5: 8 he hath *d* the faith
2 Tim. 2:12 if we *d* him, he will *d* us
2 Pet. 2: 1 *d* the Lord that bought them
Rev. 2:13 and hast not *d* my faith
DEPART (DEPARTED, DEPARTETH, DEPARTING, DEPARTS)
2 Sam.22:22 have not wickedly *d* from my God
Job 21:14 they say unto God, *d* from us
28:28 *d* from evil is understanding
Ps. 18:21 not wickedly *d* from my God
34:14 *d* from evil and do good
119:102 have *d* from thy judgments
Prov. 14:16 feareth and *d* from evil
16:17 the upright is to *d* from evil
Is. 59:15 that *d* from evil maketh himself prey
Hos. 9:12 woe also to them when I *d*
Mat. 7:23 *d* from me, ye that work
25:41 *d* from me, ye cursed, into
Luke 2:29 lettest thy servant *d* in peace
5: 8 saying, *d* from me, for I am a
Acts 20:29 after my *d* shall grievous wolves
Phil. 1:23 having a desire to *d* and
Heb. 3:12 unbelief, in *d* from the living God
1 Tim. 4: 1 some shall *d* from faith
DEPARTURE
Ezek. 26:18 shall be trouble at thy *d*
DEPTH (DEPTHS)
Ex. 15: 5 the *d* have covered them
Ps. 68:22 from the *d* of the sea
130: 1 out of the *d* have I cried
Prov. 8:27 upon the face of the *d*
Mark 4: 5 because it had no *d* of earth
Rom. 8:39 neither height nor *d* nor any other
Eph. 3:18 breadth, length, *d* and height
DERISION
Job 30: 1 younger than I have me in *d*
Ps. 2: 4 Lord shall have them in *d*
119: 51 have had me greatly in *d*
DESCEND (DESCENDED, DESCENDING)
Gen. 28:12 angels of God ascending and *d*
Ex. 19:18 Lord *d* upon it in fire
33: 9 the cloudy pillar *d*, and stood
Ps. 49:17 glory not *d* after him
Is. 5:14 rejoiceth shall *d* into it
Mat. 3:16 the Spirit of God *d* like a dove
Mark 1:10 like a dove *d* upon him
John 1:32 saw the spirit *d* from heaven
1:51 angels of God ascending and *d*
1 Thes. 4:16 Lord shall *d* from heaven

DESERT (DESERTS)
Ps. 102: 6 like an owl of the *d*
Is. 13:21 wild beasts of the *d* shall lie
35: 1 and the *d* shall rejoice
35: 6 break out and streams in the *d*
40: 3 in the *d* a highway for our God
43:19 and rivers in the *d*
51: 3 her *d* like the garden
Ezek. 13: 4 like the foxes in the *d*
Mark 1:45 but was without in *d* places
John 6:31 fathers did eat manna in the *d*
Heb. 11:38 wandered in *d* and
DESIRE
Gen. 3:16 *d* shall be to thy husband
Ex. 34:24 nor any man *d* thy land
Deut. 18: 6 come with all the *d* of his mind
2 Chr. 15:15 and sought him with their whole *d*
Neh. 1:11 who *d* to fear thy name
Job 21:14 we *d* not knowledge of thy ways
Ps. 145:16 satisfieth the *d* of every living
Prov. 10:24 *d* of righteous shall be granted
11:23 *d* of the righteous is only good
13:19 *d* accomplished is sweet
Is. 26: 8 *d* of our soul is to thy name
Hag. 2: 7 the *d* of all nations shall
Jas. 4: 2 *d* to have and cannot obtain
Rev. 9: 6 *d* to die, and death shall flee
DESIRED (DESIRES, DESIREST, DESIRETH)
Job 7: 2 servant earnestly *d* the shadow
Ps. 19:10 more to be *d* are they than gold
27: 4 one thing have I *d* of the Lord
34:12 what man *d* life and loveth
37: 4 give thee the *d* of thine heart
51: 6 thou *d* truth in the inward parts
51:16 thou *d* not sacrifice, else would
Prov. 12:12 wicked *d* the net of evil men
21:10 soul of wicked *d* evil
Jer. 17:16 neither have I *d* the woeful day
Hos. 6: 6 I *d* mercy, not sacrifice
Eph. 2: 3 fulfilling *d* of the flesh
DESOLATE
Job 16: 7 thou hast made *d* all my company
Ps. 25:16 I am *d* and afflicted
Is. 49:21 I have lost my children, and am *d*
Mat. 23:38 behold your house is left unto you *d*
Rev. 17:16 and shall make her *d* and naked
DESOLATIONS
Jer. 25:12 and will make it perpetual *d*
DESPAIR
Eccl. 2:20 to cause my heart to *d*
2 Cor. 4: 8 we are perplexed, but not in *d*
DESPISE (DESPISED, DESPISEST, DESPISETH, DESPISING)
Gen. 16: 4 her mistress was *d* in her eyes
Lev. 26:15 if ye shall *d* my statutes
1 Sam. 2:30 they that *d* me be lightly
2 Sam. 6:16 she *d* him in her heart
Job 5:17 *d* not the chastening of the Almighty
36: 5 God is mighty and *d* not any
Ps. 102:17 destitute and will not *d* their
Prov. 11:12 void of wisdom *d* his neighbour
13:13 whoso *d* the word shall be destroyed
15:32 refuseth instruction *d* his soul
19:16 he that *d* his ways shall die
23:22 *d* not thy mother when she is old
Is. 53: 3 he is *d* and rejected
Zech. 4:10 who *d* the day of small things
Mat. 6:24 hold to one, and *d* the other
Luke 10:16 he that *d* you, *d* me, and he that
Rom. 2: 4 *d* thou the riches of goodness
14: 3 that eateth *d* him that eateth not
1 Tim. 4:12 no man *d* thy youth
Heb. 10:28 he that *d* Moses' law died without
DESPISERS
Acts 13:41 behold, ye *d*, and wonder, and perish
2 Tim. 3: 3 *d* of those that are good
DESTROY (DESTROYED)
Gen. 19:13 for we will *d* this place
Esth. 4:14 thy father's house shall be *d*
Ps. 37:38 transgressors shall be *d* together
Prov. 1:32 prosperity of fools shall *d* them
13:20 a companion of fools shall be *d*
Dan. 2:44 kingdom which shall never be *d*

Hos. 4: 6 are *d* for lack of knowledge
Mat. 5:17 not come to *d* but to fulfil
John 2:19 *d* this temple, and in three days
Rom. 14:15 *d* not him with thy meat
1 Cor. 3:17 defile the temple of God shall God *d*
2 Cor. 4: 9 cast down, but not *d*
Jas. 4:12 who is able to save and to *d*
1 John 3: 8 might *d* the works of the devil

DESTRUCTION
Deut. 7:23 shall destroy them with a mighty *d*
Job 5:22 at *d* and famine shall laugh
Ps. 90: 3 thou turnest man to *d*
91: 6 *d* that wasteth at noonday
Prov. 10:29 *d* shall be to workers of iniquity
15:11 Hell and *d* are before the Lord
16:18 pride goeth before *d*, and an
18:12 before the heart of man is haughty
27:20 hell and *d* are never full
Mat. 7:13 the way, that leadeth to *d*
Rom. 3:16 *d* and misery are in their ways
1 Thes. 5: 3 sudden *d* cometh on them
2 Pet. 2: 1 bring upon themselves swift *d*
3:16 scriptures unto their own *d*

DEVIL
Mat. 4: 1 wilderness to be tempted of the *d*
John 6:70 twelve, and one of you is a *d*
8:44 ye are of your father the *d*
Eph. 4:27 neither give place to the *d*
1 Tim. 3: 6 fall into condemnation of the *d*
2 Tim. 2:26 recover out of the snare of the *d*
Jas. 4: 7 resist the *d* and he will flee
1 Pet. 5: 8 because your adversary the *d*
1 John 3: 8 to destroy the works of the *d*
3:10 children of God and children of the *d*
Rev. 2:10 the *d* shall cast some of you

DEVILS
Lev. 17: 7 offer their sacrifices unto *d*
Ps. 106:37 sacrificed their sons to *d*
Mat. 4:24 which were possessed with *d*
Mark 16: 9 out of whom he had cast seven *d*
Luke 8:36 he that was possessed of the *d*
10:17 even *d* are subject to us

DEVISE (DEVISETH)
Prov. 3:29 *d* not evil against thy neighbour
16: 9 a man's heart *d* his ways

DEVOUR (DEVOURED)
Gen. 49:27 he shall *d* the prey
Is. 9:12 they shall *d* Israel with open mouth
Prov. 30:14 to *d* the poor off the earth
Is. 24: 6 hath curse *d* the earth
Jer. 3:24 shame hath *d* the labour
Hos. 7: 7 and have *d* their judges
Mat. 23:14 for ye *d* widows' houses, and
Gal. 5:15 if ye bite and *d* one another
Heb. 10:27 which shall *d* the adversaries
1 Pet. 5: 8 seeking whom he may *d*

DEVOURING
Ex. 24:17 like *d* fire on top of the mount
Is. 29: 6 and the flame of *d* fire

DEVOUT
Acts 2: 5 dwelling at Jerusalem Jews, *d* men
10: 2 a *d* man, and one that feared God
17: 4 and of the *d* Greeks a great multitude
22:12 Ananias, a *d* man according to the law

DEW
Gen. 27:28 God give thee of the *d* of heaven
Deut. 32: 2 my speech shall distill as the *d*
Is. 26:19 thy *d* is as the *d* of herbs
Hos. 6: 4 goodness is as the early *d*

DIE
Gen. 2:17 thereof thou shalt surely *d*
3: 4 ye shall not surely *d*
Ex. 20:19 let not God speak with us, lest we *d*
Job 14:14 if a man *d* shall he live again?
Ps. 82: 7 but ye shall *d* like men
Prov. 23:13 with the rod, he shall not *d*
Eccl. 3: 2 born and a time to *d*
Is. 22:13 for tomorrow we shall *d*
Jer. 26: 8 him, saying Thou shalt surely *d*
Ezek. 3:18 wicked man shall *d* in his iniquity
18:31 why will ye *d* O house of Israel
Jonah 4: 3 better for me to *d* than to live
Mat. 26:35 though I should *d* with thee

Luke 20:36 neither can they *d* any more
John 8:21 ye shall *d* in your sins
11:50 that one man should *d* for the people
Rom. 14: 8 we *d* we *d* unto the Lord
1 Cor. 9:15 better for me to *d* than
Phil. 1:21 to live is Christ, to *d* is gain
Heb. 9:27 appointed unto men once to *d*

DIED (DIETH, DYING)
Rom. 5: 6 Christ *d* for the ungodly
5: 8 while we were yet sinners, Christ *d*
6: 9 being raised from the dead *d* no more
6:10 for in that he *d* he *d* unto sin
14: 7 no man *d* to himself
1 Cor. 15: 3 Christ *d* for our sins
2 Cor. 4:10 the *d* of the Lord Jesus
5:15 he *d* for all, that they
1 Thes. 5:10 who *d* for us that whether
Heb. 11:13 these all *d* in faith, not
11:21 By faith, Jacob, when he was *d*

DILIGENCE
Prov. 4:23 keep thy heart with all *d*
2 Pet. 1: 5 giving all *d*, add to your faith
1:10 give *d* to make your calling

DILIGENT (DILIGENTLY)
Ex. 15:26 if thou wilt *d* hearken to
Deut. 4: 9 keep thy soul *d*, lest thou forget
6:17 *d* keep the commandments of the Lord
28: 1 thou shalt hearken *d* unto the voice
Ps. 64: 6 they accomplish a *d* search
Prov. 10: 4 hand of the *d* maketh rich
12:24 hand of the *d* shall bear rule
13: 4 soul of the *d* shall be made fat
21: 5 thoughts of the *d* tend to plenty
Jer. 17:24 if ye *d* hearken unto me
Zech. 6:15 if ye will *d* obey the voice
Luke 15: 8 seek *d* till she find it
2 Pet. 3:14 be *d* to be found of him

DINNER
Prov. 15:17 better is a *d* of herbs

DIRECT (DIRECTED)
Ps. 5: 3 will I *d* my prayer to thee
119: 5 my ways were *d* to keep
Prov. 3: 6 he shall *d* thy paths
Eccl. 10:10 but wisdom is profitable to *d*
Is. 40:13 who hath *d* the spirit of the Lord
Jer. 10:23 walketh to *d* his steps

DISCERN (DISCERNED, DISCERNETH, DISCERNING)
Eccl. 8: 5 a wise man's heart *d* both time
Mal. 3:18 *d* between the righteous and the
1 Cor. 2:14 because they are spiritually *d*
11:29 not the Lord's body
12:10 to another *d* of spirits
Heb. 5:14 to *d* both good and evil

DISCIPLE (DISCIPLES)
Mat. 10:24 *d* is not above his master
10:42 cup of water in the name of a *d*
Luke 14:26 life also he cannot be my *d*
John 8:31 then are ye my *d* indeed
19:38 Joseph of Arimathaea, being a *d*

DISEASES
Ex. 15:26 I will put none of these *d*
Ps. 38: 7 are filled with a loathsome *d*
103: 3 who healeth all thy *d*

DISHONOUR (DISHONOURETH)
Prov. 6:33 a wound and *d* shall he get
Mic. 7: 6 for the son *d* his father
Rom. 1:24 to *d* their own bodies
1 Cor. 15:43 it is sown in *d* it is raised
2 Cor. 6: 8 by honour and *d*, by evil report

DISOBEDIENCE
Rom. 5:19 by one man's *d* many were made
2 Cor. 10: 6 readiness to revenge all *d*
Eph. 2: 2 worketh in the children of *d*
Col. 3: 6 cometh upon the children of *d*
Heb. 2: 2 if every *d* received just

DISOBEDIENT
Luke 1:17 to the wisdom of the just
Rom. 1:30 of evil things *d* to parents
2 Tim. 3: 2 *d* to parents, unthankful, unholy
1 Pet. 3:20 which sometime were *d* which once

DISPENSATION
1 Cor. 9:17 a *d* of the gospel is committed

Eph. 1:10 in the *d* of the fulness of time
3: 2 the *d* of the grace of God
Col. 1:25 according to the *d* of God

DISPLEASURE
Deut. 9:19 afraid of the anger and hot *d*
Ps. 2: 5 and vex them in his sore *d*

DISSENSION
Acts 15: 2 Paul and Barnabas had no small *d*
23:10 when there arose a great *d*

DISSOLVED (DISSOLVEST)
Is. 24:19 the earth is clean *d*
2 Pet. 3:11 all these things shall be *d*

DISTRESS
Gen. 35: 3 answered me in the day of my *d*
2 Sam.22: 7 in my *d* I called upon the Lord
1 Ki. 1:29 redeemed thy soul out of *d*
Ps. 4: 1 enlarged me when I was in *d*
120: 1 In my *d* I cried unto the Lord
Prov. 1:27 when *d* and anguish cometh
Is. 25: 4 strength to the needy in his *d*
Zeph. 1:15 day of trouble and *d*, a day of
Luke 21:25 upon the earth *d* of nations
Rom. 8:35 shall tribulation, or *d*, or persecution

DISTRESSED
Gen. 32: 7 Then Jacob was greatly afraid and *d*
2 Sam. 1:26 I am *d* for thee, my brother Jonathan

DISTRIBUTE (DISTRIBUTING, DISTRIBUTETH)
Luke 18:22 and *d* unto the poor, and thou
Rom. 12:13 *d* to the necessity of saints
1 Tim. 6:18 ready to *d*, willing to communicate

DIVIDE (DIVIDED, DIVIDING)
Gen. 1: 6 *d* the waters from the waters
1:14 to *d* the day from the night
Ex. 14:16 thine hand over the sea, and *d* it
Josh. 19:51 *d* for an inheritance land by lot
Ps. 55: 9 destroy O Lord and *d* their tongues
Is. 53:12 will I *d* him a portion
Mat. 12:25 city or house *d* against
1 Cor. 1:13 is Christ *d*? was Paul
12:11 *d* to every man severally as he will
2 Tim. 2:15 rightly *d* the word of truth
Heb. 4:12 to the *d* asunder of soul and spirit

DIVINE
1 Sam.28: 8 *d* unto me by the familiar spirit
Prov. 16:10 a *d* sentence is in the lips
Heb. 9: 1 had also ordinances of *d* service
2 Pet. 1: 3 his *d* power hath given

DIVINATION
Num. 22: 7 the rewards of *d* in their hand
Deut. 18:10 or that useth *d* or an observer
Acts 16:16 possessed with a spirit of *d*

DIVORCE (DIVORCED)
Lev. 22:13 Priest's daughter be a widow, or *d*
Jer. 3: 8 and given her a bill of *d*

DIVORCEMENT
Deut. 24: 1 let him write her a bill of *d*
Is. 50: 1 where is the bill of your mother's *d*
Mat. 5:31 let him give her a writing of *d*

DO
Gen. 18:25 not the Judge of all the earth *d* right
Mat. 7:12 men *d* to you, *d* ye even so
John 15: 5 without me ye can *d* nothing
Rom. 7:15 what I would that I *d* not
Phil. 4:13 I can *d* all things all through Christ

DOERS
Jas. 1:22 be ye *d* of word and not"

DOING (DOINGS)
Ps. 64: 9 they shall wisely consider of his *d*
Prov. 20:11 even a child is known by his *d*
Rom. 2: 7 by patient continuance in well *d*
Gal. 6: 9 let us not be weary in well *d*
2 Thes. 3:13 brethren, be not weary in well *d*
1 Pet. 2:15 that with well *d* ye may put

DOCTOR (DOCTORS)
Luke 5:17 there were Pharisees and *d* of the law
Acts 5:34 Gamaliel, a *d* of the law

DOCTRINE
Deut. 32: 2 my *d* shall drop as the rain
Is. 28: 9 whom shall he make to understand *d*?
Jer. 10: 8 the stock is a *d* of vanities
Mat. 7:28 the people were astonished at his *d*
Mark 1:27 what new *d* is this? for

John 7:17 he shall know of the *d*
Acts 2:42 in the apostles' *d* and fellowship
Rom. 16:17 contrary to the *d* ye have learned
Eph. 4:14 about with every wind of *d*
1 Tim. 6: 3 *d* which is according to godliness
2 Tim. 3:16 and is profitable for *d*, for
Tit. 2: 7 in *d* showing uncorruptness, gravity
     2:10 may adorn the *d* of God our Saviour
Heb. 6: 1 principles of the *d* of Christ
Rev. 2:14 that hold the *d* of Balaam

DOCTRINES
Mat. 15: 9 teaching for *d* the commandments of
     men
Col. 2:22 after the commandments and *d* of men
1 Tim. 4: 1 giving heed to the *d* of the devils
Heb. 13: 9 carried about with divers strange *d*

DOG (DOGS)
Ex. 11: 7 shall not a *d* move his tongue
Prov. 26:11 as a *d* to his vomit
Eccl. 9: 4 living *d* better than a dead lion
Mat. 7: 6 give not that which is holy to *d*
Phil. 3: 2 beware of *d*, beware of evil

DOMINION
Gen. 1:26 let them have *d* over
Num. 24:19 he that shall have *d*
Ps. 8: 6 *d* over the works of thy hands
     72: 8 shall have *d* from sea to sea
     145: 13 thy *d* endureth through all
Dan. 4: 3 his *d* is from generation to generation
Zech. 9:10 his *d* shall be from sea even to sea
Rom. 6: 9 death hath no more *d* over
2 Cor. 1:24 not have *d* over your faith

DOMINIONS
Col. 1:16 thrones or *d* or principalities

DOOR (DOORS)
Gen. 4: 7 sin lieth at the *d*
Ex. 12:23 Lord will pass over the *d*
Deut. 11:20 thou shalt write them upon the *d* posts
Ps. 24: 7 be ye lift up ye everlasting *d*
     84:10 *d* keeper in the house of my God
     141: 3 keep the *d* of my lips
Prov. 26:14 as the *d* turneth upon his hinges
Is. 6: 4 posts of the *d* moved
Hos. 2:15 valley of Achor for a *d* of hope
Mat. 6: 6 when thou hast shut thy *d*
John 10: 1 entereth not by the *d*
     10: 7 I am the *d* of the sheep
Acts 14:27 opened the *d* of faith to the Gentiles
Col. 4: 3 would open unto us a *d* of utterance
Jas. 5: 9 judge standeth before the *d*
Rev. 3: 8 set before thee an open *d*

DOUBLE
Gen. 43:12 and take *d* money in your hand
Ex. 22: 4 or sheep he shall restore *d*
Deut. 21:17 giving him a *d* portion of all
2 Ki. 2: 9 *d* portion of thy spirit be upon me
1 Chr. 12:33 they were not of *d* heart
Is. 40: 2 Lord's hand *d* for her sins
Jas. 1: 8 minded man is unstable in all
Rev. 18: 6 *d* to her, fill to her *d*

DOUBT (DOUBTETH)
Deut. 28:66 thy life shall hang in *d*
Mat. 21:21 have faith and *d* not
John 10:24 how long dost thou make us to *d*
Rom. 14:23 he that *d* is damned

DOUBTFUL
Luke 12:29 neither be ye of *d* mind
Rom. 14: 1 but not to *d* disputations

DOVE (DOVES)
Ps. 55: 6 that I had wings like a *d*
     74:19 deliver not the soul of thy turtle*d*
Is. 38:14 I did mourn as a *d*
Ezek. 7:16 mountains, like *d* of the valleys
Hos. 7:11 Ephraim is like a silly *d*
Mat. 3:16 the Spirit of God descending like a *d*
     10:16 wise as serpents and harmless as *d*
John 1:32 Spirit descending from heaven like a *d*

DRAGON (DRAGONS)
Deut. 32:33 their wine is the poison of *d*
Ps. 44:19 broken us in the place of *d*
     74:13 thou brakest the heads of the *d*
     91:13 the *d* shalt thou trample under foot

Is. 13:22 and *d* in their pleasant palaces
     51: 9 cut Rahab and wounded the *d*
Jer. 9:11 and a den of *d*, and I will
Ezek. 29: 3 the great *d* that lieth in the midst
Mal. 1: 3 waste for the *d* of the wilderness
Rev. 12: 3 the *d* gave him his power
     20: 2 the *d*, that old serpent

DRAW (DRAWN, DREW)
Ps. 18:16 *d* me out of many waters
     73:28 good for me to *d* near to God
     29:13 *d* near me with their mouth
Jer. 31: 3 with lovingkindness have I *d* thee
Jas. 4: 8 *d* nigh to God, he will *d*

DREAD
Gen. 9: 2 *d* of you shall be upon
Deut. 2:25 I put the *d* of thee and the fear

DREADFUL
Dan. 9: 4 the great and *d* God
Mal. 1:14 my name is *d* among the heathen
     4: 5 great and *d* day of the Lord

DREAM
Gen. 20: 3 God came to Abimelech in a *d*
     37: 5 and Joseph dreamed a *d*
Num. 12: 6 will speak unto him in a *d*
Job 33:15 in a *d* in a vision of the night
Ps. 126: 1 we were like them that *d*
Is. 29: 7 shall be as a *d* of night vision
Jer. 23:28 hath a *d* let him tell a *d*
Dan. 2:28 thy *d* and the visions of they head
Joel 2:28 your old men shall *d* dreams
Mat. 1:20 angel appeared in a *d*
     2:12 warned of God in a *d*
Acts 2:17 your old men shall *d* dreams

DRINK
Lev. 10: 9 not *d* wine nor strong *d*
Job 21:20 *d* of the wrath of the Almighty
Ps. 36: 8 *d* of the river of thy pleasures
     60: 3 *d* the wine of astonishment
     69:21 they gave me vinegar to *d*
     80: 5 givest them tears to *d*
     110: 7 *d* of the brook in the way
Prov. 4:17 *d* the wine of violence
     5:15 *d* out of thine own cistern
Is. 22:13 let us eat and *d*, for tomorrow
Mat. 20:22 able to *d* of the cup that I shall
     25:35 thirsty, and ye gave me *d*
     26:29 I will not *d* henceforth of this fruit
     27:34 gave him vinegar to *d*
Luke 1:15 shall *d* neither wine nor strong *d*
John 6:55 and my blood is *d* indeed
     7:37 let him come unto me and *d*, for in
Rom. 12:20 if he thirst give him *d*
     14:17 kingdom of God is not meat and *d*
1 Cor. 10: 4 did all *d* the same spiritual *d*
     10:21 cannot *d* the cup of Lord and devils
     11:25 as often as ye *d* it in remembrance
     15:32 let us eat and *d*: for tomorrow

DRINKETH
Job 15:16 which *d* iniquity like water
John 6:54 *d* my blood hath eternal life
1 Cor. 11:29 eateth and *d* unworthily
Heb. 6: 7 earth which *d* in rain

DRUNKARD (DRUNKARDS)
Deut. 21:20 he is a glutton and *d*
Ps. 69:12 I was the song of the *d*
Prov. 23:21 *d* and glutton shall come to poverty
     26: 9 thorn goeth up into the hand of a *d*
1 Cor. 5:11 idolator, or a railer, or a *d*

DRUNK (DRUNKEN)
Is. 29: 9 they are *d* but not with wine
1 Cor. 11:21 one is hungry, another *d*
1 Thes. 5: 7 be *d* are *d* in the night
Rev. 17: 2 *d* with the wine of her fornication

DRUNKENNESS
Deut. 29:19 to add *d* to thirst
Luke 21:34 be overcharged with surfeiting, and *d*
Rom. 13:13 not in rioting and *d*

DROSS
Ps. 119:119 all the wicked of the earth like *d*
Is. 1:25 purely purge away thy *d*
Ezek. 22:18 the house of Israel is to me become *d*

DRY
Judg. 6:37 if it be *d* upon all the earth
Prov. 17: 1 better is a *d* morsel
     56: 3 behold, I am a *d* tree
Hos. 9:14 a miscarrying womb and *d* breasts

DUE
Deut. 32:35 foot shall slide in *d* time
Ps. 104:27 meat in *d* season
Prov. 3:27 good from them to whom it is *d*
     15:23 a word spoken in *d* season
Eccl. 10:17 thy princes eat in *d* season
Mat. 24:45 to give them their meat in *d* season
Luke 12:42 their portion of meat in *d* season
     23:41 we receive the *d* reward of our deeds
Rom. 13: 7 tribute to whom tribute is *d*
Gal. 6: 9 in *d* season we shall reap
1 Cor. 15: 8 as one born out of *d* time

DUMB
Ps. 38:13 I was as a *d* man
Is. 35: 6 tongue of the *d* to sing
     53: 7 as a sheep before her shearers is *d*
Ezek. 3:26 that thou shalt be *d*, and shalt
Mat. 9:33 devil was cast out, the *d* spake
Mark 9:25 thou *d* and deaf spirit
Luke 1:20 behold, thou shalt be *d*

DUST
Gen. 3:19 unto *d* thou shalt return
     13:16 thy seed as the *d* of the earth
     28:14 seed shall be as the *d* of the earth
Ex. 8:17 smote the *d* of the land
Num. 23:10 who can count the *d* of Jacob
2 Chr. 1: 9 like the *d* of the earth in multitude
Job 30:19 I am become like *d* and ashes
     42: 6 repent in *d* and ashes
Ps. 7: 5 lay mine honour in the *d*
     30: 9 shall the *d* praise thee
     103: 14 remembereth that we are *d*
     104: 29 they die, and return to their *d*
Eccl. 12: 7 shall the *d* return to the earth
Is. 26:19 awake and sing, ye that dwell in *d*
Dan. 12: 2 sleep in the *d* of the earth
Amos 2: 7 that pant after the *d* of the earth
Mat. 10:14 shake off the *d* of your feet
Acts 13:51 they shook off the *d* of their feet

DUTY
Eccl. 12:13 this is the whole of *d* of man

DWELL (DWELLETH, DWELT)
Ps. 15: 1 who shall *d* in thy holy hill
     23: 6 *d* in house of Lord for ever
     84:10 than to *d* in the tents of wickedness
     120: 5 that I *d* in the tents of Kedar
Is. 33:14 who *d* with devouring fire
     33:16 he shall *d* on high
Ezek. 43: 7 I will *d* in the midst of the children
John 1:14 Word made flesh and *d*
     6:56 *d* in me, and I in him
     14:10 Father that *d* in me, he doeth
Acts 13:17 they *d* as strangers in the land of
2 Cor. 6:16 I will *d* in them, and walk in
Eph. 3:17 that Christ may *d* in your hearts
Col. 1:19 that in him should all fulness *d*
     2: 9 in Christ *d* all the fulness of
     3:16 let the word of Christ *d* in you richly
2 Tim. 1:14 Holy Ghost which *d* in us
Jas. 4: 5 spirit which *d* in us lusteth
2 Pet. 3:13 wherein *d* righteousness
1 John 3:17 how *d* the love of God in him
     4:12 God in us, and his love is
2 John 1: 2 truth's sake which *d* in us
Rev. 21: 3 he will *d* with them, and

EAGLE (EAGLES)
Ex. 19: 4 I bare you on *e* wings
Deut. 28:49 as swift as the *e* flieth
2 Sam. 1:23 they were swifter than *e*, stronger
Job 39:27 doth the *e* mount up
Ps. 103: 5 thy youth is renewed like the *e*
Prov. 30:17 the young *e* shall eat it
Is. 40:31 they shall mount up with wings as *e*
Jer. 49:16 thy nest as high as the *e*
Ezek. 10:14 the fourth the face of an *e*
Dan. 7: 4 like a lion and had *e* wings
Rev. 4: 7 beast was like a flying *e*
     12:14 given two wings of a great *e*

EAR

Deut.	32: 1	Give *e* O ye heavens
Job	36:10	God openeth man's *e*
Ps.	5: 1	give *e* to my words, O Lord
	17: 6	incline thine *e* unto me
	49: 1	give *e*, all ye inhabitants
	54: 2	give *e* to the words of my mouth
	78: 1	give *e*, O my people, to my law
	86: 6	give *e*, O Lord, unto my prayer
	94: 9	He that planted the *e* shall
Prov.	15:31	*e* that heareth reproof
	20:12	The hearing *e* and seeing eye
	25:12	wise reprover on an obedient *e*
Is.	1: 2	hear, O heavens, and give *e*
	48: 8	time thine *e* was not opened
	50: 5	Lord God hath opened mine *e* and
Jer.	6:10	*e* is uncircumcised and they cannot
Joel	1: 2	hear this, ye old men, and give *e*
1 Cor.	2: 9	eye hath not seen nor *e* heard

EARS

Deut.	29: 4	eyes to see and *e* to hear
Job	33:16	He openeth the *e* of men
Ps.	49: 4	I will incline mine *e* to a parable
	78: 1	incline your *e* to the words
	115: 6	they have *e* but they hear not
Is.	35: 5	the *e* of the deaf shall be unstopped
	55: 3	incline your *e* and come unto me
Ezek.	3:10	and hear with thine *e*
	23:25	shall take away thy nose and thine *e*
Zech.	7:11	and stopped their *e* that they
Mat.	11:15	*e* to hear, let him hear
Mark	7:33	Jesus put his fingers into his *e*
	8:18	having *e* hear ye not?
Luke	9:44	let sayings sink into your *e*
Rev.	2: 7	he that hath an *e*, let him hear

EARLY

Ps.	90:14	satisfy us *e* with thy mercy
Is.	26: 9	within me will I seek thee *e*
Hos.	5:15	in affliction will seek me *e*
Jas.	5: 7	receive *e* and latter rain

EARNEST (EARNESTLY)

Mic.	7: 3	do evil with both hands *e*
Luke	22:44	in agony, he prayed more *e*
1 Cor.	12:31	covet *e* the best gifts
2 Cor.	1:22	given the *e* of the Spirit in our hearts
	5: 2	in this we groan, *e* desiring
Eph.	1:14	which is the *e* of our inheritance
Jude	1: 3	ye should *e* contend for the faith

EARTH

Gen.	6:11	the *e* also was corrupt
	11: 1	whole *e* of one language
Ex.	9:29	that the *e* is the Lord's
Num.	16:32	*e* opened her mouth
Deut.	10:14	the *e* also, with all that therein is
	28:23	*e* under thee be iron
	32: 1	hear O the words of my mouth
Judg.	5: 4	the *e* trembled and the heavens
1 Sam.	2: 8	pillars of the *e* are the Lord's
1 Chr.	16:30	and let the *e* rejoice: and let
Job	9: 6	shaketh the *e* out of her place
	11: 9	longer than the *e*, broader than the sea
	26: 7	and hangeth the *e* upon nothing
	38: 4	I laid the foundations of the *e*
Ps.	24: 1	the *e* is the Lord's
	33: 5	*e* is full of the goodness of the Lord
	65: 9	visitest the *e* and waterest it
	72:19	let the whole *e* be filled
	89:11	are thine, the *e* also is thine
	97: 4	the *e* saw and trembled
	104:24	the *e* is full of thy riches
	106:17	the *e* opened and swallowed up Dathan
	115:16	*e* hath he given to the children
	139:15	in lowest parts of the *e*
Prov.	25: 3	heaven for height and *e* for depth
Eccl.	1: 4	but the *e* abideth for ever
	5: 2	God is in heaven and thou upon *e*
	7:20	not a just man upon *e* that doeth good
Is.	6: 3	the whole *e* is full of his glory
	13:13	*e* shall remove out of her place
	24: 1	Lord maketh the *e* empty
	26:19	*e* shall cast out the dead
	66: 1	*e* is my footstool, where is
Jer.	22:29	O *e*, *e*, *e*, hear the word

Ezek.	34:27	*e* shall yield her increase
	43: 2	the *e* shined with his glory
Hab.	2:14	for the *e* shall be filled
	3: 3	and *e* was full of his praise
Luke	5:24	Son of man power upon *e* to forgive
John	3:31	he that is of *e* is earthly
1 Cor.	10:28	the *e* is the Lord's
Heb.	6: 7	*e* which drinketh in the rain that
Rev.	12:16	and the *e* helped the woman

EARTHLY

2 Cor.	4: 7	we have this treasure in *e* vessels
	5: 1	if our *e* house of this tabernacle
Phil.	3:19	their shame who mind *e* things

EARTHQUAKE (EARTHQUAKES)

Is.	29: 6	with thunder, and with *e*
Mat.	24: 7	and *e* in divers places
	27:54	with him, watching Jesus, saw the *e*
	28: 2	behold, there was a great *e*
Acts	16:26	suddenly there was a great *e*
Rev.	11:19	and an *e*, and great hail
	16: 8	and there was a great *e*

EASE

Job	12: 5	the thought of him that is at *e*
Is.	1:24	I will *e* me of adversaries
Amos	6: 1	woe to them that are at *e*
Luke	12:19	take thine *e* and be merry

EASY (EASIER, EASILY)

Prov.	14: 6	knowledge is *e* to him
Mat.	11:30	my yoke is *e*, and my burden
Luke	16:17	*e* for heaven and earth to pass
Heb.	12: 1	sin which doth so *e* beset
Jas.	3:17	gentle, *e* to be entreated

EAST

Ps.	103:12	as far as the *e* is from the west
Is.	43: 5	bring thy seed from the *e*
Hab.	1: 9	faces shall sup up as the *e* wind
Mat.	2: 1	there came wise men from the *e*
	8:11	many shall come from the *e*

EAT

Gen.	2:16	tree of the garden thou mayest freely *e*
	3:14	dust shalt thou *e* all the days
	9: 4	the blood thereof, shall ye not *e*
Ex.	12:48	no uncircumcised person shall *e* thereof
	16:35	Israel did *e* manna forty years, until
Lev.	7:21	and *e* of the flesh of the sacrifice
	17:14	*e* the blood of no manner of flesh
	26:38	land of your enemies shall *e* you up
Num.	6: 3	nor *e* moist grapes, or dried
Deut.	14:21	shall not *e* anything that dieth
	28:55	flesh of his children whom he shall *e*
1 Ki.	13: 9	*e* no bread, drink no water
	21:23	dogs shall *e* Jezebel
2 Ki.	4:43	give the people that they may *e*
Neh.	8:10	*e* the fat, drink the sweet
Ps.	22:26	meek shall *e* and be satisfied
	53: 4	*e* up my people as bread
	78:25	man did *e* angels' food
	128: 2	*e* the labour of thine hands
Prov.	13: 2	*e* good by the fruit of his mouth
Eccl.	9: 7	*e* thy bread with joy
Is.	1:19	if obedient ye shall *e*
	3:10	shall *e* the fruit of their doings
	7:15	butter and honey shall he *e*
	11: 7	and the lion shall *e* straw
	51: 8	worm shall *e* them as wool
	55: 1	buy and *e*, yea, come buy
	61: 6	ye shall *e* the riches of the Gentiles
Jer.	15:16	words were found and I did *e*
Ezek.	3: 1	*e* this roll, and go speak
	5:10	fathers shall *e* the sons
Dan.	4:33	and did *e* grass as oxen
Amos	7:12	there *e* bread, and prophesy
Mic.	3: 3	the flesh of my people
Mat.	6:25	no thought what ye shall *e*
	26:26	Jesus said, Take *e* this is my body
Mark	1: 6	*e* locusts and wild honey
	7: 5	*e* bread with unwashen hands
	7:28	dogs *e* of the children's crumbs
	14:22	as they did *e*, Jesus took bread
Luke	15:23	let us *e*, and be merry
	22:30	ye may *e* and drink at my table
John	4:31	I have meat to *e* that ye
	6:26	because ye did *e* of the loaves

	6:53	except ye *e* the flesh of the Son
Acts	2:46	did *e* their meat with gladness
1 Cor.	8: 7	*e* it as a thing offered unto an idol
	10:31	whether therefore ye *e* or drink
	11:24	take, *e*: this is my body
2 Thes.	3:10	not work, neither should he *e*
Jas.	5: 3	*e* your flesh as it were fire
Rev.	2: 7	will I give to *e* of the tree
	17:16	*e* her flesh, and burn

EATEN (EATETH, EATING)

Num.	13:32	is a land that *e* up the inhabitants
Ps.	69: 9	zeal of thine house hath *e* me up
Prov.	9:17	bread *e* in secret is pleasant
Mat.	9:11	why *e* your master with publicans and
	11:18	John came neither *e* nor drinking.
	24:38	were *e* and drinking, marrying and
Luke	13:26	*e* and drunk in thy presence
John	2:17	the zeal of thine house hath *e* me up
	6:54	whoso *e* my flesh and drinketh
	6:58	he that *e* this bread shall live
Acts	12:23	he was *e* of worms
Rom.	14: 6	he that *e* to the Lord
1 Cor.	11:29	*e* and drinketh unworthily, *e* and

EDIFY (EDIFIED, EDIFIETH)

Rom.	14:19	wherewith one may *e* another
1 Cor.	8: 1	knowledge puffeth up, but charity *e*
	10:23	but all things *e* not
	14:17	but the other is not *e*

EDIFICATION

Rom.	15: 2	please his neighbour for his good to *e*
1 Cor.	14: 3	speaketh unto men to *e*
2 Cor.	10: 8	which the Lord hath given us for *e*

EDIFYING

1 Cor.	14:12	may excel to the *e* of the church
Eph.	4:12	for the *e* of the body of Christ
	4:29	but that which is good to the use of *e*
1 Tim.	1: 4	questions rather than godly *e*

EFFECT

Is.	32:17	*e* of righteousness quietness
Mat.	15: 6	commandment of God of none *e*
Mark	7:13	making the word of God of none *e*
Rom.	3: 3	make the faith of God without *e*
	9: 6	word of God had taken none *e*
1 Cor.	1:17	cross of Christ be made of none *e*
Gal.	5: 4	Christ is become of no *e* to you

EFFECTUAL

1 Cor.	16: 9	great door and *e* is opened unto
Eph.	3: 7	by the *e* working of his power
Jas.	5:16	*e* fervent prayer of a righteous

EGG (EGGS)

Deut.	22: 6	whether they be young ones, or *e*
Is.	10:14	as one gathereth *e* that are left
Jer.	17:11	the partridge sitteth on *e*
Luke	11:12	or if he shall ask an *e*

ELDER (ELDERS)

Gen.	25:23	the *e* shall serve the younger
Acts	14:23	ordained them *e* in every church
	20:17	Ephesus, and called the *e* of the church
Rom.	9:12	the *e* shall serve the younger
1 Tim.	5: 1	rebuke not an *e* but entreat
	5: 2	the *e* women as mothers
Tit.	1: 5	ordain *e* in every city
Jas.	5:14	let him call for the *e* of the church
1 Pet.	5: 1	which are among you I exhort
	5: 5	younger, submit yourselves unto the *e*
Rev.	4: 4	four and twenty *e* sitting
	11:16	and the four and twenty *e*, which sat

ELECT

Is.	42: 1	in whom my soul delighteth
	65: 9	mine *e* shall inherit it
Mat.	24:22	for the *e*'s sake those days shall shortened
	24:24	if possible deceive the very *e*
Luke	18: 7	God avenge his own *e*
Rom.	8:33	to the charge of God's *e*
2 Tim.	2:10	I endure all things for the *e*'s sake
Tit.	1: 1	according to the faith of God's *e*
1 Pet.	1: 2	according to the foreknowledge of God
	2: 6	corner stone, *e*, precious

ELECTION

Rom.	9:11	according to *e* might stand
	11: 5	remnant according to the *e* of grace

11: 7 but the *e* hath obtained it
1 Thes. 1: 4 brethren beloved, your *e* of God
2 Pet. 1: 10 make your calling and *e* sure

END
Gen. 6:13 *e* of all flesh is come
Deut. 8:16 to do thee good at thy latter *e*
32:20 see what their *e* shall
Ps. 37:37 the *e* of that man is peace
39: 4 make me to know mine *e*
102: 27 thy years shall have no *e*
119: 96 seen an *e* of all perfection
Prov. 5: 4 her *e* is bitter as wormwood
19:20 thou mayest be wise in thy latter *e*
Eccl. 4: 8 there is no *e* of his labour
7: 2 for that is the *e* of all men
Is. 9: 7 of his government there shall be no *e*
Jer. 4:27 yet will I not make a full *e*
Lam. 4:18 our *e* is come, our *e* is near
Ezek. 11:13 wilt thou make a full *e* of the remnant
21:25 when iniquity shall have an *e*
Dan. 6:26 dominion shall be even unto the *e*
Amos 8: 2 *e* is come upon my people of Israel
Mat. 13:39 harvest is the *e* of the world
24:13 he that shall endure unto the *e*
28:20 even unto the *e* of the world
Luke 21: 9 but the *e* is not by and by
John 13: 1 he loved them unto the *e*
Rom. 6:21 the *e* of those things is death
14: 9 to this *e* Christ both died and rose
1 Cor. 1: 8 who shall also confirm you unto the *e*
1 Tim. 1: 5 *e* of the commandment is charity
Heb. 3:14 beginning of our confidence stedfast unto the *e*
6: 8 whose *e* is to be burned
7: 3 beginning of days, nor *e* of life
1 Pet. 1: 9 receiving the *e* of your faith
4: 7 the *e* of all things is at hand
Rev. 1: 8 Alpha and Omega, the beginning and the *e*
21: 6 Omega, the beginning and the *e*
22:13 Alpha and Omega, the beginning and the *e*

ENDS
Ps. 67: 7 all the *e* of the earth shall fear him
Is. 45:22 be ye saved, all the *e* of the earth
Acts 13:47 salvation unto the *e* of the earth
1 Cor. 10: 11 upon whom the *e* of the world are come

ENDURE (ENDURED)
Gen. 33:14 children are able to *e*
Ps. 9: 7 the Lord shall *e* forever
30: 5 weeping may *e* for a night
72:17 His name shall *e* forever
89:36 seed shall *e* forever,
Prov. 27:24 crown *e* to every generation
Mat. 24:13 he that shall *e* to the end
Mark 4:17 no root, and *e* but for a time
2 Tim. 2: 3 *e* hardness as a good soldier
Heb. 12: 2 that was set before him *e* the cross
12: 7 if ye *e* chastening, God dealeth
Jas. 5: 11 we count them happy which *e*

ENDURETH
1 Chr. 16:34 his mercy *e* for ever
Ezra 3: 11 for his mercy *e* forever toward Israel
Ps. 30: 5 his anger *e* but a moment
100: 5 his truth *e* to all generations
106: 1 his mercy *e* forever
112: 3 his righteousness *e* for
117: 2 the truth of the Lord *e* for ever
119: 160 thy righteous judgments *e*
145: 13 thy dominion *e* throughout
Mat. 10:22 that *e* to end shall be saved
John 6:27 meat which *e* unto life
1 Cor. 13: 7 hopeth all things, *e* all things
Jas. 1:12 blessed is the man that *e* temptation
1 Pet. 1:25 word of the Lord *e* for

ENEMY
Ex. 23:22 I will be an *e* unto thine enemies
Job 33:10 he counteth me for his *e*
Ps. 7: 5 let the *e* persecute my soul
8: 2 mightest still the *e* and avenger
Prov. 27: 6 kisses of an *e* are deceitful
Mic. 7: 8 rejoice not against me, O mine *e*
1 Cor. 15:26 the last *e* destroyed is death

Gal. 4:16 am I therefore become your *e*
2 Thes. 3:15 count him not as an *e*,
Jas. 4: 4 friend of the world is the *e* of God

ENEMIES
Gen. 22:17 seed shall possess the gate of his *e*
Deut. 28:48 therefore shalt thou serve thine *e*
132: 18 his *e* will I clothe with shame
Prov. 16: 7 he maketh even his *e* to be at peace
Is. 66: 6 that rendereth recompence to his *e*
Mic. 7: 6 man's *e* are the men of his own house
Mat. 22:44 till I make thine *e* thy footstool
Rom. 5: 10 if when we were *e* we were reconciled
Heb. 1:13 until I make thine *e* thy footstool

ENMITY
Gen. 3:15 I will put *e* between thee and
Rom. 8: 7 carnal mind is *e* against God
Eph. 2:15 abolished in his flesh the *e*

ENJOY
Lev. 26:34 shall the land *e* her sabbaths
Heb. 11:25 *e* the pleasures of sin for a season

ENLIGHTEN (ENLIGHTENED)
Ps. 18:28 the Lord my God will *e* my darkness
Eph. 1: 18 eyes of your understanding being *e*
Heb. 6: 4 impossible for those who were once *e*

ENSIGN (ENSIGNS)
Ps. 74: 4 set up their *e* for signs
Is. 5:26 he will lift up an *e* to the nations
11: 10 stand for an *e* to the people
Zech. 9: 16 lifted up as an *e* upon his land

ENTER
Num. 20:24 for he shall not *e* into the land
Job 22: 4 will he *e* with thee into judgment
Ps. 100: 4 *e* his gates with thanksgiving
Prov. 4:14 *e* not into the path of the wicked
23:10 *e* not into the fields of the fatherless
Is. 26:20 *e* into thy chambers, and shut
57: 2 he shall *e* into peace
Mat. 5:20 no case *e* into the kingdom
6: 6 when thou prayest, *e* into thy closet
7: 21 shall *e* into the kingdom of heaven
18: 8 it is better to *e* into life halt
19:24 than for rich men to *e* into the kingdom
25:21 *e* thou into the joy of thy Lord
26:41 that ye *e* not into temptation
Mark 14:38 watch and pray, lest ye *e* into temptation
Luke 24:26 things and to *e* into his glory
John 3: 4 can he *e* the second time into his
3: 5 he cannot *e* into the kingdom of God
10: 9 I am the door; by me if any man *e*
Acts 14:22 tribulation *e* into the kingdom of God
Heb. 4: 3 believed do *e* into rest
10:19 *e* into the holiest by the blood of Jesus

ENTERED (ENTERETH)
Ex. 33: 9 as Moses *e* into the tabernacle
John 4:38 ye are *e* into their labours
10: 1 *e* not by the door, but climbeth up
Rom. 5:12 by one man sin *e* into the world
5:20 law *e* that offence might abound
Heb. 4: 6 *e* not because of unbelief

ENTERTAIN
Heb. 13: 2 be not forgetful to *e* strangers

ENTREAT (ENTREATED)
Ex. 9:28 *e* the Lord (for it is enough)
1 Cor. 4:13 being defamed, we *e*: we are made
1 Tim. 5: 1 not an elder but *e* him as a father
Jas. 3:17 easy to be *e*, full of mercy

ENTREATY (ENTREATIES)
Prov. 18:23 the poor useth *e*, but the rich

ENVY (ENVIES)
Job 5: 2 *e* slayeth the silly one
Prov. 3: 31 *e* thou not the oppressor, and
14:30 *e* is the rottenness of bones
23:17 let not thy heart *e* sinners
27: 4 who is able to stand before *e*
Phil. 1:15 some indeed preach Christ even of *e*
1 Tim. 6: 4 whereof cometh *e*, strife, railings
Tit. 3: 3 living in malice, *e*, hateful and
Jas. 4: 5 spirit in us lusteth to *e*
1 Pet. 2: 1 hypocrisies and *e* and all evil

ENVIED (ENVYING)
Gen. 26:14 the Philistines *e* him

Ps. 106: 16 they *e* Moses also in the camp
Rom. 13:13 wantonness, not in strife and *e*
1 Cor. 3: 3 *e* and strife, and divisions, are ye
Gal. 5:26 provoking one another, *e* one

ENVIOUS
Ps. 37: 1 neither be thou *e*

EPHOD
Ex. 39: 2 made the *e* of gold, blue, and purple
Judg. 8:27 and Gideon made an *e* thereof
1 Sam. 2:18 girded with a linen *e*
21: 9 wrapped in a cloth behind the *e*
2 Sam. 6:14 David was girded with a linen *e*
Hos. 3: 4 without an image, and without an *e*

EPISTLE
Acts 15:30 together they delivered the *e*
2 Cor. 7: 8 the same *e* hath made you sorry
2 Thes. 2:15 whether by word, or our *e*

EQUAL (EQUALS)
Ezek. 18:25 ye say, the way of the Lord is not *e*
Mat. 20:12 thou hast made them *e* unto us
Luke 20:36 for they are *e* unto the angels
John 5:18 making himself *e* with God
Gal. 1:14 my *e* in mine own nation
Phil. 2: 6 it not robbery to be *e* with God

EQUITY
Ps. 98: 9 and the people with *e*
Prov. 1: 3 wisdom, justice, judgment, *e*
Eccl. 2: 21 labour is in wisdom, knowledge, *e*
Is. 11: 4 reprove with *e* for the meek
59:14 truth fallen, *e* cannot enter
Mic. 3: 9 princes that pervert all *e*
Mal. 2: 6 Levi walked with me in *e*

ERR (ERRED)
1 Sam. 26: 21 the fool, and have *e* exceedingly
Ps. 95: 10 do *e* in their heart
119: 21 which do *e* from thy commandments
119: 110 I *e* not from thy precepts
Prov. 14:22 do they not *e* that devise evil
Is. 35: 8 wayfaring men, though fools, shall not *e*
63:17 why hast thou made us to *e* from thy
Jer. 23:13 and caused my people Israel to *e*
Mat. 22:29 ye do *e* not knowing the scripture
1 Tim. 6: 10 have *e* from the faith, and pierced
6: 21 professing have *e* concerning the faith
Jas. 5:19 if any of you *e* from the truth

ERROR (ERRORS)
2 Sam. 6: 7 God smote him there for his *e*
Ps. 19:12 who can understand his *e*
Is. 32: 6 utter *e* against the Lord
Dan. 6: 4 neither was any *e* or fault
Jas. 5:20 sinner from the *e* of his way
1 John 4: 6 spirit of truth and the spirit of *e*
Jude 1: 11 after the *e* of Balaam for reward

ESCAPE (ESCAPED)
Gen. 19:22 haste thee, *e* thither, for I cannot
Ezra 9: 8 to leave us a remnant to *e*
Ps. 56: 1 shall they *e* by iniquity
71: 2 deliver me and cause me to *e*
124: 7 our soul is as a bird *e*
Prov. 19: 5 that speaketh lies shall not *e*
Jer. 11: 11 which they shall not be able to *e*
Ezek. 17:15 shall he *e* that doeth such things
Mat. 23:33 can ye *e* the damnation of hell
Luke 21:36 accounted worthy to *e* all these
Rom. 2: 3 thou shalt *e* the judgment of God
1 Cor. 10:13 temptation also make a way to *e*
1 Thes. 5: 3 child; and they shall not *e*
Heb. 2: 3 how shall we *e* if we neglect
12:25 *e* not who refused him that spake
2 Pet. 1: 4 the corruption that is in the
2: 18 allure those that were clean *e*

ESTABLISH
Gen. 9: 9 *e* my covenant with you, and
17: 7 I will *e* my covenant between me and
Lev. 26: 9 and *e* my covenant with you
Deut. 8:18 that he may *e* his covenant which he sware
1 Sam. 1:23 the Lord *e* his word
2 Sam. 7:12 I will *e* his kingdom
2 Chr. 9: 8 God loved Israel to *e* them
Ps. 7: 9 *e* the just: for the righteous
48: 8 our God: God will *e* it
89: 2 faithfulness shalt thou *e* in heaven

89: 4 thy seed will I *e* for
90:17 *e* the work of our hands
Prov. 15:25 will *e* the border of the widow
Is. 9: 7 order it, and to *e* it with judgment
49: 8 to *e* the earth, to cause
62: 7 no rest till he *e* Jerusalem
Ezek. 16:60 I will *e* unto thee an everlasting
covenant
Rom. 3:10 to *e* their own righteousness
1 Thes. 3:13 *e* your hearts

ESTABLISHED
Ex. 6: 4 I have also *e* my covenant with them
15:17 which thy hands have *e*
Ps. 40: 2 upon a rock, he *e* my goings
78: 5 he *e* a testimony in Jacob
93: 2 thy throne is *e* of old
119: 90 hast *e* the earth, and it abideth
Prov. 3:19 by understanding hath he *e* the heavens
4:26 let all thy ways be *e*
16: 5 in mercy shall the throne be *e*
Jer. 10:12 hath *e* the world by his wisdom
Hab. 1:12 thou hast *e* them for correction
Mat. 18:16 or three witnesses every word may be *e*
Acts 16: 5 so were the churches *e* in the faith
Rom. 1:11 gift to the end ye may be *e*
Heb. 8: 6 *e* upon better promises
13: 9 that the heart be *e* with grace
2 Pet. 1:12 and be *e* in the present truth

ESTATE
Ps. 136:23 who remembered us in our low *e*
Luke 1:48 the low *e* of his handmaiden
Jude 1: 6 angels that kept not their first *e*

ESTEEM (ESTEEMED, ESTEEMETH, ESTEEMING)
Deut. 32:15 and lightly *e* the rock of his salvation
1 Sam. 2:30 they that despise me shall be lightly *e*
Job 23:12 *e* the words of his mouth more than
Ps. 119:128 I *e* all thy precepts concerning
Is. 53: 4 we did *e* him stricken of God
Rom. 14: 5 one man *e* one day above another
Phil. 2: 3 each other better than themselves
1 Thes. 5:13 *e* them very highly in love for
Heb. 11:26 *e* the reproach of Christ

ETERNAL
Deut. 33:27 the *e* God is thy refuge
Is. 60:15 make thee an *e* excellency
Mat. 19:16 that I may have *e* life
Mark 3:29 is in danger of *e* damnation
10:17 that I may inherit *e* life
Luke 10:25 what shall I do to inherit *e* life
John 3:15 should not perish but have *e* life
4:36 wages, gathereth fruit unto *e* life
6:54 hath *e* life and I will raise him up
17: 3 this is life *e*, that they might
Acts 13:48 ordained to *e* life believed
Rom. 1:20 even his *e* power and Godhead
2: 7 honour, immortality, and *e* life
6:23 the gift of God is *e* through Jesus
2 Cor. 4:17 exceeding and *e* weight of glory
Eph. 3:11 according to the *e* purpose
1 Tim. 1:17 unto the King *e* immortal, invisible
Tit. 1: 2 in hope of life which God
3: 7 heirs according to the hope of life
Heb. 5: 9 author of *e* salvation
9:12 obtained *e* redemption
1 Pet. 5:10 called us unto his *e* glory
1 John 1: 2 *e* life which was with the Father
5:11 God has given to us *e* life

EUNUCH (EUNUCHS)
2 Ki. 20:18 they shall be *e* in the palace
Is. 56: 3 neither *e* say, I am a dry tree
Mat. 19:12 themselves *e* for the kingdom of
heaven's sake
Acts 8:27 *e* of great authority under Candace

EVEN (EVENING)
Gen. 1: 5 the *e* and the morning were the first
1 Ki. 18:29 offering of the *e* sacrifice
Zeph. 3: 3 her judges are *e* wolves

EVER
Gen. 3:22 and eat and live for *e*
Ex. 15:18 Lord reigneth for *e* and *e*
Deut. 32:40 to heaven and say, I live for *e*
Josh. 4:24 fear the Lord your God for *e*
1 Ki. 10: 9 the Lord loved Israel for *e*

Ps. 5:11 let them *e* shout for joy
9: 7 for the Lord shall endure for *e*
10:16 the Lord is king for *e*
22:26 heart shall live for *e*
23: 6 dwell in the house of the Lord for *e*
25:37 he is *e* merciful and lendeth
30:12 I will give thanks unto thee for *e*
45: 6 thy throne, O God, is for *e*
48:14 God is our God for *e*
51: 3 my sin is *e* before me
74:19 the congregation of thy poor for *e*
92: 7 that they shall be destroyed for *e*
103: 9 neither will he keep his anger for *e*
111: 8 commandments stand fast for *e*
119: 111 have I taken as an heritage for *e*
Is. 26: 4 trust in the Lord for *e*
32:17 and assurance for *e*
57:16 I will not contend for *e*
Jer. 3: 5 will he reserve anger for *e*
Lam. 3:31 the Lord will not cast off for *e*
Mic. 7:18 retaineth not his anger for *e*
Zech. 1: 5 prophets, do they live for *e*
Luke 15:31 son, thou art with me
John 8:35 but the son abideth *e*
Rom. 1:25 the Creator who is blessed for *e*
2 Cor. 9: 9 his righteousness remaineth for *e*
1 Thes. 4: 5 *e* follow that which is good
2 Tim. 3: 7 *e* learning, and never able to
Heb. 7:25 he *e* liveth to make intercession
13: 8 the same, yesterday today and for *e*
1 Pet. 1:23 the word of God abideth for *e*
1 John 2:17 doeth the will of God abideth for *e*
Rev. 1: 6 to him be glory and dominion for *e* and *e*

EVERLASTING
Gen. 17: 8 land of Canaan, an *e* possession
Ex. 40:15 *e* priesthood throughout their
generations
Deut. 33:27 and underneath are the *e* arms
Ps. 24: 7 ye lift up ye *e* doors
90: 2 from *e* to *e* thou art
112: 6 the righteous shall be in *e* remembrance
145: 13 thy kingdom is an *e*
Prov. 10:25 righteous is an *e* foundation
Is. 9: 6 The mighty God, the *e* Father
35:10 songs and *e* joy upon their heads
55:13 to the Lord for a name, an *e* sign
56: 5 I will give them an *e* name
60:19 the Lord shall be an *e* light
Jer. 10:10 he is the living God, and an *e* King
31: 3 I have loved thee with an *e* love
Dan. 12: 2 awake some to *e* life, and some
Mic. 5: 2 goings forth of old, from *e*
Hab. 1:12 art thou not from *e*, O Lord my God
Mat. 18: 8 to be cast into *e* fire
25:46 shall go into *e* punishment
Luke 16: 9 may receive you into *e* habitations
18:30 in the world to come *e* life
John 3:36 believeth on the Son hath *e* life
4:14 well of water springing up into *e* life
5:24 that heareth my word hath *e* life
6:27 meat which endureth to *e* life
12:50 his commandment is *e* life
Acts 13:46 yourselves unworthy of *e* life
Gal. 6: 8 shall of the Spirit reap *e* life
2 Thes. 1: 9 shall be punished with *e* destruction
1 Tim. 1:16 believe on him to life *e*
6:16 to whom be honour and power *e*

EVIL
Gen. 6: 5 thoughts of his heart only *e*
Josh. 24:15 if it seem *e* unto you to serve the
Job 2:10 shall we not receive *e*
5:19 there shall no *e* touch thee
30:26 looked for good then *e* came
Ps. 23: 4 I will fear no *e* for thou
51: 4 have done this *e* in thy sight
52: 3 thou lovest *e* more than good
91:10 shall no *e* befall thee, neither
Prov. 12:21 there shall no *e* happen to the just
14:19 the *e* bow before the good
15: 3 beholding the *e* and the good
15:15 all the days of the afflicted are *e*
31:12 will do him good and not *e*
Eccl. 9: 3 heart of the sons of men is full of *e*
Is. 5:20 them that call *e* good, and good *e*

7:15 know to refuse the *e*, and choose
45: 7 I make peace and create *e*
Jer. 17:17 my hope in the day of *e*
29:11 thoughts of peace and not of *e*
Lam. 3:38 most High proceedeth not *e* and good
Ezek. 7: 5 an *e*, an only *e*, behold is come
Amos 5:14 seek good and not *e*,
9: 4 set eyes on them for *e*,
Hab. 1:13 purer eyes than to behold *e*, and
Mat. 5:11 all manner of *e* against you falsely
5:45 his sun to rise on the *e*
6:34 sufficient to the day is the *e* thereof
7: 11 ye, being *e*, know how
John 3:19 light because their deeds were *e*
Rom. 7:19 *e* which I would not that I do
7: 21 I would do good *e* is present with me
12:17 recompense to no man *e* for *e*
12: 21 be not overcome of *e* but overcome *e*
1 Cor. 13: 5 not easily provoked, thinketh no *e*
Eph. 5:16 because the days are *e*
1 Thes. 5:15 none render *e* for *e* unto any man
5:22 abstain from all appearance of *e*
1 Tim. 6:10 love of money is the root of all *e*
Heb. 5:14 exercised discern both good and *e*

EXALT (EXALTED, EXALTETH)
Ex. 15: 2 my father's God, I will *e*
Num. 24: 7 his kingdom shall be *e*
1 Sam. 2:10 *e* the horn of his anointed
2 Sam.22:47 *e* be the God of my salvation
Ps. 34: 3 let us *e* his name together
99: 5 *e* ye the Lord our God
118: 28 my God, I will *e* thee
Prov. 14:34 righteousness *e* a nation, but sin
Is. 2:11 Lord alone shall be *e* in that day
40: 4 every valley shall be *e*
Ezek. 21:26 *e* him that is low, and abase
Mat. 23:12 humbleth himself shall be *e*
Luke 1:52 their seats and *e* them of low degree
14: 11 *e* himself shall be abased
Acts 5:31 Him hath God *e* with his right hand
Phil. 2: 9 God hath highly *e* him
1 Pet. 5: 6 that he may *e* you in due time

EXAMINE (EXAMINED)
Ps. 26: 2 *e* me, O Lord, and prove me
1 Cor. 11:28 and so let a man *e* himself
2 Cor. 13: 5 *e* yourselves, whether ye be in the faith

EXAMPLE (EXAMPLES)
Mat. 1:19 not make her a public *e*
1 Thes. 1: 7 ye were *e* to all that believe
1 Tim. 4:12 an *e* of the believers in word
Heb. 8: 5 serve unto the *e* and shadow
Jas. 5:10 for an *e* of suffering affliction
1 Pet. 5: 3 but being *e* to the flock

EXCEEDING (EXCEEDINGLY)
Gen. 17: 6 I will make thee *e* fruitful
1 Ki. 4:29 gave Solomon wisdom *e* much
1 Chr. 22: 5 builded for the Lord must be *e*
magnifical
Ps. 43: 4 I will go to God my *e* joy
119:167 thy testimonies I love *e*
Eph. 1:19 *e* greatness of his power to us-ward
2: 7 might show *e* riches of his grace
3:20 him that is able to do *e* abundantly
1 Thes. 3:10 praying *e* that we might see your face
1 Tim. 1:14 grace was *e* abundant with faith
Jude 1:24 presence of his glory with *e* joy

EXCEL (EXCELLEST)
Ps. 103:20 angels that *e* in strength
Prov. 31:29 virtuously but thou *e* them all

EXCELLENCY
Gen. 49: 3 *e* of dignity and the *e*
Ex. 15: 7 in the greatness of thine *e*
Deut. 33:26 rideth in his *e* on sky
Job 37: 4 thunders with the voice of his *e*
40:10 deck thyself now with *e*
Ps. 47: 4 *e* of Jacob, whom he loved
68:34 his *e* is over Israel, and his
Is. 35: 2 see glory and *e* of our God
Amos 6: 8 I abhor the *e* of Jacob, and hate
1 Cor. 2: 1 not with *e* of speech or of wisdom
2 Cor. 4: 7 *e* of the power may be of God, and
Phil. 3: 8 loss for the *e* of the knowledge of Christ

EXCELLENT
Esth.　1:　4 the honour of his e majesty
Ps.　　8:　1 how e is thy name in all the earth
　　　 16:　3 saints, e in whom my delight
　　　 36:　7 how e is thy lovingkindness
　　 148: 13 the Lord, for his name alone is e
Prov.　12:26 the righteous is more e than his
　　 17:27 man of understanding is of e spirit
Is.　　12:　5 Lord hath done e things
Ezek.　16:　7 and thou art come to e ornaments
Dan.　　5:12 an e spirit and knowledge and
Rom.　　2:18 the things that are more e
1 Cor.　12:31 I show unto you a more e way
Phil.　　1:10 approve things that are e
Heb.　　1:　4 obtained a more e name than they
　　 11:　4 offered a more e sacrifice
2 Pet.　1:17 such a voice from the e glory

EXCUSE (EXCUSING)
Luke　14:18 with one consent began to make e
Rom.　　1:20 so that they are without e
　　　 2:15 while accusing or else e one another

EXECUTE
Ex.　　12:12 I will e judgment; I am the Lord
Num.　　5:30 priest shall e upon her all this law
　　　 8:11 they may e the service of the Lord
Ps.　 119:84 when wilt thou e judgment on them
Is.　　16:　3 take counsel, e judgment; make thy
Hos.　 11:　9 not e the fierceness of mine anger
Mic.　　7:　9 plead my cause, and e judgment for me
Zech.　 8:16 e the judgment of truth and peace
John　　5:27 hath given him authority to e judgment
Jude　　1:15 to e judgment upon all

EXHORT (EXHORTED, EXHORTING)
2 Cor.　9:　5 thought it necessary to e the brethren
1 Thes.　2:11 how we e and comforted and charged
2 Thes.　3:12 e by our Lord Jesus Christ
2 Tim.　4:　2 e with all longsuffering and doctrine
Tit.　　1:　9 e and to convince the gainsayers
Heb.　　3:13 e one another daily
　　 10:25 but e one another, and so much the
Jude　　1:　3 e you that ye should earnestly contend

EXHORTATION
Rom.　12:　8 or he that exhorteth, on e
1 Cor.　14:　3 to edification, and e, and comfort
1 Thes.　2:　3 for our e was not of deceit
1 Tim.　4:13 give attendance to reading, to e, to
　　　　 doctrine
Heb.　12:　5 ye have forgotten the e which

EXPECTATION
Ps.　　9:18 e of the poor shall not perish for
Prov.　10:28 the e of the wicked shall perish
　　 11:23 the e of the wicked is wrath
　　 23:18 thine e shall not be cut off
Acts　 12:11 from all the e of the people
Rom.　　8:19 e of the creature waiteth for the
Phil.　　1:20 according to my earnest e and my

EXPEDIENT
John　11:50 nor consider that it is e for us
　　 16:　7 e for you that I go away
1 Cor.　6:12 but all things are not e
　　 12:　1 it is not e for me to glory

EXTOL (EXTOLLED)
Ps.　　30:　1 I will e thee, O Lord
　　　 68:　4 e him that rideth upon the heavens
　　 145:　1 I will e thee, my God, O king
Is.　　52:13 he shall be exalted and e

EXTORTION
Ezek.　22:12 gained of thy neighbors by e
Mat.　23:25 within they are full of e

EXTORTIONER
Ps.　 109:11 Let the e catch all that he hath
Is.　　16:　4 for the e is at an end,
1 Cor.　5:11 or a drunkard, or an e;

EXTORTIONERS
Luke　18:11 not as other men are, e, unjust
1 Cor.　6:10 nor revilers, nor e, shall inherit

EYE
Ex.　　21:24 e for e, tooth for tooth
Deut.　32:10 kept him as the apple of his e
Job　　24:15 no e shall see me, and
Ps.　　17:　8 keep me as the apple of thine e
　　　 33:18 the e of the Lord is upon them

Prov.　20:12 seeing e, the Lord hath
　　　 23:　6 bread of him that hath an evil e
Eccl.　　1:　8 the e is not satisfied with seeing
Is.　　64:　4 neither hath the e seen, O God
Mat.　　5:38 an e for an e, and a tooth
　　　 6:22 light of the body is the e
　　 18:　9 if thine e offend thee, pluck it out
Mark　 7:22 an evil e, blasphemy, pride
Luke　11:34 the light of the body is the e
1 Cor.　2:　9 e hath not seen nor ear heard
Rev.　　1:　7 and every e shall see him, and they

EYELIDS
Job　　16:16 on my e is the shadow of death
Prov.　 4:25 let thine e look straight before thee
Jer.　　9:18 our e gush out with waters

EYEWITNESSES
2 Pet.　1:16 but were e of his majesty

EYES
Gen.　　3:　5 then your e shall be opened and ye
　　　 6:　8 Noah found grace in the e of the Lord
Deut.　12:　8 whatsoever is right in his own e
Judg.　17:　6 which was right in his own e
2 Sam.15:25 find favour in the e of the Lord
1 Ki　22:43 which was right in the e of the Lord
2 Chr.　16:　9 e of the Lord run to and fro
Ps.　　15:　4 whose e a vile person is condemned
　　　25:15 mine e are ever towards the Lord
　　　34:15 e of the Lord are upon the righteous
　　 101:　6 mine e shall be upon the faithful
　　 119:148 mine e prevent the night watches
　　 139:16 thine e did see my substance
　　 141:　8 mine e are unto thee, O God
　　 145:15 the e of all wait upon thee and thou
Prov.　 5:21 ways of man before the e of the Lord
　　 15:　3 the e of the Lord are in every place
　　 22:12 the e of the Lord preserve knowledge
Is.　　1:15 I will hide mine e from you
　　　 3:16 stretched forth necks and wanton e
　　 29:18 e of the blind see out of obscurity
　　 35:　5 e of the blind shall be opened
　　 43:　8 Blind people that have e
　　 49:　5 be glorious in the e of the Lord
Jer.　　5:　3 are not thine e upon the truth
　　　 9:　1 that mine e were a fountain of tears
　　 14:17 let mine e run down with tears
　　 24:　6 set mine e upon them for good
Ezek.　24:16 take away the desire of thine e
Amos　 9:　8 the e of the Lord God are upon
Hab.　　1:13 art of purer e than to behold evil
Zech.　 3:　9 on one stone shall be seven e
Mat.　13:16 blessed are your e for they see
　　 18:　9 having two e to be cast into hell fire
　　 20:33 that our e may be opened
Mark　 8:18 having e see ye not
Luke　　2:30 mine e have seen thy salvation
　　 10:23 blessed are the e which see
John　　9:　6 anointed the e of blind man
Rom.　11:　8 e that they should not see, and ears
Eph.　　1:18 e of your understanding being
2 Pet.　2:14 e full of adultery, and that cannot
1 John　1:　1 which we have seen with our e
　　　 2:16 lust of the e and pride
Rev.　　1:14 his e were as a flame of fire
　　　 2:18 who hath his e like unto a flame
　　　 3:18 and anoint thine e with eyesalve
　　　 4:　6 four beasts full of e before and behind
　　 19:12 His e were as a flame of fire

FACE
Lev.　19:32 honour the f of the old
Num.　　6:25 the Lord make his f shine upon thee
2 Chr.　6:42 turn not the f of thine anointed
Ps.　　17:15 behold thy f in righteousness
　　 119:135 make thy f to shine upon thy
Ezek.　 1:10 the f of a lion
Dan.　　9:17 cause thy f to shine upon
1 Cor.　13:12 glass darkly but then f to f
2 Cor.　3:18 with open f beholding as in a glass
Jas.　　1:23 his natural f in a glass
Rev.　　4:　7 third beast had a f like a man

FADE (FADETH)
Is.　　64:　6 we all do f as a leaf
Jas.　　1:11 rich man f away in his ways
1 Pet.　1:　4 inheritance that f not away

　　　　 5:　4 crown of glory that f

FAIL (FAILED, FAILETH)
Deut.　31:　6 Lord will not f nor forsake
1 Chr.　28:20 he will not f thee, nor forsake
Ps.　　12:　1 faithful f from among the children of
　　　　 men
　　　31:10 strength f because of mine iniquity
　　　71:　9 forsake me not when my strength f
　　　77:　8 doth his promise f for evermore
　　 143:　7 my spirit f; hide not thy face
Sol.　　5:　6 soul f when he spake,
Lam.　　3:22 because his compassions f not
Luke　12:33 treasure in heaven that f not
　　 16:17 than one tittle of the law to f
　　 22:32 prayed that thy faith f not
1 Cor.　13:　8 charity never f, but
Heb.　12:15 lest any f of the grace

FAINT (FAINTED, FAINTETH)
Ps.　　84:　2 even f for the courts of the Lord
Is.　　1:　5 head is sick, and the whole heart f
　　　40:30 youths shall f and be weary
2 Cor.　4:　1 we have received mercy we f not
Heb.　12:　5 nor f when thou art rebuked of him
Rev.　　2:　3 hast laboured and hast not f

FAIR (FAIRER)
Ps.　　45:　2 f than the children of men
Sol.　　1:15 behold thou art f; thou hast
Dan.　　1:15 their countenances appeared f and
　　　　 fatter
Acts　　7:20 Moses was born and was exceeding f

FAITH
Deut.　32:20 children in whom is no f
Hab.　　2:　4 just shall live by f
Mat.　　6:30 clothe you, O ye of little f
　　　 8:26 are ye fearful, O ye of little f
　　　 9:22 thy f hath made thee whole
　　 14:31 O thou of little f,
　　 15:28 O woman, great is thy f be it unto
　　 17:20 f as a grain of mustard
　　 21:21 have f and doubt not, ye shall not
Mark　 4:40 how is it ye have no f
Luke　　7:　9 I have not found so great f
　　　 7:50 thy f hath saved thee
　　 17:　5 unto the Lord, increase our f
　　 18:　8 shall he find f on the earth
　　 22:32 I have prayed that thy f fail not
Acts　　3:16 the f which is by him hath given him
　　　 6:　5 Stephen, a man full of f
　　 15:　9 purifying their hearts by f
　　 16:　5 churches established in the f
Rom.　　1:17 righteousness of God revealed from f to f
　　　 2:19 I know thy works and f
　　　 3:　3 make the f of God without effect
　　　 3:25 propitiation through f in his blood
　　　 4:　5 his f is counted for righteousness
　　　 4:11 circumcision, a seal of righteousness
　　　 4:20 strong in f giving glory to God
　　　 5:　1 being justified by f we have peace
　　　 9:32 not by f but by the works of the law
　　 10:17 f cometh by hearing, and hearing
　　 12:　3 to every man the measure of f
1 Cor.　12:　9 to another f by the same spirit
　　 13:　2 though I have all f to remove
　　 13:13 now abideth f, hope, charity
2 Cor.　1:24 of your joy; for by f ye stand
　　　 4:13 having the same Spirit of f
　　　 5:　7 we walk by f and not by sight
　　 10:15 when your f is increased, we
　　 13:　5 examine whether ye be in f
Gal.　　1:23 preacheth the f which once he
　　　 2:16 by the works of the law, but by f
　　　 2:20 I live by the f of the Son of God
　　　 3:　2 Spirit by the hearing of f
　　　 3:　8 God would justify the heathen through f
　　　 3:11 The just shall live by f
　　　 3:14 receive the promise of the Spirit
　　　　 through f
　　　 3:23 before f came, we were under the law
　　　 5:　6 but f which worketh by love
　　　 5:22 but the fruit of the Spirit is . . . f
Eph.　　1:15 heard of your f in the Lord Jesus
　　　 2:　8 by grace ye are saved through f
　　　 3:17 Christ dwell in your hearts by f

4:   5 one Lord, one f, one baptism
6:16 above all taking the shield of f
Phil.   1:25 for your furtherance and joy of the f
2:17 sacrifice and service of your f
Col.   1:23 if ye continue in f grounded
2:12 through the f of the operation of God
1 Thes. 1:   3 remember your work of f
1:   8 your f to God-ward is spread
3:10 perfect that which is lacking in your f
5:   8 putting on the breastplate of f
2 Thes. 1:   4 for your patience and f in all
3:   2 for all men have not f
1 Tim. 1:   4 godly edifying which is in f
1:   5 charity out of unfeigned
1:14 exceeding abundant with f and love
2:15 if they continue in f an.J charity
3:   9 holding the mystery of the f
4:   6 nourished up in the words of f
5:   8 he hath denied the f and is worse
6:12 fight the good fight of f
2 Tim. 1:   5 unfeigned f that is in thee
1:13 in f and love which is in Christ Jesus
2:22 follow righteousness, f, charity
Tit.   1:13 that they may be sound in f
3:15 greet them that love us in f
Heb.   4:   2 not being mixed with f in them
6:   1 dead works and of f toward God
6:12 through f and patience inherit promises
10:22 draw near in assurance of f
11:   1 f is the substance of things hoped
11:   6 without f it is impossible to please him
12:   2 Jesus the finisher of our f
Jas.   1:   3 trying of your f worketh patience
1:   6 ask in f, nothing wavering
2:   5 poor of this world rich in f
2:17 f if it hath not works, is dead
2:18 show me thy f without thy works
5:15 prayer of f shall save the sick
1 Pet. 1:   5 kept by the power of God through f
1:21 that your f and hope might be in God
2 Pet. 1:   5 add to your f virtue, and to virtue
1 John 5:   4 overcometh the world, even our f
Jude   1:   3 contend earnestly for the f
1:20 building up yourselves on holy f
Rev.   14:12 which keep the f of Jesus

FAITHLESS
Mat.   17:17 O f and perverse generation
John   20:27 be not f but believing

FAITHFUL
Num.   12:   7 who is f in all my house
Deut.   7:   9 God, the f God which keepeth covenant
1 Sam. 2:35 I will raise me up a f priest
Neh.   7:   2 a f man, and feared God
Ps.   31:23 Lord preserveth the f,
89:37 a f witness in heaven
119:   86 thy commandments are f
Prov.   11:13 He that is of a f spirit
13:17 a f ambassador is health
14:   5 a f witness will not lie
20:   6 a f man who can find?
27:   6 f are the wounds of a friend
28:20 f man shall abound with blessings
Is.   49:   7 Lord is the Holy One of Israel
Jer.   42:   5 Lord be a f witness
Mat.   25:21 well done thou good and f servant
25:23 f over a few things, I will
Luke   12:42 who is that f steward
16:10 f in least is f also in
1 Cor. 1:   9 God is f by whom ye were called
4:   2 required in stewards, a man f
10:13 God is f who will not suffer
Eph.   6:21 f minister in the Lord, shall make
1 Thes. 5:24 f is he that calleth you
1 Tim. 1:12 for he counted me f, putting me
1:15 a f saying and worthy of all acceptation
2 Tim. 2:   2 same commit thou to f men, who shall
2:11 it is a f saying: for if we be
Tit.   1:   6 one wife, having f children
1:   9 holding fast the f word as taught
3:   8 this is a f saying, and these things
Heb.   10:23 f is he that promised
1 Pet. 4:19 well doing as unto a f Creator
1 John 1:   9 he is f and just to forgive
Rev.   1:   5 f witness and the first begotten

21:   5 for these words are true and f

FAITHFULNESS
Ps.   36:   5 thy f reacheth to the clouds
40:10 I have declared thy f and thy
89:   1 make known thy f to all generations
89:   5 praise thy f in the congregation
89:   8 who is like to thy f round about thee
89:33 nor suffer my f to fail
92:   2 to show forth thy f every night
119:   75 thou in f hast afflicted me
119:   90 thy f is unto all generations
Is.   11:   5 f the girdle of his reins
Lam.   3:23 new every morning, great is thy f
Hos.   2:20 I will betroth thee to me in f

FALL
Ps.   37:24 though he f he shall not
141:   10 let the wicked f into their own nets
145:   14 the Lord upholdeth all that f
Prov.   11:   5 wicked shall f by his own wickedness
26:27 whoso diggeth a pit shall f therein
28:14 hardeneth his heart shall f
Eccl.   4:10 if they f one will lift up
Dan.   11:35 them of understanding shall f
Hos.   10:   8 and to the hills f on us
Mat.   7:27 great was the f of it
10:29 sparrow not f on the ground
15:14 blind lead the blind, both shall f into
Luke   23:30 say to the mountains, f on us
Rom.   11:11 stumbled that they should f
1 Cor. 10:12 take heed lest he f
1 Tim. 6:   9 will be rich f into temptation
Heb.   4:11 f after the same example of unbelief
6:   6 if they shall f away, to renew them
10:31 f into the hands of the living God
Jas.   1:   2 when ye f into divers temptations
2 Pet. 1:10 things, ye shall never f
Rev.   6:16 f on us and hide us from the face

FALLEN (FALLING)
Ps.   16:   6 f unto me in pleasant places
56:13 wilt not thou deliver my feet from f
116:   8 and my feet from f
Gal.   5:   4 by the law, ye are f from grace
Jude   1:24 able to keep you from f

FALSE
Ex.   20:16 not bear f witness against thy neighbour
23:   1 thou shalt not raise a f report
Deut.   5:20 shalt thou bear f witness
Ps.   119:104 therefore I hate every f way
Prov.   6:19 a f witness that speaketh lies
11:   1 a f balance is abomination to the
21:28 a f witness shall perish
Jer.   23:32 against them that prophesy f dreams
Zech.   8:17 love no f oath: for all these
Mal.   3:   5 against f swearers, and against
Mat.   7:15 beware of f prophets which come to
19:18 thou shalt not bear f witness
24:24 arise f Christs and f prophets
Rom.   13:   9 thou shalt not bear f witness
1 Cor. 15:15 and we are found f witnesses of God
2 Cor. 11:13 for such are f apostles, deceitful
Gal.   2:   4 because of f brethren unawares brought
in
2 Pet. 2:   1 there were f prophets also among the
people

FALSELY
Lev.   19:12 ye shall not swear by my name f
Ps.   44:17 neither have we dealt f in thy covenant
Jer.   6:13 unto the priest, every one dealeth f
Zech.   5:   4 house of him that sweareth f
Mat.   5:11 evil against you f or my sake
Luke   3:14 neither accuse any f, and be content
1 Pet. 3:16 be ashamed that f accuse

FAMILY (FAMILIES)
Gen.   10:   5 after their f, in their nations
Ps.   68:   6 God setteth the solitary in f
Amos   3:   2 known of all the f of the earth
Eph.   3:15 whole f in heaven and earth is named

FAMINE
Gen.   12:10 there was a f in the land
41:27 be seven years of f
Job   5:20 in f he shall redeem
Ps.   33:19 keep them alive in f
37:19 the days of f they shall be satisfied

Ezek.   5:16 evil arrows of f, which shall be
Amos   8:11 not a f of bread, nor a thirst for

FAR
Ex.   23:   7 keep thee f from a false matter
Ps.   73:27 that are f from thee shall perish
Mark   12:34 not f from the kingdom of God
Eph.   2:13 were f off are made nigh by the

FASHION (FASHIONED, FASHIONETH, FASHIONING)
Job   10:   8 made me and f me
Ps.   33:15 he f their hearts alike,
119:   73 thy hands have made me and f me
1 Cor. 7:31 for the f of this world passeth away
Phil.   2:   8 being found in f as a man
3:21 be f like his glorious body
1 Pet. 1:14 as obedient children, not f yourselves

FAST
2 Sam. 12:21 thou didst f and weep for the child
1 Ki.   21:   9 saying, proclaim a f,
2 Chr. 20:   3 proclaimed a f throughout all Judah
Ezra   8:21 then I proclaimed a f
Esth.   4:16 and f ye for me and neither eat
Is.   58:   5 is it such a f that I have chosen
Jer.   14:12 when they f I will not hear
Joel   1:14 sanctify ye a f, call a
Jonah   3:   5 Nineveh believed God, and proclaimed
a f
Zech.   7:   5 did ye at all f unto me
8:19 the f of the fourth month
Mat.   6:16 ye f be not as the hypocrites
9:14 why do we f but thy disciples f not
9:15 taken from them and then shall they f
Luke   18:12 I f twice in the week

FASTED
2 Sam. 12:16 David f and lay all night on
Mat.   4:   2 when he had f forty
Acts   13:   2 ministered to the Lord, and f and

FASTING (FASTINGS)
Neh.   9:   1 of Israel were assembled with f
Esth.   4:   3 great mourning among the Jews and f
Ps.   109:24 my knees are weak through f
Jer.   36:   6 in the Lord's house upon the f day
Dan.   6:18 palace and passed the night f
9:   3 to seek by prayer and supplication with f
Joel   2:12 all your hearts and f
Luke   2:37 with f and prayers night and day
1 Cor. 7:   5 give yourselves to f and prayer
2 Cor. 6:   5 in tumults, in labours, in watchings, in f
11:27 in hunger and thirst, in f often

FAT
Lev.   3:16 all the f is the Lord's
Prov.   11:25 liberal soul shall be made f
13:   4 soul of the diligent shall be made f
15:30 good report maketh the bones f
28:25 trust in the Lord shall be made f
Is.   25:   6 f things full of marrow

FATNESS
Ps.   36:   8 satisfied with the f of thy house
65:11 goodness, and thy paths drop f
Rom.   11:17 root and f of the olive tree

FATHER
Gen.   2:24 a man shall leave his f
17:   4 be a f of many nations
Ex.   15:   2 my f's God, and I will exalt
Num.   11:12 as a nursing f beareth the sucking child
2 Sam. 7:14 I will be his f, and he
Job   29:16 I was a f to the poor,
38:28 hath the rain a f or
Ps.   68:   5 a f of the fatherless
103:   13 a f pitieth his children
Is.   9:   6 the everlasting f,
Mal.   2:10 Have we not all one f?
Mat.   5:16 glorify your f in
23:   9 call no man your f on
John   5:20 the F loveth the Son
5:21 as the F raiseth up the dead and
8:18 f that sent me beareth witness of me
8:29 F hath not left me alone
10:30 I and my f are one
14:20 that I am in my F and ye in me
16:32 I am not alone, because the F is
20:17 I ascend to my F
Acts   1:   4 wait for the promise of the F
Rom.   4:11 the f of all that believe

1 Cor. 8: 6 *F* of whom are all things, and we
2 Cor. 6:18 I will be a *F* to you
1 Tim. 5: 1 intreat him as a *f*
Heb.   1: 5 I will be to him a *f*
        12: 9 subjection to the *F* of spirits
Jas.   1:17 and cometh down from the *F* of lights

FATHERS
Neh.   9:16 our *f* dealt proudly, and hardened
Ps.   22: 4 our *f* trusted in thee,
Acts 15:10 our *f* nor we were able to bear

FATHERLESS
Ex.   22:22 not afflict any widow, or *f* child
Ps.   10:14 thou art the helper of the *f*
  146:   9 he relieveth the *f* and widow
Hos. 14: 3 in thee the *f* findeth mercy
Jas.   1:27 visit the *f* in affliction

FAULT (FAULTS)
Ps.   19:12 cleanse thou me from secret *f*
Mat. 18:15 tell him his *f* between thee and him
Luke 23: 4 I find no *f* in this man
John 18:38 I find in him no *f* at all
1 Cor. 6: 7 utterly a *f* among you
1 Pet. 2:20 if when ye be buffeted for your *f*

FAVOUR
1 Sam. 2:26 in *f* both with the Lord
Ps.   30: 5 in his *f* is life; weeping may endure
Prov. 31:30 is deceitful, and beauty is vain
Luke 2:52 in *f* with God and man

FEAR
Gen. 15: 1 *f* not I am thy shield
      42:18 do and live, for I *f* God
Ex.   18:21 *f* God, men of truth
Num. 14: 9 Lord is with us, *f* not
Deut. 1:21 *f* not, neither be discouraged
       4:10 learn to *f* me all the days that
       5:29 such a heart that would *f* me
       6:13 thou shalt *f* the Lord thy God
     28:58 *f* this glorious name
Josh. 8: 1 *f* not, neither be thou dismayed
    24:14 *f* the Lord and serve him
1 Sam.12:24 *f* the Lord and serve him in truth
1 Ki. 18:12 thy servant did *f* the Lord
2 Chr. 6:31 that they may *f* thee, to walk in
Neh.   1:11 servants, desire to *f* thy name
Job 28:28 the *f* of the Lord, that is wisdom
Ps.   2:11 serve the Lord with *f*,
     15: 4 he honoureth them that *f* the Lord
     19: 9 the *f* of the Lord is clean, enduring
     23: 4 I will *f* no evil, for
     31:19 goodness laid up for those that *f*
     33: 8 let all the earth *f* the Lord
     34:11 children, I will teach you the *f* of the
             Lord
     36: 1 there is no *f* of God before his eyes
     53: 5 in great *f* where no *f*
     56: 4 I will not *f* what flesh
     66:16 come and hear, all that *f* God
     86:11 unite my heart to *f* thy name
   103: 13 Lord pitieth them that *f* him
  119:120 flesh trembleth for *f* of thee
  135: 20 ye that *f* the Lord, bless the Lord
  147:11 Lord taketh pleasure in them that *f*
Prov. 1:29 they did not choose the *f* of the Lord
    10:27 the *f* of the Lord prolongeth days
    14:26 the *f* of the Lord is strong confidence
    15:33 the *f* of the Lord is instruction of wisdom
    19:23 the *f* of the Lord tendeth to life
    22: 4 by the *f* of the Lord are riches
    24:21 my son, *f* the Lord and meddle not
    29:25 the *f* of man bringeth a snare
Eccl. 5: 7 vanities, *f* thou God
    12:13 *f* God and keep his
Is.   8:12 neither *f* ye their *f* nor be afraid
    33: 6 the *f* of the Lord is his treasure
    41:10 *f* thou not for I am with thee
Jer.   10: 7 who would not *f* thee, O king of
    32:39 heart that may *f* me for ever
Jonah 1: 9 I *f* the Lord the God of heaven
Mat. 10:28 *f* thou not them that kill the body
Luke 1:50 his mercy on them that *f* him to
    12: 5 *f* him, which after he hath killed
    12:32 *f* not little flock, for it
Rom. 8:15 the spirit of bondage again to *f*

    13: 7 render *f* to whom *f*, honour to
2 Cor. 7: 1 perfecting holiness in the *f* of God
Phil.   2:12 work out your own salvation with *f*
2 Tim. 1: 7 spirit of *f* but of power
Heb. 12:28 with reverence and godly *f*
    13: 6 I will not *f* what man shall do
1 John 4:18 there is no *f* in love, but perfect

FEARED (FEAREST, FEARETH)
Gen. 22:12 I know that thou *f* God
Neh.   7: 2 faithful man and *f* God above many
Job   1: 1 that *f* God and eschewed evil
Ps.   25:12 what man is he that *f* the Lord
    76: 7 even thou art to be *f*
    96: 4 Lord is to be *f* above all gods
  112:   1 blessed is the man that *f* the Lord
Prov. 28:14 happy man that *f* always
Acts 10: 2 one that *f* God with all his house
    10:35 that *f* God and worketh righteousness

FEARFUL (FEARFULLY)
Ex.   15:11 glorious in holiness, *f* in praises
Ps. 139:14 I am *f* and wonderfully made
Mat.   8:26 *f*, O ye of little faith
Heb. 10:31 *f* thing to fall into the hands
Rev. 21: 8 *f* and unbelieving shall have their part

FEAST
Prov. 15:15 merry heart hath a continual *f*
Eccl. 10:19 a *f* is made for laughter, and wine
1 Cor. 5: 8 let us keep the *f*, not

FEEBLE
Ps. 105:37 not one *f* person among
Is.   35: 3 weak hands and confirm the *f* knees
1 Thes. 5:14 comfort the *f* minded, support the
Heb. 12:12 hang down and lift up the *f* knees

FEED (FEEDETH, FED)
Ps.   28: 9 *f* them also and lift them up for
    49:14 death shall *f* on them;
Prov. 10:21 lips of the righteous *f* many
    30: 8 *f* me with food convenient for me
Sol.   2:16 I am his; he *f* among the lilies
Is.   44:20 he *f* on ashes: a deceived heart
    58:14 *f* thee with the heritage of Jacob
Jer.   3:15 pastors *f* you with knowledge
Mic.   7:14 *f* thy people with thy rod
John 21:15 he saith unto him *f* my lambs
Rom. 12:20 if thine enemy hunger, *f* him
Acts 20:28 to *f* the church of God, which he
1 Cor. 3: 2 I have *f* you with milk,
    13: 3 give my goods to *f* the poor

FEET
Job 29:15 and *f* was I to the lame
Ps.   73: 2 as for me, my *f* were almost gone
  116:   8 delivered my *f* from falling
  119: 105 thy word is a lamp to my *f*
Prov. 4:26 ponder the path of thy *f*
Is.   59: 7 their *f* run to evil, and
Luke 1:79 guide our *f* into the way of
Eph.   6:15 *f* shod with the preparation of
Heb. 12:13 and make straight paths for your *f*

FELLOWSHIP
Ps.   94:20 throne of iniquity have *f* with thee
Acts 2:42 stedfastly in the apostles' doctrine and *f*
1 Cor. 1: 9 called unto the *f* of his Son
    10:20 should have *f* with devils
2 Cor. 6:14 what *f* hath righteousness with
              unrighteousness
     8: 4 of the ministering to the saints
Eph.   5:11 and have no *f* with works of
Phil.   1: 5 for your *f* in the gospel
     2: 1 if there be any *f* of the spirit
     3:10 know him and the *f* of his sufferings
1 John 1: 6 we have *f* with him

FERVENT (FERVENTLY)
Acts 18:25 and being *f* in the spirit
Rom. 12:11 *f* in spirit, serving the Lord
Jas.   5:16 *f* prayer of a righteous man availeth
1 Pet. 1:22 love one another with a pure heart *f*
     4: 8 have *f* charity among yourselves
2 Pet. 3:10 the elements shall melt with *f* heat

FEW
Mat. 20:16 many be called, but *f* chosen

FIERY
Num. 21: 6 Lord sent *f* serpents among the people

Ps.   21: 9 thou shalt make them as a *f* oven
Eph.   6:16 quench all the *f* darts of the wicked
Heb. 10:27 *f* indignation which shall devour
1 Pet. 4:12 not strange concerning the *f* trial

FIGHT
Ex.   14:14 the Lord shall *f* for you
Acts 23: 9 let us not *f* against God
1 Tim. 6:12 *f* the good *f* of faith
2 Tim. 4: 7 I have fought a good *f*
Heb. 10:32 a great *f* of afflictions

FIG (FIGS)
Gen.   3: 7 they sewed *f* leaves together
Judg. 9:10 to the *f* tree, come thou and
1 Ki.   4:25 vine and under his *f* tree
Is.   34: 4 as a falling *f* from the *f* tree
Jer. 24: 2 one basket had very good *f*
Nah.   3:12 strong holds shall be like *f* trees
Mat.   7:16 grapes of thorns or *f* of thistles?
    21:19 presently the *f* tree withered away
Luke 13: 7 I come seeking fruit on this *f* tree
John 1:50 I saw thee under the *f* tree
Rev.   6:13 even as a *f* tree casteth her

FILTHINESS
Ezek. 36:25 from all *f* will I cleanse you
2 Cor. 7: 1 cleanse ourselves from all *f* of
Jas.   1:21 lay apart all *f* and superfluity of

FILTHY
Ps.   14: 3 they are altogether become *f*
Is.   64: 6 our righteousness as *f* rags
Col.   3: 8 *f* communication out of your mouth
1 Tim. 3: 3 not greedy of lucre
Tit.   1:11 they ought not, for lucre's sake
Rev. 22:11 that is *f* let him be *f*

FIND (FINDETH)
Prov. 1:28 me early but they shall not *f* me
     8:35 whoso *f* me *f* life
    18:22 whoso *f* a wife *f* a good thing
Jer.   6:16 ye shall *f* rest for your souls
    29:13 shall seek me and *f* me, when ye
Mat.   7: 7 seek and ye shall *f*,
     7:14 way to life, few there be that *f* it
    10:39 that *f* his life shall lose
    11:29 ye shall *f* rest unto your souls
Luke 11:10 receiveth and he that seeketh *f*
John 7:34 shall seek me, and shall not *f* me
Heb.   4:16 grace to help in time of need
Rev.   9: 6 seek death and shall not *f* it

FINGER (FINGERS)
Ex.   8:19 this is the *f* of God
    31:18 written with the *f* of God
Ps.   8: 3 the work of thy *f* fingers
Luke 11:20 with the *f* of God cast
John 20:27 reach hither thy *f*

FINISH (FINISHED)
John 17: 4 I have *f* the work which thou
    19:30 he said, It is *f*
Acts 20:24 I might *f* my course with joy
2 Cor. 8: 6 he would *f* in you the same grace
2 Tim. 4: 7 I have *f* my course
Jas.   1:15 sin when it is *f* bringeth death

FINISHER
Heb. 12: 2 author and *f* of faith

FIRE
Gen. 19:24 Lord rained brimstone and *f*
Ex.   3: 2 unto him in a flame of *f*
    40:38 *f* was on it by night
Lev. 10: 1 offered a strange *f* before the Lord
Ps.   11: 6 rain *f* and brimstone on the wicked
Prov. 25:22 heap coals of *f* on head
Is.   9:18 wickedness burneth as a *f*
    31: 9 Lord whose *f* is in Zion
    43: 2 walkest through the *f* thou shalt
Jer. 23:29 is not my word like *f*
Amos 5: 6 lest the Lord break out like *f*
Zech. 2: 5 I will be a wall of *f*
Mal.   3: 2 he is like a refiner's *f*
Mat.   3:10 hewn down, and cast into the *f*
Mark 9:43 into the *f* that never shall be quenched
Luke 3:17 he will burn with *f* unquenchable
    12:49 am come to send *f* on earth
Rom. 12:20 thou shalt heap coals of *f* on his head
Heb. 12:29 our God is a consuming *f*

FIRST
Is. 44: 6 I am the *f* and I am the last
Mat. 6:33 seek ye *f* the kingdom of God
19:30 many that are *f* shall be last
Acts 26:23 Christ should be the *f* to rise
1 John 4:19 because he *f* loved us
Rev. 20: 5 this is the *f* resurrection

FIRSTBORN
Mat. 1:25 brought forth her *f*
Luke 2: 7 brought forth her *f*
Rom. 8:29 might be the *f* among many brethren
Col. 1:15 God, the *f* of every creature
1:18 beginning the *f* from the dead
Heb. 12:23 assembly and church of the *f*

FIRSTFRUIT (FIRSTFRUITS)
Prov. 3: 9 with the *f* of all thine increase
Rom. 8:23 which have the *f* of the Spirit
11:16 if the *f* be holy the lump also
1 Cor. 15:20 Christ is the *f* of them that slept
Jas. 1:18 we should be a kind of *f*
Rev. 14: 4 being the *f* unto God

FISHERS
Mat. 4:19 I will make you *f* of men

FLAME
Ex. 3: 2 appeared unto him in a *f*
Is. 10:17 his Holy One for a *f*
Heb. 1: 7 his ministers a *f* of fire

FLATTER (FLATTERETH, FLATTERING)
Ps. 78:36 they did *f* him with
Prov. 20:19 not with him that *f* with his lips
1 Thes. 2: 5 at any time used we *f* words

FLEE (FLED)
Mat. 3: 7 who warned you to *f* from the wrath
1 Cor. 6:18 beloved *f* from fornication
10:14 *f* from idolatry
2 Tim. 2:22 *f* also youthful lusts
Jas. 4: 7 resist the devil, he will *f*

FLESH
Gen. 2:23 and *f* of my *f*: she shall
2:24 they shall be one *f*
Job 19:26 in my *f* shall I see God
Ps. 56: 4 not fear what *f* can do to me
65: 2 to thee shall all *f* come
63: 1 my *f* longeth for thee in a day
78:39 remember they are but *f*
Is. 40: 6 all *f* is grass, and all the
49:26 all *f* know I am thy Redeemer
Jer. 32:27 I am the Lord, God of all *f*
Joel 2:28 I will pour my Spirit on all *f*
Mat. 16:17 *f* and blood hath not revealed
19: 5 they twain shall be one *f*
26:41 is willing, but the *f* is weak
Luke 3: 6 all *f* shall see the salvation of God
John 1:13 born not of will but of the *f*
1:14 the Word was made *f*
3: 6 which is born of the *f* is *f*
6:53 eat the *f* of the Son of man
Rom. 7: 5 when we were in the *f*
8: 1 walk not after the *f*
9: 5 of whom concerning the *f* Christ
13:14 make not provision for the *f*
1 Cor. 1:26 not many wise men after the *f*
6:16 saith he, shall be one *f*
15:50 *f* and blood cannot inherit the
2 Cor. 1:17 purpose according to the *f*
10: 2 walked according to the *f*
Gal. 5:19 works of the *f* are manifest
6: 8 shall of the *f* reap corruption
Eph. 2: 3 *f* fulfilling the desires
5:30 members of his body, of his *f*
6: 5 masters according to the *f*
6:12 we wrestle not against *f* and blood
1 Pet. 1:24 for all *f* is as grass,
3:18 he was put to death in the *f*
2 Pet. 2:10 after the *f* in lust of uncleanness
1 John 2:16 lust of the *f* lust of the eyes

FLESHLY
2 Cor. 1:12 not with *f* wisdom but
Col. 2:18 puffed up by his *f* mind
1 Pet. 2:11 abstain from *f* lusts

FLOCK (FLOCKS)
Ps. 77:20 leddest thy people like a *f*
Is. 40:11 he shall feed his *f* like

1 Pet. 5: 2 feed the *f* of God among you

FOLLOW (FOLLOWED)
Num. 32:12 for they have wholly *f* the Lord
Deut. 16:20 is altogether just shalt thou *f*
Josh. 14: 8 I wholly *f* the Lord
Ps. 23: 6 goodness and mercy shall *f* me
Is. 51: 1 that *f* after righteousness
Mat. 4:19 *f* me and I will make
9: 9 saith unto him, *f* me
16:24 take up his cross and *f*
Luke 18:22 sell all thou hast, and *f* me
John 12:26 if any serve me let him *f* me
Rom. 14:19 *f* things that make for peace
1 Cor. 14: 1 *f* after charity, and desire spiritual
1 Thes. 5:15 *f* that which is good
1 Tim. 6:11 *f* after righteousness, godliness, faith
2 Tim. 2:22 *f* righteousness, faith, charity, peace
Heb. 12:14 *f* peace with all men,

FOLLY
Josh. 7:15 hath wrought *f* in Israel
Ps. 49:13 their way is their *f*
Prov. 26: 5 answer a fool according to his *f*

FOOD
Gen. 3: 6 saw that the tree was good for *f*
Ps. 78:25 men did eat the angels' *f*
146: 7 which giveth *f* to the hungry
Acts 14:17 filling our hearts with *f*

FOOL (FOOLS)
Ps. 14: 1 the *f* hath said in his heart
Prov. 13:20 companion of *f* shall be destroyed
14: 8 folly of the *f* is deceitful
Eccl. 5: 4 he hath no pleasure in *f*
Mat. 5:22 say to brother, Thou *f*
Luke 12:20 thou *f* this night thy soul
Rom. 1:22 professing to be wise became *f*
1 Cor. 4:10 we are *f* for Christ's sake
Eph. 5:15 circumspectly, not as *f*, but as wise

FOOLISH (FOOLISHLY)
Gen. 31:28 thou hast done *f* in so doing
Deut. 32: 6 Lord, requite *f* people and unwise
2 Sam. 24:10 I have done very *f*
Ps. 5: 5 *f* shall not stand in thy sight
Prov. 14:17 He that is soon angry dealeth *f*
Mat. 7:26 likened unto a *f* man which built
25: 2 them were wise and five were *f*
Rom. 1:21 and their *f* heart darkened
Eph. 5: 4 neither filthiness, nor *f* talking

FOOLISHNESS
Prov. 12:23 heart of fools proclaimeth *f*
14:24 *f* of fools is their *f*
15:14 mouth of fools feedeth on *f*
22:15 *f* is bound in the heart of a child
1 Cor. 1:18 cross to them that perish *f*
3:19 wisdom of this world is *f* with God

FOOT
Prov. 3:23 thy *f* shall not stumble
Is. 58:13 turn away thy *f* from the sabbath
Mat. 18: 8 if thy *f* offend thee,
Heb. 10:29 trodden under *f* the Son of God

FORBID (FORBIDDING)
Mark 10:14 and *f* them not: for of such is
Luke 18:16 and *f* them not: for of such is
1 Tim. 4: 3 *f* to marry, and commanding to abstain

FOREHEAD (FOREHEADS)
Ex. 28:38 it shall be on Aaron's *f*
Rev. 9: 4 the seal of God on their *f*
22: 4 his name shall be in their *f*

FOREKNOW (FOREKNEW)
Rom. 8:29 whom he did *f*, he also did

FOREKNOWLEDGE
Acts 2:23 determinate counsel, and *f* of God
1 Pet. 1: 2 according to the *f* of God

FOREORDAINED
1 Pet. 1:20 who was verily *f* before the foundation

FORGET (FORGETTETH, FORGETTING, FORGOTTEN)
Deut. 32:18 thou hast *f* God that formed
Ps. 9:12 he *f* not the cry of the humble
10:11 God hath *f*. he hideth
42: 9 why hast thou *f* me
77: 9 hath God *f* to be gracious
103: 2 *f* not all his benefits
119: 61 I have not *f* thy law

Is. 17:10 *f* the God of thy salvation
49:15 can a woman *f* her sucking child
Jer. 50: 5 covenant that shall not be *f*
Phil. 3:13 *f* those things which are behind
Heb. 12: 5 ye have *f* the exhortation which
13:16 to do good and to communicate *f* not

FORGIVE (FORGAVE, FORGAVEST, FORGIVEN, FORGIVETH, FORGIVING)
Ex. 32:32 if thou wilt *f* their sin
Ps. 32: 1 transgression is *f*, whose sin is
78:38 *f* their iniquity, and destroyed
86: 5 good and ready to *f*
103: 3 *f* thine iniquities; who healeth
Is. 2: 9 humbleth himself therefore *f* them not
Jer. 31:34 for I will *f* their iniquity
Mat. 6:12 *f* us our debts, as we *f*
6:14 if ye *f* men their trespasses
9: 6 Son of man hath power on earth to *f*
18:27 and loosed him, *f* him the debt
Luke 6:37 *f* and ye shall be *f*
7:47 to whom little is *f* the same loveth
17: 3 if he repent, *f* him
23:34 Father, *f* them, they know not
Rom. 4: 7 are those whose iniquities are *f*
Eph. 4:32 as God for Christ's sake hath *f* you
Col. 3:13 as Christ *f* you, so also do ye
1 John 1: 9 faithful to *f* us our sins
2:12 because your sins are *f* you

FORGIVENESS (FORGIVENESSES)
Dan. 9: 9 to the Lord our God belong mercies and *f*
Acts 26:18 may receive *f* of sins by faith
Col. 1:14 redemption, even the *f* of sins

FORM
Gen. 1: 2 the earth was without *f*
Is. 45: 7 I *f* the light and create darkness
53: 2 hath no *f* nor comeliness
Rom. 2:20 which hast the *f* of knowledge
6:17 from the heart that *f* of doctrine
Phil. 2: 6 who being in the *f* of God
2: 7 took upon him the *f* of a servant
2 Tim. 1:13 hold the *f* of sound words
3: 5 having the *f* of godliness

FORMED
Ps. 94: 9 that *f* the eye shall he not see?
Prov. 26:10 great God that *f* all things both
Is. 44: 2 *f* thee from the womb
54:17 no weapon *f* against thee shall prosper
Rom. 9:20 thing *f* say to him that *f*

FORNICATION (FORNICATIONS)
2 Chr. 21:11 inhabitants of Jerusalem to commit *f*
Ezek. 16:15 pouredst out thy *f* on
Mat. 15:19 adulteries, *f*, thefts
John 8:41 we be not born of *f*
Acts 15:20 from *f*, and from things strangled
1 Cor. 5: 1 there is *f* among you, and such *f* as
6:13 Now the body not for *f*, but
7: 2 to avoid *f* have his own wife
10: 8 neither let us commit *f*
2 Cor. 12:21 not repented of their *f*
Gal. 5:19 works of flesh, adultery, *f*
Eph. 5: 3 But *f* and all uncleanness,
1 Thes. 4: 3 should abstain from *f*
Rev. 14: 8 the wine of the wrath of her *f*
17: 4 abominations and filthiness of her *f*

FORNICATORS
1 Cor. 6: 9 be not deceived: neither *f*, nor
Heb. 12:16 Lest there be any *f* or profane

FORSAKE (FORSAKEN, FORSAKETH, FORSOOK)
Deut. 4:31 will not *f* thee neither destroy thee
32:15 then he *f* God which made him
Josh. 1: 5 I will not fail thee nor *f* thee
1 Sam. 8:57 let him not leave nor *f* us
12:22 Lord will not *f* his people
Ps. 22: 1 my God, why hast thou *f* me
71:11 God hath *f* him;
94:14 neither will he *f* the inheritance
119: 87 I *f* not thy precepts
Prov. 2:17 the guide of her youth
28:13 *f* them shall have mercy
Is. 41:17 God of Israel will not *f*
49:14 But Zion said, the Lord hath *f* me
Jer. 2:13 *f* me the fountain of living waters

17:13 *f* thee shall be ashamed
Mat. 19:27 we have *f* all, and followed thee
27:46 my God, why hast thou *f* me
2 Cor. 4: 9 Persecuted but not *f*,
Heb. 13: 5 never leave thee, nor *f* thee

FORTRESS
2 Sam.22: 2 my rock, and my *f*
Ps. 18: 2 The Lord is my rock and my *f*
91: 2 He is my refuge and my *f*; my God
144: 2 my goodness, and my *f*; my high tower
Jer. 16:19 my strength, and my *f*,

FOUND
Is. 55: 6 seek the Lord while he may be *f*
Dan. 5:27 in the balance and *f* wanting

FOUNDATION (FOUNDATIONS)
Ps. 104: 5 Who laid the *f* of the earth
Prov. 8:29 appointed the *f* of the earth
10:25 righteous is an everlasting *f*
Is. 28:16 I lay in Zion a sure *f*
John 17:24 before the *f* of the world
Rom. 15:20 build on another man's *f*
Eph. 2:20 built on the *f* of prophets
1 Tim. 6:19 a good *f* against the time to come
2 Tim. 2:19 the *f* of God standeth sure
Heb. 11:10 looked for a city which hath *f*
Rev. 21:14 the city hath twelve *f*

FOUNTAIN (FOUNTAINS)
Gen. 7:11 the *f* of the great deep broken up
Ps. 36: 9 with thee is the *f* of life
Prov. 5:18 let thy *f* be blessed
13:14 law of the wise is a *f* of life
14:27 fear of the Lord is a *f* of life
Eccl. 12: 6 a pitcher broken at the *f*
Sol. 4:12 a spring shut up, a *f* sealed
Jer. 2:13 forsaken me, the *f* of living waters
Joel 3:18 a *f* out of the house of
Zech. 13: 1 a *f* opened to the house of David
Jas. 3:12 can a *f* both yield salt
Rev. 21: 6 the *f* of the water of life

FOX (FOXES)
Ps. 63:10 they shall be a portion for *f*
Sol. 2:15 take us the *f*, the little
Ezek. 13: 4 prophets are like *f* in the deserts
Mat. 8:20 the *f* have holes, and

FRAME (FRAMED)
Ps. 103:14 For he knoweth our *f*
Heb. 11: 3 the worlds were *f* by the word

FREE
Ex. 21: 2 he shall go out *f* for nothing
Ps. 51:12 uphold with thy *f* spirit
John 8:32 truth shall make you *f*
8:36 Son make you *f* you shall be *f* indeed
Rom. 5:15 so also is a *f* gift
5:18 the *f* gift came on all
1 Cor. 7:22 he that is called, being *f*
Gal. 3:28 neither bond nor *f*
Col. 3:11 bond nor *f*, but Christ
1 Pet. 2:16 *f* and not using liberty

FREELY
Hos. 14: 4 I will love them *f*
Mat. 10: 8 *f* ye have received, *f* give
Rom. 3:24 justified *f* by his grace
8:32 with him *f* give us all
Rev. 21: 6 fountain of the water of life *f*

FRIEND (FRIENDS)
Deut. 13: 6 *f* which is as his own soul
Prov. 17:17 *f* loveth at all times
18:24 a *f* closer than a brother
Sol. 5:16 and this is my *f*, O daughters
Jer. 6:21 neighbor and his *f* shall perish
Mic. 7: 5 trust ye not in a *f*
John 15:13 lay down his life for his *f*
Jas. 2:23 he was called the *f* of God

FRIENDSHIP
Prov. 22:24 make no *f* with an angry man
Jas. 4: 4 *f* of the world is enmity with God

FROWARD
Deut. 32:20 for they are a very *f* generation
Prov. 4:24 put away from thee a *f* mouth
11:20 are of a *f* heart are abomination
1 Pet. 2:18 good and gentle, but also to the *f*

FRUIT
Gen. 4: 3 brought of the *f* of the ground
30: 2 withheld from thee the *f* of the womb
Lev. 19:24 all the *f* thereof shall be holy
2 Ki. 19:30 bear the *f* upward
Ps. 92:14 shall bring forth *f* in old age
127: 3 the *f* of the womb is his reward
Prov. 11:30 *f* of the righteous tree of life
Is. 57:19 I create the *f* of the lips
Hos. 10: 1 he bringeth *f* unto himself
Mic. 6: 7 of my body for the sin of my soul
Mat. 7:17 good tree bringeth forth good *f*
12:33 make his tree corrupt and his *f* corrupt
26:29 drink henceforth this *f* of the vine
Luke 1:42 blessed is the *f* of thy womb
15: 2 branch beareth not *f* he taketh away
Rom. 7: 4 should bring forth *f* unto God
Gal. 5:22 of the Spirit is love, joy
Eph. 5: 9 of Spirit is in all goodness
Phil. 4:17 I desire *f* that may abound
Heb. 12:11 peaceable *f* of righteousness

FRUITS
Sol. 7:13 all manner of pleasant *f*
Mat. 3: 8 therefore *f* meet for repentance
Phil. 1:11 filled with the *f* of righteousness
Jas. 3:17 full of mercy and good *f*

FULL
Prov. 30: 9 lest I be *f* and deny thee
Luke 6:25 woe to you that are *f*
Phil. 4:12 know both to be *f* and

FULFILL (FULFILLED, FULFILLING)
Luke 21:24 until the times of the Gentiles be *f*
Eph. 2: 3 the desires of the flesh,
Phil. 2: 2 *f* ye my joy, that ye be
Jas. 2: 8 if ye *f* the royal law

FULNESS
Job 20:22 in the *f* of his sufficiency
Gal. 4: 4 when the *f* of the time was come
Eph. 1:23 *f* of him that filleth all in all
3:19 filled with the *f* of God
4:13 the stature of the *f* of Christ
Col. 1:19 in him should all *f* dwell
2: 9 all the *f* of the Godhead

FURNACE
Ps. 12: 6 tried in a *f* of the earth
Is. 31: 9 Zion, his *f* in Jerusalem
48:10 chosen thee in a *f* of affliction
Dan. 3:11 into the midst of a burning fiery *f*
Mat. 13:50 cast them into the *f*

GAIN (GAINED)
Mat. 16:26 if he shall *g* the whole world
Luke 19:16 Lord, thy pound hath *g* ten pounds
Phil. 1:21 to live is Christ, to die is *g*

GALL
Deut. 29:18 root beareth *g* and wormwood
Job 16:13 poureth out my *g* upon the earth
Ps. 69:21 gave me *g* for meat
Mat. 27:34 vinegar drink mixed with *g*
Acts 8:23 in the *g* of bitterness

GARDEN
Gen. 3:23 sent him forth from the *g*
Sol. 4:12 a *g* enclosed is my sister
Is. 58:11 thou shalt be like a watered *g*
Jer. 31:12 their soul shall be as a watered *g*

GARMENT (GARMENTS)
Ezra 3: 4 rent my *g*, and my mantle
Ps. 22:18 part my *g* among them
Is. 59:17 put on *g* of vengeance
Joel 2:13 rend your hearts not *g*
Rev. 3: 4 have not defiled their *g*

GATE (GATES)
Gen. 22:17 shall possess the *g* of his enemies
Ps. 9:13 lifteth me up from the *g* of death
24: 7 lift up your heads, O ye *g*
100: 4 enter his *g* with thanksgiving
118: 19 open to me the *g* of righteousness
Is. 38:10 go to the *g* of the grave
Mat. 7:13 enter ye at the strait *g*
16:18 the *g* of hell shall not
Heb. 13:12 suffered without the *g*

GATHER (GATHERED)
Deut. 30: 3 *g* thee from all the nations

Ps. 26: 9 *g* not my soul with sinners
Jer. 29:14 I will *g* you from all the nations
Mat. 3:12 *g* his wheat into garner
7:16 do men *g* grapes of thorns
23:37 would I have *g* thy children together
John 4:36 *g* fruit unto life eternal
Eph. 1:10 *g* in one all things in Christ

GAVE (GAVEST)
Ps. 21: 4 asked life of thee, thou *g* it
81:12 *g* them up unto their own hearts' lust
John 1:12 *g* he power to become the sons
3:16 God *g* his only begotten Son
17: 4 The work which thou *g* me to do
18: 9 of them which thou *g* me
Gal. 1: 4 who *g* himself for our sins
2:20 who loved me *g* himself for me
Tit. 2:14 who *g* himself for us

GENEALOGIES
1 Tim. 1: 4 heed to fables and endless *g*
Tit. 3: 9 avoid foolish questions and *g*

GENERATION (GENERATIONS)
Gen. 2: 4 these are the *g* of the heavens
6: 9 These are the *g* of Noah
Deut. 32: 5 perverse and crooked *g*
Ps. 14: 5 God is in the *g* of righteous
24: 6 this is the *g* of them that seek
33:11 the thoughts of his heart to all *g*
72: 5 sun and moon endure, throughout all *g*
89: 4 build thy throne to all *g*
100: 5 his truth endureth to all *g*
102: 24 thy years are throughout all *g*
112: 2 *g* of upright shall be blessed
145: 4 one *g* shall praise thy works
Mat. 3: 7 O *g* of vipers, who
Acts 13:36 had served his own *g* by the will
Col. 1:26 mystery hid from ages and *g*
1 Pet. 2: 9 ye are a chosen *g* a royal

GENTILES
Gen. 10: 5 the isles of the *G* divided
Is. 42: 6 the people, for a light of the *G*
60: 3 *g* shall come to thy light
60:62 *g* shall see thy righteousness
Mat. 6:32 after these things do the *g* seek
Luke 2:32 A light to lighten the *G*
21:24 till the times of the *g*
John 7:35 among the *g*, teach the *g*
Acts 13:46 lo, we turn to the *g*
13:47 to be a light to the *G*
14:27 opened the door of faith unto the *g*
Rom. 2:14 *g* which have not the law
11:25 until the fulness of the *g* become
Eph. 3: 6 that the *g* should be fellowheirs
1 Tim. 2: 7 teacher of the *g* in faith
3:16 God in flesh, preached to the *g*

GENTLE (GENTLY)
Is. 40:11 *g* lead those with young
1 Thes. 2: 7 we were *g* among you
2 Tim. 2:24 servant of the Lord must be *g*
Tit. 3: 2 be *g* showing all meekness
Jas. 3:17 wisdom from above is *g*
1 Pet. 2:18 not only to the *g* but

GENTLENESS
2 Cor. 10: 1 by the meekness and *g* of Christ
Gal. 5:22 longsuffering, *g*, goodness

GIFT (GIFTS)
Ex. 23: 8 take no *g* for a *g* blindeth the wise
Ps. 68:18 thou hast received *g* for men
21:14 a *g* in secret pacifieth anger
Eccl. 7: 7 a *g* destroyeth the heart
Mat. 7:11 to give good *g* unto your children
John 4:10 if thou knewest the *g* of God
Rom. 6:23 *g* of God is eternal life
11:29 for the *g* and calling of God are
1 Cor. 1: 7 ye come behind in no *g*
12: 7 every man hath his proper *g*
Eph. 2: 8 it is the *g* of God
4: 8 captivity captive gave *g* to men
Heb. 6: 4 have tasted of the heavenly *g*

GIRD (GIRDED, GIRDETH, GIRT)
Ps. 18:32 God that *g* me with strength
30:11 sackcloth, and *g* me with gladness
Eph. 6:14 have your loins *g* about with truth
1 Pet. 1:13 *g* up the loins of the mind

GIVE (GIVEN, GIVETH)

Ps.	37: 21	righteous showeth mercy and g
	84: 11	Lord will g grace and glory
Prov.	28: 27	he that g to the poor
Jer.	17: 10	to g every man according to his works
Mat.	13: 12	whosoever hath, to him shall be g
	13: 11	it is g to you to know mysteries
Luke	6: 38	g and it shall be given
	12: 48	to whomsoever much is g
Acts	20: 35	more blessed to g than to receive
Rom.	8: 32	not with him also freely g us all
Eph.	4: 28	have to g to him that needeth
1 Tim.	6: 17	g us richly all things
Jas.	1: 5	that g to all men liberally

GIVER

2 Cor.	9: 7	God loveth the cheerful g

GLAD

Ps.	16: 9	therefore, my heart is g
	31: 7	I will be g and rejoice in
	64: 10	righteous shall be g in the Lord
	104: 34	I will be g in the Lord
	122: 1	I was g when they said unto me

GLADNESS

Ps.	4: 7	thou hast put g in my heart
	45: 7	anointed thee with the oil of g
	51: 8	make me to hear joy and g come before
	100: 2	serve the Lord with g,
	106: 5	rejoice in the g of thy nation
Is.	35: 10	obtain joy and g
Acts	2: 46	eat their meat with g
	14: 17	filling our hearts with food and g

GLASS

1 Cor.	13: 12	now we see through a g, darkly
2 Cor.	3: 18	beholding as in a g
Jas.	1: 23	beholding a natural face in g
Rev.	4: 6	a sea of g like unto crystal
	21: 18	the city of pure gold like clear g

GLORY

Ex.	16: 7	ye shall see the g of the Lord
1 Chr.	16: 10	G ye in his holy name:
Job	29: 20	my g was fresh in me
Ps.	8: 5	crowned him with g
	19: 1	declare the g of God
	57: 8	Awake up my g;
	64: 10	upright in heart shall g
	72: 19	filled with his g;
	89: 17	art the g of their strength
	104: 31	g of the Lord shall endure forever
	145: 11	speak of the g of thy kingdom
Prov.	3: 35	the wise shall inherit g
	16: 31	hoary head is a crown of g
	25: 27	to search their own g is not g
Is.	4: 5	the g shall be a defence
	6: 3	the whole earth is full of his g
	23: 9	to stain the pride of all g
	24: 16	heard songs, even g to
	28: 5	Lord shall be for a crown of g
	40: 5	g of the Lord shall be revealed
	41: 16	shalt g in the Holy One of
	45: 25	seed of Israel be justified, and g
	48: 11	not give my g unto another
	60: 1	the g of the Lord is risen
Jer.	2: 11	my people have changed their g
Ezek.	43: 5	the g of the Lord filled the house
Hos.	4: 7	will I change their g into shame
Hab.	3: 3	his g covered the heavens
Hag.	2: 7	I will fill this house with g
Zech.	2: 5	will be the g in the
	6: 13	build the temple and bear the g
Mat.	6: 2	that they may have g
	6: 13	thine is the kingdom, the power the g
	25: 31	son of man shall come in his g
Luke	2: 9	the g of the Lord shone round
	2: 14	g to God in the highest
	2: 32	light of Gentiles, g of thy people
John	1: 14	his g, g as of the only begotten Son
	17: 22	g which thou gavest me I have
	17: 24	I am; that they may behold my g
Rom.	2: 7	seek for g and honour
	5: 2	rejoice in the hope and g of God
	16: 27	wise be the g through Christ
1 Cor.	10: 31	do all to the image and g of God
	11: 7	is the image and g of God

	15: 43	sown in dishonour, raised in g
2 Cor.	3: 18	as in a glass, the g of the Lord
	4: 17	exceeding and eternal weight of g
	5: 12	occasion to g on our behalf
	12: 1	it is not expedient for me to g
Gal.	6: 14	God forbid I should g
Eph.	1: 6	praise of the g of his grace
	3: 13	my tribulation for you is your g
Phil.	3: 19	whose g is in their shame
Col.	1: 27	Christ in you, the hope of g
	3: 4	ye also appear with him in g
1 Thes.	2: 12	called you to his kingdom and g
1 Tim.	3: 16	The world received up into g
Heb.	1: 3	who, being the brightness of his g
1 Pet.	1: 8	joy unspeakable, full of g
	4: 13	when his g shall be revealed
2 Pet.	1: 3	called us to g and virtue
	1: 17	came a voice from excellent g
Rev.	4: 11	and worthy, O lord, to receive g
	5: 12	and g, and blessing
	21: 11	having the g of God

GLORIFY (GLORIFIED)

Lev.	10: 3	before all I will be g
Is.	60: 7	I will g the house of my glory
Mat.	5: 16	g your Father in heaven
John	7: 39	Jesus was not yet g
	12: 23	Son of man should be g
	12: 28	Father, g thy name
	15: 8	herein is my Father g
	17: 1	g thy Son that the Son g thee
	17: 10	mine are thine, I am g
	21: 19	by what death he should g God
Acts	3: 13	God of our fathers hath g his Son
Rom.	1: 21	they g him not as God
1 Cor.	6: 20	g God in your body
Gal.	1: 24	they g God in me
2 Thes.	1: 10	come to be g in his saints
	3: 1	word have free course and be g
Heb.	5: 5	Christ g not himself
1 Pet.	2: 12	g God in the day of visitation
Rev.	15: 4	who shall not fear thee, and g

GLORIOUS

Ex.	15: 6	Lord, is become g in power
	15: 11	who is like thee, g in holiness
Deut.	28: 58	this g and fearful name
Ps.	45: 13	king's daughter is all g within
	72: 19	blessed be his g name
	87: 3	g things spoken of thee
	111: 3	his work is honourable and g
	145: 5	speak of the g honour of thy
	145: 12	the majesty of his kingdom
Is.	4: 2	branch of Lord shall be g
	11: 10	his rest shall be g
	30: 30	cause his g voice to be heard
	60: 13	make the place of my feet g
	63: 12	hand of Moses with his g arm
Jer.	17: 12	a g high throne from the beginning
Rom.	8: 21	g liberty of the children of God
2 Cor.	3: 7	written and engraves in stone, was g
	4: 4	light of the g gospel should shine
Eph.	5: 27	present it to himself a g church
Phil.	3: 21	fashioned like unto his g body
Col.	1: 11	according to his g power
1 Tim.	1: 11	according to the g gospel of
Tit.	2: 13	and the g appearing of the great

GLUTTON

Prov.	23: 21	the drunkard and the g

GOAT (GOATS)

Lev.	3: 12	if his offering be a g,
Is.	1: 11	of bullocks or of lambs, or of he g
Ezek.	34: 17	judge between rams and g
Zech.	10: 3	I punished the g
Mat.	25: 32	set g on his left hand
Heb.	9: 12	Neither by the blood of g

GOD

Job	33: 12	G is greater than man
Ps.	18: 31	who is G save the Lord
	86: 10	wondrous things, thou art G alone
Dan.	11: 36	marvelous things against the G of gods
Mic.	7: 18	who a G like thee
Mat.	6: 24	cannot serve G and mammon
	19: 17	none good but one, that is G
Mark	12: 32	one G and none other

John	1: 1	with G, and the Word was G
	17: 3	know thee the only true G
Rom.	8: 31	if G be for us, who can be against
	15: 5	G of patience and consolation
	15: 13	G of hope fill you with all joy
1 Cor.	15: 28	that G may be all in all
2 Cor.	1: 3	mercies, and the G of all comfort
1 Tim.	3: 16	G was manifest in the flesh
1 Pet.	5: 10	G of all grace, who hath called
1 John	4: 12	no man hath seen G at any time
	5: 20	This is the true G

GODHEAD

Acts	17: 29	G is like unto gold
Rom.	1: 20	his eternal power and G
Col.	2: 9	the fulness of the G bodily

GODLY

Ps.	32: 6	every one that is g pray
Mal.	2: 15	he might seek a g seed
2 Cor.	1: 12	in simplicity and g sincerity
Tit.	2: 12	live soberly, righteously and g
Heb.	12: 28	with reverence and g fear

GODLINESS

1 Tim.	2: 2	quiet and peaceable life in all g
	3: 16	great is the mystery of g
	4: 7	exercise thyself rather unto g
	6: 3	doctrine which is according to g
2 Tim.	3: 5	having a form of g but
Tit.	1: 1	truth which is after g
2 Pet.	1: 3	all that pertain to life and g
	3: 11	in all holy conversation and g

GOLD

Ps.	19: 10	more desired than g,
	119: 127	love thy commandments above g
Prov.	8: 19	my fruit is better than g
Is.	13: 12	man more precious than fine g
Zech.	13: 9	and will try them as g
1 Tim.	2: 9	not with braided hair, or g
1 Pet.	1: 7	trial of faith more precious than g
	3: 3	the hair and of wearing of g
Rev.	3: 18	buy of me g tried in the fire

GOOD

Gen.	1: 31	every thing was very g
	2: 18	not g for man to be alone
	50: 20	God meant it unto g
2 Ki.	20: 19	g is the word of the Lord
Ps.	34: 8	taste and see that the Lord is g
	73: 1	truly God is g to Israel
	86: 5	Lord, art g, ready to forgive
	145: 9	Lord is g to all; and his tender
Lam.	3: 25	Lord g to them that wait
Mic.	6: 8	shown thee what is g
Mat.	19: 17	Why callest thou me g?
John	10: 32	many g works have I
Acts	9: 36	Dorcas was full of g
Rom.	3: 8	evil that g may come
	7: 18	that which is g I find not
2 Cor.	9: 8	abound to every g work
Eph.	2: 10	in Jesus Christ unto g works
Phil.	1: 6	begun a g work will finish it
1 Thes.	5: 15	follow that which is g
2 Thes.	2: 17	establish you in every g word
1 Tim.	5: 10	have diligently followed every g work
Tit.	1: 16	and unto every g work reprobate
	3: 1	to be ready to every g work
Heb.	10: 24	provoke unto love and to g works
1 Pet.	2: 12	may by your g works which

GOODNESS

Ex.	34: 6	God abundant in g and truth
Neh.	9: 25	delight themselves in g
	9: 35	not served thee in thy great g
Ps.	23: 6	g and mercy shall follow me
	27: 13	believed to see the g of the Lord
	33: 5	earth full of the g of the Lord
	52: 1	the g of God endureth continually
	52: 11	crownest the year with thy g
Hos.	3: 5	fear the Lord and his g
Rom.	2: 4	g of God leadeth to repentance
	11: 22	behold the g and severity of God
Gal.	5: 22	longsuffering, gentleness, g
Eph.	5: 9	fruit of Spirit in all g

GOSPEL

Mat.	4: 23	preaching the g of the kingdom
Mark	16: 15	preach the g to every creature

Acts 20:24 testify the *g* of the grace of God
Rom. 1: 1 separated unto *g* of God
1 Cor. 4:15 begotten you through the *g*
2 Cor. 4: 3 if our *g* hid, it is hid
     11: 4 another *g* which ye have not accepted
Eph. 1:13 truth, the *g* of your salvation
     6:15 preparation of the *g* of peace
Phil. 1:27 as it becometh the *g* of Christ
Col. 1: 5 the word of truth of the *g*
1 Tim. 1:11 according to the glorious *g*
Heb. 4: 2 unto us was the *g* preached
1 Pet. 4: 6 *g* was preached to the dead
Rev. 14: 6 having the everlasting *g* to preach

GOVERNMENT (GOVERNMENTS)
Is. 9: 6 *g* shall be upon his shoulder
1 Cor. 12:28 gifts of healing, helps *g*
2 Pet. 2:10 uncleanliness, and despise *g*

GRACE
Ps. 84:11 Lord will give *g* and glory
Prov. 3:34 he giveth *g* to the lowly
Zech. 4: 7 with shoutings, crying, *g g* unto it
     12:10 spirit of *g* and supplications
Luke 2:40 *g* of God was upon
Acts 18:27 which we had believed through *g*
Rom. 3:24 justified freely by his *g*
     5:20 did much more abound
     6:14 not under law, but *g*
     11: 5 according to the election of *g*
     16:20 *g* of our Lord Jesus Christ
2 Cor. 1:12 by the *g* of God our conversation
     6: 1 receive not the *g* of God in vain
     8: 1 *g* of God bestowed on the churches
     9:14 for the exceeding *g* of God in you
     12: 9 my *g* sufficient for thee
     13:14 *g* of the Lord Jesus Christ
Gal. 2:21 I do not frustrate the *g* of God
Eph. 2: 5 by *g* ye are saved
     2: 7 show exceeding riches of his *g*
     4:29 minister *g* to the hearers
Phil. 4:23 *g* of our Lord Jesus Christ
1 Thes. 5:28 *g* of our Lord Jesus Christ
Heb. 4:16 come boldly to the throne of *g*
     13: 9 heart be established with *g*
Jas. 4: 6 he giveth more *g* unto the humble
1 Pet. 3: 7 heirs of the *g* of life
     4:10 stewards of the manifold *g* of God
     5: 5 and giveth *g* to the humble
     5:12 this the true *g* of God wherein ye stand
2 Pet. 3:18 grow in *g* and knowledge

GRACIOUS (GRACIOUSLY)
Gen. 33: 5 which God hath *g* given thy servant
Ex. 22:19 I will be *g* to whom I will be *g*
Num. 6:25 and be *g* unto thee
Neh. 9:31 thou art a *g* and merciful God
Ps. 77: 9 hath God forgotten to be *g*
     86:15 full of compassion and *g*
     103: 8 Lord is merciful and *g*
     119: 29 grant me thy law *g*
Hos. 14: 2 all iniquity, and receive us *g*
Amos 5:15 the Lord God of hosts will be *g*
Jonah 4: 2 thou art a *g* God
1 Pet. 2: 3 tasted that the Lord is *g*

GRAPES
Sol. 2:13 the tender *g* give a good smell
Ezek. 18: 2 fathers have eaten sour *g*
Mic. 7: 1 fruits, as the *g* gleanings of vintage

GRASS
Ps. 103:15 as for man his days are like *g*
Mat. 6:30 if God so clothe the *g*
Jas. 1:11 but it withereth the *g*
1 Pet. 1:24 for all flesh is as *g*

GRAVE
1 Sam. 2: 6 Lord bringeth down to the *g*
Job 5:26 come to thy *g* in full age
Ps. 6: 5 in the *g* who shall give thanks
Is. 38:18 the *g* cannot praise thee
Hos. 13:14 ransom them from the power of the *g*
1 Cor. 15:55 O *g* where is thy victory

GRAVEN
Jer. 17: 1 it is sin *g* upon table of their heart

GREAT
Gen. 12: 2 make of thee a *g* nation
     30: 8 with *g* wrestlings have I wrestled

Job 5: 9 *g* things and unsearchable
Ps. 47: 2 a *g* king over all the earth
     48: 2 the city of the *g* king
   147: 5 *g* is our Lord, and of *g* power
Nah. 1: 3 slow to anger and *g* in power
Mal. 1:14 I am a *g* king
Luke 1:49 hath done to me *g* things

GREATER
Job 33:12 God is *g* than man
Mat. 12:42 *g* than Solomon is here
John 1:50 see *g* things than these
     10:29 gave them me, is *g* than all
     14:28 my father is *g* than I
1 Cor. 14: 5 *g* is he that prophesieth
1 John 4: 4 *g* he that is in you

GREATLY
1 Chr. 16:25 and *g* to be praised
Ps. 28: 7 my heart *g* rejoiceth
     89: 7 God is *g* to be feared
   145: 3 great is the Lord, and *g* to be praised

GREATNESS
Num. 14:19 according to the *g* of thy mercy
Deut. 32: 3 ascribe ye *g* to our God
Ps. 66: 3 through the *g* of thy power
   145: 3 and his *g* is unsearchable
Is. 63: 1 travelling in *g* of strength
Eph. 1:19 the exceeding *g* of his power

GREEDY
Prov. 15:27 he that is *g* of gain troubleth
Is. 56:11 they are *g* dogs, never
1 Tim. 3: 3 not *g* of filthy lucre

GREEDINESS
Eph. 4:19 to work all uncleanness with *g*

GRIEF
Is. 53: 3 sorrows, and acquainted with *g*
Heb. 13:17 with joy, and not with *g*

GRIEVE (GRIEVED)
Gen. 6: 6 earth, and it *g* him at his heart
Ps. 119:158 I beheld transgressors and was *g*
Jer. 5: 3 stricken, they have not *g*
Lam. 3:33 nor *g* the children of men
Amos 6: 6 they are not *g* for affliction
Rom. 14:15 if thy brother be *g* with thy meat

GRIEVIOUS
Ps. 10: 5 His ways are always *g*; thy judgments
1 John 5: 3 his commandments are not *g*

GROAN (GROANED, GROANETH)
John 11:33 *g* in spirit, and was troubled
Rom. 8:22 whole creation *g* and travaileth
2 Cor. 5: 4 we that are in this tabernacle do *g*

GROANING (GROANINGS)
Ps. 6: 6 I was weary with my *g*
     38: 9 my *g* is not hid from thee
Rom. 8:26 *g* which cannot be uttered

GROW (GROWETH)
Eph. 2:21 *g* unto an holy temple
     4:15 *g* up into him in all things
1 Pet. 2: 2 milk of word that ye may *g*
2 Pet. 3:18 *g* in grace, and in knowledge

GUIDE
Ps. 48:14 he will be our *g* even unto death
Prov. 2:17 forsaketh the *g* of youth
Is. 58:11 Lord shall *g* thee continually
Jer. 3: 4 Father, thou art the *g* of my youth
Luke 1:79 *g* our feet into the way of peace
John 16:13 he will *g* you into all truth

GUILE
Ps. 32: 2 in whose spirit is no *g*
     34:13 keep thy lips from speaking *g*
John 1:47 Israelite indeed in whom is no *g*
1 Thes. 2: 3 nor of uncleanliness, nor in *g*

GUILTY
Ex. 34: 7 will by no means clear the *g*
1 Cor. 11:27 *g* of the body and blood of
Jas. 2:10 offend in one point, *g* of all

GUILTLESS
Ex. 20: 7 not hold him *g* that taketh

HABITATION (HABITATIONS)
Deut. 26:15 look down from thy holy *h*
Ps. 68: 5 God in his holy *h*
     74:20 earth full of *h* of cruelty
Is. 63:15 behold from the *h* of thy holiness

Jer. 31:23 Lord bless thee, O *h* of justice
Zech. 2:13 out of his holy *h*
Luke 16: 9 receive into everlasting *h*
Jude 1: 6 angels which left their own *h*
Rev. 18: 2 Babylon is become the *h* of

HAIR (HAIRS)
Ps. 40:12 more than the *h* of mine head
Mat. 5:36 not make one *h* white or
     10:30 *h* of your head are all numbered
1 Cor. 11:14 if a man hath long *h*
1 Tim. 2: 9 not with braided *h*, or gold

HAND
Num. 11:23 is the Lord's *h* waxed short
Deut. 33: 3 all his saints are in thy *h*
2 Sam. 24:14 fall now into the *h* of the Lord
Ezra 7: 9 *h* of his God on him
     8:22 *h* of our God is upon
Job 2:10 good at the *h* of God and not evil
Ps. 16: 8 he is at my right *h*
     16:11 at thy right *h* are pleasures for
     31: 5 into thy *h* I commend my spirit
     48:10 thy right *h* is full of righteousness
   110: 5 Lord at thy right *h* shall strike
   137: 5 let my right *h* forget her cunning
   139: 10 thy *h* lead and thy right *h*
   145: 16 thou openest thy *h* and satisfiest
Prov. 3:16 length of days is in her right *h*
     10: 4 *h* of the diligent maketh rich
     30:32 lay thy *h* upon thy mouth
Eccl. 9: 1 wise and their works in the *h* of God
     10: 2 wise man's heart at his right *h*
Sol. 2: 6 his right *h* doth embrace me
Is. 1:12 who required this at your *h*
     40: 2 received of the *h* of the Lord double
     59: 1 *h* of the Lord is not shortened
Mat. 5:30 if thy right *h* offend
     6: 3 left *h* know what thy right *h*
     18: 8 if thy *h* or thy foot
     20:21 one on the right *h*, the other on
     25:33 sheep on the right *h*, goats on left
Mark 14:62 sitting on right *h* of power
Luke 1:74 out of the *h* of our enemies
Acts 2:33 the right *h* of God exalted
     7:55 Jesus standing on the right *h*
Rom. 8:34 even at the right *h* of God
Col. 3: 1 sitteth on the right *h* of God
1 Pet. 3:22 is on the right *h* of God
     5: 6 under the mighty *h* of God

HANDS
Gen. 27:22 *h* are the *h* of Esau
Ex. 17:12 Moses' *h* were heavy,
Job 17: 9 clean *h* shall be stronger
Ps. 24: 4 clean *h* and a pure
   119: 73 thy *h* have made me and fashioned
Prov. 31:20 reacheth thy *h* to the needy
     31:31 give her of the fruit of her *h*
Mic. 7: 3 do evil with both *h*
Luke 23:46 into thy *h* I commend my spirit
John 13: 3 given all things into his *h*
2 Cor. 5: 1 house not made with *h*
Eph. 4:28 let him labour, working with his *h*
1 Tim. 2: 8 pray every where, lifting up holy *h*
Heb. 10:31 fall into the *h* of the living God
Jas. 4: 8 cleanse your *h* ye sinners

HANG (HANGED, HANGETH)
Deut. 21:23 that is *h* is accursed of God
     28:66 thy life shall *h* in doubt
Josh. 8:29 he *h* on a tree until eventide
Job 26: 7 he *h* the earth on nothing
Ps. 137: 2 we our harps upon the willows
Mat. 18: 6 millstone were *h* about his neck
     22:40 commandments *h* all the law and the
Gal. 3:13 everyone that *h* on a tree
Heb. 12:12 lift up the hands which *h* down

HAPPY
Deut. 33:29 *h* art thou, O Israel
Job 5:17 *h* the man whom God correcteth
Ps. 127: 5 *h* the man who hath his quiver
   128: 2 *h* shalt thou be, and
Prov. 3:13 *h* is the man that findeth wisdom
     14:21 that hath mercy on poor, *h* is he
     16:20 who trusteth in Lord, *h* is he
     28:14 *h* is man that feareth

29:18 he that keepeth the law, *h* is he
Mal. 3:15 now we call the proud *h*
John 13:17 are ye if ye do them
Rom. 14:22 *h* is he that condemneth not
1 Pet. 3:14 suffer for righteousness' sake, *h* are ye

HARD
Gen. 18:14 any thing too *h* for the Lord
2 Ki. 2:10 hast asked a *h* thing
Ps. 60: 3 shown thy people *h* things
Prov. 13:15 way of transgressors is *h*
Jer. 32:17 nothing too *h* for thee
Mark 10:24 how *h* is it for them that trust
Acts 9: 5 *h* for thee to kick against the pricks
2 Pet. 3:16 things too *h* to be understood

HARDEN (HARDENED)
Ex. 4:21 I will *h* his heart
Deut. 15: 7 shalt not *h* thy heart
Josh. 11:20 was of the Lord to *h* their hearts
Ps. 95: 8 *h* not your heart, as in the provocation
Is. 63:17 *h* our heart from thy fear
Mark 6:52 loaves; for their heart was *h*
Heb. 3: 8 *h* not your hearts, as
3:13 *h* through the deceitfulness of sin

HARDNESS
Mat. 19: 8 *h* of your hearts suffered you
2 Tim. 2: 3 endure *h* as a good soldier

HARLOT (HARLOTS)
Gen. 34:31 sister as with a *h*
Prov. 7:10 woman with the attire of an *h*
Is. 1:21 the faithful city become as an *h*
Jer. 2:20 thou wanderest, playing the *h*
Ezek. 16:15 own beauty, and playedst the *h*
Hos. 2: 5 mother hath played the *h*
4:15 though thou Israel, play the *h*
Mat. 21:31 *h* into the kingdom of God
1 Cor. 6:16 joined to a *h* is one body

HARMLESS
Mat. 10:16 as serpents and *h* as doves

HARVEST
Gen. 8:22 seedtime and *h*
Ex. 34:21 in *h* thou shalt rest
Is. 9: 3 according to the joy in *h*
Jer. 5:24 unto us the appointed weeks of the *h*
8:20 *h* is past, summer is
Joel 3:13 sickle for the *h* is ripe
Mat. 9: 3 pray ye the Lord of the *h*
13:39 *h* is the end of the world
Rev. 14:15 for the *h* of earth is ripe

HASTE
Ex. 12:33 out of the land in *h*
Ps. 38:22 make *h* to help me, O Lord
Sol. 8:14 make *h*, my beloved
Is. 52:12 ye shall not go out with *h*

HASTY (HASTILY)
Prov. 20:21 inheritance may be gotten *h*
29:20 a man that is *h* in words?

HATE
Gen. 24:60 the gate of those which *h* them
Lev. 19:17 shall not *h* thy brother
Deut. 7:10 repayeth them that *h* him
Ps. 68: 1 let them that *h* him flee
97:10 ye that love the Lord, *h* evil
119:104 I *h* every false way
139:21 do not I *h* them that *h*
Prov. 8:13 fear of Lord is to *h* evil
8:36 all they that *h* me love death
Amos 5:15 *h* the evil, and love the good
Luke 14:26 and *h* not his father
Rom. 7:15 what I *h* that do I
1 John 3:13 marvel not if the world *h*
Rev. 17:16 these shall *h* the whore

HATED (HATEST, HATETH)
Ex. 23: 5 ass of him that *h* thee lying
Deut. 21:15 one beloved, and another *h*
Ps. 5: 5 thou *h* all workers of iniquity
50:17 seeing thou *h* instruction
Prov. 1:29 for that they *h* knowledge
5:12 how have I *h* instruction
13:24 spareth rod, *h* his son
Mal. 1: 3 I *h* Esau, and laid his mountains
Mat. 10:22 shall be *h* of all men
Luke 19:14 his citizens *h* him, and

John 12:25 *h* his life in this world
15:24 *h* both seen, and me and my Father
Rom. 9:13 loved, but Esau have I *h*
Eph. 5:29 no man *h* his own flesh
1 John 2: 9 *h* his brother is in darkness
3:15 *h* his brother is a murderer

HATERS
Rom. 1:30 backbiters, *h* of God

HAUGHTY
Ps. 131: 1 Lord, my heart is not *h*
Prov. 16:18 and an *h* spirit before a fall

HAUGHTINESS
Is. 2:11 *h* of men shall be bowed down
16: 6 he is very proud: even of his *h*

HEAD
Gen. 3:15 it shall bruise thy *h* and
Ezra 9: 6 iniquity increased over thy *h*
Ps. 38: 4 iniquities gone over my *h*
Prov. 16:31 hoary *h* is a crown of glory
20:29 beauty of the old men is a gray *h*
25:22 heap coals of fire upon his *h*
Sol. 5:11 his *h* is as most fine gold
Is. 1: 5 whole *h* is sick and
Jer. 9: 1 O that my *h* were waters
48:37 every *h* shall be bald
Ezek. 16:43 thy way upon thy *h*
Dan. 2:28 visions of thy *h* on a bed
2:38 thou art this *h* of gold
Mat. 8:20 where to lay his *h*
14: 8 give me the *h* of John Baptist
Rom. 12:20 coals of fire on his *h*
Eph. 1:22 gave him to be *h* over
4:15 which is the *h* even Christ
5:23 husband is the *h* of the wife
Col. 1:18 he is the *h* of the body
2:19 holding the *h* from which all
Rev. 19:12 on his *h* were many crowns

HEADS
Gen. 2:10 was parted and became into four *h*
Ps. 24: 7 lift up your *h*, O ye
Is. 35:10 everlasting joy upon their *h*
Luke 21:28 look up, and lift up your *h*
Rev. 13: 1 having seven *h* and ten horns

HEAL (HEALED, HEALETH)
Ex. 15:26 I the Lord that *h* thee
Num. 12:13 Lord, saying, *h* her
Deut. 32:39 I wound, and I *h*
2 Chr. 7:14 and will *h* their land
30:20 Hezekiah, and *h* the people
Ps. 6: 2 *h* me, for my bones
30: 2 unto thee and thou hast *h* me
103: 3 who *h* all thy diseases
147: 3 he *h* the broken in heart
Is. 6:10 convert and be *h*
30:26 *h* the stroke of their wound
53: 5 with his stripes we are *h*
Jer. 3:22 I will *h* your backslidings
17:14 *h* me, and I shall be
Mat. 4:24 had the palsy, and he *h* them
12:15 he *h* them all
Luke 4:18 sent me to *h* the brokenhearted
4:23 will say, Physician, *h* thyself
John 12:40 converted and I should *h*
Acts 28:27 and I should *h* them
Jas. 5:16 pray that ye may be *h*
1 Pet. 2:24 by whose stripes ye were *h*

HEALING
Jer. 14:19 for the time of *h*, and behold
Mal. 4: 2 righteousness arise with *h* in his wings
1 Cor. 12: 9 to another the gifts of *h*
Rev. 22: 2 tree were for the *h* of the nations

HEALTH
Ps. 42:11 *h* of countenance, and my God
Prov. 3: 8 shall be *h* to thy navel, and marrow
12:18 the tongue of the wise is *h*
Jer. 8:15 looked for a time of *h*
30:17 I will restore *h* and

HEAP (HEAPED, HEAPETH)
Job 36:13 hypocrites in heart *h* up wrath
Prov. 25:22 shalt *h* coals of fire on

HEAR
1 Ki. 8:30 *h* thou in heaven thy dwellingplace

Job 5:27 *h* it and know it for good
Ps. 4: 1 mercy upon me, and *h* my prayer
39:12 mercy upon me, and *h* my prayer oh Lord
51: 8 make me to *h* joy and
84: 8 Lord God of hosts, *h* my prayer
115: 6 have ears, but *h* not
143: 1 *h* my prayer, O Lord, give ear
Prov. 19:27 cease to *h* instruction
Is. 55: 3 *h* and your soul shall live
Mat. 13:17 to *h* those things which ye *h*
18:17 if he neglect to *h* them
John 5:25 they that *h* shall live
Jas. 1:19 every man be swift to *h*
Rev. 3:20 if any *h* my voice, and open

HEARD
Ps. 6: 9 Lord hath *h* my supplication
34: 4 I sought the Lord, and he *h*
5: God, hast *h* my vows
1 Cor. 2: 9 eye hath not seen nor ear *h*
Heb. 5: 7 was *h* in that he feared
Rev. 3: 3 thou hast received and *h*

HEARER (HEARERS)
Rom. 2:13 not the *h* of the law
Eph. 4:29 minister grace unto the *h*
Jas. 1:22 doers of the word, and not *h* only

HEARETH
1 Sam. 3: 9 speak, Lord; for thy servant *h*
Mat. 7:24 whoso *h* these sayings of mine
John 9:31 God *h* not sinners, but
Rev. 22:17 let him that *h* say, Come

HEARING
Prov. 20:12 the *h* ear, and the seeing eye
Rom. 10:17 faith cometh by *h*
Heb. 5:11 seeing ye are dull of *h*

HEARKEN
Deut. 28: 1 if thou *h* diligently
28:15 if thou wilt not *h* unto the voice
Ps. 103:20 angels *h* to the voice of his word
Is. 46:12 *h* unto me, ye stouthearted

HEART
Ex. 35: 5 whosoever is of a willing *h*
Deut. 6: 5 love God with all thy *h* and soul
Josh. 22: 5 serve him with all your *h*
1 Sam. 10: 9 God gave him another *h*
16: 7 but the Lord looketh on the *h*
1 Chr. 16:10 let the *h* of them rejoice
2 Chr. 30:19 prepareth his *h* to seek God
Ps. 22:26 your *h* shall live for ever
24: 4 clean hands and a pure *h*
37:31 law of his God is in his *h*
51:17 a broken and contrite *h*, O God
57: 7 my *h* is fixed, O God
64: 6 every one of them, and the *h*, is deep
73:26 my flesh and my *h* faileth, but
84: 2 my *h* and my *h* crieth for the
Prov. 4:23 keep thy *h* with diligence
14:10 *h* knoweth its own bitterness
16: 9 a man's *h* deviseth his way
Eccl. 7: 4 *h* of the wise is in the house
Sol. 3:11 the gladness of his *h*
Is. 6:10 make the *h* of this people fat
57:15 to revive the *h* of the contrite ones
Jer. 17: 9 *h* is deceitful above all things
24: 7 I will give them an *h* to know
29:13 search for me with all your *h*
32:39 And I will give them one *h*
Ezek. 11:19 I will give them an *h* of flesh
18:31 make you a new *h*, and a new spirit
36:26 I will take away the stony *h*
Mal. 4: 6 turn the *h* of the fathers
Mat. 5: 8 blessed are the pure in *h*
6:21 there will your *h* be also
12:35 of good treasure of the *h*
15:19 out of the *h* proceed evil thoughts
22:37 Lord thy God with all thy *h*
Luke 2:19 pondered them in her *h*
2:51 mother kept all these sayings in her *h*
10:27 love the Lord thy God, with all thy *h*
John 14: 1 let not your *h* be troubled
Acts 11:23 with the purpose of *h* they would cleave
13:22 found a man after mine own *h*
2 Cor. 3: 3 in fleshy tables of the *h*
1 Tim. 1: 5 charity out of a pure *h*

2 Tim. 2:22 call on the Lord out of a pure *h*
1 Pet. 1:22 love one another with pure *h*
1 John 3:20 if *h* condemn us, God

HEATHEN
Ps. 2: 1 why do the *h* rage
Gal. 3: 8 justify the *h* through faith

HEAVEN
2 Chr. 6:18 behold, *h*, and the *h* of heavens
Ps. 73:25 whom have I in *h* but
103: 11 as *h* is high above the
115: 16 *h* even the heavens are the Lord's
Prov. 25: 3 *h* for height, and earth
Eccl. 5: 2 God is in *h* thou upon earth
Is. 66: 1 *h* is my throne, and
Jer. 31:37 if *h* can be measured
Hag. 1: 10 *h* is stayed from dew
John 1: 51 you shall see *h* open
Acts 7:49 *h* is my throne, and the earth
Heb. 10:34 have in *h* a better substance
1 Pet. 1: 4 inheritance reserved in *h*
Rev. 21: 1 saw a new *h* and a

HEAVENS
Ps. 8: 3 when I consider thy *h*
19: 1 the *h* declare the glory of God
89: 11 the *h* are thine, and earth also
Is. 65:17 I create new *h* and a new earth
Eph. 4: 10 ascended far above all *h*
2 Pet. 3:12 *h* being on fire shall be dissolved

HEAVENLY
Mat. 6:14 your *h* Father will also
John 3:12 if I tell you of *h* things
Eph. 1: 3 all spiritual blessings in *h* places
2: 6 in *h* places in Christ
2 Tim. 4:18 will preserve me unto his *h* kingdom
Heb. 3: 1 partakers of the *h* calling

HEAVY
Prov. 31: 6 wine to those of *h* hearts
Mat. 11:28 that labour and are *h* laden

HEAVINESS
Ps. 119:28 my soul melteth for *h*
Prov. 12:25 *h* in the heart maketh it stoop
14:13 end of that mirth is *h*

HEEL (HEELS)
Gen. 3:15 thou shalt bruise his *h*
Ps. 41: 9 lifted his *h* against me
John 13:18 lifted up his *h* against me

HEIR (HEIRS)
Gen. 21:10 bondwoman shall not be *h*
Rom. 4: 13 should be *h* of the world
8:17 *h* of God, joint *h* with Christ
Gal. 3:29 Abraham's seed and *h* according to
4: 7 if a son, then an *h* of
Eph. 3: 6 Gentiles should be fellow *h*
Heb. 1: 2 whom he hath appointed *h* of all
6:17 willing to show *h* of promise
11: 7 became *h* of the righteousness
1 Pet. 3: 7 together of the grace of life

HELL
Deut. 32:22 shall burn to the lowest *h*
Job 26: 6 *h* is naked before him
Ps. 9:17 wicked shall be turned into *h*
55:15 let them go down quick into *h*
139: 8 make my bed in *h*
Prov. 5: 5 her steps take hold on *h*
9:18 her guests are in the depths of *h*
23:14 shalt deliver his soul from *h*
27:20 *h* and destruction are never full
Is. 5:14 *h* hath enlarged herself, and opened
Amos 9: 2 though they dig into *h*
Jonah 2: 2 out of the belly of *h* cried I
Hab. 2: 5 enlargeth his desire as *h*
Mat. 5:22 be in danger of *h* fire
10:28 destroy soul and body in *h*
11:23 heaven shalt be brought down to *h*
16:18 gates of *h* shall not prevail
23:15 twofold more than the child of *h*
Mark 9:45 to be cast into *h*
Luke 12: 5 power to cast into *h*
Acts 2:27 wilt not leave my soul in *h*
Jas. 3: 6 tongue set on the fire of *h*
2 Pet. 2: 4 cast them down to *h*
Rev. 1:18 have the keys of *h* and
6: 8 Death, and *H* followed

20: 13 death and *h* delivered up the dead

HELMET
Eph. 6:17 take the *h* of salvation
1 Thes. 5: 8 an *h*, hope of salvation

HELP
Gen. 2:18 make him an *h* meet
Ps. 27: 9 thou hast been my *h*
33:20 he is our *h* and shield
40:13 make haste to *h* me
46: 1 God a very present *h* in trouble
60: 11 vain is the *h* of man
71:12 my God, make haste for my *h*
115: 9 Lord is our *h* and shield
124: 8 our *h* is in the name of Lord
Is. 63: 5 there was none to *h*
Heb. 4:16 find grace to *h* in time

HELPER (HELPERS)
Ps. 10:14 art the *h* of the fatherless
2 Cor. 1:24 faith, but are the *h* of your joy
3 John 1: 8 we might be fellow *h* to the truth

HEM
Mat. 9:20 touched the *h* of his garment
14:36 touch the *h* of his garment

HEN
Mat. 23:37 even as a *h* gathereth
Luke 13:34 as a *h* gathereth her brood

HERESY (HERESIES)
Acts 24:14 way which they call *h*
Gal. 5:20 strife, seditions, *h*
2 Pet. 2: 1 shall bring in damnable *h*

HERITAGE
Ps. 61: 5 *h* of those that fear thy name
119: 111 testimonies taken as *h*
Is. 54:17 *h* of the servant of the Lord's
Joel 2:17 give not thine *h* to reproach
1 Pet. 5: 3 not as lords over God's *h*

HEWED
Jer. 2:13 *h* them out cisterns, broken cisterns

HIDE (HID, HIDDEN, HIDEST, HIDETH)
Gen. 3: 8 Adam and his wife *h* themselves
18:17 shall I *h* from Abraham that thing
Job 33:17 and *h* thy pride from man
42: 3 who is he that *h* counsel
Ps. 17: 8 *h* me under the shadow
27: 5 in time of trouble he shall *h* me
31:20 shalt *h* them in the secret
44:24 wherefore *h* thou thy face
51: 9 *h* thy face from my sins
119: 11 thy word have I *h* in mine heart
139: 12 the darkness *h* not
Is. 8:17 I will wait on the Lord that *h*
45:15 thou art a God that *h* thyself
Mat. 11:25 hast *h* these things from the wise
1 Cor. 4: 5 bring to light *h* things
2 Cor. 4: 3 if the gospel be *h* it is *h* to
Col. 2: 3 in whom are *h* all the treasures
3: 3 your life is *h* with Christ in God
Jas. 5:20 and shall *h* a multitude of sins
1 Pet. 3: 4 let it be the *h* man of heart
Rev. 2:17 give to eat of the *h* manna
6:16 *h* us from the face of him

HIGH
Num. 24:16 the knowledge of the most *h*
Deut. 26:19 make thee *h* above all
1 Ki. 9: 8 at this house which is *h*
1 Chr. 17:17 estate of a man of *h* degree
Job 11: 8 It is as *h* as heaven,
Ps. 49: 2 both low and *h*, rich
47: 2 the Lord most *h* is terrible
83:18 Jehovah art most *h* over all earth
89:13 strong hand, and *h* is his right hand
97: 9 Lord art *h* above all the earth
103: 11 as heaven is *h* above
107: 41 setteth the poor on *h*
113: 5 like our God who dwelleth on *h*
131: 1 or in things too *h* for me
Is. 14:14 I will be like the most *h*
57:15 I dwell in the *h* and holy place
Ezek. 21:26 is low, and abase him that is *h*
Luke 24:49 be endued with power from on *h*
Acts 7:48 most *h* dwelleth not in temples
Rom. 12:16 mind not *h* things, but condescend

2 Cor. 10: 5 every *h* thing that exalteth itself
Phil. 3:14 the prize of the *h* calling of God

HIGHER (HIGHEST)
Ps. 18:13 *H* gave his voice;
Eccl. 5: 8 he that is *h* than the *h*
Is. 55: 9 as the heavens are *h*
Luke 1:35 power of the *H* shall overshadow
2:14 glory to God in the *h*
6:35 shall be the children of the *H*
Heb. 7:26 *h* than the heavens

HEIGHT
Rom. 8:39 nor *h* nor depth nor any other creature
Eph. 3:18 length, and depth and *h*, nor any other

HILL (HILLS)
Gen. 49:26 utmost bound of everlasting *h*
Num. 23: 9 from the *h* I beheld him
Ps. 2: 6 set the King on the holy *h* of Zion
65:12 little *h* rejoice on every side
68:16 why leap ye, ye high *h*
98: 8 let the *h* be joyful
99: 9 worship at his holy *h*
114: 4 little *h* skipped like lambs
Hos. 10: 8 and to the *h* fall on us
Luke 23:30 and to the *h*, cover us

HOLD (HOLDETH, HOLDING)
Ex. 20: 7 will not *h* him guiltless
Job 2: 3 still he *h* fast integrity
17: 9 righteous shall *h* on to the way
Ps. 66: 9 *h* our soul in life
Prov. 17:28 fool when he *h* his peace counted wise
Is. 41:13 God will *h* thy right hand
62: 1 for Zion's sake will I not *h* my peace
Jer. 2:13 cisterns that can *h* no water
6: 11 I am weary with *h* in;
Mat. 6:24 *h* to one, despise the other
Phil. 2:16 *h* forth the word of life
1 Thes. 5:21 *h* fast to that which is good
1 Tim. 3: 9 *h* mystery of faith in a pure conscience
2 Tim. 1:13 *h* fast to the form of sound words
Tit. 1: 9 *h* fast the faithful
Heb. 3: 6 if we *h* fast the confidence
4:14 let us *h* fast our profession
Rev. 2:25 what ye have *h* fast till I come
3: 3 received and heard *h* fast and repent

HOLY
Ex. 3: 5 thou standest is *h* ground
19: 6 of priests, and an *h* nation
26:33 the *h* place, and the most *h*
29: 6 the crown upon the mitre
30:25 make it an oil of *h* ointment
31:15 Sabbath of rest *h* to the Lord
Lev. 11:45 be *h* for I am *h*
20: 3 to profane my *h* name
21:22 both of the most *h* and
27:14 sanctify his house to be *h*
Num. 5:17 priest shall take *h* water
Deut. 28: 9 an *h* people unto himself
33: 8 Urim be with the *h*
1 Sam. 2: 2 there is none as *h* Lord
21: 5 vessels of the young men are *h*
Ps. 5: 7 I worship toward the *h* temple
16: 10 thou suffer thine *H* one
87: 1 foundation is in the *h* mountains
99: 5 worship at his footstool, for he is *h*
Is. 11: 9 nor destroy in all my *h* mountain
49: 7 redeemer of Israel, and his *H* one
Ezek. 36:20 profaned my *h* name
Dan. 4:13 an *h* one came down from heaven
Hos. 11: 9 the *H* one in the midst of thee
Obad. 1:16 drunk upon my *h* mountain
Hab. 1:12 O Lord my God, mine *H* one
2:20 the Lord is in his *h* temple
Mat. 7: 6 give not that which is *h* unto the dogs
Acts 3:14 denied the *H*, and the Just
Rom. 7:12 wherefore the law is *h*
11:16 for if the firstfruit is *h*
12: 1 sacrifice, *h*, acceptable to God
1 Cor. 7:14 children unclean, now *h*
Eph. 2: 21 unto an *h* temple in the Lord
2 Tim. 1: 9 called us with *h* calling
Tit. 1: 8 sober, just, *h*, temperate
1 Pet. 1:15 be ye *h* in all manner of conversation
2: 5 a *h* priesthood, to offer up

2: 9 an *h* nation, a peculiar
1 John 2:20 have an unction from the *H* one
Jude 1:20 building yourselves in most *h* faith
Rev. 3: 7 he that is *h*, he that is true
4: 8 *h. h. h.* Lord God Almighty
15: 4 fear thee for thou only art *h*
22:11 he that is *h* let him be *h* still

HOLINESS

Ex. 15:11 like thee glorious in *h*
1 Chr. 16:29 worship the Lord in the beauty of *h*
2 Chr. 20:21 praise the beauty of his *h*
Ps. 29: 2 worship the Lord in the beauty of *h*
47: 8 God sitteth upon the throne of his *h*
93: 5 *h* becometh thine house, O Lord
110: 3 in the beauties of *h*; from the
Is. 35: 8 shall be called the way of *h*
62: 9 drink it in the courts of my *h*
63:18 the people of thy *h* have possessed
Jer. 2: 3 Israel was *h* unto the Lord
Obad. 1:17 deliverance and there shall be *h*
Zech. 14:20 on horse bells, *h* to Lord
Acts 3:12 by your own power or *h*
Rom. 1: 4 according to the Spirit of *h*
6:22 ye have your fruit unto *h*
2 Cor. 7: 1 perfecting *h* in the fear of God
Eph. 4:24 in righteousness and true *h*
1 Thes. 3:13 unblameable in *h* before God
1 Tim. 2:15 charity, *h* with sobriety
Tit. 2: 3 behaviour as becometh *h*
Heb. 12:10 we might be partakers of his *h*

HOLY GHOST

Mat. 1:18 was found with child of the *H*
3:11 ye shall be baptize you with the *H*
3:12 blasphemy against the *H*
Mark 12:36 for David himself said by the *H*
13:11 not ye that speak, but the *H*
Luke 1:15 *H* shall come upon thee
3:22 *H* descended in bodily shape
12:12 *H* shall teach you what to say
John 7:39 for the *H* was not yet given
14:26 Comforter, which is the *H*
20:22 unto them receive ye the *H*
Acts 1: 8 after that the *H* is come upon you
2:38 receive the gift of the *H*
5: 3 filled thine heart to lie to the *H*
5:32 and so is also the *H*
7:51 ye do always resist the *H*
9:31 walking in the comfort of the *H*
10:44 the *H* fell on all them which
11:16 be baptized with the *H*
13: 2 and fasted, the *H* said; Separate me
15:28 it seemed good to the *H* and us
16: 6 forbidden of the *H* to preach in
20:23 save that the *H* witnesseth
21:11 thus saith the *H* so shall the Jews
Rom. 5: 5 by the *H* which is given
9: 1 conscience bearing witness in the *H*
14:17 righteousness, peace, joy in the *H*
15:16 being sanctified by the *H*
1 Cor. 2:13 in words the *H* teacheth
6:19 your body is the temple of the *H*
2 Cor. 6: 6 by the *H* love unfeigned
13:14 communion of the *H* be with you
1 Thes. 1: 5 in power and in the *H*
Tit. 3: 5 by the renewing of the *H*
Heb. 2: 4 with gifts of the *H*
3: 7 as the *H* saith, today if
1 Pet. 1:12 preached gospel with the *H*
2 Pet. 1:21 they were moved by the *H*
1 John 5: 7 Father, Word, and the *H*
Jude 1:20 holy faith praying in the *H*

HOLY SPIRIT

Ps. 51:11 take not thy *H* from me
Is. 63:10 rebelled and vexed his *H*
Luke 11:13 give the *H* to them that ask
Eph. 1:13 sealed with the *H*
4:30 grieve not the *H* of God
1 Thes. 4: 8 God, who hath given his *H*

HOME

Ruth 1:21 Lord hath brought me *h* again empty
Eccl. 12: 5 man goeth to his long *h*
2 Cor. 5: 6 whilst at *h* in body, absent
Tit. 2: 5 chaste, keepers at *h*, good

HONEST (HONESTLY)

Luke 8:15 which in an *h* and good heart
Rom. 12:17 provide things *h* in the sight
13:13 let us walk as in the day
2 Cor. 8:21 Providing for *h* things not only
13: 7 should do that which is *h*
Phil. 4: 8 are true whatsoever things are *h*
1 Thes. 4:12 ye may walk *h* toward them
Heb. 13:18 in all things willing to live *h*
1 Pet. 2:12 having your conversation *h* among

HONEY

Gen. 43:11 and a little *h*, spices myrrh
Ex. 16:31 taste was like wafers made with *h*
Judg. 14:18 what is sweeter than *h*
Ps. 19:10 fine gold sweeter also than *h*
81:16 with *h* out of the rock should I
Sol. 4:11 *h* and milk under thy tongue
Is. 7:15 butter and *h* shall he eat
Mat. 3: 4 his meat locusts and wild *h*
Rev. 10: 9 shall be in thy mouth sweet as *h*

HONOUR

Ex. 14:17 I will get me *h* upon Pharaoh
1 Sam. 2:30 that *h* me I will *h*
1 Chr. 29:12 both riches and *h* come of thee
2 Chr. 26:18 shall it be for thine *h*
Ps. 7: 5 lay mine *h* in the dust
8: 5 crowned him with glory and *h*
49:20 man in *h* understandeth not
Prov. 3: 9 *h* the Lord with substance
3:16 her left hand riches and *h*
14:28 the people is the king's *h*
15:33 wisdom: and before *h* is humility
20: 3 it is an *h* to cease from strife
25: 2 *h* of kings to search a matter
26: 1 *h* is not seemly for a fool
29:23 *h* shall uphold the humble
Is. 29:13 with their lips do me *h*
Mat. 13:57 prophet is not without *h*
John 5:23 the Son as they *h* the Father
12:26 serve me, him will my Father *h*
Rom. 2: 7 in well doing seek glory, *h*
9:21 make one vessel to *h*, and another
12:10 in *h* preferring one another
1 Tim. 5: 3 *h* widows that are widows indeed
1 Pet. 2:17 *h* all men. Love thy brotherhood
3: 7 giving *h* unto the wife

HOPE

Job 11:20 *h* shall be as giving up
31:24 if I have made gold my *h*
Ps. 16: 9 my flesh shall rest in *h*
22: 9 didst make me *h* on my mother's
39: wait I for my *h* is in thee
42: 5 *h* thou in God, for I
119: 49 thou hast caused me to *h*
Prov. 10:28 *h* of the righteous shall be gladness
11: 7 *h* of unjust men perisheth
14:32 righteous hath *h* in his death
19:18 chasten thy son while there is *h*
Is. 57:10 saidst thou not, There is no *h*
Jer. 14: 8 the *h* of Israel, the Saviour
17: 7 blessed whose the Lord is *h*
Lam. 3:26 good that a man should *h*
Ezek. 37:11 bones are dried and our *h* is lost
Hos. 2:15 valley of Achor for the door of *h*
Zech. 9:12 to the strong hold, ye prisoners of *h*
Rom. 5: 4 patience experience; experience, *h*
8:24 we are saved by *h*: but *h*
15: 4 comfort of scriptures, have *h*
1 Cor. 13:13 now abideth faith, *h*, charity
Eph. 2:12 having no *h* and without God
1 Thes. 4:13 as others which have no *h*
5: 8 for the helmet, the *h* of salvation
1 Tim. 1: 1 Jesus Christ who is our *h*
Tit. 2:13 looking for that blessed *h*
Heb. 6:11 to the full assurance of *h*
6:19 which *h* we have as an anchor
1 Pet. 1: 3 begotten again to lively *h*
3:15 asketh a reason of *h* in you

HORN (HORNS)

1 Sam. 2: 1 my *h* is exalted in the Lord
Ps. 18: 2 and the *h* of my salvation
92:10 my *h* is as the *h* of a unicorn
Rev. 5: 6 as it had been slain having seven *h*

13: 1 having seven heads and ten *h*

HORSE (HORSES)

Ex. 15:21 the *h* and his rider hath he thrown
Ps. 147:10 delighteth not in the strength of the *h*
Jer. 12: 5 canst thou contend with *h*
Zech. 1: 8 there red *h* speckled and white
Rev. 6: 8 and behold a pale *h*

HOSPITALITY

Rom. 12:13 necessity of saints; given to *h*
1 Tim. 3: 2 of good behavior, given to *h*
Tit. 1: 8 but a lover of *h*,
1 Pet. 4: 9 use *h* one to another

HOST (HOSTS)

Ps. 27: 3 an *h* should encamp against me
103: 21 Bless ye the Lord, all ye his *h*
Luke 2:13 multitude of the heavenly *h*

HOT

Ps. 38: 1 chasten me in thy *h* displeasure
39: 3 my heart was *h* within me
Prov. 6:28 can one go upon *h* coals
1 Tim. 4: 2 seared with a *h* iron
Rev. 3:15 thou art neither cold nor *h*

HOUR

Mat. 10:19 given you in that same *h*
24:36 day and *h* knoweth no man
25:13 know neither day nor *h*
Luke 12:12 Holy Ghost shall teach you that same *h*
John 2: 4 mine *h* is not yet come
7:30 his *h* was not yet come
Rev. 3: 3 not know what *h* I come
17:12 power as kings one *h* with the beast

HOUSE

Gen. 28:17 is none other but the *h* of God
Deut. 6: 7 when thou sittest in thine *h*
Josh. 24:15 as for me and my *h*
Job 30:23 *h* appointed for all living
Ps. 23: 6 in the *h* of the Lord
26: 8 I loved the habitation of thine *h*
36: 8 satisfied with the fatness of thine *h*
55:14 unto the *h* of God in
112: 3 wealth and riches shall be in his *h*
Eccl. 7: 2 go to the *h* of mourning
12: 3 when keepers of the *h* tremble
Sol. 2: 4 brought me to the banqueting *h*
Is. 2: 3 to the *h* of the God of Jacob
5: 8 woe to them that join *h* to *h*
38: 1 set thine *h* in order,
64: 11 our holy and beautiful *h*
Mic. 4: 2 to the *h* of the God of Jacob
Mat. 10:13 if the *h* be worthy, let your peace
12:25 a *h* divided against itself shall not
12:44 I will return into my *h*
23:38 *h* is left unto you desolate
Luke 11:17 and a *h* divided against a *h*
11:24 I will return unto my *h*
John 4:53 believed and his whole *h*
14: 2 in my Father's *h* are many
Acts 11:14 thou and all thine *h* saved
1 Tim. 3:15 behave thyself in the *h* of God
5: 8 specially for those of his own *h*
1 Pet. 4:17 begin at the *h* of God

HOUSES

Job 4:19 dwell in *h* of clay
Prov. 19:14 *h* and riches are the inheritance
Mat. 11: 8 wear soft clothing are in king's *h*
19:29 everyone that hath forsaken *h*
23:14 hypocrites! for ye devour widows' *h*
Mark 10:29 no man that hath left the *h*
Luke 20:47 which devour widows *h*, and for a
1 Tim. 3:12 their children and their own *h* well

HOUSEHOLD

Acts 16:15 baptized and her whole *h*
Gal. 6:10 who are of the *h* of faith

HUMBLE (HUMBLED)

Ex. 10: 3 thou refuse to *h* thyself
Lev. 26:41 if uncircumcised hearts be *h*
2 Ki. 22:19 hast *h* thyself before the Lord
2 Chr. 7:14 shall *h* themselves
12:12 And when he *h* himself the wrath
33:23 *h* not himself before the Lord
Ps. 9:12 forgetteth not the cry of the *h*
34: 2 *h* shall hear thereof, and be glad
35:13 I *h* my soul with fasting

Prov. 16:19 to be of an *h* spirit
Is. 5:15 *h* and eyes of the lofty shall be *h*
10:33 haughty shall be *h*
57:15 *h* spirit, to revive the spirit of
Jer. 44:10 they are not *h* unto this day
Mat. 18:4 whosoever therefore shall *h* himself
23:12 he that shall *h* himself
2 Cor. 12:21 my God will *h* me
Phil. 2:8 *h* himself and became obedient
Jas. 4:6 But giveth grace unto the *h*
4:10 *h* yourselves in the sight of Lord
1 Pet. 5:5 giveth grace to the *h*
5:6 *h* yourselves under the mighty hand

HUMILITY
Prov. 15:33 wisdom: and before honour is *h*
22:4 by *h* are riches and honour
Acts 20:19 serving the Lord with all *h*
Col. 2:18 of your reward in a voluntary *h*
1 Pet. 5:5 be clothed with *h*: For God resisteth

HUNGER
Deut. 8:3 suffered thee to *h*, and fed thee
Ps. 34:10 do lack, and suffer *h*
Prov. 19:15 idle soul shall suffer *h*
Is. 49:10 shall not *h* nor thirst
Lam. 4:9 sword better than slain with *h*
Mat. 5:6 blessed are they which do *h*
Luke 6:21 blessed are ye that *h*
John 6:35 cometh to me shall never *h*
Rom. 12:20 if thine enemy *h* feed
1 Cor. 4:11 we both *h* and thirst,
11:34 if any man *h* let him eat at

HUNGRY
Ps. 107:9 filleth the *h* soul with goodness
146:7 God giveth food to the *h*
Prov. 25:21 if thine enemy be *h* give him
27:7 to the *h* soul every bitter thing is sweet
Is. 58:7 to deal thy bread to the *h*
58:10 if thou draw out thy soul to the *h*
Ezek. 18:7 hath given his bread to the *h*
Luke 1:53 filled the *h* with good
Phil. 4:12 how to be full and to be *h*

HUSBAND (HUSBANDS)
Gen. 3:16 to thy *h*, and he shall rule over
29:32 therefore my *h* will love me
Ex. 4:25 a bloody *h* art thou
Is. 54:5 for thy Maker is thine *h*
Mark 10:12 if a woman put away her *h*
John 4:17 I have no *h*. Jesus said
1 Cor. 7:14 unbelieving *h* is sanctified by
7:34 careth how she may please her *h*
14:35 let them ask the *h* at
Eph. 5:23 the *h* is the head of wife
5:25 *h*, love your wives, as Christ
Col. 3:19 *h* love your wives, and be not bitter
1 Pet. 3:1 ye wives be in subjection to your own *h*
3:7 likewise ye *h*, dwell

HYMN (HYMNS)
Eph. 5:19 in psalms and *h*, and spiritual psalms
Col. 3:16 admonishing one another in psalms and *h*

HYPOCRISY
1 Tim. 4:2 speaking lies in *h* having their conscience
Jas. 3:17 without partiality and without *h*
1 Pet. 2:1 and all guile and *h*

HYPOCRITE (HYPOCRITES)
Job 8:13 the *h's* hope shall perish
15:34 congregation of *h* shall be desolate
20:5 joy of the *h* for a moment
Is. 9:17 every one is a *h* and
33:14 fearfulness hath surprised the *h*
Mat. 6:2 as the *h* do in the synagogues
7:5 thou *h*, first cast out the beam
24:51 appoint him portion with *h*

IDLE
Prov. 19:15 an *i* soul shall suffer
Mat. 12:36 every *i* word that men shall speak
Luke 24:11 words seemed as *i* tales

IDLENESS
Prov. 31:27 eateth not the bread of *i*

IDOL (IDOLS)
Is. 2:8 land is full of *i*; they worship

Zech. 11:17 woe to the *i* shepherd
Acts 15:20 abstain from the pollutions of *i*
Rom. 2:22 thou that abhorrest *i* dost thou commit
1 Cor. 8:1 touching things offered to *i*
1 John 5:21 keep yourselves from *i*
Rev. 2:14 eat things sacrificed to *i*

IDOLATER (IDOLATERS)
1 Cor. 5:11 or an *i*, or a railer
10:7 neither be ye *i*, as
Eph. 5:5 covetous man, who is an *i*
Rev. 21:8 and sorcerers, and *i*,
22:15 and *i*, and whosoever loveth

IDOLATRY
Acts 17:16 city wholly given to *i*
1 Cor. 10:14 beloved, flee from *i*
Col. 3:5 covetousness, which is *i*

IGNORANCE
Lev. 4:13 congregation of Israel sin through *i*
Eph. 4:18 alienated from God through *i*

IGNORANT (IGNORANTLY)
Rom. 10:3 for being *i* of God's righteousness
Acts 17:23 when therefore ye *i* worship
1 Cor. 14:38 if man be *i* let him be *i*
Heb. 5:2 can have compassion on the *i*

IMAGE
Gen. 1:26 let us make man in our *i*
5:3 in his own likeness after his *i*
Lev. 26:1 set up any *i* of stone
Dan. 2:31 this great *i* whose brightness
Mat. 22:20 whose is this *i* and superscription
Rom. 8:29 conformed to the *i* of the Son
2 Cor. 4:4 Christ who is the *i* of God
Col. 1:15 the *i* of the invisible God
Heb. 1:3 express the *i* of his person

IMMORTAL
1 Tim. 1:17 the King *i*, invisible

IMMORTALITY
Rom. 2:7 seek for glory, honour, *i*
1 Cor. 15:53 mortal must put on *i*
2 Tim. 1:10 brought life and *i* to light

IMPOSSIBLE
Mat. 17:20 nothing shall be *i* unto you
19:26 with men this is *i* but
Luke 1:37 with God nothing shall be *i*
Heb. 6:4 *i* for those once enlightened
11:6 without faith it is *i* to please

IMPUTED (IMPUTETH, IMPUTING)
Lev. 7:18 shall it be *i* unto him that offereth
17:4 blood shall be *i* unto that man
Ps. 32:2 whom the Lord *i* not iniquity
Rom. 4:6 God *i* righteousness without work
5:13 sin is not *i* when there is no law
2 Cor. 5:19 not *i* their trespasses
Jas. 2:23 *i* unto him for righteousness

INCLINE (INCLINED)
Josh. 24:23 *i* your heart unto the God
1 Ki. 8:58 that he may *i* our hearts unto him
Ps. 40:1 he *i* unto me and
119:36 *i* my heart unto thy testimonies
Prov. 2:2 *i* thine ear unto wisdom
Is. 55:3 *i* your ear and come unto me
Jer. 7:26 nor *i* their ear, but hardened
44:5 nor *i* their ear to turn

INCORRUPTIBLE (UN-)
Rom. 1:23 the glory of the *i* God
1 Cor. 9:25 corruptible crown; but we an *i*
15:52 dead shall be raised *i*,
1 Pet. 1:4 to an inheritance *i* and
1:23 not of corruptible seed, but of *i*

INCORRUPTION
1 Cor. 15:50 neither doth corruption inherit *i*

INCREASE (INCREASED)
Lev. 25:36 take no usury of him nor *i*
Deut. 16:15 bless thee in all thine *i*
Ps. 62:10 if riches *i* set not your heart
67:6 shall the earth yield her *i*
Prov. 9:9 will hear, and will *i* learning
Is. 9:7 of the *i* of his government
29:19 meek shall *i* their joy
Luke 2:52 Jesus *i* in wisdom and
17:5 said unto the Lord, *i* our faith
John 3:30 he must *i* but I decrease

1 Cor. 3:6 Apollos watered; but God gave the *i*
Col. 2:19 increaseth with the *i* of God

INDIGNATION
Esth. 5:9 full of *i* against Mordecai
Mic. 7:9 I will bear the *i* of the Lord
Nah. 1:6 who can stand before his *i*
Rom. 2:8 *i* and wrath,
Heb. 10:27 fiery *i* which shall devour
Rev. 14:10 poured into the cup of his *i*

INFINITE
Job 22:5 and thine iniquities, *i*
Ps. 147:5 his understanding is *i*

INFIRMITY (INFIRMITIES)
Ps. 77:10 this is my *i*: but
Prov. 18:14 spirit of man will sustain *i*
Mat. 8:17 himself took our *i*, and
Rom. 8:26 the Spirit helpeth our *i*
2 Cor. 12:9 I rather glory in my *i*
Heb. 5:2 himself is compassed with *i*

INHERIT
Gen. 15:8 shall I know that I shall *i* it
Ps. 37:11 the meek shall *i* the earth
82:8 O God, thou shalt *i* all nations
Prov. 3:35 wise shall *i* glory; but
8:21 that love me to *i* substance
Mat. 5:5 they shall *i* the earth
25:34 *i* the kingdom prepared for you
Mark 10:17 what shall I do that I may *i* eternal
1 Cor. 6:9 unrighteous shall not *i* the kingdom
15:50 flesh and blood cannot *i* the kingdom
Gal. 5:21 shall not *i* the kingdom of God
Heb. 6:12 faith and patience *i* the promises
Rev. 21:7 overcometh shall *i* all

INHERITANCE
Deut. 18:2 the Lord is their *i*
1 Ki. 8:36 hast given to thy people for an *i*
Ps. 16:5 Lord is a portion of mine *i*
28:9 save thy people and bless thine *i*
94:14 neither will he forsake his *i*
106:40 that he abhorred his own *i*
Prov. 19:14 riches are the *i* of fathers
Eccl. 7:11 wisdom is good with an *i*
Acts 20:32 and to give you an *i*
Eph. 5:5 any *i* in the kingdom of Christ
Col. 3:24 shall receive the reward of *i*
Heb. 9:15 the promise of eternal *i*
1 Pet. 1:4 to an *i* incorruptible and undefiled

INIQUITY
Ex. 20:5 visiting the *i* of the fathers upon
34:7 forgiving *i*, and transgression
Lev. 26:41 accept the punishment of their *i*
Num. 23:21 hath not beheld *i* in Jacob
Job 4:8 they that plow *i* and sow wickedness
5:16 *i* stoppeth her mouth
15:16 man which drinketh *i* like water
34:22 workers of *i* may hide
34:32 if I have done *i* I will
Ps. 5:5 thou hatest all workers of *i*
18:23 kept myself from mine *i*
32:5 mine *i* have I not hid
51:5 I was shapen in *i*
66:18 if I regard *i* in my heart
92:7 workers of *i* do flourish
119:133 let not any *i* have dominion
Prov. 21:15 be to the workers of *i*
Is. 27:9 by this shall the *i* of Jacob be purged
53:6 Lord laid on him the *i* of us all
Jer. 3:13 only acknowledge thine *i*
31:30 every one shall die for his own *i*
Ezek. 18:30 so *i* shall not be your ruin
33:8 that wicked man shall die in his *i*
Mic. 7:18 that pardoneth *i* and passeth by the
Mat. 7:23 depart from me, ye that work *i*
24:12 because *i* shall abound, the love of
Acts 8:23 and in the bond of *i*
Rom. 6:19 uncleanness and to *i* unto *i*
1 Cor. 13:6 rejoiceth not in *i* but rejoices in
2 Thes. 2:7 mystery of *i* doth already work
Tit. 2:14 he might redeem us from all *i*
Jas. 3:6 tongue is a fire, a world of *i*

INIQUITIES
Lev. 26:39 and also in the *i* of their fathers
Ezra 9:6 our *i* are increased over our head

Neh. 9: 2 confessed *i* of the fathers
Job 13:26 to possess the *i* of my youth
Ps. 38: 4 mine *i* are gone over my head
51: 9 my sins, and blot out all mine *i*
79: 8 remember not against us former *i*
90: 8 thou hast set our *i* before thee
130: 3 if thou, Lord, mark *i*
130: 8 he shall redeem Israel from all *i*
Is. 43:24 hast wearied me with thine *i*
Dan. 4:27 thine *i* by showing mercy to the
Acts 3:26 every one of you from his *i*
Rom. 4: 7 blessed are they whose *i* are forgiven
Rev. 18: 5 God hath remembered her *i*

INNOCENT
Ps. 19:13 and I shall be *i* from the great
Prov. 28:20 rich shall not be *i*

INNOCENCY
Ps. 26: 6 I will wash my hands in *i*

INNUMERABLE
Ps. 40:12 *i* evils have compassed me
Heb. 11:12 which is by the sea shore *i*
12:22 an *i* company of angels

INQUIRE (INQUIRED, INQUIREST)
Judg. 20:27 children of Israel *i* of the Lord
1 Sam.30: 8 David *i* at the Lord,
Ps. 78:34 returned and *i* early after God
27: 4 Lord and to *i* in his temple
Is. 21:12 if ye will *i* ye: return
Jer. 21: 2 I pray thee of the Lord
Zeph. 1: 6 have not sought the Lord, nor *i* for him
1 Pet. 1: 10 of which salvation prophets have *i*

INSPIRATION
2 Tim. 3:16 scripture is given by *i*

INSTRUCT (INSTRUCTED)
Deut. 4:36 hear his voice that he might *i* thee
Job 40: 2 contendeth with the Almighty *i* him
Ps. 16: 7 my reins *i* me in the night
Sol. 8: 2 mother's house who would *i* me
Is. 8: 11 *i* me that I should not walk
28:26 his God doth *i* him to discretion
Phil. 4:12 in all things I am *i* both

INSTRUCTION
Job 33:16 men and sealeth their *i*
Ps. 50:17 hatest *i* and castest my words
Prov. 19:27 cease to hear *i* that causeth
23:12 apply thine heart to *i* and
2 Tim. 3:16 correction, for *i* in righteousness

INSTRUCTOR (INSTRUCTORS)
1 Cor. 4:15 ye have ten thousand *i* in Christ

INSTRUMENTS
Gen. 49: 5 *i* of cruelty are in their habitations
Ps. 7:13 prepared for him *i* of death
Rom. 6:13 neither yield members as *i* of unrighteousness

INTEGRITY
Gen. 20: 5 didst this in the *i* of my heart
Job 27: 5 I will not remove mine *i*
Ps. 7: 8 according to my *i* that is
25:21 let *i* and uprightness preserve me
26: 1 I have walked in mine *i*
Prov. 11: 3 *i* of upright shall guide

INTERCESSION
Is. 53:12 and made *i* for the transgressors
Jer. 27:18 now make *i* to the Lord
Rom. 8:26 Spirit maketh *i* for us
8:34 who also maketh *i* for us
Heb. 7:25 he ever liveth to make *i*

INTERCESSOR
Is. 59:16 there was no *i*: therefore his

INTERPRETATION
Gen. 40: 5 according to the *i* of his dream
Dan. 2:36 we will tell the *i* thereof
1 Cor. 12:10 another the *i* of tongues
14:26 revelation, hath an *i*
2 Pet. 1:20 scripture is of any private *i*

INVISIBLE
Rom. 1:20 the *i* things of him from the
Col. 1:16 visible, and *i*, whether they be
1 Tim. 1:17 King eternal, immortal, *i*
Heb. 11:27 endured as seeing him who is *i*

INWARD (INWARDLY)
Job 19:19 my *i* friends abhorred me

Ps. 51: 6 desireth truth in the *i* parts
Jer. 31:33 my law in their *i* parts
Mat. 7:15 *i* they are ravening wolves
Luke 11:39 your *i* part is full of ravening
Rom. 2:29 he is a Jew which is one *i*
7:22 Law of God after the *i* man
2 Cor. 4:16 the *i* man is renewed day by day

IRON
Prov. 27:17 *i* sharpeneth *i*; so a man
Dan. 5:23 gods of silver, and gold, of brass, *i*
1 Tim. 4: 2 conscience seared with a hot *i*

ISSUES
Ps. 68:20 belong the *i* from death
Prov. 4:23 for out of it are the *i* of life

IVORY
1 Ki. 10:18 made a great throne of *i*
Rev. 18:12 all manner vessels of *i*

JEALOUS (JEALOUSY)
Ex. 20: 5 am a *j* God, visiting the iniquity
34:14 name is *j*, is a *j* God
Deut. 6:15 thy God is a *j* God among you
Josh. 24:19 he is a *j* God; he will not forgive
Ps. 79: 5 shall thy *j* burn like fire
Prov. 6:34 *j* is the rage of a man
Ezek. 39:25 be *j* for my holy name
Nah. 1: 2 God is *j* and the Lord
Zech. 1:14 I am *j* for Jerusalem and for Zion
Rom. 10:19 provoke you to *j* by
1 Cor. 10:22 we provoke the God to *j*
2 Cor. 11: 2 *j* over you with godly jealousy

JERUSALEM
Is. 24:23 reign in mount Zion, and in *J*
Zech. 12:10 upon the inhabitants of *J*
Gal. 4:26 *J* which is above is free
Heb. 12:22 living God, the heavenly *J*
Rev. 3:12 which is new *J*, which
21: 2 the holy city, new *J*

JESUS
Mat. 1:21 thou shalt call his name *J*
8:29 do with thee *J* thou
27:37 This is *J* the King of the Jews
1 Cor. 12: 3 Spirit of God calleth *J*
Eph. 4:21 taught by him as the truth is in *J*
Heb. 2: 9 But we see *J*, who was made a little
12: 2 looking unto *J* the author and
Rev. 22:16 I *J* have sent my angel

JEW (JEWS)
Rom. 2:10 *J* first, and also to the Gentile
1 Cor. 9:20 to Jews I became as a *J*
Gal. 3:28 there is neither *J* nor Greek, there

JOIN (JOINED)
Prov. 11:21 hand *j* in hand, the wicked shall
Eccl. 9: 4 for him that is *j* to the living
Is. 5: 8 woe to them that *j* house to house
Jer. 50: 5 let us *j* ourselves to the Lord
Mat. 19: 6 what God hath *j* together let not
1 Cor. 1:10 that ye be perfectly *j* together
Eph. 5:31 shall be *j* to his wife

JOY
2 Chr. 20:27 go again to Jerusalem with *j*
Neh. 8:10 *j* of the Lord is your strength
Job 20: 5 of the hypocrite but for
Ps. 16:11 thy presence is fulness of *j*
43: 4 unto God my exceeding *j*
51:12 restore to me the *j* of thy salvation
126: 5 that sow in tears shall reap in *j*
Eccl. 9: 7 eat thy bread with *j*
Is. 9: 3 according to the *j* in harvest
35:10 with songs and everlasting *j*
61: 3 give them the oil of *j* for mourning
61: 7 everlasting *j* shall be to them
Zeph. 3:17 will *j* over thee with singing
Mat. 13:20 hear the word, and with *j*
Luke 1:44 babe leaped in the womb for *j*
15: 7 *j* shall be in heaven over one
John 16:20 your sorrow be turned into *j*
16:24 that your *j* may be full
17:13 my *j* fulfilled in themselves
Acts 20:24 finish my course with *j*
Rom. 15:13 you with all *j* and peace
2 Cor. 2: 3 my *j* is the *j* of you all
Gal. 5:22 fruit of the Spirit is love, *j*
Phil. 4: 1 my *j* and crown, so stand fast in

1 Thes. 1: 6 receive the word with *j* of
Heb. 12: 2 who for the *j* set before
Jas. 1: 2 count it all *j* when ye
1 Pet. 4:13 be glad with exceeding *j*
1 John 1: 4 that your *j* may be full

JOYFUL (JOYFULLY)
Ps. 35: 9 my soul shall be *j* in the Lord
Eccl. 9: 9 live *j* with the wife whom thou
Is. 56: 7 make them *j* in my house
2 Cor. 7: 4 exceeding *j* in all our tribulation

JOYFULNESS
Deut. 28:47 servedst not the Lord thy God with *j*
Col. 1: 11 all patience longsuffering with *j*

JOYOUS
Heb. 12: 11 for the present seemeth to be *j*

JUDGE
Gen. 16: 5 Lord *j* between me and thee
18:25 shall not the *J* of the earth
Deut. 32:36 the Lord shall *j* his people
1 Sam.24:12 Lord *j* between me and thee
Ps. 9: 8 Lord shall *j* the world in righteousness
68: 5 father of the fatherless and *j* of widows
Is. 33:22 The Lord is our *j*, the
Mat. 7: 1 *j* not, that ye be not
Luke 12:14 who made me a *j* or a
John 5:30 as I hear I *j* and my judgment
12:47 I came not to *j* the world
Acts 7:27 made thee ruler and a *j*
10:42 to be the *J* of the quick and dead
17:31 in which he will *j* the
Rom. 2:16 when God shall *j* the secrets of men
14:10 why dost thou *j* thy brother
1 Cor. 4: 3 I *j* not mine own self
6: 3 know ye not that we shall *j* angels
14:29 two or three and let the other *j*
Col. 2:16 let no man *j* you in meat
2 Tim. 4: 1 who shall *j* the quick and the dead
4: 8 Lord the righteous *j*, shall give me
Heb. 10:30 Lord shall *j* his people
Jas. 5: 9 the *j* standeth before the door

JUDGETH (JUDGING)
Deut. 1:17 ye shall not respect persons in *j*
Ps. 7:11 God *j* the righteous
58:11 he is a God that *j* in earth
Luke 22:30 sit on thrones, *j* the twelve
1 Cor. 2:15 but he that is spiritual *j* all things

JUDGMENT
Deut. 1:17 for the *j* is God's: and the cause
Ps. 1: 5 ungodly not stand in *j*
9:16 Lord is known by the *j*
143: 2 enter not into *j* with thy servant
Prov. 21:15 it is joy to the just to do *j*
29:26 every man's *j* cometh from the Lord
Eccl. 11: 9 God will bring thee into *j*
Is. 1:27 Zion shall be redeemed with *j*
28:17 *j* also will I lay to the
30:18 the Lord is a God of *j*
42: 1 he shall bring *j* to the Gentiles
61: 8 I the Lord love *j*,
Jer. 5: 1 if there be any that executeth *j*
10:24 correct me, but with *j*;
Dan. 4:37 whose works are truth and his ways *j*
Amos 5:24 let *j* run down as waters,
Mat. 5: 21 kill shall be in danger of the *j*
John 5:27 and given him authority to execute *j*
9:39 for *j* I am come into the world
16: 8 and of righteousness, and of *j*
Acts 24:25 temperance, and *j* to
Rom. 5:18 *j* came upon all men to condemnation
14:10 must all stand before the *j* seat
1 Pet. 4:17 *j* begin at the house of God
Rev. 17: 1 show thee *j* of a great whore

JUDGMENTS
Ps. 19: 9 *j* of the Lord are true and righteous
36: 6 thy *j* are a great deep
119: 75 I know, O Lord, that thy *j* are right
119: 108 O Lord, teach me thy *j*
Is. 26: 8 in the way of thy *j*, O Lord, have
26: 9 when thy *j* are in the earth
Jer. 12: 1 let me talk with thee of thy *j*
Rom. 11:33 how unsearchable are his *j*, and his

JUST
Gen. 6: 9 Noah was a *j* man and

Deut. 25:15 shalt have a perfect and *j* weight
2 Sam. 23: 3 he that ruleth men must be *j*
Prov. 4:18 path of the *j* is as a shining
10: 6 blessings are on the head of the *j*
11: 1 but a *j* weight is his delight
12:21 no evil shall happen to the *j*
18:17 in his own cause seemeth *j*
20: 7 the *j* man walketh in his integrity
24:16 *j* man falleth seven
Eccl. 7:20 is not a *j* man on earth
Is. 26: 7 way of the *j* is uprightness
Ezek. 18: 9 he is *j*, he shall live
Hab. 2: 4 *j* shall live by his faith
John 5:30 I judge and my judgment is *j*
Acts 7:52 coming of the *J* One
24:15 both of the *j* and the unjust
Rom. 1:17 *j* shall live by faith
3:26 he might be *j* and the
7:12 commandment holy, *j*
Gal. 3:11 *j* shall live by faith
Phil. 4: 8 whatsoever things are *j*
Heb. 2: 2 received a *j* recompence
10:38 *j* shall live by faith
Rev. 15: 3 *j* and true are thy ways

JUSTLY
Mic. 6: 8 to do *j* and love kindness

JUSTICE
Gen. 18:19 to do *j* and judgment,
Ps. 89:14 *j* and judgment are the habitation
Jer. 50: 7 O habitation of *j*, and

JUSTIFICATION
Rom. 4:25 was raised again for our *j*

JUSTIFIED
Job 13:18 I know that I shall be *j*
25: 4 how can man be *j* with God?
Ps. 51: 4 mightest be *j* when thou speakest
Is. 45:25 the seed of Israel be *j*
Jer. 3:11 hath *j* herself more than Judah
Mat. 11:19 wisdom is *j* of her children
12:37 by thy words thou shalt be *j*
Luke 7:29 *j* God, being baptized of
Rom. 2:13 doers of the law shall be *j*
3:24 being *j* freely by his grace
4: 2 if Abraham were *j* by works
5: 1 being *j* by faith, we
8:30 whom he *j* them he
1 Cor. 6:11 ye are *j* in the name of the Lord
Gal. 2:16 not *j* by the works of law
3:11 no man is *j* by the law
3:24 that we might be *j* by faith
5: 4 *j* by the law, ye are fallen
1 Tim. 3:16 in flesh, *j* in spirit
Tit. 3: 7 that being *j* by his grace
Jas. 2:21 Abraham *j* by works when

JUSTIFY (JUSTIFIETH)
Ex. 23: 7 will not *j* the wicked
Job 9:20 if I *j* myself, mine own
33:32 speak, for I desire to *j* thee
Luke 16:15 ye are they which *j* yourselves
Rom. 3:30 God shall *j* circumcision
4: 5 him that *j* the ungodly
8:33 it is God that *j*

KEEP
Gen. 18:19 *k* the way of the Lord
28:15 I am with thee and will *k* thee
Ex. 23: 7 *k* thee far from a false matter
Num. 6:24 Lord bless thee and *k*
Deut. 29: 9 *k* the words of this covenant
Ps. 17: 8 *k* me as the apple of the eye
39: 1 *k* my mouth with a bridle
91:11 angels to *k* thee in all
106: 3 blessed are they that *k* judgment
119: 4 commanded us to *k* thy precepts
127: 1 except the Lord *k* the city
141: 3 before my mouth; *k* the door of my
Eccl. 3: 7 a time to *k* silence,
Is. 26: 3 thou wilt *k* him in perfect
Jer. 3:12 I will not *k* anger for ever
Hab. 2:20 let the earth *k* silence
1 Cor. 14:34 let your women *k* silence
Eph. 4: 3 endeavouring to *k* unity of the
Phil. 4: 7 shall *k* your hearts and minds through
2 Thes. 3: 3 Lord shall stablish you and *k* you

1 Tim. 6:20 *k* that which is committed
2 Tim. 1:12 able to *k* that which I have
Jude 1:24 that is able to *k* you
Rev. 22: 9 them which *k* the sayings

KEEPEST (KEEPETH, KEEPING)
Ex. 34: 7 *k* mercy for thousands, forgiving
Ps. 19:11 in *k* of them is great reward
121: 3 he that *k* thee will not slumber
Prov. 13: 3 he that *k* his mouth *k* his life
1 Pet. 4:19 *k* of their souls to him
Rev. 16:15 that watcheth and *k* his garments

KEEPER (KEEPERS)
Ps. 121: 5 the Lord is thy *k*: the Lord
Eccl. 12: 3 when *k* of the house shall
Sol. 1: 6 made me the *k* of vineyards
Tit. 2: 5 chaste, *k* at home, good, obedient

KEPT
2 Sam. 22:22 *k* the ways of the Lord
Ps. 50:21 and I *k* silence; thou thoughtest
Luke 2:19 Mary *k* all these things
John 15:20 if they have *k* my sayings
17:12 that thou gavest me I have *k*
Rom. 16:25 *k* secret since the world
2 Tim. 4: 7 I have *k* the faith

KEY (KEYS)
Mat. 16:19 the *k* of the kingdom
Rev. 1:18 have the *k* of hell and
3: 7 he that hath the *k* of David
20: 1 the *k* of the bottomless pit

KILL (KILLED, KILLETH)
Ex. 20:13 thou shalt not *k*
Eccl. 3: 3 time to *k* and a time to
Mat. 10:28 *k* the body, but are not able to *k*
Mark 3: 4 lawful to save life, or *k*
John 16: 2 who *k* you will think he doeth
2 Cor. 3: 6 letter *k* but the spirit giveth life
Rev. 13:10 that *k* with sword must be *k*

KIND
Gen. 1:11 yielding fruit after his *k*
Luke 6:35 he is *k* to the unthankful
1 Cor. 13: 4 charity suffereth long and is *k*

KINDNESS
2 Sam. 9: 3 may show the *k* of God
Neh. 9:17 slow to anger and of great *k*
141: 5 smite me; it shall be a *k*
Prov. 19:22 the desire of a man is his *k*
31:26 in her tongue is the law of *k*
Is. 54: 8 with everlasting *k* will I have mercy
Col. 3:12 put on bowels of mercies, *k*
2 Pet. 1: 7 brotherly *k* to brotherly *k* charity

KINDLE (KINDLED)
2 Sam. 22: 9 devoured: coals were *k* by it
Ps. 2:12 when his wrath is *k* but a little
Prov. 26:21 a contentious man to *k* strife
Is. 30:33 stream of brimstone, doth *k* it

KING
Gen. 14:18 Melchizedek *k* of Salem
Job 18:14 bring him to the *k* of terrors
Ps. 10:16 the Lord is *k* forever
24: 7 *K* of glory shall come
47: 7 God is *K* of all the earth
74:12 God is my *k* of old
Prov. 30:31 a *k* against whom there is no
Eccl. 8: 4 where the word of the *k* is there
Is. 32: 1 a *k* shall reign in righteousness
33:22 the Lord is our *k* he will save
43:15 Creator of Israel, your *K*
Hos. 3: 5 Lord their God and David their *k*
13:11 I gave thee a *k* in mine anger
Zech. 9: 9 behold, thy *K* cometh
Luke 23: 2 himself is Christ, a *k*
John 6:15 by force to make him *k*
1 Tim. 1:17 now unto the *K* eternal
6:15 *K* of kings, and Lord of lords
1 Pet. 2:17 fear God, honour thy *k*
Rev. 17:14 Lord of Lords, and *k*
19:16 *k* of kings, and Lord

KINGS
Ps. 102:15 *k* of the earth be thy glory
Prov. 8:15 by me *k* reign, and princes
Luke 22:25 *k* of Gentiles exercise authority
1 Tim. 2: 2 *k* and for all that are in authority

Rev. 1: 6 made us *k* and priests to God
5:10 unto our God, *k* and priests

KINGDOM
Ex. 19: 6 be a *k* of priests, and an
1 Chr. 29:11 thine is the *k*, O Lord
Dan. 2:44 God of heaven set up a *k*
7:27 whose *k* is an everlasting *k*
Mat. 3: 2 for the *k* of heaven is at hand
5: 3 theirs is the *k* of heaven
6:13 for thine is the *k* and the
6:33 seek ye first the *k* of God
11:12 *k* of heaven suffereth violence
12:25 every *k* divided against itself
12:28 the *k* of God is come
13:38 good seed are the children of the *k*
16:19 the keys of the *k* of heaven
23:13 shut up the *k* of heaven against men
25: 1 *k* of heaven be likened unto ten
25:34 inherit the *k* prepared
Mark 11:10 blessed be the *k* of our father David
Luke 10:11 *k* of God is come nigh unto you
12:32 good pleasure to give you the *k*
17:21 *k* of God is within you
21:31 *k* of God is nigh at hand
22:29 I appoint unto you a *k*
John 3: 3 he cannot see the *k* of God
18:36 my *k* is not of this world
Rom. 14:17 *k* of God is not meat and drink
1 Cor. 4:20 *k* of God is not in word
6: 9 shall not inherit the *k* of God
15:24 delivered up the *k* to God
Eph. 5: 5 hath any inheritance in the *k* of God
Col. 1:13 translated us into the *k* of
2 Thes. 1: 5 be counted worthy of the *k* of God
Jas. 2: 5 rich in faith, heirs of the *k*
2 Pet. 1:11 into the everlasting *k* of our Lord
Rev. 1: 9 in the *k* and patience of Jesus
17:17 to give their *k* to the beast

KISS (KISSED)
Ps. 2:12 *k* the son lest he be angry
85:10 peace have *k* each other
Luke 7:38 *k* his feet and anointed
Rom. 16:16 salute one another with an holy *k*
1 Pet. 5:14 with the *k* of charity

KISSES
Prov. 27: 6 *k* of an enemy are deceitful

KNEE (KNEES)
Is. 35: 3 confirm the feeble *k*
45:23 to God every *k* shall
Mat. 27:29 they bowed the *k* before him
Rom. 14:11 every *k* shall bow to
Eph. 3:14 I bow my *k* unto the Lord

KNOCK
Mat. 7: 7 *k* and it shall be opened
Rev. 3:20 I stand at the door and *k*

KNEW (KNEWEST)
Gen. 3: 7 they *k* they were naked
4: 1 Adam *k* Eve his wife,
Deut. 34:10 whom the Lord *k* face to face
Mat. 7:23 I never *k* you: depart
John 4:10 if thou *k* the gift of God

KNOW
1 Sam. 3: 7 Samuel did not yet *k* Lord
2 Ki. 19:27 I *k* thy abode and thy going
1 Chr. 28: 9 *k* thou the God of thy father
Job 5:27 *k* thou it for thy good
13:23 make me to *k* my transgression
19:25 I *k* that my Redeemer liveth
Ps. 9:10 that *k* thy name will trust in
41:11 by this I *k* thou favourest
46:10 be still, and *k* that I am God
51: 6 thou shalt make me to *k* wisdom
139: 23 search me O God and *k* my heart
Is. 58: 2 seek me daily and delight to *k*
Jer. 29:11 I *k* the thoughts that I think
Mic. 3: 1 is it not for you to *k* judgment
Mat. 6: 3 let not the left hand *k* what
7:11 how to give good gifts
25:12 say unto ye, I *k* you not
John 10:14 and *k* my sheep and am known
13:18 I *k* whom I have chosen
13:35 by this shall all men *k*
Acts 1: 7 it is not for you to *k* the times

1 Cor. 13:12 now I *k* in part; but then
Eph. 3:19 to *k* the love of Christ
Phil. 4:12 I *k* both how to be abased
2 Tim. 1:12 I *k* whom I have believed
Rev. 2: 2 I *k* thy works and thy labor
3: 1 I *k* thy works, that thou hast

KNOWETH (KNOWN)
Ps. 1: 6 Lord *k* the way of the righteous
94:11 Lord *k* the thoughts of man that
103: 14 he *k* our frame, that
138: 6 the proud he *k* afar off
Zeph. 3: 5 the unjust *k* no shame
Mat. 6: 8 Father *k* things ye have need of
10:26 hid that shall not be *k*
1 Cor. 8: 3 love God, the same is *k* of him
13:12 even as I am also *k*
Gal. 4: 9 *k* God, or rather are *k* of God
2 Tim. 2:19 Lord *k* them that are his
1 John 3: 1 the world *k* us not

KNOWLEDGE
Gen. 2:17 of the tree of *k* of good and evil
1 Sam. 2: 3 the Lord is a God of *k*
Ps. 19: 2 night unto night showeth *k*
139: 6 such *k* is too wonderful
Prov. 8:12 I find out *k* of witty inventions
9:10 *k* of the holy is understanding
30: 3 nor have the *k* of the holy
Eccl. 9:10 nor device nor *k* nor wisdom
Jer. 3:15 feed you with *k* and understanding
Hos. 4: 6 are destroyed for lack of *k*
Rom. 2:20 hast the form of *k* and
10: 2 a zeal of God, but not according to *k*
1 Cor. 8: 1 all have *k k* puffeth
Eph. 3:19 love of Christ which passeth *k*
Col. 2: 3 treasures of wisdom and *k*
3:10 renewed in *k* after the image
1 Pet. 3: 7 dwell with them according to their *k*
2 Pet. 1: 5 faith virtue and to virtue *k*
3:18 grow in grace and in the *k* of the

LABOUR
Ps. 128: 2 thou shalt eat the *l* of
Prov. 14:23 in all *l* there is profit
23: 4 *l* not to be rich; cease
Eccl. 4: 8 no end of all his *l*
Is. 55: 2 ye spend your *l* for that which
Mat. 11:28 ye that *l* and are heavy laden
John 4:38 reap that whereon ye bestowed no *l*
6:27 *l* not for the meat that
1 Cor. 15:58 your *l* is not in vain in
1 Thes. 1: 3 work of faith, *l* of love
Heb. 4: 11 let us *l* to enter into

LABOURED
Is. 49: 4 I have *l* in vain
John 4:38 other men *l* and ye are
Phil. 2:16 not run in vain, neither *l* in vain

LABOURER (LABOURERS)
Mat. 9:37 plenteous but the *l* are
Luke 10: 2 send forth *l* into his harvest
1 Cor. 3: 9 for we are *l* together with God
1 Tim. 5:18 the *l* is worthy of his reward

LACK (LACKING)
1 Thes. 3: 10 which is *l* in your faith
Jas. 1: 5 If any of you *l* wisdom

LAMB (LAMBS)
Gen. 22: 8 God will provide himself a *l*
Is. 11: 6 wolf shall dwell with the *l*
53: 7 brought as a *l* to slaughter
John 1:29 behold the *L* of God
21:15 Jesus said to Peter, Feed my *l*
1 Pet. 1:19 as a *l* without blemish
Rev. 5:12 worthy is the *L* that was slain
7:14 white in the blood of the *L*
13: 8 *L* slain from the foundation

LAME
Lev. 21:18 a blind man, or a *l*, or
Job 29:15 eyes to the blind, feet to the *l*
Prov. 26: 7 legs of the *l* are not equal
Is. 35: 6 shall the *l* man leap as an hart

LAMP
2 Sam.22:29 thou art my *l* O Lord
1 Ki. 15: 4 give him a *l* in Jerusalem
Ps. 119:105 thy word a *l* to my feet
132: 17 I have ordained a *l* for mine

Prov. 6:23 the commandment is a *l* and the law
13: 9 *l* of wicked shall be put out
Is. 62: 1 salvation as the *l* that
Mat. 25: 1 which took their *l* went forth

LANGUAGE
Gen. 11: 1 earth was of one *l*
Ps. 81: 5 I heard a *l* that I understood not

LASCIVIOUSNESS
Mark 7:22 deceit, *l*, an evil eye
2 Cor. 12: 21 fornication and *l*, which they have
Gal. 5:19 fornication, uncleanness, *l*
1 Pet. 4: 3 when we walked in *l*
Jude 1: 4 turning the grace of God into *l*

LAUGH (LAUGHING)
Gen. 18:15 he said, Nay, but thou didst *l*
Job 8: 21 till he fill thy mouth with *l*
Ps. 2: 4 he that sitteth in heavens shall *l*
52: 6 righteous shall see and fear and *l*
Prov. 1:26 I will *l* at your calamity
Luke 6: 21 weep now for ye shall *l*

LAUGHTER
Ps. 126: 2 was our mouth filled with *l*
Prov. 14:13 in *l* the heart is sorrowful
Eccl. 7: 3 sorrow is better than *l*
Jas. 4: 9 let *l* be turned to mourning

LAW
Neh. 9:26 cast thy *l* behind their backs
Ps. 19: 7 *l* of the Lord is perfect
40: 8 thy *l* is within my heart
94:12 teachest him out of thy *l*
119: 70 I delight in thy *l*
119: 97 how I love thy *l*
Prov. 7: 2 keep my *l* as the apple of thine eye
13:14 the *l* of the wise is a fountain
29:18 keepeth the *l* happy is
Is. 2: 3 out of Zion shall go forth the *l*
8:16 seal the *l* among my disciples
51: 7 people in whose heart is my *l*
Jer. 31:33 I will put the *l* in inward parts
John 1:17 *l* was given by Moses
19: 7 we have a *l* and by our *l* he
Acts 13:39 not justified by the *l* of Moses
Rom. 2:13 not hearers of the *l*
3:31 do we make void the *l?*
4:15 *l* worketh wrath; where no *l*
5:13 sin is not imputed where no *l*
7:12 the *l* is holy, just, and good
7:22 I delight in the *l* of God
8: 2 made me free from the *l* of sin
1 Cor. 6: 1 go to *l* before the unjust
Gal. 2:16 man not justified by works of the *l*
2:19 I through the *l* am dead to the *l*
5:23 love, faith, against such is no *l*
Phil. 3: 9 righteousness which is of the *l*
1 Tim. 1: 9 that *l* is not made for the righteous
Heb. 7:19 for the *l* made nothing perfect
Jas. 1:25 whoso looketh into the perfect *l*
1 John 3: 4 sin transgresseth the *l*

LAWFUL
Ezek. 18: 5 do that which is *l* and
1 Cor. 6:12 all things are *l* unto
10:23 All things are *l* for me

LAY
Eccl. 7: 2 the living will *l* it to heart
Mat. 6: 20 *l* up for yourselves treasure
John 10:15 I *l* down my life for the sheep
1 Tim. 5:22 *l* hands suddenly on no man
6:12 *l* hold on eternal life
Heb. 6:18 *l* hold upon the hope set before
12: 1 *l* aside every weight
1 John 3:16 we ought to *l* down our lives

LAID (LAYETH, LAYING)
Ps. 62: 9 to be *l* in the balance
Prov. 2: 7 *l* up sound wisdom for the righteous
26:24 and *l* up deceit within him
Is. 53: 6 Lord hath *l* on him the iniquity
Luke 1:66 *l* up in their hearts
12:19 much goods *l* up for many years
1 Cor. 3: 10 I have *l* the foundation
Col. 1: 5 hope which is *l* up for you
2 Tim. 4: 8 *l* up for me a crown of
Heb. 6: 2 *l* on of hands, and of resurrection
1 Pet. 2: 1 *l* aside all malice and all guile

LEAD (LEADETH, LED)
Ps. 5: 8 *l* me O Lord in thy righteousness
23: 2 *l* me beside still waters
61: 2 *l* me to the rock that is higher
139: 24 *l* me in the way everlasting
Is. 11: 6 a little child shall *l* them
40: 11 gently *l* those with young
Zech. 5: 8 weight of *l* upon the mouth
Mat. 7:13 broad is the way that *l*
15:14 blind *l* the blind, both shall fall
John 10: 3 calleth sheep and *l* them out
Rev. 7:17 and shall *l* them unto living

LEAN
Prov. 3: 5 *l* not unto thine own understanding
Mic. 3: 11 yet will they *l* on the Lord

LEAP (LEAPED, LEAPING)
Sol. 2: 8 cometh *l* upon the mountains
Is. 35: 6 shall the lame man *l*
Luke 1: 41 the babe *l* in her womb
6:23 rejoice in that day and *l* for joy

LEARN (LEARNED)
Deut. 4: 10 that they may *l* to fear
Ps. 119: 71 that I might *l* thy statutes
Prov. 22:25 lest thou *l* his ways
Is. 26: 10 yet will he not *l* righteousness
50: 4 given me the tongue of the *l*
Mat. 11:29 *l* of me, for I am meek
John 6:45 hath *l* of Father cometh unto me
Eph. 4: 20 ye have not so *l* Christ
Heb. 5: 8 he were a Son, yet *l* he obedience

LEARNING
Acts 26:24 much *l* doth make thee mad
2 Tim. 3: 7 ever *l* and never able

LEAVE
Gen. 2:24 man shall *l* his father and mother
Ps. 16: 10 not *l* my soul in hell
27: 9 *l* me not, neither forsake me
Mat. 5:24 there thy gift before the altar
19: 5 shall a man *l* father and mother
John 14:18 will not *l* you comfortless
14:27 peace I *l* with you, my
Acts 2:27 not *l* my soul in hell
Eph. 5: 31 man *l* his father and mother
Heb. 13: 5 I will never *l* thee, nor forsake

LEAVEN
Ex. 12:15 put away *l* our of your houses
Mat. 13:33 heaven is like unto *l* which a woman
16: 6 beware of the *l* of the Pharisees
Luke 12: 1 beware ye of the *l* of the Pharisees
1 Cor. 5: 6 a little *l* leaveneth a whole lump

LEND (LENDER, LENDETH)
Ex. 22:25 *l* money to any of my people
Deut. 23:20 stranger thou mayest *l* upon usury
Ps. 112: 5 showeth favour and *l*, he will guide
Prov. 19:17 hath pity upon the poor *l* to Lord
Prov. 22: 7 borrower is servant to the *l*

LEVIATHAN
Job 41: 1 draw out *l* with an hook
Ps. 74:14 breakest the heads of *l*

LIAR (LIARS)
Ps. 116: 11 All men are *l*
Is. 44:25 frustrateth the tokens of *l*
John 8:44 he is a *l* and the father
Rom. 3: 4 let God be true, every man a *l*
Tit. 1:12 the Cretians are always *l*
1 John 1: 10 we make him a *l*, and his word
2: 4 keepeth not his commandments is a *l*
Rev. 2: 2 not and hast found them *l*

LIBERTY
Lev. 25: 10 and proclaim *l* throughout all the land
Ps. 119:45 I will walk at *l* for I seek
Is. 61: 1 proclaim *l* to the captives
Luke 4: 18 to set at *l* the bruised
Rom. 8: 21 glorious *l* of the children of God
Gal. 5: 1 stand fast in the *l* wherewith Christ
Jas. 1:25 looketh into the perfect law of *l*
2:12 be judged by the law of *l*

LIE
Num. 23:19 God is not a man, that he should *l*
Col. 3: 9 *l* not one to another, seeing
Tit. 1: 2 God that cannot *l* hath promised
Heb. 6:18 it was impossible for God to *l*

LYING
Ps.   119:163 I hate and abhor / but love thy law
Prov.   12:19 a / tongue is but for a moment
Jer.   7: 4 trust ye not in / words, saying
Hos.   4: 2 by swearing and / and killing and
Eph.   4:25 wherefore putting away /

LIFE
Gen.   2: 9 tree of / also in the midst
          30:15 before thee this day, / and good
1 Ki.   19: 4 O Lord, take away my /
Job   2: 4 hath will he give for his /
Ps.   21: 4 asked / of thee and thou gavest
          36: 9 with thee is the fountain of /
          63: 3 lovingkindness better than /
          91:16 with long / will I satisfy
Prov.   8:35 whoso findeth me findeth /
          15:24 way of / is above to the wise
          18:21 death and / are in the power of the
Mat.   6:25 take no thought for your /
          10:39 findeth his / shall lose it
          20:28 to give his / a ransom for many
John   1: 4 in him was / and the / was
           3:36 believeth on the Son hath everlasting /
           5:40 come to me, that ye might have /
           6:35 I am the bread of /
           8:12 but shall have the light of /
          10:10 I am come that they might have /
          11:25 I am the resurrection and the /
          14: 6 I am the way, the truth, and the /
Rom.   5:10 reconciled shall be saved by his /
           8: 2 law of the Spirit of / in Christ
2 Cor.   2:16 to the other, the savour of / unto /
           3: 6 letter killeth, the spirit giveth /
Gal.   2:20 the / which I now live in the flesh
Col.   3: 3 your / is hid with Christ
1 Tim.   4: 8 having the promise of the / that
2 Tim.   1:10 brought / and immortality to light
1 John   5:12 he that hath the Son hath /

LIFT UP (LIFTED, LIFTING)
Num.   6:26 / his countenance upon thee
Ps.   4: 6 Lord / the light of countenance
          24: 7 / your heads, O ye gates
          25: 1 to thee I / my soul
          75: 4 wicked / not the horn
         102: 10 thou hast / and cast me down
         121: 1 mine eyes unto the hills
Eccl.   4:10 one will / his fellow
Is.   26:11 Lord, when thy hand is /
Lam.   3:41 let us / our hearts with
John   3:14 so must the Son of man be /
           8:28 when ye have / the Son of man
          12:32 if I be / will draw all men
1 Tim.   2: 8 / holy hands, without wrath
Heb.   12:12 / the hands which hang
Jas.   4:10 Lord and he shall / you up

LIGHT
Gen.   1: 3 let there be /
Job   18: 5 / of the wicked put out
          25: 3 on whom doth not his / arise
Ps.   4: 6 lift up the / of thy countenance
          36: 9 in thy / shall we see /
          43: 3 O send out thy / and
          97:11 / is sown for the righteous
         119:105 and a / unto my path
Prov.   4:18 path of the just is as shining /
          15:30 / of the eyes rejoiceth the
Eccl.   11: 7 / is sweet and a pleasant
Is.   5:20 darkness for / and / for
           9: 2 in darkness have seen a great /
          30:26 / of the moon shall be as the /
          42: 6 a / of the Gentiles
          58: 8 thy / break forth as morning
          60: 1 shine; for thy / is come
Mat.   5:14 ye are the / of the world
           5:16 let your / so shine before men
          11:30 my yoke easy, my burden /
Luke   2:32 a / to lighten the Gentiles
John   1: 4 the life was the / of men
           1: 7 came to bear witness of the /
           3:19 loved darkness rather than /
           8:12 I am the / of the world
           8:12 shall have the / of life
          12:35 walk while ye have the /

LIGHTS
Phil.   2:15 ye shine as / in the world
Jas.   1:17 down from the father of /

LIGHTNING (LIGHTNINGS)
Ex.   19:16 there were thunders and /
Mat.   24:27 as the / cometh out of the
          28: 3 his countenance was like /
Luke   10:18 Satan as / fall from heaven

LIKENESS
Gen.   1:26 in our image, after our /
Rom.   6: 5 in the / of his death
           8: 3 in the / of sinful flesh
Phil.   2: 7 made in the / of men

LION (LIONS)
Gen.   49: 9 Judah is a / whelp
Ps.   22:13 ravening and a roaring /
Prov.   28: 1 righteous are bold as a /
Is.   11: 6 calf and young / and the fatling
          35: 9 no / shall be there, nor
Ezek.   10:14 face of a /, on the right
Hos.   5:14 and as a young / to the house
2 Tim.   4:17 delivered out of the mouth of the /
1 Pet.   5: 8 the devil as a roaring /
Rev.   4: 7 beast was like a /
           5: 5 L of the tribe of Judah

LIPS
Ps.   12: 3 cut off all flattering /
          45: 2 grace is poured into thy /
          63: 3 my / shall praise thee
         141: 3 keep the door of my /
Prov.   10:18 hideth hatred with lying /
          26:23 burning / and a wicked heart
Is.   6: 5 I am a man of unclean /

LITTLE
Ps.   2:12 his wrath is kindled but a /
           8: 5 a / lower than the angels
          37:16 a / that a righteous man hath
Prov.   6:10 a / sleep, a / slumber,
          16: 8 better is a / with righteousness
Is.   28:10 here a / and there a /
Mat.   6:30 O ye of / faith
          14:31 O thou of / faith
Luke   19:17 been faithful in a very /
1 Tim.   4: 8 bodily exercise profiteth /
Heb.   2: 7 a / lower than the angels

LIVE
Job   14:14 if a man die, shall he / again
Ps.   55:23 men shall not / out half their days
         146: 2 while I / will I praise
Is.   55: 3 hear, and your soul shall /
Hab.   2: 4 the just shall / by faith
Mat.   4: 4 man shall not / by bread alone
Acts   17:28 in him we / and move
Rom.   8:13 if ye / after the flesh
          14: 8 whether we /, we / unto the Lord
2 Cor.   5:15 which / should not / to themselves
          13:11 be of one mind, / in peace
Gal.   2:20 / in the flesh, I / by the faith
           5:25 if we / in Spirit, walk
Phil.   1:21 to / is Christ, and to die is
Heb.   13:18 willing to / honestly

LIVED (LIVETH)
Job   19:25 for I know that my Redeemer /
Acts   23: 1 / in all good conscience before God
Rom.   6:10 in that he /, he / unto God
Heb.   7:25 he ever / to make intercession
Jas.   5: 5 ye have / in pleasure on the earth
Rev.   1:18 he that / and was dead

LIVELY
1 Pet.   1: 3 begotten again to a / hope
           2: 5 ye, as / stones, are built

LIVING
Is.   38:19 the /, the / shall praise

Jer.   2:13 fountain of / waters, and hewed them
Mat.   22:32 God of the dead, but of the /
John   7:38 shall flow rivers of / water
Rom.   12: 1 present your bodies a / sacrifice
Heb.   10:20 by a new and / way, which he hath
1 Pet.   2: 4 coming as to a / stone

LOINS
Prov.   31:17 she girdeth her / with strength
Luke   12:35 let your / be girded
Eph.   6:14 / girt about with truth
1 Pet.   1:13 gird up the / of your mind

LONG (LONGED, LONGETH)
Job   6: 8 the thing that I / for
Ps.   63: 1 my flesh / for thee
          84: 2 my soul /, yea, even fainteth
         119:131 I have / for thy commandments
         119:174 I have / for thy salvation

LONGSUFFERING
Ex.   34: 6 gracious, /, and abundant
Num.   14:18 the Lord is / and of great mercy
Ps.   86:15 compassion, and gracious, /
Rom.   2: 4 goodness, and forbearance, and /
           9:22 endured with much / the vessels
Gal.   5:22 joy peace, /, gentleness
Eph.   4: 2 meekness, with /, forbearing one
1 Tim.   1:16 Christ might show forth all /
2 Tim.   3:10 purpose, faith, /, charity, patience
2 Pet.   3: 9 but is / to us-ward

LOOK (LOOKED)
Gen.   29:32 the Lord / on my affliction
Sol.   1: 6 / not upon me, because I am black
Is.   45:22 / unto me and be saved
Jer.   8:15 we / for peace, but no good came
Mic.   7: 7 I will / unto the Lord
2 Cor.   4:18 we / not at things seen
Phil.   2: 4 / not every man on his own
Heb.   11:10 for he / for a city which hath
1 Pet.   1:12 things the angels desire to / into

LOOKETH (LOOKING)
1 Sam.   16: 7 / on outward appearance, but the
Mat.   5:28 whosoever / on a woman to lust after
Luke   9:62 / back is fit for the kingdom of God
Tit.   2:13 / for that blessed hope
Heb.   12: 2 / to Jesus, the author
2 Pet.   3:12 / for and hasting unto the coming
Jude   1:21 / for the mercy of our

LOOSE (LOOSED, LOOSETH)
Josh.   5:15 / thy shoe from thy foot
Ps.   102:20 to / those appointed to death
Eccl.   12: 6 or ever the silver cord be /

LORD
Ex.   34: 6 L, the L God, merciful
Deut.   4:35 L he is God; there is none else
           6: 4 O Israel, the L our God is one L
          10:17 the L your God is God of gods
Neh.   9: 6 art thou, even thou L alone; thou
Ps.   4: 5 put your trust in the L
          34: 2 soul make her boast in the L
          37: 4 delight thyself in the L
          97:12 rejoice in the L, ye righteous
         100: 3 the L, he is God, it is he that
         104: 34 will be glad in the L
Prov.   3: 5 trust in the L with
Is.   45:17 Israel shall be saved in the L
          45:24 in the L have I righteousness
          61:10 greatly rejoice in the L
Dan.   2:47 and a L of kings, and a revealer
Joel   2:23 rejoice in the L your God
Mark   2:28 Son of man is L of the sabbath
Acts   2:36 crucified, both L and Christ
Rom.   10:12 same L over all is rich
          14: 9 L of the dead and of the living
          16:12 labour in the L
1 Cor.   2: 8 have crucified the L of glory
           8: 6 one God, one L Jesus Christ
          15:47 second man is the L from heaven
          15:58 abounding in the work of the L
Eph.   4: 5 one L, one faith, one baptism
Phil.   3: 1 rejoice in the L
1 Tim.   6:15 king of kings and L of lords
Rev.   14:13 dead which die in the L
          17:14 he is the L of lords, and king

LOSE (LOST)
Prov.   23:   8   and / thy sweet words
Eccl.   3:   6   and a time to /; a time
Mat.   5:13   if salt have / his savour
            10:   6   to the / sheep of the
            10:42   in no wise / his reward
            16:26   and / his own soul
            18:11   save that which was /
Luke   15:   4   hundred sheep, if he /
            19:10   save that which is /
            15:32   thy brother was / and is found
2 Cor.   4:   3   gospel be hid, hid to them that are /

LOT (LOTS)
Lev.   16:10   on which the / fell
Prov.   18:18   / causeth contentions to cease
Mat.   27:35   parted his garments, casting /
Mark   15:24   casting / upon them

LOVE
Lev.   19:18   thou shalt / thy neighbour as thyself
Deut.   6:   5   shalt / the Lord thy
            10:12   to / him and to serve
Ps.   18:   1   I will / thee, oh Lord
            31:23   / the Lord, all ye his saints
           119:   97   O, how / I thy law
           145:   20   Lord preserveth them that / him
Sol.   2:   5   I am sick of /
             8:   6   / is strong as death
Jer.   31:   3   loved thee with everlasting /
Zech.   8:19   / the truth and peace
Mat.   5:44   / your enemies, bless
            19:19   / thy neighbor as
            22:37   the Lord thy God
            22:39   / thy neighbor as
            24:12   / of many shall wax cold
John   5:42   have not the / of God
            13:34   that ye also / one another
            14:23   if a man / me, he will keep
            15:13   greater / hath no man
            15:17   that ye / one another
Rom.   5:   5   / of God is shed abroad in our
             8:35   separate us from the / of Christ
            13:10   / is the fulfilling of the law
Gal.   5:   6   faith which worketh by /
             5:14   / thy neighbor as
             5:22   fruit of the Spirit is /, joy, peace
Eph.   3:17   rooted and grounded in /
             4:15   speaking truth in /
             5:   2   walk in / as Christ hath loved
             5:25   / your wives, even as Christ
Col.   2:   2   knit together in / and
             3:19   Husbands, / your wives
1 Thes.   1:   3   your labour of /, and
             3:12   abound in / toward one another
             5:   8   breastplate of faith and /
2 Thes.   3:   5   hearts into the / of God
Heb.   13:   1   let brotherly / continue
Jas.   2:   8   / thy neighbor as
1 Pet.   1:22   see that ye / one another
             2:17   / the brotherhood
1 John   2:   5   in him is the / of God perfected
             3:   1   what manner of / the Father hath
             3:23   and / one another
             4:   7   for / is of God
             4:   8   knoweth not God, for God is /
             4:12   If we / one another
             4:18   there is no fear in /
             4:19   we / him because he first
2 John   1:   1   whom I / in the truth
Rev.   2:   4   thou hast left thy first /

LOVED
Hos.   11:   1   Israel was a child, then I / him
Mal.   1:   2   yet I have / Jacob
Mark   10:21   Jesus beholding him, / him
Luke   7:47   are forgiven, for she / much
John   3:16   God so / the world that
            13:   1   having / his own, which were in
            14:28   if ye / me, ye would rejoice
            15:   9   as my Father / me, so have I /
            16:27   Father loveth you because ye / me
            21:   7   whom Jesus / saith unto Peter
Rom.   8:37   conquerors through him that / us
             9:13   Jacob I /, Esau I hated
Gal.   2:20   Son of God, who / me

Eph.   2:   4   great love wherewith he / us
             5:   2   walk in love, as Christ / us
             5:25   wives as Christ / the church
2 Tim.   4:10   / this present world, and is
Heb.   1:   9   hast / righteousness and hated
2 Pet.   2:15   who / the wages of unrighteousness
1 John   4:10   that we / God, but that he / us
Rev.   5:   1   that / us and washed us

LOVETH
Ps.   146:   8   the Lord / the righteous
Prov.   3:12   whom the Lord / he correcteth
            17:17   a friend / at all times
Mat.   10:37   / father or mother more than me
John   3:35   Father / the Son and
2 Cor.   9:   7   God / a cheerful giver
Heb.   12:   6   whom the Lord /, he chasteneth

LOVINGKINDNESS
Ps.   36:   7   how excellent is thy /
            63:   3   thy / is better than life
           103:        who crowneth thee with /
Jer.   32:18   thou showest / to thousands

LOW
Job   40:12   that is proud and bring him /
Ps.   49:   2   both / and high, rich and
Prov.   29:23   man's pride shall bring him /
Luke   1:48   he hath regarded the / estate
             3:   5   every mountain and hill shall be
                     brought /

LOWLINESS
Eph.   4:   2   with all / and meekness
Phil.   2:   3   but in / of mind let

LOWLY
Prov.   3:34   he giveth grace unto the /
Mat.   11:29   learn of me, I am meek and /

LUCRE
1 Tim.   3:   3   not greed of filthy /
Tit.   1:   7   not given to filthy /

LUST (LUSTETH)
Ex.   15:   9   my / shall be satisfied
Mat.   5:28   looketh on a woman to / after her
Rom.   7:   7   I had not known / except the law
1 Cor.   10:   6   not / after evil things
Gal.   5:16   shall not fulfil the / of the flesh
Jas.   4:   2   Ye / and have not: ye
1 John   2:16   / of the flesh, and / of

LUSTS
Mark   4:19   / of other things entering in
John   8:44   / of your father ye will
Rom.   6:12   ye should obey it in the / thereof
            13:14   for the flesh, to fulfil the /
            13:24   crucified flesh with affections and /
2 Tim.   2:22   flee also youthful /
Tit.   2:12   denying ungodliness and worldly /
Jas.   4:   3   ye may consume it upon your /
1 Pet.   2:11   abstain from fleshly /
             4:   2   no longer live to the /
Jude   1:18   walk after their own ungodly /

MAD
1 Sam.   21:13   feigned himself / in
Hos.   9:   7   prophet is a fool, spiritual man is /
John   10:20   hath a devil and is /
Acts   26:24   much learning doth make thee /

MADNESS
Deut.   28:28   Lord shall smite thee with /
Luke   6:11   they were filled with /

MAGNIFY (MAGNIFIED)
2 Sam.   7:26   let thy name be / for
Job   7:17   man, that thou shouldest / him
Ps.   34:   3   / the Lord with me
            69:30   / him with thanksgiving
Luke   1:46   my soul doth / the Lord
Acts   19:17   name of Lord Jesus was /
Phil.   1:20   Christ be / in my body

MAJESTY
Job   40:10   deck thyself now with /
Ps.   21:   5   honour and / hast thou laid
            29:   4   voice of the Lord is full of /
            93:   1   he is clothed with /; the Lord
           145:   5   of the glorious honour of thy /
Is.   2:10   for glory of his /
Heb.   8:   1   throne of the M in the
2 Pet.   1:16   eyewitnesses of his /

Jude   1:25   be glory and /, dominion and power

MAKE (MADE)
Gen.   1:26   Let us / man in our
Ps.   104:24   in wisdom hast thou / them all
           139:   14   fearfully and wonderfully /
Prov.   16:   4   Lord hath / all things for himself
John   1:   3   all things were / by
Gal.   4:   4   / of a woman, / under the law
Phil.   2:   7   / in the likeness of

MAKER
Prov.   14:31   the poor, reproacheth his /
            22:   2   Lord is the / of them
Is.   45:   9   unto him that striveth with his /
            51:13   forgettest the Lord thy /
            54:   5   thy / is thy husband
Heb.   11:10   whose builder and / is God

MALE
Gen.   1:27   / and female created he them
Num.   5:   3   both / and female shall ye put out
Mat.   19:   4   made them / and female
Gal.   3:28   there is neither / nor female

MALICE
1 Cor.   5:   8   with the leaven of /
            14:20   in / be children, but in
Eph.   4:31   away from you, with all /
Col.   3:   8   anger, wrath, /, blasphemy
1 Pet.   2:   1   laying aside all /

MAMMON
Mat.   6:24   you cannot serve God and /
Luke   16:   9   friends of the / of righteousness

MAN
Gen.   1:27   God created / in his own image
Ex.   15:   3   the Lord is a / of war
Num.   23:19   God is not a / that he
2 Ki.   9:11   know the /, and his communication
Job   7:17   what is /, that thou shouldest be
            14:   1   / born of woman is of few days
            15:14   What is /, that he should be clean?
            25:   6   much less / that is a worm
Ps.   8:   4   what is / that thou art mindful
            10:18   / of the earth may no more oppress
            25:12   what is he that feareth the Lord
            90:   3   thou turnest / to destruction
           104:   23   / goeth forth to his work
           118:        6   not fear; what can / do
Prov.   9:   8   rebuke a wise / and he will love thee
            14:16   a wise / feareth and departeth
Eccl.   7:29   God made / upright, but
            10:   2   a wise / heart is at his right hand
            12:   5   / goeth to his long home
Is.   2:22   cease ye from / whose breath
            53:   3   a / of sorrows and acquainted
Jer.   9:23   let not the wise / glory in wisdom
            31:22   a woman shall compass a /
Zech.   13:   7   awake against the / that
Mat.   4:   4   / shall not live by bread
             8:   9   I am a / under the authority
            16:26   what shall a / give in exchange
John   3:   3   except a / be born again
Rom.   6:   6   old / crucified with him
             7:22   in the law of God after the inward /
1 Cor.   2:11   / knoweth the things of a /
            11:   8   / is not of the woman, but the
2 Cor.   4:16   though outward / perish, yet inward /
                     is renewed
            12:   2   I knew a / in Christ
Eph.   4:24   put on the new /
Phil.   2:   8   in fashion as a / he humbled
Col.   3:10   put on the new /
2 Tim.   3:17   the / of God may be perfect
Jas.   3:13   who is a wise / and endued with
1 Pet.   3:   4   be the hidden / of the heart

MANIFEST (MANIFESTED)
Eccl.   3:18   that God might / them
John   2:11   / forth his glory, and his
            14:21   love him and will / myself to him
            17:   6   I have / thy name unto men
1 Cor.   5:   5   make the counsels of the hearts
Gal.   5:19   works of the flesh are /
1 Tim.   3:16   God was / in the flesh
1 John   3:10   in this children of God are /
             4:   9   in this was / the love of God

MANIFOLD
Ps.   104:24 how *m* are thy works
Luke   18:30 receive *m* more in this present time
Eph.   3:10 known by the church the *m* wisdom of
God

MANNA
Ex.   16:15 It is *m*; for they wist
Deut.   8:16 fed thee in the wilderness with *m*
Neh.   9:20 withheldest not thy *m* from their
Ps.   78:24 rained down *m* upon
John   6:31 fathers did eat *m* in
Rev.   2:17 to eat of the hidden *m*

MARK
Ps.   130: 3 if thou shouldest *m* iniquity
Ezek.   9: 4 set thy *m* on the foreheads
Phil.   3:14 I press toward the *m*
Rev.   13:17 save he that had the *m*

MARRIAGE
Mat.   22: 2 king made a *m* for his
25:10 that were ready went into the *m*
John   2: 1 there was a *m* in Cana
Heb.   13: 4 *m* is honourable in all
Rev.   19: 7 of Lamb is come

MARRY (MARRIED)
Deut.   25: 5 the wife of the dead shall not *m*
Jer.   3:14 I am *m* to you, saith Lord
Luke   14:20 I have *m* a wife, and
1 Cor.   7: 9 better to *m* than to burn
1 Tim.   4: 3 forbidding to *m* and
5:14 that younger women *m* and

MARTYR (MARTYRS)
Acts   22:20 the blood of thy *m* Stephen
Rev.   17: 6 the blood of the *m* of Jesus

MARVEL (MARVELLED)
Mat.   8:10 when Jesus heard it, he *m*
Mark   6: 6 he *m* because of their unbelief
John   5:28 *M* not at this: for the hour
Acts   3:12 why *m* ye at this

MARVELLOUS
1 Chr.   16:12 remember his *m* works
Ps.   17: 7 show thy *m* kindness
98: 1 for he hath done *m* things
139: 14 *m* are thy works; and that my soul
Mic.   7:15 show unto him *m* things
1 Pet.   2: 9 out of darkness into his *m* light
Rev.   15: 3 Great and *m* are thy works

MASTER (MASTERS)
Mat.   6:24 no man can serve two *m*
23:10 neither be ye called *m*
John   13:13 ye call me *M* and Lord
Eph.   6: 9 ye *m* do the same thing unto them
Col.   4: 1 *m* give unto your servants that
Jas.   3: 1 be not many *m*, knowing we shall

MEASURE
Job   11: 9 the *m* is longer than the earth
Ps.   39: 4 the *m* of my days, what it is
Mat.   7: 2 with what *m* ye mete
23:32 fill up the *m* of your fathers
John   3:34 giveth not the Spirit by *m*
2 Cor.   1: 8 that we were pressed out of *m*
Eph.   4:13 unto the *m* of the stature of

MEAT
Ps.   42: 3 my tears have been my *m*
104: 27 give them their *m* in due season
Prov.   6: 8 provideth her *m* in the summer
Mat.   6:25 is not life more than *m*
John   4:32 I have *m* to eat ye know
4:34 my *m* is to do the will of him
6:55 my flesh is *m* indeed
Rom.   14:17 kingdom of God is not *m* and drink
1 Cor.   6:13 *m* for the belly, and the belly
10: 3 did all eat the same spiritual *m*

MEDIATOR
Gal.   3:19 by angels in the hand of a *m*
1 Tim.   2: 5 one *m* between God and men
Heb.   8: 6 he is the *m* of a better covenant
12:24 to Jesus the *m* of a new covenant

MEDICINE
Prov.   17:22 merry heart doeth good like a *m*

MEDITATE
Ps.   1: 2 in his law doth he *m* day and night
77:12 I will also of all thy work

Luke   21:14 not *m* before what ye shall answer
1 Tim.   4:15 *m* upon these things

MEDITATION
Ps.   5: 1 words, O Lord, consider my *m*
49: 3 *m* of my heart shall be of understanding
119: 97 thy law! It is my *m* all the day

MEEK
Ps.   22:26 *m* shall eat and be satisfied
37:11 *m* shall inherit the earth
147: 6 the Lord lifteth up the *m*
149: 4 beautify the *m* with salvation
Is.   29:19 *m* shall increase their joy
61: 1 preach good tidings to the *m*
Mat.   5: 5 blessed are the *m*: for they shall
11:29 I am *m* and lowly in heart
1 Pet.   3: 4 ornament of the *m* and quiet spirit

MEEKNESS
Ps.   45: 4 because of truth and *m*
Zeph.   2: 3 seek righteousness, seek *m*
1 Cor.   4:21 love, and in the spirit of *m*
2 Cor.   10: 1 beseech you by the *m* and gentleness
Gal.   6: 1 one in the spirit of *m*
Eph.   4: 2 walk with lowliness, *m*
2 Tim.   2:25 in *m* instructing those that oppose
Tit.   3: 2 showing all *m* unto all men
Jas.   1:21 receive with the engrafted word
1 Pet.   3:15 hope that is in you with *m* and fear

MEET
Gen.   2:18 make him an help *m* for him
Amos   4:12 prepare to *m* thy God
Mat.   3: 8 therefore fruits *m* for repentance
Acts   26:20 do works *m* for repentance
1 Thes.   4:17 caught up to *m* the Lord

MEMBER (MEMBERS)
Ps.   139:16 book all my *m* were written
Mat.   5:29 that one of thy *m* should perish
Rom.   6:13 neither yield ye your *m* as
1 Cor.   6:15 your bodies *m* of Christ
12:12 body is one, and hath many *m*
Jas.   3: 5 tongue is a little *m*
5:30 *m* of his body, his flesh and
Col.   3: 5 mortify your *m* on earth

MEMORIAL
Ex.   3:15 this is my *m* to all generations
17:14 write this for a *m* in the book
Hos.   12: 5 God of hosts; the Lord is his *m*
Mat.   26:13 hath done, be told for a *m* of her
Acts   10: 4 alms are come up for a *m* before God

MENTION
Ps.   71:16 make *m* of thy righteousness
Eph.   1:16 making *m* of you in my prayers

MERCY
Ex.   34: 7 keeping *m* for thousands, forgiving
Num.   14:18 and of great *m*, forgiving iniquity
Deut.   7: 9 which keepeth covenant and *m*
Ps.   23: 6 goodness and *m* shall follow me
52: 8 I trust in the *m* of God
57: 3 God shall send forth his *m*
101: 1 I will sing of his *m*
103: 8 slow to anger and plenteous in *m*
103: 17 *m* of the Lord is from everlasting
107: 1 his *m* endureth forever
Prov.   16: 6 by *m* and truth iniquity is purged
20:28 *m* and truth preserve the king and
Hos.   6: 6 I desired *m* and not sacrifice
14: 3 in thee the fatherless findeth *m*
Mic.   6: 8 to do justly, and love *m*
7:18 because he delighteth in *m*
Luke   1:50 his *m* is on them that fear him
1:78 through the tender *m* of our God
Rom.   9:15 *m* on whom I will have *m*
11:31 through your *m* they obtain *m*
2 Cor.   4: 1 as we have received *m*
1 Tim.   1:13 I obtained *m* because I
Heb.   4:16 we may obtain *m* and
Jas.   2:13 shall have judgment without *m*
5:11 Lord is very pitiful and of tender *m*

MERCIES
1 Chr.   21:13 for very great are his *m*
Ps.   25: 6 thy tender *m* and thy lovingkindness
51: 1 the multitude of thy tender *m*
Rom.   12: 1 I beseech you by the *m* of God
2 Cor.   1: 3 Father of *m* and God of

Col.   3:12 put on bowels of *m*

MERCIFUL
Ex.   34: 6 Lord God *m* and gracious
2 Chr.   30: 9 God is *m* and gracious
Ps.   18:25 thou wilt show thyself *m*
117: 2 his *m* kindness is great toward us
Jer.   3:12 I am *m*, saith the Lord
Jonah   4: 2 thou a gracious God, and *m*
Mat.   5: 7 blessed are the *m*, for they shall
Luke   6:36 *m*, as your Father also
Heb.   2:17 a *m* and faithful high priest
8:12 I will be *m* to their unrighteousness

MIGHT
Deut.   6: 5 all thy soul, and with all thy *m*
2 Chr.   20:12 no *m* against this great company
Ps.   145: 6 speak of the *m* of thy terrible acts
Zech.   4: 6 not by *m*, nor by power, but
Eph.   3:16 strengthened with *m* by his Spirit
Col.   1:11 strengthened with all *m*, according

MIGHTY (MIGHTILY)
Deut.   10:17 a great God, a *m* and
Judg.   5:23 help of the Lord against the *m*
Ps.   24: 8 Lord strong and *m*, the Lord of
Jer.   32:19 great in counsel, *m* in work
19:20 so *m* grew the word of God
1 Cor.   1:26 many *m*, not many noble are called
Col.   1:29 which worketh in me *m*

MILK
Job   10:10 hast poured me out as *m*
Is.   55: 1 buy wine and *m* without
Joel   3:18 the hills shall flow with *m*
Heb.   5:12 such as have need of *m*
1 Pet.   2: 2 desire the sincere *m* of the word

MIND
Neh.   4: 6 people had a *m* to work
Is.   26: 3 whose *m* is stayed on thee
Luke   12:29 neither be ye of doubtful *m*
Acts   20:19 serving Lord with all humility of *m*
Rom.   8: 7 carnal *m* is enmity
11:34 who hath known the *m* of the Lord
1 Cor.   1:10 joined together in the same *m*
2:16 we have the *m* of Christ
2 Cor.   13:11 be of one *m*, live in peace
Phil.   2: 2 being of one accord, of one *m*
2 Tim.   1: 7 of love and of sound *m*
Tit.   1:15 their *m* and conscience is defiled
1 Pet.   3: 8 be ye all of one *m*

MINDS
2 Cor.   3:14 their *m* were blinded
Phil.   4: 7 keep your hearts and *m* through
Heb.   10:16 in their *m* will I write
2 Pet.   3: 1 stir up your pure *m* by

MINDED
Rom.   8: 6 to be carnally *m* is death

MINDFUL
Ps.   8: 4 man that thou art *m* of him?
111: 5 he will be ever *m* of his covenant

MINISTER (MINISTERS)
Ps.   103:21 *m* of his that do his pleasure
Mat.   20:26 among you, let him be your *m*
Luke   1: 2 eyewitnesses and *m* of
4:20 he gave it again to the *m*
Acts   26:16 to make thee a *m* and
Rom.   13: 6 they are God's *m*, attending
15: 8 Christ was the *m* of circumcision
15:16 *m* of Jesus Christ to the Gentiles
15:25 to *m* unto the saints
1 Cor.   4: 1 account of us as *m* of Christ
2 Cor.   3: 6 made us able *m* of the new testament
6: 4 approved ourselves as *m* of God
11:23 are they *m* of Christ?
Eph.   3: 7 was made a *m* according to the gift
Heb.   1: 7 his *m* a flame of fire
8: 2 *m* of the sanctuary, and of the
1 Pet.   4:11 if any man *m*, let him

MINISTERED (MINISTERING)
Mat.   4:11 angels came and *m* unto him
Gal.   3: 5 he that *m* to you the spirit
Heb.   1:14 all *m* spirits sent forth
6:10 ye have *m* to the saints

MINISTRATIONS
Luke   1:23 days of his *m* were accomplished

MINISTRY
Acts 6: 1 were neglected in the daily *m*
2 Cor. 9:13 the experiment of this *m* they glorify

MINISTRY
Acts 6: 4 to prayer and to the *m* of the word
2 Cor. 5:18 given to us the *m* of reconciliation
Col. 4:17 take heed to the *m* which thou hast
1 Tim. 1:12 faithful putting me into the *m*

MIRACLE (MIRACLES)
Mark 6:52 they considered not the *m*
9:39 shall do a *m* in my name
John 2:11 this beginning of *m* did Jesus in
11:47 this man doeth many *m*
Acts 2:22 by *m* and wonders and signs
19:11 special *m* by the hands of Paul
1 Cor. 12:10 to another the working of *m*
12:29 are all workers of *m*
Gal. 3: 5 worketh *m* among you, doeth he it

MISCHIEF
Ps. 10:23 *m* is in their hearts
36: 4 he deviseth *m* upon his bed
Prov. 10:23 sport to a fool to do *m*
24:16 wicked shall fall into *m*

MISERY
Job 3:20 to him that is in *m*
Prov. 31: 7 drink and remember his *m* no more
Eccl. 8: 6 the *m* of man is great
Rom. 3:16 destruction and *m* are in their ways

MISERABLE
1 Cor. 15:19 we are of all men most *m*
Rev. 3:17 thou art wretched and *m*

MOCK (MOCKED, MOCKETH)
1 Ki. 18:27 that Elijah *m* them, and said
Prov. 14: 9 fools make a *m* at sin
17: 5 whoso *m* the poor reproacheth his

MOCKER (MOCKERS)
Prov. 20: 1 wine is a *m*, strong drink
Jude 1:18 there should be *m* in the last

MOMENT
Ps. 30: 5 his anger endureth but a *m*
1 Cor. 15:52 in a *m*, in the twinkling

MONEY
Is. 55: 1 he that hath no *m*, come
Mic. 3:11 the prophets divine for *m*
Acts 8:20 thy *m* perish with thee because
1 Tim. 6:10 love of *m* is the root of

MORTAL
Rom. 6:12 let not sin reign in your *m* body
8:11 quicken your *m* bodies by his
1 Cor. 15:53 this *m* must put on immortality

MOTH
Ps. 39:11 beauty to consume away like a *m*
Is. 50: 9 the *m* shall eat them up
Mat. 6:20 where neither *m* nor rust doth corrupt
Luke 12:33 thief approacheth, neither *m* corrupteth

MOTHER (MOTHER'S)
Gen. 3:20 she was the *m* of all living
Ps. 27:10 when father and *m* forsake me
71: 6 out of my *m* bowels
139: 13 covered me in my *m* womb
Mat. 12:49 behold my *m* and my brethren

MOVE (MOVED)
Ps. 15: 5 doeth these things shall never be *m*
46: 5 she shall not be *m*: God shall help
121: 3 will not suffer thy foot to be *m*
Prov. 12: 3 the righteous shall not be *m*
Acts 17:28 in him we live and *m*
Col. 1:23 be not *m* away from hope
Heb. 12:28 kingdom which cannot be *m*

MOURN (MOURNED)
Is. 61: 2 to comfort all that *m*
Mat. 5: 4 blessed are they that *m*
11:17 we have *m* unto you
1 Cor. 5: 2 and have not rather *m*
Jas. 4: 9 be afflicted and *m* and

MOURNING
Ps. 30:11 for me my *m* into dancing
Is. 61: 3 the oil of joy for *m*, the garment
Jer. 31:13 I will turn their *m* into joy
Joel 2:12 with fasting and with weeping and with *m*
Jas. 4: 9 laughter be turned to *m*

MOUTH
Ps. 8: 2 out of the *m* of babes
37:30 *m* of righteous speaketh wisdom
103: 5 who satisfieth thy *m* with good
Prov. 10:31 *m* of the just bringeth forth wisdom
18: 7 a fool's *m* is his destruction
Lam. 3:29 putteth his *m* in dust
Mat. 12:34 out of abundance of heart the *m* speaketh
21:16 out of the *m* of babes
Luke 21:15 will give you a *m* and
Rom. 10:10 with the *m* confession is made

MULTITUDE
Ps. 5: 7 in the *m* of thy mercy
51: 1 unto the *m* of thy tender mercies
94:19 in the *m* of my thoughts
106: 45 to the *m* of his mercies
Prov. 15:22 in the *m* of counsellors
24: 6 in *m* of counsellors there is
Eccl. 5: 3 voice is known by *m* of words
Jas. 5:20 hide a *m* of sins
1 Pet. 4: 8 cover the *m* of sins

MURDER (MURDERS)
Mat. 15:19 proceed evil thoughts, *m*
Rom. 1:29 full of envy, *m*, debate
Gal. 5:21 envyings, *m*, drunkenness
Rev. 9:21 repented they of their *m*

MURDERER
Job 24:14 *m* rising with the light killeth
Hos. 9:13 forth his children to the *m*
John 8:44 was a *m* from the beginning
1 Pet. 4:15 none suffer as a *m*, or

MYSTERY (MYSTERIES)
Mark 4:11 know the *m* of the kingdom
Rom. 11:25 ye should be ignorant of this *m*
16:25 according to revelation of the *m*
1 Cor. 2: 7 wisdom of God in a *m*, even the
13: 2 prophecy and understand all *m*
Eph. 1: 9 made known the *m* of
3: 4 my knowledge in the *m* of Christ
6:19 make known the *m* of the gospel
Col. 1:26 *m* which hath been hid
4: 3 to speak the *m* of Christ
2 Thes. 2: 7 *m* of iniquity doth already work
1 Tim. 3: 9 holding the *m* of the faith
Rev. 10: 7 *m* of God should be finished

NAKED
Gen. 2:25 they were both *n*, the
3: 7 knew that they were *n*
Ex. 32:25 when Moses saw the people were *n*
Job 1:21 *n* came I out of my mother's womb
Mat. 25:36 *n* and ye clothed me: I was
1 Cor. 4:11 hunger and thirst and are *n*
2 Cor. 5: 3 clothed we shall not be found *n*
Rev. 16:15 keepeth his garments, lest he walk *n*

NAME (NAME'S)
Ex. 34:14 whose *n* is Jealous, is a jealous
Ps. 8: 1 how excellent is thy *n* in all
72:17 his *n* shall endure for ever
106: 8 he saved them for his *n* sake
138: 2 praise thy *n* for thy lovingkindness
Prov. 22: 1 a good *n* is rather to be chosen
Eccl. 7: 1 good *n* better than precious ointment
Is. 9: 6 his *n* shall be called Wonderful
55:13 shall be to the Lord for a *n*
62: 2 thou shalt be called by a new *n*
Jer. 32:20 made thee a *n* as at this day
Mal. 1:14 my *n* is dreadful among the
Mat. 10:22 hated of all for my *n* sake
10:41 receive prophet in the *n* of
Luke 6:22 cast out your *n* as evil
John 14:13 ask in my *n*, that will I do
15:16 ask of the father in my *n*
16:24 asked nothing in my *n*
20:31 ye might have life through his *n*
Acts 9:15 a chosen vessel to bear my *n*
Eph. 1:21 every *n* that is named
Phil. 2: 9 a *n* above every *n*
Col. 3:17 do all in the *n* of the Lord
1 Pet. 4:14 reproached for the *n* of Christ
1 John 3:23 believe on the *n* of the Son
Rev. 2:17 new *n* written, which no man
3: 8 and hast not denied my *n*

3:12 write on him the *n* of my God
14: 1 his Father's *n* written in their

NAMES
Luke 10:20 your *n* are written in heaven
Rev. 3: 4 hast a few *n* in Sardis which have

NARROW
Prov. 23:27 strange woman is a *n* pit
Mat. 7:14 and *n* is the way which leadeth

NATION (NATIONS)
Gen. 17: 6 I will make *n* of thee and kings
Ex. 19: 6 priests, and an holy *n*
Ps. 9:20 *n* may know themselves to be but
33:12 *n* whose God is the Lord
Is. 2: 4 *n* shall not lift the sword against *n*
40:17 *n* before him are as nothing
55: 5 *n* that knew thee not shall
Mat. 25:32 before him be gathered all *n*
Luke 7: 5 he loveth our *n* and he hath built
Acts 10:35 in every *n* he that feareth
14:16 suffered all *n* to walk
Rom. 10:19 by a foolish *n* I will
Phil. 2:15 midst of a crooked and perverse *n*
1 Pet. 2: 9 ye are an holy *n*, a peculiar people
Rev. 5: 9 kindred and tongue, and people and *n*
21:24 *n* of them that are saved

NATURAL (NATURALLY)
1 Cor. 2:14 the *n* man receiveth not
2 Tim. 3: 3 without *n* affection, trucebreakers
Jas. 1:23 beholding his *n* face in a glass

NATURE
1 Cor. 11:14 doth not even *n* itself teach
Gal. 4: 8 them which by *n* are no gods
Eph. 2: 3 by *n* the children of wrath
Heb. 2:16 on him the *n* of angels
Jas. 3: 6 setteth on fire the course of *n*
2 Pet. 1: 4 might be partakers of the divine *n*

NEED (NEEDETH)
Mat. 6:32 ye have of all these things
Heb. 4:16 grace to help in time of *n*
Rev. 22: 5 and they *n* no candle

NEEDFUL
Luke 10:42 one thing is *n*, and Mary hath

NEEDY
Ps. 9:18 *n* shall not always be forgotten
72:12 he shall deliver the *n*
113: 7 lifteth the *n* out of the dunghill

NEGLECT
1 Tim. 4:14 *n* not the gift that is in thee
Heb. 2: 3 if we *n* so great a salvation

NEIGHBOUR
Ex. 20:16 not bear false witness against thy *n*
Lev. 19:18 shalt love thy *n* as thyself
Ps. 15: 3 nor doeth evil to his *n*
Prov. 27:10 better is a *n* that is near
Jer. 31:34 teach no more every man his *n*
Mat. 19:19 love thy *n* as thyself
Luke 10:29 Jesus, and who is my *n*
Rom. 13: 9 love thy *n* as thyself
15: 2 let every one of us please his *n*
Jas. 2: 8 love thy *n* as thyself

NEST (NESTS)
Ps. 84: 3 the swallow a *n* for herself
Hab. 2: 9 set his *n* on high, that
Mat. 8:20 birds of the air have *n*

NET (NETS)
Ps. 31: 4 Pull me out of the *n*
Hab. 1:16 they sacrifice unto their *n*
Mat. 13:47 heaven is like unto a *n*

NEW
Ps. 33: 3 sing unto him a *n* song
Eccl. 1: 9 there is no *n* thing under the sun
Is. 42:10 sing unto the Lord a *n* song
62: 2 be called by a *n* name
65:17 *n* heavens and a *n* earth
Jer. 31:22 created a *n* thing in the earth
Ezek. 11:19 put a *n* spirit within you
36:26 a *n* heart also will I give
Mat. 9:16 putteth *n* cloth unto an old garment
John 13:34 a *n* commandment I give unto you
1 Cor. 5: 7 that ye may be a *n* lump
2 Cor. 5:17 *n* creature; behold, all things are become *n*

Gal.   6:15 nor uncircumcision, but a *n* creature
Eph.   4:24 put on the *n* man
Col.   3:10 put on the *n* man
2 Pet.   3:13 *n* heavens and a *n*
1 John   2: 8 a *n* commandment I write unto you
Rev.   2:17 a *n* name written
         5: 9 they sung a *n* song
        21: 1 a *n* heaven and a *n*

NEWNESS
Rom.   6: 4 should walk in the *n* of life
         7: 6 should serve in the *n* of spirit

NIGH
Ps.   34:18 Lord is *n* unto them that are
       145:18 Lord is *n* them that call on
Rom.   10: 8 the word is *n* thee
Eph.   2:13 made *n* by the blood of Christ

NIGHT
Gen.   1: 5 and the darkness he called *n*
Ps.   19: 2 *n* unto *n* showeth knowledge
        30: 5 weeping may endure for a *n*
        42: 8 in the *n* his song shall be
        77: 6 I call to remembrance my song in the *n*
       134: 1 which by *n* stand in the house
Is.   30:29 ye shall have a song as in the *n*
        59:10 stumble at noonday as in the *n*
Luke   12:20 this *n* thy soul shall be required
John   3: 2 the same came to Jesus by *n*
         9: 4 *n* cometh when no man can work
        11:10 if a man walk in the *n* he stumbleth
Rom.   13:12 *n* is far spent; the day is at hand
1 Thes. 5: 7 sleep in the *n* and they
Rev.   21:25 shall be no *n* there

NOTHING
Luke   1:37 with God *n* shall be impossible
John   15: 5 without me ye can do *n*
1 Cor. 13: 2 and have not charity, I am *n*
2 Cor.   6:10 having *n* yet possessing all
1 Tim.   6: 7 we brought in *n* into world

NUMBER (NUMBERED, NUMBEREST, NUMBERS)
Job   14:16 for now thou *n* my steps
Ps.   90:12 teach us to *n* our days
Is.   53:12 *n* with the transgressors, and he
Rev.   7: 9 multitude no man could *n*

NURSE (NURSING)
Is.   49:23 *n* fathers and their queens *n* mothers
1 Thes. 2: 7 a *n* cherisheth her children

OBEY (OBEYED)
Deut.   11:27 blessing if ye *o*
Josh.   24:24 his voice will we *o*
1 Sam.15:22 to *o* is better than sacrifice
Acts   5:29 ought to *o* God rather than men
Rom.   2: 8 contentious, and do not *o* truth
Eph.   6: 1 children, *o* your parents in the Lord
Col.   3:20 Children, *o* your parents in all things
2 Thes. 3:14 if any man *o* not our word
Tit.   3: 1 to *o* magistrates, to be ready to
Heb.   5: 9 salvation to all them that *o*
1 Pet.   3: 1 if any *o* not the word

OBEDIENCE
Rom.   5:19 by the *o* of one shall many be
        16:26 to all nations for the *o* of faith
1 Cor. 14:34 they are commanded to be under *o*
2 Cor.   7:15 he remembereth the *o* of you
        10: 5 every thought to the *o* of Christ
Heb.   5: 8 learned *o* by things suffered
1 Pet.   1: 2 sanctification of the Spirit to *o*

OBEDIENT
Deut.   8:20 perish; because ye would not be *o*
Rom.   15:18 to make Gentiles *o* by word
2 Cor.   2: 9 whether ye be *o* in all
Eph.   6: 5 servants, be *o* to them
Phil.   2: 8 he became *o* unto death
Tit.   2: 9 exhort servants to be *o*

OBSERVE (OBSERVED)
Ex.   12:42 it is a night to be much *o*
Jonah   2: 8 they that *o* lying vanities
Mat.   28:20 teaching them to *o* all things
Mark   6:20 man and an holy, and *o* him
        10:20 all these I *o* from my youth
Gal.   4:10 ye *o* days and months and times

OBTAIN (OBTAINED)
Prov.   8:35 and shall *o* favour of the Lord

Is.   35:10 they shall *o* joy and gladness, and
Hos.   2:23 her that had not *o* mercy
1 Cor.   9:24 so run, that ye may *o*
Eph.   1:11 whom also we have *o* an inheritance
1 Tim.   1:13 but I *o* mercy, because
Heb.   1: 4 inheritance *o* a more excellent name
         4:16 we may *o* mercy and find grace
         9:12 *o* eternal redemption for us
        11:35 they might *o* a better resurrection
Jas.   4: 2 ye desire to have, and cannot *o*

OFFENCE (OFFENCES)
Is.   8:14 rock of *o* to both the houses of Israel
Acts   24:16 conscience void of *o*
Rom.   4:25 who was delivered for our *o* and
         5:17 by one man's *o* death reigned
         9:33 a stumblingstone and rock of *o*
2 Cor.   6: 3 giving no *o* in any thing
Gal.   5:11 then is the *o* of the cross ceased
Phil.   1:10 without *o* till the day of Christ
1 Pet.   2: 8 and a rock of *o*, even to them

OFFEND (OFFENDED)
Prov.   18:19 a brother *o* is harder to be won
Mat.   5:29 if thy right eye *o* thee
        11: 6 whosoever shall not be *o* in me
        17:27 yet lest we should *o* them, go
        18: 6 should *o* one of these little ones
        26:33 yet will I never be *o*
Mark   4:17 immediately they are *o*
         9:43 if thy hand *o* thee, cut
Rom.   14:21 thy brother stumbleth or is *o*
Jas.   2:10 yet *o* in one point he is guilty
         3: 2 in many things we *o*

OFFER (OFFERED)
Mat.   5:24 then come and *o* thy gift
2 Tim.   4: 6 I am now ready to be *o*, and the time
Heb.   9:14 Spirit *o* himself without spot to God
         9:28 Christ was once *o* to bear sins
        11: 4 by faith Abel *o* unto God a more
        13:15 let us *o* the sacrifice of praise

OFFERING
Eph.   5: 2 an *o* and a sacrifice to God
Heb.   10: 5 sacrifice and *o* thou wouldest not
        10:14 by one *o* he hath perfected for ever

OIL
Ps.   45: 7 anointed thee with the *o* of gladness
Is.   61: 3 *o* of joy for mourning, the garment
Mic.   6: 7 with ten thousands of rivers of *o*
Mat.   25: 3 and took no *o* with
Luke   7:46 head with *o* didst not anoint
        10:34 pouring in *o* and wine, and set him
Heb.   1: 9 anointed thee with the *o* of gladness

OINTMENT (OINTMENTS)
Ps.   133: 2 it is like precious *o* upon the head
Eccl.   7: 1 good name is better than precious *o*
Mat.   26:12 she hath poured this *o* on my body
Luke   7:37 brought an alabaster box of *o*
John   12: 5 why was not this *o* sold

OLD
Ps.   71: 9 me not off in the time of *o* age
        92:14 still bring forth fruit in *o* age
Prov.   22: 6 when he is *o* he will not depart from
Jer.   6:16 ask for the *o* paths
Rom.   6: 6 our *o* man is crucified
1 Cor.   5: 7 purge out the *o* leaven
2 Cor.   5:17 *o* things are passed away
Eph.   4:22 the former conversation the *o* man
Col.   3: 9 ye have put off the *o* man

OMEGA
Rev.   1: 8 I am the Alpha and the *O*
        21: 6 Alpha and *O*, the beginning and the end
        22:13 Alpha and *O*, the beginning and the end

ONE
Gen.   2:24 they shall be *o* flesh
Eccl.   4: 9 two are better than *o*
Mat.   19: 5 and they twain shall be *o* flesh
John   10:30 I and my Father are *o*
1 Cor.   8: 4 there is none other God but *o*
        10:17 we being many are *o* bread and *o* body
Gal.   3:20 not mediator of *o*, but God is *o*
1 John   5: 7 and these three are *o*

OPEN (OPENED, OPENEST)
Gen.   3: 7 eyes of them both were *o*

Ps.   51:15 O Lord, *o* thou my lips: and my
       145:16 thou *o* thine hand, and
Is.   35: 5 eyes of the blind shall be *o*
        42: 7 to *o* the blind eyes, to bring out
        53: 7 yet he *o* not his mouth
Mat.   7: 7 knock, and it shall be *o*
        25:11 saying, Lord, Lord, *o* to us
Acts   14:27 the door of faith to the Gentiles
1 Cor. 16: 9 great door and effectual is *o*
Col.   4: 3 *o* to us a door of utterance
Rev.   5: 2 who is worthy to *o* the book

OPPORTUNITY
Mat.   26:16 he sought *o* to betray
Gal.   6:10 as we have therefore, let us do
Phil.   4:10 were also careful, but ye lacked *o*

OPPRESS (OPPRESSED)
Ps.   9: 9 Lord also will be a refuge for the *o*
Prov.   22:22 neither *o* the afflicted in the gate
Is.   1:17 relieve the *o*, judge the fatherless
Zech.   7:10 *o* not the widow, nor the fatherless
Mal.   3: 5 witness against those that *o*
Acts   10:38 healing all that were *o* of the devil
Jas.   2: 6 do not rich men *o*

OPPRESSION (OPPRESSIONS)
Ps.   12: 5 for the *o* of the poor
Eccl.   4: 1. considered all the *o* that are done

OPPRESSOR (OPPRESSORS)
Ps.   54: 3 and *o* seek after my soul
        72: 4 shall break in pieces the *o*
Prov.   3:31 envy thou not the *o*
Is.   3:12 children are their *o*
        51:13 because of the fury of the *o*

ORACLES
Acts   7:38 who received the lively *o* to give
Rom.   3: 2 unto them were committed the *o* of
1 Pet.   4:11 let him speak as the *o* of God

ORDAIN (ORDAINED)
Ps.   8: 2 hast thou *o* strength because of
Is.   26:12 Lord, thou wilt *o* peace for us
Acts   13:48 as many as were *o* to eternal life
Rom.   7:10 the commandment which was *o* to life
        13: 1 powers that be are *o* of God
Eph.   2:10 God hath before *o* that we should
1 Tim.   2: 7 *o* a preacher and an apostle
Tit.   1: 5 and *o* elders in every city
Heb.   5: 1 *o* for men in things pertaining to
Jude   4 before of old *o* to this condemnation

OUTSTRETCHED
Deut.   26: 8 and with an *o* arm and with
Jer.   27: 5 my great power and by my *o* arm

OUTWARD (OUTWARDLY)
1 Sam.16: 7 man looketh on the *o* appearance
Mat.   23:28 even so ye also *o* appear righteous
Rom.   2:28 not a Jew, which is one *o*
2 Cor.   4:16 though our *o* man perish

OVERCOME (OVERCOMETH)
John   16:33 good cheer, I have *o* the world
1 John   2:13 ye have *o* the wicked one
         5: 4 born of God *o* the world
Rev.   2: 7 to him that *o* I will give
         3:12 him that *o* will I make a pillar
         3:21 him that *o* will I grant
        17:14 the Lamb shall *o* them: for he is

OVERSEER (OVERSEERS)
Prov.   6: 7 which having no guide, *o*, or ruler
Acts   20:28 the Holy Ghost hath made you *o*

OVERTHROW (OVERTHROWETH, OVERTHROWN)
Ps.   140:11 hunt the violent man to *o* him
Prov.   13: 6 but wickedness *o* the sinner
Acts   5:39 be of God, ye cannot *o*

OWE (OWED)
Mat.   18:24 which *o* him ten thousand talents
Rom.   13: 8 *o* no man anything, but to love

OWN
John   1:11 his *o* and his *o* received him not
1 Cor.   6:19 and ye are not your *o*
        10:24 let no man seek his *o*
Phil.   2: 4 look not every man on his *o* things

OX (OXEN)
Prov.   7:22 as an *o* goeth to the slaughter
Mat.   22: 4 my *o* and my fatlings are killed
Luke   14:19 I have bought five yoke of *o*

John 2:14 in the temple those that sold *o*
1 Cor. 9: 9 doth God take care for *o*

PAIN (PAINS)
Is. 66: 7 before her *p* came, she was delivered
Jer. 6:24 and *p*, as of a woman in travail
Acts 2:24 loosed the *p* of death
Rev. 21: 4 neither shall there be any more *p*

PARABLE (PARABLES)
Ps. 49: 4 incline mine ear to a *p*
Prov. 26: 9 is a *p* in the mouth of fools
Mat. 13: 3 spake many things unto them in *p*
Luke 5:36 spake also a *p* unto them; no man
13: 6 he spake also this *p*; a certain man

PARADISE
Luke 23:43 today shalt thou be with me in *p*
2 Cor. 12: 4 he was caught up into *p*

PARDON (PARDONED, PARDONETH)
Ex. 34: 9 *p* our iniquity, and our
Neh. 9:17 thou art a God ready to *p*
Job 7:21 why dost thou not *p* my transgression
Ps. 25:11 thy name's sake O Lord *p* my iniquity
Is. 40: 2 that her iniquity is *p*
55: 7 to our God, for he will abundantly *p*
Mic. 7:18 who is God like unto thee that *p*

PARENTS
Mat. 10:21 children rise up against their *p*
Luke 18:29 no man hath left house, or *p*
21:16 ye shall be betrayed both by *p*
Rom. 1:30 of evil things, disobedient to *p*
2 Cor. 12:14 the *p* but the *p* for the children
1 Tim. 5: 4 to requite their *p*: for
2 Tim. 3: 2 disobedient to *p*, unthankful, unholy

PART
Luke 10:42 Mary hath chosen that good *p*
1 Cor. 13: 9 know in *p* and we prophesy in *p*

PARTAKER (PARTAKERS)
Ps. 50:18 thou hast been *p* with adulterers
1 Cor. 9:10 in hope should be *p* of his hope
10:17 we are all *p* of that one bread
10:30 if I by grace be a *p* why am I
Eph. 5: 7 be ye not therefore *p* with them
1 Tim. 5:22 be not *p* of other men's sins
Heb. 3:14 for we are made *p* of Christ
6: 4 and were made *p* of the Holy Ghost
12:10 might be *p* of his holiness
1 Pet. 5: 1 a *p* of the glory that shall be revealed

PASS (PASSED, PASSETH)
Is. 43: 2 when thou *p* through the waters
Mark 14:35 the hour might *p* from him
Luke 16:17 easier for heaven and earth to *p*
1 Cor. 7:31 fashion of this world *p* away
Phil. 4: 7 peace of God *p* all understanding
1 John 2:17 world *p* away and the lust thereof

PASSOVER
Ex. 12:11 it is the Lord's *p*
Deut. 16: 2 therefore sacrifice the *p* unto the Lord
1 Cor. 5: 7 Christ our *p* is sacrificed

PASTOR (PASTORS)
Jer. 3:15 I will give you *p* according
Eph. 4:11 and some, *p* and teachers

PASTURE (PASTURES)
Ps. 23: 2 maketh me to lie down in green *p*
95: 7 we are the people of his *p*
100: 3 his people and the sheep of his *p*
John 10: 9 shall go in and out, and find *p*

PATH (PATHS)
Ps. 16:11 wilt show me the *p* of life
119: 35 go in the *p* of thy commandments
Prov. 3:17 all her *p* are peace
Is. 59: 8 they have made them crooked *p*
Mat. 3: 3 way of the Lord make his *p* straight
Heb. 12:13 make straight *p* for your feet

PATIENCE
Mat. 18:29 have *p* with me, and I will pray
Luke 8:15 bring forth fruit with *p*
Rom. 5: 3 knowing that tribulation worketh *p*
15: 5 now the God of *p* and consolation
Col. 1:11 unto all *p* and longsuffering
2 Thes. 1: 4 for your *p* and faith in
1 Tim. 6:11 godliness, faith, love *p* meekness
Tit. 2: 2 sound in faith, in charity, in *p*
Heb. 6:12 through faith and *p* inherit the promises

10:36 have need of *p*, that after ye have
12: 1 run with *p* the race that is set before us
Jas. 1: 3 trying of your faith worketh *p*
2 Pet. 1: 6 and to temperance *p*, and to *p*
Rev. 1: 9 in the kingdom and *p* of Jesus
13:10 here is the *p* of saints

PATIENT
Rom. 2: 7 by *p* continuance in well doing
12:12 *p* in tribulation, instant in
1 Tim. 3: 3 not greedy of filthy lucre, but *p*
2 Tim. 2:24 gentle unto all men, apt to teach, *p*
Jas. 5: 7 *p* therefore, brethren, unto the coming of the

PATIENTLY
Ps. 37: 7 in the Lord, and wait *p* for him
40: 1 I waited *p* for the Lord
1 Pet. 2:20 for your faults, ye shall take it *p*

PEACE
Num. 6:26 countenance upon thee, and give thee *p*
Ps. 34:14 do good; seek *p* and pursue it
85: 8 he will speak *p* unto his people
122: 6 pray for the *p* of Jerusalem
Prov. 16: 7 his enemies to be at *p* with him
Is. 9: 6 everlasting Father, Prince of *P*
26: 3 thou wilt keep him in perfect *p*
45: 7 I make *p* and create evil
48:18 had thy *p* been as a river
66:12 extend *p* to her like a river
Jer. 6:14 saying, *p*, when there is no *p*
29: 7 seek the *p* of the city
Mat. 10:34 I came not to send *p* but a sword
Luke 2:14 on earth *p*, good will towards
2:29 lettest thou thy servant depart in *p*
John 14:27 *p* I leave with you; my *p* I give
16:33 that in me ye might have *p*
Rom. 5: 1 we have *p* with God through Jesus Christ
14:17 righteousness, and *p* and joy in the
1 Cor. 7:15 God hath called us to *p*
2 Cor. 13:11 live in *p*, and the God
Gal. 5:22 fruit of the Spirit is love, joy, *p*
Eph. 2:14 he is our *p*, who hath made both
Phil. 4: 7 the *p* of God, which passeth all
1 Thes. 5:13 and be at *p* among yourselves
Heb. 12:14 follow *p* with all men and holiness
Jas. 3:18 fruit of righteousness is sown in *p*
1 Pet. 3:11 let him seek *p* and ensue
2 Pet. 3:14 ye may be found of him in *p*

PEACEABLE (PEACEABLY)
Rom. 12:18 lieth in you live *p* with all men
1 Tim. 2: 2 that we may lead a quiet and *p* life
Jas. 3:17 from above is first pure, then *p*

PEARL (PEARLS)
Mat. 7: 6 cast not *p* before swine
13:46 found one *p* of great price

PECULIAR
Ex. 19: 5 ye shall be a *p* treasure unto me
Deut. 14: 2 chosen thee to be a *p* people
Tit. 2:14 purify unto himself a *p* people
1 Pet. 2: 9 an holy nation, a *p* people

PEOPLE
Ps. 100: 3 we are his *p* and the sheep of his
144: 15 happy is that *p* whose God
Is. 1: 4 a *p* laden with iniquity, a seed of
27:11 a *p* of no understanding
Jer. 31:33 their God, and they shall be my *p*
Ezek. 36:28 and ye shall be my *p*, and I will
Hos. 1: 9 Lo-ammi: for ye are not my *p*
Mat. 1:21 Jesus shall save his *p* from their sins
2 Cor. 6:16 their God and they shall be my *p*
Heb. 4: 9 remaineth a rest to the *p* of God
1 Pet. 2:10 now the *p* of God

PERDITION
John 17:12 is lost but the son of *p*
Phil. 1:28 to them an evident token of *p*
2 Thes. 2: 3 be revealed, the son of *p*
2 Pet. 3: 7 judgment and *p* of ungodly men

PERFECT
Job 1: 1 and that man was *p* and upright
Ps. 19: 7 law of the Lord is *p*
Mat. 5:48 *p* even as your Father which is in
19:21 if thou wilt be *p* go and sell
1 Cor. 2: 6 among them that are *p*
2 Cor. 12: 9 my strength is made *p* in weakness

Eph. 4:13 a *p* man, unto the measure of
Col. 1:28 present every man *p* in Christ
4:12 may stand *p* and complete
2 Tim. 3:17 man of God may be *p*
Heb. 2:10 make the captain of their salvation *p*
13:21 make you *p* in every good work
Jas. 1: 4 let patience have her *p* work
1:17 good gift and every *p* gift is from above
1 John 4:18 *p* love casteth out fear
Rev. 3: 2 I have not found thy works *p*

PERFECTION
Luke 8:14 bring no fruit to *p*
2 Cor. 13: 9 this also we wish, even your *p*
Heb. 6: 1 let us go on unto *p*

PERISH (PERISHED)
Esth. 4:16 if I *p*, I *p*
Prov. 29:18 there is no vision, the people *p*
Mat. 8:25 him, saying Lord, save us, we *p*
John 3:15 believeth in him should not *p*
3:16 should not *p* but have everlasting life
1 Cor. 8:11 the weak *p* for whom Christ died
2 Pet. 3: 9 not willing that any *p*

PERSECUTE (PERSECUTED, PERSECUTEST)
Job 19:22 why *p* me as God
Ps. 10: 2 wicked in his pride doth *p* the poor
109: 16 *p* the poor and needy man
Mat. 5:11 when men shall revile you and *p* you
5:44 despitefully use you and *p* you
10:23 when they *p* you in this city
John 15:20 they *p* me they will persecute you
Acts 9: 4 Saul, Saul, why *p* thou me?
Rom. 12:14 bless them which *p* you: bless and
1 Cor. 4:12 we bless; being *p* we suffer it
15: 9 because I *p* the church of God
2 Cor. 4: 9 *p* but not forsaken
Gal. 1:13 I *p* the church of God
4:29 *p* him born after the Spirit

PERSON (PERSONS)
Deut. 10:17 which regardeth not *p*, nor taketh
Mat. 22:16 thou regardest not the *p* of men
Acts 10:34 God is no respecter of *p*
Gal. 2: 6 God accepteth no man's *p*
Eph. 6: 9 neither is there respect of *p* with him
Col. 3:25 and there is no respect of *p*
Heb. 1: 3 and the express image of his *p*
1 Pet. 1:17 who without respect of *p* judgeth

PERSUADE (PERSUADED)
Acts 21:14 when he would not be *p*
Rom. 8:38 I am *p* that neither death
2 Cor. 5:11 we *p* men, but we are made manifest
Gal. 1:10 do I *p* men, or God

PERVERSE
Deut. 32: 5 they are a *p* and crooked generation
Prov. 17:20 he that hath a *p* tongue falleth
Mat. 17:17 O faithless and *p* generation
Phil. 2:15 in the midst of a crooked and *p* nation
1 Tim. 6: 5 *p* disputings of men or corrupt minds

PESTILENCE (PESTILENCES)
2 Sam. 24:15 so the Lord sent a *p* upon Israel
Ps. 78:50 but gave their life over to the *p*
Amos 4:10 I have sent among you the *p*
Mat. 24: 7 there shall be famines, and *p*

PHYSICIAN
Job 13: 4 ye are all *p* of no value
Jer. 8:22 is there no *p* there
Mat. 9:12 that be whole need not a *p*
Luke 4:23 say unto me, *P* heal thyself

PIERCE (PIERCED, PIERCING)
Ps. 22:16 they *p* my hands and my feet
Luke 2:35 sword shall *p* through
1 Tim. 6:10 *p* themselves through with many sorrows
Heb. 4:12 even to the dividing asunder of
Rev. 1: 7 they also which *p* him

PILGRIMS
Heb. 11:13 were strangers and *p* on the earth
1 Pet. 2:11 I beseech you as strangers and *p*

PILLAR (PILLARS)
Gen. 19:26 she became a *p* of salt
Ex. 13:21 by day in a *p* of cloud
Num. 14:14 and in a *p* of fire by night
Job 26:11 the *p* of heaven tremble

Ps.　　99:　7 spake unto them in the cloudy *p*
1 Tim.　3:15 God the *p* and ground of the truth

PIT
Gen.　37:20 cast him into some *p*
Job　　33:24 deliver him from going down to the *p*
Ps.　　28:　1 like them that go down to the *p*
　　　143:　7 unto them that go down into the *p*
Is.　　38:17 it from the *p* of corruption
Rev.　　20:　1 having the key of the bottomless *p*

PITIETH
Ps.　　103:13 *p* his children, so the Lord *p*

PITIFUL
Jas.　　5:11 that the Lord is very *p*
1 Pet.　3:　8 as brethren be *p*, be courteous

PITY
Job　　6:14 *p* should be shown from his friend
Is.　　63:　9 in his *p* he redeemed them
Mat.　18:33 as I had *p* on thee

PLACE (PLACES)
Ex.　　3:　5 the *p* whereon thou standest is holy
Ps.　　6:　1 lines fallen unto me in pleasant *p*
　　　32:　7 thou art my hiding *p*; thou shalt
　　　90:　1 Lord, thou hast been our dwelling *p*
Prov.　15:　3 eyes of the Lord are in every *p*
Is.　　40:　4 and the rough *p* plain
John　8:37 my word hath no *p* in you
1 Cor.　4:11 and have no certain dwelling *p*
Eph.　　1:　3 all spiritual blessings in heavenly *p*
　　　3:10 principalities and powers in heavenly *p*
　　　6:12 against spiritual wickedness in high *p*

PLANT (PLANTED, PLANTETH, PLANTS)
Ps.　　1:　3 a tree *p* by the rivers
　　　92:13 *p* in the house of the Lord
　　　128:　3 thy children like olive *p* around
Jer.　　18:　9 kingdom, to build it and to *p* it
　　　24:　6 *p* them and not pluck
Mat.　15:13 my heavenly Father hath not *p*
　　　21:33 *p* a vineyard and hedged it
Rom.　6:　5 we have been *p* together
1 Cor.　3:　6 I have *p*, Apollos watered

PLEAD
Job　　13:19 who will *p* with me
　　　16:21 might *p* for man with God
Is.　　1:17 the fatherless; *p* for the widow
　　　43:26 let us *p* together: declare thou
Jer.　　2:29 wherefore will ye *p* with me
Hos.　　2:　2 *p* with your mother, *p*

PLEASE
Ps.　　69:31 this also shall *p* the Lord
Prov.　16:　7 when man's ways *p* the Lord
Rom.　8:　8 that are in flesh cannot *p* God
　　　15:　2 let every one of us *p* his neighbour
1 Cor.　7:32 how he may *p* the Lord
　　　10:33 I *p* men in all things
Gal.　　1:10 do I seek to *p* men
1 Thes.　4:　1 how ye ought to walk, and to *p* him
Heb.　　11:　6 without faith it is impossible to *p*

PLEASED (PLEASETH, PLEASING)
Eccl.　7:26 whoso *p* God shall escape
Is.　　53:10 it *p* the Lord to bruise him
Mic.　　6:　7 will the Lord be *p* with thousands
Mat.　　3:17 Son, in whom I am well *p*
　　　17:　5 in whom I am well *p*, hear ye him
Rom.　15:　3 for even Christ *p* not himself
Col.　　1:10 worthy of the Lord unto all *p*
1 Thes.　2:　4 not as *p* men, but God
Heb.　　11:　5 he had this testimony, that he *p* God
　　　13:16 with such sacrifices God is well *p*
1 John　3:22 do things *p* in his sight

PLEASANT
Gen.　　2:　9 every tree that is *p* to the sight
Ps.　　16:　6 lines fallen to me in *p* places
　　　133:　1 how *p* for brethren to dwell
Prov.　9:17 bread eaten in secret is *p*

PLEASURE
Ps.　　5:　4 not a God that hath *p* in
　　　51:18 do good in thy good *p* unto Zion
　　　103:21 ministers of his that do his *p*
　　　147:11 Lord taketh *p* in them
Prov.　21:17 he that loveth *p* shall be poor
Eccl.　　5:　4 for he hath no *p* in fools
Is.　　53:10 the *p* of the Lord shall prosper in

Ezek.　18:32 no *p* in the death of him that dieth
Mal.　　1:10 I have no *p* in you, saith the Lord
Luke　12:32 it is your Father's good *p*
2 Cor.　12:10 I take *p* in infirmities
Eph.　　1:　5 according to the good *p* of
2 Thes.　1:11 fulfil all good *p* of his
Heb.　10:38 my soul shall have no *p*
Rev.　　4:11 for thy *p* they are and were created

PLEASURES
Ps.　　16:11 at thy right hand *p* for evermore
2 Tim.　3:　4 lovers of *p* more than lovers of God
Tit.　　3:　3 serving divers lusts and *p*
Heb.　11:25 to enjoy the *p* of sin

PLENTEOUS
Ps.　103:　8 slow to anger, and *p* in mercy
　　　130:　7 with him is *p* redemption
Mat.　　9:37 harvest is *p*, but the labourers

PLOUGH (PLOW, PLOWED, PLOWETH)
Ps.　129:　3 the plowers *p* on my back: they made
Jer.　26:18 Zion shall be *p* like a field
Hos.　10:13 ye have *p* wickedness, ye have
Luke　9:62 having put his hand to the *p*
1 Cor.　9:10 he that *p* should *p* in hope

PLOWMAN
Is.　　61:　5 shall be your *p* and your vinedressers
Amos　9:13 the *p* shall overtake the reaper

PLOWSHARES
Is.　　2:　4 they shall beat their swords into *p*
Joel　　3:10 beat your *p* into swords

POLLUTIONS
Acts　15:20 they abstain from *p* of idols
2 Pet.　2:20 they have escaped the *p* of the world

PONDERED
Luke　2:19 *p* them in her heart

POOR
Deut.　15:11 for the *p* shall never cease out
1 Sam.　2:　7 Lord maketh *p* and maketh rich
Job　　5:16 so the *p* hath hope, and iniquity
Ps.　　10:14 *p* committeth himself to thee
　　　69:33 the Lord heareth the *p* and
　　　132:15 satisfy her *p* with bread
Prov.　13:　7 there is that maketh himself *p*
　　　14:31 oppresseth the *p* reproacheth his Maker
　　　22:22 rob not the *p* because he is *p*
Is.　　14:32 *p* of his people shall trust
Mat.　　5:　3 blessed are the *p* in spirit
　　　11:　5 *p* have the gospel preached to
　　　26:11 ye have the *p* always with you
Luke　6:20 blessed be ye *p*: for yours is the
2 Cor.　6:10 as *p*, yet making many rich
　　　8:　9 for your sakes he became *p*
Gal.　　2:10 we should remember the *p*
Jas.　　2:　5 God chosen the *p* of this world

PORTION
2 Ki.　2:　9 double *p* of thy spirit
Ps.　16:　5 Lord is the *p* of mine inheritance
　　　73:26 of my heart and my *p* for ever
Is.　　61:　7 they shall rejoice in their *p*
Zech.　2:12 Lord shall inherit Judah his *p*

POSSIBLE
Mat.　19:26 with God all things are *p*
Mark　9:23 all things are *p* to him
　　　14:36 Father, all things are *p* to thee
Luke　18:27 impossible with men are *p* with God
Rom.　12:18 if it be *p*, as much as lieth in you

POTTER (POTTER'S)
Is.　29:16 shall be esteemed as the *p* clay
　　　64:　8 and thou our *p*, and we all are
Lam.　　4:　2 the work of the hands of the *p*
Rom.　9:21 hath not the *p* power over the clay
Rev.　　2:27 as the vessels of the *p* shall they

POUR (POURED, POURETH)
Job　16:20 mine eye *p* out tears unto God
Ps.　　45:　2 grace is *p* into thy lips
　　　62:　8 *p* out your heart before him
Is.　32:15 the Spirit be *p* upon us from on high
Rev.　16:　1 *p* vials of the wrath of God

POVERTY
Prov.　10:15 destruction of the poor is their *p*
　　　20:13 love not sleep lest thou come to *p*
　　　30:　8 give me neither *p* nor riches
2 Cor.　8:　2 their deep *p* abounded

　　　　　8:　9 ye through his *p* might be rich
Rev.　　2:　9 I know thy works, and tribulation, and *p*

POWER
2 Sam.22:33 God is my strength and *p*
Job　26:14 thunder of his *p* who can
Ps.　　62:11 that the *p* belongeth unto God
Prov.　18:21 and life are in the *p* of the tongue
Is.　　40:29 he giveth *p* to the faint
Jer.　10:12 he hath made the earth by his *p*
Mic.　　3:　8 I am full of *p* by the Spirit
Zech.　4:　6 not by might, nor by *p*
Mat.　　9:　6 hath *p* on earth to forgive sins
　　　22:29 the scriptures nor the *p* of God
　　　28:18 all *p* is given unto me in heaven
Mark　9:　1 kingdom of God come with *p*
Luke　1:35 *p* of the Highest shall overshadow
　　　24:49 till ye be endued with *p*
John　1:12 gave he *p* to become the sons of God
　　　10:18 *p* to lay it down and *p*
　　　19:10 that I have *p* to crucify thee
Rom.　1:16 gospel is the *p* of God unto salvation
　　　13:　1 there is no *p* but of God
1 Cor.　1:24 Christ the *p* of God, and the wisdom
　　　5:　4 together with the *p* of our Lord
2 Cor.　4:　7 excellency of the *p* may be of God
　　　13:10 according to the *p* which the Lord hath
Eph.　　1:19 exceeding greatness of his *p*
Phil.　　3:10 know the *p* of his resurrection
Col.　　1:11 according to his glorious *p*
1 Tim.　6:16 to whom be honour and *p* everlasting
2 Tim.　3:　5 form of godliness, denying *p*
Heb.　　1:　3 all things by the word of his *p*
　　　2:14 destroy him that had the *p* of death
1 Pet.　1:　5 kept by the *p* of God through faith
2 Pet.　1:　3 divine *p* hath given
Jude　1:25 be glory and majesty, dominion and *p*
Rev.　　2:26 him will I give *p* over nations
　　　5:13 blessing and honour and glory and *p*
　　　7:12 and *p* and might be unto our God
　　　11:17 hast taken to thee thy great *p*
　　　19:　1 honour and *p*, unto the Lord our God

POWERS
Eph.　　6:12 against principalities, against *p*
Col.　　1:16 or dominions or principalities, or *p*
1 Pet.　3:22 authorities and *p* being made subject

PRAISE (PRAISED)
Judg.　5:　3 I will sing *p* to the Lord God
Ps.　　7:17 I will *p* the Lord according to his
　　　33:　1 *p* is comely for the upright
　　　63:　3 my lips shall *p* thee
　　　65:　1 *p* waiteth for thee
　　　96:　4 great and greatly to be *p*
　　　145:　3 Lord, and greatly to be *p*
　　　145:10 all thy works shall *p* thee
Prov.　31:31 her own works *p* her in the gates
Is.　　38:18 the grave cannot *p* thee
　　　60:18 walls Salvation and thy gates *P*
Hab.　　3:　3 earth was full of his *p*
John　12:43 *p* of men more than the *p* of God
Rom.　2:29 whose *p* is not of men
Eph.　　1:　6 *p* of the glory of his grace
Phil.　　4:　8 if there be any *p*, think on
Heb.　13:15 offer the sacrifice of *p* to God

PRAISES (PRAISING)
Ps.　78:　4 generation to come the *p* of the
　　　84:　4 they will still be *p* thee
　　　149:　6 high *p* of God be in their mouth
Is.　　60:　6 shall show forth the *p* of the Lord
Luke　2:13 multitude of the heavenly host *p* God
1 Pet.　2:　9 ye should show forth the *p* of him

PRAY
Ps.　　5:　2 my God: to thee will I *p*
　　　122:　6 *p* for the peace of Jerusalem
Mat.　26:41 watch and *p* that ye enter not
Mark　11:24 things ye desire when ye *p*
Luke　11:　1 teach us to *p* as John also
　　　18:　1 end, that men ought always to *p*
　　　21:36 watch ye and *p* always
John　16:26 I will *p* the Father for
　　　17:　9 I *p* for them: I *p* not
Rom.　8:26 know not what we should *p* for
1 Cor.　14:15 I will *p* with the spirit
Col.　　1:　9 do not cease to *p* for

1 Thes. 5:17 *p* without ceasing
2 Thes. 3: 1 finally, brethren, *p* for
1 Tim. 2: 8 that men *p* every where lifting up
Heb. 13:18 *p* for us, for we trust
Jas. 5:13 any afflicted? let him *p*

PRAYING (PRAYED)
Luke 22:32 I have *p* for thee that thy faith
Eph. 6:18 *p* always with all prayer and
Jas. 5:17 he *p* earnestly that it might not rain

PRAYER
Ps. 65: 2 thou that hearest *p* unto thee
        102: 17 he will regard the *p* of the destitute
Prov. 15: 8 *p* of the upright is his delight
Is. 56: 7 an house of *p* for all people
Mat. 17:21 this kind goeth not out but by *p*
        23:14 for a pretence, make long *p*
Luke 6:12 continued all night in *p* to God
Acts 1:14 continued with one accord in *p* and
        6: 4 give ourselves continually to *p*
        12: 5 *p* was made without ceasing
Rom. 12:12 continuing instant in *p*
1 Cor. 7: 5 may give yourselves to *p*
2 Cor. 1:11 ye also helping together by *p* for us
Phil. 4: 6 in every thing by *p* and supplication
1 Tim. 4: 5 sanctified by the word of God and *p*
Jas. 5:16 effectual fervent *p* of a righteous
1 Pet. 4: 7 be ye therefore sober and watch unto *p*

PRAYERS
1 Tim. 2: 1 first of all that supplications, *p*
1 Pet. 3: 7 that your *p* be not hindered
Rev. 5: 8 which are the *p* of saints

PREACH
Mat. 10:27 what ye hear in thine ear, that *p* ye
Mark 1: 4 and *p* the baptism of repentance for
Luke 4:18 to *p* deliverance to the captives
        9:60 go and *p* the kingdom of God
Rom. 10:15 how shall they *p* except they
1 Cor. 1:23 we *p* Christ crucified, unto the
2 Cor. 4: 5 we *p* not ourselves but Christ
Phil. 1:15 some indeed *p* Christ even of envy
2 Tim. 4: 2 *p* the word; be instant in season

PREACHED (PREACHETH, PREACHING)
Mark 6:12 he *p* that men should repent
Luke 24:47 remission of sins should be *p* in his
Acts 10:36 *p* peace by Jesus Christ: (he is Lord)
1 Cor. 1:18 *p* of the cross is to them
        2: 4 my *p* was not with enticing words
        15: 1 gospel which I *p* unto you
        15:12 if Christ be *p* that he rose
Gal. 1:23 *p* the faith he once destroyed
Col. 1:23 which was *p* to every creature
1 Tim. 3:16 *p* unto the Gentiles believed on
1 Pet. 3:19 went and *p* unto the spirits in prison

PREACHER
Eccl. 1: 1 the words of the *p*, the son of
1 Tim. 2: 7 ordained a *p*, and an apostle
2 Tim. 1:11 whereunto I am appointed a *p*

PRECEPTS
Ps. 119:15 I will meditate in thy *p*
        119: 110 I erred not from thy *p*
        119: 141 I do not forget thy *p*
Is. 28:10 *p* upon *p*, *p* upon *p*

PRECIOUS
1 Sam. 26:21 my soul was *p* in thine eyes
Ps. 116:15 *p* in the sight of the Lord
        126: 6 forth and weepeth, bearing *p* seed
        139: 17 how *p* are thy thoughts
Is. 13:12 I will make a man more *p* than gold
        43: 4 since thou wast *p* in my sight
1 Pet. 1:19 redeemed with the *p* blood of Christ
        2: 4 stone chosen of God and *p*

PREDESTINATE (PREDESTINATED)
Rom. 8:30 whom he did *p* them he also called
Eph. 1: 5 having *p* us unto the adoption

PREPARE
Ps. 61: 7 O *p* mercy and truth, which may
Is. 40: 3 *p* ye the way of the Lord
Amos 4:12 *p* to meet thy God, O Israel
Mat. 11:10 shall *p* thy way before thee
John 14: 2 I go to *p* a place for you

PREPARED (PREPAREST)
2 Chr. 19: 3 hast *p* thine heart to seek God

Ps. 23: 5 thou *p* a table before me in the
Is. 64: 4 what he hath *p* for him
Mat. 20:23 to them for whom it is *p*
        25:34 inherit the kingdom *p* for you
Luke 1:17 ready a people *p* for the Lord
        12:47 knew his lord's will, and *p* not
Rom. 9:23 of mercy which he had afore *p* to
2 Tim. 2:21 *p* and unto every good work
Rev. 21: 2 *p* as a bride adorned for her husband

PRESENT
Ps. 46: 1 a very *p* help in trouble
Acts 10:33 all here *p* before God
Rom. 8:38 nor things *p* nor things to come
        12: 1 *p* your bodies a living sacrifice
1 Cor. 3:22 or thing *p*, or things to
        5: 3 absent in body, but *p* in spirit
2 Cor. 5: 8 to be *p* with the Lord
Gal. 1: 4 deliver us from this *p* evil world
Col. 1:22 to *p* you holy and unblameable and
2 Tim. 4:10 having loved this *p* world
Jude 1:24 *p* you faultless before the presence

PRESENCE
Ps. 16:11 in thy *p* is fulness of joy
        51: 11 cast me not away from thy *p*
        100: 2 come before his *p* with singing
        139: 7 whither shall I flee from thy *p*
Jonah 1:10 fled from the *p* of the Lord
1 Cor. 1:29 no flesh glory in his *p*
Rev. 14:10 *p* of the holy angels and in *p* of

PRESERVE (PRESERVED, PRESERVETH)
Ps. 16: 1 *p* me, O God, for in thee
        25:21 let integrity and uprightness *p* me
        32: 7 thou shalt *p* me from trouble
        41: 2 Lord will *p* and keep him alive
        64: 1 *p* my life from fear of the enemy
        116: 6 the Lord *p* the simple: I was brought
        121: 7 Lord shall *p* thee from all evil
        145: 20 Lord *p* all them that love him
Luke 17:33 shall lose his life shall *p* it
1 Thes. 5:23 soul and body be *p* blameless unto
2 Tim. 4:18 *p* me to his heavenly kingdom
Jude 1: 1 and *p* in Jesus Christ

PRESS (PRESSED)
Luke 6:38 good measure, *p* down, and shaken
Acts 18: 5 Paul was *p* in the spirit and
2 Cor. 1: 8 were *p* out of measure, above
Phil. 3:14 I *p* towards the mark

PRETENCE
Mat. 23:14 and for a *p* make long prayer
Phil. 1:18 whether in *p*, or in truth, Christ is

PREVAIL (PREVAILED, PREVAILEST)
1 Sam. 2: 9 by strength shall no man *p*
Ps. 9:19 arise, O Lord, let not man *p*
Eccl. 4:12 if one *p* against him, two shall
Mat. 16:18 gates of hell shall not *p*
Acts 19:20 mightily grew the word of God and *p*

PRICE
Is. 55: 1 and milk without money and without *p*
Mat. 13:46 pearl of great *p*, went and sold
1 Cor. 6:20 for ye are bought with a *p*
1 Pet. 3: 4 in the sight of God of great *p*

PRIDE
Ps. 10: 2 wicked in his *p* doth persecute
Prov. 8:13 hate evil, *p* and arrogancy
        11: 2 when *p* cometh, then cometh shame
        13:10 by *p* cometh contention: but with
        16:18 *p* goeth before destruction
        29:23 man's *p* shall bring him low
Dan. 4:37 those that walk in *p*
Obad. 1: 3 *p* of thine heart hath deceived thee
1 Tim. 3: 6 lest being lifted up with the *p* fall
1 John 2:16 lust of the eyes, and the *p* of life

PRIEST
Heb. 2:17 a merciful and faithful high *p*
        5: 6 thou art a *p* for ever after the
        6:20 Jesus, made an high *p* for ever
        7:26 for such an high *p* became us
        9:11 Christ being come an high *p* of good

PRIESTS
Is. 61: 6 ye be named *P* of the Lord
Mat. 12: 5 *p* in the temple profane the sabbath
Rev. 1: 6 kings and *p* unto God and his Father

        5:10 made us unto our God kings and *p*

PRIESTHOOD
1 Pet. 2: 5 an holy *p*, to offer up spiritual
        2: 9 ye are a chosen generation, a royal *p*

PRINCE
Is. 9: 6 everlasting Father, *P* of Peace
John 12:31 now shall the *p* of this world
        14:30 *p* of this world cometh and hath
Acts 3:15 And killed the *P* of life, whom God
        5:31 to be a *P* and a Saviour
Eph. 2: 2 *p* of the power of the
Rev. 1: 5 the *p* of the kings of the earth

PRINCES
Ps. 45:16 thou mayest make *p* in earth
        118: 9 than to put confidence in *p*
Mat. 20:25 *p* of Gentiles exercise dominion over
1 Cor. 2: 6 nor of the *p* of this world

PRINCIPALITY (PRINCIPALITIES)
Rom. 8:38 nor angels, nor *p*, nor powers
Eph. 1:21 far above all *p*, and power and might
        6:12 but against *p*, against powers
Col. 2:10 which is the head of all *p* and power
Tit. 3: 1 be subject to *p* and powers

PRISON
Is. 53: 8 he was taken from *p*
        61: 1 opening of *p* to them that are bound
Mat. 5:25 and thou be cast into *p*
        18:30 cast into *p* till he should pay
        25:36 I was in *p* and ye came
1 Pet. 3:19 preached unto the spirits in *p*
Rev. 2:10 devil cast some of you into *p*

PRISONER (PRISONERS)
Ps. 79:11 let the sighing of the *p* come before
        146: 7 the Lord looseth the *p*
Zech. 9:12 turn to the stronghold, ye *p* of hope
Eph. 4: 1 I a *p* of the Lord beseech you

PRIVATE (PRIVATELY)
Gal. 2: 2 but *p* to them which were of reputation
2 Pet. 1:20 scripture is of any *p* interpretation

PRIZE
1 Cor. 9:24 run all, but one receiveth the *p*
Phil. 3:14 for the *p* of the high calling

PROCEED (PROCEEDED, PROCEEDETH)
Deut. 8: 3 by every word that *p* out of the mouth
Mat. 4: 4 word that *p* out of the mouth of God
        15:19 out of the heart *p* evil thoughts
John 8:42 I *p* forth and came from God
        15:26 Spirit of truth, which *p* from the
Eph. 4:29 no corrupt communication *p* out
Jas. 3:10 out of the same mouth *p* blessing
Rev. 11: 5 fire *p* out of their mouth

PROFANE (PROFANED, PROFANING)
Lev. 18:21 shalt thou *p* the name of thy God
Mal. 2:10 *p* the covenant of our fathers
Mat. 12: 5 priests in the temple *p* the sabbath
1 Tim. 1: 9 law is for the unholy and *p*
        6:20 avoiding *p* and vain babblings

PROFESSION
1 Tim. 6:12 and hast professed a good *p*
Heb. 3: 1 High Priest of our *p*, Christ Jesus
        4:14 Son of God, let us hold fast our *p*
        10:23 let us hold fast the *p* of our faith

PROFIT (PROFITETH)
Prov. 10: 2 treasures of wickedness *p* nothing
        14:23 in all labour there is *p*
Eccl. 7: 11 by it there is *p* to them
Is. 30: 5 not *p* then nor be an help nor *p*
Jer. 2: 8 walked after things that do not *p*
John 6:63 the flesh *p* nothing: the words that
1 Cor. 13: 3 have not charity, it *p* me nothing
Gal. 5: 2 Christ shall *p* you nothing
Heb. 4: 2 the word preached did not *p* them
        12:10 but he for our *p* that we might

PROFITABLE
1 Tim. 4: 8 godliness is *p* unto all things
2 Tim. 3:16 inspiration of God, and is *p* for doctrine
Tit. 3: 8 these things are good and *p* unto men
Philem. 1: 11 now *p* to thee and to

PROMISE (PROMISES)
Ps. 77: 8 doth his *p* fail for evermore
Luke 24:49 the *p* of my Father upon you
Acts 1: 4 wait for the *p* of the Father

Rom.   4:16 *p* might be sure to all the seed
      9: 8 children of the *p* are counted for
2 Cor. 1:20 all the *p* of God in him are yea
Gal.   3:21 is the law against the *p*
     4:28 as Isaac was, are the children of *p*
Eph.   1:13 with that holy Spirit of *p*
1 Tim. 4: 8 *p* of the life that now is, and
Heb.   6:12 through faith and patience inherit the *p*
     8: 6 which was established upon better *p*
     9:15 receive the *p* of eternal inheritance
2 Pet. 1: 4 us exceeding great and precious *p*
     3: 4 where is the *p* of his coming?
1 John 2:25 *p* that he promised us, even eternal

PROMISED
Rom.   1: 2 which he had *p* afore by his prophets
Tit.   1: 2 which God, that cannot lie, *p* before
Heb. 10:23 for he is faithful that *p*
    11:11 she judged him faithful who had *p*

PROPHECY
1 Cor. 12:10 the working of miracles; to another *p*
1 Tim. 4:14 which was given thee by *p*
2 Pet. 1:20 no *p* of the scripture is of any
Rev.   1: 3 they that hear the words of this *p*
    22: 7 keepeth the sayings of the *p* of

PROPHESY (PROPHESIED)
Joel   2:28 thy sons and thy daughters shall *p*
Amos 2:12 commanded the prophets, saying *p* not
Mat.   7:22 have we not *p* in thy name
    11:13 prophets and the law *p* until John
John 11:51 *p* that Jesus should die
1 Cor. 13: 9 know in part and we *p* in part
    14: 1 but rather that ye may *p*
1 Pet. 1:10 *p* of the grace that should come

PROPHET
Deut. 18:18 raise them up a *p* from among
Hos.   9: 7 *p* is a fool, the spiritual man
Mat. 10:41 he that receiveth a *p* in the name
    13:57 a *p* is not without honour save in
Luke 7:28 there is not a greater *p*
    24:19 *p* mighty in deed and word
John 7:40 said, Of a truth this is the *P*
2 Pet. 2:16 forbad the madness of the *p*

PROPHETS
Num. 11:29 all the Lord's people were *p*, and
Jer.   5:13 the *p* shall become wind, and the
Mat.   5:17 come to destroy the law, or *p*
    7:12 this is the law and the *p*
    22:40 on these hang all the law and the *p*
Luke 1:70 spake by the mouth of his holy *p*
    6:23 so did their fathers unto the *p*
    16:29 they have Moses and the *p*
    24:44 *p*, and in the psalms, concerning me
John 8:52 Abraham is dead, and the *p*
Acts   3:18 by the mouth of all his *p*
    10:43 to him give all the *p* witness
    26:22 things which the *p* and Moses
Rom.   1: 2 promised afore by his *p*
1 Cor. 12:28 first apostles, secondarily *p*
    14:32 spirits of the *p* are subject to the *p*
Eph.   2:20 the foundation of the apostles and *p*
1 Thes. 2:15 killed the Lord Jesus and their own *p*
Heb.   1: 1 spake in the past unto the fathers by
       the *p*
Rev. 18:20 rejoice, ye apostles and *p*
    22: 6 Lord God of the holy *p* sent his

PROPITIATION
Rom.   3:25 God hath set forth to be a *p*
1 John 2: 2 he is the *p* for our sins
    4:10 his Son to be the *p* for our sins

PROSPER (PROSPERED)
Deut. 29: 9 that ye may *p* in that all ye do
Ps.   1: 3 whatsoever he doeth shall *p*
   122: 6 they shall *p* that love thee
Is.   53:10 the pleasure of the Lord shall *p*
    54:17 no weapon against thee shall *p*
1 Cor. 16: 2 as God hath *p* him, that there be

PROSPERITY
Ps.   30: 6 in my *p* I said I shall never
    73: 3 when I saw the *p* of the wicked
   122: 7 walls, and *p* be in thy palaces
Eccl. 7:14 in the day of *p* be joyful

PROUD
Ps.   12: 3 the tongue that speaketh *p* things

    40: 4 respecteth not the *p* nor
   138: 6 the *p* he knoweth afar off
Prov. 6:17 *p* look, a lying tongue, and hands
    21: 4 high look and a *p* heart, and the
Mal.   3:15 now we call the *p* happy; yea
Luke 1:51 the *p* in the imagination of their
Jas.   4: 6 God resisteth the *p*, but giveth grace
1 Pet. 5: 5 for God resisteth the *p*, and giveth

PROVE (PROVED)
Ps.   17: 3 thou hast *p* mine heart
    26: 2 examine me, O Lord, *p* me
    66:10 thou, O God, hast *p* us as
Rom. 12: 2 that ye may *p* what is that good and
2 Cor. 8: 8 to *p* the sincerity of your love
Gal.   6: 4 let every man *p* his work
1 Thes. 5:21 *p* all things; hold fast
Heb.   3: 9 your father tempted me, *p* me

PROVERB (PROVERBS)
1 Ki.   4:32 he spake three thousand *p*
Ps.   69:11 and I became a *p* to them
Eccl. 12: 9 he set in order many *p*
Is.   14: 4 thou shalt take up this *p* against
Jer. 24: 9 to be a reproach and a *p*
Ezek. 14: 8 will make him a sign and a *p*
John 16:25 things have I spoken unto you in *p*

PROVIDE (PROVIDETH)
Gen. 22: 8 God will *p* himself a lamb
Rom. 12:17 *p* things honest in the sight of all
1 Tim. 5: 8 if any *p* not for his own

PROVOKE (PROVOKED)
Deut. 31:20 and *p* me, and break my covenant
Ps.   78:40 how oft did they *p* him
   106: 7 *p* him at the sea, even at the Red
Jer.   7:19 do they *p* me to anger
Luke 11:53 to *p* him to speak of many things
Rom. 10:19 will *p* you to jealousy
1 Cor. 10:22 do we *p* the Lord to jealousy
2 Cor. 9: 2 and your zeal hath *p* very many
Heb. 10:24 to *p* unto love and good works

PRUDENT
Prov. 12:16 known but a *p* man covereth shame
    13:16 *p* man dealeth with knowledge
    15: 5 he that regardeth reproof is *p*
    16:21 wise in heart shall be called *p*
    18:15 heart of the *p* getteth knowledge
    19:14 a *p* wife is from the Lord
Mat. 11:25 hid these things from the wise and *p*
1 Cor. 1:19 the understanding of the *p*

PSALM (PSALMS)
1 Chr. 16: 7 David delivered first this *p* to thank
Ps.   95: 2 joyful noise unto him with *p*
    98: 5 and with the voice of a *p*
Acts 13:33 it is also written in the second *p*
1 Cor. 14:26 every one of you hath a *p*
Eph. 5:19 speaking to yourselves in *p*
Jas   5:13 merry? let him sing *p*

PUBLICAN (PUBLICANS)
Mat.   5:46 do not even the *p* the same
    11:19 a friend of *p* and sinners
    18:17 unto thee as an heathen man and a *p*
    21:31 *p* and harlots go into the kingdom
Luke 3:12 came also *p* to be baptized
    7:29 the *p*, justified God, being baptized
    18:13 and the *p*, standing afar off

PUBLISH (PUBLISHED)
Is.   52: 7 bringeth good tidings, that *p* peace
Acts 13:49 word of the Lord was *p*

PUFFED (PUFFETH)
1 Cor. 4:19 the speech of them which are *p* up
    8: 1 knowledge *p* up, but charity edifieth
    13: 4 charity vaunteth not itself, is not *p* up
Col.   2:18 vainly *p* up by his fleshly mind

PUNISH (PUNISHED)
Hos. 12: 2 will *p* Jacob according to his ways
2 Thes. 1: 9 be *p* with everlasting destruction
2 Pet. 2: 9 unto the day of judgment to be *p*

PUNISHMENT
Amos 1: 3 I will not turn away the *p*
Mat. 25:46 go into everlasting *p*
2 Cor. 2: 6 sufficient to such a man is this *p*
Heb. 10:29 of how much sorer *p*, suppose

PURCHASED
Acts   8:20 the gift of God may be *p* with money
    20:28 which he hath *p* with his own blood
Eph.   1:14 until the redemption of the *p* possession

PURE
2 Sam.22:27 with the *p* thou wilt show thyself *p*
Job   4:17 man can be more *p* than his Maker
Ps.   12: 6 words of the Lord are *p* words
    24: 4 clean hands and a *p* heart
Prov. 15:26 words of the *p* are pleasant
Acts 20:26 I am *p* from the blood
Phil.   4: 8 are just, whatsoever things are *p*
1 Tim. 3: 9 faith in a *p* conscience
Tit.   1:15 to the *p* all things are *p*
Heb. 10:22 our bodies washed with *p* water
Jas.   1:27 *p* religion and undefiled before God
    3:17 wisdom from above is first *p*

PURGE (PURGED)
Ps.   51: 7 *p* me with hyssop, and
    65: 3 transgressions, thou shalt *p*
Is.   6: 7 iniquity is taken, and sin *p*
Mal.   3: 3 purify and *p* them as gold
1 Cor. 5: 7 *p* out therefore the old leaven
2 Tim. 2:21 if a man therefore *p* himself from
Heb. 9:14 *p* your conscience from dead works
2 Pet. 1: 9 he was *p* from old sins

PURIFY (PURIFIED, PURIFIETH, PURIFYING)
Mal.   3: 3 and he shall *p* the sons of Levi
Acts 15: 9 *p* their hearts by faith
Heb.   9:13 sanctifieth to the *p* of the flesh
Tit.   2:14 *p* unto himself a peculiar
Jas.   4: 8 *p* your hearts, ye double
1 Pet. 1:22 *p* your souls in obeying the truth
1 John 3: 3 *p* himself, even as he is pure

PURPOSE (PURPOSED)
Eccl. 3:17 a time there for every *p* and for
Rom. 8:28 called according to his *p*
Eph.   1: 9 which he hath *p* in himself
    3:11 according to the eternal *p* which

PUT
Gen.   3:15 I will *p* enmity between thee and
Ps.   8: 6 *p* all things under his feet
    59:17 *p* on righteousness as a breastplate
Jer. 31:33 *p* my law in their inward parts
Ezek. 11:19 *p* a new spirit within you
    36:27 I will *p* my Spirit in you
Mat.   5:15 *p* it under a bushel, but on a
Luke 1:52 *p* down the mighty from their seats
Rom. 13:12 *p* on the armour of light
    13:14 *p* on the Lord Jesus Christ
Gal.   3:27 baptized into Christ have *p* on Christ
    6:11 *p* on the whole armour of God
Col.   3: 9 that ye have *p* off the old man
    3:14 above all things *p* on charity
2 Pet. 1:14 I must *p* off this tabernacle

PUTTETH (PUTTING)
Eph.   4:25 *p* away lying, speak
Col.   2:11 in *p* off the body of
1 Thes. 5: 8 *p* on the breastplate of faith
1 Pet. 3: 3 wearing of gold or *p*
    3:21 *p* away of the filth

QUEEN (QUEENS)
Jer. 44:25 to burn incense to the *q* of heaven
Mat. 12:42 the *q* of the south shall rise up
Rev. 18: 7 I sit a *q*, and am no widow

QUENCH (QUENCHED)
Sol.   8: 7 many waters cannot *q* love
Is.   42: 3 smoking flax shall he not *q*
Mark 9:43 fire that never shall be *q*
Eph.   6:16 to *q* the fiery darts of
1 Thes. 5:19 *q* not the Spirit

QUESTION (QUESTIONS)
1 Tim. 1: 4 which minister *q*, rather than godly

QUICK (QUICKLY)
Eccl. 4:12 threefold cord is not *q* broken
Is.   11: 3 of *q* understanding in fear
Acts 10:42 to be the Judge of *q*
2 Tim. 4: 1 who shall judge the *q* and dead
Rev. 11: behold, I come *q*: hold

QUICKEN (QUICKENED, QUICKENETH, QUICKENING)
Ps.   80:18 *q* us, and we will call on thy name
   119: 25 *q* thou me according to thy word

119: 40 *q* me in thy righteousness
119: 149 *q* me according to thy judgment
John 5: 21 even so the Son *q* whom he will
6: 63 it is the Spirit that *q*
Rom. 8: 11 *q* your mortal bodies
1 Cor. 15: 45 last Adam was made a *q* spirit
Col. 2: 13 hath he *q* together with him
1 Pet. 3: 18 in the flesh, but *q* by the Spirit

QUIET
Eccl. 9: 17 words of the wise are heard in *q*
Is. 7: 4 take heed and be *q*, fear not
1 Thes. 4: 11 study to be *q* and to do your own
1 Tim. 2: 2 lead a *q* and peaceable life in all
1 Pet. 3: 4 ornament of a meek and *q* spirit

QUIETNESS
Job 34: 29 when he giveth *q* who
Eccl. 4: 6 better is a handful with *q*
Is. 30: 15 in *q* and confidence
32: 17 effect of righteousness shall be *q*
2 Thes. 3: 12 exhort that with *q* they work

QUIVER
Ps. 127: 5 the man that hath his *q* full of them

RACE
Ps. 19: 5 strong man to run a *r*
Eccl. 9: 11 that the *r* is not to the swift
1 Cor. 9: 24 they which run in a *r*
Heb. 12: 1 run with patience the *r* that is set

RAGE (RAGED, RAGETH, RAGING)
Ps. 46: 6 the heathen *r*, the
89: 9 rulest the *r* of the sea
Prov. 6: 34 jealousy is the *r* of a
14: 16 the fool *r* and is confident
20: 1 wine is a mocker, strong drink is *r*
Jude 1: 13 *r* waves of the sea, foaming out

RAGS
Prov. 23: 21 drowsiness shall clothe a man with *r*
Is. 64: 6 our righteousnesses are as filthy *r*

RAIMENT
Mat. 6: 25 meat, and the body more than *r*
11: 8 man clothed in soft *r*?
17: 2 his *r* was white as the light
1 Tim. 6: 8 having food and *r* let us be therewith
Rev. 3: 5 shall be clothed in white *r*

RAIN
Lev. 26: 4 I will give you *r* in due season
2 Chr. 7: 13 that there be no *r*, or
Job 5: 10 who giveth *r* on the earth
38: 26 cause it to *r* on the earth
Ps. 11: 6 upon the wicked he shall *r* snares
68: 9 didst send a plentiful *r*
147: 8 who prepareth *r* for
Prov. 16: 15 favour is as a cloud of the latter *r*
Eccl. 12: 2 nor clouds return after *r*
Sol. 2: 11 winter is past; the *r* is
Is. 55: 10 as the *r* cometh down
Hos. 10: 12 till he come and *r* righteousness
Amos 4: 7 withholden the *r* from
Zech. 14: 17 even upon them shall be no *r*
Mat. 5: 45 sendeth *r* on the just
Heb. 6: 7 earth which drinketh in *r*
Jas. 5: 18 prayed again, the heaven gave *r*

RAISE (RAISED, RAISETH)
Deut. 18: 18 I will *r* them up a Prophet
Ps. 113: 7 he *r* up the poor out of
145: 14 *r* up those that are bowed down
Is. 44: 26 *r* up the decayed places thereof
58: 12 *r* up the foundations of many
Hos. 6: 2 third day he will *r* us
Mat. 11: 5 deaf hear, the dead are *r* up
Luke 1: 69 *r* up an horn of salvation
John 6: 40 I will *r* him up at the last day
Rom. 4: 25 *r* again for our justification
1 Cor. 6: 14 God hath both *r* up the Lord
2 Cor. 4: 14 he which *r* up the Lord Jesus
Eph. 2: 6 hath *r* us up together and made us

RANSOM
Ex. 30: 12 give every man a *r* for
Ps. 49: 7 nor give to God a *r* for him
Prov. 13: 8 *r* of man's life are his riches
21: 18 the wicked shall be a *r* for the
Mat. 20: 28 to give his life a *r* for
1 Tim. 2: 6 gave himself a *r* for all

READ (READEST, READETH)
Neh. 13: 1 they *r* in the book of Moses
Acts 8: 30 understandest thou what thou *r*
1 Thes. 5: 27 epistle be *r* unto all

READY
Neh. 9: 17 thou art a God *r* to pardon
Ps. 45: 1 tongue is the pen of a *r* writer
Mark 14: 38 spirit is *r* but the flesh
1 Tim. 6: 18 do good, *r* to distribute
Tit. 3: 1 to be *r* to every good work
Rev. 3: 2 that are *r* to die: for I have

REAP (REAPED, REAPETH)
Hos. 10: 12 *r* in mercy, break up your fallow
10: 13 plowed wickedness, ye have *r* iniquity
Mat. 6: 26 sow not, neither do they *r*
John 4: 36 he that *r* receiveth wages
1 Cor. 9: 11 a great thing if we *r*
Gal. 6: 7 that shall he also *r*
6: 9 shall *r* if we faint not
Rev. 14: 16 and the earth was *r*

REASON
Dan. 4: 36 my *r* returned unto
1 Pet. 3: 15 asketh a *r* of the hope

REASONABLE
Rom. 12: 1 which is your *r* service

REBELLIOUS
Is. 30: 9 this is a *r* people,
Jer. 4: 17 she hath been *r*
Ezek. 2: 5 for they are a *r* house

REBUKE
2 Ki. 19: 3 a day of trouble, *r* and
Ps. 6: 1 *r* me not in thine anger, nor
Prov. 9: 8 *r* a wise man, he will love
27: 5 open *r* is better than secret love
Mat. 16: 22 Peter took him and began to *r* him
Luke 17: 3 brother trespass against thee *r* him
Phil. 2: 15 sons of God, without *r*
1 Tim. 5: 1 *r* not an elder, entreat
5: 20 them that sin *r* before

RECEIVE
Job 2: 10 shall we *r* good at the hand of God
Ps. 6: 9 the Lord will *r* my prayer
73: 24 and afterward *r* me to glory
Mat. 10: 41 shall *r* a prophet's reward; and he
18: 5 *r* one such little child in my name
19: 11 all men cannot *r* this saying
21: 22 ask in prayer, believing, ye shall *r*
Mark 4: 16 heard the word, immediately *r* it with
11: 24 believe that ye *r* them, and ye shall
Luke 16: 9 *r* you into everlasting habitations
John 3: 27 man can *r* nothing
5: 44 which *r* honour one of another
16: 24 ask, and ye shall *r*, that your joy
Acts 2: 38 shall *r* the gift of the Holy Ghost
7: 59 Lord Jesus, *r* my spirit
10: 43 whosoever believeth shall *r* remission
20: 35 more blessed to give than to *r*
26: 18 may *r* forgiveness of sins
Rom. 14: 1 him that is weak in faith *r* ye
1 Cor. 3: 8 every man *r* his own reward
2 Cor. 5: 10 may *r* things done in the body
Gal. 3: 14 *r* the promise of the Spirit
Eph. 6: 8 same shall he *r* of the Lord
Col. 3: 24 *r* the reward of inheritance
Jas. 1: 21 *r* with meekness the engrafted word
3: 1 we shall *r* the greater condemnation
1 Pet. 5: 4 shall *r* a crown of glory
1 John 3: 22 whatsoever we ask, we *r*
2 John 1: 8 but that we *r* a full reward

RECEIVED (RECEIVETH, RECEIVING)
Jer. 7: 28 nor *r* correction, truth
Mat. 7: 8 every one that asketh *r*
10: 8 freely ye have *r*, freely
10: 40 he that *r* you *r* me
Luke 6: 24 ye have *r* your consolation
John 1: 11 own, and his own *r* him not
3: 32 no man *r* his testimony
12: 48 rejecteth me, and *r* not my words
Acts 8: 17 them, and they *r* the Holy Ghost
Rom. 5: 11 by whom we have *r* atonement
8: 15 have *r* the spirit of adoption
14: 3 him that eateth, for God hath *r* him
15: 7 ye one another, as Christ also *r* us

1 Cor. 2: 14 natural man *r* not the
11: 23 For I have *r* of the Lord
Phil. 4: 15 as concerning giving and, *r*, but ye
1 Tim. 3: 16 in the world *r* up into glory
Heb. 11: 13 in faith not having *r* promises
12: 28 wherefore we *r* a kingdom
1 Pet. 1: 9 *r* the end of your faith

RECOMPEN(C)SE
Is. 66: 6 render *r* to his enemies
Hos. 9: 7 the days of *r* are come
Luke 14: 12 again and a *r* be made
Rom. 12: 17 *r* to no man evil for
Heb. 2: 2 disobedience received just *r* of reward
10: 35 confidence, which hath great *r* of
11: 26 he had respect unto *r*

RECOMPENSED
Prov. 11: 31 the righteous shall be *r*
Jer. 18: 20 shall evil be *r* for good
Rom. 11: 35 it shall be *r* unto him again

RECONCILE (RECONCILED)
Mat. 5: 24 first be *r* to thy brother
Rom. 5: 10 when we were enemies we were *r*
2 Cor. 5: 18 God, who hath *r* us to himself
5: 20 in Christ's stead, be ye *r* to God
Col. 1: 20 to *r* all things to himself

RECONCILIATION
2 Chr. 29: 24 they made *r* with their blood
2 Cor. 5: 18 given to us the ministry of *r*
Heb. 2: 17 make *r* for the sins of the people

RED
Ps. 75: 8 and the wine is *r*; it is full of
Is. 1: 18 though they be *r* like crimson
63: 2 wherefore art thou *r* in thine apparel
Zech. 1: 8 a man riding upon a *r* horse
Rev. 6: 4 went out another horse that was *r*
12: 3 behold a great *r* dragon

REDEEM (REDEEMED, REDEEMETH)
Gen. 48: 16 angel which *r* me from all evil
Ex. 6: 6 I will *r* you with a stretched out arm
Ps. 34: 22 the Lord *r* the soul of his servants
49: 15 God will *r* my soul from power
103: 4 who *r* thy life from destruction
136: 24 *r* us from our enemies:
Is. 52: 3 shall be *r* without money
63: 9 love and in his pity he *r* them
Hos. 13: 14 I will *r* them from death
Luke 1: 68 he hath visited and *r* his people
24: 21 which should have *r* Israel
Gal. 3: 13 Christ hath *r* us from the curse of
Eph. 5: 16 *r* the time because the days are evil
Col. 4: 5 that are without, *r* the time
Tit. 2: 14 might *r* us from all iniquity
1 Pet. 1: 18 not *r* with corruptible things as
Rev. 5: 9 hast *r* us to God by thy blood
14: 4 these were *r* from among men

REDEEMER
Job 19: 25 I know that my *r* liveth
Ps. 19: 14 O Lord, my strength and my *r*
Prov. 23: 11 their *r* is mighty
Is. 63: 16 our father and *r*; he shall plead
Jer. 50: 34 their *R* is strong; the Lord of hosts

REDEMPTION
Ps. 49: 8 *r* of their soul is precious
111: 9 he sent *r* unto his people
Luke 2: 38 looked for *r* in Jerusalem
21: 28 heads, for your *r* draweth nigh
Rom. 3: 24 through *r* that is in Christ Jesus
8: 23 waiting for the *r* of our body
1 Cor. 1: 30 righteousness, and sanctification, and *r*
Eph. 1: 7 in whom we have *r* through his blood
1: 14 until the *r* of the purchased possession
4: 30 sealed unto the day of *r*
Col. 1: 14 in whom we have *r* through his blood
Heb. 9: 12 obtained eternal *r* for us

REFINE (REFINED)
Is. 48: 10 behold, I have *r* thee,
Zech. 13: 9 and will *r* them as silver is refined

REFINER
Mal. 3: 3 he shall sit as a *r* and purifier

REFUGE
Deut. 33: 27 the eternal God is thy *r*
Ps. 9: 9 the Lord also will be a *r*

46: 1 God is our *r* and strength; a
57: 1 thy wings will I make my *r*, until
59:16 hast been my defence and *r* in the
62: 7 my strength and my *r*
Is.   4: 6 and for a place of *r*,
Jer.   16:19 Lord my strength my fortress and my *r*
Heb.   6:18 fled for *r* to lay hold

REFUSE (REFUSED)
Ps.   118:22 the stone which the builders *r*
Jer.   5: 3 have *r* to receive correction
     31:15 *r* to be comforted for her children
Lam.   3:45 made us as the offscouring and *r*
1 Tim.   4: 4 nothing to be *r* if it be received
Heb.   12:25 *r* him that spake on earth

REGARD (REGARDED, REGARDEST, REGARDETH)
Ps.   66:18 if I *r* iniquity in my heart
    102: 17 will *r* the prayer of the destitute
    106: 44 he *r* their affliction
Prov.   13:18 he that *r* reproof shall
     15: 5 he that *r* reproof is prudent
Is.   5:12 that *r* not the work of the Lord
Mat.   22:16 thou *r* not the person
Luke   1:48 *r* the low estate of his handmaiden
Rom.   14: 6 he that *r* the day *r* it

REGENERATION
Tit.   3: 5 saved us by the washing of *r*

REIGN (REIGNED, REIGNEST, REIGNETH)
Ex.   15:18 Lord shall *r* for ever
1 Chr. 29:12 thou *r* over all; and in
Ps.   93: 1 the Lord *r*, he is clothed with majesty
     99: 1 the Lord *r*, let the people tremble
    146: 10 the Lord shall *r* for
Prov.   8:15 by me kings *r* and princes
Is.   52: 7 saith unto Zion, Thy God *r*
Rom.   5:14 nevertheless death *r* from Adam to Moses
     5: 21 that as sin *r* unto death so
2 Tim.   2:12 if we suffer, we shall *r*
Rev.   5: 10 we shall *r* on the earth
     19: 6 for the Lord God omnipotent *r*
     20: 4 *r* with Christ a thousand years
     22: 5 they shall *r* for ever

REINS
Ps.   16: 7 my *r* also instruct me
Prov.   23:16 my *r* shall rejoice, when thy lips
Jer.   17:10 search the heart, I try the *r*
Rev.   2:23 I am he which searcheth the *r* and

REJECT (REJECTED)
2 Ki.   17:20 and the Lord *r* all the seed of Israel
Is.   53: 3 despised and *r* of men
Jer.   6:30 because the Lord hath *r* them
     8: 9 they *r* the word of the
Lam.   5:22 thou hast utterly *r* us
Mark   7: 9 ye *r* the commandment of God
Luke   7:30 *r* the counsel of God
John   12:48 he that *r* me, and receiveth not
Gal.   4:14 ye despised not, nor *r*
Heb.   12:17 he was *r* for he found
Tit.   3: 10 after the first and second admonition *r*

REJOICE
Deut.   28:63 Lord will *r* over you
1 Sam.   2: 1 because I *r* in thy salvation
2 Chr.   6: 41 let thy saints *r* in goodness
Ps.   2:11 Lord with fear and *r* with trembling
     9:14 I will *r* in thy salvation
     51: 8 bones which thou hast broken may *r*
     65: 8 evening to *r*
     68: 3 let them *r* before God
     86: 4 *r* the soul of thy servant
    105: 3 heart of them *r* that seek the
Prov.   5:18 *r* with the wife of thy youth
Is.   29:19 poor among men shall *r* in the Holy
     41:16 thou shalt *r* in the Lord
     62: 5 shall thy God *r* over
Jer.   32:41 I will *r* over them to
Joel   2:23 *r* in the Lord your God
Hab.   3:18 Yet I will *r* in the Lord
Zeph.   3:17 *r* over thee with joy
Luke   6:23 *r* ye in that day; leap
     10:20 rather *r* because your names
John   14:28 if ye loved me ye would *r*
Rom.   5: 2 *r* in hope of the glory of God
     12:15 *r* with them that do *r*

1 Cor.   7:30 that *r*, as though they rejoiced not
Phil.   3: 3 and *r* in Christ Jesus,
     4: 4 *r* in the Lord always:
Col.   1:24 *r* in my sufferings for
1 Thes. 5:16 *r* evermore
Jas.   1: 9 brother of low degree *r* in that he
1 Pet.   1: 8 *r* with joy unspeakable and full

REJOICED (REJOICETH)
Ps.   28: 7 my heart greatly *r*:
    119: 14 I have *r* in the way of
Prov.   13: 9 the light of the righteous *r*
Is.   62: 5 bridegroom *r* over the bride
Luke   1:47 my spirit hath *r* in God my
     10:21 Jesus *r* in spirit and
John   8:56 father Abraham *r* to see my day
1 Cor.   7:30 as though they *r* not;
     13: 6 *r* not in iniquity but *r* in
Jas.   2:13 mercy; and mercy *r* against judgment

REJOICING
Ps.   19: 8 statutes of Lord are right, *r* the heart
Jer.   15:16 thy word was the joy and *r* of my
Acts   5:41 *r* that they were counted worthy
     8:39 he went on his way *r*
2 Cor.   1:12 our *r* is this, the testimony
Heb.   3: 6 *r* of hope firm unto the end

RELIGION
Jas.   1:27 pure *r* and undefiled before God and

REMEMBER
Gen.   9:16 look upon it that I may *r*
Ex.   13: 3 *r* this day in which ye came out of Egypt
Deut.   7:18 shalt well *r* what the Lord thy God did
     8:18 thou shalt *r* the Lord thy God
Neh.   13:14 *r* me O my God, concerning
Ps.   20: 7 we will *r* the name of the Lord
     25: 6 *r* O Lord thy tender mercies
     63: 6 when I *r* thee upon my bed
     77: 11 I will *r* the works of the Lord
Eccl.   12: 1 *r* now thy Creator in days of
Sol.   1: 4 we will *r* thy love
Is.   43:25 I will not *r* thy sins
Jer.   2: 2 for I *r* thee, the kindness of thy youth
     31:34 I will *r* their sin no
Ezek.   16:60 I will *r* my covenant
     36: 31 shall ye *r* your own evil ways
Hab.   3: 2 in wrath *r* mercy
Luke   1:72 to *r* his holy covenant
     17:32 *r* Lot's wife
Gal.   2: 10 we should *r* the poor
Col.   4:18 *r* my bonds. Grace be
Heb.   8:12 iniquities will I *r* no more
     13: 3 *r* them that are in bonds

REMEMBERED (REMEMBERETH)
Gen.   8: 1 God *r* Noah and every living thing
Num.   10: 9 ye shall be *r* before the Lord
Ps.   77: 3 I *r* God and was
     98: 3 hath *r* his mercy and truth
    119: 52 I *r* thy judgments of old
    136: 23 who *r* us in our low estate
Luke   24: 8 and they *r* his words
John   2:17 disciples *r* that it was written
Rev.   18: 5 God hath *r* her iniquities

REMEMBRANCE
Ps.   6: 5 in death is no *r* of
Is.   26: 8 to thy name, and to the *r* of thee
Lam.   3:20 my soul hath them still in *r*
Mal.   3:16 a book of *r* was written
Luke   22:19 for you: this do in *r* of me
John   14:26 bring all things to your *r*
Acts   10: 31 thine alms are had in *r*
1 Cor.   11:25 ye drink it, in *r* of me
2 Pet.   3: 1 stir up your pure minds by way of *r*
Jude   1: 5 I will put you in *r*
Rev.   16:19 Babylon came in *r* before God

REMISSION
Mat.   26:28 shed for many for the *r* of sins
Mark   1: 4 baptism of repentance for the *r* of
Luke   1:77 by the *r* of their sins
Acts   2:38 of Jesus Christ for the *r* of sins
     10:43 shall receive *r* of sins
Rom.   3:25 his righteousness for the *r* of sins
Heb.   9:22 without shedding of blood is no *r*
     10:18 where *r* of these is,

REMNANT
2 Ki.   19: 4 lift up thy prayer for the *r*
Ezra   9: 8 leave us a *r* to escape
Is.   1: 9 unto us a very small *r*
     10: 21 the *r* shall return,
Jer.   23: 3 I will gather the *r* of my flock
Ezek.   6: 8 yet will I leave a *r*
Rom.   9:27 a *r* shall be saved
     11: 5 *r* according to the election of grace

REMOVE (REMOVED)
Ps.   103:12 so far hath he *r* our transgressions
    119: 29 *r* from me the way of lying
Prov.   4:27 *r* thy foot from evil
     10:30 righteous shall never be *r*
Luke   22:42 if thou be willing, *r* this cup
Rev.   2: 5 I will *r* thy candlestick

REND
Is.   64: 1 thou wouldest *r* the heavens
Joel   2:13 *r* your heart and not your garments

RENDER
2 Chr.   6:30 *r* to every man according to his ways
Job   33:26 he will *r* to man his righteousness
Ps.   116:12 what shall I *r* to the Lord
Prov.   26:16 seven men that can *r* a
Mat.   22: 21 *r* therefore unto Caesar the things
Rom.   13: 7 *r* therefore to all their
1 Thes. 5:15 that none *r* evil for evil

RENEW (RENEWED, RENEWEST, RENEWING)
Ps.   51: 10 *r* a right spirit in me
    103: 5 thy youth is *r* like the eagle's
    104: 30 *r* the face of the earth
Is.   40:31 upon the Lord shall *r* their strength
Rom.   12: 2 transformed by the *r* of your mind
2 Cor.   4:16 inward man is *r* day by day
Eph.   4:23 be *r* in the spirit of
Heb.   6: 6 *r* them again unto repentance

REPAY (REPAID)
Deut.   7: 10 he will *r* him to his face
Is.   59:18 to their deeds accordingly he will *r*
Rom.   12:19 I will *r*, saith the Lord

REPENT
Job   42: 6 I abhor myself and *r* in dust
Ps.   135:14 will *r* himself concerning
Jer.   18: 8 I will *r* of the evil I thought
Jonah   3: 9 if God will turn and *r*
Mat.   3: 2 *r* ye, for the kingdom of heaven is
Mark   1:15 *r* and believe the gospel
     6:12 preached that men should *r*
Luke   13: 3 except ye *r* ye shall all
     16:30 went unto them from dead, they will *r*
     17: 3 if he *r* forgive him
Acts   2:38 *r* and be baptized
     3:19 *r* and be converted,
     8:22 *r* of this thy wickedness
     17:30 commandeth all men everywhere to *r*
     26:20 should *r* and turn to God
Rev.   2: 5 thou art fallen, and *r*
     2:16 *r*, or I will come unto
     3:19 be zealous therefore, and *r*

REPENTANCE
Mat.   3: 8 fruits meet for *r*
     3: 11 baptize you with water unto *r*
     9:13 not righteous but sinners to *r*
Mark   1: 4 and preach the baptism of *r*
Luke   15: 7 just persons which need no *r*
Acts   5: 31 give *r* to Israel and forgiveness of
     13:24 preached the baptism of *r* to all
Rom.   2: 4 goodness of God leadeth to *r*
     11:29 gifts and calling of God without *r*
2 Cor.   7: 10 godly sorrow worketh *r* to salvation
Heb.   6: 1 not laying again the foundation of *r*
2 Pet.   3: 9 that all should come to *r*

REPENTED (REPENTETH)
Gen.   6: 6 and it *r* the Lord that
Ex.   32:14 the Lord *r* of the evil
Jer.   8: 6 no man *r* him of his wickedness
Mat.   21:29 but afterward he *r* and
     27: 3 *r* himself, and brought again the
Luke   15: 7 one sinner that *r*, more than over

REPROACH (REPROACHED, REPROACHES)
Josh.   5: 9 have I rolled away the *r* of Egypt
Ps.   15: 3 up a *r* against his neighbour
     69: 7 for thy sake I have borne *r*

69:20 *r* hath broken my heart
Prov. 14:34 sin is a *r* to any people
18: 3 also contempt, and with ignominy *r*
Is. 51: 7 fear ye not the *r* of men
Jer. 31:19 I did bear the *r* of my youth
2 Cor. 12:10 I take pleasure in infirmities, in *r*
Heb. 11:26 esteeming the *r* of Christ greater riches
13:13 without the camp, bearing his *r*
1 Pet. 4:14 if ye be *r* for the name of Christ

REPROBATE (REPROBATES)
Rom. 1:28 God gave them over to a *r* mind
2 Tim. 3: 8 corrupt minds, *r* concerning the faith
Tit. 1:16 unto every good work *r*

REPROOF
Prov. 1:23 turn you at my *r*: behold I will
10:17 he that refuseth *r* erreth
13:18 he that regardeth *r* shall be honoured
15: 5 he that regardeth *r* is prudent
15:32 heareth *r* getteth understanding
17:10 entereth more into a wise
2 Tim. 3:16 is profitable for doctrine, for *r*

REPROVE (REPROVED, REPROVETH)
Prov. 9: 7 that a *r* scorner getteth
15:12 a scorner loveth not one that *r*
29: 1 he that being often *r* hardeneth
Is. 29:21 that *r* in the gate, and turn aside
Hos. 4: 4 let no man strive nor *r*
John 16: 8 *r* the world of sin, righteousness
3:20 lest his deeds should be *r*

REPUTATION
Eccl. 10: 1 that is in *r* for wisdom
Acts 5:34 had in *r* among all the people
Gal. 2: 2 privately to them which were of *r*
Phil. 2: 7 made himself of no *r*, and took

REQUEST (REQUESTS)
Ps. 106:15 he gave them their *r*; but sent
Phil. 4: 6 let your *r* be made known unto God

REQUIRE (REQUIRED)
Gen. 42:22 also his blood is *r*
Deut. 10:12 what doth the Lord *r*
Prov. 30: 7 two things have I *r* of
Mic. 6: 8 what doth the Lord *r*
Luke 12:20 shall be *r* of thee
12:48 of him shall much be *r*

REQUITE (REQUITING)
Deut. 32: 6 do ye thus *r* the Lord
2 Chr. 6:23 by *r* the wicked, by recompensing
1 Tim. 5: 4 and to *r* their parents:

RESERVE (RESERVED, RESERVETH)
Jer. 50:20 will pardon them whom I *r*
Nah. 1: 2 he *r* wrath for his enemies
1 Pet. 1: 4 not away, *r* in heaven for you
2 Pet. 2: 9 and to *r* the unjust unto the day
Jude 1: 6 *r* in everlasting chains

RESIST (RESISTED, RESISTETH)
Mat. 5:39 I say unto you that ye *r* not evil
Acts 7:51 ye do always *r* the Holy Ghost
Rom. 9:19 who hath *r* his will?
2 Tim. 3: 8 so do these *r* the truth
Heb. 12: 4 have not yet *r* unto blood
Jas. 4: 6 God *r* the proud, but giveth grace
4: 7 *r* the devil, and he will
1 Pet. 5: 5 God *r* the proud, and giveth grace

RESPECT (RESPECTETH)
2 Chr. 19: 7 nor *r* of persons, nor
Ps. 40: 4 *r* not the proud, nor
119: 6 *r* to all thy commandments
138: 6 yet hath he *r* unto the lowly
Prov. 24:23 not good to have *r* of persons
Rom. 2:11 there is no *r* of persons
Eph. 6: 9 neither is there of *r*
Col. 3:25 there is no *r* of
Jas. 2: 1 Lord of glory, with *r* of persons
2: 9 if ye have *r* to persons, ye commit

REST
Ex. 16:23 the *r* of the holy sabbath
Deut. 12: 9 as yet come to the *r*
Ps. 9: My flesh shall *r* in hope
95:11 they should not enter into my *r*
125: 3 rod of the wicked shall not *r*
132:14 this is my *r* for ever: here will I
Is. 11:10 his *r* shall be glorious

30:15 in returning and *r* shall ye be saved
57:20 the troubled sea, when it cannot *r*
Jer. 6:16 ye shall find *r* for your souls
Hab. 3:16 I might *r* in the day of trouble
Heb. 4: 9 a *r* to the people of God
Rev. 14:13 they may *r* from their labours

RESTEST (RESTETH)
Prov. 14:33 wisdom *r* in the heart of him
Eccl. 7: 9 anger *r* in bosom of fools
1 Pet. 4:14 glory and of God *r* upon you

RESTING
Num. 10:33 search out a *r* place for them
Is. 32:18 and in quiet *r* places
Jer. 50: 6 they have forgotten their *r* place

RESTORE (RESTORED, RESTORETH)
Ps. 23: 3 He *r* my soul: he
51:12 *R* unto me the joy of
Gal. 6: 1 *r* such an one in the spirit

RESTITUTION
Ex. 22: 3 he should make full *r*;
Acts 3:21 until the times of *r* of all things

RESURRECTION
Mat. 22:23 Sadducees which say that there is no *r*
Luke 20:36 being the children of the *r*
John 5:29 done good unto the *r* of life
11:25 I am the *r* and the life
Acts 17:18 preached unto them Jesus and the *r*
24:15 there shall be a *r* of the dead
Rom. 6: 5 together in the likeness of his *r*
1 Cor. 15:12 is no *r* of the dead
Phil. 3:10 and the power of his *r*,
Heb. 6: 2 and of *r* of the dead,
11:35 that they might obtain a better *r*
Rev. 20: 5 This is the first *r*

RETURN
Gen. 3:19 till thou *r* unto the ground
1 Ki. 8:48 to thee with all their heart
Job 1:21 naked shall I *r* thither
Eccl. 12: 7 dust shall *r* to the earth
35:10 the ransomed of the Lord shall *r*
55:11 shall not *r* unto me void
Jer. 3:12 *r*, thou backsliding Israel, saith
5: 3 they have refused to *r*
15:19 let them *r* unto thee, but *r*
Hos. 2: 1 I will go and *r* to my first husband
7:16 they *r*, but not to the Most High
11: 9 I will not *r* to destroy Ephraim
Mal. 3: 7 *r* to me, and I will *r* to

RETURNED (RETURNING)
Ps. 78:34 they *r* and inquired early after God
Is. 30:15 in *r* and rest shall ye be
Amos 4: 6 yet have ye not *r* unto me
1 Pet. 2:25 but are now *r* unto the Shepherd

REVEAL (REVEALED, REVEALETH)
Deut. 29:29 things which are *r* belong unto us
Job 20:27 heaven shall *r* his iniquity
Dan. 2:19 then was the secret *r* unto Daniel
Mat. 11:25 and hast *r* them unto babes
16:17 flesh and blood hath not *r*
Rom. 1:17 righteousness of God *r* from faith to
8:18 glory which shall be *r* in us
1 Cor. 2:10 God hath *r* them to us
2 Thes. 1: 7 when the Lord Jesus shall be *r*
2: 3 and that man of sin be *r*; the Son

REVELATION (REVELATIONS)
Rom. 2: 5 wrath and *r* of the righteous
16:25 according to the *r* of the mystery
Gal. 1:12 taught it, but by the *r* of Jesus
Eph. 3: 3 by *r* he made known unto me the
1 Pet. 1:13 unto you at the *r* of Jesus Christ
Rev. 1: 1 the *r* of Jesus Christ, which God

REVENGE (REVENGETH)
Jer. 15:15 *r* me of my persecutors; take me
Nah. 1: 2 the Lord *r* and is furious
2 Cor. 7:11 what zeal, yea, what *r*

REVERENCE
Ps. 89: 7 to be had in *r* of all them
Eph. 5:33 wife see that she *r* her
Heb. 12:28 serve God acceptably with *r*

REVILE (REVILED)
Ex. 22:28 shalt not *r* the gods, nor curse the
Mat. 5:11 when men shall *r* you, and persecute

1 Cor. 4:12 being *r* we bless; being persecuted
1 Pet. 2:23 when he was *r r* not

REVILERS
1 Cor. 6:10 nor drunkards, nor *r*,

REVIVE (REVIVED)
Ps. 85: 6 wilt thou not *r* us
Is. 57:15 the spirit of the humble, to *r*
Hos. 6: 2 after two days will he *r* us
Rom. 14: 9 Christ both died and rose, and *r*

REVOLT (REVOLTING)
Is. 1: 5 ye will *r* more and
Jer. 5:23 hath a *r* and a rebellious heart

REWARD
Ps. 19:11 in keeping them is great *r*
58:11 there is a *r* for the righteous
127: 3 fruit of the womb is his *r*
Prov. 11:18 righteousness shall be sure *r*
Is. 3:11 *r* of his hands shall be
Mic. 7: 3 the judge asketh for a *r*
Mat. 5:12 great is your *r* in heaven
6: 2 I say unto you, They have their *r*
10:41 shall receive a prophet's *r*
Rom. 4: 4 is the *r* not reckoned
1 Cor. 3: 8 every man shall receive his own *r*
Col. 2:18 no man beguile you of your *r*
3:24 receive the *r* of inheritance
1 Tim. 5:18 labourer is worthy of his *r*
2 Tim. 4:14 Lord *r* him according to his works
Heb. 2: 2 received a just recompence of *r*
Rev. 22:12 I come quickly; and my *r* is with

REWARDED (REWARDETH)
Ps. 103:10 nor *r* us according to our iniquities

REWARDER
Heb. 11: 6 of them that diligently seek

RICH
Ex. 30:15 the *r* shall not give
Prov. 10: 4 hand of the diligent maketh *r*
14:20 but the *r* hath many friends
22: 2 *r* and poor meet together
23: 4 labour not to be *r*: cease from
28:20 that maketh haste to be *r* shall
Eccl. 5:12 abundance of the *r* will not suffer
Jer. 9:23 let not the *r* man glory
Mat. 19:23 *r* man shall hardly enter into the
Luke 1:53 *r* he hath sent empty away
6:24 woe unto you that are *r*
16: 1 certain *r* man which
18:23 sorrowful: for he was very *r*
2 Cor. 6:10 as poor yet making many *r*
8: 9 though he was *r* yet for your sakes
Eph. 2: 4 God, who is *r* in mercy
1 Tim. 6:18 that they be *r* in good works
Jas. 2: 5 poor of this world *r* in faith
Rev. 2: 9 thy poverty, (but thou art *r*)
3:17 because thou sayest, I am *r*

RICHES
1 Chr. 29:12 both *r* and honour come of thee
Ps. 49: 6 boast themselves in multitude of their *r*
52: 7 trusted in the abundance of his *r*
104: 24 the earth is full of thy *r*
Prov. 11:28 that trusteth in his *r* shall fall
14:24 crown of the wise is their *r*
27:24 *r* are not for ever, nor
30: 8 give me neither poverty nor *r*
Jer. 17:11 so he that getteth *r*
Mat. 13:22 deceitfulness of *r*, choke the word
11:12 the fall of them be the *r* of
2 Cor. 8: 2 unto the *r* of their liberality
Eph. 1: 7 according to the *r* of his
2: 7 show exceeding *r* of grace
Col. 1:27 the *r* of the glory of this mystery
1 Tim. 6:17 not trust in uncertain *r*
Jas. 5: 2 your *r* are corrupted,

RICHLY
Col. 3:16 word of Christ dwell in you *r*
1 Tim. 6:17 who giveth us *r* all things to enjoy

RIDE (RIDETH)
Deut. 33:26 who *r* upon thy heaven
Ps. 68:33 that *r* upon the heavens of heavens
Is. 19: 1 Lord *r* upon a stiff cloud

RIGHT
Gen. 18:25 Judge of all the earth do *r*

Deut. 21:17 the *r* of the firstborn is
Ps. 19: 8 the statutes of the Lord are *r*
51:10 renew a *r* spirit within
Prov. 12: 5 thoughts of the righteous are *r*
14:12 a way which seemeth *r* to
21: 2 way of man is *r* in his
Is. 30:10 prophesy not unto us *r* things
Hos. 14: 9 ways of the Lord are *r*
Amos 3:10 they know not to do *r*
Luke 12:57 judge ye not what is *r*
Acts 4:19 whether it be *r* in the sight of God
8:21 heart is not *r* in the sight of
Eph. 6: 1 parents in the Lord: for this is *r*
Rev. 22:14 have a *r* to the tree of life

RIGHTLY
2 Tim. 2:15 *r* dividing the word of truth

RIGHTEOUS
Gen. 18:23 also destroy the *r* with the wicked
Ps. 1: 6 Lord knoweth the way of the *r*
5:12 thou, Lord, wilt bless the *r*
32:11 glad in the Lord and rejoice, ye *r*
34:17 *r* cry, and the Lord
37:25 have I not seen the *r* forsaken
55:22 never suffer the *r* to be moved
58:11 there is a reward for the *r*
64:10 *r* shall be glad in the Lord
92:12 the *r* shall flourish like a palm tree
97:11 light is sown for the *r*, and gladness
145:17 the Lord is *r* in all his ways
146: 8 the Lord loveth the *r*
Prov. 3:32 his secret is with the *r*
10:21 the lips of the *r* feed
10:30 the *r* shall never be removed
11: 8 *r* is delivered out of trouble
11:28 the *r* shall flourish as a branch
12:26 *r* is more excellent than his
13: 9 the light of the *r* rejoiceth
15: 6 in the house of the *r* is
15:19 the way of the *r* is made plain
28: 1 the *r* are bold as a lion
Eccl. 7:16 be not *r* over much,
Is. 3:10 say ye to *r*, it shall be well
60:21 thy people also shall be all *r*
Ezek. 3:20 when a *r* man doth turn
Mat. 9:13 not come to call the *r*,
10:41 shall receive the *r* man's reward
25:46 but the *r* into life eternal
Luke 1: 6 they were both *r* before God
18: 9 that they were *r* and despised
Rom. 3:10 there is none *r*, no not
5: 7 scarcely for a *r* man
1 Tim. 1: 9 law is not made for a *r*
Jas. 5:16 fervent prayer of the *r* man
Rev. 22:11 he that is *r* let him be *r*

RIGHTEOUSLY
Tit. 2:12 live soberly, *r*, and

RIGHTEOUSNESS
Gen. 15: 6 and he counted it to him for *r*
Deut. 6:25 it shall be our *r* if
1 Ki. 8:32 give him according to his *r*
Job 36: 3 and will ascribe *r* to my Maker
Ps. 11: 7 righteous Lord loveth *r*
15: 2 walketh uprightly and worketh *r*
40:10 I have not hid thy *r* within my
50: 6 heavens shall declare his *r*
85:10 *r* and peace have kissed each other
97: 2 *r* and judgment are the habitation
106: 31 that was counted unto him for *r*
Prov. 11: 5 *r* of the perfect shall direct his way
11:18 to him that soweth *r* a sure
13: 6 *r* keepeth him that is upright in
14:34 *r* exalteth a nation: but sin
15: 9 he loveth him that followeth *r*
16:12 the throne is established by *r*
Is. 11: 5 *r* shall be the girdle of his loins
26: 9 inhabitants of the world will learn *r*
28:17 to line and *r* to the plummet
32:17 work of *r* shall be peace
46:13 I bring near my *r*, it shall not
57:12 I will declare thy *r*, and the works
61:10 covered me with the robe of *r*
64: 6 and all our *r* are as filthy rags
Jer. 23: 6 be called THE LORD OUR *R*

Dan. 9: 7 O Lord, *r* belongeth unto thee
Zeph. 2: 3 seek *r*, seek meekness: it may be
Mal. 4: 2 Sun of *r* arise with healing
Mat. 3:15 it becometh us to fulfil all *r*
5: 6 which do hunger and thirst after *r*
6:33 God, and his *r*; and all
Luke 1:75 in holiness and *r*
John 16: 8 the world of sin, and of *r*
Acts 10:35 worketh *r*, is accepted,
13:10 thou enemy of all *r*
Rom. 1:17 is the *r* of God revealed
3:22 even *r* of God which is by faith of
4: 5 his faith is counted for *r*
4:22 it was imputed to him for *r*
5:18 by the *r* of one the free gift came
5:21 grace reign through *r* unto eternal
6:13 members as instruments of *r*
9:30 have attained to *r*, even *r*, 31.
10: 3 ignorant of God's *r*,
10:10 heart of man believeth unto *r*
14:17 but *r*, and peace, and joy
1 Cor. 1:30 made unto us wisdom and *r*
15:34 awake to *r* and sin not
2 Cor. 5:21 might be made the *r* of God in him
6: 7 armour of *r* on the right hand
11:15 transformed as ministers of *r*
Gal. 2:21 if *r* come by the law,
3: 6 and it was accounted to him for *r*
Eph. 6:14 having on the breastplate of *r*
Phil. 1:11 being filled with fruits of *r*
3: 6 *r* which is in the law blameless
1 Tim. 6:11 follow after *r*, godliness, faith
Heb. 12:11 peaceable fruit of *r* unto them
Jas. 1:20 man worketh not the *r* of God
3:18 fruit of *r* is sown in peace
1 Pet. 3:14 if ye suffer for *r* sake
2 Pet. 1: 1 through the *r* of God
3:13 new earth, wherein dwelleth *r*
1 John 2:29 one that doeth *r* is born of him
Rev. 19: 8 fine linen is the *r* of saints

RIOTOUS
Prov. 23:20 winebibbers; among *r* eaters of flesh
Luke 15:13 wasted his substance with *r* living

RIPE
Jer. 24: 2 like the figs that are first *r*
Joel 3:13 the sickle, for the harvest is *r*
Rev. 14:15 harvest of the earth is *r*

RISE
Sol. 3: 2 I will *r* now, and go
Is. 26:14 deceased, they shall not *r*
43:17 together, they shall not *r*
54:17 every tongue that shall *r* against thee
1 Thes. 4:16 dead in Christ shall *r* first

RIVER (RIVERS)
Ex. 1:22 is born ye shall cast into the *r*
Job 20:17 he shall not see the *r*
Ps. 36: 8 drink of the *r* of thy pleasures
46: 4 There is a *r*, the streams whereof
119:136 *R* of water run down mine eyes
Prov. 21: 1 of the Lord, as the *r* of water
Is. 48:18 then had thy peace been as a *r*
66:12 I will extend peace to her like a *r*
Mic. 6: 7 or with ten thousands of *r* of oil
John 7:38 belly shall flow *r* of living water
Rev. 22: 2 on either side of the *r*

ROAR
Is. 42:13 he shall cry, yea *r*; he shall
Joel 3:16 Lord also shall *r* out of Zion
Amos 1: 2 Lord will *r* from Zion, and utter

ROB
Prov. 22:22 *R* not the poor, because he is poor
Mal. 3: 8 Will a man *r* God? Yet ye have

ROBBERY
Prov. 21: 7 *r* of the wicked shall destroy
Amos 3:10 who store up violence and *r*
Phil. 2: 6 thought it not *r* to be equal

ROBE (ROBES)
Is. 61:10 covered me with the *r* of righteousness
Rev. 7:14 and have washed their *r*

ROCK (ROCKS)
Ex. 17: 6 thou shalt smite the *r*
Num. 20:11 with his rod he smote the *r* twice
Deut. 32: 4 He is the *R*, his work is perfect

Ps. 18: 2 the Lord is my *r*
31: 3 thou art my *r* and my fortress
61: 2 lead me to the *r* that is higher than
62: 2 he only is my *r* and my salvation
89:26 and the *r* of my salvation
94:22 God is the *r* of my refuge
Mat. 7:24 wise man, which built his house on a *r*
16:18 on this I will build my church
1 Cor. 10: 4 them: and that *R* was Christ

ROD
Ex. 4:20 Moses took the *r* of God
Ps. 23: 4 thy *r* and staff they comfort
125: 3 of the wicked shall not rest upon
Prov. 13:24 spareth his *r* hateth his son
23:14 shalt beat him with the *r*
Mic. 7:14 feed thy people with thy *r*
Rev. 2:27 he shall rule with a *r* of iron

ROOT
Deut. 29:18 among you a *r* that beareth gall
Is. 11:10 there shall be *r* of Jesse
Mat. 3:10 laid to the *r* of the trees
Luke 17: 6 be thou plucked up by the *r*
Rom. 11:16 if the *r* be holy, so are
1 Tim. 6:10 love of money is the *r* of all

ROOTED
Mat. 15:13 not planted, shall be *r* up
Eph. 3:17 being *r* and grounded in love
Col. 2: 7 and built up in him,

ROSE
Sol. 2: 1 I am the *r* of Sharon
Is. 35: 1 shall rejoice and blossom as the *r*

ROYAL
Jas. 2: 8 if ye fulfil the *r* law
1 Pet. 2: 9 a *r* priesthood, an holy nation

RUBIES
Job 28:18 Price of wisdom is above *r*
Prov. 3:15 she is more precious than *r*
8:11 for wisdom is better than *r*
31:10 for her price is far above *r*

RULE (RULETH)
Ps. 103:19 his kingdom *r* over all
Prov. 16:23 he that *r* his spirit
25:28 that hath no *r* over his own spirit
Gal. 6:16 walk according to this *r*
Phil. 3:16 let us walk by the same *r*
Col. 3:15 let the peace of God *r*
1 Tim. 3: 5 man know not how to *r* his own house
Rev. 12: 5 man child who was to *r* all

RULER (RULERS)
Mic. 5: 2 unto me that is to be *r* in Israel
Mat. 25:21 I will make thee *r* over
Rom. 13: 3 *r* are not a terror to good works
Eph. 6:12 *r* of the darkness of this world

RUN (RUNNETH)
1 Sam. 8:11 some shall *r* before his chariots
2 Chr. 16: 9 eyes of the Lord *r* to
Ps. 19: 5 rejoiceth as a strong man to *r* a race
23: 5 my head with oil; my cup *r* over
Is. 40:31 shall *r* and not be weary
Rom. 9:16 nor of him that *r* but of God
Gal. 2: 2 *r*, or had *r* in vain
Heb. 12: 1 *r* with patience the race

SABBATH (SABBATHS)
Ex. 20: 8 Remember the *s* day, to keep it holy
Lev. 23: 3 seventh day is the *s* of rest
26: 2 Ye shall keep my *s*, and reverence
Is. 56: 4 Eunuchs that keep my *s*
58:13 call the *s* a delight, the holy
Ezek. 20:13 my *s* they greatly polluted
Mat. 12: 5 priests in the temple profane the *s*
28: 1 end of the *s*, as it began to dawn
Acts 13:42 preached to them the next *s* every *s*

SACKCLOTH
Job 16:15 I have sewed *s* upon my skin
Ps. 30:11 thou hast put off my *s*,
Rev. 11: 3 threescore days, clothed in *s*

SACRIFICE
1 Sam.15:22 to obey is better than *s*
Ps. 50: 5 made covenant with me by *s*
107:22 *s* the sacrifices of thanksgiving
141: 2 up of my hands as the evening *s*
Prov. 21: 3 more acceptable to Lord than *s*

Dan. 9: 27 cause s and oblation to cease
Hos. 6: 6 for I desired mercy and not s
Mat. 9: 13 I will have mercy, and not s
Mark 9: 49 and every s be salted with salt
Rom. 12: 1 present your bodies a living s
Eph. 5: 2 a s to God for a sweetsmelling
Phil. 2: 17 offered on the s and
       4: 18 a s acceptable, wellpleasing to God
Heb. 9: 26 put away sin by s of himself

SACRIFICED (SACRIFICES)
Ps. 51: 17 s of God are a broken spirit
1 Cor. 5: 7 Christ our passover is for us
Heb. 13: 15 offer the s of praise to God
1 Pet. 2: 5 priesthood, to offer up spiritual s

SAINTS
Deut. 33: 3 all his s are in thy hand
1 Sam. 2: 9 he will keep the feet of his s
Ps. 50: 5 gather my s together unto me
       89: 5 in the congregation of the s
       97: 10 he preserveth the souls of his s
       116: 15 is the death of his s
Prov. 2: 8 preserveth the way of his s
Rom. 8: 27 beloved of God, called to be s
       8: 27 intercession for the s, according
1 Cor. 1: 2 called to be s, with all that
       16: 1 concerning the collection for the s
2 Cor. 8: 4 of the ministering to the s
       9: 12 supplieth the want of the s
Eph. 3: 8 less than the least of all s
       6: 18 supplication for all s
Heb. 6: 10 ye have ministered to the s
Rev. 5: 8 which are the prayers of the s
       11: 18 to the s and them that fear
       13: 7 to make war with the s
       14: 12 here is the patience of the s
       15: 3 thy ways, thou King of s
       16: 6 shed the blood of the s and prophets
       19: 8 fine linen is the righteousness of s
       20: 9 compassed the camp of the s

SALT
Gen. 19: 26 she became a pillar of s
Mat. 5: 13 ye are the s of the earth: but if
Mark 9: 50 Have s in yourselves, and have peace
Col. 4: 6 grace, seasoned with s, that ye may

SALVATION
Ex. 15: 2 he is become my s: he
2 Sam. 23: 5 this is all my s, and all
Ps. 3: 8 s belongeth to the Lord
       18: 2 the horn of my s, and
       27: 1 my light and my s;
       37: 39 s of the righteous is of the Lord
       50: 23 I will show him the s of God
       51: 14 thou God of my s, and
       68: 20 God is the God of s
       85: 9 his s is nigh them that fear him
       89: 26 God, and the rock of my s
       118: 14 and song, and is become my s
       119: 155 s is far from the wicked
       140: 7 Lord, the strength of my s
       149: 4 will beautify the meek with s
Is. 12: 2 Behold, God is my s; I will trust
       25: 9 be glad and rejoice in his s
       45: 17 Lord with an everlasting s
       46: 13 I will place in Zion
       52: 10 shall see the s of our God
       59: 16 his arm brought s unto him
       60: 18 call thy walls S, thy gates
       61: 10 clothed me with garments of s
Jer. 3: 23 in vain is s hoped for
Lam. 3: 26 quietly wait for the s of the Lord
Jonah 2: 9 have vowed S is of the Lord
Mic. 7: 7 I will wait for the God of my s
Hab. 3: 18 I will joy in the God of my s
Luke 19: 9 this day is s come to this house
John 4: 22 worship: for s is of the Jews
Rom. 1: 16 it is the power of God to s
       11: 11 through their fall s is come
       13: 11 now is our s nearer
2 Cor. 6: 2 it is for your consolation and s
       6: 2 behold, now is the day of s
Eph. 6: 17 take the helmet of s
Phil. 2: 12 work out your own s
1 Thes. 5: 8 for an helmet, the hope of s

2 Thes. 2: 13 from the beginning chosen you to s
       3: 15 able to make thee wise unto s
Tit. 2: 11 grace of God that bringeth s
Heb. 2: 3 escape, if we neglect so great s
       5: 9 he became the author of eternal s
1 Pet. 1: 5 through faith to s, ready to be
Rev. 7: 10 S to our God, which sitteth upon
       12: 10 Now is come s, and strength, and
       19: 1 S, and glory, and honour

SANCTIFY
Ex. 13: 2 s unto me all the firstborn
       31: 13 I am the Lord that doth s
Lev. 20: 7 s yourselves therefore and be ye holy
Is. 8: 13 s the Lord of hosts himself
Joel 2: 16 s the congregation, assemble the
John 17: 17 s them through thy truth
1 Thes. 5: 23 very God of peace s you wholly
Heb. 13: 12 that he might s the people
1 Pet. 3: 15 s the Lord God in your hearts

SANCTIFIED (SANCTIFIETH)
Gen. 2: 3 blessed seventh day and s it
Is. 5: 16 God that is holy shall be s
Jer. 1: 5 I s thee, and I ordained thee
Mat. 23: 17 or the temple that s the gold
John 10: 36 him whom the Father hath s
Acts 20: 32 among all them which are s
Rom. 15: 16 being s by the holy ghost
1 Cor. 6: 11 ye are washed, but ye are s
       7: 14 unbelieving husband is s by the wife
1 Tim. 4: 5 s by the word of God
Heb. 10: 14 perfected for ever them that are s

SANCTIFICATION
1 Thes. 4: 4 possess his vessel in s and honour
2 Thes. 2: 13 chosen you to salvation through s
1 Pet. 1: 2 s of the spirit, unto obedience

SANCTUARY
Ps. 63: 2 seen thee in the s
       73: 17 I went into the s of God
Is. 8: 14 he shall be for a s
Ezek. 11: 16 be to them as a little s
Heb. 9: 2 the showbread; which is called the s

SAND
Gen. 22: 17 s which is upon the seashore
       32: 12 thy seed as the s of the sea
Is. 10: 22 Israel be as the s of the sea
Mat. 7: 26 built his house upon the s

SATAN
1 Chr. 21: 1 S stood up against Israel
Job 1: 6 S came also among
Ps. 109: 6 let S stand at his right
Mat. 4: 10 get thee hence, S: for it is
       16: 23 unto Peter, Get thee behind me S
Luke 10: 18 I beheld S as lightning fall
       22: 3 then entered S into Judas
Acts 26: 18 turn from the power of S
Rom. 16: 20 God of peace shall bruise S
1 Cor. 5: 5 deliver such an one to S
2 Cor. 12: 7 messenger of S to buffet me
1 Tim. 1: 20 I have delivered unto S, that they
Rev. 2: 24 have not known the depths of S

SATISFY (SATISFIETH, SATISFIED)
Ps. 17: 15 when I awake s with thy likeness
       22: 26 The meek shall eat and be s
       63: 5 my soul shall be s as with marrow
       65: 4 s with the goodness of thy house
       90: 14 O s us early with thy mercy
       91: 16 with long life will I s him
       103: 5 who s thy mouth with good
       107: 9 he s the longing soul and filleth
       132: 15 s her poor with bread
Prov. 5: 19 let her breasts s thee at all times
       27: 20 eyes of man are never s
       30: 15 there are three things never s
Eccl. 5: 10 loveth silver shall not be s
Is. 53: 11 see travail of his soul and be s
       66: 11 be s with the breasts of her

SAVE
Gen. 45: 7 s your lives by a great deliverance
Job 22: 29 he shall s the humble person
Ps. 6: 4 s me for thy mercies' sake
       18: 27 wilt s the afflicted people; but
       69: 35 God will s Zion and build the
       72: 4 shall s the children of the needy

       109: 31 those that condemn to s him from
       145: 19 hear their cry and will s them
Is. 25: 9 and he will s us
       35: 4 he will come and s
       45: 20 pray unto a god that cannot s
Jer. 17: 14 s me and I shall be saved
Ezek. 18: 27 he shall s his soul alive
       36: 29 s you from all your uncleanness
Zeph. 3: 17 of thee is mighty; he will s
Zech. 8: 7 I will s my people from the east
Mat. 1: 21 s his people from their
       16: 25 whosoever will s his life shall lose
       18: 11 Son of man is come to s that which
Mark 3: 4 to s life or to kill? But
John 12: 27 s me from this hour
       12: 47 judge the world but to s the world
1 Cor. 1: 21 preaching to s them that believe
       9: 22 that I might by all means s some
1 Tim. 1: 15 to s sinners, of whom I am chief
Heb. 7: 25 able to s them to the uttermost
Jas. 1: 21 word which is able to s
       2: 14 works? can faith s him?
       5: 15 prayer of faith shall s the sick
1 Pet. 3: 21 baptism doth also now s us
Jude 1: 23 others s with fear, pulling

SAVED
Ps. 44: 7 thou hast s us from our enemies
       80: 3 face to shine, we shall be s
Is. 45: 17 Israel shall be s in the Lord
Jer. 4: 14 that thou mayest be s
Mat. 19: 25 saying, who then can be s
Mark 16: 16 believeth and is baptized shall be s
Luke 1: 71 be s from our enemies
       7: 50 woman, thy faith hath s thee
       18: 42 thy sight: thy faith hath s thee
       23: 35 he s others, let him save himself
John 3: 17 world through him might be s
Acts 2: 47 daily such as should be s
       4: 12 none other name whereby we must be s
       16: 30 what must I do to be s
Rom. 5: 10 shall be s by his life
       8: 24 we are s by hope: but hope that
       10: 1 for Israel is that they might be s
       11: 26 all Israel shall be s
1 Cor. 1: 18 to us which are s it is the power
Eph. 2: 5 by grace ye are s
1 Tim. 2: 15 she shall be s in childbearing
Tit. 3: 5 according to his mercy he s us

SAVIOUR
2 Sam. 22: 3 my refuge, my s; thou
2 Ki. 13: 5 Lord gave Israel a s so that
Is. 43: 3 I am thy S: I gave Egypt for
       45: 15 O God of Israel, the S
       60: 16 thy s and thy Redeemer
Hos. 13: 4 there is no s beside
Luke 1: 47 my spirit hath rejoiced in God my S
       2: 11 a S which is Christ the
Eph. 5: 23 he is the s of the body
       4: 10 who is the s of all men
Tit. 2: 13 God and our s Jesus
       3: 4 love of God our S toward man
2 Pet. 2: 20 knowledge of the Lord and S
Jude 1: 25 only wise God our S be glory

SAVOUR (SAVOUREST)
Gen. 8: 21 and the Lord smelled a sweet s
Ex. 29: 18 it is a sweet s, an offering
Lev. 1: 9 by fire, a sweet s unto the Lord
Sol. 1: 3 of the s of thy good ointments thy
2 Cor. 2: 15 are to God a sweet s of Christ
Eph. 5: 2 sacrifice to God for a sweetsmelling s

SCATTER (SCATTERED, SCATTERETH)
Gen. 49: 7 in Judah, and s them in Israel
Ezek. 34: 5 s, because there is no shepherd
Mat. 9: 36 abroad as sheep, having no shepherd
Luke 1: 51 s the proud in the imagination of

SCEPTRE
Gen. 49: 10 s shall not depart from Judah
Num. 24: 17 s shall rise out of Israel
Ps. 45: 6 s of thy kingdom is a right s
Heb. 1: 8 righteousness is the s of thy kingdom

SCOFFERS
2 Pet. 3: 3 come in the last days of s

SCORN
Job	16:20	My friends s me: but mine eye
Ps.	44:13	a s and a derision to them

SCORNER (SCORNERS)
Prov.	1:22	the s delight in their scorning
	9:8	reprove not a s, lest
	14:6	a s seeketh wisdom and findeth

SCORNFUL
Ps.	1:1	sitteth in the seat of the s
Prov.	29:8	S men bring a city into a snare
Is.	28:14	s men, that rule this people

SCRIPTURE (SCRIPTURES)
Dan.	10:21	which is noted in the s of truth
Mat.	22:29	ye do err not knowing the s
John	5:39	Search the s; for in
Acts	17:11	searched the s daily
Rom.	15:4	through the comfort of the s
2 Tim.	3:15	thou hast known the holy s
	3:16	all s is given by inspiration
2 Pet.	3:16	wrest, as they do also other s

SEA
Ps.	72:8	dominion also from s to s
Prov.	8:29	gave to the s his decree
Is.	48:18	righteousness as the waves of the s
	57:20	wicked are like the troubled s
Zech.	9:10	his dominion shall be from s to s
Rev.	4:6	there was a s of glass
	10:2	set his right foot upon the s
	15:2	a s of glass mingled with fire
	21:1	and there was no more s

SEAL
Sol.	8:6	Set me as a s upon thine heart
John	3:33	set to his s that God is true
Rom.	4:11	s of the righteousness of the faith
1 Cor.	9:2	s of my apostleship

SEALED
John	6:27	for him hath God the Father s
2 Cor.	1:22	who hath also s us and given the
Eph.	1:13	ye were s with that Holy Spirit
Rev.	5:1	a book s with seven seals
	7:3	s the servants of our God

SEARCH (SEARCHED, SEARCHEST, SEARCHETH)
1 Chr.	28:9	the Lord s all hearts
Job	10:6	iniquity, and s after my sin
Ps.	139:23	s me, O God, and
Prov.	25:27	men to s their own glory is
Jer.	17:10	I the Lord s the heart
Zeph.	1:12	I will s Jerusalem with candles
John	5:39	s the scriptures; for in
Acts	17:11	these s the scriptures daily
1 Cor.	2:10	for the spirit s all things, yea

SEASON (SEASONS)
Ps.	1:3	bringeth forth his fruit in his s
Luke	4:13	he departed from him for a s
John	5:35	willing for a s to rejoice
Acts	1:7	for you to know the times or s
2 Tim.	4:2	be instant in s, out of s
Heb.	11:25	enjoy the pleasures of sin for a s
1 Pet.	1:6	greatly rejoice, though now for a s

SEASONED
Col.	4:6	speech be always with grace s

SECRET (SECRETS)
Job	11:6	he would show thee the s of wisdom
	15:8	hast thou heard the s of God
Ps.	25:14	s of the Lord is with them that
	44:21	he knoweth the s of the heart
	139:15	when I was made in s, and curiously
Prov.	9:17	bread eaten in s is pleasant
	11:13	A talebearer revealeth s, but he
Amos	3:7	revealeth his s to his
Mat.	6:4	thine alms may be in s: and thy
Rom.	2:16	God shall judge the s of men by

SEE (SEEN, SEETH)
Ps.	34:8	O taste and s that the Lord is good
Mat.	5:8	in heart: for they shall s God
	6:1	before men to be s of them
	13:17	which ye s and have not s them
	23:5	their works they do to be s of men
John	1:18	no man hath s God at any time
	12:45	he that s me s him that
	14:9	he that hath s me hath s the Father
	16:22	I will s you again, and

	20:29	blessed are they that have not s
2 Cor.	4:18	things which are s are temporal
1 Tim.	6:16	whom no man hath s, nor can s
	11:1	the evidence of things not s
1 Pet.	1:8	not having s, ye love
1 John	3:2	we shall s him as he is
Rev.	1:7	and every eye shall s him
	22:4	they shall s his face:

SEED (SEEDS)
Gen.	1:11	whose s is in itself upon the earth
	17:7	between me and thee and thy s
Ps.	37:28	s of wicked shall be cut off
	126:6	bearing precious s shall doubtless
Prov.	11:21	s of righteous shall be
Eccl.	11:6	morning, sow thy s
Is.	53:10	see his s, he shall prolong his days
	55:10	that it may give s to the sower
Mat.	13:38	good s are the children of the kingdom
Luke	8:11	the s is the word of God
Rom.	9:8	children of promise are counted for s
1 John	3:9	his s remaineth in him

SEEK
Deut.	4:29	thou s him with all thy heart
1 Chr.	28:9	thou s him, he will be found
Ezra	8:21	to s of him a right way
Ps.	9:10	not forsake them that s
	10:15	s out his wickedness till thou
	63:1	my God, early will I s
	69:32	heart shall live that s God
	119:2	blessed are they that s
Prov.	8:17	that s me early shall find
Is.	26:9	within me will I s thee early
Jer.	29:13	ye shall s me and find
Amos	5:4	s ye me, ye shall live
Zeph.	2:3	s righteousness, s meekness
Mat.	6:33	s ye first the kingdom of God
	7:7	s and ye shall find; knock
Luke	13:24	many will s to enter in
	19:10	s and to save that which was lost
John	8:21	ye shall s me and shall die in your
Rom.	2:7	s for glory and honour
1 Cor.	10:24	let no man s his own
Phil.	2:21	all s their own, not the things
Col.	3:1	s those things which are above
1 Pet.	3:11	let him s peace, and ensue it

SEEKETH (SEEKING)
John	4:23	Father s such to worship
1 Cor.	13:5	s not her own, is not
1 Pet.	5:8	s walketh about s whom he may devour

SELL (SELLETH)
Gen.	25:31	S me this day thy birthright
Prov.	23:23	buy truth and s it not
Mat.	13:44	s all that he hath and buyeth
	19:21	go, and s that thou

SEND
Ps.	43:3	O s out thy light and
Mat.	9:38	s forth labourers into his harvest
John	14:26	whom the Father will s in my name
	16:7	if I depart I will s him unto
2 Thes.	2:11	God shall s them strong delusion

SEPARATE (SEPARATED)
Gen.	49:26	him that was s from his brethren
Is.	59:2	iniquities have s between you and
Acts	13:2	s me Barnabas and Saul for the work
Rom.	8:35	who shall s us from love of Christ
2 Cor.	6:17	and be ye s, saith the Lord
Gal.	1:15	who s me from my mother's womb

SERAPHIMS
Is.	6:2	above it stood the s

SERPENT (SERPENTS)
Gen.	3:1	the s was more subtle
Num.	21:6	Lord sent fiery s among the people
Prov.	23:32	at last it biteth like a s
Mat.	7:10	will he give him a s
	10:16	be ye wise as s, harmless as
John	3:14	as Moses lifted up the s in the
2 Cor.	11:3	as the s beguiled Eve through his
Rev.	12:9	that old s, called the Devil

SERVE
Deut.	10:20	him thou shalt s, and to him
Josh.	22:5	s him with all your heart
	24:15	choose you this day whom ye will s
1 Sam.	12:20	s the Lord with all your heart

1 Chr.	28:9	s him with a perfect heart
Ps.	2:11	s Lord with fear,
Mat.	6:24	ye cannot s God and mammon
Luke	1:74	s him without fear in
	12:37	will come forth and s them
John	12:26	if any man s me let him
Acts	6:2	leave the word of God and s the tables
Rom.	1:9	whom I s with my spirit
	7:6	we should s in newness of spirit
	16:18	they s not the Lord Jesus Christ
Gal.	5:13	but by love s one another
Col.	3:24	for ye s the Lord
1 Thes.	1:9	to s the living and true God
Heb.	9:14	from dead works to s the living God
Rev.	7:15	s him day and night in

SERVANT (SERVANTS)
Is.	42:1	behold my s whom I uphold
	49:3	thou art my s, O Israel,
	52:13	my s shall deal prudently
Mat.	20:27	let him be your s
	25:21	well done, good and faithful s
John	8:34	committeth sin is the s of sin
	13:16	s not greater than the lord
Rom.	6:17	ye were the s of sin
1 Cor.	7:21	art thou called, being a s
	9:19	made myself a s to
Gal.	1:10	should not be the s of Christ
Phil.	1:1	the s of Jesus Christ, to all the
	2:7	took on him the form of a s
2 Tim.	2:24	the s of the Lord must not strive
1 Pet.	2:16	but as the s of God
2 Pet.	2:19	themselves are the s of corruption
Rev.	7:3	we have sealed the s of our God

SERVICE
Jer.	22:13	useth his neighbour's s without
Rom.	12:1	which is your reasonable s

SERVING
Luke	10:40	Martha was cumbered about much s
Acts	20:19	s the Lord with all humility
Rom.	12:11	fervent in spirit; s the Lord

SETTLE (SETTLED)
Luke	21:14	S it therefore in your hearts
Col.	1:23	in faith grounded and s
1 Pet.	5:10	stablish, strengthen, s

SHADOW (SHADOWS)
1 Chr.	29:15	days on the earth are as a s
Job	8:9	days upon earth are a s
Ps.	17:8	under the s of thy wings
	57:1	in the s of thy wings
	144:4	his days are as a s
Eccl.	8:13	his days which are as a s
Is.	49:2	in the s of his hand hath he hid
Jas.	1:17	no variableness, neither s of

SHAKE (SHAKEN)
Hag.	2:7	I will s all nations and
Mat.	10:14	s off the dust of your feet
	11:7	a reed s with the wind

SHAME
Ex.	32:25	made them naked to their s
Prov.	11:2	when pride cometh, then cometh s
	18:13	it is folly and s unto
Is.	22:18	thy glory shall be the s
Hos.	4:7	change their glory to s
Zeph.	3:5	the unjust knoweth no s
Acts	5:41	worthy to suffer s for his
Heb.	12:2	endured the cross, despising the s
Rev.	16:15	naked, and they see his s

SHARP (SHARPER)
Is.	49:2	my mouth like a s sword
Heb.	4:12	s then any twoedged sword

SHARPENETH
Job	16:9	s his eyes upon me
Prov.	27:17	Iron s iron; so a man

SHED
Mat.	26:28	which is s for many for the
Rom.	5:5	love of God is s abroad
Tit.	3:6	Which he s on us abundantly

SHEEP
Ps.	44:22	are counted as s for slaughter
	78:52	people to go forth like s
	95:7	pasture, and the s of his hand
	100:3	people, and the s of his pasture

Is. 53: 6 all we like s have gone astray
Zech. 13: 7 smite the shepherd, and the s shall
Mat. 9:36 as s having no shepherd
10: 6 to the lost s of the house of Israel
18:12 If a man have an hundred s
25:32 divideth his s from the goats
John 10:27 My s hear my voice
21:16 unto him, feed my s
1 Pet. 2:25 were as s going astray

SHEPHERD
Gen. 49:24 the s, the stone of Israel
Num. 27:17 as sheep that have no s
1 Ki. 22:17 as sheep that have no s
Ps. 23: 1 the Lord is my s' l
80: 1 give ear, O S of Israel
Ezek. 34: 5 were scattered because there is no s
37:24 they all shall have one s
Zech. 13: 7 awake, O sword, against my s
Mark 6:34 as sheep not having a s
John 10: 11 I am the good s: the good s
Heb. 13:20 Jesus, that great s
1 Pet. 2:25 returned unto the S and bishop
5: 4 the chief S shall appear

SHEPHERDS (SHEPHERDS')
Ezek. 34: 2 prophesy against the s of Israel
Mic. 5: 5 raise against him seven s

SHIELD
Gen. 15: 1 I am thy s, and thy
Deut. 33:29 Lord the s of thy help
Ps. 3: 3 thou, O Lord art a s for me
33:20 he is our help and our s
115: 9 he is their help and their s
Eph. 6:16 above all, taking the s of faith

SHINE
Num. 6:25 Lord make his face s upon thee
Job 10: 3 s on the counsel of the wicked
22:28 light shall s upon thy ways
37:15 the lights of his cloud to s
Ps. 31:16 face to s upon thy servant
Mat. 5:16 let your light so s before
13:43 righteous s forth as the sun
2 Cor. 4: 6 who commanded light to s
Phil. 2:15 among whom ye s as lights

SHORT
Num. 11:23 Lord's hand waxed s
Rom. 3:23 and come s of the glory of God

SHORTENED
Prov. 10:27 years of the wicked shall be s
Is. 50: 2 is my hand s at all,
Mat. 24:22 except those days be s

SHOUT
Ps. 47: 5 God is gone up with a s
1 Thes. 4:16 Lord shall descend with a s

SHOW (SHOWETH, SHOWING)
Ps. 4: 6 who will s us any good?
91:16 I will s him my salvation
Luke 20:47 for a s make long prayers
John 5:20 and s him all things
1 Cor. 11:26 s the Lord's death till he come
Tit. 2: 7 s thyself a pattern of good works

SICK
Sol. 2: 5 for I am s of love
Is. 1: 5 whole head is s and
Jas. 5:14 is any s among you?
5:15 prayer of faith shall save the s

SICKNESS (SICKNESSES)
Ex. 23:25 I will take s away
Mat. 8:17 infirmities, and bare our s

SIFT
Is. 30:28 to s the nations with a sieve
Amos 9: 9 I will s the house of Israel
Luke 22:31 he may s you as wheat

SIGHT
2 Cor. 5: 7 we walk by faith, not by s

SILENCE
Ps. 31:18 lying lips be put to s
50:21 hast thou done, and I kept s
83: 1 Keep not thou s, O God
Jer. 8:14 God hath put us to s
Amos 5:13 the prudent shall keep s
1 Cor. 14:34 Let your women keep s in the
1 Tim. 2:12 over the man, but to be in s

1 Pet. 2:15 ye may put to s the ignorance
Rev. 8: 1 there was s in heaven

SIMPLE
Ps. 19: 7 sure, making wise the s
116: 6 Lord preserveth the s
119:130 giveth understanding to the s
Prov. 8: 5 O ye s, understand wisdom
14:18 The s inherit folly: but
21: 11 the s is made wise
Rom. 16:18 deceive the hearts of the s

SIN
Gen. 4: 7 doest not well, s lieth at the door
Job 10: 6 searchest after my s
Ps. 4: 4 stand in awe and s not
32: 1 is forgiven, whose s is covered
51: 3 my s is ever before me
Prov. 14:34 s is a reproach to any
Is. 30: 1 that they may add s to s
53:10 make his soul an offering for s
John 1:29 taketh away the s of the world
Rom. 5:12 by one man s entered into the world
6:14 s shall not have dominion
7: 9 s revived, and I died
7:13 but s, that it might appear s
7:25 with the flesh the law of s
8: 2 made me free from the law of s
2 Cor. 5:21 him to be s for us, who knew no s
Eph. 4:26 be ye angry and s not
Jas. 1:15 lust bringeth forth s, and s
1 Pet. 2:22 who did no s, neither was guile
1 John 1: 8 if we say we have no s
2: 1 ye s not; if any man s we have
3: 9 he cannot s because he is born of God

SINS
Ps. 19:13 thy servant from presumptuous s
90: 8 our secret s in the light
103: 10 dwelt with us after our s
Is. 43:25 and will not remember thy s
59: 2 your s have hid his face
59:12 our s testify against us
Dan. 9:24 to make an end of s
John 8:21 shall die in your s: whither I go
1 Cor. 15: 3 Christ died for our s
15:17 ye are yet in your s
Gal. 1: 4 gave himself for our s
2 Tim. 3: 6 silly women laden with s
1 Pet. 2:24 bare our s in his own body
1 John 2: 2 propitiation for our s
Rev. 1: 5 and washed us from our s

SINNED (SINNETH)
Ex. 32:33 whosoever hath s against me, him
Josh. 7:20 I have s against the Lord God
Job 1:22 in all this Job s not
33:27 I have s and perverted
Ps. 51: 4 thee only have I s, and done this evil
106: 6 we have s with our fathers
Eccl. 7:20 man that doeth good, and s not
Is. 42:24 he against whom we have s
Jer. 3:25 we have s against the Lord
Lam. 1: 8 Jerusalem hath grievously s
Ezek. 18: 4 soul that s it shall die
Dan. 9: 5 We have s, and have committed iniquity
Mat. 27: 4 s in that I have betrayed
Luke 15:18 Father, I have s against heaven
Rom. 2:12 many as s without the law
3:23 all have s and come short
1 John 1: 10 if we say we have not s
5:18 whosoever is born of God s not

SINNER (SINNERS)
Gen. 13:13 wicked and s before the Lord
Ps. 1: 1 nor standeth in the way of s
25: 8 therefore will he teach s in the way
Is. 33:14 the s in Zion are afraid
Mat. 9:13 I am not come to call righteous, but s
Luke 13: 2 were s above all the Galilaeans
15: 7 joy in heaven over one s that
18:13 God be merciful to me a s
John 9:31 we know that God heareth not s
Rom. 5: 8 while we were yet s Christ died
1 Tim. 1:15 came into world to save s
Jas. 4: 8 cleanse your hands, ye s
5:20 converteth the s from the error

SINCERITY
Josh. 24:14 serve him in s and in truth
1 Cor. 5: 8 with the unleavened bread of s
2 Cor. 1:12 in simplicity and godly s we have
8: 8 to prove the s of your love
Eph. 6:24 that love our Lord Jesus Christ in s

SINEW (SINEWS)
Job 10: 11 fenced me with bones and s
Is. 48: 4 thy neck is an iron s

SING
Ex. 15: 1 I will s unto the Lord
15:21 S ye to the Lord for he hath
1 Chr. 16:23 S unto the Lord all the earth
Ps. 9: 11 S praises to the Lord which
30: 4 S unto the Lord O ye saints
47: 7 of all the earth: s ye praises
57: 7 I will s and give praise
92: 1 s praises unto thy name, O most
95: 1 let us s unto the Lord
144: 9 I will s a new song unto thee
145: 7 and shall s of thy righteousness
147: 1 it is good to s praises
Prov. 29: 6 the righteous doth s and rejoice
Is. 5: 1 I will s to my wellbeloved
12: 5 S unto the Lord; for he hath
65:14 my servants shall s for joy
1 Cor. 14:15 I will s with the spirit
Jas. 5:13 is any merry? let him s

SINGING
Eph. 5:19 and making melody in your heart

SINGLENESS
Acts 2:46 with gladness and s of heart
Eph. 6: 5 trembling, in s of your heart
Col. 3:22 in s of heart, fearing God

SKIN (SKINS)
Job 2: 4 s for s, yea all that a man
19:26 after my s, worms destroy this body
Jer. 13:23 Can the Ethiopian change his s

SLACK
Zeph. 3:16 Let not thine hands be s
2 Pet. 3: 9 The Lord is not s concerning

SLAY (SLAIN)
Lev. 14:13 he shall s the lamb in the place
Job 13:15 Though he s me, yet
Ps. 139:19 thou wilt s the wicked
Eph. 2:16 having s in his flesh the enmity
Rev. 5: 9 wast s and hast redeemed
13: 8 of the Lamb s from the foundation

SLEEP
Gen. 2:21 caused a deep s to fall upon
Ps. 76: 6 are cast into a dead s
127: 2 giveth his beloved s
132: 4 will not give s to mine eyes
Prov. 19:15 Slothfulness casteth into a deep s
20:13 love not s lest thou come to poverty
Eccl. 5:12 s of the labouring man is sweet
Jer. 31:26 beheld: and my s was sweet to me
Luke 9:32 with him were heavy with s
1 Cor. 11:30 sickly among you, and many s
15:51 we shall not all s but shall
1 Thes. 4:14 them also which s in Jesus died
5: 6 let us not s as others; but

SLEEPEST
1 Cor. 15:20 firstfruits of them that s
Eph. 5:14 he saith, awake, thou that s

SLIP (SLIPPETH)
Ps. 18:36 under me, that my feet did not s
94:18 I said, My foot s; thy mercy

SLOTHFUL (SLOTHFULNESS)
Prov. 12:24 but the s shall be under tribute
15:19 way of the s man is as a hedge of
18: 9 s in his work is the brother to
19:15 s casteth into a deep sleep
21:25 desire of the s killeth
Heb. 6:12 be not s but followers

SLOW
Prov. 14:29 He that is s to wrath is of great
Luke 24:25 fools s of heart to believe
Jas. 1:19 s to speak, s to wrath

SLUGGARD
Prov. 6: 6 Go to the ant, thou s
13: 4 the soul of the s desireth

SLUMBER (SLUMBERED, SLUMBERETH)
Ps.   132: 4 mine eyes, or *s* to mine eyelids
Rom.   11: 8 given them the spirit of *s*
2 Pet.   2: 3 not, and their damnation *s* not

SMITE (SMITEST, SMITTEN)
Ps.   141: 5 let the righteous *s* me; it shall
Is.   53: 4 him stricken, *s* of God, and
Mat.   5:39 thee on thy right cheek

SMOKE (SMOKING)
Deut. 29:20 his jealousy shall *s* against
Ps.   74: 1 why doth thine anger *s* against
Is.   42: 3 *s* flax shall he not quench
Rev.   14:11 *s* of their torment ascendeth

SNARE (SNARES)
Ex.   23:33 it will surely be a *s*
Ps.   18: 5 the *s* of death prevented me
      91: 3 deliver thee from the *s* of
     119: 110 wicked have laid a *s* for me
     124: 7 *s* is broken, and we are escaped
Prov. 13:14 depart from the *s* of death
2 Tim.   2:26 out of the *s* of the devil

SNOW
Ps.   51: 7 shall be whiter than *s*
Is.   1:18 shall be as white as *s*
Dan.   7: 9 whose garment was white as *s*
Mat.   28: 3 lightning, and his raiment white as *s*
Rev.   1:14 white like wool, as white as *s*

SOBER
1 Thes. 5: 6 let us watch and be *s*
1 Tim.   3:11 wives be grave, not slanderers, *s*
Tit.   1: 8 *s*, just, holy, temperate
         2: 2 that the aged men be *s*, grave
1 Pet.   1:13 up the loins of your mind, be *s*
         4: 7 be ye therefore *s* and watch unto prayer
         5: 8 be *s*, be vigilant:

SOBERLY
Rom.   12: 3 but to think *s*, according as God
Tit.   2:12 worldly lusts, we should live *s*

SOFT
Job   23:16 for God maketh my heart *s*
Prov. 15: 1 *s* answer turneth away wrath: but
Mat.   11: 8 to see? A man clothed in *s* raiment

SOJOURNER (SOJOURNERS)
Lev.   25:23 are strangers and *s*
1 Chr. 29:15 strangers before thee, and *s*
Ps.   39:12 with thee, and a *s*

SOLD
1 Ki. 21:20 hast *s* thyself to work evil
2 Ki. 17:17 *s* themselves to do evil
Rom.   7:14 I am carnal, *s* under sin

SON
Num.   23:19 neither the *s* of man,
2 Sam. 18:33 O Absalom, my *s*, my *s*
Ps.   2:12 kiss the *S* lest he be angry
         8: 4 *s* of man, that thou visitest
        80:17 upon the *s* of man whom thou
Prov. 10: 1 a wise *s* maketh a glad father
Dan.   3:25 is like the *S* of God
         7:13 like the *S* of man came
Mat.   4: 3 thou be the *S* of God
       11:27 no man knoweth the *S*, but the Father
       16:16 the *S* of the living God
Luke   10: 6 if the *s* of peace be
John   1:18 only begotten *S*, which is in the
         3:16 gave his only begotten *s*
         5:21 *S* quickeneth whom he will
         8:36 if the *S* shall make you free
Acts   3:13 hath glorified his *s* Jesus
Rom.   1: 3 concerning his *S* Jesus
         5:10 by the death of his *s*
         8: 3 sending his own *S* in the likeness
         8:32 spared not his own *s*
Gal.   1:16 To reveal his *S* in me, that I
         4: 4 God sent forth his *S*, made of a
1 Thes. 1:10 wait for his *S* from heaven
Heb.   5: 8 though he were a *S* yet learned he
1 John   3:23 believe on the name of his *S*
         5:11 and this life is in his *S*

SONS
Gen.   6: 2 *s* of God saw the daughters

         38: 7 all the *s* of God shouted for joy
Ps.   144:12 that our *s* may be as plants
Mal.   3: 3 purify the *s* of Levi
John   1:12 become the *s* of God, even to them
Rom.   8:14 they are the *s* of God
Gal.   4: 6 because ye are *s*, God hath sent
Heb.   2:10 bringing many *s* to glory
       12: 7 God dealeth with you as with *s*
1 John   3: 1 we should be called the *s* of God

SONG (SONGS)
Ex.   15: 2 Lord is my strength and my *s*
Job   35:10 giveth *s* in the night
Ps.   33: 3 sing unto him a new *s*
        42: 8 his *s* shall be with me
        96: 1 sing unto the Lord a new *s*
       149: 1 Sing unto the Lord a new *s*
Is.   42:10 Sing unto the Lord a new *s*
Eph.   5:19 in psalms and hymns and spiritual *s*
Rev.   5: 9 they sung a new *s*
       14: 3 no man could learn that *s*

SORCERER (SORCERERS)
Jer.   27: 9 nor to your *s*, which
Rev.   21: 8 whoremongers, and *s*, and idolaters

SORRY
Ps.   38:18 I will be *s* for my sin
2 Cor. 2: 2 if I make you *s*, who is he then
         7: 8 the same epistle hath made you *s*

SORROW (SORROWS)
Ps.   18: 4 *s* of death compassed me
        90:10 is their strength, labour and *s*
       127: 2 sit up late to eat the bread of *s*
Prov. 15:13 by *s* of the heart the spirit
Eccl.   1:18 is better than laughter
Is.   35:10 *s* and sighing shall flee away
        53: 3 man of *s*, and acquainted with
Jer.   31:12 shall not *s* any more at all
Lam.   1:12 there be any *s* like unto my *s*
Mat.   24: 8 all these are the beginning of *s*
       16:20 your *s* shall be turned into joy
2 Cor. 2: 7 swallowed up with overmuch *s*
         7:10 for godly *s* worketh repentance
Phil.   2:27 lest I should have *s* upon *s*
1 Thes. 4:13 *s* not, as others which have no hope
1 Tim. 6:10 and pierced through with many *s*
Rev.   21: 4 no more death, neither *s*

SORROWFUL
Job   6: 7 to touch as my *s* meat
Prov. 14:13 in laughter the heart is *s*
Jer.   31:25 replenished the *s* soul
Mat.   19:22 that saying, he went away *s*
       26:22 they were exceeding *s*

SOUGHT
Ps.   34: 4 I *s* the Lord, and he heard
        78:34 then they *s* him: and they returned
Eccl.   7:29 they have *s* out many inventions
Is.   62:12 shall be called, *S* out, a city not
        65: 1 found of them that *s* me not
Rom.   9:32 *s* it not by faith, but

SOUL
Ex.   30:12 every man a ransom for his *s*
Deut.   6: 5 and with all thy *s*, and with all
         1:13 heart and with all your *s*
Josh. 22: 5 your heart and with all your *s*
1 Sam. 18: 1 of Jonathan knit with the *s*
1 Chr. 22:19 *s* to seek the Lord your God
Job   27: 8 God taketh away his *s*
Ps.   16:10 not leave my *s* in hell
        31: 7 hast known my *s* in adversities
        35: 9 my *s* shall be joyful in
        42: 5 why cast down, O my *s*
        62: 1 Truly my *s* waiteth upon God
        63: 1 my *s* thirsteth for thee, my flesh
       107: 9 filleth the hungry *s* with goodness
Prov. 10: 3 not suffer the *s* of the righteous
        27: 7 the full *s* loatheth an honeycomb
Is.   26: 9 with my *s* have I desired thee
        55: 3 hear and your *s* shall live
        58:10 and satisfy the afflicted *s*
        61:10 my *s* shall be joyful in my God
Jer.   31:25 I have satiated the weary *s*
Ezek.   3:19 but thou hast delivered thy *s*
Mat.   10:28 not able to kill the *s*: but rather
       16:26 gain the whole world, and lose his *s*

         22:37 and with all thy *s*, and
        26:38 My *s* is exceedingly sorrowful
Mark   12:33 and with all the *s*, and
Luke   1:46 my *s* doth magnify the Lord
       12:20 this night thy *s* shall
John   12:27 Now is my *s* troubled;
Rom.   13: 1 let every *s* be subject
1 Thes. 5:23 *s* and body be preserved blameless
Heb.   10:39 believe to the saving of the *s*

SOULS
Prov. 11:30 that winneth *s* is wise
Jer.   6:16 ye shall find rest for your *s*
Mat.   11:29 ye shall find rest unto your *s*
1 Pet. 2:25 Shepherd and Bishop of your *s*
         4:19 commit the keeping of their *s* to him
Rev.   6: 9 *s* of them that were slain for the
        20: 4 *s* of them that were beheaded for

SOUND
Job   15:21 dreadful *s* is in his ears
Ps.   47: 5 Lord with the *s* of a trumpet
        89:15 people that know joyful *s*
Amos   6: 5 that chant to the *s* of the viol
1 Tim. 1:10 thing that is contrary to *s* doctrine
2 Tim. 1: 7 and of love and of a *s* mind
Tit.   2: 2 temperate, *s* in faith, in charity

SOW (SOWETH, SOWN)
Job   4: 8 *s* wickedly, reap the
Ps.   126: 5 *s* in tears shall reap in joy
Prov. 11:18 to him that *s* righteousness
        22: 8 *s* iniquity shall reap vanity
Jer.   31:27 I will *s* the house of Israel
Hos.   8: 7 *s* wind, they shall reap whirlwind
Mic.   6:15 thou shalt *s* but thou
Mat.   13: 3 Behold, a sower went forth to *s*
Luke   12:24 the ravens; for they neither *s* nor
       19:22 reaping that I did not *s*
John   4:37 true, and one *s*, another reapeth
1 Cor. 9:11 have *s* to you spiritual
       15:42 it is *s* in corruption; it is raised
2 Cor. 9: 6 *s* sparingly shall reap
Gal.   6: 7 whatsoever a man *s*, that shall
Jas.   3:18 fruit of righteousness *s* in peace
Ps.   39:13 *s* me that I may recover strength
Prov. 13:24 he that *s* the rod hateth his
Joel   2:17 *s* thy people O Lord and give not
Mal.   3:17 I will *s* them, as a man
Rom.   8:32 that *s* not his own Son
       11:21 if God *s* not the natural branches
2 Pet. 2: 4 God *s* not angels that sinned

SPARKS
Job   5: 7 trouble, as the *s* fly upward
Is.   50:11 that compass yourself about with *s*

SPARROW (SPARROWS)
Ps.   102: 7 am as a *s* along upon the house
Mat.   10:29 two *s* sold for a farthing

SPEAK
1 Sam. 3: 9 S, Lord, for thy servant heareth
Ps.   85: 8 he will *s* peace to his people
Mat.   10:19 how or what ye shall *s*
Luke   6:26 when all men *s* well of
Acts   4:20 cannot but *s* the things which we
1 Cor. 1:10 ye all *s* the same thing
Tit.   3: 2 to *s* evil of no man to
Jas.   1:19 swift to hear, slow to *s*
2 Pet. 2:10 not afraid to *s* evil of dignities

SPEAKETH (SPEAKING)
Mat.   6: 7 shall be heard for their much *s*
       12:34 abundance of the heart the mouth *s*
Eph.   4:15 But *s* the truth in love
         4:31 evil *s*, be put away from you, with
         5:19 *s* to yourselves in psalms
1 Tim. 4: 2 *s* lies in hypocrisy
Heb.   12:24 better things than that of Abel
Rev.   13: 5 a mouth *s* great things

SPEECH (SPEECHES)
Gen.   11: 1 one language and of one *s*
Mat.   26:73 them; for thy *s* betrayeth thee
Rom.   16:18 by fair *s* deceive the hearts
1 Cor. 2: 1 with excellency of *s*
2 Cor. 3:12 use great plainness of *s*
Col.   4: 6 let your *s* be always with grace
Tit.   2: 8 sound *s*, that cannot be condemned

SPEND (SPENT)
Job	21:13	they s their days in wealth
Ps.	90: 9	s our years as a tale
Is.	55: 2	s money for that which is
Rom.	13:12	night is far s, the day is at
2 Cor.	12:15	gladly spend and be s

SPEW (SPEWING)
Lev.	18:28	the land s not you out
Jer.	25:27	be drunken, and s and
Hab.	2:16	shameful s shall be on thy glory
Rev.	3:16	I will s thee out

SPIRIT
Gen.	1: 2	the s of God moved upon the face
	6: 3	my s shall not always strive
Num.	11:17	take of the s which is
2 Ki.	2: 9	double portion of thy s
2 Chr.	15: 1	s of God came upon Azariah
Job	26:13	by his s he garnished
	32:18	the s within constraineth me
Ps.	31: 5	to thine hand I commit my s
	32: 2	in whose s there is no guile
	34:18	such as be of a contrite s
	51:10	renew a right s within
	51:17	sacrifices of God are a broken s
	78: 8	s was not stedfast with God
	139: 7	whither should I go from thy s
	142: 3	when my s was overwhelmed within
	143: 7	O Lord, my s faileth
Prov.	15:13	by sorrow of heart the s is broken
	16:18	and an haughty s before a fall
	18:14	a wounded s who can bear?
	20:27	s of man is the candle of the Lord
Eccl.	3:21	knoweth the s of man
	12: 7	the s shall return to God
Is.	32:15	the s be poured upon us
	34:16	his s it hath gathered them
	57:15	to revive the s of the humble
	66: 2	that is poor and of a contrite s
Ezek.	36:27	I will put my s within
Mic.	2:11	walking in s and falsehood
Zech.	4: 6	but by my s, saith the Lord
	12:10	s of grace and supplication
	13: 2	the prophets of the unclean s
Mat.	3:16	S of God descending like a dove
	12:28	cast out devils by the s
	12:43	when the unclean s is gone out of a
	22:43	doth in s call him Lord
	26:41	s is willing, but the flesh weak
Luke	1:47	my s hath rejoiced in God my
	1:80	child grew, and waxed strong in s
	2:27	he came by the S into the temple
	23:46	into thy hands I commend my s
	24:39	s hath not flesh and
John	3: 5	born of water and of s he cannot
	4:24	God is a S: and they
	6:63	it is the s that quickeneth
Acts	6:10	resist the wisdom and the s
	7:59	Lord Jesus, receive my s
	16: 7	the S suffered them
Rom.	1: 9	whom I serve with my s in the
	8: 1	not after flesh, but after the S
	8: 9	if any have not the S of Christ, he
	8:14	as many as are led by the S of God
	8:16	S beareth witness with our s
1 Cor.	2:10	s: for the S searcheth
	2:14	things of the S of God
	3:16	the S of God dwelleth in you
	6:11	Jesus, and by the S of our God
	12: 3	speaking by the S of God
	12:13	all made to drink into one S
	14:14	unknown tongue, my s prayeth
2 Cor.	3: 6	not of the letter but of the s
	3:17	S of the Lord is, there is liberty
	7: 1	from filthiness of flesh and s
Gal.	3: 3	begun in S are ye now
	4: 6	sent forth the S of his Son into your
	5:22	fruit of the S is love, joy, peace
	5:25	live in the S let us also walk in
Eph.	4: 4	there is one body, and one S even
	4:23	be renewed in the s of your mind
	4:30	grieve not the holy S of God
	5: 9	fruit of S is in all goodness
	6:18	prayer and supplication in the s
Col.	2: 5	yet am I with you in the s

1 Thes.	5:23	whole s be preserved blameless unto
Heb.	9:14	through the eternal S offered himself
Jas.	4: 5	s that dwelleth in us lusteth
1 Pet.	3: 4	the ornament of a meek and quiet s
	3:18	in flesh, but quickened by the S
	4:14	s of glory and of God resteth
1 John	4: 1	not every s, but try
Rev.	1:10	I was in the S on the Lord's day
	11:11	S of life from God entered

SPIRITS
Prov.	16: 2	but the Lord weigheth the s
Mat.	10: 1	gave them power against unclean s
Luke	10:20	rejoice not that the s are subject to you
Acts	5:16	them which were vexed with unclean s
	8: 7	unclean s, crying with loud voice
1 Cor.	14:32	s of the prophets are subject
1 Pet.	3:19	preached unto the s in prison
Rev.	16:14	they are the s of devils

SPIRITUAL
Rom.	1:11	impart unto you some s gift
	7:14	that the law is s, but I am carnal
	15:27	partakers of their s things
1 Cor.	2:13	comparing s things with s
	3: 1	not speak unto you as unto the s
	9:11	if we have sown unto you s things
	10: 3	did all eat the same s meat
	15:44	natural body, it is raised a s body
Gal.	6: 1	ye which are s restore
Eph.	1: 3	blessed us with all s blessings
	5:19	psalms and hymns and s songs
	6:12	against s wickedness in high places
Col.	3:16	psalms and hymns and s songs
1 Pet.	2: 5	are built up a s house,

SPIRITUALLY
Rom.	8: 6	to be s minded is life and peace
1 Cor.	2:14	they are s discerned

SPOT
Deut.	32: 5	s is not the s of his children
Sol.	4: 7	there is no s in thee
1 Tim.	6:14	keep this commandment without s
Heb.	9:14	offered himself without s to God
1 Pet.	1:19	lamb without blemish and without s
2 Pet.	3:14	peace, without s, and blameless

SPRING (SPRINGING, SPRUNG)
Ps.	85:11	Truth shall s out of the earth
Mat.	13: 7	and the thorns s up, and choked
John	4:14	s up into everlasting life
Heb.	12:15	root of bitterness s up

SPRINKLE (SPRINKLED, SPRINKLING)
Is.	52:15	so shall he s many nations
Ezek.	36:25	then will I s clean water upon you
Heb.	10:22	hearts s from an evil conscience
	12:24	to blood of s, that speaketh
1 Pet.	1: 2	s of the blood of Jesus Christ

SPY
Num.	13:16	which Moses sent out to s the land
Josh.	2: 1	men to s secretly, saying
Gal.	2: 4	to s out our liberty

STAFF
Ps.	23: 4	thy rod and thy s they
Is.	3: 1	from Judah the stay and the s
	9: 4	the s of his shoulder
	10: 5	s in their hand is mine indignation
Zech.	11:10	took my s, even Beauty

STAND
Ex.	14:13	s still, and see the salvation of
1 Sam.	6:20	is able to s before his holy Lord
Job	19:25	s at the latter day upon the earth
Ps.	76: 7	who may s in thy sight
	130: 3	iniquities, O Lord, who shall s
Prov.	19:21	the counsel of the Lord, that shall s
Is.	46:10	my counsel shall s, and I will
Nah.	1: 6	who can s before his indignation
Mal.	3: 2	who shall s when he appeareth?
Mat.	12:25	against itself shall not s
Luke	21:36	s before the Son of
Rom.	5: 2	this grace wherein we s
	14:10	shall all s before the judgment seat
1 Cor.	16:13	s fast in the faith quit
2 Cor.	1:24	your joy: for by faith ye s
Gal.	5: 1	s fast in liberty
Phil.	1: 4	s fast in the Lord, dearly beloved
1 Thes.	3: 8	we live, if ye s fast in Lord

2 Thes.	2:15	s fast, and hold the traditions
1 Pet.	5:12	grace of God wherein ye s
Rev.	3:20	I s at the door and knock
	20:12	small and great, s before God

STANDETH
Ps.	1: 1	nor s in the way of sinners
	33:11	counsel of the Lord s forever
Rom.	14: 4	to his own master he s or falleth
1 Cor.	10:12	s take heed lest he fall
2 Tim.	2:19	the foundation of God s sure, having
Jas.	5: 9	the Judge s before the door

STAR (STARS)
Num.	24:17	there shall come a S out of Jacob
Judg.	5:20	the s in their courses
Mat.	2: 2	we have seen his s in the east
Rev.	12: 1	on her head a crown of twelve s

STATURE
Mat.	6:27	one cubit unto his s
Eph.	4:13	measure of the s of the fulness of

STATUTES
Ex.	15:26	and keep all his s, I
Ps.	19: 8	s of the Lord are right
	105: 45	that they might observe his s
Ezek.	33:15	walk in the s of life
Mic.	6:16	the s of Omri are kept

STEAL (STOLE, STOLEN)
Ex.	20:15	Thou shalt not s
Prov.	6:30	thief, if he s to satisfy his soul
	9:17	s waters are sweet,
Mat.	6:19	thieves break through and s
	27:64	come by night, and s him away
Eph.	4:28	let him that s, steal no

STEDFAST
Ps.	78: 8	whose spirit was not s with God
Dan.	6:26	God, and s forever
1 Cor.	15:58	be ye s unmoveable, always abounding
Heb.	3:14	confidence s to the end
1 Pet.	5: 9	whom resist s in the faith, knowing

STEPS
Ps.	18:36	thou hast enlarged my s under me
	37:23	s of a good man are
	119:133	order my s in thy word
Prov.	16: 9	but the Lord directeth his s
Jer.	10:23	man that walketh to direct his s
Rom.	4:12	who also walk in the s of that faith
1 Pet.	2:21	that ye should follow his s

STEWARD (STEWARDS)
Luke	12:42	that faithful and wise s
1 Cor.	4: 1	and s of the mysteries of God
Tit.	1: 7	must be blameless, as the s of God
1 Pet.	4:10	as good s of the manifold grace

STIFFNECKED
Ex.	34: 9	it is a s people; and
Deut.	10:16	heart, and be no more s
Acts	7:51	s and uncircumcised in heart

STILL (STILLETH)
Ps.	4: 4	own heart upon your bed, and be s
	8: 2	s the enemy and the avenger
	46:10	be s and know that I am God
	65: 7	which s the noise of the seas
	139: 18	I awake, I am s with thee
Is.	30: 7	their strength is to sit s
Mark	4:39	Peace, be s And the wind

STIR
Ps.	35:23	s up thyself, and awake to my
	78:38	away, and did not s up all his wrath
2 Tim.	1: 6	s up the gift of God that is

STONE (STONES)
Gen.	49:24	is the shepherd, the s of Israel
Ps.	118:22	s which the builders refused
Is.	8:14	s of stumbling and for a rock
	28:16	a s, a tried s, a precious corner s
Dan.	2:34	s cut out without hands
Mat.	3: 9	God is able of these s to raise
	7: 9	ask for bread, will he give him a s
Luke	19:40	the s would immediately cry out
Rom.	9:33	lay in Zion, a stumbling s
1 Pet.	2: 4	whom coming, as unto a living s
	2: 6	chief corner s, elect, precious

STORM
Ps.	107:29	he maketh the s a
Is.	4: 6	for a covert from s

25: 4 refuge from the *s*, a shadow
Nah. 1: 3 in the whirlwind, and in the *s*
Mark 4:37 arose a great *s* of wind

STRAIGHT
Ps. 5: 8 thy way *s* before my face
Eccl. 1:15 which is crooked cannot be made *s*
Is. 40: 3 make in the desert a highway for our
45: 2 make the crooked places *s*
Luke 3: 4 Lord, make his paths *s*
3: 5 crooked shall be made *s*
Heb. 12:13 make *s* paths for your

STRAIT
Mat. 7:13 enter in at the *s* gate
Phil. 1:23 I am in a *s* betwixt two

STRANGE
Lev. 10: 1 and offered *s* fire
Judg. 11: 2 for thou art the son of a *s* woman
Ezra 10:11 the land, and from the *s* wives
Ps. 81: 9 there shall no *s* god be
Hos. 8:12 they were counted as a *s* thing
Zeph. 1: 8 such as are clothed with *s* apparel
Luke 5:26 we have seen *s* things
Heb. 11: 9 as in a *s* country
13: 9 about with divers and *s* doctrines
1 Pet. 4:12 think it not *s* concerning the fiery
Jude 1: 7 going after *s* flesh are set forth

STRANGER (STRANGERS)
1 Chr. 29:15 For we are *s* before thee
Ps. 39:12 for I am a *s* with thee, and
105: 12 very few and *s* in it
119: 19 I am a *s* in the earth
146: 9 the Lord preserveth the *s*
Mat. 25:35 was a *s* and ye took me
John 10: 5 a *s* will they not follow
Eph. 2:19 are no more *s* and foreigners
Heb. 11:13 confessed that they were *s* and
13: 2 be not forgetful to entertain *s*
1 Pet. 2:11 beseech you as *s* and

STREAM (STREAMS)
Ps. 46: 4 There is a river the *s*
Is. 30:25 rivers and *s* of waters in the day
35: 6 and *s* in the desert
66:12 Gentiles like a flowing *s*
Amos 5:24 and righteousness as a mighty *s*
Luke 6:48 the *s* beat vehemently

STREET (STREETS)
Prov. 1:20 uttereth her voice in the *s*
Luke 14:21 Go out quickly into the *s*
Rev. 21:21 *s* of the city was pure gold
22: 2 In the midst of the *s* of

STRENGTH
Gen. 49: 3 the beginning of my *s*, the
Ex. 15: 2 Lord is my *s* and song
1 Sam. 2: 9 by *s* shall no man prevail
15:29 the *S* of Israel will not lie
Job 6:12 Is my *s* the *s* of stones
12:13 with him is wisdom and *s*
Ps. 18: 2 my *s*, in whom I will trust
18:32 It is God that girdeth me with *s*
27: 1 Lord is the *s* of my life
28: 7 Lord is my *s* and my shield
29:11 Lord will give *s* to his people
43: 2 thou art the God of my *s*
46: 1 God is our refuge and *s*, a very
68:35 he that giveth *s* and power unto his
73:26 God is the *s* of my heart
84: 5 blessed is the man whose *s* is in
93: 1 the Lord is clothed with *s*
96: 6 *s* and beauty are in his sanctuary
118: 14 Lord is my *s* and song
138: 3 strengthenedst me with *s* in my soul
Eccl. 9:16 wisdom is better than *s*
Is. 12: 2 Jehovah is my *s* and
25: 4 a *s* to the poor, a *s* to the needy
40:29 that have no might he increaseth *s*
49: 5 my God shall be my *s*
Jer. 16:19 O Lord, my *s*, and my fortress
Hab. 3:19 the Lord God is my *s*,
Luke 1:51 he hath shown *s* with his arm
1 Cor. 15:56 is sin; and *s* of sin is the law
2 Cor. 12: 9 my *s* is made perfect in weakness
Rev. 5:12 wisdom, and *s*, and
12:10 now is come salvation and *s*

STRENGTHEN (STRENGTHENED, STRENGTHENEDST, STRENGTHENETH)
Ps. 27:14 he shall *s* thine heart
41: 3 *s* him on the bed of languishing
104: 15 bread which *s* man's heart
138: 3 *s* me with strength in my soul
Is. 35: 3 *s* ye the weak hands, and confirm
54: 2 lengthen thy cords, and *s* thy stakes
Zech. 10:12 I will *s* them in the
Luke 22:32 thou art converted, *s* thy brethren
Eph. 3:16 to be *s* with might by
Phil. 4:13 through Christ which *s* me
Col. 1: 11 *s* with all might according to
2 Tim. 4:17 Lord stood with me and *s* me
1 Pet. 5:10 make you perfect, stablish, *s*
Rev. 3: 2 watchful and *s* the things which remain

STRETCH (STRETCHED, STRETCHETH)
1 Ki. 17:21 *s* himself upon the child three times
Job 15:25 he *s* out his hand against God
Prov. 31:20 she *s* out her hand to the poor
Is. 40:22 *s* out the heavens as a curtain
51:13 that hath *s* forth the heavens
Zech. 12: 1 which *s* forth the heavens
Mat. 12:13 *s* forth thy hand. And he *s*
John 21:18 shalt *s* forth thy hands
Rom. 10:21 all day I have *s* forth my hands

STRIFE (STRIFES)
Ps. 80: 6 makest us a *s* to our neighbours
Prov. 10:12 hatred stirreth up *s*,
15:18 wrathful man stirreth up *s*
20: 3 honour for a man to cease from *s*
28:25 a proud heart stirreth up *s*
30:33 forcing of wrath bringeth *s*
Luke 22:24 there was also a *s* among them
1 Cor. 3: 3 there is among you envying, *s*
Gal. 5:20 wrath, *s*, seditions,
Phil. 2: 3 let nothing be done through *s*
1 Tim. 6: 4 whereof cometh envy, *s*, railings
2 Tim. 2:23 that they do gender *s*
Jas. 3:14 if ye have bitter envying and *s*

STRIPES
Prov. 17:10 hundred *s* into a fool
Is. 53: 5 his *s* we are healed
Luke 12:48 commit things worthy of *s*
1 Pet. 2:24 by whose *s* ye were healed

STRIVE (STRIVETH, STRIVING)
Gen. 6: 3 Spirit shall not always *s*
Prov. 3:30 *s* not with a man without cause
Is. 45: 9 woe to him that *s* with his Maker
Mat. 12:19 he shall not *s* nor cry
Luke 13:24 *s* to enter in at the strait gate
Phil. 1:27 one mind *s* together for the faith
2 Tim. 2:24 the servant of Lord must not *s*
Heb. 12: 4 resisted unto blood, *s* against sin

STRONG
Josh. 14:11 I am as *s* this day as I
Ps. 24: 8 The Lord *s* and mighty, the Lord
31: 2 be thou my *s* rock, for
71: 7 but thou art my *s* refuge
Prov. 14:26 fear of the Lord is *s* confidence
18:10 name of the Lord is a *s* tower
24: 5 a wise man is *s*; yea, a
Eccl. 9:11 the swift, nor the battle to the *s*
Sol. 8: 6 love is as *s* as death; jealousy
Is. 26: 1 we have a *s* city
35: 4 Be *s*, fear not: behold, your God
53:12 shall divide the spoil with the *s*
Jer. 50:34 their Redeemer is *s*,
Joel 3:10 let the weak say, I am *s*
Luke 11:21 *s* man armed keepeth his palace
Rom. 4:20 was *s* in faith, giving
15: 1 we that are *s* ought to bear the
infirmities
1 Cor. 16:13 quit you like men, be *s*
2 Cor. 12:10 when I am weak, then am I *s*
Eph. 6:10 be *s* in the Lord, and
2 Tim. 2: 1 be *s* in the grace that
Heb. 11:34 out of weakness were made *s*

STRONGER
Job 17: 9 clean hands shall be *s* and *s*
1 Cor. 1:25 weakness of God is *s* than men

STUBBORN (STUBBORNNESS)
Deut. 21:18 *s* and rebellious son

1 Sam. 15:23 and *s* is as iniquity and idolatry
Ps. 78: 8 a *s* and rebellious generation

STUDY (STUDIETH)
Prov. 24: 2 their heart *s* destruction and their
Eccl. 12:12 much *s* is a weariness of the flesh
1 Thes. 4:11 that ye *s* to be quiet
2 Tim. 2:15 *S* to show thyself approved

STUMBLE (STUMBLED, STUMBLETH)
Prov. 3:23 thy foot shall not *s*
4:12 runnest, thou shalt not *s*
Is. 8:15 many among them shall *s* and fall
28: 7 err in vision, *s* in judgment
Rom. 9:32 they *s* at that stumblingstone
14:21 whereby thy brother *s* or is offended
1 Pet. 2: 8 even to them which *s* at the word

STUMBLING
Is. 8:14 but for a stone of *s* and for a
Rom. 9:32 stumbled at the *s* stone
1 Pet. 2: 8 stone of *s*, and a rock of offense

STUMBLINGBLOCK (STUMBLINGBLOCKS)
Lev. 19:14 put a *s* before the blind
Is. 57:14 take up the *s* out of the way
Jer. 6:21 I will lay *s* before this
Rom. 11: 9 a trap, snare, and a *s*,
14:13 put a *s* or an occasion
1 Cor. 1:23 unto the Jews a *s*, and
Rev. 2:14 taught Balac to cast a *s*

SUBDUE (SUBDUED)
Phil. 3:21 able to *s* all things unto himself
Heb. 11:33 who through faith *s* kingdoms

SUBJECT
Luke 10:20 spirits are *s* unto you;
Rom. 8: 7 not *s* to the law of God
8:20 creature was made *s* to vanity
13: 1 every soul be *s* unto the higher powers
1 Cor. 14:32 spirits of the prophets are *s* to
15:28 shall be *s* unto him
Eph. 5:24 church is *s* to Christ
Heb. 2:15 all their lifetime *s* to bondage
Jas. 5:17 Elias was a man *s* to like passions
1 Pet. 2:18 be *s* to your masters
5: 5 be *s* one to another

SUBJECTION
1 Cor. 9:27 body, and bring it into *s*
1 Tim. 2:11 woman learn in silence with all *s*
3: 4 having his children in *s*
Heb. 2: 8 put all in *s* under him
12: 9 be in *s* unto the father
1 Pet. 3: 5 in *s* unto their own

SUBMIT (SUBMITTED, SUBMITTING)
Ps. 68:30 till everyone *s* himself
Rom. 10: 3 have not *s* unto the righteousness of
1 Cor. 16:16 that ye *s* yourselves unto such
Eph. 5:21 *s* yourselves one to another
Col. 3:18 *s* yourselves unto your
Heb. 13:17 rule over you, and *s* yourselves
Jas. 4: 7 *S* yourselves therefore to God
1 Pet. 5: 5 *s* yourselves unto the elder

SUBSTANCE
Deut. 33:11 bless, Lord, his *s* and
Ps. 139:15 my *s* was not hid from
Prov. 3: 9 honour the Lord with thy *s*
Heb. 10:34 and an enduring *s*
11: 1 faith is the *s* of things hoped for

SUCK (SUCKED, SUCKING)
Deut. 32:13 made him to *s* honey
Job 20:16 he shall *s* the poison of asps
Is. 11: 8 the *s* child shall play on the hole
49:15 a woman forget her *s* child
Lam. 4: 4 the tongue of the *s* child cleaveth
Mat. 24:19 to them that give *s* in
Luke 11:27 blessed are paps which thou hast *s*
23:29 paps which never gave *s*

SUFFER
Ps. 55:22 never *s* the righteous to be moved
89:33 nor *s* my faithfulness to fail
121: 3 not *s* thy foot to be moved
Mat. 16:21 many things of the elders and
17:17 how long shall I *s* you?
19:14 *s* little children, and
1 Cor. 4:12 being persecuted, we *s* it
10:13 God will not *s* you to be tempted

Phil.   1:29 but also to *s* for his
2 Tim.   2:12 if we *s* we shall also reign
Heb.   11:25 choosing rather to *s* affliction
1 Pet.   4:15 none of you *s* as a murderer

SUFFERED (SUFFERETH)
Ps.   105:14 he *s* no man to do them wrong
Mat.   11:12 kingdom of heaven *s* violence
Acts   14:16 *s* all nations to walk in their own
  16: 7 the Spirit *s* them not
1 Cor. 13: 4 Charity *s* long, and is kind
Phil.   3: 8 for whom I *s* loss of
Heb.   5: 8 obedience by the things which he *s*
1 Pet. 2:21 Christ also *s* for us,
  5:10 after that ye have *s* a while

SUFFERINGS
Rom.   8:18 the *s* of this present times
2 Cor.   1: 6 enduring of the same *s*
Phil.   3:10 the fellowship of his *s*
Col.   1:24 now rejoice in my *s* for you
Heb.   2:10 of their salvation perfect through *s*
1 Pet.   1:11 testified beforehand the *s* of Christ
  4:13 ye are partakers of Christ's *s*

SUFFICIENT
Mat.   6:34 *s* unto the day is the evil
2 Cor.   2:16 who is *s* for these things?
  3: 5 not that we are *s* of ourselves
  12: 8 my grace is *s* for thee

SUMMER
Gen.   8:22 heat, and *s* and winter, and day
Ps.   74:17 thou hast made *s* and
Zech. 14: 8 in *s* and in winter shall it be

SUN
Josh.   10:12 *s*, stand thou still upon Gibeon
Ps.   74:16 prepared the light and the *s*
  104: 19 *s* knoweth his going down
  121: 6 *s* shall not smite thee by day
  136: 8 *s* to rule the day:
Is.   60:19 *s* shall be no more thy light by day
  60:20 thy *s* shall no more go down
Mal.   4: 2 *S* of righteousness arise
Mat.   5:45 his *s* to rise on evil
  13:43 shine forth as the *s* in the kingdom
Eph.   4:26 let not the *s* go down
Rev.   7:16 neither shall the *s* light on them
  10: 1 his face was as it the *s*
  21:23 city had no need of the *s*

SUPPER
Luke 14:16 A certain man made a great *s*
  22:20 also the cup after *s*,
1 Cor. 11:20 is not to eat the Lord's *s*
Rev.   19: 9 the marriage *s* of the Lamb

SUPPLICATION (SUPPLICATIONS)
Job   8: 5 and make thy *s* to the almighty
Ps.   6: 9 Lord hath heard my *s*; the Lord
  55: 1 hide not thyself from my *s*
Zech. 12:10 the spirit of grace and of *s*
Eph.   6:18 prayer and *s* in the spirit
Phil.   4: 6 prayer and *s* with thanksgiving
1 Tim. 5: 5 continueth in *s* and prayers
  2: 1 first of all *s*, prayers, intercessions
Heb.   5: 7 offered up prayers and *s*

SUPPLY (SUPPLIETH)
2 Cor.   9:12 *s* the want of the saints
Eph.   4:16 by that which every joint *s*
Phil.   1:19 the *s* of the Spirit of
  4:19 my God shall *s* all your need

SURE
Ps.   19: 7 testimony of the Lord is *s*
  93: 5 thy testimonies are very *s*
Prov. 11:18 righteousness shall be a *s* reward
Is.   28:16 a *s* foundation: he that
  55: 3 even the *s* mercies of David
John   6:69 are *s* that thou art that Christ
Acts 13:34 give you the *s* mercies of David
Rom.   4:16 promise might be *s* to
2 Tim. 2:19 foundation of God standeth *s*
2 Pet.   1:10 to make your calling and election *s*

SWALLOW (SWALLOWED)
Ex.   15:12 thy right hand, the earth *s* them
Ps.   84: 3 the *s* a nest for herself
Jer.   8: 7 the *s* observe the time
Is.   25: 8 will *s* up death in victory

Mat.   23:24 strain at a gnat, *s* a camel
2 Cor.   2: 7 should be *s* up with overmuch sorrow
  5: 4 mortality be *s* up of life

SWEAR (SWEARETH)
Ps.   15: 4 he that *s* to his own hurt
Is.   45:23 shall bow, every tongue shall *s*
  65:16 shall *s* by the God of truth
Mat.   5:34 *s* not at all; neither by
Jas.   5:12 *s* not, neither by heaven, neither

SWEAT
Gen.   3:19 In the *s* of thy face shalt thou
Luke 22:44 *s* was as it were great drops

SWEET
Ps.   104:34 meditation of him shall be *s*
  119: 103 how *s* are thy words unto my taste
Prov.   9:17 stolen waters are *s*,
Eccl.   5:12 sleep of the labouring man is *s*
Sol.   5:16 his mouth is most *s*;
Is.   5:20 bitter for *s* and *s* for
Phil.   4:18 an odour of a *s* smell
Rev.   10: 9 in thy mouth *s* as honey

SWIFT
Deut. 28:49 as *s* as the eagle flieth
Eccl.   9:11 the race is not to the *s*
Rom.   3:15 their feet are *s* to shed blood
Jas.   1:19 *s* to hear, slow to speak
2 Pet.   2: 1 bring on themselves *s* destruction

SWORD (SWORDS)
Gen.   3:24 cherubims and a flaming *s*
Lev.   26: 6 shall the *s* go through
2 Sam. 12:10 *s* shall never depart from thine
Ps.   17:13 from the wicked, which is thy *s*
  59: 7 are in their lips: for
Prov. 30:14 whose teeth are as *s*
Is.   2: 4 beat their *s* into plowshares
Jer.   9:16 I will send a *s* after
  15: 2 such as are for the *s* to the *s*
Joel   3:10 Beat your plowshares into *s*
Mat.   10:34 not to send peace, but the *s*
Luke   2:35 a *s* shall pierce through
Rom. 13: 4 he beareth not the *s* in vain
Eph.   6:17 *s* of the Spirit which is the word
Heb.   4:12 sharper than any twoedged *s*
Rev.   1:16 mouth went a sharp twoedged *s*
  19:15 out of his mouth goeth a sharp *s*

SYNAGOGUE (SYNAGOGUES)
Mat.   6: 5 love to pray standing in the *s*
Luke   7: 5 he hath built us a *s*
John   9:22 should be put out of the *s*
Rev.   2: 9 are not but are the *s* of Satan

TABERNACLE (TABERNACLES)
Ex.   29:43 the *t* shall be sanctified
Ps.   15: 1 who shall abide in thy *t*
  84: 1 how amiable are thy *t*
  118: 15 salvation is in the *t* of
Is.   33:20 a *t* that shall not be taken down
Acts 15:16 will build again the *t* of David
2 Cor.   5: 4 we that are in this *t* do groan
Heb.   8: 2 sanctuary and the true *t*, which the
2 Pet.   1:13 as long as I am in this *t*
  1:14 knowing I must put off this my *t*
Rev.   21: 3 the *t* of God is with men

TABLE (TABLES)
Deut. 10: 4 he wrote on the *t* according to
2 Chr.   4:19 *t* whereon the showbread was set
Ps.   23: 5 Thou preparest a *t* before me
  69:22 let their *t* become a snare
Prov.   3: 3 write them on the *t* of
Jer.   17: 1 is graven on the *t* of their heart
Mat.   15:27 which fall from the masters' *t*
1 Cor. 10:21 partakers of the Lord's *t*
2 Cor.   3: 3 not in *t* of stone, but fleshy *t*
Heb.   9: 4 budded, and the *t* of the covenant

TAKE
Ex.   20: 7 not *t* the name of the Lord in vain
Ps.   51:11 not thy holy spirit
  116: 13 I will *t* the cup of salvation
Mat.   16:24 *t* up his cross and
  20:14 *T*, that thine is, and go
  26:26 said, *T*, eat; this is my body
Luke 12:19 *t* thine ease, eat, drink
John 10:17 my life, that I might *t* it again
1 Cor. 11:24 *T* eat, this is my body

Eph.   6:13 *t* unto you the whole armour
Rev.   3: 11 that no man *t* thy crown

TAKEN (TAKING)
Ps.   119:111 thy testimonies have I *t*
  119: 143 trouble and anguish have *t* hold of
Is.   16:10 gladness is *t* away and joy out of
Mat.   6:27 which of you by *t* thought can
  21:43 kingdom of God shall be *t* from
  24:40 one shall be *t*, the other left
Mark   4:25 shall be *t* even that which he hath
Acts   1: 9 he was *t* up; and a cloud
Rom.   7: 8 sin, *t* occasion by the commandment
2 Cor.   3:16 Lord, the veil shall be *t* away
Eph.   6:16 *t* the shield of faith

TALE (TALES)
Ps.   90: 9 our years as a *t* that is told
Luke 24:11 seemed to them as idle *t*

TALEBEARER
Lev.   19:16 go up and down as a *t*
Prov. 11:13 A *t* revealeth secrets: but he that
  18: 8 The words of a *t* are as wounds
  20:19 goeth about as a *t* revealeth secrets
  26:22 words of a *t* are as wounds

TALENT (TALENTS)
Mat.   18:24 which owed him ten thousand *t*
  25:25 hid thy *t* in the earth

TALK (TALKETH, TALKING)
Deut.   6: 7 of them when thou sittest
Ps.   71:24 my tongue shall *t* righteousness
  105: 2 *t* ye of all his wondrous works
Eph.   5: 4 nor foolish *t*, nor jesting

TARRY (TARRIED)
Ps.   68:12 she that *t* at home divided the spoil
  101: 7 telleth lies shall not *t* in my sight
Prov. 23:30 that *t* long at wine;
Jer.   14: 8 turneth aside to *t* for a night
Hab.   2: 3 though it *t* wait for it
Mat.   25: 5 bridegroom *t*, they all slumbered
  26:38 *t* ye here and watch
Luke   2:43 child Jesus *t* behind in Jerusalem
John 21:22 that he *t* till I come what is that
1 Cor. 11:33 together to eat, *t* one for another

TASTE (TASTED)
Ex.   16: 31 the *t* was like wafers
Ps.   34: 8 O *t* and see that the Lord is good
Mat.   16:28 shall not *t* of death till they see
Luke 14:24 were bidden shall *t* of my supper
John   8:52 keep my saying shall never *t* death
Col.   2:21 touch not, *t* not,
Heb.   2: 9 of God should *t* death for every man
  6: 4 *t* of the heavenly gift
1 Pet.   2: 3 if ye have *t* that the Lord is gracious

TAUGHT
2 Chr. 30:22 *t* the good knowledge of the Lord
Ps.   71:17 hast *t* me from my youth
Is.   54:13 children shall be *t* of the Lord
John   6:45 shall be all *t* of God
Acts 20:20 I have *t* you publicly, and from house to
Gal.   6: 6 let him that is *t* in the word
1 Thes. 4: 9 yourselves are *t* of God to love

TEACH
Deut.   4: 9 *t* them thy sons, and thy sons' sons
1 Sam. 12:23 I will *t* you the good
Job   22:22 shall any *t* God knowledge
Ps.   25: 5 lead me in thy truth, and *t* me
  27:11 *T* me thy way, O Lord
  34:11 I will *t* you the fear of
  51:13 will I *t* transgressors
  90:12 so *t* us to number our days
  119: 66 *T* me good judgment and knowledge
  143: 10 *T* me to do thy will;
Is.   2: 3 he will *t* us of his ways
Jer.   31:34 *t* no more every man his neighbour
Mat.   28:19 go ye therefore and *t* all nations
John   9:34 and dost thou *t* us?
  14:26 he shall *t* you all
1 Cor.   4:17 as I *t* every where in every church
1 Tim. 2:12 I suffer not a woman to *t*
  3: 2 given to hospitality, apt to *t*
2 Tim. 2: 2 be able to *t* others
Heb.   5:12 have need that one *t*
1 John 2:27 need not that any man *t* you

TEACHER (TEACHERS)

Ps.	119:99	more understanding than all my *t*
Hab.	2:18	and a *t* of lies, that the maker
John	3: 2	thou art a *t* come from God
Rom.	2:20	a *t* of babes which hast the
1 Tim.	2: 7	a *t* of the Gentiles in faith
2 Tim.	1:11	and a *t* of the Gentiles
	4: 3	heap to themselves *t*, having itching
Tit.	2: 3	to much wine *t* of good things
Heb.	5:12	ye ought to be *t* ye have need

TEACHEST (TEACHETH, TEACHING)

Ps.	34:11	*t* my hands to war so that a
	94:12	O Lord, and *t* him out of thy law
Mat.	15: 9	*t* for doctrines the commandments
	22:16	*t* the way of God in truth
	28:20	*t* them to observe all things
Rom.	2:21	*t* another, *t* thou not thyself
Col.	1:28	*t* every man in all wisdom
Tit.	2:12	*t* us that denying ungodliness
1 John	2:27	same anointing *t* you of all things

TEARS

Job	16:20	mine eye poureth out *t*
Ps.	6: 6	water my couch with my *t*
	56: 8	put thou my *t* in thy bottle
	126: 5	they that sow in *t* shall reap in joy
Is.	25: 8	wipe away all *t* from off all faces
Luke	7:38	to wash his feet with *t*
Acts	20:31	warn everyone night and day with *t*
2 Cor.	2: 4	I wrote unto you with many *t*
Heb.	5: 7	with strong crying and *t* unto him
Rev.	7:17	wipe all *t* from their

TEETH

Ps.	3: 7	broken the *t* of the ungodly
	112: 10	he shall gnash with his *t*
Sol.	4: 2	like a flock of sheep
Jer.	31:29	his *t* shall be set on
Ezek.	18: 2	children's *t* are set on
Mat.	8:12	shall be weeping and gnashing of *t*
	24:51	shall be weeping and gnashing of *t*

TELL

Ps.	48:13	*t* it to the generation following
Prov.	30: 4	name, if thou canst *t*
Mat.	8: 4	see thou *t* no man; but go
	18:15	go and *t* him his fault
John	4:25	when he is come he will *t* us all
2 Cor.	12: 2	out of the body, I cannot *t*

TEMPERANCE

Acts	24:25	as he reasoned of righteousness, *t*
Gal.	5:23	*t*: against such there is
2 Pet.	1: 6	knowledge *t*, and to *t*

TEMPERATE

1 Cor.	9:25	mastery is to *t* in all
Tit.	1: 8	sober, just, holy, *t*
	2: 2	men be sober, grave, *t*

TEMPLE (TEMPLES)

Ps.	29: 9	in his *t* doth every one speak of
Mal.	3: 1	suddenly come to his *t*, even the
Mat.	12: 6	place is one greater than the *t* is
John	2:19	destroy this *t* and in three days
1 Cor.	3:16	ye are the *t* of God
	6:19	body is the *t* of the Holy Ghost
	9:13	live of the things of the *t*
2 Cor.	6:16	hath the *t* of God with idols
Rev.	7:15	serve him day and night in the *t*
	11:19	*t* of God was opened in heaven
	21:22	God and the Lamb are the *t*

TEMPT (TEMPTED, TEMPTING)

Gen.	22: 1	God did *t* Abraham, and said unto
Deut.	6:16	ye shall not *t* the Lord
Ps.	78:18	they *t* God in their heart by asking
Is.	7:12	not ask, neither will I *t* the Lord
Mat.	4: 1	to be *t* of the devil
	16: 1	*t* desired him that he
	22:18	why *t* ye me, ye hypocrites
	22:35	asked him a question, *t* him
Luke	10:25	stood up, and *t* him,
	11:16	others, *t* him, sought of him
John	8: 6	This they said, *t* him
Acts	5: 9	have agreed together to *t* the Spirit
	15:10	why *t* ye God to put a yoke
1 Cor.	7: 5	that Satan *t* you not
	10:13	not suffer you to be *t*
Gal.	6: 1	lest thou also be *t*

TEMPTATION (TEMPTATIONS)

Ps.	95: 8	as in the day of *t* in the wilderness
Mat.	6:13	lead us not into *t*, but deliver us
Luke	4:13	devil had ended all *t*
	8:13	in time of *t* fall away
	22:28	have continued with me in my *t*
Acts	20:19	with many tears and *t*
1 Cor.	10:13	no *t* taken you but
Gal.	4:14	*t* which was in my flesh
Heb.	3: 8	day of *t* in the wilderness
Jas.	1:12	blessed is man that endureth *t*
1 Pet.	1: 6	heaviness through manifold *t*
2 Pet.	2: 9	deliver the godly out of *t*
Rev.	3:10	keep thee from the hour of *t*

TEMPTER

Mat.	4: 3	the *t* came to him
1 Thes.	3: 5	*t* have tempted you

TENDER

2 Ki.	22:19	Because thine heart was *t*
Luke	1:78	Through the *t* mercy of our God

TENDERHEARTED

Eph.	4:32	be ye kind to one another, *t*

TERRIBLE

Deut.	7:21	is among you, a mighty God and *t*
Neh.	1: 5	the great and *t* God
Ps.	45: 4	hand shall teach thee *t* things
	47: 2	for the Lord most high is *t*
	66: 3	how *t* art thou in thy works
	76:12	he is *t* to the kings of
	99: 3	praise thy great and *t* name
Jer.	20:11	is with me as a mighty *t* one
Joel	2:11	Lord is great and very *t*
Zeph.	2:11	The Lord will be *t* unto them: for

TERROR

Jer.	17:17	be not a *t* unto me:
Ezek.	26:21	I will make thee a *t*,
Rom.	13: 3	rulers are not a *t* to good
2 Cor.	5: 1	knowing therefore the *t* of the Lord

TESTAMENT

Mat.	26:28	my blood of the new *t*
Luke	22:20	This cup is the new *t*
1 Cor.	11:25	This cup is the new *t*
Heb.	7:22	Jesus made a surety of a better *t*
Rev.	11:19	in his temple the ark of his *t*

TESTIFY (TESTIFIED, TESTIFYING)

Ps.	81: 8	I will *t* unto thee: O Israel
Is.	59:12	our sins *t* against us:
Jer.	14: 7	our iniquities *t* against us
John	3:11	*t* that we have seen
Acts	20:24	*t* the gospel of the grace of God
Heb.	11: 4	God *t* of his gifts
1 Pet.	5:12	*t* that it is the true grace
1 John	4:14	*t* that the Father sent

TESTIMONY (TESTIMONIES)

Ps.	25:10	keep his covenant and his *t*
	93: 5	Thy *t* are very sure:
	119: 2	Blessed are they that keep his *t*
Is.	8:16	bind up the *t*, seal the law
Mat.	10:18	for a *t* against them
John	3:32	testifieth, and no man receiveth his *t*
Acts	14: 3	to the word of his grace
2 Cor.	1:12	the *t* of our conscience
Heb.	11: 5	before his translation he had this *t*
Rev.	1: 9	God, and for the *t* of Jesus Christ
	11: 7	shall have finished their *t*
	19:10	the *t* of Jesus is the spirit

THANK

Mat.	11:25	I *t* thee, O Father, Lord of heaven
Luke	17: 9	Doth he *t* that servant because he
	18:11	God, I *t* thee, that I am not
John	11:41	I *t* thee that thou hast heard
Rom.	7:25	I *t* God through Jesus
1 Cor.	1: 4	I *t* my God always on your behalf
1 Tim.	1:12	I *t* Jesus Christ our

THANKFUL

Ps.	100: 4	be *t* unto him, and
Rom.	1:21	as God, neither were *t*

THANKS

Col.	3:15	and be ye *t*
Mat.	26:27	took the cup and gave *t*
Luke	22:17	took the cup and gave *t*
1 Cor.	15:57	But *t* be to God which giveth
2 Cor.	8:16	But *t* be to God which
	9:15	*t* be to God for his unspeakable
Eph.	5: 4	but rather giving of *t*
1 Thes.	3: 9	what *t* can we render to God
	5:18	In every thing, give *t*
2 Thes.	2:13	we are bound to give *t*
1 Tim.	2: 1	giving of *t*, be made for all men
Heb.	13:15	our lips giving *t* to his name

THANKSGIVING

Ps.	26: 7	publish with the voice of *t*
	100: 4	Enter his gates with *t*
	116: 17	offer to thee the sacrifice of *t*
Phil.	4: 6	by prayer and supplication with *t*
1 Tim.	4: 3	created to be received with *t*
Rev.	7:12	wisdom, and *t*, and

THINK

Rom.	12: 3	*t* of himself more highly
1 Cor.	8: 2	if any man *t* that he knoweth
Gal.	6: 3	if a man *t* himself to be something
Eph.	3:20	above all that we ask or *t*
Phil.	4: 8	be any praise, *t* on these things

THOUGHT

Gen.	50:20	As for you, ye *t* evil
Ps.	48: 9	we have *t* of thy lovingkindness
	139: 2	understandest my *t* afar
Mat.	6:25	take no *t* for your life
	6:34	take therefore no *t* for the morrow
Mark	13:11	take no *t* beforehand
	14:72	when he *t* thereon he wept
Luke	12:22	take no *t* for your life
1 Cor.	13:11	*t* as a child, but when
2 Cor.	10: 5	bringeth into captivity every *t*
Phil.	2: 6	*t* it not robbery to be equal

THOUGHTS

Gen.	6: 5	imagination of the *t* of his heart
Judg.	5:15	were great *t* of the heart
Ps.	10: 4	God is not in all his *t*
	94:11	Lord knoweth the *t* of man
	139: 17	how precious are thy *t* to me
	139: 23	know my heart, try me, and know my *t*
Prov.	12: 5	The *t* of the righteous are right
	16: 3	thy *t* shall be established
Is.	55: 8	my *t* are not your *t*
	59: 7	their *t* are *t* of iniquity
	66:18	I know their works and their *t*
Mat.	15:19	out of heart proceed evil *t*
Luke	2:35	the *t* of many hearts may be revealed
Rom.	2:15	witness and their *t* the mean while
1 Cor.	3:20	the Lord knoweth the *t* of the wise
Heb.	4:12	a discerner of the *t* and intents
Jas.	2: 4	and are become judges of evil *t*

THIRST (THIRSTETH)

Ps.	42: 2	my soul *t* for God, for the living
Is.	49:10	shall not hunger nor *t*
	55: 1	Ho, every one that *t*,
Mat.	5: 6	do hunger and *t* after righteousness
John	4:14	shall never *t*, but the water that
	6:35	believeth on me shall never *t*
	7:37	if any man *t*, let him come unto me
Rom.	12:20	feed him; if he *t* give him drink
Rev.	7:16	neither *t* any more;

THORNS

Gen.	3:18	*t* also thistles shall it bring
Mat.	7:16	do men gather grapes of *t*?
	13: 7	some fell among *t*; and the *t*

THREE

Prov.	30:15	*t* things that are never satisfied
	30:29	*t* things which go well, yea, four
1 Cor.	14:27	or at the most by *t*,
1 John	5: 7	For there are *t* that bear record in

THRESH (THRESHETH)

Hab.	3:12	thou didst *t* the heathen in anger
1 Cor.	9:10	that he that *t* in hope

THRONE

Ps.	11: 4	the Lord's *t* is heaven:
	45: 6	Thy *t*, O God, is for ever
	89:14	are the habitation of thy *t*

Prov.	25: 5 *t* shall be established in righteousness
Dan.	7: 9 his *t* was like a fiery
Mat.	19:28 shall sit in the *t* of his glory
	25:31 shall sit on the *t* of his glory
Heb.	1: 8 Thy *t*, O God, is for ever
	4:16 boldly to the *t* of grace
Rev.	20:11 And I saw a great white *t*
	22: 3 *t* of God and the Lamb shall be in

THUNDER (THUNDERETH)

Job	26:14 but the *t* of his power who can
	40: 9 canst thou *t* with a voice
Ps.	29: 3 the God of glory *t*: the Lord is
	81: 7 in the secret place of *t*
Mark	3:17 Boanerges, which is, The sons of *t*

TIDINGS

Ps.	112: 7 not be afraid of evil *t*
Luke	1:19 and to show thee these glad *t*
	2:10 I bring you good *t* of great joy
	8: 1 preaching and showing the glad *t*
Acts	13:32 we declare unto you glad *t*
Rom.	10:15 bring glad *t* of good things

TIME

Ps.	32: 6 in a *t* when thou mayest be found
	41: 1 deliver him in *t* of trouble
	89:47 remember how short my *t* is
Eccl.	3: 1 and a *t* to every purpose
	9:11 *t* and chance happeneth to them all
Ezek.	16: 8 thy *t* was the *t* of love
	22: 7 that it shall be for a *t*
Luke	19:44 knewest not the *t* of thy visitation
John	7: 6 my *t* is not yet come: your *t*
Acts	17:21 spent their *t* in nothing else
Rom.	13:11 it is high *t* to awake out of sleep
2 Cor.	6: 2 Behold, now is the accepted *t*
Eph.	5:16 redeeming the *t*, because the days
Col.	4: 5 are without, redeeming the *t*
1 Pet.	1:17 pass the *t* of your sojourning
Rev.	12:14 times, and a half *t*

TIMES

Ps.	31:15 my *t* are in thy hand
	34: 1 bless the Lord at all *t*
	62: 8 trust in him at all *t*; ye people
Prov.	17:17 a friend loveth at all *t*
Luke	21:24 till the *t* of the Gentiles
Acts	1: 7 not for you to know the *t*
	3:19 *t* of refreshing shall come
	17:26 determined the *t* before appointed
1 Tim.	4: 1 that in the latter *t* some shall
2 Tim.	3: 1 in the last days perilous *t*

TITHE (TITHES)

Gen.	14:20 he gave him *t* of all
Mal.	3: 8 robbed thee? In *t* and offerings
Mat.	23:23 ye pay *t* of mint and
Luke	18:12 I give *t* of all that I

TONGUE

Job	5:21 be hid from the scourge of the *t*
	20:12 though he hide it under his *t*
Ps.	34:13 keep thy *t* from evil, and thy lips
	35:28 *t* shall speak of thy righteousness
	45: 1 my *t* is the pen of a ready
	137: 6 let my *t* cleave to the roof
Prov.	12:18 but the *t* of the wise is health
	15: 4 wholesome *t* is a tree of life
	18:21 death and life are in power of the *t*
	21: 6 getting of treasures by a lying *t*
	25:15 a soft *t* breaketh the bone
Is.	30:27 his *t* as a devouring fire
	50: 4 Lord hath given me the *t* of the learned
Acts	2:26 heart rejoice and my *t* was glad
Jas.	1:26 and bridleth not his *t*
	3: 5 *t* is a little member and boasteth
1 Pet.	3:10 refrain his *t* from evil

TONGUES

Ps.	55: 9 O Lord, and divide their *t*
Mark	16:17 they shall speak with new *t*
Acts	2: 4 spake with *t* and prophesied
1 Cor.	12:10 to another divers kinds of *t*
	14:23 and all speak with *t*, another come

TORMENT (TORMENTED)

Mat.	8:29 art thou come hither to *t* us
Luke	16:24 for I am *t* in this flame
Heb.	11:37 being destitute, afflicted, *t*
Rev.	14:11 smoke of their *t* ascendeth up for

	18: 7 so much *t* and sorrow give her: for

TOSS (TOSSED)

Ps.	109:23 I am *t* up and down like a locust
Is.	22:18 violently turn and *t* thee like a
Jas.	1: 6 driven with the wind and *t*
Eph.	4:14 be no more children *t* to and fro

TOUCH (TOUCHED, TOUCHETH)

1 Sam.	10:26 men whose hearts God had *t*
Job	19:21 hand of God hath *t* me
Ps.	105:15 *T* not mine anointed and do my
Is.	52:11 *t* no unclean thing; go ye out of
Mat.	9:21 If I may but *t* his garment
	14:36 only *t* the hem of his garment
Mark	10:13 that he should *t* them: and his
John	20:17 *t* me not, for I am not yet
1 Cor.	7: 1 good for a man not to *t* a woman
2 Cor.	6:17 *t* not the unclean thing; and I
Col.	2:21 *t* not, taste not, handle not

TOWER

Ps.	61: 3 a strong *t* from the enemy
	144: 2 my high *t*, and my deliverer
Mat.	21:33 winepress in it, and built a *t*

TRADITION (TRADITIONS)

Mat.	15: 3 commandment of God by your *t*
Gal.	1:14 exceedingly jealous of the *t*
Col.	2: 8 after the *t* of men after the
2 Thes.	2:15 hold the *t* which ye have been taught
	3: 6 disorderly, and not after the *t*
1 Pet.	1:18 received by *t* from your fathers

TRAIN

Prov.	22: 6 *T* up a child in the way

TRANSFIGURED

Mat.	17: 2 And was *t* before them: and his
Mark	9: 2 themselves: and he was *t* before them

TRANSFORMED

Rom.	12: 2 be ye *t* by the renewing of your
2 Cor.	11:15 *t* as the ministers of rightousness

TRANSGRESS (TRANSGRESSED, TRANSGRESSETH)

1 Sam.	2:24 make the Lord's people to *t*
2 Chr.	24:20 why *t* ye the commandments of the Lord?
Ps.	17: 3 my mouth shall not *t*
	25: 3 be ashamed which *t* without cause
Prov.	28:21 piece of bread that man will *t*
Is.	43:27 teachers have *t* against
Jer.	2: 8 pastors also *t* against
Lam.	3:42 we have *t* and have rebelled
Dan.	9:11 Israel have *t* thy law
Amos	4: 4 come to Bethel and *t*;
Mat.	15: 2 do thy disciples *t* the traditions
Rom.	2:27 and circumcision dost *t* the law

TRANSGRESSION

Ex.	34: 7 forgiving iniquity, *t*,
Job	13:23 make me to know my *t*
Ps.	32: 1 blessed he whose *t* is forgiven
	107: 17 Fools because of their *t* are afflicted
Prov.	17: 9 that covereth *t* seeketh love
Is.	53: 8 the *t* of my people was he stricken
	59:20 them that turn from *t* in Jacob
Mic.	6: 7 shall I give my firstborn for my *t*
Rom.	4:15 where no law is, there is no *t*
1 John	3: 4 sin is the *t* of the law

TRANSGRESSIONS

Josh.	24:19 will not forgive your *t*
Job	31:33 If I covered my *t* as Adam
Ps.	25: 7 sins of my youth, nor my *t*
	32: 5 I will confess my *t*
	39: 8 deliver me from all my *t*
	51: 3 I acknowledge my *t*
	103: 12 so far hath he removed our *t*
Is.	43:25 I am he that blotteth out thy *t*
	44:22 blotted out as a thick cloud thy *t*
	53: 5 was wounded for our *t*
Heb.	9:15 for the redemption of the *t*

TRANSGRESSOR (TRANSGRESSORS)

Ps.	51:13 Then will I teach *t* thy
	59: 5 be not merciful to any wicked *t*
Prov.	13:15 way of the *t* is hard
Is.	48: 8 called a *t* from the womb
	53:12 made intercession for the *t*
Jas.	2:11 if thou kill, thou art become a *t*

TRAVAIL (TRAVAILED, TRAVAILETH, TRAVAILING)

Job	15:20 wicked man *t* with pain all his
Eccl.	1:13 sore *t* hath God given
	5:14 those riches perish by evil *t*
Is.	13: 8 pain as a woman that *t*
	66: 7 before she *t*, she brought forth
Jer.	31: 8 her that *t* with child
Hos.	13:13 The sorrows of a *t* woman
Gal.	4:19 children, of whom I *t*
2 Thes.	3: 8 labour and *t* night and
Rev.	12: 2 being with child, *t* in

TREACHEROUS (TREACHEROUSLY)

Is.	21: 2 treacherous dealer dealeth *t*
Jer.	9: 2 an assembly of *t* men
Hos.	5: 7 they have dealt *t* against Lord
Mal.	2:15 none deal *t* against the wife

TREAD (TREADETH)

Job	40:12 *t* down the wicked
Ps.	7: 5 let him *t* down my life
	44: 5 through thy name will we *t* them under
Is.	63: 3 *t* them in mine anger
1 Cor.	9: 9 ox that *t* out the corn
1 Tim.	5:18 ox that *t* out the corn
Rev.	11: 2 holy city shall they *t*

TREASURE (TREASURES)

Ex.	19: 5 be a peculiar *t* unto me
Deut.	28:12 Lord shall open to thee his good *t*
Ps.	135: 4 and Israel for his peculiar *t*
Prov.	2: 4 searchest for her as for hid *t*
	10: 2 *t* of wickedness profit nothing
	21: 6 getting *t* by a lying tongue
	21:20 there is *t* to be desired
Is.	33: 6 fear of the Lord is his *t*
Mat.	6:19 not up for yourselves *t* on earth
	6:21 where your *t* is, there
	12:35 a good man out of the good *t* of
	13:52 bringeth forth out of his *t*
	19:21 thou shalt have *t* in heaven
Luke	12:21 layeth up *t* for himself, and is not
2 Cor.	4: 7 we have this *t* in earthen vessels
Col.	2: 3 hid all the *t* of wisdom
Heb.	11:26 greater riches than *t*

TREE (TREES)

Gen.	2:16 Of every *t* of the garden
	3:22 take also the *t* of life
Ps.	1: 3 like a *t* planted by rivers
	52: 8 I am like a green olive *t*
	104: 16 *t* of the Lord are full of sap
Prov.	3:18 she is a *t* of life to
	11:30 fruit of the righteous is the *t* of
Is.	61: 3 might be called *t* of righteousness
Jer.	17: 8 a *t* planted by the waters
Ezek.	47:12 grow all *t* for meat whose leaf
Mat.	7:17 good *t* bringeth forth good fruit
	12:33 *t* is known by his fruit
Mark	8:24 I see men as *t* walking
Rev.	22: 2 in midst of street was the *t* of life
	22:14 may have right to the *t* of life

TREMBLE (TREMBLED, TREMBLING)

1 Sam.	4:13 for his heart *t* for the ark of God
Ezra	9: 4 every one that *t* at the words of God
Ps.	2:11 fear, and rejoice with *t*
Eccl.	12: 3 keepers of the house shall *t*
Jer.	10:10 at his wrath the earth shall *t*
Dan.	6:26 men *t* and fear before
Zech.	12: 2 make Jerusalem a cup of *t*
Acts	24:25 as he reasoned Felix *t*
1 Cor.	2: 3 in fear, in weakness, and in much *t*
Phil.	2:12 your own salvation with fear and *t*
Jas.	2:19 devils also believe and *t*

TRESPASS (TRESPASSES)

Ezra	9: 6 our *t* is grown up unto the heavens
Mat.	6:14 if ye forgive men their *t*
	18:15 thy brother *t* against thee
	18:35 every one his brother their *t*
Luke	17: 3 If thy brother *t* against thee, rebuke
2 Cor.	5:19 not imputing their *t* to
Eph.	2: 1 who were dead in *t*
Col.	2:13 having forgiven you all *t*

TRIAL

Job	9:23 laugh at the *t* of the innocent
Heb.	11:36 others had a *t* of cruel mockings
1 Pet.	1: 7 the *t* of your faith

4:12 strange concerning the fiery *t*

TRIBES
Ps.   105:37 not one feeble person among their *t*
Mat.   24:30 shall all the *t* of the earth
Acts   26: 7 promise our twelve *t* instantly

TRIBULATION
Judg. 10:14 in the time of your *t*
Mat.   24:29 immediately after the *t* of those days
John   16:33 in the world ye shall have *t*
Acts   14:22 we must through much *t* enter into
Rom.   2: 9 *t* and anguish upon every soul
        5: 3 knowing that *t* worketh patience
        8:35 from the love of Christ? shall *t*
      12:12 hope, patient in *t*
2 Cor. 1: 4 comforteth us in all our *t*
        7: 4 exceeding joyful in all our *t*
2 Thes. 1: 6 to recompense *t* to them that trouble
Rev.   1: 9 brother and companion in *t*
        2:10 shall have *t* ten days
        2:22 into great *t* except they repent

TRIBULATIONS
1 Sam. 10:19 of all your adversities and your *t*
Rom.   5: 3 glory in *t* also: knowing that *t*
Eph.   3:13 faint not at my *t* for

TRIBUTE
Prov. 12:24 slothful shall be under *t*
Mat.   17:24 doth not the master pay *t*
      22:17 is it lawful to give *t* to Caesar
Rom.   13: 7 *t* to whom *t* is due;

TRIUMPH (TRIUMPHED, TRIUMPHING)
Ex.   15: 1 he hath *t* gloriously: the horse
2 Sam. 1:20 daughters of the uncircumcised *t*
Job   20: 5 the *t* of the wicked is short
Ps.   25: 2 let not mine enemies *t* over me
      92: 4 *t* in the works of thy hands
2 Cor. 2:14 God, which always causeth us to *t*

TRODDEN
Ps.   119:118 *t* down all them that err
Is.   63: 3 I have *t* the winepress
Luke   21:24 Jerusalem shall be *t* down of the
Heb.   10:29 who hath *t* under foot the Son of God

TROUBLE (TROUBLES)
Job   5: 7 man is born to *t* as sparks fly
      14: 1 few days and full of *t*
Ps.   9: 9 oppressed a refuge in times of *t*
      27: 5 time of *t* he shall hide
      34:17 deliver them out of all their *t*
      37:39 their strength in the time of *t*
      46: 1 a very present help in *t*
      91:15 I will be with him in *t*
    143: 11 bring my soul out of *t*
Prov. 11: 8 righteous delivered out of *t*
Is.   33: 2 our salvation also in time of *t*
Jer.   14: 8 saviour thereof in time of *t*
Dan.   12: 1 shall be a time of *t*
1 Cor. 7:28 shall have *t* in the flesh

TROUBLED (TROUBLETH)
Ps.   30: 7 hide thy face, and I was *t*
      77: 3 I remembered God, and was *t*
Prov. 11:17 he that is cruel *t* his own flesh
Is.   57:20 wicked are like the *t* sea
John   5: 4 *t* the water: whosoever then first
      12:27 now is my soul *t*; and what shall
      14: 1 let not your heart be *t*
Gal.   5:10 he that *t* you shall bear his judgment
2 Thes. 1: 7 to you who are *t* rest

TRUE
Ps.   19: 9 the judgments of the Lord are *t*
      119:160 thy word is *t* from beginning
Mat.   22:16 we know that thou art *t* and
Luke   16:11 commit to your trust *t* riches
John   1: 9 That was the *t* Light, which lighteth
      4:23 *t* worshippers worship the Father
      6:32 giveth you *t* bread from heaven
      7:28 but he that sent me is *t*
      15: 1 I am the *t* vine, and
2 Cor. 1:18 as God is *t*, our word
      6: 8 as deceivers and yet *t*
Phil.   4: 8 whatsoever things are *t*
1 John 5:20 may know him that is *t*
Rev.   3: 7 holy, he that is *t*
      19: 11 upon him was called Faithful and *T*

TRUMPET (TRUMPETS)
Josh.   6: 4 bear before the ark seven *t*
Ps.   81: 3 Blow up the *t* in the new moon
      98: 6 With *t* and sound of cornet
Is.   27:13 great *t* shall be blown
      58: 1 lift up thy voice like a *t*
Mat.   6: 2 do not sound a *t* before thee
Rev.   8: 6 which had seven *t* prepared

TRUST
1 Chr. 5:20 they put their *t* in him
Job   13:15 he slay me, yet will I *t*
Ps.   4: 5 put your *t* in the Lord
      37: 3 *t* in the Lord, and do
      37: 5 *t* also in him; and he shall bring it
      37:40 save them because they *t* in him
      40: 4 that maketh the Lord his *t*
      55:23 but I will *t* in thee
      62: 8 in him at all times,
      71: 5 thou art my *t* from my youth
     115: 9 *t* thou in the Lord: he
     118: 8 it is better to *t* in the Lord
     119: 42 for I *t* in thy word
     125: 1 they that *t* in the Lord shall
Prov. 22:19 thy *t* may be in the Lord
Is.   26: 4 *t* ye in the Lord for
      50:10 *t* in the name of the Lord
Jer.   7: 4 *t* ye not in lying words
Mic.   7: 5 *t* ye not in a friend,
Mark 10:24 hard for them that *t* in riches
2 Cor. 1: 9 should not *t* in ourselves
Phil.   3: 4 might *t* in the flesh

TRUSTED (TRUSTETH)
Ps.   22: 4 our fathers *t* in thee: they *t*
      28: 7 my heart *t* in him, and
      32:10 he that *t* in the Lord, mercy shall
      34: 8 blessed is the man that *t* in him
      52: 7 *t* in the abundance of his riches
      57: 1 for my soul *t* in thee
      84:12 blessed is man that *t* in thee
      86: 2 save thy servant that *t* in thee
Jer.   17: 7 blessed is man that *t* in the Lord
Luke   18: 9 who certainly which *t* in themselves

TRUTH
Ex.   34: 6 abundant in goodness and *t*
Deut. 32: 4 a God of *t* and without iniquity
Ps.   15: 2 and speaketh the *t* in his heart
      25: 5 Lead me in thy *t*, and
      51: 6 desirest *t* in the inward parts
      91: 4 his *t* shall be thy shield
     117: 2 *t* of the Lord endureth
     119: 30 I have chosen the way of *t*
Prov. 12:19 lip of *t* shall be established
      16: 6 by mercy and *t* iniquity is purged
Is.   59:14 *t* is fallen in the street
Jer.   4: 2 The Lord liveth, in *t*
Dan.   4:37 all whose works are *t*
Zech. 8:16 speak every man *t* to
John   1:14 full of grace and *t*
      8:32 know the *t*, and the *t* shall
      14: 6 I am the way, the *t*, and the life
      14:17 Spirit of *t*; whom the world
      16:13 guide you into all *t*
      17:17 through thy *t*: thy word is *t*
      18:37 I should bear witness unto the *t*
Acts   26:25 forth the words of *t*
Rom.   1:25 changed the *t* of God into a lie
      2: 2 judgment of God is according to *t*
1 Cor. 5: 8 bread of sincerity and *t*
2 Cor. 13: 8 nothing against the *t*
Gal.   3: 1 should not obey the *t*,
Eph.   4:15 but speaking the *t* in love
      5: 9 goodness, and rightousness, and *t*
      6:14 having your loins girt about with *t*
2 Thes. 2:10 received not the love of *t*
1 Tim. 3:15 God, the pillar and ground of the *t*
2 Tim. 2:18 who concerning the *t* have erred
      3: 7 come to the knowledge of the *t*
      4: 4 turn away their ears from *t*
1 Pet. 1:22 purified your souls in obeying the *t*
2 Pet. 1:12 and be established in the present *t*
1 John 1: 8 and the *t* is not in us
      5: 6 because the Spirit is *t*

TRY
Job   7:18 morning, and *t* him every moment
Ps.   11: 4 his eyelids *t* the children of men
     139: 23 *t* me, and know my thoughts
Lam.   3:40 search and *t* our ways, and turn
Zech. 13: 9 will *t* them as gold is tried
1 Cor. 3:13 fire shall *t* every man's work
1 Pet. 4:12 fiery trial which is to *t* you
1 John 4: 1 *t* the spirits whether they are of

TRIED (TRIEST, TRIETH, TRYING)
Ps.   7: 9 the righteous God *t* the heart
      11: 5 Lord *t* the righteous
      66:10 thou hast *t* us as silver is *t*
Dan.   12:10 shall be purified and *t*
1 Thes. 2: 4 God, which *t* our hearts
Heb.   11:17 by faith, Abraham, when he was *t*
Jas.   1: 3 *t* of your faith worketh patience
1 Pet. 1: 7 though it be *t* with fire
Rev.   3:18 buy of me gold *t* in the fire

TURN
Deut. 4:30 if thou *t* to the Lord thy God
1 Ki.   8:35 and *t* from their sin,
2 Chr. 15: 4 in their trouble but *t*
Ps.   22:27 remember, and *t* unto
      80: 3 *T* us again, O God,
Is.   31: 6 *t* ye not unto him
      58:13 If thou *t* away thy foot
Jer.   18: 8 *t* from their evil, I will repent
Lam.   3:40 and *t* again to the Lord
Ezek. 18:32 *t* yourselves, and live
Hos.   12: 6 *t* thou to thy God;
Joel   2:13 and *t* unto the Lord
Mic.   7:19 he will *t* again, he will have compassion
Luke   1:16 children of Israel shall he *t*
Acts   26:20 repent, and *t* to God
2 Cor. 3:16 when it shall *t* to the Lord
Gal.   4: 9 how *t* ye again to the weak
2 Tim. 3: 5 power thereof: from such *t* away
Heb.   12:25 if we *t* away from him that speaketh
2 Pet. 2:21 to *t* from the holy commandment

TURNED
Ps.   30: 11 *t* for me my mourning into dancing
      44:18 heart is not *t* back
Is.   42:17 They shall be *t* back,
      44:20 a deceived heart hath *t* him
      53: 6 *t* every one to his own
Jer.   2:27 for they have *t* their back unto me
      8: 6 every one *t* to his course
Hos.   7: 8 Ephraim is a cake not *t*
John 16:20 sorrow shall be *t* to joy
1 Thes. 1: 9 how ye *t* to God from idols to serve
Jas.   4: 9 let your laughter be *t* to mourning
2 Pet. 2:22 dog is *t* to his own vomit again

TURNETH (TURNING)
Prov. 15: 1 A soft answer *t* away wrath
Is.   9:13 the people *t* not unto
Jer.   14: 8 *t* aside to tarry for a night
Jas.   1:17 variableness, neither shadow of *t*
Jude   1: 4 *t* the grace of God into lasciviousness

TWINKLING
1 Cor. 15:52 in the *t* of an eye, at

UNAWARES
Ps.   35: 8 destruction come upon him at *u*
Luke   21:34 day come upon you *u*
Heb.   13: 2 some have entertained angels *u*
Jude   1: 4 certain men crept in *u*

UNBELIEF
Mat.   13:58 works there because of their *u*
Mark   6: 6 marvelled because of their *u*
      9:24 I believe; help thou mine *u*
      16:14 upbraided them with their *u*
Rom.   4:20 promise of God through *u*
      11:20 because of *u* they were broken off
1 Tim. 1:13 I did it ignorantly in *u*
Heb.   3:12 you an evil heart of *u*, in departing

UNBELIEVERS
Luke   12:46 his portion with the *u*
1 Cor. 14:23 are unlearned or *u*, will they not
2 Cor. 6:14 unequally yoked together with *u*

UNBELIEVING
1 Cor. 7:14 the *u* husband is sanctified by the
Tit.   1:15 defiled and *u* is nothing pure
Rev.   21: 8 fearful, and *u*, and the

UNCIRCUMCISED
Ex.   6: 30 I am of *u* lips, and
Jer.   6: 10 behold, their ear is *u*
Acts   7: 51 Ye stiffnecked and *u* in heart

UNCIRCUMCISION
Rom.   4: 10 he was in circumcision, or in *u*
1 Cor. 7: 19 and *u* is nothing, but the keeping
Gal.   2: 7 gospel of *u* was committed
Col.   2: 13 dead in your sins and the *u*

UNCLEAN
Lev.   5: 2 a soul touch any *u* thing
Is.   6: 5 I am a man of *u* lips
Rom.   14: 14 there is nothing *u* of itself
1 Cor. 7: 14 else were your children *u*
Eph.   5: 5 nor *u* person, nor covetous man

UNCLEANNESS
Mat.   23: 27 dead men's bones, and of all *u*
Rom.   6: 19 members servants to *u*, and to
Eph.   4: 19 to work all *u* with greediness
        5: 3 all *u* let it not once be named
1 Thes. 4: 7 hath not called us to *u*

UNDEFILED
Ps.   119: 1 Blessed are the *u*, in the way
Heb.   7: 26 holy, harmless, *u*, separate from
       13: 4 honourable in all, and the bed *u*
Jas.   1: 27 pure religion and *u* before God and
1 Pet. 1: 4 to an inheritance incorruptible, *u*

UNDERSTAND (UNDERSTANDEST,
    UNDERSTANDETH, UNDERSTOOD)
Gen.   11: 7 they may not *u* one another's speech
1 Chr. 28: 9 *u* all the imaginations of the thoughts
Ps.   19: 12 who can *u* his errors?
      107: 43 shalt *u* the lovingkindness of the Lord
      139: 2 thou *u* my thought afar off
Prov.   2: 5 shalt thou *u* the fear of the Lord
        8: 5 O ye simple, *u* wisdom: and, ye
       19: 25 understanding and he will *u* knowledge
       28: 5 that seek the Lord *u* all things
Is.   32: 4 heart also of the rash shall *u*
Mat.   13: 19 and *u* it not, then cometh the
       13: 51 have ye *u* all these
John   12: 16 *u* not his disciples at
Acts   8: 30 *u* thou what thou readest?
Rom.   13: 11 I *u* as a child, I
2 Pet. 3: 16 are some things hard to be *u*

UNDERSTANDING
Deut.   4: 6 is your wisdom and your *u*
Job   12: 13 and strength, he hath counsel and *u*
       32: 8 Almighty giveth them *u*
       38: 36 who hath given *u* to the heart
Ps.   47: 7 sing ye praises with *u*
       49: 3 meditation of my heart be of *u*
      119: 34 give me *u* and I shall
      119: 104 through thy precepts I get *u*
      147: 5 his *u* is infinite
Prov.   2: 2 apply thine heart to *u*
        3: 5 lean not unto thine own *u*
        3: 13 happy is the man that getteth *u*
        8: 5 ye fools, be ye of an *u* heart
        9: 6 and go in the way of *u*
       14: 29 slow to wrath is of great *u*
       16: 22 *u* is a wellspring of life
       21: 30 *u* nor counsel against the Lord
       30: 2 I have not the *u* of a
Is.   11: 2 spirit of wisdom and *u*, the spirit
       27: 11 it is a people of no *u*
       40: 28 is no searching of his *u*
Jer.   51: 15 stretched out heaven by his *u*
Mark   12: 33 with all the heart and with all the *u*
Luke   2: 47 were astonished at his *u* and answers
       24: 45 then opened he their *u*
1 Cor. 1: 19 bring to nothing the *u* of the prudent
       14: 14 spirit prayeth, but *u* is unfruitful
       14: 20 Brethren, be not children in *u*
Eph.   1: 18 eyes of your *u* being enlightened
        4: 18 the *u* darkened, being alienated
Phil.   4: 7 peace of God which passeth all *u*
Col.   1: 9 in all wisdom and spiritual *u*
        2: 2 riches of the full assurance of *u*
2 Tim. 2: 7 give thee *u* in all things

UNFEIGNED
2 Cor. 6: 6 by the Holy Ghost, by love *u*
1 Tim. 1: 5 conscience, and of faith *u*

2 Tim. 1: 5 the *u* faith that is in
1 Pet. 1: 22 through the Spirit unto *u* love

UNFRUITFUL
Mat.   13: 22 choke the word, and he becometh *u*
Eph.   5: 11 fellowship with the *u* works
2 Pet. 1: 8 barren nor *u* in the knowledge

UNGODLY
Ps.   1: 1 walketh not in the counsel of the *u*
        1: 5 *u* shall not stand in the judgment
        3: 7 hast broken the teeth of the *u*
       43: 1 plead my cause against an *u* nation
Prov. 16: 27 An *u* man diggeth up evil
       19: 28 an *u* witness scorneth judgment
Rom.   4: 5 him that justifieth the *u*
        5: 6 in due time Christ died for the *u*
1 Tim. 1: 9 disobedient for the *u* and for sinners
1 Pet. 4: 18 where shall the *u* and the sinner
2 Pet. 2: 5 the flood upon the world of the *u*
        3: 7 day of judgment and perdition of *u* men
Jude   1: 4 *u* men, turning the grace of God
        1: 15 all their *u* deeds, which they have

UNGODLINESS
Rom.   1: 18 against all *u* and unrighteousness
       11: 26 turn away the *u* from Jacob
Tit.   2: 12 denying *u* and worldly

UNITY
Ps.   133: 1 brethren to dwell together in *u*
Eph.   4: 3 Endeavouring to keep *u* of the Spirit
        4: 13 till we all come in *u* of faith

UNJUST
Ps.   43: 1 from the deceitful and *u* man
Prov. 11: 7 hope of *u* men perisheth
       29: 27 *u* man is an abomination to
Zeph.   3: 5 the *u* knoweth no shame
Mat.   5: 45 rain on the just and the *u*
Luke   16: 8 lord commended the *u* steward
       18: 6 hear what the *u* judge saith
       18: 11 other men are, extortioners, *u*,
Acts   24: 15 both of the just and *u*
1 Pet. 3: 18 suffered for sins, the just for *u*
2 Pet. 2: 9 reserve the *u* to the day of

UNKNOWN
Acts   17: 23 this inscription, To the *u* god
1 Cor. 14: 27 If any man speak in an *u* tongue
2 Cor. 6: 9 as *u* and yet well known

UNLEAVENED
Ex.   12: 39 and they baked *u*
1 Cor. 5: 7 be a new lump, as ye are *u*

UNPROFITABLE
Mat.   25: 30 cast ye the *u* servant to the outer
Luke   17: 10 we are *u* servants
Rom.   3: 12 are together become *u*
Tit.   3: 9 they are *u* and vain
Heb.   13: 17 for that is *u* for you

UNRIGHTEOUS
Luke   16: 11 not been faithful in *u* mammon
Rom.   3: 5 is God *u* who taketh vengeance?
1 Cor. 6: 9 *u* shall not inherit the
Heb.   6: 10 God is not *u* to forget

UNRIGHTEOUSNESS
Jer.   22: 13 woe to him that buildeth his house by *u*
John   7: 18 is true, and no *u* in him
Rom.   6: 13 members as instruments of *u*
        9: 14 is there *u* with God? God forbid
2 Cor. 6: 14 what fellowship hath righteousness
                  with *u*
2 Thes. 2: 10 all deceivableness of *u*
Heb.   8: 12 will be merciful to their *u*
2 Pet. 2: 15 loved the wages of *u*
1 John 1: 9 to cleanse us from all *u*

UNSEARCHABLE
Job   5: 9 doeth great things and *u*
Ps.   145: 3 praised; and his greatness is *u*
Eph.   3: 8 Gentiles the *u* riches of Christ

UNSPEAKABLE
2 Cor. 9: 15 unto God for his *u* gift
       12: 4 and heard *u* words, which it is
1 Pet. 1: 8 rejoice with joy *u* and full of

UNSTABLE
Jas.   1: 8 man is *u* in all his ways
2 Pet. 3: 16 they that are unlearned and *u* wrest

UNWORTHY (UNWORTHILY)
Acts   13: 46 judge yourselves *u* of everlasting
1 Cor. 6: 2 are ye *u* to judge the smallest
       11: 27 drink this cup of the Lord *u*

UPHOLD (UPHOLDEST, UPHOLDETH, UPHOLDING)
Ps.   37: 17 but the Lord *u* the righteous
       41: 12 thou *u* me in my integrity
       51: 12 *u* me with thy free spirit
       63: 8 thy right hand *u* me
      119: 116 *u* me according unto thy word
      145: 14 The Lord *u* all that fall
Prov. 29: 23 honour shall *u* the humble
Is.   41: 10 I will *u* thee with the right hand
Heb.   1: 3 *u* all things by word of

UPRIGHT
Ps.   7: 10 saveth the *u* in heart
       11: 7 his countenance doth behold the *u*
       18: 25 *u* man thou wilt show
       25: 8 good and *u* is the Lord
       64: 10 all the *u* in heart shall glory
      112: 2 generation of the *u* shall be blessed
      140: 13 *u* shall dwell in thy presence
Prov.   2: 21 *u* shall dwell in the land
       10: 29 way of Lord is strength to the *u*
       11: 3 integrity of the *u* shall
       13: 6 righteousness keepeth him that is *u*
       28: 10 *u* shall have good

UPRIGHTLY
Ps.   15: 2 He that walketh *u*, and worketh
       58: 1 do ye judge *u*, O ye sons of
Prov. 15: 21 man of understanding walketh *u*
Is.   33: 15 righteously, and speaketh *u*.,
Gal.   2: 14 I saw they walked not *u*

UPRIGHTNESS
Job   33: 23 to show unto man his *u*
Ps.   25: 21 let integrity and *u* preserve me
      143: 10 lead me into the land of *u*
Is.   26: 7 the way of the just is *u*

URIM
Ex.   28: 30 breastplate of judgment the *U*
Num.   27: 21 for him after the judgment of *U*
1 Sam. 28: 6 neither by dreams nor by *U*
Ezra   2: 63 a priest with *U* and Thummim

USURY
Lev.   25: 37 give him thy money upon *u*
Neh.   5: 10 let us leave off this *u*
Ps.   15: 5 putteth not out his money to *u*
Prov. 28: 8 by *u* and unjust gain increaseth
Ezek. 22: 12 thou hast taken *u* and increase
Mat.   25: 27 should have received mine own with *u*

UTTER (UTTERED, UTTERETH)
Ps.   19: 2 day to day *u* speech, and
       78: 2 I will *u* dark sayings
       94: 4 they *u* and speak hard things
Rom.   8: 26 groanings which cannot be *u*
2 Cor. 12: 4 words not lawful for man to *u*
Heb.   5: 11 to say and hard to be *u*

UTTERANCE
Acts   2: 4 as Spirit gave them *u*
Col.   4: 3 God would open unto us the door of *u*

VAIN
Ex.   20: 7 the name of the Lord thy God in *v*
1 Sam. 12: 21 should ye go after *v* things
Job   11: 12 for a *v* man would be wise
Ps.   39: 6 they are disquieted in *v*
       60: 11 for *v* is the help of man
       73: 13 cleansed my heart in *v*
      127: 1 the watchman waketh but in *v*
Is.   45: 19 seek ye me in *v*: I the
Jer.   3: 23 in *v* is salvation hoped for from
Mat.   15: 9 in *v* do they worship me
Rom.   1: 21 but became *v* in their imaginations
       13: 4 beareth not the sword in *v*
1 Cor. 3: 20 thoughts of the wise are *v*
2 Cor. 6: 1 receive not the grace of God in *v*
Eph.   5: 6 deceive you with *v* words
Jas.   1: 26 this man's religion is *v*

VANITY (VANITIES)
Job   7: 16 let me along; for my days are *v*
Ps.   12: 2 speak *v* every one with his neighbour
       31: 6 hated them that regard lying *v*
       39: 5 his best state is altogether *v*

39: 11	surely every man is v
62: 9	men of low degree are v
94: 11	thoughts of man that they are v
119: 37	turn away mine eyes from beholding v
144: 4	man is like to v: his days as a

Eccl.
1: 2	v of v, all is v
3: 19	above a beast: for all is v
12: 8	saith the preacher; all is v

Is. 40: 17 less than nothing and v
Jonah 2: 8 that observe lying v
Acts 14: 15 turn from these v unto the
Rom. 8: 20 creature was made subject to v
Eph. 4: 17 walk in the v of their mind
2 Pet. 2: 18 great swelling worlds of v

VALIANT (VALIANTLY)
Ps. 60: 12 Through God we shall do v
118: 16 hand of the Lord doeth v
Jer. 9: 3 they are not v for the truth
Heb. 11: 34 waxed v in fight, turned to

VEIL
Is. 25: 7 the v that is spread over all
Mat. 27: 51 v of the temple was rent
2 Cor. 3: 13 Moses put a v over his
Heb. 6: 19 entereth into that within the v

VENGEANCE
Gen. 4: 15 v shall be taken on him
Deut. 32: 35 to me belongeth v and recompence
Ps. 58: 10 rejoice when he seeth v
94: 1 God, to whom v belongeth
Is. 34: 8 the day of the Lord's v
Jer. 51: 6 time of the Lord's v
Luke 21: 22 these be days of v,
Rom. 12: 19 V is mine; I will repay,
Heb. 10: 30 V belongeth unto me, I will recompense
Jude 1: 7 suffering the v of eternal fire

VESSEL (VESSELS)
Ps. 2: 9 pieces like a potter's v
31: 12 I am like a broken v
Acts 9: 15 he is a chosen v unto
Rom. 9: 21 make one v unto honour and another
2 Cor. 4: 7 we have this treasure in earthen v
1 Thes. 4: 4 possess his v in sanctification
2 Tim. 2: 21 be a v unto honour,
1 Pet. 3: 7 honour to the wife as to the weaker v

VEXED
Ps. 6: 2 heal me; for my bones are v
6: 10 enemies be ashamed and sore v

VICTORY
1 Chr. 29: 1 glory, and the v, and the majesty
Ps. 98: 1 his holy arm hath gotten him v
Is. 25: 8 He will swallow up death in v
1 Cor. 15: 15 death is swallowed up in v
15: 55 O grave, where is thy v?
1 John 5: 4 the v that overcometh

VILE
Ps. 15: 4 whose eyes a v person is contemned
Is. 32: 6 v person will speak villany
Rom. 1: 26 gave them up to v affections
Phil. 3: 21 shall change our v body

VINE
Ps. 128: 3 wife shall be as a fruitful v
Hos. 10: 1 Israel is an empty v
Mic. 4: 4 sit every man under his v
Mat. 26: 29 not drink of this fruit of the v
John 15: 1 I am the true v and my Father

VINEYARD
Ps. 80: 15 v which thy right hand hath planted
Is. 5: 1 My wellbeloved hath a v
Mat. 20: 1 hire labourers into his v
21: 33 householder which planted a v
Luke 13: 6 planted in his v; and
1 Cor. 9: 7 who planteth a v, and eateth not

VIOLENCE
Gen. 6: 11 earth was filled with v
Ps. 72: 14 redeem their soul from deceit and v
73: 6 v covereth them as a garment
Mat. 11: 12 kingdom of heaven suffereth v
Luke 3: 14 do v to no man, and
Heb. 11: 34 quenched the v of fire

VIRGIN (VIRGINS)
Sol. 1: 3 therefore do the v love
Is. 7: 14 Behold a v shall conceive

Mat. 1: 23 Behold, a v shall be with child
2 Cor. 11: 2 present you as a chaste v
Rev. 14: 4 for they are v. These

VIRTUE
Luke 6: 19 there went v out of him
Phil. 4: 8 if there be any v,
2 Pet. 1: 3 called us to glory and v

VIRTUOUS
Prov. 12: 4 A v woman is a crown
31: 10 Who can find a v woman

VISION
Prov. 29: 18 where there is no v the people perish
Ezek. 13: 16 see v of peace for her,
Hos. 12: 10 I have multiplied v,
Joel 2: 28 young men shall see v
Hab. 2: 3 the v is yet for an appointed time
Mat. 17: 9 Tell the v to no man
Acts 2: 17 young men shall see v
10: 19 Peter thought on the v
16: 9 a v appeared to Paul in the night

VISIT (VISITED, VISITING)
Ex. 20: 5 v the iniquity of the fathers
Deut. 5: 9 v the iniquity of the fathers
Ps. 17: 3 thou hast v me in the
106: 4 v me with thy salvation
Hos. 8: 13 and v their sins: they
Mat. 25: 36 I was sick and ye v
Luke 1: 68 he hath v and redeemed his people
1: 78 dayspring from on high hath v us
Acts 7: 23 v his brethren the children of
15: 14 did v the Gentiles, to
15: 36 v our brethren in every city
Jas. 1: 27 to v the fatherless and

VOICE
Gen. 4: 10 v of thy brother's blood
Ps. 5: 3 my v shalt thou hear in the morning
42: 4 God, with the v of
95: 7 today, if ye will hear his v
103: 20 hearkening to the v of his word
Is. 30: 19 unto thee at the v of thy cry
John 5: 25 dead shall hear the v
10: 3 sheep hear his v: and he calleth
Gal. 4: 20 to change my v; for I
1 Thes. 4: 16 v of the archangel
Rev. 3: 20 if any man hear my v

VOID
Ps. 119: 126 for they have made v thy law
Is. 55: 11 it shall not return to me v
1 Cor. 9: 15 man should make my glorying v

VOMIT
Job 20: 15 he shall v them up
Prov. 23: 8 thou hast eaten shalt thou v up
26: 11 dog returneth to his v
2 Pet. 2: 22 dog is turned to his own v

VOW (VOWED, VOWS, VOWEDST)
Gen. 28: 20 Jacob v a v, saying, if God
Num. 6: 2 to v a v of a Nazarite
Ps. 50: 14 pay thy v to the most High
56: 12 thy v are upon me, O
61: 5 O God, hast heard my v
65: 1 unto thee shall the v be performed
Prov. 20: 25 after v to make inquiry
Is. 19: 21 they shall v a v unto the Lord
Jonah 1: 16 to the Lord, and made v

WAGES
Hag. 1: 6 earneth w to put into the bag
Mal. 3: 5 oppress the hireling in his w
Luke 3: 14 be content with your w
Rom. 6: 23 the w of sin is death

WAIT
Ps. 25: 5 on thee do I w all the day
27: 14 w on the Lord: be of good
62: 5 w thou only upon God
130: 5 I w for the Lord, my soul doth w
145: 15 eyes of all w upon
Prov. 20: 22 w on the Lord and he will save
Is. 30: 18 blessed are all they that w for him
40: 31 that w on Lord shall renew
Lam. 3: 25 good to them that w
Hos. 12: 6 w on thy God continually
Mic. 7: 7 w for the God of my salvation
Luke 12: 36 men that w for their

1 Thes. 1: 10 to w for his Son from

WAITED (WAITETH, WAITING)
Ps. 33: 20 our soul w for the Lord
40: 1 I w patiently for the Lord
130: 6 my soul w for the Lord more
Is. 25: 9 our God, we have w for him
33: 2 O Lord, we have w for thee
64: 4 prepared for him that w for him
Mark 15: 43 which also w for the kingdom of God
Luke 2: 25 w for the consolation of Israel
Rom. 8: 23 within ourselves w for the adoption
1 Cor. 1: 7 w for the coming of our Lord
2 Thes. 3: 5 into the patient w for Christ
1 Pet. 3: 20 longsuffering of God w in the days

WAKETH (WAKENETH)
Ps. 127: 1 watchman w but in vain
Is. 50: 4 he w morning by morning, he w my

WALK
Gen. 17: 1 w before me and be thou perfect
Lev. 26: 12 I will w among you
26: 21 if ye w contrary unto me
Deut. 5: 33 w in all the ways which the Lord
Ps. 23: 4 though I w through the valley
84: 11 withhold from them that w uprightly
116: 9 I will w before the Lord
Eccl. 11: 9 w in the ways of thine heart
Is. 2: 3 and we will w in his paths
40: 31 they shall w and not faint
Amos 3: 3 can two w together except they
Mic. 6: 8 w humbly with thy God
John 8: 12 not w in darkness, but shall have
11: 9 w in day he stumbleth
12: 35 w while ye have light
Rom. 6: 4 should w in newness of life
8: 1 w not after the flesh
13: 13 let us w honestly as in the day
2 Cor. 5: 7 we w by faith, not by sight
10: 3 though we w in the flesh, we do not war
Gal. 5: 16 w in the Spirit, and not fulfil the
6: 16 as many as w according to this rule
Eph. 2: 10 ordained that we should w in
4: 1 that ye w worthy of the vocation
5: 2 w in love, as Christ also hath loved
5: 8 w as children of light
Phil. 3: 16 let us w by the same rule
Col. 1: 10 that ye might w worthy
2: 6 Lord, so w ye in him
4: 5 w in wisdom toward
1 Thes. 2: 12 ye would w worthy of God, who
4: 1 how ye ought to w and to please
1 John 1: 7 if we w in the light, as
2: 6 so to w as he walked
3 John 1: 4 my children w in truth
Rev. 3: 4 shall w with me in white
21: 24 shall w in the light of it

WALKED (WALKEST, WALKETH, WALKING)
Gen. 3: 8 voice of Lord God w in the garden
Ps. 15: 2 he that w uprightly and worketh
55: 14 we w unto the house of God
81: 13 and Israel had w in my ways
Is. 9: 2 people that w in darkness
57: 2 each one w in his uprightness
Luke 1: 6 God, w in all the commandments and
Acts 9: 31 w in the fear of the
Rom. 14: 15 thy meat, now w thou not charitably
2 Cor. 10: 2 as if we w according to the flesh
12: 18 w we not in the same spirit
Eph. 2: 2 in time past ye w according to the
Col. 3: 7 ye also w some time, when ye lived
1 Pet. 4: 3 w about, seeking whom he may
2 Pet. 3: 3 w after their own lusts
Rev. 2: 1 w in the midst of seven golden

WANT
Job 31: 19 any perish for w of clothing
Ps. 23: 1 is my shepherd; I shall not w
2 Cor. 8: 14 a supply for your w: that there may
Phil. 4: 11 not that I speak in respect of w

WAR
Ps. 18: 34 He teacheth my hands to w
27: 3 though w should rise against me
Is. 2: 4 neither shall they learn w any more
2 Cor. 10: 3 we do not w after the flesh
1 Tim. 1: 18 them mightest w a good warfare

1 Pet.   2: 11 fleshly lusts which *w*
Rev.   11: 7 pit shall make *w* against them, and
      12: 7 there was *w* in heaven: Michael
      19: 11 he doth judge and make *w*

WARS (WARRETH)
Ps.   46: 9 he maketh *w* to cease unto the end
Mat.   24: 6 hear of *w* and rumours of *w*
Jas.   4: 1 from whence come *w* and fightings

WARFARE
Is.   40: 2 that her *w* is accomplished
2 Cor. 10: 4 weapons of *w* are not carnal

WARN (WARNED, WARNING)
Ps.   19: 11 by them is thy servant *w*
      33: 3 blow trumpet, *w* the people
Mat.   3: 7 who hath *w* you to flee
Acts   10: 22 *w* from God by an holy angel
      20: 31 I ceased not to *w* every one night
1 Cor.   4: 14 my beloved sons I *w*
Col.   1: 28 *w* every man
1 Thes. 5: 14 *w* them that are unruly comfort

WASH (WASHED, WASHING)
Job   9: 30 if I *w* myself with snow water
Ps.   51: 2 *w* me thoroughly from mine iniquity
      51: 7 *w* me and I shall be whiter than
Is.   1: 16 *w* you, make you clean
Jer.   4: 14 *w* thy heart from wickedness
Luke   7: 38 to *w* his feet with tears
John   13: 14 ought to *w* one another's feet
Acts   22: 16 be baptized and *w* away
Eph.   5: 26 *w* of water by the word
Tit.   3: 5 saved us, by the *w* of regeneration
Heb.   10: 22 our bodies *w* with pure water
Rev.   1: 5 *w* us from our sins in his own blood
      7: 14 their robes, and made them white

WATCH
Job   7: 12 thou settest a *w* over
Ps.   102: 7 I *w* and am as a sparrow
      130: 6 they that *w* for morning
      141: 3 set a *w*, O Lord, before my mouth
Mat.   24:42 *w* therefore, for ye know not
Mark 13:33 take ye heed, *w* and
1 Cor. 16:13 *w* ye, stand fast in the
1 Thes. 5: 6 let us *w* and be sober
2 Tim.   4: 7 *w* thou in all things
1 Pet.   4: 7 be sober, *w* unto

WATCHED (WATCHETH)
Ps.   37:32 the wicked *w* the righteous
Jer.   31:28 like as I have *w* over
Eph.   6:18 *w* thereunto with all perseverance

WATCHMAN (WATCHMEN)
Is.   21: 11 *W*, what of the night
      52: 8 Thy *w* shall lift up thy voice
      62: 6 I have set *w* upon thy walls
Jer.   31: 6 that the *w* upon the mount
Ezek.   3:17 I have made thee a *w*
      33: 7 I have set thee a *w*

WATER
Job   15:16 drinketh iniquity like *w*
Ps.   22:14 I am poured out like *w*
Is.   12: 3 draw *w* out of wells of salvation
      27: 3 I will *w* it every moment
      30:20 *w* of affliction, yet shall not thy
      41:17 when the poor and needy seek *w* and
      44: 3 pour *w* on him that is thirsty
      58: 11 a spring of *w*, whose waters fail
Ezek. 36:25 will I sprinkle clean *w* upon you
Amos   8: 11 nor a thirst for *w*, but of hearing
Mat.   3: 11 I indeed baptize you with *w*
      10:42 cup of cold *w* only in the name of a
Luke   16:24 dip the tip of his finger in *w*
John   3: 5 except a man be born of *w*
      3:23 baptized because there was much *w*
      4:14 shall be in him a well of *w*
      7:38 flow rivers of living *w*
      19:34 came there out blood and *w*
Acts   8:38 went down both into the *w*
Eph.   5:26 cleanse it with the washing of *w*
1 John   5: 6 he that came by *w* and blood, even
Jude   1: 12 clouds they are without *w*
Rev.   21: 6 fountain of the *w* of life
      22:17 take the *w* of life freely

WATERS
Ps.   23: 2 leadeth me beside still *w*

      124: 4 *w* had overwhelmed
Prov.   9:17 stolen *w* are sweet, and bread
Eccl.   11: 1 cast thy bread upon the *w*
Is.   35: 6 in the wilderness shall *w* break forth
      54: 9 this is as the *w* of Noah unto me
      58: 11 a spring of water, whose *w* fail not
Jer.   2:13 fountain of living *w*
      9: 1 O that my head were *w*
Ezek. 47: 1 *w* issued out from
Hab.   2:14 Lord, as the *w* cover
Rev.   1:15 sound of many *w*
      19: 6 his voice as the sound of many *w*

WAY
Ex.   13: 21 to lead them the *w*;
1 Sam. 12:23 teach you the good and right *w*
1 Ki.   2: 2 I go the *w* of all the earth
Ezra   8: 21 seek of him a right *w*
Job   17: 9 righteous shall hold on his *w*
Ps.   1: 6 *w* of the ungodly shall perish
      18:30 his *w* is perfect
      25: 8 teach sinners in the *w*
      37:23 delighteth in his *w*
      67: 2 that thy *w* may be known
      119: 9 shall a young man cleanse his *w*
      119: 30 I have chosen the *w* of truth
      139: 24 lead me in the *w* everlasting
Prov.   2: 8 Lord preserveth the *w* of his saints
      10:29 *w* of the Lord is strength
      14:12 a *w* which seemeth right
      15: 9 *w* of the wicked is abomination
      16: 9 man's heart deviseth his *w*
Eccl.   11: 5 knowest not what is the *w* of the
Is.   26: 7 *w* of the just is uprightness
      35: 8 shall be called The *w* of holiness
      55: 7 let the wicked forsake his *w*
      59: 8 *w* of peace they know not
Jer.   10:23 *w* of man is not in himself
      21: 8 the *w* of life and the *w* of death
Mat.   7:13 broad is the *w*, that leadeth
      21:32 John came in the *w* of righteousness
Luke   1:79 guide our feet in the *w* of peace
John   1:23 straight is the *w* of the Lord
      14: 6 I am the *w*, the truth,
Acts   16:17 show unto us the *w* of salvation
1 Cor. 10:13 make a *w* to escape,
      12:31 show I unto you a more excellent *w*
2 Pet.   2: 2 the *w* of truth shall be evil spoken

WAYS
Ps.   84: 5 in whose heart are the *w* of
      91: 11 keep thee in all thy *w*
      145: 17 Lord is righteous in all his *w*
Prov.   3:17 Her *w* are *w* of pleasantness
      5: 21 *w* of man are before the eyes of the
      16: 7 when a man's *w* please the Lord
Is.   2: 3 he will teach us of his *w*
Lam.   3:40 let us search and try our *w*
Mic.   4: 2 he will teach us of his *w*
Rom.   11:33 his *w* past finding
Rev.   15: 3 just and true are thy *w*

WEAK
Ps.   6: 2 O Lord; for I am *w*;
Is.   35: 3 strengthen ye the *w* hands
Mat.   26: 41 willing, but the flesh is *w*
Rom.   4: 19 being not *w* in faith
      14: 1 him that is *w* in the faith receive
1 Cor.   4: 10 we are *w* but ye are strong
      9:22 to the *w* became I as *w*
      11:30 for this cause many are *w* and sickly
      12: 10 I am *w* then am I strong
1 Thes. 5:14 support the *w*, be

WEAKER
1 Pet.   3: 7 the wife, as unto the *w* vessel

WEAKNESS
1 Cor.   1:25 the *w* of God is stronger
      2: 3 I was in you with *w*
      15:43 it is sown in *w*; it is raised
2 Cor. 12: 9 my strength is made perfect in *w*
      4 he was crucified through *w*
Heb.   11:34 out of *w* were made strong

WEALTH
Deut.   8:17 mine hand hath gotten me this *w*
Job   21:13 They spend their days in *w*
Ps.   49: 6 They that trust in their *w*

      112: 3 *w* and riches shall be in his
Prov.   10:15 rich man's *w* is his strong city
      13: 11 *w* gotten by vanity
      19: 4 *w* maketh many friends

WEARY
Gen.   27:46 I am *w* of my life
Job   10: 1 my soul is *w* of my life;
Prov.   3: 11 nor be *w* of his correction
Is.   40:31 shall run and not be *w*
Jer.   6: 11 I am *w* with holding in:
      31:25 I have satiated the *w* soul
Gal.   6: 9 let us not be *w* in well doing
2 Thes. 3:13 brethren, be not *w* in

WEDDING
Mat.   22: 3 them that were bidden to the *w*
Luke   14: 8 any man to a *w*, sit not down in

WEEP (WEEPEST, WEEPETH)
Job   30:25 Did not I *w* for him
Ps.   126: 6 he that goeth forth and *w*
Is.   30:19 thou shalt *w* no more
Jer.   9: 1 I might *w* day and night
Lam.   1: 2 she *w* sore in the night
Luke   6: 21 blessed are ye that *w* now: for ye
      23:28 *w* not for me, but *w* for yourselves
John   20:13 say unto her Woman, why *w* thou
Rom.   12:15 *w* with them that *w*
1 Cor.   7:30 that *w* as though they wept not
Jas.   5: 1 rich men, *w* and howl

WEEPING
Ps.   30: 5 *w* may endure for a night
Is.   22:12 Lord God of hosts call to *w* and
Joel   2:12 with fasting and with *w*
Mat.   8:12 *w* and gnashing of teeth
      22:13 be *w* and gnashing of teeth
      25:30 be *w* and gnashing of teeth

WEIGH (WEIGHED, WEIGHETH)
Job   31: 6 let me be *w* in an even balance
Prov.   16: 2 but the Lord *w* the spirits
Is.   26: 7 doth *w* the path of the just
Dan.   5: 27 art *w* in the balances

WEIGHT (WEIGHTS)
Prov.   11: 1 just *w* is his delight
      20:23 Divers *w* are an abomination
2 Cor.   4:17 exceeding and eternal *w* of glory
Heb.   12: 1 let us lay aside every *w*

WELLS (WELLS)
Ps.   84: 6 valley of Baca make it a *w*
Prov.   10: 11 righteous man is a *w* of life
Sol.   4: 15 a *w* of living waters and streams
Is.   12: 3 ye draw water out of *w*
John   4: 14 a *w* of water springing up
2 Pet.   2: 17 These are *w* without water

WEPT
Neh.   1: 4 I sat down and *w*, and mourned
Ps.   69:10 When I *w*, and chastened
Mat.   26:75 went out and *w* bitterly
Luke   19: 41 beheld the city, and *w* over it
John   11:35 Jesus *w*

WHEAT
Ps.   81:16 with the finest of the *w*
Mat.   3: 12 gather his *w* into the garner
Luke   22: 31 that he may sift you as *w*
John   12:24 except a corn of *w* fall

WHIRLWIND
2 Ki.   2: 11 went up by a *w* into heaven
Prov.   1:27 destruction cometh as a *w*
      10:25 As the *w* passeth, so is the wicked
Is.   66:15 his chariots like a *w*
Nah.   1: 3 Lord hath his way in the *w*
Hab.   3: 14 came out as a *w* to scatter me

WHITE (WHITER)
Num.   12:10 Miriam became leprous, *w* as snow
Ps.   51: 7 I shall be *w* than snow
Eccl.   9: 8 thy garments be always *w*
Sol.   5: 10 my beloved is *w* and ruddy
Is.   1:18 they shall be as *w* as snow; though
Dan.   12: 10 many shall be purified and be made *w*
Mat.   17: 2 his raiment was *w* as the light
Rev.   2:17 and will give him a *w* stone
      4: 4 elders sitting clothed in *w* raiment
      15: 6 clothed in pure and *w* linen
      19:14 clothed in fine linen, *w* and clean

WHOLE
Job　　5:18　he woundeth and his hands make w
Ps.　　9: 1　with my w heart; I will show
Is.　　54: 5　The God of the w earth
Mat.　　9:21　touch thy garment, I shall be w
Mark　　5:34　thy faith hath made thee w
John　　5: 4　w of whatsoever disease
Acts　　9:34　Jesus Christ maketh thee w: arise
1 John　2: 2　for the sins of the w world
　　　　5:19　the w world lieth in wickedness

WHOLESOME
Prov.　15: 4　A w tongue is a tree
1 Tim.　6: 3　consent not to w words

WHOLLY
1 Thes.5:23　God of peace sanctify you w
1 Tim.　4:15　give thyself w to them

WHORE
Lev.　　21: 9　profane herself by playing the w
Deut.　22:21　the w in her father's
Ezek.　16:28　thou hast played the w also with
Rev.　　17: 1　judgment of the great w that sitteth
　　　　17:16　these shall hate the w

WHOREDOM (WHOREDOMS)
Jer.　　3: 9　through the lightness of her w
Hos.　　2: 4　be the children of w
　　　　4:12　spirit of w hath caused them to
　　　　5: 4　spirit of w is in the midst

WHOREMONGER (WHOREMONGERS)
Eph.　　5: 5　no w, nor unclean person
Heb.　　13: 4　w and adulterers God will judge
Rev.　　21: 8　murderers, and w, and
　　　　22:15　sorcerers, and w, and

WICKED
Gen.　　18:25　slay the righteous with the w
Deut.　15: 9　a thought in thy w heart
　　　　25: 1　righteous, and condemn the w
Ps.　　7:11　God is angry with the w
　　　　11: 6　on the w he shall rain snares
　　　　119:155　salvation is far from the w
　　　　145:20　but all the w will he destroy
Prov.　21:12　God overthroweth the w for their
　　　　28: 1　w flee when no man pursueth
Is.　　55: 7　let the w forsake his
Jer.　　17: 9　heart is deceitful and desperately w
Ezek.　3:18　warn the w from his w way

WICKEDNESS
Gen.　　6: 5　God saw that the w
　　　　39: 9　how can I do this great w
1 Sam.24:13　w proceedeth from the
Ps.　　7: 9　w of the wicked come to an end
Prov.　8: 7　w is an abomination to my lips
　　　　10: 2　treasures of w profit nothing
Jer.　　2:19　thine own w shall correct thee
　　　　14:20　we acknowledge, O Lord, our w
Acts　　8:22　repent therefore of this thy w
1 John　4:19　whole world lieth in w

WIDOW (WIDOWS)
Deut.　10:18　judgment of the fatherless and w, and
Ps.　　68: 5　a judge of the w, is God in his
　　　　146: 9　he relieveth the fatherless and w
Jer.　　49:11　and let the w trust in
Mat.　　23:14　for ye devour w houses
Mark　　12:42　there came a certain poor w
Luke　　18: 3　there was a w in that city
1 Tim.　5: 3　honour w that are w indeed
Jas.　　1:27　fatherless and w in their affliction

WIFE (WIVES)
Ex.　　20:17　not covet thy neighbor's w
Prov.　5:18　rejoice with the w of thy youth
　　　　18:22　findeth a w findeth a good thing
　　　　19:14　a prudent w is from the Lord
Eccl.　9: 9　live joyfully with the w
1 Cor.　7:29　w be as though they
Eph.　　5:28　love their w their own bodies
Col.　　3:19　love your w
1 Tim.　3:11　even so must their w be grave
1 Pet.　3: 1　ye w, be in subjection
Rev.　　19: 7　his w hath made herself ready
　　　　21: 9　show the bride, the Lamb's w

WILL
Deut.　33:16　the good w of him that
Ezra　　7:18　do after the w of your God

Ps.　　40: 8　I delight to do thy w,
Mat.　　7:21　doeth the w of my Father
　　　　6:10　Thy w be done in earth
　　　　26:42　I drink it, thy w be done
Mark　　3:35　shall do the w of God
Luke　　22:42　not my w, but thine,
John　　1:13　w of flesh, nor of the w of man
　　　　4:34　my meat is to do the w of him that
　　　　7:17　any man w do his w
　　　　17:24　I w that they also, whom thou hast
　　　　21:14　the w of the Lord be done
　　　　22:14　thou shouldest know his w
Rom.　　1:10　journey by the w of God
　　　　8:27　according to the w of God
　　　　12: 2　and perfect, w of God
1 Cor.　1: 1　through the w of God
2 Cor.　8: 5　unto us by the w of God
Gal.　　1: 4　according to the w of God
Eph.　　1: 9　known unto us, the mystery of his w
　　　　6: 6　doing the w of God
Phil.　　2:13　worketh both to w and to do
Col.　　1: 9　knowledge of his w in all wisdom
　　　　4:12　complete in all the w of God
1 Thes.4: 3　this is the w of God
2 Tim.　2:26　captive by him at his w
Heb.　　10: 9　I come to do thy w, O
　　　　10:36　ye have done the w of God
　　　　13:21　in every good work to do his w
1 Pet.　4:19　according to the w of God
1 John　2:17　doeth the w of God abideth for ever
　　　　5:14　any thing according to his w
Rev.　　17:17　in their hearts to fulfil his w

WILLING (WILLINGLY)
Ex.　　35: 5　whosoever is of a w heart
1 Chr.28: 9　with a perfect heart and with a w mind
Mat.　　26:41　spirit is indeed w but the flesh
Luke　　22:42　if thou be w., remove this cup
2 Cor.　5: 8　w rather to be absent from the body
2 Pet.　3: 9　not w that any should perish

WIN (WINNETH)
Prov.　11:30　and he that w souls is wise
Phil.　　3: 8　them but dung, that I may w Christ

WIND (WINDS)
Job　　7: 7　O remember that my life is w
Ps.　　103:16　w passeth over it, and it is gone
　　　　135: 7　he bringeth the w out
Eccl.　11: 4　he that observeth the w
Ezek.　37: 9　come from the four w, O breath
Hos.　　8: 7　sown the w, and they shall reap
Mat.　　8:26　rebuked the w and the sea
Luke　　8:25　commandeth even the w and the water
John　　3: 8　w bloweth where it listeth
Eph.　　4:14　with every w of doctrine,

WINDOWS
Gen.　　7:11　w of heaven were opened

WINE
Ps.　　104:15　w maketh glad the heart
Prov.　20: 1　w is a mocker, strong drink is
　　　　23:31　look not thou upon the w when it is red
　　　　31: 6　and w to those that be of heavy heart
Sol.　　1: 2　love is better than w
Is.　　5:11　till w inflame them
　　　　55: 1　buy w and milk without money and
Hos.　　3: 1　look to other gods, love flagons of w
Eph.　　5:18　be not drunk with w
1 Tim.　3: 3　not given to w, no striker, not
　　　　5:23　use a little w for thy stomach's sake
Tit.　　1: 7　not given to w, no

WINEBIBBER (WINEBIBBERS)
Prov.　23:20　Be not among w
Mat.　　11:19　a man gluttonous, and a w

WINGS
Ruth　　2:12　under whose w thou art come to trust
Ps.　　17: 8　hide me under the shadow of thy w
　　　　18:10　fly upon the w of the wind
　　　　36: 7　trust under the shadow of thy w
　　　　91: 4　under his w shalt thou trust
Mal.　　4: 2　with healing in his w

WINTER
Sol.　　2:11　For, lo, the w is past, the rain

WISE
Job　　32: 9　great men are not always w
Ps.　　2:10　Be w, now therefore,

　　　　19: 7　Lord is sure, making w the simple
　　　　107:43　whoso is w and will observe
Prov.　3: 7　be not w in thine own eyes
　　　　3:35　the w shall inherit glory
　　　　13:20　walketh with w men shall be w
　　　　26:12　a man w in his own conceit
Eccl.　7: 4　heart of the w is in the house of
　　　　9: 1　the w and their work
Is.　　5:21　are w in their own eyes, and prudent
Dan.　　12: 3　w shall shine as brightness
Hos.　　14: 9　who is w and he shall understand
Mat.　　10:16　be ye therefore w as serpents
　　　　11:25　hid these things from the w
Rom.　　1:22　professing themselves to be w
1 Cor.　4:10　but ye are w in Christ
Eph.　　5:15　circumspectly not as fools but as w

WISDOM
1 Ki.　　4:29　God gave Solomon w, and
　　　　　　　　understanding
Job　　28:28　the fear of the Lord, that is w
Ps.　　111:10　Lord is the beginning of w
Prov.　4: 5　get w, get understanding: forget
　　　　9:10　Lord is the beginning of w
　　　　16:16　better is it to get w than gold
　　　　19: 8　he that getteth w loveth his own soul
　　　　23: 4　cease from thine own w
Eccl.　1:18　in much w is much grief
　　　　8: 1　a man's w maketh his face
Mat.　　11:19　But w is justified of her children
1 Cor.　1:24　power of God, and the w of God
　　　　1:30　who of God is made unto us w
　　　　2: 6　we speak w among them that are
　　　　　　　　perfect
　　　　3:19　w of this world is foolishness
Col.　　1: 9　in all w and spiritual understanding
Jas.　　1: 5　you lack w let him ask of God
　　　　3:17　w from above is first pure
Rev.　　5:12　worthy is the Lamb to receive w
　　　　13:18　here is w: Let him that
　　　　17: 9　is the mind which hath w

WITCHCRAFT
Gal.　　5:20　Idolatry, w, hatred, variance

WITHHOLD (WITHHOLDETH, WITHHELD)
Gen.　　22:12　thou hast not w thy son
Job　　31:16　If I have w the poor from their
Ps.　　40:11　W not thou thy tender mercies
　　　　84:11　no good thing will he w
Prov.　3:27　w no good from them to whom it is
　　　　11:24　w more than is meet but it tendeth
　　　　23:13　w not correction from child
2 Thes.2: 6　now ye know what w that he might

WITNESS
Gen.　　31:48　This heap is a w between me and thee
Deut.　17: 6　at the mouth of one w
Judg.　11:10　Lord be w, between us
1 Sam.12: 5　The Lord is w against
Job　　16:19　my w is in heaven,
Ps.　　89:37　as a faithful w in heaven
Is.　　55: 4　him for a w to the people
Jer.　　42: 5　true and faithful w between us
Mic.　　1: 2　the Lord God be w against you
Mal.　　2:14　Lord hath been w between thee
　　　　3: 4　I will be a swift w against
John　　5:37　sent me hath borne w of me
Acts　　14:17　left not himself without w
1 John　5:10　believeth on the Son of God hath w
Rev.　　1: 5　Christ, who is the faithful w
　　　　20: 4　beheaded for the w of Jesus

WITNESSES
Josh.　24:22　w against yourselves
Is.　　43:10　ye are my w, saith the Lord
Mat.　　18:16　mouth of two or three w
2 Cor.　13: 1　two or three w shall every word be
1 Thes.2:10　ye are w and God also
1 Tim.　5:19　but before two or three w
　　　　12: 1　so great a cloud of w
Rev.　　11: 3　power unto my two w,

WOMAN
Gen.　　2:23　she shall be called W
　　　　3:15　enmity between thee and the w
Prov.　11:16　gracious w retaineth honour
　　　　12: 4　a virtuous w is a crown to her
　　　　14: 1　every wise w buildeth her house

31: 10 who can find a virtuous *w*
31: 30 a *w* that feareth the Lord, she shall
Is.   49: 15 can a *w* forget her sucking child
54: 6 called thee as a *w* forsaken
Mat.   5: 28 looketh on a *w* to lust
John   8: 3 brought unto him a *w* taken in adultery
Rom.   1: 27 the natural use of *w*
1 Cor. 11: 7 the *w* is the glory of the man
Gal.   4: 4 sent forth his Son, made of a *w*
1 Tim. 2: 11 let *w* learn in silence
2: 12 I suffer not a *w* to
Rev. 12: 1 *w* clothed with the sun, and the moon

WOMEN
Prov. 31: 3 give not thy strength to *w*
Is.   32: 11 tremble, ye *w* that are
Lam.   4: 10 *w* have sodden their own children
Mat. 11: 11 born of *w*, there hath not risen
Luke   1: 28 blessed art thou among *w*
1 Cor. 14: 34 let your *w* keep silence in the
1 Tim. 2: 9 *w* adorn themselves in modest apparel
5: 14 therefore that the younger *w* marry
2 Tim. 3: 6 lead captive silly *w*
1 Pet. 3: 5 in the old time holy *w*
Rev. 14: 4 were not defiled with *w*

WOMB (WOMBS)
Gen. 25: 23 Two nations are in thy *w*
29: 31 he opened her *w*: but Rachel was
Ps.   22: 9 he that took me out of the *w*
127: 3 fruit of the *w* is his reward
139: 13 covered me in my mother's *w*
Eccl. 11: 5 how the bones do grow in the *w*
Is.   44: 2 formed thee from the *w*, which will
66: 9 to bring forth, and shut the *w*
Luke   1: 42 blessed is fruit of thy *w*
11: 27 blessed is *w* that bare thee
23: 29 barren, and the *w* that never bare

WONDER (WONDERED)
Ps.   71: 7 I am as a *w* unto many; but thou
Is.   29: 14 marvelous work and a *w*
Luke   4: 22 *w* at the gracious words
Acts 13: 41 ye despisers, and *w*
Rev. 12: 1 And there appeared a great *w*

WONDERFUL
Job   42: 3 things too *w* for me,
Ps. 119: 129 thy testimonies are *w*:
139: 6 such knowledge is too *w* for me
Prov. 30: 18 three things which are too *w* for
Is.   9: 6 his name shall be called *W*
25: 1 thou hast done *w* things

WONDERS
Ex.   7: 3 multiply my signs and my *w*
Ps.   77: 14 thou art the God that doest *w*
88: 10 wilt thou show *w* to the dead?
136: 4 who alone doeth great *w*
Joel   2: 30 And I will show *w* in the heavens
John   4: 48 except ye see signs and *w*
Acts   2: 43 many *w* and signs
Rom. 15: 19 mighty signs and *w* by the power of
Rev. 13: 13 he doeth great *w*, so

WORD
Deut.   8: 3 every *w* that proceedeth out
30: 14 the *w* is nigh unto thee
Ps.   18: 30 *w* of the Lord is tried:
68: 11 Lord gave the *w*: great
119: 11 thy *w* have I hid in mine heart
119: 105 thy *w* is a lamp unto my feet
130: 5 in his *w* do I hope
147: 19 showeth his *w* unto Jacob
Prov. 25: 11 a *w* fitly spoken is like apples
30: 5 Every *w* of God is pure
Is.   40: 8 *w* of our God shall stand
50: 4 how to speak a *w* in season
Jer.   20: 9 his *w* was in mine heart as fire
Mat.   8: 8 speak the *w* only and
12: 36 every idle *w* that men shall speak
Mark   7: 13 Making the *w* of God of none effect
John   1: 1 in the beginning was the *W*
1: 14 the *W* was made flesh, and dwelt
5: 38 have not his *w* abiding in you
8: 31 If ye continue in my *w*, then
15: 3 clean through the *w*
17: 17 through thy truth: thy *w* is truth
Acts   2: 41 that gladly received his *w*

13: 15 any *w* of exhortation for the people
13: 26 to you is the *w* of this salvation sent
17: 11 received the *w* with all readiness
Rom. 10: 17 hearing by the *w* of God
1 Cor. 4: 20 kingdom of God is not in *w*, but
Gal.   6: 6 taught in the *w* communicate unto
Eph.   5: 26 washing of water by the *w*
Col.   3: 16 let the *w* of Christ dwell in
1 Thes. 2: 13 truth, the *w* of God, which effectually
2 Thes. 2: 17 stablish you in every good *w*
3: 1 *w* of the Lord may have free course
Tit.   1: 9 holding fast the faithful *w*
Heb.   4: 2 the *w* preached did not profit
4: 12 For the *w* of God is quick
13: 22 suffer the *w* of exhortation
Jas.   1: 21 receive with meekness the engrafted *w*
3: 2 if any man offend not in *w*
1 Pet. 3: 1 if any obey not the *w*
2 Pet. 1: 19 also a more sure *w* of prophecy
1 John 1: 1 hands have handled of the *W*
Rev.   8 and hast kept my *w*,
12: 11 overcame by the *w* of their testimony

WORDS
Prov. 15: 26 *w* of the pure are pleasant *w*
22: 17 bow down thine ear, hear the *w*
Eccl. 10: 12 the *w* of a wise man's mouth
12: 11 *w* of the wise are as goads
Jer.   7: 4 trust ye not in lying *w*
Hos.   6: 5 slain them by the *w* of my mouth
Mic.   2: 7 do not my *w* do good
Zech. 1: 13 good *w* and comfortable *w*
Mark   8: 38 ashamed of me and of my *w*
13: 31 my *w* shall not pass away
Luke   4: 22 the gracious *w* which proceeded
John   5: 47 how shall ye believe my *w*
15: 7 my *w* abide in you, ye shall ask
Acts   7: 22 was mighty in *w* and in deeds
15: 24 troubled you with *w*, subverting
20: 35 remember the *w* of the Lord
26: 25 speak forth the *w* of truth and soberness
2 Tim. 1: 13 hold fast the form of sound *w*
2: 14 strive not about *w* to no profit
Rev. 22: 18 the *w* of the prophesy of this book

WORK
Gen.   2: 3 rested from all his *w* which God
Ex.   20: 10 in it thou shalt not do any *w*
Deut. 33: 11 and accept the *w* of his hands
Job   1: 10 thou hast blessed the *w* of his hands
10: 3 shouldest despise the *w* of thine hands
Ps.   8: 3 heavens, the *w* of thy fingers
9: 16 wicked is snared in the *w* of his own
Eccl. 8: 17 I beheld all the *w* of God
12: 14 God shall bring every *w* into judgment
Is.   10: 12 whole *w* upon mount Zion
28: 21 do his *w*, his strange *w*
64: 8 we all are the *w* of thy hand
Jer. 18: 3 potter wrought a *w* on
John   6: 28 might *w* the works of God
9: 4 I must *w* the works of him
17: 4 finished the *w* which thou gavest
Acts   5: 38 if this *w* be of men it
13: 2 for the *w* whereto I have called
1 Cor. 3: 13 every man's *w* shall be made
9: 1 are not ye my *w* in the Lord?
Eph.   4: 12 for the *w* of the ministry
1 Thes. 4: 11 and to *w* with your own hands, as we
2 Thes. 1: 11 goodness, and the *w* of faith with
2: 17 stablish you in every good *w*
3: 10 if any would not *w*, neither should he eat
2 Tim. 4: 5 do the *w* of an evangelist
Jas.   1: 4 let patience have her perfect *w*
1: 25 doer of the *w* this man shall be blessed
1 Pet. 1: 17 judgeth according to every man's *w*

WORKS (WORKS)
Job   37: 14 consider the wondrous *w* of God
Ps.   40: 5 are thy wonderful *w* which thou hast
78: 4 wonderful *w* that he
92: 4 triumph in the *w* of thy hands
107: 8 wonderful *w* to the children
138: 8 forsake not the *w* of thine own hands
Prov. 31: 31 let her own *w* praise
Eccl. 11: 5 knowest not the *w* of God
Is.   26: 12 wrought all our *w* in

Mat.   7: 22 thy name done many wonderful *w*
John   5: 20 will show him greater *w* than these
9: 3 *w* of God should be made manifest in
10: 38 believe the *w* that ye
14: 12 greater *w* than these shall he do
Acts   2: 11 our tongues the wonderful *w* of God
26: 20 God, and do *w* meet for repentance
Rom.   4: 6 God imputeth righteousness without *w*
9: 32 but as it were by the *w* of the law
11: 6 then is it no more of *w*
Gal.   2: 16 by the *w* of the law
3: 10 as many as are of the *w* of the law
5: 19 *w* of the flesh are manifest
Eph.   2: 9 not of *w*, lest any man should
5: 11 with the unfruitful *w* of darkness
1 Thes. 5: 13 highly in love for their *w* sake
2 Tim. 1: 9 not according to our *w*, but according
Tit.   1: 16 in *w* they deny him, being abominable
3: 5 not by *w* or righteousness which
Heb.   6: 1 repentance from dead *w*
9: 14 conscience from dead *w* to serve the
Jas.   2: 14 and have not *w*? can faith save
2: 24 by *w* a man is justified
1 John 3: 8 he might destroy the *w* of the devil
Rev.   9: 20 repented not of the *w* of their
20: 13 judged every man according to their *w*

WORKETH
Prov. 11: 18 wicked *w* a deceitful work
John   5: 17 my Father *w* hitherto,
Acts 10: 35 and *w* righteousness, is accepted with
1 Cor. 12: 6 same God which *w* all
Gal.   5: 6 but faith which *w* by love
Eph.   1: 11 *w* all things after the counsel of
Phil.   2: 13 God which *w* in you
1 Thes. 2: 13 effectually *w* also in you that

WORKING
Rom.   7: 13 sin, *w* death in me by
Eph.   1: 19 according to the *w* of his mighty
4: 28 *w* with his hands the
Phil.   3: 21 according to *w* whereby he is able
2 Thes. 3: 11 *w* not at all, but are busybodies
Heb. 13: 21 *w* in you that which is well pleasing

WORKERS
2 Cor. 6: 1 as *w* together with him beseech you
11: 13 are false apostles, deceitful *w*
Phil.   3: 2 beware of evil *w*, beware of the

WORKMAN
Mat. 10: 10 for the *w* is worthy of his meat
2 Tim. 2: 15 *w* that needeth not to be ashamed

WORKMAMSHIP
Ex.   31: 3 knowledge, and in all manner of *w*
Eph.   2: 10 we are his *w*, created in Christ

WORLD
Ps.   50: 12 *w* is mine and the fulness
96: 10 *w* also shall be established
Eccl. 3: 11 hath set the *w* in their heart
Jer. 10: 12 established the *w* by his wisdom
Mat. 12: 32 neither in the *w* to come
16: 26 gain the whole *w* and lose his
Mark 16: 15 go ye into all the *w* and
Luke 20: 35 accounted worthy to obtain that *w*
John   1: 29 which taketh away the sin of the *w*
3: 16 God so loved the *w* that he gave
8: 23 ye are of this *w*; I am
12: 47 to judge the *w* but to save the *w*
14: 17 whom the *w* cannot receive
14: 31 *w* may know that I love the Father
15: 18 if the *w* hate you, ye
16: 28 I leave the *w* and go to the Father
17: 9 I pray not for the *w*, but for them
17: 11 I am no more in the *w*, but these
17: 23 *w* may know that thou hast sent
Rom.   3: 19 all the *w* may become guilty
12: 2 But be not conformed to this *w*
Gal.   6: 14 *w* is crucified unto me, and I unto
1 Tim. 6: 7 brought nothing into this *w*
Tit.   1: 2 promised before the *w* began
Heb.   2: 5 put in subjection the *w* to come
11: 38 of whom the *w* was not worthy
1 John 2: 2 for the sins of the whole *w*
2: 17 *w* passeth away and the lust
3: 1 the *w* knoweth us not,
5: 19 the whole *w* lieth in wickedness

Rev.   3:10 temptation shall come on all the *w*
      13: 3 all the *w* wondered after the beast

WORM (WORMS)
Job   25: 6 How much less man, that is a *w*
Ps.   22: 6 I am a *w* and no man
Is.   41:14 fear not, thou *w* Jacob
      66:24 their *w* shall not die,
Mark   9:48 their *w* dieth not, and

WORMWOOD
Lam.   3:19 my misery, the *w* and
      8:11 the name of the star is called *W*

WORSHIP (WORSHIPPED)
1 Chr. 16:29 *w* the Lord in the beauty of holiness
      29:20 *w* the Lord, and the king
Ps.   96: 9 *w* the Lord in the beauty of holiness
      99: 5 *w* at his footstool; for he is
Jer.   1:16 *w* the works of their own hands
Mat.   4:10 Thou shalt *w* the Lord thy God, and
      15: 9 in vain do they *w* me,
John   4:24 *w* him must *w* him in spirit
Acts   17:23 whom therefore ye ignorantly *w*
      24:14 so *w* I the God of my fathers
Rom.   1:25 and *w* and served the creature
Rev.   5:14 fell down and *w* him
      7:11 on their faces, and *w* God
      13: 4 they *w* the dragon which gave power
      22: 9 sayings of this book: *w* God

WORTHY
Gen.   32:10 I am not *w* of the least
Mat.   8: 8 not *w* that thou shouldest come
      10:10 workman is *w* of his meat
      22: 8 which were bidden were not *w*
Luke   3: 8 forth therefore fruits *w* of repentance
      7: 4 *w* for whom he should do this
      10: 7 labourer is *w* of his hire
      15:19 no more *w* to be called thy son
      20:35 accounted *w* to obtain that world
      21:36 *w* to escape all these things
Acts   5:41 counted *w* to suffer shame
Rom.   8:18 not *w* to be compared with the glory
Eph.   4: 1 walk *w* of the vocation wherewith
1 Thes. 2:12 walk *w* of God, who hath called you
      1:11 God would count you *w* of this calling
1 Tim.   1:15 *w* of all acceptation, that Christ
      5:18 labourer is *w* of his reward
      6: 1 count their masters *w* of all honour
Heb.   3: 3 *w* of more glory than Moses
      10:29 sorer punishment shall he be thought *w*
Rev.   3: 4 in white, for they are *w*
      5:12 *w* is the Lamb that was slain
      16: 6 blood to drink; for they are *w*

WOUND (WOUNDED, WOUNDETH, WOUNDS)
Ex.   21:25 *w* for *w*, stripe for stripe
Deut.   32:39 I *w* and I heal:
Job   5:18 he *w* and his hands make whole

Ps.   109:22 my heart is *w* within me
Prov.   18:14 a *w* spirit who can bear?
      27: 6 Faithful are the *w* of a friend
      53: 5 But he was *w* for our transgressions
Jer.   15:18 pain perpetual, and my *w* incurable
      30:17 heal thee of thy *w*,
1 Cor.   8:12 and *w* their weak conscience, ye sin
Rev.   13: 3 his deadly *w* was healed: and all the

WRATH
Ps.   76:10 *w* of man shall praise
      78:38 did not stir up all his *w*
Is.   54: 8 in a little *w* I hid my face
      60:10 in my *w* I smote thee,
Ezek.   7:14 my *w* is upon all the multitude
Hab.   3: 2 make known; in *w* remember mercy
Mat.   3: 7 flee from the *w* to come
Rom.   2: 5 *w* against the day of *w*
      5: 9 saved from *w* through him
      12:19 but rather give place unto *w*
Eph.   2: 3 by nature children of *w*
      4:26 let not the sun go down on your *w*
1 Thes. 1:10 delivered us from the *w* to come
      5: 9 For God hath not appointed us to *w*
1 Tim.   2: 8 holy hands without *w*
Jas.   1:19 slow to speak, slow to *w*
Rev.   6:16 from the *w* of the Lamb
      14: 8 wine of *w* of her fornication

WRESTLE (WRESTLED)
Gen.   32:24 and there *w* with a
Eph.   6:12 we *w* not against flesh

WRETCHED
Rom.   7:24 O *w* man that I am!
Rev.   3:17 thou art *w*, and miserable, and poor

WRITE (WRITTEN)
Ex.   34:27 *W* thou these words: for after the
Deut.   6: 9 *w* them upon the posts of thy house
Ps.   69:28 not be *w* with the righteous
      102: 18 shall be *w* for the generation to come
Prov.   3: 3 *w* them on table of thine heart
Jer.   30: 2 *W* thee all the words
1 Cor.   10:11 and they are *w* for our admonition
2 Cor.   3: 2 ye are our epistle *w* in our hearts
Heb.   12:23 are *w* in heaven, and to God
1 John   2: 1 these things I *w* unto you that ye
      2: 7 I *w* no new commandment unto
      2:13 I *w* unto you, fathers
      2:21 I have not *w* unto you because ye

WRONG (WRONGED, WRONGETH)
Prov.   8:36 *w* his own soul: all they that
Jer.   22: 3 and do no *w*,do no violence
2 Cor.   7: 2 we have *w* no man, we have corrupted
Col.   3:25 he that doeth *w* shall receive
Philem. 1:18 If he hath *w* thee or oweth thee

WROUGHT
1 Sam.14:45 hath *w* this great salvation

Ps.   139:15 curiously *w* in the lowest parts
Is.   26:12 thou also hast *w* all our works in us
John   3:21 that they are *w* in God
Rom.   7: 8 *w* in me all manner of concupiscence
1 Pet.   4: 3 have *w* the will of Gentiles

YEAR (YEARS)
Ps.   90: 4 a thousand *y* in thy sight are but
Is.   61: 2 proclaim the acceptable *y* of the Lord
Luke   4:19 preach the acceptable *y* of the Lord
2 Pet.   3: 8 a thousand *y* as one day
Rev.   20: 2 Satan, and bound him a thousand *y*

YESTERDAY
Job   8: 9 we are but of *y*, and
Heb.   13: 8 the same *y*, and today, and for ever

YIELD (YIELDED, YIELDETH)
Ps.   67: 6 shall the earth *y* her increase
Rom.   6:13 *y* ye your members as instruments
      6:19 ye have *y* your members servants to
Heb.   12:11 *y* the peaceable fruit of righteousness

YOKE (YOKED)
Deut.   28:48 shall put a *y* of iron upon thy neck
1 Ki.   12: 4 Thy father made our *y* grievous
Is.   9: 4 broken the *y* of his burden
Mat.   11:29 take my *y* upon you,
2 Cor.   6:14 be ye not unequally *y*
Gal.   5: 1 entangled again with the *y* of bondage

YOUNG
Ps.   37:25 I have been *y*, and now am
Is.   40:11 gently lead those that are with *y*

YOUTH
Gen.   8:21 imagination of man is evil from his *y*
Ps.   25: 7 sins of my *y*, nor my transgressions
Eccl.   11:10 childhood and *y* are vanity
Jer.   2: 2 the kindness of thy *y*,
1 Tim.   4:12 let no man despise thy *y*

ZEAL
2 Ki.   10:16 with me, and see my *z* for the Lord
Ps.   119:139 my *z* hath consumed me because
Is.   9: 7 *z* of the Lord of hosts
      63:15 where is thy *z* and thy
Rom.   10: 2 record that they have a *z* of God
Phil.   3: 6 concerning *z*, persecuting the church

ZEALOUS (ZEALOUSLY)
Acts   22: 3 and was *z* toward God
Gal.   4:18 *z* affected always in a
Tit.   2:14 peculiar people *z* of good works
Rev.   3:19 be *z* therefore and

ZION
Ps.   2: 6 my king upon my holy hill of *Z*
      9:11 to the Lord, which dwelleth in *Z*
      48: 2 joy of the whole earth is mount *Z*
Is.   60:14 The *Z* of the Holy One of Israel
Heb.   12:22 But ye are come unto mount *Z*

Index to Color Maps

KJV Prophecy
Marked Reference Study Bible

Project management and editorial by Gary Knapp

Editorial assistance by Sally M. Hupp

Production management by Mark Luce

Interior design by Sharon Wright, Belmont, MI

Art direction by Cindy Davis

Cover design by Christine Gannon

Interior proofreading by Peachtree Editorial and Proofreading
Service, Peachtree City, GA

Interior typesetting by Auto-Graphics, Inc., Pomona, CA

Printing and binding by R.R. Donnelley, Crawfordsville, IN

Guarantee

Care

*We suggest loosening the binding of your new Bible by gently
pressing on a small section of pages at a time from the center.
To ensure against breakage of the spine, it is best not to bend
the cover backward around the spine or to carry study notes,
church bulletins, pens, etc., inside the cover. Because a felt-
tipped marker will "bleed" through the pages, we recommend
use of a ball-point pen or pencil to underline favorite passages.
Your Bible should not be exposed to excessive heat, cold, or
humidity. Protecting the gold or silver edges of the paper from
moisture will avoid spotting, streaking, or fading.*

Definitions

*Bonded leather: no less than 90% leather fibers with latex base.
Top-Grain leather: 100% pigskin
Cowhide: 100% cowhide*

Map 1: WORLD OF THE PATRIARCHS

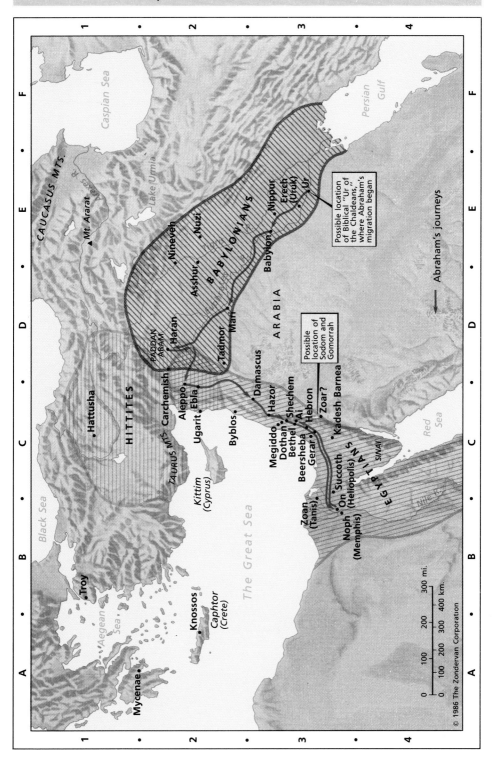

Caspian Sea

CAUCASUS MTS.

Mt Ararat

Lake Urmia

Black Sea

Troy

Aegean Sea

Mycenae

Knossos

Caphtor (Crete)

The Great Sea

HITTITES

Hattusha

TAURUS MTS.

Carchemish

Aleppo

Ugarit Ebla

Byblos

Kittim (Cyprus)

PADDAN ARAM

Haran

Tadmor

Mari

Damascus

Hazor

Megiddo

Dothan Shechem

Bethel Ai

Beersheba

Gerar Hebron

Zoar?

Kadesh Barnea

SINAI

Red Sea

Zoan (Tanis)

On (Heliopolis)

Noph (Memphis)

Succoth

EGYPTIANS

Nile R.

Nineveh

Asshur

Nuzi

BABYLONIANS

Babylon

Nippur

Erech (Uruk)

Ur

ARABIA

Persian Gulf

Possible location of Biblical "Ur of the Chaldeans," where Abraham's migration began

Possible location of Sodom and Gomorrah

→ Abraham's journeys

0   100   200   300 mi.

0   100   200   300   400 km.

© 1986 The Zondervan Corporation

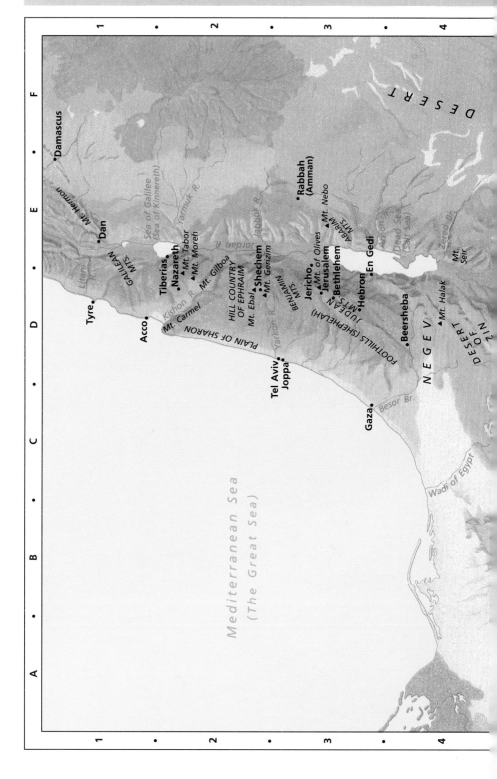

Damascus

DESERT

Mt. Hermon

Sea of Galilee
(Sea of Kinnereth)

Yarmuk R.

Rabbah
(Amman)

Mt. Nebo

Litani R.

Dan

GALILEAN MTS

Jordan R.

Jabbok R.

ABARIM MTS

Tyre

Tiberias
Nazareth
Mt. Tabor
Mt. Moreh

Mt. Gilboa

Shechem
Mt. Ebal
Mt. Gerizim

HILL COUNTRY
OF EPHRAIM

BENJAMIN MTS

Mt. of Olives
Jericho
Jerusalem
Bethlehem

En Gedi

Arnon R.

Dead Sea
(Salt Sea)

Zered Br.

Mt. Seir

Acco

Mt. Carmel

Kishon R.

PLAIN OF SHARON

Yarkon R.

JUDEAN MTS

FOOTHILLS (SHEPHELAH)

Hebron

Beersheba

Mt. Halak

DESERT OF ZIN

Tel Aviv
Joppa

NEGEV

Gaza

Besor Br.

Wadi of Egypt

Mediterranean Sea
(The Great Sea)

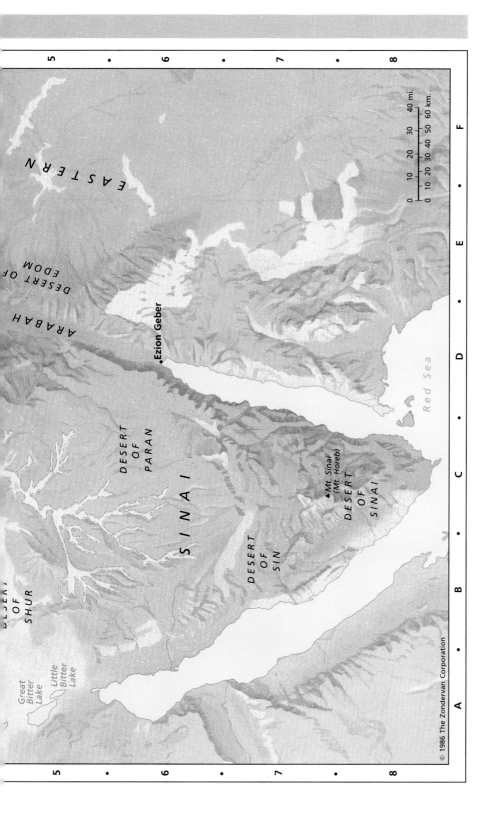

© 1986 The Zondervan Corporation

Map 3: **EXODUS AND CONQUEST OF CANAAN**

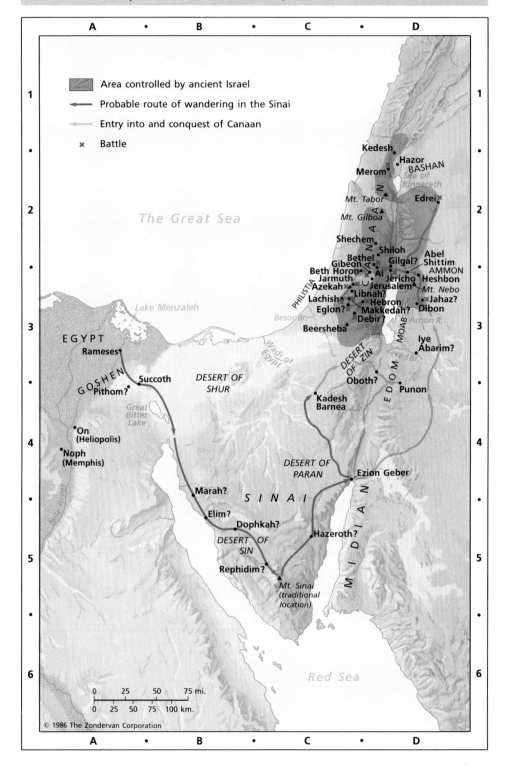

Area controlled by ancient Israel

Probable route of wandering in the Sinai

Entry into and conquest of Canaan

× Battle

The Great Sea

Kedesh

Hazor
BASHAN
Merom
Sea of
Kinnereth

Mt. Tabor
Edrei ×
Mt. Gilboa

Shechem
Shiloh
Bethel
Gibeon Gilgal?
Abel
Shittim
Beth Horon
Ai
Jericho
AMMON
Jarmuth
Heshbon
Azekah
Jerusalem
Mt. Nebo
Lachish
Libnah?
Jahaz?
Eglon?
Hebron
Dibon
Makkedah?
Debir?
MOAB
Beersheba
Arnon R.

Iye
Abarim?

EGYPT
Rameses

DESERT
OF ZIN

DESERT OF
SHUR
Oboth?
Punon

Lake Menzaleh
Besor Br.

GOSHEN
Succoth
Pithom?

Wadi of Egypt

EDOM

Great
Bitter
Lake
Kadesh
Barnea

On
(Heliopolis)

Noph
(Memphis)

DESERT OF
PARAN
Ezion Geber

Marah?
S I N A I
M
I
D
I
A
N

Elim?

Dophkah?

DESERT OF
SIN
Hazeroth?

Rephidim?

Mt. Sinai
(traditional
location)

Red Sea

0   25   50   75 mi.
0 25 50 75 100 km.
© 1986 The Zondervan Corporation

Map 4: LAND OF THE TWELVE TRIBES

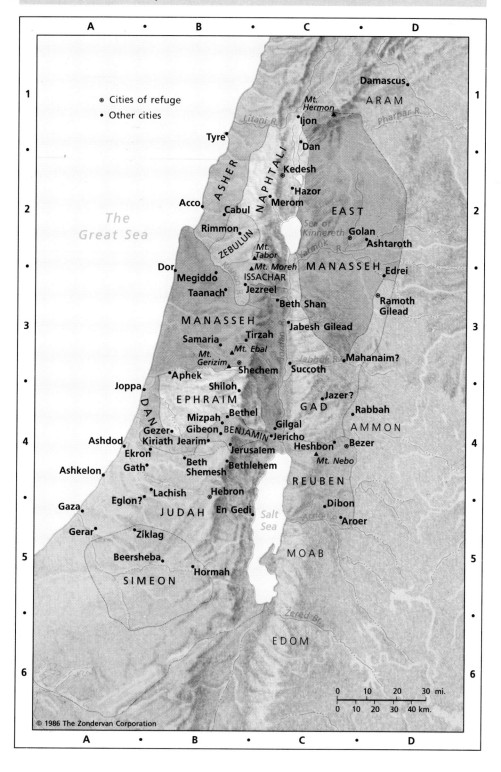

A • B • C • D

⊚ Cities of refuge
• Other cities

Damascus•

ARAM

Mt. Hermon▲
Ijon•

Litani R.   *Pharpar R.*

Tyre•

Dan•

ASHER

NAPHTALI

Kedesh⊚

•Hazor
Acco•   •Merom
Cabul•

EAST

The Great Sea

Rimmon•

Sea of Kinnereth

ZEBULUN   Golan⊚
                  •Ashtaroth
Dor•   Mt. Tabor▲   Yarmuk R.

Megiddo•   ▲Mt. Moreh   MANASSEH   •Edrei
         ISSACHAR
Taanach•   Jezreel•
                              •Beth Shan   Ramoth⊚ Gilead

MANASSEH   •Jabesh Gilead

Samaria•   Tirzah•
         ▲Mt. Ebal   Jabbok R.   •Mahanaim?
Mt. Gerizim▲ ⊚Shechem   •Succoth

Joppa•   •Aphek

DAN   Shiloh•   •Jazer?

EPHRAIM   GAD   •Rabbah

Mizpah•   •Bethel
Gezer•   Gibeon•   •Gilgal   AMMON
Ashdod• Kiriath Jearim• BENJAMIN •Jericho
Ekron•   •Jerusalem   Heshbon• •Bezer
Gath• •Beth   •Bethlehem   ▲Mt. Nebo
Ashkelon• Shemesh

REUBEN

•Lachish   Hebron⊚
Gaza• Eglon?•   En Gedi•   •Dibon
Gerar•   •Ziklag   JUDAH   •Aroer

Beersheba•

MOAB
Hormah•

SIMEON

Salt Sea

Zered Br.

EDOM

0   10   20   30 mi.
0   10 20 30 40 km.

© 1986 The Zondervan Corporation

A • B • C • D

Map 5: **KINGDOM OF DAVID AND SOLOMON**

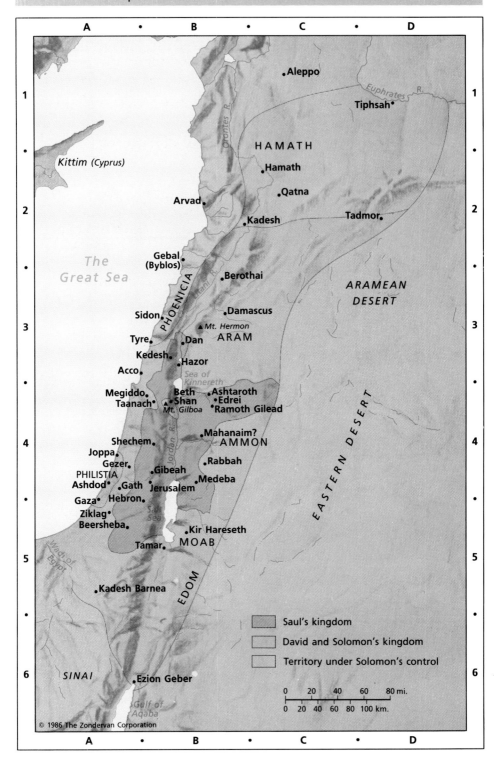

Aleppo

Euphrates R.

Tiphsah

HAMATH

Orontes R.

Kittim (Cyprus)

Hamath

Qatna

Arvad

Tadmor

Kadesh

ARAMEAN
DESERT

Gebal
(Byblos)

The
Great Sea

PHOENICIA

Berothai

Damascus

Sidon

▲ Mt. Hermon

Tyre

Dan

ARAM

Kedesh

Hazor

Acco

Sea of
Kinnereth

Megiddo

Beth

Ashtaroth

Taanach

Shan

Edrei

▲ Mt. Gilboa

Ramoth Gilead

EASTERN DESERT

Mahanaim?

Shechem

AMMON

Joppa

Jordan R.

Gezer

Rabbah

PHILISTIA

Gibeah

Ashdod

Gath

Medeba

Gaza

Hebron

Jerusalem

Ziklag

Salt Sea

Beersheba

Kir Hareseth

Tamar

MOAB

EDOM

Wadi of Egypt

Kadesh Barnea

Saul's kingdom

David and Solomon's kingdom

Territory under Solomon's control

0   20   40   60   80 mi.

0 20 40 60 80 100 km.

SINAI

Ezion Geber

Gulf of
Aqaba

© 1986 The Zondervan Corporation

Map 6: PROPHETS IN ISRAEL AND JUDAH

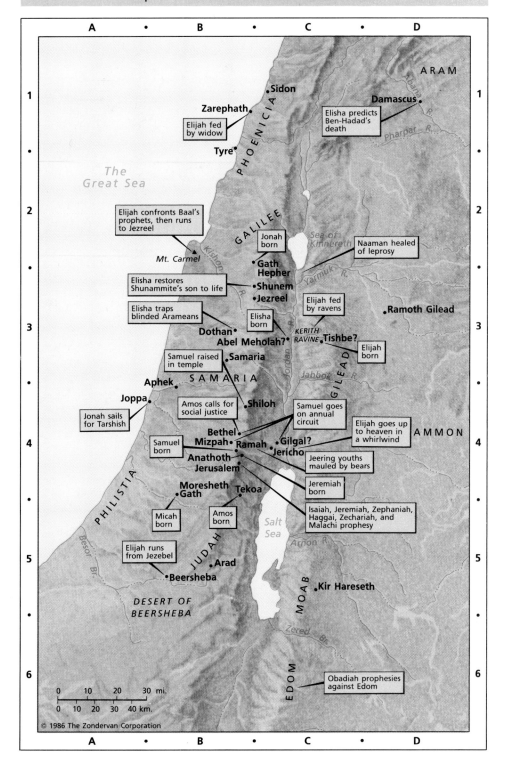

ARAM

Sidon

Zarephath

Elijah fed by widow

Damascus

Elisha predicts Ben-Hadad's death

PHOENICIA

Tyre

The Great Sea

GALILEE

Elijah confronts Baal's prophets, then runs to Jezreel

Mt. Carmel

Kishon

Jonah born

Sea of Kinnereth

Naaman healed of leprosy

Gath Hepher

Yarmuk R.

Elisha restores Shunammite's son to life

Shunem

Jezreel

Elijah fed by ravens

Ramoth Gilead

Elisha traps blinded Arameans

Elisha born

KERITH RAVINE

Tishbe?

Elijah born

Dothan

Abel Meholah?

Jordan

GILEAD

Samuel raised in temple

Samaria

Jabbok R.

S A M A R I A

Aphek

Joppa

Amos calls for social justice

Shiloh

Samuel goes on annual circuit

Elijah goes up to heaven in a whirlwind

AMMON

Jonah sails for Tarshish

Bethel

Mizpah

Ramah

Gilgal?

Jericho

Jeering youths mauled by bears

Samuel born

Anathoth

Jerusalem

Jeremiah born

PHILISTIA

Moresheth Gath

Tekoa

Isaiah, Jeremiah, Zephaniah, Haggai, Zechariah, and Malachi prophesy

Micah born

Amos born

Salt Sea

JUDAH

Elijah runs from Jezebel

Arad

Arnon R.

Beersheba

MOAB

Kir Hareseth

Besor Br.

DESERT OF BEERSHEBA

Zered Br.

EDOM

Obadiah prophesies against Edom

0   10   20   30 mi.
0 10 20 30 40 km.

© 1986 The Zondervan Corporation

Abana R.

Pharpar R.

Map 7: ASSYRIAN AND BABYLONIAN EMPIRES

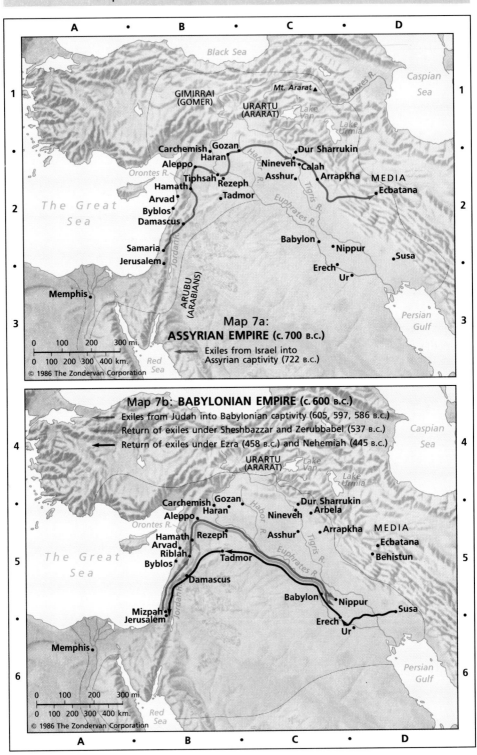

Map 7a:
ASSYRIAN EMPIRE (c. 700 B.C.)
← Exiles from Israel into Assyrian captivity (722 B.C.)

0   100   200   300 mi.
0   100 200 300 400 km.
© 1986 The Zondervan Corporation

Map 7b: BABYLONIAN EMPIRE (c. 600 B.C.)
← Exiles from Judah into Babylonian captivity (605, 597, 586 B.C.)
Return of exiles under Sheshbazzar and Zerubbabel (537 B.C.)
← Return of exiles under Ezra (458 B.C.) and Nehemiah (445 B.C.)

0   100   200   300 mi.
0   100 200 300 400 km.
© 1986 The Zondervan Corporation

Map 8: JERUSALEM IN JESUS' TIME

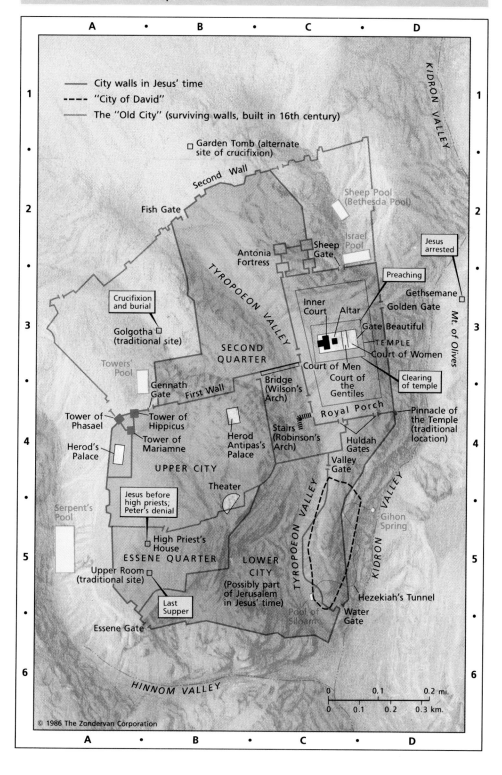

City walls in Jesus' time
---- "City of David"
The "Old City" (surviving walls, built in 16th century)

KIDRON VALLEY

Garden Tomb (alternate site of crucifixion)

Second Wall

Fish Gate

Sheep Pool (Bethesda Pool)

Israel Pool

Jesus arrested

Antonia Fortress

Sheep Gate

Preaching

Gethsemane

Golden Gate

Crucifixion and burial

TYROPOEON VALLEY

Inner Court

Altar

Gate Beautiful

Golgotha (traditional site)

SECOND QUARTER

TEMPLE
Court of Women

Mt. of Olives

Court of Men

Clearing of temple

Towers' Pool

Gennath Gate

First Wall

Bridge (Wilson's Arch)

Court of the Gentiles

Royal Porch

Pinnacle of the Temple (traditional location)

Tower of Phasael

Tower of Hippicus

Stairs (Robinson's Arch)

Huldah Gates

Herod's Palace

Tower of Mariamne

Herod Antipas's Palace

Valley Gate

UPPER CITY

KIDRON VALLEY

Theater

Jesus before high priests; Peter's denial

TYROPOEON VALLEY

Gihon Spring

Serpent's Pool

High Priest's House

ESSENE QUARTER

LOWER CITY
(Possibly part of Jerusalem in Jesus' time)

Upper Room (traditional site)

Hezekiah's Tunnel

Last Supper

Pool of Siloam

Water Gate

Essene Gate

HINNOM VALLEY

0   0.1   0.2 mi.
0   0.1   0.2   0.3 km.

Map 9: JESUS' MINISTRY

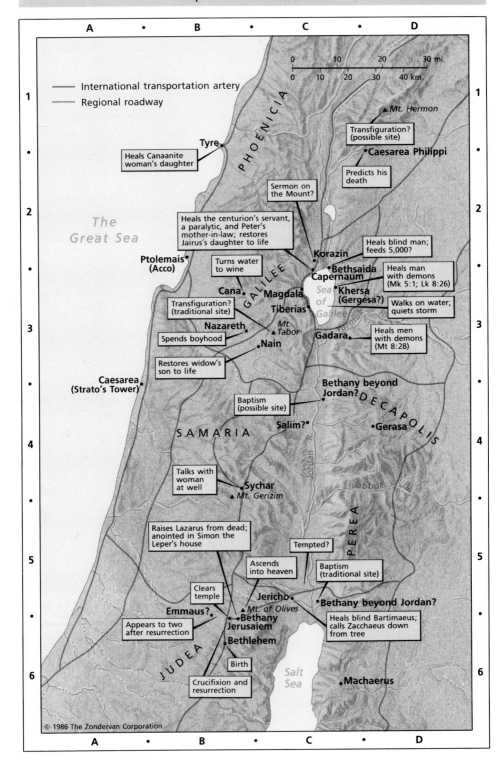

International transportation artery
Regional roadway

0   10   20   30 mi.
0   10   20   30   40 km.

A   •   B   •   C   •   D

PHOENICIA

Mt. Hermon

Tyre

Heals Canaanite woman's daughter

Transfiguration? (possible site)

Caesarea Philippi

Predicts his death

Sermon on the Mount?

The Great Sea

Heals the centurion's servant, a paralytic, and Peter's mother-in-law; restores Jairus's daughter to life

Heals blind man; feeds 5,000?

Korazin

Ptolemais (Acco)

Turns water to wine

GALILEE

Bethsaida
Capernaum

Heals man with demons (Mk 5:1; Lk 8:26)

Cana   Magdala   Sea of Galilee   Khersa (Gergesa?)

Transfiguration? (traditional site)

Tiberias

Walks on water; quiets storm

Nazareth

Mt. Tabor

Gadara

Heals men with demons (Mt 8:28)

Spends boyhood

Nain

Restores widow's son to life

Caesarea (Strato's Tower)

Bethany beyond Jordan?

Baptism (possible site)

DECAPOLIS

SAMARIA

Salim?

Gerasa

Talks with woman at well

Sychar
Mt. Gerizim

PEREA

Raises Lazarus from dead; anointed in Simon the Leper's house

Tempted?

Ascends into heaven

Baptism (traditional site)

Clears temple

Jericho

Emmaus?

Mt. of Olives

Bethany beyond Jordan?

Appears to two after resurrection

Bethany
Jerusalem

Heals blind Bartimaeus; calls Zacchaeus down from tree

Bethlehem

JUDEA

Birth

Salt Sea

Crucifixion and resurrection

Machaerus

© 1986 The Zondervan Corporation

A   •   B   •   C   •   D

Map 10: APOSTLES' EARLY TRAVELS

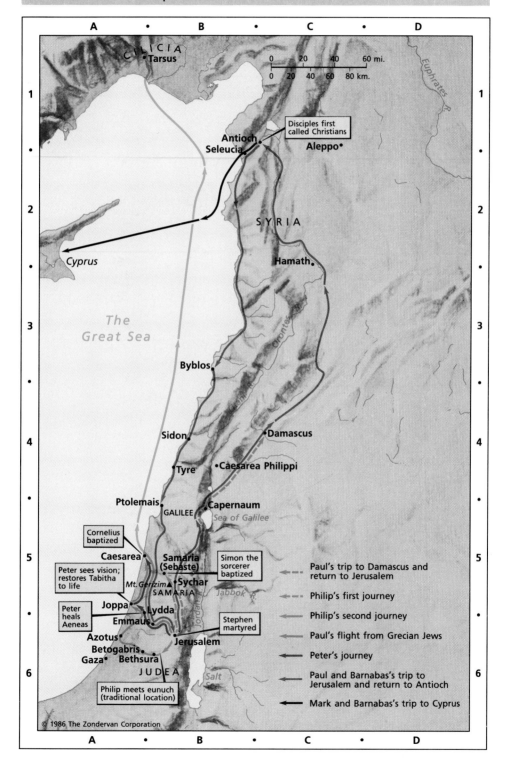

CILICIA
Tarsus

0   20   40   60 mi.
0 20 40 60 80 km.

Antioch
Seleucia

Disciples first
called Christians

Aleppo

Cyprus

SYRIA

Hamath

The
Great Sea

Byblos

Sidon

Damascus

Tyre

Caesarea Philippi

Ptolemais

Capernaum
GALILEE   Sea of Galilee

Cornelius
baptized

Caesarea

Samaria
(Sebaste)

Simon the
sorcerer
baptized

Peter sees vision;
restores Tabitha
to life

Mt. Gerizim   Sychar
SAMARIA   Jabbok

Joppa

Lydda

Peter
heals
Aeneas

Emmaus

Stephen
martyred

Azotus

Betogabris

Gaza   Bethsura

Jerusalem

JUDEA   Salt

Philip meets eunuch
(traditional location)

Euphrates R.

Orontes R.

Jordan

Paul's trip to Damascus and
return to Jerusalem

Philip's first journey

Philip's second journey

Paul's flight from Grecian Jews

Peter's journey

Paul and Barnabas's trip to
Jerusalem and return to Antioch

Mark and Barnabas's trip to Cyprus

© 1986 The Zondervan Corporation

GERMANIA

GALLIA

DALMATIA

Adriatic Sea

ITALY

Corsica

Rome
Forum of Appius
Three Taverns
Puteoli

MACED

Berea

Sardinia

EPIRUS

Tyrrhenian
Sea

Rhegium

Ionian
Sea

ACH

Sicily
Syracuse

NUMIDIA

Malta

AFRICA

The

TRIPOLITANIA

◄─── First Missionary Journey (A.D. 46–48)

─── Second Missionary Journey (A.D. 49–52)

─── Third Missionary Journey (A.D. 53–57)

─── Trip to Rome (A.D. 59–60)

© 1986 The Zondervan Corporation

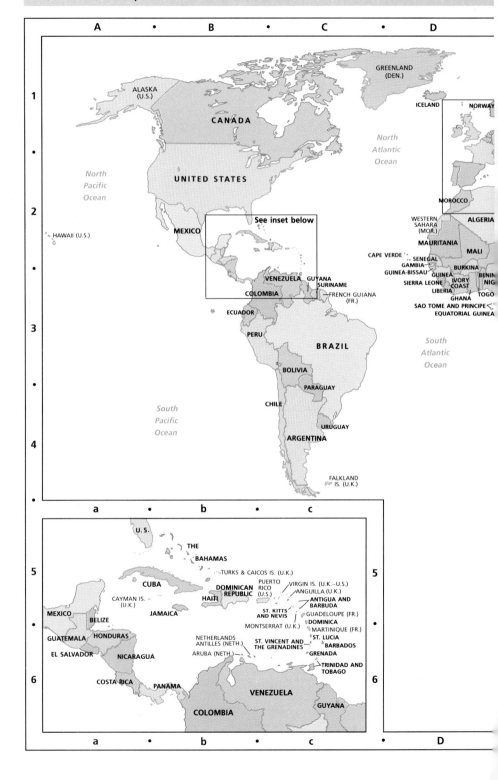

E • F • G • H

SVALBARD
(NOR.)

FINLAND   See inset below
SWEDEN

RUSSIA

1

KAZAKSTAN
MONGOLIA

North
Pacific
Ocean

UZBEKISTAN KYRGYZSTAN
TURKEY TURKMENISTAN TAJIKISTAN
NORTH
KOREA
JAPAN

UNISIA   IRAQ   AFGHANISTAN
IRAN   PAKISTAN   NEPAL
CHINA
SOUTH
KOREA

LIBYA   EGYPT   QATAR   BHUTAN
SAUDI
ARABIA
BANGLADESH
TAIWAN

2

IGER   UNITED ARAB
EMIRATES   OMAN   INDIA   BURMA
(MYANMAR)   LAOS

CHAD   SUDAN   ERITREA YEMEN   THAILAND
CAMBODIA   VIETNAM   PHILIPPINES

RIA   CENTRAL
AFRICAN
REPUBLIC   DJIBOUTI
ETHIOPIA   SRI LANKA   BRUNEI
MALAYSIA

CAMEROON   UGANDA   SOMALIA   MALDIVES
CONGO   RWANDA   KENYA   SINGAPORE
INDONESIA   PAPUA
NEW
GUINEA

ABON   BURUNDI
ZAIRE   TANZANIA   SEYCHELLES   Indian Ocean

3

ANGOLA   COMOROS   SOLOMON
ISLANDS
VANUATU

MALAWI
ZAMBIA   MOZAMBIQUE
NAMIBIA   ZIMBABWE   MAURITIUS
BOTSWANA   MADAGASCAR   RÉUNION (FR.)
AUSTRALIA   NEW
CALEDONIA
(FR.)

SWAZILAND
SOUTH
AFRICA   LESOTHO

NEW
ZEALAND

4

© 1996 The Zondervan Corporation

f • g • h

FAEROE IS.
(DEN.)   NORWAY   FINLAND
SWEDEN   EST.
LATVIA
LITH.   RUSSIA

UNITED
KINGDOM   DENMARK
IRELAND   NETHERLANDS   BELARUS   KAZAKSTAN

5

BELGIUM   GERMANY   POLAND
LUXEMBOURG   CZECH
REPUBLIC   SLOVAKIA   UKRAINE
SWITZERLAND   AUSTRIA   HUNGARY   MOLDOVA
FRANCE   LIECH.   SLOV.   ROMANIA
CROATIA   BOS.&
HERZ.
MONACO   SAN
MARINO   YUGO.   BULGARIA   GEORGIA
ANDORRA   ITALY   ALBANIA   F.Y.R.
MACED.   ARMENIA

PORTUGAL   SPAIN   GREECE   TURKEY   AZERBAIJAN

GIBRALTAR (U.K.)

6

MALTA   CYPRUS   SYRIA
MOROCCO   TUNISIA   LEBANON
WEST BANK
ISRAEL   IRAQ
ALGERIA   LIBYA   JORDAN   KUWAIT
EGYPT

E • f • g • h

Map 13: ROMAN EMPIRE

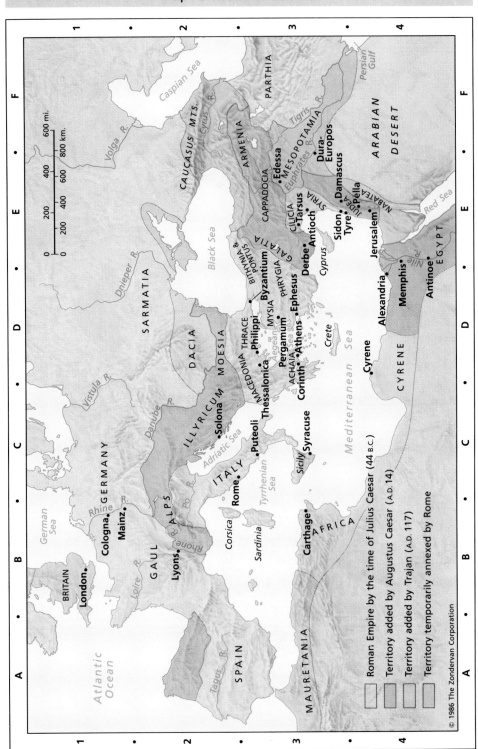

Roman Empire by the time of Julius Caesar (44 B.C.)

Territory added by Augustus Caesar (A.D. 14)

Territory added by Trajan (A.D. 117)

Territory temporarily annexed by Rome

© 1986 The Zondervan Corporation

600 mi.

800 km.

BRITAIN

London

GAUL

Lyons

Cologne

Mainz

GERMANY

ALPS

Rhine R.

Rhone R.

Loire R.

German Sea

Atlantic Ocean

SPAIN

Tagus R.

Corsica

Sardinia

ITALY

Rome

Puteoli

Po R.

Tyrrhenian Sea

Adriatic Sea

Sicily

Syracuse

Carthage

AFRICA

MAURETANIA

ILLYRICUM

Solona

MOESIA

DACIA

SARMATIA

Vistula R.

Danube R.

Dnieper R.

Volga R.

Caspian Sea

CAUCASUS MTS.

Cyrus R.

ARMENIA

PARTHIA

Tigris R.

Euphrates R.

MESOPOTAMIA

Dura-Europos

Edessa

CAPPADOCIA

Tarsus

CILICIA

Antioch

SYRIA

Damascus

Pella

NABATEA

JUDEA

Jerusalem

Sidon

Tyre

Cyprus

ARABIAN DESERT

Persian Gulf

Red Sea

EGYPT

Nile R.

Antinoe

Memphis

Alexandria

CYRENE

Cyrene

Mediterranean Sea

Crete

Thessalonica

MACEDONIA

THRACE

Philippi

Byzantium

BITHYNIA & PONTUS

GALATIA

PHRYGIA

MYSIA

Pergamum

Ephesus

Athens

ACHAIA

Corinth

Derbe

Aegean Sea

Black Sea

600

400

400

200

200

0

0

200

400

600